UNDERSTANDING CRIME IN CANADA

An Introduction to Criminology

Edited by NEIL BOYD

 emond · Toronto, Canada · 2015

Emond Montgomery Publications Limited
60 Shaftesbury Avenue
Toronto ON M4T 1A3
http://www.emond.ca/highered

Printed in Canada on FSC-certified paper.
Reprinted February 2018.

We acknowledge the financial support of the Government of Canada through the Canada Book Fund for our publishing activities.

Emond Montgomery Publications has no responsibility for the persistence or accuracy of URLs for external or third-party Internet websites referred to in this publication, and does not guarantee that any content on such websites is, or will remain, accurate or appropriate.

Acquisitions and development editor: Mike Thompson
Director, editorial and production: Jim Lyons
Editorial assistant: Katy Littlejohn
Copy editor: Claudia Forgas
Proofreader: Joe Cottercio-Milligan
Assistant production editor: Jamie Bush
Indexer: Paula Pike
Text designer: Tara Wells
Cover designers: Stephen Cribbin & Simon Evers
Cover image: Sally Davies

Library and Archives Canada Cataloguing in Publication

Boyd, Neil, 1951-, author
   Understanding crime in Canada : an introduction in criminology / Neil Boyd.

Includes bibliographical references and index.
ISBN 978-1-55239-605-6 (pbk.)

   1. Criminology—Canada—Textbooks.   2. Crime—Canada—Textbooks.   3. Crime—Canada—Case studies.   I. Title.

HV6807.B67 2014   364.971   C2014-900661-6

Brief Contents

PART ONE Approaching Criminology

PART TWO Foundations of Canadian Criminology

PART THREE Theories of Crime

PART FOUR   Types of Crime

Contents

Selected Figures and Tables

Preface

For the past 35 years I have taught in the School of Criminology at Simon Fraser University. During that time I have seen criminology studied from many different vantage points. I have seen a range of psychological, sociological, and biological analyses of crime; I have seen crime conceptualized as a matter of choice, and I have seen, in quite a different vein, feminist and critical analyses of both crime and the creation of law.

All of these perspectives have helped me to improve my understanding of crime, and it is, accordingly, a breadth of perspectives that I am hoping to convey within this textbook. When I first began teaching criminology courses in the late 1970s, I was somewhat more narrowly focused, mostly interested in the continuing evolution of law and attempts to understand its twists and turns, sometimes over centuries, and sometimes within the space of a decade.

But the great benefit of having spent virtually all of my professional life in the School of Criminology at Simon Fraser has been the exposure to a range of theories and studies of substantive types of crime. I suppose that this text reflects my education over more than three decades, and if there is a message in its content, it is that criminology is a realm of study that can usefully house many disparate perspectives.

My colleague Rob Gordon, the former director of the School of Criminology, has always been fond of referring to a "big tent" approach to the study of crime, noting that all credible forms of inquiry are to be welcomed. But, he has always been quick to add, please don't burn the tent down—if you try that approach, you will no longer be welcome within it.

Professor Gordon's admonition flows from his knowledge of the many conflicts that have emerged within criminology: positivist versus critical criminology, quantitative versus qualitative methodologies, crime control versus due process, and so on. Most of these conflicts have been healthy and stimulating—depending, of course, on the tolerances of those who hold opposing points of view.

I am indebted to the many authors who have contributed to this text, bringing carefully constructed overviews of their topics to introductory students and reflecting a substantial range of viewpoints. My message to students is that there is no singular criminology, and that you will benefit from understanding different theoretical perspectives, different methodological approaches, and different types of crime. This book will have accomplished its purpose if you, the student, emerge from your reading of it with the sense that the world of crime is not black or white, but is better analyzed and understood as flowing from a rich and, I hope, satisfying mix of competing values, perspectives, theories, and methodologies.

Neil Boyd
Professor and Director
School of Criminology
Simon Fraser University
May 2014

Acknowledgments

The publisher and author wish to thank the following people for providing reviewer feedback, suggestions, or other assistance during the development of this book: Walter DeKeseredy (UOIT), Lisa Gerrard (Algonquin College), Jonathan Heidt (University of the Fraser Valley), Catherine Huth (Langara College), Fiona Kay (Queen's University), Paul Millar (Nipissing University), Bastien Quirion (University of Ottawa), and Michael Seredycz (Grant MacEwan University). Special thanks to Barry Cartwright (Simon Fraser University) for his editorial assistance.

For Instructors

For additional information and resources, please visit the accompanying website for this book at **www.emp.ca/CRIM**. The "Updates" tab on this site provides links to current news stories, commentary, legislation, cases, and other relevant information to enhance and update the content of this book.

For information on obtaining the teaching resources available to instructors who have chosen this book for their courses, visit the "For Instructors" tab on this book's website. These resources include PowerPoint slides, test bank, sample syllabus, image bank, and more. An online student tutorial package, featuring additional lectures, quizzes, self-assessment tools, and flash cards, is also available to supplement this book. See the "For Instructors" tab or contact your Emond Montgomery representative for more information.

About the Authors

Neil Boyd is professor and director of the School of Criminology at Simon Fraser University.

Valerie Steeves is an associate professor in the Department of Criminology at the University of Ottawa. **Trevor Scott Milford** is a PhD candidate in the Department of Sociology and Anthropology at Carleton University.

Craig Jones is a professor in the Faculty of Law at Thompson Rivers University.

Hilary Kim Morden is a sessional lecturer and graduate researcher in the School of Criminology at Simon Fraser University. **Ted Palys** is a professor in the School of Criminology at Simon Fraser University.

Hannah Scott is a professor in the Faculty of Social Science and Humanities at the University of Ontario Institute of Technology.

Barry Cartwright is a senior lecturer in the School of Criminology at Simon Fraser University.

Jonathan Heidt is an assistant professor in the School of Criminology at the University of the Fraser Valley.

Gail Anderson is professor and associate director of undergraduate programs in the School of Criminology at Simon Fraser University.

Laura Huey is an associate professor in the Department of Sociology at Western University.

Fiona Kay is a professor in the Department of Sociology at Queen's University.

Graham Farrell is professor and research chair in environmental criminology at the Institute for Canadian Urban Research Studies (ICURS) and the School of Criminology at Simon Fraser University. **Tarah Hodgkinson** is a PhD candidate in the School of Criminology at Simon Fraser University.

Sara Thompson is an assistant professor in the Department of Criminology at Ryerson University.

Lisa Murphy is coordinator of the Sexual Behaviours Clinic, Integrated Forensic Program, at the Royal Ottawa Mental Health Centre. **J.P. Fedoroff** is director of the Sexual Behaviours Clinic at the Royal Ottawa Mental Health Care Group and head of the Division of Forensic Psychiatry at the University of Ottawa.

Bill O'Grady is a professor in the Department of Sociology and Anthropology at the University of Guelph.

Andrew Hathaway is an associate professor in the Department of Sociology and Anthropology at the University of Guelph. **Amir Mostaghim** is a PhD candidate in the Department of Sociology and Anthropology at the University of Guelph.

Scot Wortley is an associate professor of criminology at the Centre for Criminology and Sociolegal Studies at the University of Toronto.

Poonam Puri is associate dean and professor at Osgoode Hall Law School, York University. **Simon Kupi**, JD, is counsel at the National Energy Board in Calgary.

PART ONE
Approaching Criminology

Criminology in Action: The Exoneration of David Milgaard

David Milgaard at a press conference in 1995, prior to his exoneration. He is flanked by his mother, Joyce, and DNA expert Dr. Edward Blake.
Source: John Mahler/GetStock.com.

A little after 6:30 a.m. on the morning of January 31, 1969, 16-year-old David Milgaard drove into the city of Saskatoon with his two teenage companions, Nichol John and Ron Wilson. There were ice crystals in the air; the temperature hovered just below −40 degrees Celsius. Milgaard and his friends were looking for the home of their friend Albert Cadrain, but became lost, first stopping at a motel to obtain directions, and then becoming stuck in ice in a back alley, a few miles from the Cadrain home. They knocked on the door of a home in the neighbourhood where they had become stuck, and a local couple invited them in, allowing them to make arrangements to get their car out of the back alley. The three friends spent about a half hour in the home, chatting amicably with the couple, and then finally made their way to Cadrain's, arriving about 9 a.m.

On the same morning, Gail Miller, a 20-year-old nursing assistant, left her rooming house a little before 7 a.m. to walk a few blocks to her bus stop. She never arrived. She was dragged into a back alley, stabbed repeatedly in the back and chest with a small paring knife, and sexually assaulted. Her body was found about an hour later, face down in a snow bank. Her underwear was down around her ankles, and there were 11 stab wounds in her back, above her breast, and on the left side of her neck.

The police initially believed that the killing was the work of a predatory rapist who had committed three sexual assaults on women in the same neighbourhood during the previous six months; these crimes all involved the use of a knife, and dragging the victims into a back alley, before perpetrating the attacks.

Police interviews in the local neighbourhood after the killing were turning up little of value, although there was some forensic evidence of note. A trail of Gail Miller's belongings was found, going from the crime scene a few blocks away, to the Cadrain home. Albert Cadrain told police in early March that he had seen blood on David Milgaard on the morning of the murder. Cadrain had already been interviewed by Regina police in February, strip-searched, and subjected to a rectal examination for drugs. At that time he had laughed at police suggestions that he, Milgaard, or Wilson could be responsible for such a crime. The police charged him with vagrancy; he was convicted and sentenced to a week in jail.

Saskatoon police, after receiving this information from Cadrain, interviewed Milgaard, John, and Wilson repeatedly. They began to think that one of these three young hippie kids from Regina, likely David Milgaard, was responsible for the rape and murder of Gail Miller. Within a few months, the police had statements from both Wilson and John, implicating Milgaard. The two teens finally said that Milgaard had left the car that morning after being stuck in a back alley, and before arriving at the motel; they claimed he had gone out of sight, and stabbed and raped a young woman before returning to the car.

In January 1970, David Milgaard was convicted of capital murder and sentenced to hang. His appeals against the conviction were unsuccessful, but his sentence was commuted to life imprisonment.

Fast-forward to 1990. David Milgaard had been in federal penitentiaries for more than 20 years, but his mother, Joyce, had always believed in his innocence. Two important developments took place during that year. First, the Milgaards learned that someone had been convicted in 1970 for the rapes in Saskatoon that occurred in the months prior to the Gail Miller murder. That person was Larry Fisher, who had a history of violent rape with knives, and was serving a 12-year sentence for raping and stabbing a woman in Saskatchewan and leaving her for dead. Fisher had also been living in the basement of the Cadrain home in 1970 with his wife, Linda; the trail of belongings leading from Gail Miller's body to Cadrain's now had a different interpretation attached to it. Second, a private investigator tracked down Ron Wilson. Over a few beers, Wilson confessed that he and John had decided to "sink" Milgaard to get police investigators off their backs—and that Milgaard had never left the car at all.

A Personal Perspective on the Milgaard Case

Neil Boyd

In that same year, 1990, I was supervising a directed studies on homicide with Kim Rossmo, who was in the process of developing his now globally renowned technique of geographic profiling, a tool that permits police officers to focus on the likely residence of offenders in cases of serial crimes. Kim and I received a grant for an academic study of the Milgaard conviction, and we set to work. It was an example of what might best be called "criminology in action": we read law in the form of hundreds of pages of trial transcripts and appeal transcripts; we visited the crime scene and timed the movements that were behind the theory of the Crown; and we interviewed all of the witnesses at trial who would talk to us, most notably David Milgaard, Ron Wilson, and Linda Fisher (the former wife of Larry Fisher).

Criminology had come a long way since 1969. We knew in 1990 that the statistical likelihood of having two predatory sex offenders active in the same neighbourhood in Saskatoon in 1969 was extremely small. We also knew, in large measure from Kim's geographic profiling, that Larry Fisher was a much better bet for this crime; he had a lengthy history of predatory sexual assault; David Milgaard had no criminal history at all. By 1990 we knew that wrongful convictions occur for a variety of reasons: tunnel vision by the police, lying by individuals in custody (or in debt to police in some way), a lack of relevant DNA evidence, false confessions, and erroneous forensic evidence at trial.

The Milgaard convictions had all of these variables in play. The police never backed away from their initial tunnel vision: their view that Milgaard was guilty persisted, quite surprisingly, even after 1990, when Fisher surfaced as an alternative suspect and Wilson recanted his testimony. Both John and Wilson had spent time in police custody before offering up false statements regarding Milgaard's guilt. Cadrain had been a police informer prior to the murder of Gail Miller; four years after his testimony against Milgaard, he was committed to a psychiatric institution for mental health difficulties.

Our own careful reconstruction of the timeline of the homicide, available from the trial transcript, revealed to us that the theory of the Crown was not tenable. There simply was not enough time for David Milgaard to rape and kill Gail Miller. And it was almost beyond belief to think that this teenage boy would be chatting amicably with a motel operator and a couple in Saskatoon just minutes after raping and stabbing a young woman to death. We learned something important from this case: individuals can be reluctant to admit having made tragic mistakes and, instead, may run away from those life-changing errors, as Ron Wilson and Nichol John did.

In April 1992, after the Milgaard case had been referred to the Supreme Court of Canada, the court came down with its unanimous decision. The court could not conclude beyond a reasonable doubt that Milgaard was not guilty, and for reasons that are still hard to fathom today, it could not even conclude that Milgaard's innocence was more probable than his guilt. They simply concluded that the new evidence regarding Larry Fisher might lead to a different outcome, and so they ordered a new trial. The province of Saskatchewan decided not to prosecute, given the time lag between the events of 1969 and the present, and so David Milgaard was set free, but not without a cloud still over his head. Was he guilty or innocent? There was no answer.

But in 1997 we finally received a verdict, not from the fallible realm of human justice, but from the science of DNA testing. New developments in DNA testing in Britain had made it possible to determine the DNA link between the spermatozoa found on Gail Miller's clothing and the DNA of the two suspects, David Milgaard and Larry Fisher. The results exonerated David Milgaard and clearly matched Larry Fisher. Today, David Milgaard is a free man, and was awarded $12 million in compensation for spending 23 years in jail for a crime he did not commit. And Larry Fisher, now in his 60s, is serving a 25-year term for the first-degree murder of Gail Miller. This case is a reminder of the progress of criminology over time. Ultimately, it was science, in this case, that led to justice, providing an important reminder of both human fallibility and the need to continually expand our understanding of crime.

Before You Read Chapter 1

- How many different kinds of criminological study are mentioned in this case study?
- Why is this a worthwhile case study for criminologists to examine? What larger questions or issues does it raise for anyone studying crime?
- What reasons might account for "tunnel vision" on the part of police?
- In what ways has our understanding of crime expanded since Gail Miller's murder?

What Is Criminology?

Introduction

The *Oxford Reference Dictionary* defines *criminology* simply as the "scientific study of crime." And *crime*, in turn, is defined as "an act punishable by law; an evil act; a shame, a senseless act."

The behaviours that are at the heart of crime have been a part of human conduct for as long as *Homo sapiens* have existed. Pre-state societies saw assaults, robberies, thefts, and homicides—the kinds of activities that we regard today as criminal and punishable by the state.

But **criminology** as a field of serious academic and scientific study is a relatively recent development. Although one can point to the Code of Hammurabi in ancient Babylon or the pronouncements of the Roman Republic as examples of early codifications of crime, or to the work of 18th-century philosopher Cesare Beccaria on punishment, the study of crime did not really begin in any systematic way until the 19th century (Rafter, 2009). Even then, there was not a great deal of coherence within the field, a phenomenon that arguably continues in the present. German psychiatrist Richard von Krafft-Ebing wrote of sexual deviations, Italian anthropologist Cesare Lombroso wrote of "criminal man," and French sociologist Émile Durkheim wrote much more broadly of the normalcy of crime in all human societies.

criminology
The study of crime and criminal behaviour, which are defined by reference to criminal law.

Criminology as an Academic Discipline

In Canada the study of crime in universities began during the 1950s, at the University of British Columbia. The new program in criminology was announced in 1951, housed within the Department of Social Sciences. The development of the new program was spurred by an emerging sense that correctional efforts—the rehabilitation of offenders—would be assisted by an accumulating body of knowledge (Parkinson, 2008). The proponents of the program argued that offenders could no longer be seen as "born criminals," and they pointed to the local Haney Correctional Institution as the site of an emerging progressive correctional administration, concerned about developing educational and vocational programs, maintaining family and community ties for offenders, and developing programs of probation and parole.

Although this program was short-lived, closing in 1959, with criminology courses becoming part of the School of Social Work, the impetus for the study of crime in Canada, and in other Western nation-states, was clearly building. In 1963, criminologist Denis Szabo declared the arrival of "a new discipline" and "a new profession" when the School of Criminology was created at the Université de Montréal. In the same year, J.L.J. Edwards established the Centre of Criminology at the University of Toronto as a research entity; and in 1967, Tadeusz Grygier established the Department of Criminology at the University of Ottawa as an applied interdisciplinary program, with courses in both English and French. And in 1973, Simon Fraser University's School of Criminology, led by Ezzat Fattah (a former faculty member of the Université de Montréal), began to offer its program, again interdisciplinary in structure. From the 1960s to the present, criminology programs emerged within departments of sociology at many universities, focused on understanding crime as a form of **deviance** and then studying the processes of defining criminal law, the social precursors to involvement in crime, and the potential range of appropriate and/or effective responses to lawbreakers.

deviance
Behaviour that differs from accepted social norms; may include acts that violate specific rules (crime), sexual behaviours, or non-criminal acts that challenge accepted values.

The Emergence of Criminology in the Postwar Era: The Social Backdrop

These developments necessarily raise the question of why, during the 1960s and 1970s, the study of crime emerged as a subject of scholarly inquiry, no longer limited to the relatively exclusive purview of philosophers, theologians, and politicians. Canada was not the only country where this kind of rapid growth of the discipline occurred. In both the United States and the United Kingdom, the study of crime emerged as both a burgeoning and contested form of academic inquiry (Laub, 2004; Taylor, Walton, & Young, 1973).

Urbanization and industrialization were key features of social life in Canada, the United Kingdom, and the United States during the late 19th and early 20th centuries. Substantial migration took place from rural areas to urban areas, and new categories of crime arose, often related to the behaviours of the urban poor: for example, new proscriptions were enacted against vagrancy, drunkenness, and prostitution. The early 20th century also witnessed the beginnings of globalization—immigration in the form of inexpensive labour arriving from China, Japan, and the developing world. These new immigrants represented an economic threat to the established labour force. They also brought long-standing parts of their cultures with them to their new world—opium from China, hashish from India, and coca and cocaine from South America. These alternatives to tobacco and alcohol were resisted, and criminally prohibited, and laws were passed to aid deportation of "foreign drug peddlers" and to restrict immigration.

Put differently, the culture was changing. It was more urban and more global, and the changes created tensions. Along with the growth in literacy and greater access to information came challenges to traditional institutions and ways of thinking. The practice of capital punishment began to be criticized, public executions moved behind closed doors (out of sight of the population), and reformers began to advocate for more humane treatment of lawbreakers and more economic support for the urban poor.

By the end of the Second World War, social conflicts had become social threats. Global annihilation now appeared as a possibility, underlined by the Cold War between two dominant world powers, the United States and the Soviet Union. And so began the 1960s. Crime rates began to escalate in a time of youth rebellion. Young people were urged to make love, not war, in the wake of the US entry into Vietnam, while countercultural leaders such as Timothy Leary championed experimentation with mind-active drugs with the rallying cry, "tune in, turn on, and drop out."

A **demographic** shift of some relevance also took place. Beginning in the mid-1960s, the percentage of young men within the populations of Canada, the United States, and the United Kingdom increased dramatically. As well, the postwar baby boomers, born between 1946 and 1964, entered their crime-prone years (between the ages of 15 and 34) in the mid-1960s. In every era of human history and in every part of the world today, young men commit a disproportionate amount of crime, relative to other age cohorts. It was perhaps not surprising, then, that in the postwar era, with this explosion of young men in national populations, that crime rates should rise—although considerable debate exists within criminological literature as to the statistical importance of this demographic shift (Fox, 2000; Marvell & Moody, 1991).

demographics
Statistical data relating to characteristics of a population, such as relative size of age groups, gender balance, or any other measurable information.

correlation
The finding that two measurable phenomena occur together, suggesting a relationship, but not necessarily one of direct cause and effect.

BOX 1.1

Correlates of Crime

As we will see in Chapter 4, Measuring Crime, a full understanding of the prevalence of crime is highly dependent on how crime is defined, and how it is then reported to, processed, and counted by police. It is safe to say, however, that young men—not just in Canada today, but in most times and places throughout history—tend to commit a disproportionate amount of crime, as Figure 1.1 illustrates. Both age and sex can be seen in this figure as important **correlates** of crime; that is, they are factors that do not *cause* crime, but they are strongly linked to criminal behaviour. Simply put, young men make contributions to crime statistics that are remarkably disproportionate to the size of their population in Canada, the United States, the United Kingdom, and elsewhere.

Several other correlates of crime will be discussed at relevant points in this book, including, for example, the disproportionate representation of poverty, race, and income inequality within certain criminal justice statistics. The difficult task for criminologists is to try to understand the significance of these correlations. They do not express cause-and-effect relationships; but responding to this information, and understanding the meanings of these relationships, is important in the construction of an effective criminal justice policy.

FIGURE 1.1   Cases Completed in Adult Criminal Court, by Age Group and Sex of the Accused, Canada, 2010–11

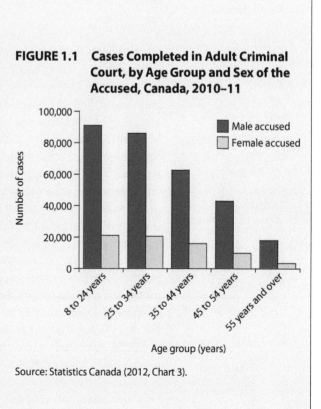

Source: Statistics Canada (2012, Chart 3).

The decade from 1966 to 1975 was a time of social upheaval. During that time, alcohol consumption (which is closely tied to criminal behaviour) had increased dramatically, by approximately 50 percent per capita. The birth control pill had also fundamentally changed male–female relationships when it emerged in the mid-1960s, allowing women to experiment with sex without the risk of pregnancy, and outside of marriage. Not surprisingly, the divorce rate, aided by greater social acceptance of the dissolution of marriage, increased fourfold, again from 1966 to 1975. In addition, young women were leaving the family or marital home for the workplace. In Canada, the number of women in the labour force increased from 2.2 million in 1966 to more than 5.5 million in 1975. These were dramatic social changes for both men and women, and they were not always easy to accept, particularly for men (Boyd, 1988).

Crime rates, perhaps understandably, given this backdrop, were increasing dramatically (see Figure 11.2 on page 261 of this book). The social changes of the 20th century, particularly those of the post–Second World War era, contributed in many ways to creating the social conditions in which criminology emerged as an academic discipline. What was to be done about the use of cannabis and other drugs, flowing from the far-flung regions of the globe? What was to be done about the conflict between youth and the generation of their parents? What was to be done about the increasing disintegration of marriage and the problems of domestic violence? Would men be able to accept and embrace the continuing emancipation of women? Criminology entered the fray with multiple and sometimes conflicting agendas: controlling crime, reducing conflict, emancipating women and youth, and evaluating policies that might best respond to these new realities.

Criminology: A Discipline, or a Home for Established Disciplines?

What does it mean to be a criminologist? As the diversity of the authors of this book illustrates, the field has typically been *interdisciplinary* in its orientation, drawing on long-established disciplines such as sociology, psychology, law, geography, history, political science, and economics. More recently, with developments in the use of DNA and in **forensic entomology**, it also draws on the fields of chemistry and biology. Those educated in all of these realms tend to bring to the study of criminology both the substantive base of knowledge from their disciplines and a corresponding range of methods for undertaking academic inquiry.

forensic entomology
The study of insects to assist in legal investigations; insects found on a corpse can help identify facts about the time and place of the victim's death.

Psychology, as the study of individual behaviour, tends to focus on the criminal, often classifying this individual, trying to predict the risk of reoffending, and then evaluating the effectiveness of various forms of rehabilitation or treatment. Psychological explanations of crime have evolved over the years, moving from Freudian psychoanalysis to personality theory to theories of moral development and, more recently, to developmental conceptions of criminal involvement (Moffitt, 1993). In all of these constructions of crime, the individual is front and centre: an individual's psyche and behaviours are the focus of the study of crime.

Sociological analyses of crime, not surprisingly, focus on the *social order*—the extent to which social forces work to define crime and create conditions in which crime might either flourish or diminish. Sociological analyses of crime essentially try to understand how the social context of our lives works to create laws and certain kinds of crime and crime rates. They also point to social and structural changes that might be made in order to effectively respond to the challenges that crime presents. As Chapter 12, Socio-logical Approaches, indicates, sociology has historically been the dominant paradigm within criminology, giving rise to social control theory, labelling theory, differential association theory, and notions of *anomie*. More recently, it has developed a range of critical theories of crime: moral panics and the culture of control, Marxian and neo-Marxian analysis, Foucauldian perspectives (after French thinker Michel Foucault), and postmodern conceptions of **criminality**. For as long as criminology has been a subject of academic inquiry, social analyses of crime, law, and deviance have been pre-eminent. Crime and criminal conduct have been regarded as more likely to be driven by social conditions than by individual aberrations.

criminality
The state of being criminal; criminal acts or practices.

BOX 1.2

Understanding Deviance

All societies define some behaviours as deviant, and some of these deviant behaviours are also regarded, through the further step of criminalization by the state, as crimes. These shifting definitions of deviance and crime can differ markedly across societies. For example, some nations regard alcohol consumption as both devi-ant and criminal; others regards sexuality outside of marriage as deviant and, in some circumstances, as criminal and deserving of severe penalties.

The history of crime teaches us that deviance, and crime itself, are both malleable constructions. In late 19th-century Canada, homosexuality was illegal and pun-ishable by imprisonment. And yet today, gay marriage is legal and we have openly gay politicians, celebrities, and an ever-growing number of athletes and other public figures. (Meanwhile, in some countries, particularly sev-eral in Africa, punishment for homosexuality has recently grown *more* severe, including life imprisonment—which illustrates how tolerance and definitions of deviance can trend in the opposite direction.)

Similarly, doctors who performed abortions in 19th-century Canada were subject to criminal conviction, and even faced the possibility of a death sentence. Today, abortions are not subject to any criminal penalties. We are also currently witnessing a significant debate about whether some kinds of illegal drug use should properly be regarded as criminal and/or deviant. Many well-known politicians—that is, leaders and members of a group whom we often call "lawmakers"—openly admit to hav-ing smoked cannabis, and two US states have legalized its use. This leads one to ask: Is marijuana possession now gradually becoming more or less like alcohol and tobacco use—a potential risk to an individual's health and subject to some regulation, but not generally con-sidered a crime deserving of punishment, and ultimately perhaps not even a deviant act in the opinion of most people? Recent polling suggests that a majority of Can-adians now feel that way.

Michael Leshner and Michael Stark celebrate a court's decision allowing them to wed. In 2003, they became the first legally married same-sex couple in Canada. This landmark decision was one clear illustration of how social attitudes had shifted in recent decades.

Source: Tony Bock/GetStock.com.

The study of law is also central to criminology, as it defines the landscape of crime, setting out the specifics of prohibited behaviours and the penalties that are attached to them. The history of law provides insight into the changing nature of crime, especially the malleability of some forms of deviance and the evolving nature of what might be viewed as appropriate responses to crime. The history of criminal law, in particular, indicates how and why new forms of criminality are created. For example, historical analysis of law demonstrates that the emergence of a global prohibition of certain mind-active drugs in the early 20th century began as a moral crusade driven by racism and economic fears: this prohibition, perhaps not surprisingly, is now facing challenges to both its empirical logic and its corresponding moral underpinnings. Similarly, the study of the history of criminal law reveals changing responses to long-established and universally condemned forms of conduct. For example, in Canada in the latter half of the 19th century, capital punishment was regarded in law as an appropriate punishment, not only for murder but also for many other crimes. The study of amendments to criminal law over time and the debates surrounding these amendments reflects changes not only to the punishment of crime but also to the logic and utility of these changes.

The disciplines of history, geography, political science, and economics have, historically, been less central to the study of criminology than psychology, sociology, and law, but they have each made different kinds of contributions. Recurring patterns within the social and spatial geography of crime have been critical to the development of programs of crime prevention through environmental design (CPTED) and the tracking of serial predatory offenders across time and space (Brantingham & Brantingham, 1984; Rossmo, 1999).

Detailed histories of crime, law, and criminal behaviours have provided a greater understanding of the utility of law and various legislative and policy initiatives as well as the kinds of variables that might foster or diminish crime. More recently, economics has made important contributions to criminology, permitting evaluative analyses of the costs and benefits of various crime reduction initiatives. With recent developments in the utility of gathering DNA at crime scenes, and in studying the decomposition of bodies to determine time of death (forensic entomology), the fields of chemistry and biology have also become a significant part of criminology, providing evidence that can be both *inculpatory* and *exculpatory* (that is, pointing to one's guilt or innocence).

Is there a specific discipline of criminology that will in time displace or unite all of these long-established disciplines? Or is criminology better described simply as the study of crime and, as such, wholly dependent on the methods and literature of sociology, psychology, law, and other areas of knowledge? Today, many universities across the Western world offer MA, MSc, and PhD programs in criminology. In Canada alone, the Université de Montréal, the University of Toronto, and Simon Fraser University all offer doctoral programs in criminology. But can any of these institutions claim ownership of a new academic discipline?

The faculty in departments and schools of criminology represent a variety of disciplines: law, psychology, sociology, economics, geography, and the natural sciences. But they also include individuals with doctorates in criminology.

Perhaps for those who argue that criminology is a separate discipline, rather than simply a particular focus of study, the difficulty is in demonstrating that criminology has a set of theories and methods specific to it and separate from other disciplines. Some of

BOX 1.3

Why Study Crime?

Before embarking on an in-depth examination of the many aspects of criminology covered in the chapters that follow, it is worthwhile to stand back and consider several general questions about the *value* of studying crime. Thinking about these issues helps one appreciate the role that criminology plays in defining and shaping our society, and why it is important and beneficial—both for individuals and society—to understand crime and criminal behaviour.

What to criminalize and how to respond to crime?

First, we need to think about what we as a society should criminalize. The power to define a person as criminal, and then to be able to deprive that person of liberty, is an extraordinary power. We learn from the history of crime that its content is highly malleable—in Canada alone within the past century we have come to regard some previously criminal acts as tolerable behaviours, and some forms of punishment as inappropriately harsh and counterproductive. We also know that the powers of the police and the criminal justice system have often been abused or misapplied. The questions of how the state defines and responds to crime say a great deal about our culture, and they are deserving of careful consideration.

What does the best evidence tell us about our responses to crime and their effectiveness?

There are some forms of crime that have always been defined as such: physical offences against persons, theft, and fraud come quickly to mind. But how effective are the typical responses to these crimes? Does imprisonment for certain kinds of crime have significant impacts on crime rates—that is, is it an effective deterrent? What about probation, fines, or conditional sentences? Can neighbourhoods and communities be designed in ways that will reduce opportunities for crime, and therefore crime itself? Do the media influence our responses to crime, and do they give us an accurate understanding of crime? These are all important questions, and criminological research can provide important insights into the utility of various approaches and the creation of sound policies.

Can the study of crime help us to respond to emerging challenges?

Since the beginning of the 21st century we have witnessed significant social changes in Western society. Concerns about terrorism since the attacks of September 11, 2001 have led to expanded security measures and surveillance, which have in turn raised fears about compromised privacy and human rights. More generally, we have seen the proliferation of the Internet and of telephones that are also computers and cameras. What are the implications of these changes for crime and crime detection? We must now contend with identity theft, Internet and telephone fraud, and more, all of it within a virtual and a global context. On any given day, we all face the possibility of being victims of these new kinds of crimes. How can we effectively respond to these new challenges?

Furthermore, while crime rates have dropped in most Western nations, there is a great deal of ongoing debate about why this has happened: A simple demographic shift? A cultural shift? Improvements in technologies for combatting crime? More effective policing? Or is a large proportion of crime simply shifting to a new, virtual terrain? If we are to understand both the present and the future of our society, and determine how best to deal with these challenges, these are some of the key questions we must attempt to answer.

the most recent and arguably innovative approaches within criminology—life-course-development theory, geographic profiling, DNA profiling, and critical criminology—have origins in psychology, geography, chemistry, and sociology, respectively.

What Do Criminologists Study?

As criminology is home to a host of disciplines, it is not surprising that the questions that criminologists ask tend to vary significantly, dependent in part on the field of their training and the lens or framework through which they understand the realities of crime. This issue of *what* to study takes us back to the social and political backdrop against which the study of criminology emerged in the 1960s and 1970s. Crime rates were rising, and the social conflicts described earlier in this chapter did set the stage for a more rigorous analysis of crime. Perhaps not surprisingly, the questions of what to study and how to study produced multiple responses, reflective of the conflicts of the era, as they still do today.

criminalization

To define an act as a crime, and thereby subject that act to formal punishment.

The process of **criminalization** itself has been the subject of considerable scrutiny. The criminalization of the possession and distribution of certain kinds of drugs is an ongoing process that has produced a considerable amount of research, as has the criminalization and subsequent decriminalization of abortion, and the contested criminalization of the trade in sexual services. In each of these areas, criminologists have examined the legal history of criminalization, the effectiveness of associated laws, the intended and unintended consequences of these laws, the harms imposed by these illegal activities—and the harms imposed by the laws that control them.

How these contested terrains of criminal law are studied depends, in part, on the disciplinary background of the criminologist. A historian will canvass and catalogue the emergence of law and legal amendments in substantial detail, attempting to explain the social, political, and economic context of legal changes. A psychologist will consider the harms to the individual, not only from involvement in these typically consensual activities, but also from the law itself. An economist will consider the cost effectiveness of various sanctions. For example, would a supervised injection site for drug users reduce health-care costs by cutting down the rate of HIV and hepatitis C?

Once we move away from the contested terrains of criminal law—those realms where we consider certain behaviours to be socially tolerable and capable of regulation (rather than unacceptable and deserving imprisonment)—the focus of inquiry becomes quite different.

Crime Rates: Why Do They Go Up? Why Do They Go Down?

Since 1960, a considerable amount of data has been reported by police (through the Uniform Crime Reporting Survey), indicating the extent of particular types of crime. We are now able to look back for decades, using data from dozens of nation-states, in order to determine whether specific crimes have increased or decreased over time within specific jurisdictions. We can also compare different nation-states over time, to determine whether the trends observed cross national boundaries.

criminal justice system

The various institutions and processes through which an offender passes, such as the police, the courts, and correctional facilities and programs.

We have learned that the reliability of these police data varies: reports of homicides tend to be very closely related to the actual number of homicides committed in most jurisdictions. But police reports of theft, assault, and sexual assault represent only a minority of all such incidents; they depend on the willingness of victims to report a particular crime, the perceived significance of an incident by the victim, and both individual and societal attitudes toward involvement with police and the **criminal justice system**. Fortunately, we also have a considerable amount of data generated by surveys of individual victimization (such as the General Social Survey), which document the extent of crime experienced by a random selection of citizens in a given jurisdiction (Statistics Canada, 2013). The combination of police reports of crime and ongoing surveys of criminal victimization provides a more complete and nuanced understanding of changing crime rates.

FIGURE 1.2   Criminology, Criminal Justice, and Deviance

Criminologists study changing crime rates in order to provide explanations for increases and decreases. Put differently, what variables contribute to an increase in certain kinds of crime, and, more important, what can we do to push those rates in the opposite direction? Alternatively, once crime rates have fallen, what variables can we attribute this to? And how can we produce more of the same? Much has been written, for example, about the crime drop experienced in Canada and the United States from the 1990s to the present (Blumstein & Wallman, 2000; Farrell, Tilley, Tseloni, & Mailley, 2011; Pinker, 2011).

What we have learned is that the explanations for the increase and decrease in crime rates are not universal. For example, motor vehicle theft has dropped significantly over the past 15 years, largely because of improvements in motor vehicle alarm and access technology, making the possibility of theft much less likely (Kriven & Ziersch, 2007).

Why have homicides in Canada and the United States dropped to almost half the rates experienced in the late 1970s? Many different explanations have been offered (Pinker, 2011; Zimring, 2006), but no universally accepted account exists for this change. We can point to a vast amount of correlational data regarding crime rates and other variables, but cause–effect descriptions and conclusions are simply not possible. Nonetheless, the tracking of crime and attempts to explain increases and decreases, notably the increases of the late 1960s and the early 1970s and the decreases of the past 20 years, are a critical focus for criminology. If we are to reduce the impact that crime has on our everyday lives, we need to understand how and why particular kinds of crime increase and decrease over time. It is, for example, not surprising to learn that while many forms of personal and property crime have declined markedly over the past 20 years, online victimization, identity theft, and credit card fraud have all dramatically increased (United Nations Office on Drugs and Crime, 2013).

Studying the Criminal Pathways to Crime

An important part of criminology—beyond understanding the creation of criminal law, concomitant penalties, and changing crime rates—is the task of understanding why particular individuals commit crime and, in some circumstances, continue to do so. What, for example, are the characteristics of those convicted of crime, and why do some people commit a significant amount of crime, while others do not?

We have learned that most people convicted of crime are male, and relatively young (typically between the ages of 15 and 34). They also tend to have few resources and little education. Early criminologists such as Cesare Lombroso argued that criminality was a biological trait (that certain people are "born criminal"). William Sheldon argued in the mid-1950s that body type (or "somatotyping") is strongly linked to criminal behaviour, with well-muscled mesomorphs more likely to commit criminal offences. Neither of these conceptions linking biology to criminality were able to find much empirical support, but research in the past 20 to 30 years has begun to regard criminal conduct as a complex mix of both biology and environment.

traits
Those attributes or features that distinguish or characterize an individual.

It appears that some individuals have personality **traits** and characteristics that predispose them to crime (Raine, 2013), but biology does not predetermine criminality. However, a series of studies of adopted children and identical twins raised apart have prompted some rethinking of the relative significance of environment in predisposing individuals to involvement in crime. When Sarnoff Mednick, William Gabrielli Jr., and Barry Hutchings (1984) discovered, after considering a sample of more than 14,000 Danish adoptions, that these children were significantly more likely to commit crime if their biological fathers had criminal records—trumping the influence of the criminal records held by the adopted fathers who raised them—the findings were denounced in some quarters, and met with disbelief in others. But other research has served to confirm the thrust of this finding. Although our tendency has been to view crime as environmental in origin, research data suggest that our biology can also create challenges and predispositions that can, in some circumstances, outweigh environmental influences. Again, while biology may not determine criminality, we are learning that it is not as unimportant as was once thought. Just as intellectual and athletic abilities are widely acknowledged to have a genetic backdrop, we are now accepting that difficult personalities can also have a biological origin (Raine, 2013).

We have also begun to accept that acquired trauma can have a significant impact on predispositions to crime. Frontal lobe damage, for example, has now been clearly linked to an increase in the likelihood of impulsively aggressive behaviour (Brower & Price, 2001). And the prevalence of brain injuries in prison populations has been very clearly identified as both disproportionate to the general population and a significant risk factor for reoffending (Raine, 2013).

In studying the criminal pathways to crime, criminologists have come to appreciate the complex mix of biological predisposition and environmental influences, permitting a more nuanced analysis of the genesis of crime. We now tend to consider that the onset of crime is influenced by the interaction of biological risks and a dysfunctional environment, often characterized by physical and emotional abuse and neglect.

empirical
That which is understood or verified through experiment, measurement, or direct observation; as opposed to *theoretical*.

Further, study of the criminal has also allowed us the opportunity to understand that often little **empirical** support exists for some of our populist conceptions. Just as during the 1960s and 1970s we came to reject the simplicity of Lombroso's criminal man and

Sheldon's somatotyping, we have more recently come to realize that adult male sex offenders are not specialists in that particular kind of crime; that is, they are not men who predominantly commit a relatively narrow range of predatory sex offences.

Sex offenders are a much more diverse population, and their crimes encompass a range of offences, from incest and inappropriate touching to predatory attacks on strangers; violent predatory attacks on strangers are actually very rare events (Bonnar-Kidd, 2010; Bonnycastle, 2012). Sex offenders (with the notable exception of pedophiles) also tend not to specialize in this kind of crime; they are more accurately classified as antisocial deviants who commit a range of crimes, some of which happen to be sex offences (Lussier, Tzoumakis, Cale, & Amirault, 2010). We have also learned that most sex offenders have relatively low rates of reoffending, again contrary to populist conceptions (Hanson & Bussière, 1998). These findings raise important questions, for example, about the empirical logic of a sex offender registry. Why, we might ask, do we have a sex offender registry that includes such a varied range of offenders, particularly when the rates of reoffending for most of these kinds of crime are actually much lower than other crimes?

It is clear, then, that much can be learned through the study of offenders, sometimes leading to findings that conflict with popular misconceptions and societal biases. And although those who study the individual offender are often criticized for failing to take account of social conditions and thereby inadvertently demonizing and **stigmatizing** offenders, it can also be argued that this kind of research can serve to create a better understanding of the difficulties that offenders face, and the challenges that we have, correspondingly, in responding appropriately and humanely to their circumstances. Studies focused on offenders can also help us understand when young men and women are at risk of involvement in crime; this understanding may lead us to find ways to prevent the harms that these individuals are likely to impose on others, and on themselves.

stigmatize
To strongly disapprove of a person or behaviour; to find disgraceful.

Technologies of Crime Control: Criminology's Contributions to Crime Prevention

The study of criminology has also produced innovative and potentially valuable technologies for the control of crime. A rich academic literature has developed within this realm, documenting the techniques as well as their costs, benefits, and potential limitations.

Crime prevention through environmental design (CPTED, examined in Chapter 13, Violent Crime) is a term that originated with the late criminologist C. Ray Jeffery (Jeffery, 1971). It is essentially a multi-disciplinary approach, and almost all of its **interventions** apply to an urban environment, using, among other initiatives, landscape and lighting design to increase natural surveillance. CPTED seeks to manage crime by decreasing the opportunity and an individual's motivation for committing crime, and by increasing the risk to the offender if the crime is committed. A considerable body of empirical evidence demonstrates the utility of this approach (Casteel & Peek-Asa, 2000; Cozens, Saville, & Hillier, 2005; Felson, 1987). Further, many criminology programs now offer courses focused on the practicalities of this approach and encourage students to use it to both investigate and solve specific problems faced by local communities (Brantingham & Brantingham, 1993). Some critics of CPTED argue, however, that environmental design can only displace crime to less-protected environments, and does not address the root causes of or motivations for criminal offences. Other critics suggest that CPTED shifts the responsibility for crime prevention away from the state and onto the individual,

interventions
Strategies intended to shape the physical environment to mitigate crime; also various programs targeting individual offenders, offering alternatives to criminal behaviour.

expecting citizens "to become prudent consumers of crime prevention advice or else face moral and/or ethical sanction for not holding up their end of the proverbial bargain" (Parnaby, 2007).

Geographic profiling is aligned with CPTED; it draws on an understanding of urban environments and the behaviours of serial predatory offenders, and it uses mathematical tools to determine the likely residence of a given offender. Developed by Kim Rossmo, a former detective with Vancouver Police Department, geographic profiling focuses the investigation of serial crimes on a relatively small geographic area, looking at the spatial patterns of such crimes and the specific hunting behaviours of the offenders (Rossmo, 1999). Although geographic profiling only considers the spatial behaviour of serial offenders, it has been successful in specific cases, and has spawned a literature that builds on the accuracy of its projections (Levine & Block, 2011).

Electronic monitoring, also known as *electronic tagging*, typically involves an offender wearing an electronic device that allows his or her location to be monitored through a control centre. Electronic monitoring permits both the pretrial release of individuals back into the community and home detention, in which a sentence is served within the community. Electronic monitoring offers significant advantages: it avoids both the cost of placing the offender in a correctional facility and the well-documented negative impacts of incarceration on the individual. The concerns raised over electronic monitoring have to do with its potential for **net widening**—imposing a form of control on individuals who might otherwise not be subject to such control—and its potential for demeaning intrusions into personal privacy. Additionally, electronic monitoring must deal with the practical issue of how to respond quickly and effectively when an offender either removes the monitor or travels outside of the permitted range.

Empirical studies on the effectiveness and consequences of electronic monitoring have revealed, however, that it is a technology that does not appear to be used to widen the net of control over offenders. Rather, it seems to be an effective public safety alternative to the use of imprisonment, reducing reoffending for the individuals placed under such surveillance (Padgett, Bales, & Blomberg, 2006).

The trial of O.J. Simpson for the 1994 murder of his wife, Nicole Brown Simpson, and her friend Ronald Goldman focused global attention on the use of DNA evidence in criminal trials. Deoxyribonucleic acid is a molecule that encodes genetic instructions in all living organisms. It is akin to a fingerprint when used to identify an individual, and, in fact, is often referred to as genetic fingerprinting. The forensic science of DNA testing has made considerable advances during the past 25 years, and is now widely used in criminal trials in order to link an accused to a crime scene and a particular victim or victims (and to exclude an accused from a crime scene). In the O.J. Simpson case, the defence team poked holes in the handling of the DNA evidence, arguing that it could have been contaminated at several different points, leading to physical evidence that was unreliable. However, although police mishandling of the evidence was problematic in many ways, the evidence still pointed to Simpson's guilt—his blood was found at the crime scene, the blood of his wife was found on his sock, and Goldman's blood was found in his car.

Although DNA evidence can be mishandled and inappropriately ignored (as in the Simpson case), it has become a very valuable tool in the detection of crimes, allowing conclusions regarding guilt that are both inculpatory and exculpatory. In Canada, both

geographic profiling
A tool that permits police officers to focus on the likely residence of offenders in cases of serial crimes.

net widening
Imposing a form of control on individuals who might otherwise not be subject to such control.

Guy Paul Morin and David Milgaard have been compensated for their wrongful convictions, largely due to the contribution of DNA evidence.

The Study of Crime: What Theories, What Methods?

As the preceding sections of this chapter demonstrate, criminologists employ a significant range of approaches to study crime—from a detailed examination of the legal history of the criminal law, to an evaluation of the effectiveness of various criminal sanctions, to geographic profiling. When one looks at the content of university courses in criminology, whether at the graduate or undergraduate level, courses on theory and methods are pre-eminent. Many other courses appear in the curricula of criminology schools and departments: policing, corrections, criminal law, sentencing, penology, juvenile delinquency, drugs and crime, white collar crime, and criminal investigations. But at the heart of the criminological enterprise are courses focused on theory and methods.

What theories guide criminology and criminologists? Some theorists, who might describe themselves as *critical criminologists*, focus on the power of the state and its potential for abuse; others, who might describe themselves as *rational choice theorists*, argue that crime occurs as a consequence of rational choices made by willing (or largely willing) actors. Still others use learning theory as a guide for their scholarly analysis. One prominent department of criminology focuses on teaching theories related to anomie, differential association, social control, social disorganization, routine activities, deterrence, and developmental approaches. A theory course in another department of criminology has a somewhat overlapping agenda: "Topics may include labeling theory, differential association, Marxist theories of crime, and moral regulation."

What methods are used by criminologists? A similar breadth exists, although most discussions of methods tend to focus on a distinction between **qualitative** and **quantitative** approaches. It is a distinction that is, at least to some extent, rooted in particular disciplines. Lawyers and sociologists are more likely to employ qualitative methods of analysis. In contrast, psychologists and economists are more likely to employ quantitative methods.

These distinctions also have some elasticity; some sociologists conduct research that is very much quantitative, relying on the analysis of large sets of data. As well, some psychologists focus on qualitative approaches to crime and criminal behaviour, interviewing offenders and their victims. The combination of quantitative and qualitative methods, also known as a *mixed methods approach*, has gained popularity during the past 20 years. Adam Trahan and Daniel Stewart (2013) argue, for example, that the current divide between quantitative and qualitative research is restricting our ability to develop a coherent understanding of crime and criminal justice, and that mixed methods—combining qualitative and quantitative approaches in a single study—provides a way out of this difficulty. (See Box 1.4, below.)

But before we embark on any discussion of the relative merits of quantitative, qualitative, and mixed methods approaches, we must think first about the nature of the questions that we ask about crime, law, offenders, and their victims. Let us suppose that we want to know whether the extent, nature, and character of homicide have changed in Canada over a 50-year span—between 1964 and 2014. Statistics Canada can provide us with a substantial amount of quantitative data from police-generated forms, filled out after a homicide has been uncovered. We can document changing rates, any changes

qualitative
The study of phenomena based not on measurement but an exploration of the reasons for human behaviour and the qualities of subjective experience.

quantitative
Relating to the measurement of something—its quantity—rather than its qualities.

BOX 1.4

Qualitative and Quantitative Approaches to Studying Crime

The study of crime has been dominated by quantitative analyses of crime. Richard Tewksbury (2009) notes that only 10 to 15 percent of all articles published in peer-refereed criminological journals use qualitative methods. He goes on to make the bold claim that this is lamentable, as qualitative methods—interviews, field observations, and participant involvement—have superior value in "the creation of criminological and criminal justice knowledge" (p. 38). We do not have to agree with Tewksbury's claim, however, to see the value of both approaches, sometimes used in isolation of one another, and most profitably used in combination.

Both quantitative and qualitative methods have their limitations. With quantitative methods, the often justifiable fear is that the methods will dominate the inquiry—that increasingly sophisticated statistical manipulations of data may add little to our understanding of a particular phenomenon. Put differently, the questions we ask are at the heart of the criminological enterprise, and the responses we receive from quantitative study inevitably point to correlations, not cause–effect relationships. For example, even Mednick et al.'s (1984) startling finding that adopted male children are more likely to commit crime if their biological fathers (rather than their adopted fathers) had criminal records, is not without its limita-

tions. We do not really know what specific behaviours or attributes have been inherited, and what impact these attributes might have on the development of criminality over time. The Mednick et al. (1984) data also revealed a strong genetic link with property crime, but not with violent crime. With quantitative research, the methodology employed is always open to criticism, and our abilities to explain the variations that exist between two variables are typically limited. For example, David Weisburd and Alex Piquero (2008), after examining empirical tests of criminological theory in criminology between 1968 and 2005, concluded:

> The overall level of variance explained is often very low, with 80 or 90 per cent unexplained. There has been no improvement over time … Criminologists will need to pay much more attention to what is not explained in criminological modeling if they are to make significant advances in understanding crime. (p. 453)

What sorts of things do you believe qualitative research can tell us about crime and criminal behaviour that quantitative methods might not? Conversely, what would quantitatively-oriented criminologists cite as the shortcomings of research that is too reliant on qualitative approaches?

over time in the methods used to commit such crime, the gender and age of victims and suspects, provincial and municipal differences in prevalence, and potentially changing motivations for these killings.

A significant part of the answer to our questions depends, then, on the use of quantitative methods—engaging in a systematic empirically-based inquiry, using numerical data, and depending on mathematical, statistical, or computational techniques. But our questions could also benefit from qualitative research; for example, interviews with police officers who investigated homicides during this time span, and interviews with individuals convicted of homicides during this time span. These interviews could add much detailed and rich information about the potentially changing nature of homicide, complementing the rigour of quantitative analysis.

While the insights obtained from qualitative data may be useful contributions to building knowledge within a given field, they cannot be assumed to apply to a much larger group of individuals. In part, this is because the techniques—field observations or semi-structured interviews—are more subjective and more likely to be affected by the differing approaches and potential biases and inclinations of individual interviewers. Another factor that contributes to a lack of reliability with qualitative data is the typically small number of participants (or number of data points). The irony is this: the value of qualitative data usually increases as its similarities to quantitative data increase. For example, if one researcher conducts four interviews with consumers of crystal meth regarding the origins of their use of the drug, current patterns of consumption, reasons for using, and their hopes for the future, the results may be somewhat useful, perhaps even illuminating. But if 10 different researchers each conducted 20 interviews of a similar kind in 10 Canadian provinces, the findings would have much more relevance and utility. One might argue that this is the Achilles heel of qualitative research. In order to achieve greater legitimacy and respect within the discipline of criminology, it must begin to more closely resemble its older and more established cousin, quantitative research.

Conclusion: Toward an Inclusive Criminology

Rob Gordon, the former director of the School of Criminology at Simon Fraser University, has always been fond of referring to his "big tent" approach to criminological research, teaching, and practice. He means, through the image of a big tent, to say that all credible approaches are welcome in this area of study, including CPTED; critical analysis of the history of laws, the practices of enforcement, and sentencing rationales; and psychological research on how and why individuals commit crimes, and what can be done to decrease the likelihood of reoffending. The field of criminology can comfortably house subjects as diverse as improving our understanding of the behavioural patterns of serial sex offenders; documenting and explaining the resilience of illegal markets; understanding what drives the spatial and temporal distribution of crime in urban neigbourhoods; and using forensic entomology to determine time of death in homicide investigations.

As you read through the chapters in this book, we hope you will find work that encourages you to look at crime and criminology through many different lenses. This is the challenge that criminology offers: a problem in search of multiple solutions, with many avenues of approach available.

SUMMARY OF KEY POINTS

- Although crime has been a part of societies throughout history, the serious scientific and academic study of crime is a relatively recent development.
- Criminology has typically been a very interdisciplinary field of study, drawing on disciplines as diverse as law, sociology, psychology, geography, political science, economics, gender studies, and more.
- All societies define some behaviours as deviant, and some of these deviant behaviours become subject to criminalization by the state. These definitions of deviance and crime can differ markedly across societies, but can also be quite malleable. Consider, for example, recent changes in public attitudes and legal responses relating to marijuana and homosexuality in North America, in only the last decade.
- Criminology can play a valuable role in determining how society copes with many new 21st-century challenges, including those relating to the current revolution in communications technologies.

■ The findings of criminologists often provide information that serves to correct popular misconceptions or societal biases about the nature of crime and criminals.

■ There are two categories of methods—qualitative and quantitative—that are used to study crime, each with its own advantages and disadvantages, depending on the context or goal of the research. Many criminologists now see a fusion of quantitative and qualitative methods as a particularly compelling approach to the study of crime.

QUESTIONS FOR CRITICAL DISCUSSION

1. Can you imagine a time in which criminology will be regarded as an entirely distinct discipline, such as psychology, law, or sociology?
2. Given that most data gathered by criminologists are correlational, how much explanatory power does criminological research actually have? Does the use of correlational data represent a serious limitation for the field?
3. What do you think are the main reasons for the increase in crime rates in Canada from the late 1960s to the early 1970s? And, correspondingly, what do you think are the main reasons for the decrease in crime rates in Canada over the past 20 years?

SUGGESTED FURTHER READINGS

Canadian Journal of Criminology and Criminal Justice: https://www.ccja-acjp.ca/en/cjc.html

Criminology (journal): http://onlinelibrary.wiley.com/journal/10.1111/(ISSN)1745-9125

Journal of Law and Society: http://onlinelibrary.wiley.com/journal/10.1111/(ISSN)1467-6478

Journal of Research in Crime and Delinquency: http://jrc.sagepub.com

The Yale Law Journal: http://www.yalelawjournal.org

Websites

The American Society of Criminology: http://www.asc41.com

REFERENCES

Blumstein, A., & Wallman, J. (Eds.). (2000). *The crime drop in America*. New York: Cambridge University Press.

Bonnar-Kidd, K. (2010). Sexual offender laws and the prevention of sexual violence or recidivism. *American Journal of Public Health*, *100*(3), 412–419.

Bonnycastle, K. (2012). *Stranger rape: Rapists, masculinity and penal governance*. Toronto: University of Toronto Press.

Boyd, N. (1988). *The last dance: Murder in Canada*. Toronto: Prentice-Hall.

Brantingham, P.J., & Brantingham, P.L. (1984). *Patterns in crime*. New York: Macmillan.

Brantingham, P.L., & Brantingham, P.J. (1993). Environment, routine and situation: Toward a pattern theory of crime. *Advances in Criminological Theory*, *5*, 259–294.

Brower, M.C., & Price, B.H. (2001). Neuropsychiatry of frontal lobe dysfunction in violent and criminal behaviour: A critical review. *Journal of Neurology, Neurosurgery and Psychiatry*, *71*, 720–726.

Casteel, C., & Peek-Asa, C. (2000). Effectiveness of crime prevention through environmental design in reducing robberies. *American Journal of Preventive Medicine, 18*, 99–115.

Cozens, P., Saville, G., & Hillier, D. (2005). Crime prevention through environmental design: A review and modern bibliography. *Journal of Property Management, 23*(5), 328–356.

Farrell, G., Tilley, N., Tseloni, A., & Mailley, J. (2011). The crime drop and the security hypothesis. *Journal of Research in Crime and Delinquency, 48*(2), 147–175.

Felson, M. (1987). Routine activities and crime prevention in the developing metropolis. *Criminology, 25*, 911–931.

Fox, J.A. (2000). Demographics and U.S. homicide: Trends by age, sex and race for 1976–1998 and beyond. In A. Blumstein & J. Wallman (Eds.), *The crime drop in America* (pp. 288–318). New York: Cambridge University Press.

Hanson, R.K., & Bussière, M.T. (1998). Predicting relapse: A meta-analysis of sexual offender recidivism studies. *Journal of Consulting and Clinical Psychology, 66*(2), 348–362.

Jeffery, C.R. (1971). *Crime prevention through environmental design*. Beverly Hills, CA: Sage.

Kriven, S., & Ziersch, E. (2007). New car security and shifting vehicle theft patterns in Australia. *Security Journal, 20*(2), 111–122.

Laub, J.H. (2004). The life course of criminology in the United States: The American Society of Criminology 2003 Presidential Address. *Criminology, 42*(1), 1–26.

Levine, N., & Block, R. (2011). Bayesian journey-to-crime estimation: An improvement in geographic profiling methodology. *The Professional Geographer, 63*(2), 213–229.

Lussier, P., Tzoumakis, S., Cale, J., & Amirault, J. (2010). Criminal trajectories of adult sex offenders and the age effect: Examining the dynamic aspect of offending in adulthood. *International Criminal Justice Review, 20*(2): 147–168.

Marvell, T., & Moody, C. (1991). Age structure and crime rates: The conflicting evidence. *Journal of Quantitative Criminology, 7*, 237–273.

Mednick, S.A., Gabrielli, W.F., Jr., & Hutchings, B. (1984). Genetic influences in criminal convictions: Evidence from an adoption cohort. *Science, 224*(4651), 891–894.

Moffitt, T.E. (1993). Adolescence-limited and life-course-persistent antisocial behavior: A developmental taxonomy. *Psychological Review, 100*, 674–701.

Padgett, K., Bales, W., & Blomberg, T. (2006). Under surveillance: An empirical test of the effectiveness and consequences of electronic monitoring. *Criminology and Public Policy, 5*(1), 61–91.

Parkinson, G. (2008). Recovering the early history of Canadian criminology: Criminology at the University of British Columbia, 1951–1959. *Canadian Journal of Criminology and Criminal Justice, 50*(5), 589–620.

Parnaby, P. (2007). Crime prevention through environmental design: Financial hardship, the dynamics of power, and the prospects of governance. *Crime, Law and Social Change, 48*(1), 73–85.

Pinker, S. (2011). *The better angels of our nature: Why violence has declined*. New York: Viking.

Rafter, N. (2009). *The origins of criminology: A reader*. London, UK: Taylor and Francis.

Raine, A. (2013). *The anatomy of violence: The biological roots of crime*. New York: Pantheon.

Rossmo, D.K. (1999). *Geographic profiling*. Boca Raton, FL: CRC Press.

Statistics Canada. (2012). Adult criminal court statistics in Canada, 2010/2011. *Juristat* (Catalogue no. 85-002-X). Ottawa: Statistics Canada, Canadian Centre for Justice Statistics. Retrieved from http://www.statcan.gc.ca/pub/85-002-x/2012001/article/11646-eng.htm.

Statistics Canada. (2013). *The General Social Survey: An overview*. Ottawa: Statistics Canada.

Taylor, I., Walton, P., & Young, J. (1973). *The new criminology: For a social theory of deviance*. London, UK: Routledge.

Tewksbury, R. (2009). Qualitative versus quantitative methods: Understanding why qualitative methods are superior for criminology and criminal justice. *Journal of Theoretical and Philosophical Criminology, 1*(1), 38–58.

Trahan, A., & Stewart, D. (2013). Toward a pragmatic framework for mixed-methods research in criminal justice and criminology. *Applied Psychology in Criminal Justice, 9*(1), 59–74.

United Nations Office on Drugs and Crime. (2013, February). Comprehensive study on cybercrime. Retrieved from http://www.unodc.org/documents/commissions/CCPCJ _session22/13-80699_Ebook_2013_study_CRP5.pdf

Weisburd, D., & Piquero, A. (2008). How well do criminologists explain crime? Statistical modeling in published studies. *Crime and Justice: A Review of Research, 37*, 453–502.

Zimring, F. (2006). *The great American crime decline*. New York: Oxford University Press.

Spin, "Skunk," and Moral Panic

In October 2007, the *London Evening Standard* newspaper ran a story titled, "Deadly Skunk Floods City." Written by the newspaper's home affairs editor, Martin Bentham, the article began as follows:

> Dramatic new evidence of the dangers of cannabis emerged today as government scientists warned that the most harmful "skunk" variety is flooding our streets.

The article noted that "skunk" cannabis (i.e., strains of the plant that typically have higher concentrations of the psychoactive ingredient tetrahydrocannabinol, or THC) accounted for 75 percent of the cannabis seized by the police. Bentham then added:

> The powerful drug can cause mental illness, say medical experts, and has led to a number of killings by addicts. Prime Minister Gordon Brown has already announced a review of the drug's status.

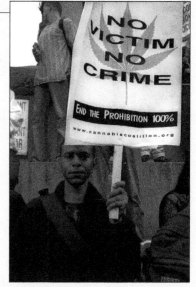

Londoners taking part in a march calling for the legalization of cannabis.
Source: Alamy.

And indeed, in early 2008, the British Labour government of Gordon Brown reclassified cannabis as a more problematic "class B" drug, despite objections from its own Advisory Council on the Misuse of Drugs.

Ironically, shortly afterward in a 2009 editorial, the very same *London Evening Standard* lamented the "moral panic" that had preceded this change in legislation:

> [T]he Government reclassified cannabis as class B ... not because of the science but largely thanks to a media hue and cry over the alleged dangers posed by strong "skunk" cannabis. If that is to be the basis of policy, it is hard to see what the point of the Advisory Council on the Misuse of Drugs is any more. The bigger worry is what this suggests about ministers' attitudes to science and to spin. ("Spin and Drugs," 2009)

And so the same media outlet that had, in the first place, helped create the moral panic over skunk cannabis flooding the streets of London was now suggesting that science and not political "spin" should be the basis for government policy.

Had the best available science been consulted in October 2007, it would have revealed that domestic production of skunk cannabis had been going on in the United Kingdom for over ten years and that monitoring of the THC levels in cannabis, in both Europe and the United Kingdom, revealed no dramatic changes with respect to the strength of cannabis over the previous decade or more. In truth, skunk was hardly a new phenomenon; it had remained widely available since it appeared in the 1970s. Perhaps just as important for the public debate on this issue, there was good evidence from a number of surveys that cannabis use was actually declining within the general population of the United Kingdom.

The claim that skunk cannabis can cause mental illness was similarly distorted, as was the suggestion that the potency of the drug had led to a number of killings by addicts. One of the most authoritative texts on the subject of cannabis concludes, on the issue of its effect on health, that "the public health impact of contemporary patterns of cannabis use are modest by comparison with those of other illicit drugs (such as the opioids) or with alcohol" (Room et al., 2008, p. 56). Similarly, that text offers no empirical support for the claim that cannabis consumption can lead users to commit violent crime; such conduct is inconsistent with both the known social and pharmacological impacts of the drug. At the same time, alcohol—which is of course legal, and much more socially acceptable—is rarely the subject of this type of false information campaign or public outcry, despite a strong correlation between its consumption and violent crime.

The work of criminologists Jock Young (1971) and Stanley Cohen (1972/1980) is highly relevant to the episode described above. They were instrumental in introducing and explaining the concept of *moral panics*: responses to conditions or circumstances thought to represent a threat to established interests. These panics are brought on by allegations that the behaviours of certain groups will jeopardize the values and the principles of a given social order. In this case, the claim that cannabis addicts could kill and that vulnerable young people could suffer from mental illness due to cannabis served to provoke widespread public fear and anxiety.

As the power and reach of the mass media have grown over the last century, so too have the media's abilities to influence public perceptions of criminal activity in cases such as this.

Before You Read Chapter 2

- Who served to gain from the misleading characterizations of cannabis described in this case? In what ways did they benefit?
- What is the purpose of this kind of media coverage? Why might a media organization report such flawed information, as was seen in this case study?
- Can you think of similar cases in which the media played a major role in influencing public opinion on a controversial issue? Do you think the media often tries to deliberately promote a certain agenda? Or are they simply "reporting the facts" as they understand them?
- What role *should* the media play in describing, reporting, or commenting on crime and the criminal justice system?

The Media: Shaping Our Understanding of Crime

Introduction

Students often come to the study of criminology with a predefined set of attitudes, beliefs, and perceptions about crime and the criminal justice system. In many cases, those ideas have been shaped by the news stories they have read, the television shows and films they have watched, and the video games they have played. Consider the following statistics: the average child spends more than five hours a day in front of a screen, watching television or movies, or playing video games (Carnagey, Anderson, & Bartholow, 2007), and more than two-thirds of what they see on that screen involves violence (Federman, 1998). By age 18, it is estimated that the average child will have seen approximately 200,000 violent acts and 16,000 murders on television alone (Senate Committee on the Judiciary, 1999). As members of a media-rich culture, we all consume a variety of media that provide us with a continuous stream of images and stories about crime, many of them violent.

Not surprisingly, attitudes about the media's depictions of crime have changed a great deal over time. In the 1940s, Canada's parliamentarians warned that crime comics would increase psychopathology among young people. As a result, they passed a law that is technically still in force today: under section 163 of the *Criminal Code*, it is a crime to make, print, publish, distribute, or sell a crime comic. This section of the *Criminal Code* may seem amusing to us in the 21st century, but it is a useful example of how the media, the law, and public attitudes toward crime can influence one another.

This chapter explores the ways in which media images and stories can inform or affect our understanding of crime and the workings of our criminal justice system. For our purposes, *the media* includes any means of mass communication—including newspapers, magazines, radio, television, film, video games, music videos, and social media. Across these media you will find both real-world crime reporting by different types of news organizations as well as countless fictional stories centred around crime, such as police television shows, forensic television dramas, and action films. Thus, before exploring the many aspects of criminology that are examined in the chapters that follow, this chapter provides an opportunity to step back and consider the ways in which many of our attitudes and opinions are formed and the often complex relationship that exists between the media and crime.

Perspectives on Media and Crime: A Brief Overview

When social scientists first began to seriously study crime and media in the 1960s and 1970s, psychologists and sociologists sought to measure the impact of media consumption on aggression. These studies, which focus on **media effects**, suggested that children who watched a lot of violence on television, for example, were more likely to act violently toward others.

media effects
The concept that exposure to media has an effect on behaviour. For example, young people exposed to violent media will behave aggressively.

Although many social scientists have rejected the media effects approach because of methodological concerns, some criminologists have continued to be interested in the effects of exposure to media violence. For example, Matt DeLisi, Michael Vaughn, Douglas Gentile, Craig Anderson, and Jeffrey Shook (2013) have argued the following:

> The consumption of violent media is far from innocuous, and when violent media consumption in the form of video games is viewed by adults as a "reward" for youth to spend their free time, it can be problematic. Youth with pre-existing psychopathology are particularly at risk for the deleterious effects of violent video games, and much more research is needed on correctional samples of youth to ascertain the severity of violent video games and related media factors as risk factors for their behavioural problems. (p. 139)

Others, such as Ray Surette (2013), suggest that media images of crime expose viewers to anti-social behaviours and that these behaviours may be copied by youth who are already pre-disposed to violence. From this perspective, "the association between exposure to media crime and criminal behavior has been more often viewed as one of instructional sources, as crime catalysts and rudders, rather than as crime generating triggers" (p. 394).

active audiences
The concept that audiences are not passive recipients of information or meanings but are instead active in the process of creating meaning.

However, many criminologists have moved away from considering the effect of the media on crime to instead examine the cultural meaning of media violence. Much of this work is based on the cultural studies concept of **active audiences**. This concept suggests that people do not passively consume media messages, as implied in some of the media effects literature. Instead, the meaning of the messages is negotiated or constructed by an interaction between the persons who produced the image and the audiences who consume it. From this perspective, audience members do not simply *absorb* a violent image; they *make* their own meaning of it according to their own perspectives and values. This approach has led to the emergence of the subdiscipline of *cultural criminology*, which explores the links between culture, crime, and crime control in contemporary social life (Ferrell, 1999). From this perspective, news media and popular culture are *social sites* where people collectively negotiate the meaning of crime, violence, victimization, justice, and community. As much as crime generates media stories, those media stories themselves also create narratives that provide the context for our understanding of criminal events. Media narratives are therefore excellent cultural artifacts for criminologists to examine, because they provide a window into the social construction of the meaning of crime.

Criminological studies of media emphasize the need for **critical thinking** in our interactions with news and other types of media (see Box 2.1). As we will see below, media narratives of crime contribute to shaping our society; they can either help promote tolerance for and public engagement with the issues of the day, or reinforce stereotypes and limit the range of public debate. These realities suggest that we must acquire the skills to interpret and understand the many messages embedded in the media we consume and critically assess our roles as audience members.

critical thinking
The process of evaluating information, claims, or arguments through careful questioning and the application of reason.

The Case of the Columbine High School Shootings

As we begin to explore the complex ways in which audiences construct the meaning of crime, let us consider a particularly well-known case.

On April 20, 1999, Eric Harris and Dylan Klebold walked into Columbine High School in Colorado and started shooting, killing 15 people before turning their guns on themselves. Within minutes of the first shot being fired, journalists were camped outside the school and graphic images of bodies, escaping students, and a grieving community began to flood the news media. At the height of the incident, over 400 reporters, between

---

BOX 2.1

Thinking Critically About Media

In order to develop an ability to think more critically about media coverage of actual crime or fictional depictions of the criminal justice system, it is important to consider the following questions:

- Who created this media product, and what is its purpose?
- What assumptions or beliefs do its creators appear to have, as reflected in the content?
- What is the commercial purpose of this media product (in other words, how will it help someone make money)? What influence might this factor have on the content, and on how it is being communicated?
- How might different people see this media product in different ways?
- Who and what is shown in a positive light? In a negative light? Why might these people or issues be shown this way?
- Who and what is not shown at all?
- What conclusions might audiences draw about an event or an issue, based on the facts being presented in this news story or narrative?

Source: MediaSmarts (2014).

A frame from the footage taken by security cameras inside Columbine High School.

75 and 90 satellite trucks, and 60 television cameras were on the scene, including at least 20 television crews from foreign countries (Jefferson County Sherriff's Department, n.d.). The coverage was so extensive that the story was ranked the largest US news story for 1999 and the seventh-largest story of the 1990s (Muschert, 2009, p. 165).

Within days, the news coverage shifted from reporting the facts and garnering reaction, to discussing root causes of the violence. The most common explanations involved the lack of gun control and, interestingly for our purposes, the role of popular media; a number of pundits argued that Harris and Klebold's actions were a result of their interest in video games, Marilyn Manson's music, and the movie *The Matrix*. A headline from a National Public Radio online article was typical of much of the discussion: "Columbine High School Shootings and How the Internet, Video Games and Violence on TV and in the Movies May Contribute to Teen-Age Violence" (Muschert, 2009, p. 167). Popular media were not only singled out as potentially responsible for causing the Columbine shootings; Columbine itself was incorporated into a variety of popular media products. Most famously, filmmaker Michael Moore's 2002 documentary *Bowling for Columbine* examined politics and power relationships, and took issue with the argument that popular media causes crime. The film cited statistics that indicate that other countries with high video game consumption, for example, do not have elevated levels of shooting violence. The film also incorporated an interview with rocker Marilyn Manson, who defended himself against the accusation that his music was central to Harris's and Klebold's motivations. In an interesting twist, Manson pointed the finger instead to a different kind of medium: advertising containing fear-based messages.

Other media creators appropriated images of the shooting for their own purposes. For example, the closed-captioned video coverage of Harris and Klebold in the school cafeteria, which was posted to the Internet shortly after the shooting, is featured in the highly controversial video game *Super Columbine Massacre RPG!* In the game, players re-enact Harris and Klebold's attack, proceeding through the school to kill students with names like "Preppy Girl" and "Jock Type." Danny Ledonne, who created the game in 2005, maintains that he did so to help explore his own experience with bullying as a teen, to explore the shooters' motivations, and to provide a social critique of the news media's sensationalization of the massacre. Many people attacked Ledonne for being insensitive to the victims' families and seeking to profit from the tragedy. However, the game does underline the power of media images, and it draws attention to the negotiation that occurs between producers and audiences about what, exactly, these media representations of violence mean.

In perhaps the most interesting example of the complex interplay between crime and media, it was discovered that Harris and Klebold had made videos of themselves before the shootings in which they reflect on how famous they will become, and wonder if

Steven Spielberg or Quentin Tarantino will direct the film that will tell their story. Klebold concluded:

> Directors will be fighting over this story. I know we're gonna have followers because we're so f…ing God-like. We're not exactly human—we have human bodies but we've evolved into one step above you, f…ing human shit. We actually have f…ing self-awareness. (Jefferson County Sheriff's Office, n.d.)

The Columbine incident is an excellent illustration of how media stories about crimes shape our understanding of those crimes, and how our understanding of crime shapes the kinds of media stories we produce. In this sense, media and crime are mutually constituted—each works to shape the other. For example, the real-world crimes committed during the Columbine shootings generated a great deal of news coverage, and that news coverage shaped our attitudes—and arguably our policies—relating to similar real-world incidents for years to come (Muschert, Henry, Bracy, & Peguero, 2014). The shooters themselves sought to impact others' perceptions of the real-world incident by creating a media record of their thoughts before the rampage began and anticipated that they would continue to "live on" in other media after the incident. In this sense, their media story shaped the way we saw the real-world incident. And others, like Danny Ledonne, created different media narratives around the incident to tell different stories. All of these narratives continue to compete for the attention of media audiences, who interpret them in a variety of ways for their own purposes. And, as we shall see below, these media narratives have also determined which issues would be widely discussed and which ones would not.

Media, Crime, and the Problem Frame

A brief perusal of a local newspaper or television news program demonstrates that crime is central to the production of Canadian news media. Clearly, journalists consider crime to be newsworthy and often focus on it to the exclusion of other kinds of stories. At the same time, crime is also a central component of entertainment; it grips the collective imagination of television viewers, theatregoers, Internet browsers, and readers of true-crime books as few other topics can (Dowler, Fleming, & Muzzatti, 2006, p. 837).

David Altheide (1997) suggested that violence is treated in this way because both news organizations and popular media producers are primarily focused on entertainment and are, accordingly, looking for clear, unambiguous stories. Ideally, these stories will garner immediate attention yet be easily resolved at some time in the future. He argues that media stories about crime are therefore cast through a **problem frame** because such a frame helps generate a narrative that is easily understood and likely to sell. The problem frame focuses on the existence of something extraordinary and "bad" that affects many people. An ideal story concerns a crime that is unambiguously bad and calls out for a solution that can be pointed to in some point in the future when an organization (usually the government, the police, or some other arm of the state) responsible for fixing the problem will do so.

Applying the problem frame to the Columbine incident, media stories focused on the exceptional nature of school shootings (the extraordinary and easily identifiable bad thing) and the horror it generated in the community, the nation, and beyond (affecting many people). An immediate response was required to fix the problem of school

problem frame
A narrative that is easily understood because it focuses on the existence of something extraordinary and "bad" that affects many people, and identifies unambiguous solutions that can be implemented in the future.

shootings, and an attempt was made to identify an unambiguous and easily resolved cause, such as violent video games. The government "solved" the problem by holding a series of consultations on youth consumption of violent media and enacting legislation requiring rating labels and content warnings for media content.

This type of morality play provides a simplistic version of events that complies with the need to quickly and easily identify and punish the bad person responsible for the crime. But it also serves to create boundaries around the event, determining what can and cannot be discussed. The Columbine incident, for example, generated a great deal of discussion about young people's consumption of violent media, but broader questions about mental health and the need for better services for young people in crisis were not a significant part of the debate.[1]

In a similar vein, any attempts by the media to focus attention on lax gun laws in the immediate aftermath of a mass shooting (of which there have been many in the United States in recent decades) are quickly criticized by various quarters—notably by powerful interest groups such as the National Rifle Association and other media outlets—for attempts to "politicize a tragedy." The result is a now-familiar pattern in which news stories focus on the grieving families or the issue of violent popular culture but tend to avoid any serious, prolonged debate about gun laws and access to guns.

A story such as the Columbine incident—which focuses on sensational and unusual events that are horrifying and likely to evoke a strong emotional reaction—may sell media stories, but it also links crime storytelling to fear, which in turn distorts our understanding of crime and deviance. Dowler, Fleming, and Muzzatti (2006) write:

> The selective nature of crime news, for example, with its emphasis on violence and sensationalism—essentially crime as a product, playing to the fears, both imagined and real, of viewers and readers—has produced a distorted picture of the world of crime and criminality. (p. 839)

Moral Panics

A distorted picture of crime and criminality can have real policy consequences. In their classic analysis of the relationship between the media and the criminal justice system, *Policing the Crisis: Mugging, the State and Law and Order*, Stuart Hall, Chas Critcher, Tony Jefferson, John Clarke, and Brian Roberts (1978) demonstrated how media stories about a new "crime wave" of muggings in London in the 1970s encouraged politicians to devote more police resources to catching the perpetrators, which led to more arrests and more convictions. Judges then quoted the news stories to justify higher sentences for offenders. After a period of time, the politicians reported that the problem was solved, so fewer resources were devoted to catching muggers, and the number of arrests dropped. However, the actual number of robberies did not change throughout the entire "war on mugging."

moral panic
Occurs when there is a gap between people's perceptions of a problem and the "fact" of the problem, and the difference can be explained ideologically (Hall et al., 1978).

Hall et al. (1978) cited Stanley Cohen's notion of **moral panic**—when a "condition, episode, person or group of persons emerges to become defined as a threat to societal values and interests" (Cohen, 1972/1980, p. 9)—to explain how the belief that a particular crime is on the rise justifies a change in activities (such as devoting more police resources to arresting perpetrators) that in turn makes it look like the crime is on the rise even when it is not. They concluded that the "rising crime rate equation" plays a conservative ideological role in maintaining the status quo by creating public support for more policing to bring the "crisis" back under control. This dynamic underlines how the narratives around crime have real consequences; they shape our understanding of who should be protected, who should protect them, and whom they should be protected from.

BOX 2.2

Cohen on Social Problems and Moral Panics

Stanley Cohen explored the relationship between the media and moral panics in his 1972 book *Folk Devils and Moral Panics: The Creation of the Mods and Rockers*. A year later, Stanley Cohen and Jock Young published *The Manufacture of News: Social Problems, Deviance, and the Mass Media*. These books, along with the 1973 book *The New Criminology: For a Social Theory of Deviance* by Ian R. Taylor, Paul Walton, and Jock Young, as well as Stuart Hall's 1978 book *Policing the Crisis: Mugging, the State and Law and Order* are considered landmark works in the field of critical criminology (a topic explored in detail in Chapter 9). The evolution of cultural criminology—and indeed, studies on the relationship between the media and crime—can be traced back to these writings of the 1970s.

In *Folk Devils and Moral Panics*, Cohen (1972/1980) drew on Edwin Lemert's 1951 book *Social Pathology*, in which Lemert discussed primary and secondary deviance. According to Lemert, *primary deviance* occurs when an individual (or group) engages in disapproved behaviour, without seeing that behaviour as necessarily "deviant" or "criminal." *Secondary deviance*, on the other hand, results from the social reaction to primary deviance. In other words, individuals may come to view themselves as "deviant" or "criminal" because they are subjected to stigmatization and social control. Cohen also drew upon Howard Becker's 1963 book *Outsiders: Studies in the Sociology of Deviance*. Becker, the most well known of the labelling theorists (discussed in Chapter 12), pinpointed the role of **moral entrepreneurs** (or "moral crusaders") in the social construction of deviance. Moral entrepreneurs are members of society who have wealth, power, and political clout, not to mention sufficient time and energy to pursue their moral crusades. Becker argued that unless a certain type of behaviour was deemed to be deviant or criminal by these moral entrepreneurs, and

as a consequence became the target of rule making and rule enforcement, then that behaviour would likely be tolerated by society or, if not, then at least ignored.

Cohen (1972/1980) identified the mass media as a crucial factor in stirring up moral panics. He said that when there is no news to report, the media engage in their own moral crusading or moral entrepreneurship, acting "as agents of moral indignation." The media, according to Cohen, actively search for social "problems" to sensationalize and individuals or groups to demonize. More often than not, the media single out youth culture—hippies, skinheads, punks—and present them as the next big threat to the social order.

The Mods and Rockers of 1960s Britain were not new, but as Cohen (1972/1980) says, they were presented as "new" by the media in order to justify their inclusion in news reports. Despite the sudden attention brought to bear on their activities by the media in the mid-1960s, these two loosely organized youth groups had been in existence for years. The Mods and Rockers dressed differently, listened to different kinds of music, and occasionally clashed in "rumbles" in seaside resort towns. The British media exaggerated and distorted the seriousness of these occasional clashes, referring to the Mods and Rockers as screaming mobs and describing their activities as "orgies of destruction." In reality, the so-called troublemakers were often outnumbered by the crowds, who turned out in the hope of seeing some action on an otherwise boring long weekend. Nobody was killed, few incidents of serious violence occurred, and relatively little property damage took place. As is the case with most moral panics, the concern about the Mods and Rockers lost momentum and quickly faded from the public imagination.

---

moral entrepreneur

A person, group, or organization that takes the lead in identifying certain behaviour as deviant and in need of legal sanctions.

The "Bad Guys"

Hall et al. (1978) also argued that crime news reflects society's shared values, linking the ideological role of the "rising crime rate equation" in 1970s London to rising racial tensions between the police and London's black community. Media-driven moral panics were used to strengthen public and political support for increased policing. Increased arrests and convictions were then used to restrict the freedom of the supposed criminals (the **folk devils** referred to by Cohen, 1972/1980) at the heart of these moral panics: black Londoners accused of mugging.

folk devils
Originating in images from folklore, this term refers to people or groups presented in media as deviant outsiders and the cause of social problems.

Media Depictions of Race and Gender

In news and entertainment media today, stories about crime often continue to reflect these deep-seated social tensions. Rodanthi Tzanelli, Majid Yar, and Martin O'Brien (2005) wrote that crime stories "as a whole can be seen to make use of, exemplify and give voice to wider assumptions, concerns and anxieties about social life, social disorder and social change" (p. 98). These assumptions, concerns, and anxieties are brought to the forefront when we consider how certain types of offenders are **stereotyped** in media representations.

stereotyping
The simplistic and often belittling representation of a person or group, using exaggerations of traits that the larger group supposedly possesses.

In popular media portrayals, people of colour are commonly represented in derogatory and unflattering ways (Dickerman, Christensen, Beatriz, & McClain, 2008). Racialized populations are often portrayed as criminal: in news media, the subjects of stories about crime are between three and four times more likely to be black than white (Coogan, 2012).

The field of sports media offers some examples of this difference in media coverage. In recent years, two NFL quarterbacks have been accused of violent criminal activity. Michael Vick was charged in 2007 with operating an illegal interstate dog-fighting ring; Ben Roethlisberger was accused of two counts of sexual assault in 2009 and 2010. Vick and Roethlisberger are both top-tier players, but one important distinction between the two men is their race: Vick is African American; Roethlisberger is Caucasian. In news coverage on ABC, CBS, and Fox News, far more coverage was dedicated to Vick's case than Roethlisberger's (in fact, Fox News ignored Roethlisberger's case entirely). News stories emphasized that Vick's case reflected a subculture of violence more than Roethlisberger's. Characterizations of Vick were visceral and dehumanizing, using words like "barbaric" and "evil." Meanwhile, characterizations of Roethlisberger were sympathetic and understanding. As one commentator pointed out, "Certainly the media have convicted Vick" (Coogan, 2012, p. 142).

While there is no doubt that white youth, such as the Mods and Rockers and Columbine shooters, can sometimes be the source of moral panic, it is more common for racialized offenders (particularly black offenders) to be portrayed as violent, aggressive "thugs and toughs" (Carter, 1988, p. 420). As Coogan (2012) writes, "In influencing perceptions and attitudes, race represents a salient factor for viewers" (p. 129). Coogan also argues that the overwhelming media portrayal of blacks as perpetrators of crime can have real social consequences, resulting in viewers or readers perceiving them as more dangerous than other groups and substantiating existing racist misconceptions of blacks as dangerous or violent.

The Media Coverage of Hurricane Katrina

One of the best-known examples of moral panics occurred in the aftermath of Hurricane Katrina, which struck the southern US coast in August 2005 and left the city of

New Orleans devastated. In their examination of the hurricane's aftermath, Timothy Brezina and Herbert E. Phipps (2010) drew on Cohen's (1972/1980) work on "folk devils and moral panics" (see Box 2.2) and Erich Goode and Nachman Ben-Yehuda's formula for evaluating moral panics (see Box 2.3) to demonstrate how the interactions between news reporters, politicians, and public officials created a media story that greatly exaggerated the urban chaos and violent crime that took place in New Orleans. Brezina and Phipps stated that this exaggeration was due to false statements from the police and public officials who were caught off guard by the extent of the damage caused by the hurricane (and the federal government's inaction in the face of the crisis has had a lasting negative effect on the reputation of then President George W. Bush). Authorities in New Orleans responded by feeding misinformation to the media, who in turn fed gruesome tales to the public, no doubt certain that they would attract huge audiences. The result was that powerless, low-status hurricane refugees had the blame shifted to them as they became cast as the "villains" by police, politicians, and media.

As the hurricane survivors congregated in their urgent search for safety and shelter, the media painted a picture of a city (including the Superdome, a football stadium *cum* shelter) rife with lawlessness and rampant murder. However, much of the crime reported in the media, including the alleged rape of babies, did not in fact occur (Brezina & Phipps, 2010, p. 100).

The media's distortion of events can be explained by several factors, including breakdowns in communication, class and racial stereotyping, and narratives that had been established, such as "civil unrest" and "urban warfare." Kathleen Tierney, Christine Bevc, and Erica Kuligowski (2006) examined the role that such narratives and "disaster myths" played in the news coverage following Hurricane Katrina:

> These reports (of rampant murder) were later found to be groundless, but they were accepted as accurate by both media organizations and consumers of news because they were consistent with the emerging, myth-inspired media narrative that characterized New Orleans as a "snake pit of anarchy," a violent place where armed gangs of black men took advantage of the disaster, not only to loot, but also to commit capital crimes. (p. 68)

Other Stereotypes

Muslim persons accused of crimes have also frequently been the subjects of discriminatory media representations, especially in the years after the September 11, 2001 attacks. Muslims are commonly constructed in various popular media as terrorists, jihadists, and sexual deviants (Puar & Rai, 2002). These constructions help incite or perpetuate deep-seated Islamophobia. They also help justify more punitive action against Muslim offenders in the name of anti-terrorism and the preservation of Western sensibilities. Consider the 2010 incident in which a small plane was flown into a government building in Austin, Texas. Initial reports speculated that this event was another case of terrorism. However, when it was revealed that the pilot was a white man with a grievance against the tax policies of the US government, the narrative of a "terror attack" quickly disappeared. This was perhaps surprising, given that the incident so clearly replicated the airplane attacks of September 11 on the World Trade Center and the Pentagon—acts that are now considered synonymous with "terrorism."

Media **discourses** also commonly represent youth and young offenders as "dangerous others" who are prone to violence and crime and do not consider the consequences

discourses
Refers to forms of language, representation, and practices and how meaning is created and shared. Discourses take place within specific cultural and historical contexts.

BOX 2.3

Goode and Ben-Yehuda on Moral Panics and Social Construction

Erich Goode and Nachman Ben-Yehuda (1994) set out criteria to distinguish between legitimate social problems worthy of public concern and moral panics stirred up by moral entrepreneurs and the media. According to Goode and Ben-Yehuda, a moral panic is characterized by the following five features (which usually appear sequentially):

1. *Concern.* A "heightened level of concern" about the "problem," often fanned by media attention, action groups, or legislative initiatives.

2. *Hostility.* An "increased level of hostility" toward the targeted group, with the group's behaviour characterized as harmful or threatening to the values, beliefs, and morals of "normal" society.

3. *Consensus.* Some sort of fairly widespread "consensus" (agreement) among members of the society that the threat posed by the wrongful behaviour is real and serious.

4. *Disproportionality.* A level of concern that is disproportionate to the actual seriousness of the threat; figures may be exaggerated, and there may be little or no evidence of a real threat.

5. *Volatility.* The sudden appearance and then disappearance of the "threat" without any valid explanation for why it became such a big problem one day and was no longer a problem the next day.

Goode and Ben-Yehuda also proposed three theories to explain why moral panics emerge.

- *Grassroots theory* suggests that moral panics begin with genuine public concern about a problem (real or imagined) and that politicians and the media become involved in response to this public concern. Most proponents of the grassroots model would acknowledge that involvement of the media, action groups, and politicians is necessary in order for a moral panic to develop fully.

- *Elite-engineered theory* suggests that small, powerful groups deliberately set out to create moral panics to divert public attention away from truly serious social problems, where the solutions to those problems might negatively impact the interests of the elite groups themselves. Goode and Ben-Yehuda point to Hall et al.'s 1978 book *Policing the Crisis* as an example of the elite-engineered model, where the wealthy and powerful in British society used the media and the legislative/law-enforcement apparatus to generate public fear about a non-existent increase in muggings.

- *Interest group theory*—based on Howard Becker's (1963) work on how moral crusades are launched by moral entrepreneurs—is the most common perspective on moral panics. It suggests that interest groups such as the media, politicians, professional groups, and religious organizations may act independently rather than in consort with one another. While the moral panics generated by these interest groups may seem self-serving, the groups might genuinely believe that they are acting in the best interests of society.

Goode and Ben-Yehuda concluded that a blend of all three theories is required in order to properly understand moral panics. Concern must be present at the grassroots (public) level, but this concern requires articulation by the media, politicians, and interest groups. The elite may be able to "engineer" a moral panic, but to do so successfully, some genuine public fear must exist. Moreover, the elite need a degree of cooperation from the media, legislators, and law enforcement officials. Interest groups may be able to focus attention on a social "problem," and argue for enhanced rule making and rule enforcement. However, to create a moral panic, they need to strike a resonant chord with the public, and with the media and politicians (who ultimately respond to public opinion).

of their actions, often allegedly led astray by violent music or video games (as was suggested in the case of the Columbine shooters) (Mahari & Conner, 2003).

Female offenders are often seen as particularly worrisome and commonly described as *predatory* or *promiscuous* (Ringrose, 2006). Women, and especially marginalized women, are often harshly judged and constructed as deviant (or as offenders) for departing from stereotypical feminine ideals such as being passive, self-restrained, or pretty. Those who do depart from these ideals face an "explosion in arrest rates and incarceration of girls and women, in spite of decreases in violent crime" (Chesney-Lind & Eliason, 2006).

The stereotypes perpetuated in media representations come together to portray society in a way that constructs certain groups as the norm and acceptable, and other groups as deviant and unacceptable. As we have seen, portrayals of criminals are more likely to include social minorities, whether in terms of ethnicity, religion, gender, or age. These portrayals have the effect of preserving majority social values and constructing the **other** as inherently transgressive. As we will see below, this has real implications for how we deal with crime and victimization in Canadian society.

other
A person or group of people defined as fundamentally different, or even deviant, by the dominant culture, often through stereotyping.

The Victim

We have established that crime media tend to reflect dominant social values. As the previous section pointed out, media influence how we think about offenders. They also affect how we think about victims. Like media representations of offenders, media representations of victims revolve around deeply entrenched social stereotypes. As Dowler, Fleming, and Muzzatti (2006) write, "[T]he common statement 'If it bleeds it leads' is not entirely truthful, as it really depends on who is bleeding" (pp. 840–841).

The concept of the "ideal victim" was first suggested by Norwegian criminologist Nils Christie (1986). According to Christie, an ideal victim is "a person or a category of individuals who, when hit by crime, most readily are given the complete and legitimate status of being a victim" (p. 18). The more characteristics of an ideal victim an individual has, the more readily victim status will be conferred upon that individual.

In media portrayals, the ideal victim intersects with values surrounding race, religion, gender, age, and other social characteristics. Portrayals of victims are often strongly affected by racism, Islamophobia, ageism, ableism, homophobia, and misogyny. As a rule, victims with a minority status are constructed as less ideal than victims with a majority status. Victims characterized as deviant—whether because they engage in deviant activities or because they come from a social minority—are also constructed as "less innocent" than other victims. As Dowler, Fleming, and Muzzatti (2006) point out, "Minority crime victims receive less attention and less sympathy" (p. 840).

Race and gender are two major components of media portrayals of victims. A crime story involving a white victim or a minority offender will commonly play on racist stereotypes; meanwhile, victims of crime who are racial minorities are frequently ignored (Dowler, Fleming, & Muzzatti, 2006). Consider the amount of press coverage typically given to a crime against a white person (such as the alleged attack by black male youth on the white female "Central Park Jogger," referred to in Box 2.4), versus the murder of a young man or woman of colour in a housing project. Clearly, crimes committed *by* racial minorities receive more news coverage than crimes committed *against* them. And crimes against white victims are almost always considered to be more newsworthy than crimes against minorities.

BOX 2.4

The Ideal Victim

According to Christie (1986), an ideal victim is

1. Weak in relation to the offender: either female, sick, very old, very young, or a combination thereof
2. Going about routine, respectable, and legitimate (read as "legal") daily activities when she or he is victimized
3. Blameless for what transpired
4. Unrelated to and unacquainted with the person who committed the offence
5. In a submissive or subordinate position to the perpetrator, who can easily be described in negative terms
6. Someone with enough influence, power, or sympathy to assert "victim status" without threatening the broader political status quo

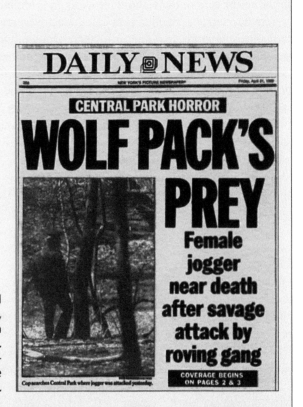

The 1989 assault and rape of the Central Park Jogger, a young white woman, caused widespread public hysteria, which was fuelled by the police and the media. Five young men—four of them African-American, one Hispanic—were wrongfully convicted in the case.

Female victims, meanwhile, are more newsworthy than male victims, provided that they can be characterized as innocent, virtuous, and honourable (Dowler, Fleming, & Muzzatti, 2006). The result is problematic and sexist media portrayals of female victims as either "innocent" or "blameworthy." "Innocent" victims are constructed as submissive and passive recipients of male violence; "blameworthy" victims are constructed as responsible for their victimization. This shift of responsibility onto the victim reduces or eliminates the responsibility of the perpetrator and portrays these victims as less deserving than victims who are "innocent." As Dowler, Fleming, and Muzzatti (2006) write, such portrayals send a message that "violence against women is devalued, while the female victim is depersonalized, objectified, and dehumanized" (p. 841).

The "Good Guys"

Media portrayals can also impact viewers' or readers' perceptions of police. Police in news media and reality television are commonly portrayed as crime-fighting, heroic, nononsense law enforcers who are hypercompetent, hard-working, and "tough on crime" (Doyle, 2003; Inciardi & Dee, 1987). As Doyle (2003) points out, crime media "offer a very particular and selective vision of policing … best seen as 'reality fiction'" (p. 34).

By portraying police as hypercompetent, depictions of police in news media and reality television can create exaggerated public expectations for real-life police performance.

At the same time, they can also conceal the darker side of policing, rarely focusing on police brutality, abuses of power, or police incompetency. A general lack of negative real-world portrayals of police can build pro-police sentiment among the public, when there is no corresponding documentation of their flaws and shortcomings. In Canada, however, a few recent high-profile portrayals of police abuse of power have also served to demonstrate that media depictions are not entirely one-sided. These include the fatal tasering of Robert Dziekański at Vancouver Airport in 2007, and the use of excessive force during mass protests at the G20 summit in Toronto in 2010.

The Effect of Social Media

As in so many other facets of modern life, technology and social media have had a profound effect on how crime is reported and interpreted. **Sousveillance** is the recording of an activity by a participant in that activity (Mann, Nolan, & Wellman, 2003). Unlike **surveillance**, which normally happens from the "top down"—where a central authority watches those "below" it, such as through the use of security cameras—sousveillance normally happens from the "bottom up." It can often be used as a way to hold those in positions of power accountable for their actions. Sousveillance can be considered a form of "watching the watchers" and is a strategy for ensuring that police do not abuse their authority.

With the explosion in use of social media tools such as Twitter, Facebook, and YouTube, sousveillance is becoming increasingly prevalent. Social media users can easily film police brutality or discrimination and publicly post it to their online accounts. In response, some American states have made it illegal to film police, even in public places.

sousveillance
The recording, by a citizen participant or witness, of an incident or activity, to hold a bureaucratic organization to account. It can be used to record incidents in which police may be seen abusing their power.

surveillance
The monitoring of individuals or populations for the purposes of control and /or care (Lyon, 2001).

In July 2013, 18-year-old Sammy Yatim was shot nine times and tasered by police while he was brandishing a knife on an empty Toronto streetcar. His death was captured by a citizen bystander and posted on social media.

Reality TV and News Media Depictions

The relationship between police and news media sources is complex. In news media, journalists can face pressures to report stories about police in a positive way since a positive relationship with police ensures access to interviews or news tips. The same constraints play out in popular media as well. In reality TV shows like *Cops*, for example, television networks give police ultimate control over what footage makes a final broadcast. Giving police editorial control is necessary to ensure that film crews continue to have access to ride-alongs, ongoing investigations, and other footage that requires police permission and cooperation. As a result, the transparency of footage that makes a final broadcast is compromised, and only footage that portrays police in a positive light makes the final cut (Doyle, 2003).

In addition to contributing to a general perception that police are hypercompetent, media portrayals can also inaccurately represent the nature of police work, misconstruing what it means to work in law enforcement. News media and reality TV (as well as fictional police dramas) "promote the idea that fighting crime is the chief function of police, as opposed to preventing crime, directing traffic, and keeping the peace" (Inciardi & Dee, 1987, p. 100). Since news media and reality TV shows function as informal recruitment and training materials for those beginning or considering careers in policing (Doyle, 2003), glamourized media portrayals of policing also have very real implications beyond general public sentiment toward police.

Courts and the CSI Effect

Since its first broadcast in 2000, *CSI: Crime Scene Investigation* and its various spinoffs (e.g., *CSI: Miami* and *CSI: New York*) have consistently been some of the top-rated dramas on American and Canadian television (Kissel, 2014). The popularity of *CSI* has inspired other forensic shows including *Bones*, *Numbers*, *NCIS*, and *Criminal Minds*. Forensic crime dramas, unlike earlier crime dramas, focus on the "howdunnit" as opposed to the "whodunnit" (Robbers, 2008), bringing forensic investigations into the mainstream.

However, shows such as *CSI* are not accurate portrayals of crime scene investigations. Police agencies are depicted as having endless resources, elaborate methods of forensic testing that seem to produce instant results, an ability (and a need) to get forensic evidence for every case, and small caseloads (Robbers, 2008). The "*CSI* effect" refers to the theory that, in the real world, "jurors hold unrealistic expectations of forensic evidence and investigation techniques, and have an increased interest in the discipline of forensic science, because of the influence of *CSI*-type television shows" (Robbers, 2008, p. 86). As a result, the Crown (or state) could have a higher burden of proof because of jurors' expectations that forensic evidence should always be discussed during a criminal trial, and jurors' beliefs that forensic evidence is infallible.

Few empirical studies have assessed the impact of a potential *CSI* effect. A recent study found no evidence of a *CSI* effect, although the researcher concluded that further research was needed (Podlas, 2006). Other criminologists have argued that the *CSI* effect is a myth and that forensic crime dramas do not affect juror expectations during trials (Shelton, Kim, & Barak, 2007; Tyler, 2006). Some have argued that while jurors may have an increased expectation of scientific evidence, this expectation is related to modern advances in science and information technology rather than the influence of shows such as *CSI* (Shelton, Kim, & Barak, 2007).

However, a recent American study found that nearly 80 percent of prosecutors, publicly funded defence lawyers, and judges believed that, in certain cases, jurors had made decisions influenced by forensic television programs (Robbers, 2008). Fifty percent of respondents believed that juries saw a lack of forensic testing as sloppy police work, even when forensic testing was not essential to a case. Slightly less than half of respondents discussed cases where irrelevant forensic evidence had been introduced in trials at the request of jurors, or where juries acquitted defendants because of a lack of forensic evidence. While the perceptions of prosecutors, public defenders, and judges could imply that there may be some truth to a *CSI* effect after all, it is important to note that these perceptions do not provide definitive evidence of a *CSI* effect. Rather, they highlight a disconnect between the meaning of crime and criminality constructed by the media and within the criminal justice system.

A CSI Effect for Judges, Prosecutors, and Defenders?

Discussions of a *CSI* effect normally refer to juror expectations. A less common application of the *CSI* effect involves the job execution of judges, prosecutors, and defenders.

In Robbers's 2008 study, prosecutors, judges, and defenders overwhelmingly wrote that they spent a lot more time carefully reviewing and critiquing forensic evidence, even after experts had discussed it. Prosecutors and defence attorneys related that they spent time considering the extent of a potential *CSI* effect during *voir dire* (in this case, the preliminary examination of prospective jurors) and would bump potential jurors who appeared to have trouble distinguishing television from reality. One-third of respondents noted that they felt the need to mention forensic television shows during trial, and that they spent more time familiarizing themselves with forensics so they could be better prepared at trial.

So, while conclusive proof that a *CSI* effect exists among jurors may not exist, the argument can be made that a *CSI* effect does exist among other actors in the legal system. It is worth considering what implications this finding has for the way trials are conducted.

BOX 2.5

Burns and Crawford on School Shootings and Moral Panics

In their 1999 article, "School Shootings, the Media and Public Fear: Ingredients for a Moral Panic," Ronald Burns and Charles Crawford asked whether the public fear generated by a series of six school shootings in the United States over a two-year period (and culminating in the 1999 Columbine High School shootings) was justified. Building upon the earlier work of Cohen (1972/1980) on folk devils and moral panics (see Box 2.2), and Goode and Ben-Yehuda's (1994) model for distinguishing be-

tween moral panics and legitimate social problems (see Box 2.3), Burns and Crawford demonstrated that many of the characteristics of a moral panic were present in the aftermath of this series of school shootings.

Burns and Crawford (1999) argued that widespread *concern* was evident: enhanced security measures were introduced in schools nationwide (with metal detectors and "drop and cover" drills); daytime television was pre-empted to provide continuous coverage; front-page coverage appeared in the major newspapers; and politicians quickly stepped into the fray, blaming the entertainment industry for promoting youth violence and promising tough legislative changes. *Hostility* was evident in the form of a $1 billion US government grant to prevent and toughen the prosecution of juvenile crime, and a proposal for a $1.5 billion grant for state and local governments that imposed corrective sanctions (i.e., prison sentences) on young, first-time offenders. Nationwide surveys indicated that *consensus* existed regarding the threat posed by the school shootings, with 75 percent of Americans saying that they "were very seriously concerned," and significant numbers of people expressing fear for their children's safety while at school. Finally, Burns and Crawford argued that *disproportionality* was evident in the severe social reaction to this rash of school shootings. They pointed out that more school shooting deaths took place in both the 1992–93 and 1993–94 school years than in the 1997–98 school year, that arrest rates for violent juvenile crime were on the decline when the moral panic erupted, and that, statistically speaking, the chances of being killed in a school shooting were less than the chances of being struck by lightning.

In particular, Burns and Crawford (1999) applied Goode and Ben-Yehuda's model of moral panics to explain how the media, politicians, and the public interacted with one another to generate a moral panic. As can be seen in Figure 2.1, which applies specifically to the then-recent school shootings in the United States, the public feeds concern to the media, while the media provides sensationalism of the issue in return. The public provides direction to politicians, who provide rhetoric in return. The media help politicians with issue identification, while politicians provide legitimation for the media coverage. An interesting aspect of this transactional diagram is that "juveniles"—whose behaviour is the real target of the debate—are left out of the loop entirely. Nobody bothers to ask them if they feel concerned or threatened, whether they support tougher security measures in schools, or whether they support new, tough-on-youth crime laws.

FIGURE 2.1   Interactions in the School Shooting Moral Panic

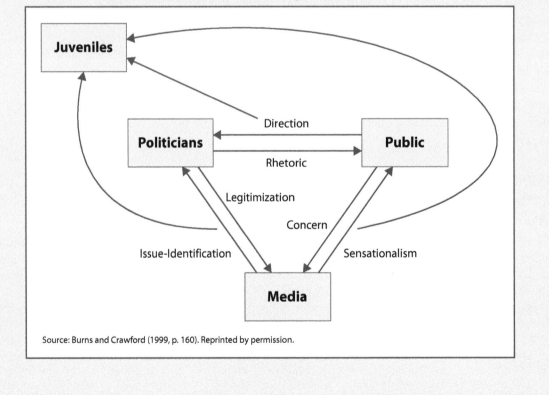

Source: Burns and Crawford (1999, p. 160). Reprinted by permission.

Conclusion

Many criminologists argue that the stories about crime we watch or read are more than news or entertainment; they are one way in which we collectively construct the meaning of criminals, victims, police, and other justice officials. They are also one way we negotiate who is part of "us" and who is the "other," or one of "them." Therefore, criminology students need to approach media representations critically to better identify the many messages about crime and criminality embedded in the media they consume, and to question the assumptions and biases the media often contain.

SUMMARY OF KEY POINTS

- *Media effects*, an early focal point in the study of media and crime, suggested that exposure to media could determine behaviour, most notably aggression. For instance, children who watched a lot of violence on television were more likely to act violently toward others. (The approach subsequently came under scrutiny from some criminologists who questioned its methodologies).
- Many criminologists shifted their focus away from the effect of the media on crime to instead examine the cultural meaning of media violence. The concept of *active audiences* suggests that people do not passively consume media messages; rather, meaning is constructed by an interaction between the persons who produced the image and the audiences who consume it.
- When examining how the media cover crime, it is essential to engage in *critical thinking*. This involves a rigorous, logical evaluation of the claims and arguments being presented, and a questioning of both the messages embedded in the media we consume, and our role as audience members.
- Crime is presented in the media not only as news content, but also as a central component in many forms of entertainment. It often takes the form of simple narratives or *problem frames*, which are often not accurate representations of complex reality.
- *Moral panics* tend to arise when a person or group of persons "become defined as a threat to societal values and interests" (Stanley Cohen). The media often play a central role in the diffusion of moral panics, along with, in some cases, politicians, the police, and *moral entrepreneurs*.
- According to Erich Goode and Nachman Ben-Yehuda, a moral panic is characterized by the following five features (which usually appear sequentially): 1. concern; 2. hostility; 3. consensus; 4. disproportionality; 5. volatility.
- As illustrated by the examples of news coverage of Hurricane Katrina, or the legal problems of NFL quarterbacks Michael Vick and Ben Roethlisberger, the media can often reflect deep-seated social tensions in society relating to race, class, or other issues.
- Nils Christie suggested that the media often confer victim status on an individual based on certain characteristics he or she possesses, relating to race, gender, class, etc.

NOTE

1. Mark Leary, Robin Kowalski, Laura Smith, and Stephen Phillips (2003) have noted that in 13 of 15 school shootings between 1995 and 2001, acute or chronic rejection of the shooter was prominent. Furthermore, all of the shooters had one or more of three risk factors: a significant interest in firearms or bombs, a fascination with death or Satanism, and psychological problems of depression, impulse control, and/or sadism.

QUESTIONS FOR CRITICAL DISCUSSION

1. Over the next several days, take note of the kinds of stories about crime that are contained in the news you read or hear, and the television shows and movies you watch. Who is the victim? Who is the perpetrator? How do the police interact with the other characters? How do these stories shape your own assumptions about who commits crime, who is victimized by crime, and how the police intervene?

2. Can you think of an example of an "ideal victim" that appeared in any media you watched or listened to recently? What made the victim seem "innocent"? How was this "innocence" conveyed? What kinds of images or words were used to describe the victim?

3. In what ways do different media outlets cover the same story? Try the following exercise: Seek out news stories from multiple sources on the policing of the G20 Summit in Toronto in 2010. You can search the CBC (www.cbc.ca), the Canadian Press (www.thecanadianpress.com), the *Toronto Sun* (www.torontosun.com) and The Media Co-op (an alternative news site run by activists from across Canada; www.mediacoop.ca). How does coverage by these different sources differ? What kinds of assumptions are made about the role of the police by each source?

4. What do the media portrayals of Michael Vick and Ben Roethlisberger say about social tensions around race? Do you think these portrayals would be different if both men had been black or if both men had been white? What if one had been Muslim or female? Does it matter that their crimes were quite different?

5. Look up section 163 of the *Criminal Code*, where it states that it is a crime to make, print, publish, distribute, or sell a crime comic. You can read the parliamentary debate at http://parl.canadiana.ca/view/oop.debates_HOC2101_01/514?r=0&s=3. Is this legislation the result of a moral panic? Why or why not? If so, which groups do you think lobbied for the legislation? Why?

6. What implications does sousveillance have for the ways we think about police? How do you think sousveillance affects the public's relationship with the police? Should it be legal to film police and post those videos online? Why or why not?

7. Do you believe jurors are as easily influenced by forensic television as other members of the legal system seem to believe? Might there be other explanations for jurors' high expectations of forensic evidence?

SUGGESTED FURTHER READINGS

Cohen, S. (1980). *Folk devils and moral panics: The creation of the mods and rockers*. Oxford, UK: Basil Blackwood. (Original work published 1972.)

Greer, C. (Ed.). (2010). *Crime and media: A reader*. Oxford, UK: Routledge.

Hall, S., Critcher, C., Jefferson, T., Clarke, J.N., & Roberts, B. (1978). *Policing the crisis: Mugging, the state and law and order.* London, UK: Macmillan.

Surette, R. (2010). *Media, crime, and criminal justice* (4th ed.). Belmont, CA: Wadsworth.

Websites

Center for Media Literacy: http://www.medialit.org

MediaSmarts: http://mediasmarts.ca

REFERENCES

Altheide, D. (1997). The news media, the problem frame, and the production of fear. *Sociological Quarterly, 38*(4), 647–668.

Becker, H. (1963). *Outsiders: Studies in the sociology of deviance.* New York: Free Press of Glencoe.

Bentham , M. (2007, October 15). Deadly skunk floods city. *London Evening Standard.* Retrieved from http://www.standard.co.uk/news/deadly-skunk-floods-city-6678202.html.

Brezina, T., & Phipps, H.E. (2010). False news reports, folk devils, and the role of public officials: Notes on the social construction of law and order in the aftermath of Hurricane Katrina. *Deviant Behavior, 31,* 97–134.

Burns, R., & Crawford, C. (1999). School shootings, the media and public fear: Ingredients for a moral panic. *Crime, Law and Social Change, 32*(2), 147–168.

Carnagey, N., Anderson, C., & Bartholow, B. (2007). Media violence and social neuroscience: New questions and new opportunities. *Current Directions in Psychological Science, 16*(4), 178–182.

Carter, S. (1988). When victims happen to be black. *Yale Law Journal, 97,* 420–447.

Chesney-Lind, M., & Eliason, M. (2006). From invisible to incorrigible: The demonization of marginalized women and girls. *Crime Media Culture, 2*(1), 29–47.

Christie, N. (1986). The ideal victim. In E. Fattah (Ed.), *From crime policy to victim policy* (pp. 17–30). London, UK: Macmillan.

Cohen, S. (1980). *Folk devils and moral panics: The creation of the mods and rockers.* Oxford, UK: Basil Blackwood. (Original work published 1972.)

Coogan, D. (2012). Race and crime in sports media: Content analysis on the Michael Vick and Ben Roethlisberger cases. *Journal of Sports Media, 7*(2), 129–151.

DeLisi, M., Vaughn, M., Gentile, D., Anderson, C., & Shook, J. (2012). Violent video games, delinquency and youth violence: New evidence. *Youth Violence and Juvenile Justice, 11*(2), 132–142.

Dickerman, C., J. Christensen, S. Beatriz, & McClain, K. (2008). Big breasts and bad guys: Depictions of gender and race in video games. *Journal of Creativity in Mental Health, 3*(1), 20–29.

Dowler, K., Fleming, T., & Muzzatti, S.L. (2006). Constructing crime: Media, crime and popular culture. *Canadian Journal of Criminology and Criminal Justice, 48*(6), 837–850.

Doyle, A. (2003). *Arresting images: Crime and policing in front of the television camera.* Toronto: University of Toronto Press.

Federman, J. (1998). *National television study* (Vol. 3). Thousand Oaks, CA: Sage.

Ferrell, J. (1999). Cultural criminology. *Annual Review of Sociology, 25*(1), 395–418.

Goode, E., & Ben-Yehuda, N. (1994). Moral panics: Culture, politics and social construction. *Annual Review of Sociology, 20*(1), 149–171.

Hall, S., Critcher, C., Jefferson, T., Clarke, J.N., & Roberts, B. (1978). *Policing the crisis: Mugging, the state and law and order.* London, UK: Macmillan Press.

Inciardi, J.A., & Dee, J.L. (1987). From the Keystone Cops to Miami Vice: Images of policing in American popular culture. *Journal of Popular Culture, 21*(2), 84–102.

Jefferson County Sheriff's Department. (n.d.). The media response [Report on Columbine High School incident]. Retrieved from http://www.cnn.com/SPECIALS/2000/columbine.cd/Pages/MEDIA_TEXT.htm.

Kissel, R. (2014, March 13). Fourteen years later, "Survivor," "CSI" still going strong for CBS. *Variety.* Retrieved from http://variety.com/2014/tv/news/fourteen-years-later-survivor-csi-still-going-strong-for-cbs-1201131575/.

Leary, M., Kowalski, R., Smith, L., & Phillips, S. (2003). Teasing, rejection and violence: Case studies of the school shootings. *Aggressive Behavior, 29*(3), 202–214.

Lemert, E. (1951). Social pathology: A systematic approach to the theory of sociopathic behaviour. New York: McGraw-Hill.

Lyon, D. (2001). *Surveillance society: Monitoring everyday life.* Buckingham, UK: Open University Press.

Mahari, J., & Conner, R. (2003). Black violence has a bad rap. *Journal of Social Issues, 59*(1), 121–140.

Mann, S., Nolan, J., & Wellman, B. (2003). Sousveillance: Inventing and using wearable computing devices for data collection in surveillance environments. *Surveillance & Society, 1*(3), 331–355.

MediaSmarts. (2014). Digital and media literacy fundamentals. Retrieved from http://mediasmarts.ca/digital-media-literacy-fundamentals.

Muschert, G.W. (2009). Frame-changing in the media coverage of a school shooting: The rise of Columbine as a national concern. *The Social Science Journal, 46,* 164–170.

Muschert, G.W., Henry, S., Bracy, N.L., & Peguero, A.A. (Eds.). (2014). *Responding to school violence: Confronting the Columbine effect.* London, UK: Lynne Rienner Publishers.

Podlas, K. (2006). The *CSI* effect: Exposing the media myth. *Fordham Intellectual Property, Media and Entertainment Law Journal, 16,* 429–465.

Puar, J., & Rai, A. (2002). Monster, terrorist, fag: The war on terrorism and the production of docile patriots. *Social Text 72, 20*(3), 117–148.

Ringrose, J. (2006). A new universal mean girl: Examining the discursive construction and social regulation of a new feminine pathology. *Feminism & Psychology, 16*(4), 405–424.

Robbers, M. (2008). Blinded by science: The social construction of reality in forensic television shows and its effect on criminal jury trials. *Criminal Justice Policy Review, 19*(1), 84–102.

Room, R., Fischer, B., Hall, W., Lenton, S., & Reuter, P. (2008). *Cannabis policy: Moving beyond stalemate—The global cannabis commission report.* Oxford, UK: Beckley Foundation. Retrieved from http://www.beckleyfoundation.org/Cannabis-Commission-Report.pdf.

Senate Committee on the Judiciary. (1999). *Children, violence and the media: A report for parents and policy makers.* n.p.

Shelton, D., Kim, Y., & Barak, G. (2007). A study of juror expectations and demands concerning scientific evidence: Does the "*CSI* effect" exist? *Vanderbilt Journal of Entertainment & Technology Law, 9,* 330–368.

Spin and drugs [Editorial]. (2009, November 2). *London Evening Standard.*

Surette, R. (2013). Cause or catalyst: The interaction of real world and media crime models. *American Journal of Criminal Justice, 38,* 392–409.

Tierney, K., Bevc, C., & Kuligowski, E. (2006). Metaphors matter: Disaster myths, media frames, and their consequences in Hurricane Katrina. *Annals of the American Academy of Political and Social Science, 604,* 57–81.

Tyler, T. (2006). Viewing *CSI* and the threshold of guilt: Managing truth and justice in reality and fiction. *Yale Law Journal, 115*(5), 1050–1085.

Tzanelli, R., Yar, M., & O'Brien, M. (2005). "Con me if you can": Exploring crime in the American cinematic imagination. *Theoretical Criminology, 9*(1), 97–117.

Young, J. (1971). The role of the police as amplifiers of deviancy, negotiators of reality and translators of fantasy: Some consequences of our present system of drug control as seen in Notting Hill. In S. Cohen (Ed.), *Images of deviance* (pp. 27–61). Harmondsworth, UK: Penguin Books.

Legislation

Criminal Code. (1985). RSC 1985, c. C-46.

PART TWO

Foundations of Canadian Criminology

The Bountiful Polygamy Case: Section 293 of the Criminal Code of Canada

Winston Blackmore of Bountiful, British Columbia.
Source: Gerry Kahrmann/Vancouver Sun.

Polygamy is the term used to describe a marriage involving more than two people. Anthropologists and historians tell us that, almost without exception, it takes the form of *polygyny* (that is, one man with more than one wife), although *polyandry* (the opposite arrangement) also occurs in some societies. Usually, polygamy is founded upon, or at least supported by, particular religious doctrines or deep cultural tradition.

Canada's concern over polygamy dates back to the early days of Confederation. In 1887, Mormon elder Charles Ora Card led a vanguard of Mormon settlers into Western Canada, fleeing persecution of the polygamous group by an increasingly intolerant US government. The federal government already held a lingering concern over polygamy as practised by some First Nations peoples in the Northwest Territory (as Canada's western provinces of today were then known). To make matters worse, a mischievous Vancouver Island politician named Anthony Maitland Stenhouse converted to Mormonism and noisily declared that no Canadian law prohibited polygamy, so he would (if he could find two willing women) marry plurally. A criminal law was seen to be the solution to polygamy, and in 1890, *An Act Further to Amend the Criminal Law* was passed.

Canada's legislative approach to polygamy seemed to deter it for a while. In fact, polygamy did not take hold in a significant way in Canada until the 1940s, when a handful of excommunicated Mormons from Card's Alberta colony moved onto a large piece of land in southern British Columbia, which became known as Bountiful. Eventually, Bountiful became a community of about 1,000, isolated and mysterious. As the decades wore on, complaints surfaced about child brides, "lost boys," and an (apparently increasingly) abusive patriarchy that served the interests of church elders and no one else.

When the *Canadian Charter of Rights and Freedoms* was introduced in 1982, it was not surprising that the polygamy prohibition was identified by constitutional lawyers as a criminal law that could not be justified. The prohibition surely was a Victorian anachronism, perpetuated through bigotry and inattention, a way to isolate and marginalize (mostly) religious minorities such as Muslims, Canada's small but persistent band of fundamentalist Mormons, and a small numbers of African immigrants from nations where this traditional practice continues. Uncertain of the constitutional validity of the prohibition, BC's attorney general openly refused to enforce it against the senior men of Bountiful, including bishop Winston Blackmore, who at one time claimed to have 24 wives.

But the problem of polygamy was not going away, and even if Bountiful remained a small outpost, newspaper stories reported that polygamy was spreading among immigrant populations in Ontario and elsewhere. Some certainty around the law was needed.

The matter finally came for adjudication before the Supreme Court of British Columbia through a constitutional reference case in 2010–11 (a *reference case* is a rare form of proceeding in which the government may ask the court to settle a controversial issue without the traditional, purely adversarial process). Would the criminal prohibition survive modern scrutiny?

After 42 days of often intense hearings and submissions, Chief Justice Robert Bauman decided that the law infringed on the religious freedoms of polygamists, which was contrary to section 2(a) of the Charter, but that the infringement was justified as reasonable, given the significant harms associated with polygamy. Relying on what he referred to as "the most comprehensive judicial record on the subject ever produced," Bauman set out in a 357-page decision his conclusions that polygamy caused harm to women and children as well as society at large (*Reference re: Section 293 of the Criminal Code of Canada*, 2011). In his reasons for judgment, Bauman referred to the international experience with polygamy and noted that in societies where the practice was most prevalent, the rights of women and children (and many men) suffered accordingly. He decided that it was likely that such negative effects were *caused* by the social structure that polygamy promotes and reinforces, and were not simply coincidental. And for every negative effect predicted by the expert witnesses, Bauman found plenty of corroborating evidence from individuals who had experienced the problems first-hand in the polygamous communities of Canada and the United States.

The polygamy reference case was unusual in many ways: it was the first reference case heard by a trial court, with live witnesses, instead of by an appeal panel relying on counsel's submissions alone; some witnesses were permitted to offer their evidence anonymously; an *amicus curiae* ("friend of the court") was hired to argue against the government's position that the law should be upheld; and a large number of groups were permitted to appear as "interested persons" to argue for or against the law. These features are not common to an ordinary criminal process.

In its exploration of the appropriate role of criminal law in addressing social harm, morality, and the clash of rights, *Reference re: Section 293 of the Criminal Code of Canada* remains a very useful takeoff point for a discussion of the ideas underlying criminal law.

Before You Read Chapter 3

- To what extent do you believe the state (via the police, the courts, or provincial or federal legislatures) has the right to impose laws on an isolated or traditional community and its unconventional family or marriage practices?
- Are there social norms or practices that should always be "off limits" for the state?
- How would you define the "crime" described in this case? What makes this case an interesting topic for exploring the intersection of criminology and the law?
- During the BC hearings, what arguments do you imagine were made by those witnesses who supported this community's right to practise polygamy?

Criminal Law in Canada

Introduction: What Is Criminal Law?

Criminology is the study of crime and criminal behaviour, which are defined by reference to **criminal law**. What is crime, and how do we decide what behaviour is criminal and what is not?

All societies have developed mechanisms for the collective enforcement of group norms in service of what might be called a "public purpose." Where these mechanisms take the shape of a **prohibition** coupled with a *penalty*, they are legitimately regarded as elements of a criminal legal system. In modern nation-states, near-universal characteristics separate criminal law from other aspects of the legal system. Unlike violations of social norms that are embodied in the law of contract or tort, criminal behaviour is addressed by state, not individual, action; and the penalties that may be imposed often, although not always, involve periods of imprisonment in state institutions.

The Origins of Criminal Law

Crime is prosecuted by the state because it is considered to be a violation of public order (which was once referred to as "the king's peace") rather than an infringement on the rights of another citizen. However, the distinction between private and public criminality has not always been so clear. For much of Western history, incarceration or state-enforced servitude could be imposed for private debts, and breaches of public obligations were generally left to be prosecuted by the affected private individuals, usually victims and their families. The ancient world's most famous recorded criminal trials were framed as private undertakings: the prosecution that led to the execution of the Greek philosopher Socrates in 399 BCE was initiated and conducted in large part by Meletus, a poet;

criminology
The study of crime and criminal behaviour, which are defined by reference to criminal law.

criminal law
The entire set of principles, procedures, and rules established by governments through the courts and criminal legislation in order to ensure public safety. It includes definitions of crimes, criminal responsibility, and punishments, and defences to a criminal charge.

prohibition
A law forbidding a specific act.

and some centuries later, Cicero's prosecution of Gaius Verres for corruption was initiated on behalf of deprived Roman citizens. Indeed, "private prosecutions" are technically available in Canada to this day.

By the Age of Enlightenment in 18th-century Europe, a number of factors had combined to create what we now recognize as a modern system of criminal law: the emergence of the government as a meaningful source of central authority and a mechanism of collective action, which supplemented and eventually displaced the Church (which, in many European countries, had its own law, its own police, and its own prisons); the growth of professional state police services; and the ever-increasing complexity of social interaction. The modern system of criminal law required a body of **penal law** that was comprehensive, codified (whether in written laws or in courts' decisions), and—in theory at least—subject to consistent enforcement.

Most of the "core" criminal prohibitions in Canada—such as murder, robbery, trespass, and assault—originate in ancient history and were inherited in more or less their modern form along with the laws of England in a process that began in the 18th century and continued until the *Statute of Westminster* in 1931 (which saw the Supreme Court of Canada become the court of last resort for criminal matters). By the time most of the remaining British North American colonies and territories merged into Canada in the late 19th century, the basic elements of the criminal justice system—police, courts, prisons, and legislation—were firmly in place. However, unlike Great Britain, where **common law** (or "judge-made") offences continued in force, Canada adopted its own *Criminal Code* in 1892. The effect of this Code was to substantially codify existing English offences. That said, Canada retained the power to create common law offences until the 1950s.

Criminal Law in Canada

We would be forgiven if we thought of the criminal process as either a provincial or a local affair. After all, provincial or municipal police forces investigate most crimes, and prosecutors working for the provincial governments prosecute most offenders. Nevertheless, by the terms of section 91(27) of Canada's *Constitution Act, 1867*, the federal Parliament determines what acts are criminal and which available punishments apply, as well as the procedures associated with investigating and prosecuting crimes.

The federal government may enact any criminal laws necessary to protect "public peace, order, security, health, and morality" (*The Canadian Federation of Agriculture v. The Attorney-General of Quebec and Others*, 1950; more recently, see *Reference re: Assisted Human Reproduction Act*, 2010). Thus, some laws that might not be regarded as truly "criminal," such as those that restrict the sale of tobacco products (*RJR-MacDonald Inc. v. Canada (Attorney General)*, 1995) have been considered by the courts to be valid exercises of the federal power.

However, the laws that most people think of as "criminal laws," and the laws that consume virtually all of the efforts of the criminal courts and the corrections systems, are found mainly in two pieces of federal legislation: the *Criminal Code* and the *Controlled Drugs and Substances Act*. Others are the *Youth Criminal Justice Act* and the *Crimes Against Humanity and War Crimes Act* (examined in Box 3.1).

Criminal offences generally fall into one of two categories: summary offences or indictable offences. A **summary offence** (known in many US states, and historically in Canada, as a "misdemeanour") is the less serious type. It generally carries a penalty of

penal law
A law that imposes punishment, as opposed to (for instance) a law that provides only the right of a victim to compensation.

common law
A body of law defined primarily through successive decisions of judges, as opposed to through legislation.

summary offence
A relatively minor offence, punishable by a fine or a maximum jail sentence of six months.

BOX 3.1

The Crimes Against Humanity and War Crimes Act

Canada's *Crimes Against Humanity and War Crimes Act* (CAHWCA) is an especially interesting criminal law statute, because it gives domestic legal effect to international criminal law. Under this Act, Canadian courts are authorized to assume jurisdiction over crimes against humanity, war crimes, genocide, and any other crime recognized under international law, even if the crime took place in another country and did not involve any Canadian citizens—a power referred to as "universal jurisdiction." The CAHWCA also allows courts to assume jurisdiction over international crimes committed within Canada or abroad by Canadian citizens and state officials. This suggests that international law can take its place alongside the common law, statutes, and the Constitution as a source of criminal law in Canada.

In 2009, Désiré Munyaneza, a Rwandan national with permanent resident status in Canada, became the first person charged and convicted under the CAHWCA. After

being recognized by members of the Rwandan diaspora in Toronto, Munyaneza was prosecuted in Quebec. The Quebec Superior Court found him guilty of genocide, war crimes, and crimes against humanity during the Rwandan genocide, and sentenced him to life imprisonment with no possibility of parole for 25 years.

In the larger international arena, the International Criminal Court (ICC), located in The Hague in the Netherlands, has a mandate under the provisions of public international law to prosecute genocide and other crimes against humanity. More than 120 countries are members of this "court of last resort," which will try serious cases in those situations where a national court proves unable or unwilling to do so. Notably, several powerful nations, including the United States, Israel, China, and Russia have refused participation in the ICC, and have often been critical of it.

---

no more than six months in prison or a $5,000 fine. More serious offences, referred to in some other countries (and historically) as "felonies," are called **indictable offences** in Canada. While the most serious crimes, such as murder, are only prosecuted by way of indictment, the majority of indictable offences may also result in summary convictions, and so are known as "hybrid offences." The distinction between summary and indictable offences has procedural consequences as well.

indictable offence

A serious offence, such as murder or rape, which carries a severe penalty. An *indictment* is the formal process of setting out a criminal charge in a document for serious, "indictable" offences.

The Criminal Courts

The adjudication of Canada's criminal cases is divided between two levels of court in the provinces and territories (with the exception of Nunavut, which has a single territorial court)—and these levels have developed considerable overlap.[1] Provincial *superior courts* are administered by the provinces, but their judges are appointed federally. These courts are tasked with the adjudication of the most serious matters, civil and criminal. They have their own powers and are independent; that is, they are not "creatures of statute" (created by Parliament). While the federal and provincial governments can legislate the processes and administration of these courts, they can't impair the courts' fundamental powers or jurisdiction (*MacMillan Bloedel Ltd. v. Simpson*, 1995).

Each province may structure its courts as it sees fit, but the common design divides the superior court into a *trial court* (called in British Columbia the Supreme Court, in Alberta the Court of Queen's Bench, and in Ontario the Superior Court of Justice) and a *court of appeal*.

Each province also has its *provincial court*, which is sometimes referred to as the "inferior court," and which again may be variously named (for example, in Ontario, it is called the Court of Justice, and in British Columbia it is called the Provincial Court).

FIGURE 3.1   Hierarchy of Courts

Provincial Court judges are appointed by the provincial government and generally have jurisdiction over matters considered to be less important than those that occupy the superior courts. However, describing the Provincial Court as "inferior" is somewhat misleading, at least with respect to criminal law, because every criminal prosecution begins in Provincial Court and the overwhelming majority are concluded there as well. In recent years, Canadian constitutional law has developed to recognize substantial, fundamental powers even in these "inferior" entities, to the point now where their independence has received constitutional recognition virtually equivalent to that of superior courts (*Reference re: Remuneration of Judges of the Provincial Court (P.E.I.)*, 1997).

At a national level, the Federal Court and the Federal Court of Appeal deal mainly with matters of exclusively federal interest, and the Supreme Court of Canada can hear and provide final decisions on appeals from all the other courts.

Criminal courts are responsible for applying the *Criminal Code* or relevant regulatory statute to the facts of a particular case. Doing so necessarily involves a substantive interpretation of the law. Moreover, because judges traditionally give written reasons for their decisions, the courts themselves are a significant source of criminal rules. As a result, commentators sometimes describe the Canadian legal regime as a common law (that is, a judge-made law) system. However, this description is incorrect, at least with respect to criminal justice. While judges can exercise varying degrees of discretion in their decisions, they remain constrained by legislation in the same way as judges in countries that use the continental European, or

civil law

A system in which the law is primarily set out in legislation, and judges' discretion is limited to interpretation and application of those written provisions.

civil law, system. The difference, if any, is only of degree. The Canadian criminal law tradition stands in stark contrast to the English tradition and its numerous "common law crimes"—that is, crimes that were defined (if not invented) by judges, often over generations and even centuries. It might surprise the North American reader to learn that the prohibition on murder, for instance, is not founded on any English statute (although legislation may establish defences, procedures, and modify punishments). Common law crimes persist in some Commonwealth jurisdictions; in Canada, however, they were abolished[2] at the time of the consolidation of the *Criminal Code* in 1953.

One way in which Canadian criminal law differs sharply from the continental European tradition is in its complete reliance on an adversarial, rather than inquisitorial, model. In many European countries, the judge may play a role as an active investigator, along with the prosecutorial lawyers of the state. In Canada and other countries based on English tradition, the judge is an impartial arbiter between the state on one hand, usually represented by a public prosecutor, and the individual and his or her lawyer on the other.

Criminal Justice Process

Typically, a crime is investigated by police officers employed by municipal or provincial police forces (or, in the case of RCMP officers, by a federal force contracted out to provinces and municipalities). When the police have gathered sufficient evidence to support a charge, then (in most provinces), they provide a report to the public prosecutor's office (a semi-independent branch of the attorney general's ministry generally known as

Crown counsel), who then approves the charge based on an assessment of whether the evidence will support a conviction and whether prosecution is in the public interest. Much is made of the fact that some jurisdictions still allow the police to "press charges" without prior approval. However, in practice, cases cannot proceed without prosecutorial support, so little practical difference exists between one approach and the other.

In all provinces, the prosecution begins by the swearing of an *information* before a justice of the peace. Usually, the swearing is done by a police officer or another public official. The police officer recounts his or her belief that a crime has been committed, and the justice of the peace orders the charge. Private prosecutions (whereby a layperson, rather than a police officer or other public official, swears the information and initiates the prosecution) are still technically possible under the Code. However, they are now almost always taken over by Crown counsel, who may pursue or (far more often) *stay* charges (that is, suspend or terminate the prosecution).

Once a person is arrested, he or she is usually released on a promise to appear in court at an appointed time. In more serious matters, the police may choose to hold the accused in custody. In such cases, the accused must be brought before a justice of the peace within 24 hours for a "bail" hearing, at which the Crown must demonstrate a reason for continued custody or the conditions for interim release. Usually the accused is granted bail, often with conditions such as the posting of a bond, a curfew, or orders that the accused avoid certain places or people.

In more serious cases, where the Crown proceeds by way of **indictment**, a preliminary inquiry is usually held at which a judge of the Provincial Court decides whether sufficient evidence exists to proceed to trial. If evidence is insufficient, then the accused is discharged (subject to the Crown's right to restart the prosecution if more evidence becomes available or, in extraordinary cases, to proceed by direct indictment). If sufficient evidence exists, a trial date is set.

indictment
A formal written accusation, usually reserved for more serious crimes.

In cases where the Crown is pursuing a summary conviction, no preliminary inquiry takes place and the matter proceeds directly to trial in the Provincial Court.

Under section 11 of the *Charter of Rights and Freedoms*, the accused has a right to choose trial by judge and jury for any offence that could result in a sentence of five years or more. In any other case, the trial will be by judge alone, whether in the superior court or Provincial Court. In jury trials, a panel of laypeople determines the accused's guilt or lack thereof (it should be noted that "innocence" is not an available verdict in Canada). The judge makes peripheral decisions such as those governing the admissibility of evidence and the setting or modification of bail conditions. The judge also guides the jury on the legal rules it is to apply through comprehensive instructions.

Throughout a trial, the accused may sit mute, exercising the right to silence and forcing the state to prove every element of the case against him or her beyond a reasonable doubt. Nonetheless, prosecutions that proceed to trial usually conclude with a conviction, either through trial or through an accused's plea of "guilty" (often the result of a pretrial bargain for a lesser sentence). Of course, a trial may also result in an acquittal (after which an accused may not be retried, unless the Crown successfully appeals), a stay of proceedings (a suspension of charges), or a mistrial (where the trial is aborted but may begin anew at a later date).

Once convicted, an accused faces a sentence that can range from an absolute or conditional discharge (whereby an accused is essentially forgiven for the offence, either

FIGURE 3.2   The Criminal Justice Process in Canada

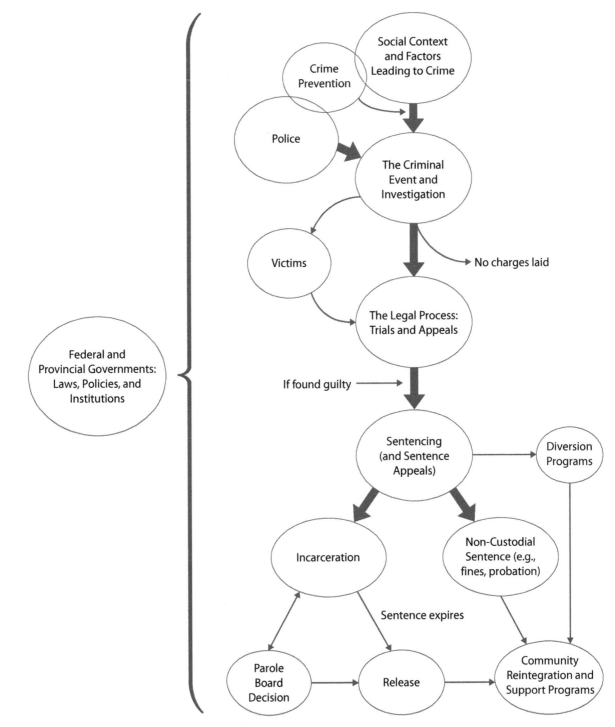

immediately or following a period of good behaviour) to imprisonment for periods up to life. However, the parole system in Canada generally releases prisoners under supervision after they have served one-third of their sentences (with the exception of murderers, who are ineligible for parole for 10 to 25 years). Sentences of less than two years are served in provincial correctional institutions. Sentences of two years or more are served in federal penitentiaries. The death penalty for murder was abolished in Canada in 1976; by that time, Canada had not carried out an execution in 14 years. Although a few attempts have been made to lobby for the reintroduction of the death penalty, Supreme Court of Canada decisions regarding the rights of accused facing extradition to death-penalty jurisdictions suggest that no such law could withstand a constitutional challenge (*United States v. Burns*, 2001).

Arthur Lucas (left) and Ronald Turpin were the last two people executed in Canada, on December 11, 1962, at Toronto's Don Jail.

The Elements of a Crime

As described above, in Canada a crime is described in a federal statute, which sets out the prohibition and the associated penalty. These provisions typically contain a description of the prohibited acts (collectively known by the Latin term **actus reus**) coupled with some element of mental culpability (**mens rea**).[3] The basic offence of theft, for instance, is described in section 322 of the *Criminal Code* as follows:

> 322(1) Every one commits theft who fraudulently and without colour of right takes, or fraudulently and without colour of right converts to his use or to the use of another person, anything, whether animate or inanimate, with intent
> (a) to deprive, temporarily or absolutely, the owner of it, or a person who has a special property or interest in it, of the thing or of his property or interest in it;

What follows in the Code are a number of clarifications designed to provide some guidance to the courts. When does the theft occur? For instance, is a person guilty of shoplifting when he picks up the item from the shelf? When he conceals it in a pocket? When he walks out of the store? Section 322(2) of the Code provides some guidance:

> 322(2) A person commits theft when, with intent to steal anything, he moves it or causes it to move or to be moved, or begins to cause it to become movable.

In theory, then, the theft has occurred when the item is taken from the shelf. However, each element of the offence must be proven by the Crown beyond a reasonable doubt. Practically speaking, how can one prove the "intent to steal" without the accused actually leaving the store without paying, or at least without him concealing the item or otherwise signalling a criminal purpose? Nevertheless, the law as it is defined allows the police to intervene and the Crown to prosecute at the earliest stages, where an intent to steal is coupled with some concrete action.

Note that criminal *intent* changes an ambiguous act (such as picking up an item from a shelf) into an act that can result in arrest and imprisonment (such as stealing). As such, the concept of a "guilty mind" (*mens rea*) is central to our understanding of most criminal sanctions. Proof beyond a reasonable doubt of mental culpability is a necessary element of every serious criminal offence and most less-serious ones. The exceptions

actus reus
The criminal act or personal conduct relating to a crime; it may include a failure to act, but does not include the mental element of a criminal offence.

mens rea
The mental element of a criminal offence or the state(s) of mind of the offender; it is the intent to commit a criminal act.

are criminal or penal negligence and "strict liability" offences (where, once the Crown has proved the prohibited acts, or *actus reus*, the onus switches to the defendant to show that he or she *did not* have a criminal intent by establishing, for instance, due diligence). In even rarer situations, "absolute liability" (where the commission of the act alone is sufficient to support conviction) may be permissible where no potential for imprisonment exists. Generally speaking, the more serious the crime and its consequences, the higher the requirement that intent be proven: murder requires proof of a subjective intent to kill a victim, or at least the reckless intent to create a situation where death is likely to occur. On the opposite end of the spectrum, some offences of a "regulatory" nature do not require intent. For example, if someone parks in a space prohibited for parking by a municipal bylaw, the only proof required is that the car was illegally parked, regardless of why, and might result in the fining of a car's registered owner even if the car had been parked by a thief.

Criminal Defences

One other significant feature of Canadian criminal law is the availability of defences. The most common criminal defence is simply that the Crown has failed to establish the elements of an offence. As described above, to prove an offence, the Crown must establish beyond a reasonable doubt that the accused committed the prohibited act or made the omission that the offence prohibits (the *actus reus*), as well as any associated mental elements of the offence (the *mens rea*). Where the prosecution fails to establish any of the elements of the offence, or the defendant can disprove an element of the offence, there will be no criminal liability. Thus, a defence such as an "alibi," or a partial defence such as **intoxication**, would be used simply to cast doubt on the Crown's proof of a required element of the offence.

> **intoxication**
> A potential defence in which drugs or alcohol may prevent an accused from forming the necessary intent to commit a particular crime.

More formal defences—often called "true defences"—are also available to an accused. A *true defence* is a set of circumstances that, if proven by the accused, will excuse him or her of the crime. The defence of insanity is one example. The Code itself sets out certain defences that, if proven on a balance of probabilities, absolve behaviour that would otherwise be considered criminal. Section 34 of the *Criminal Code*, for example, provides that a person is not guilty of a crime if he or she acts reasonably in his or her own defence or the defence of another.

> **duress**
> An unlawful threat or coercion used by one person to induce another to perform some act against his or her will.

The courts themselves have crafted still other defences—these "common law defences" are incorporated into the *Criminal Code* by virtue of section 8(3).[4] The defence of **duress** is one such "common law defence" that is available to any crime except murder. It provides that where an accused committed an act under threat of death or serious injury, and had no reasonable alternative, he or she will escape liability provided that the crime committed was not disproportional to the threat. If a defence such as duress is raised by an accused, the burden is upon the Crown to prove that one or more of its elements is not present.

The "Public Purpose" of Criminal Law

A criminal law is not simply a prohibition coupled with a penalty: to be considered valid, a criminal law must also serve a public purpose.

This public purpose may evolve over time, usually as new "mischiefs"—harms to be avoided—are perceived. But which harms does criminal law implicitly recognize? How direct must they be?

To explore this question, let's return to the idea of "theft" in a more explicitly modern context than the shoplifting example discussed earlier: What does "theft" mean in the age of telecommunications? What behaviour can the criminal law be used to control?

Almost everyone knows someone who has "stolen" cable or satellite signals. Should society treat this act as criminal "theft"? For most of Canada's history, radio (and later television) programming had been available to anyone with a receiver, free over the public airwaves. The development in the 1960s of various technologies for delivering television broadcasts only to *paying* subscribers led some to circumvent the subscription restriction and obtain the service for free (for instance, by splicing into their neighbours' cable connection). Courts might well disagree on whether this is "theft" under the traditional definition: certainly, the cable hacker is converting something to his own use (to the extent that a pattern of modulation of electrical signals is a "thing"), without the legal right to do so. But is the cable hacker truly intending to "deprive" anyone of it? In the 1970s, the following crime was added to the Code:

> 326(1) Every one commits theft who fraudulently, maliciously, or without colour of right, …
>> (b) uses any telecommunication facility or obtains any telecommunication service.

The reasons for the addition are not difficult to imagine. Cable companies and other controlled-subscription broadcasters (such as satellite TV providers) invest in an infrastructure and expect a return. Customers provide that return through their subscriptions. Allowing "free riders" to piggyback on the system deprives the service provider of income and forces paying users to effectively subsidize the system's hackers. However, these harms, even if economically significant, are indirect. Unlike murder or robbery, the moment at which telecommunications theft is committed nobody is hurt, and it is unlikely that anyone even knows the crime has occurred. But indirect harms are no less real: the innocent and obedient cable subscriber *will* pay more, even a few pennies more, as an indirect result of piracy.

Some have attempted to restrict criminal law only to areas where direct harm has occurred ("My right to swing my fist ends only where another's nose begins"). Yet courts have consistently rejected the "harm principle" as providing a clear boundary on criminal law (*R v. Malmo-Levine; R v. Caine*, 2003). In fact, the harm principle, at least to the extent that it requires some immediate, apparent, or direct harm to justify criminalization, isn't even very helpful as a descriptive, let alone prescriptive, norm. Criminal laws justified, in whole or in part, on indirect or even speculative effects are surprisingly common. How else to explain the various possession offences? The criminal law, for instance, prohibits the possession of high-capacity pistol magazines (even if never loaded), child pornography (even if computer-simulated), and burglary tools; it also controls the keeping or distribution of hundreds or even thousands of other things, from drugs to dangerous or endangered animals to some kinds of writing (*Regulations Prescribing Certain Firearms and Other Weapons, Components and Parts of Weapons, Accessories, Cartridge Magazines, Ammunition and Projectiles as Prohibited or Restricted*; *R v. Sharpe*, 2001; *Mihalchan v. The King*, 1945).

Possession offences are not the only crimes aimed at acts whose commission may not be immediately harmful to anyone. Incest is a crime almost everywhere, even when it occurs between adults raised in separate households, and even when (due to sterility, age, or contraception) there is no possibility of conception (and thus no danger of birth defects). As was discussed in Case Study 3.1 that precedes this chapter, polygamy (being in a marriage with more than one person at a time) is also a crime, even when those directly affected view the acts as harmless or even positively good. Dangerous driving and other forms of recklessness can be criminal even if no accident results. Less notoriously, and perhaps surprisingly, it is a crime in Canada to publish an advertisement offering a reward for the recovery of a lost or stolen item and promising "no questions asked" (*Criminal Code*, s. 143).

The justification for criminalizing activities with indirect or speculative effects can only be that, while they are not necessarily *individually* harmful, the acts increase the *risk* of social harm in society. For example, the proliferation of high-capacity pistol magazines or burglary tools increases the *risk* of mass shootings or breaking-and-entering incidents; permitting even consenting adults to engage in safe incestuous relationships increases the *risk* that girls (who are overwhelmingly the victims of sexual abuse in the home) will be targeted and groomed as sexual partners by male household members; and "no questions asked" reward posters create a marketplace for stolen goods and therefore increase the *risk* of thefts. In each case, the law intervenes early by criminalizing activity that *might* lead to more serious crimes or other harm.

All countries, even the most notoriously abusive, have sought to justify their laws, asserting that they serve the public good and address harms, whether real or imagined. So, naturally, there must be limits to the power to criminalize on the basis of *speculation* of indirect harm or risk. Nevertheless, Canadian courts have generally deferred to Parliament in making the determination, holding that Parliament's apprehension of future harm must only be "reasonable," not demonstrable or actual. Although there have been important exceptions with significant social repercussions (as in laws relating to abortion, homosexuality, and assisted suicide), judges have overwhelmingly accepted a parliamentary determination that a criminal prohibition is justified. It is hoped, of course, that this deference is also the result of Parliament's own respect for the limits of the criminal power, and its concomitant restraint when crafting laws.

The Purpose and Function of Criminal Law
Denunciation and Retribution

deterrence
A principle of sentencing or punishment intended to discourage citizens from offending or reoffending.

denunciation
A formal expression that conduct is unacceptable.

retribution
Punishment for transgressions.

The most frequently cited justifications for criminal penalties are **deterrence**, **denunciation**, and **retribution**. The last two, denunciation and retribution, are almost redundant in a system dedicated to imposing penalties for activities deemed objectionable by society. What benefits do denunciation and retribution offer beyond their deterrent effects?

Denunciation and retribution could be considered as social goods in themselves. Participating in denunciation and retribution—whether verbal and physical—against those who violate social norms probably increases humans' sense of positive well-being. Punishing is, as countless psychological experiments have shown, often pleasurable. But this pleasure can be achieved whether the target of social ire is guilty or innocent (consider the crowds taunting Jesus on his walk to crucifixion or the Puritans of the Salem witch trials). Presumably, we evolved (biologically and culturally) to gain satisfaction from punishing transgressors because doing so provided positive benefits to the group and, consequently, to its individual members through the elimination of group-diminishing behaviour.

The fact that our criminal law system goes to great lengths to ensure that its targets have *actually* transgressed suggests that denunciation and retribution must be directed at actual wrongdoing; in this sense, their main value would seem to lie in their ability to guide behaviour and prevent crime.

Deterrence

Whether the prospect of criminal punishment actually modifies behaviour in convicted individuals (specific deterrence) or in others who learn of it (general deterrence) has been repeatedly called into question. Some go so far as to say that the criminal law, by and large, simply codifies what people would do anyway, and so little or no deterrence actually occurs. (A good account of the deterrence debate can be found in Paternoster, 2010).

By contrast, deterrence advocates argue that most people comply with the law as they understand it, and respond to its changes. So, for instance, when the Canadian government introduced a criminal prohibition on the possession of an unregistered firearm, coupled with significant penalties for non-compliance, most gun owners registered their weapons or disposed of them through gift, sale, or surrender. Thus, the targeted activity (possession of an unregistered firearm) was undeniably—and, in the unique circumstances, measurably—deterred.

Those who contemplate engaging in criminal activities are rarely "rational actors"—that is, they are not people who make subtle cost–benefit assessments and govern themselves accordingly. Certainly, people who are only occasionally tempted to commit a crime are likely deterred by the threat of exposure, arrest, and prosecution. However, habitual criminals are a fairly distinct population—generally poor, often sick with drug addiction or underlying (often undiagnosed) mental illness, and almost always suffering from deficiencies in impulse control. They are also overwhelmingly young and male, a cohort that is, perhaps for evolutionary reasons, disproportionately driven to taking risks and inclined to violent acts as a means of improving social status. General deterrence has been shown to have little effect on habitual criminals: the path of criminality of teenaged boys, for instance, does not appear to change on the birthday they become subject to greater penalties as "adult offenders."

Some have concluded that changes to the law have no deterrent effect, but surely this is going too far for the reasons discussed earlier. Nevertheless, we might concede that

The federal government's gun registry program sparked a highly charged debate across Canada. It was supported by police, but many opponents felt it was far too costly and would have no effect on deterring criminals. The registry was eventually cancelled, although Quebec still maintains a registry. Here, Montreal police seize weapons after consulting the registry during a standoff with an armed man.

Source: Graham Hughes/Canadian Press.

for habitual criminals, the penal justice system behaves more as a regulator of opportunity to commit crime than a moral force; it acts mainly to disrupt criminal behaviour (because a prisoner is temporarily prevented from committing most crimes, and the activities of organized crime or conspiratorial criminal networks are impaired through the rotating arrest and prosecution of even a minority of its members). In this view, members of the criminal "class" are "managed" through the period of their greatest anti-social tendencies, and the public absorbs the associated expenses as a significant but acceptable social cost. These issues and related themes will be explored in greater detail in Part Three of this book, Theories of Crime.

The Limits of Criminal Law: Revolution and Evolution

Any successful society exists in a tension between the liberty of individuals and the power of the state. Individual fulfillment requires freedom to direct one's own path in life, subject to limitations in the interest of the collective good. But this borderline is a battleground. On the one side, individuals strive for their own success, even if doing so sometimes places the collective good at risk. On the other side, the group—and by extension the state—prefers the preservation of public order above almost all else, particularly where the activities it restricts are not those in which the majority of the public engages. The two sides, therefore, are constantly at odds. Nowhere is this more apparent than in the interplay between *constitutional law*, which restrains government and enforces individual rights, and *criminal law*, which provides crude coercive weight to the will of the majority.

This section provides a brief introduction to the idea of "rights" in the criminal law context and an exploration of their limits "in a free and democratic society."

The Development of the "Rights" of Criminal Defendants

The idea that criminal defendants should have "rights" has grown alongside the development of the modern nation-state and, perhaps ironically, in response to the spread of democratic power within populations.

In England after the Norman Conquest of 1066, the series of revolutions, compromises, and agreements that eroded the power of the king empowered lesser nobles and, over time, led to an increasingly representative Parliament. Not coincidentally, one of the means by which the Crown's power was diminished was through the recognition of fundamental rights of citizens faced with criminal accusations, and a number of English history's landmark legal tracts, most famously the *Magna Carta* ("great charter") in 1215, began to refer to the inalienable right of individuals to a minimum standard of due process.

Once **parliamentary supremacy**—something resembling the **rule of law**—took hold, it became clear that removing the power to arbitrarily punish from the king and transferring it to Parliament did not necessarily advance the cause of justice. Democracy alone was no defence against the abuse of prosecutorial authority. Elected assemblies had shown themselves to be just as capable of the arbitrary imposition of capital or penal sanctions as any warlord or king, and (given a legislature's sensitivity to the popular whim and will), perhaps more so. Just consider the Six Generals' trial in ancient Athens (Socrates' "other trial") and the notorious "Bills of Attainder" and "Bills of Pains and Penalties" passed by the English Parliament to effectively convict and punish named

parliamentary supremacy
The concept that the legislative body is superior to other institutions, including the executive and the courts.

rule of law
The principle that governments, individuals, and corporations must follow the law; governments may take actions that limit the activities or rights of citizens only in accordance with substantive and procedural requirements prescribed by law.

individuals. The ancient English right of ***habeas corpus*** (literally, "you have the body"), which permitted a prisoner to challenge the lawfulness of his or her confinement, didn't help if the law under which he or she was detained was itself capricious, corrupt, or unfair. The increasing popular demand to establish fundamental rights in the law became one of the forces that drove the development of constitutionalism. What was needed was a body of laws that would restrain the power of democracy itself.

The birth of the United States at the close of the 18th century, and in particular the codification of the Bill of Rights in the US Constitution, firmly and famously established the idea that the power of the collective and the state must be balanced against the rights of the individual, because only constitutional law could constrain the legislature.

England, from which Canada largely derives its criminal justice system, never adopted a written constitution. However, the notion of citizens' rights against the prosecutorial state has remained a powerful unwritten norm throughout the British Commonwealth. When Canada's *Charter of Rights and Freedoms* was introduced in 1982, it set out a number of rights specific to an accused that in large part mirror those in the then 200-year-old American Bill of Rights. The Charter produced no radical upheaval in criminal justice outcomes in this country, in part perhaps because these fundamental ideas were already so firmly entrenched (Roach, 2008).

The *Charter of Rights and Freedoms* grants a number of rights to criminal defendants. Some are extremely general, such as the guarantee in section 7 that one will not be deprived of life or liberty except in accordance with the principles of fundamental justice. Others are more specific, such as the right in section 8 "to be secure against unreasonable search or seizure," to be free from "cruel or unusual treatment of punishment," and to be tried "within a reasonable time" (pursuant to section 11). Still other rights, such as the provision of an interpreter where necessary (section 14), are very specific. Most, such as the right of *habeas corpus* and the right to remain silent upon arrest, served to enshrine long-standing, even ancient, rights of Anglo-Canadian tradition.

Limitations on Rights

The vulnerability of criminal defendants make them members of a minority for whom special protection is warranted, and so it's not surprising that defendants' rights were the earliest fundamental rights enumerated in the laws of Athens, Rome, and England (and in numerous other countries and cultures; however, our focus is on the Canadian system's most immediate legal forebears). As the law progressed, other vulnerable minorities were also recognized as worthy of legal (and later constitutional) protection: first, members of political and religious groups, then those of disadvantaged races as well as women (although not technically a minority, women were historically underrepresented in the democratic power structure so as to make them similarly vulnerable). Ideally, the goal of the law is to treat all citizens equally except where differential treatment (or differential impact) can be objectively justified (as it might be in the case of children, for instance). Efforts to build a more just and equal society, which often conflict with individuals' desire to do as they please, have strongly influenced the development of criminal law in Canada and elsewhere.

Rights, even fundamental rights, have never been without qualification. For example, although the right of free speech has often been regarded in the West as nearly absolute, it is protected in all communications except those that are immediately harmful (such

habeas corpus
The right of an accused (in the form of a *writ*) to appear before a court, and not be detained without just cause.

as in US Justice Oliver Wendell Holmes' famous example of shouting "fire" in a crowded theatre [*Schenck v. United States*, 1919]). In reality, the near-absolute right of free speech has often succumbed to criminal law as the notion of what constitutes sufficiently imminent danger changes. Criminal conspiracies may be nothing more than conversations that never manifest in damage or injury, but their prohibition has never been seriously controversial. Even mildly critical speech in wartime has been deemed "seditious" and has resulted in imprisonment of notional traitors in the United States (which had constitutional protections for free speech), no less than in England and Canada (which didn't have such protections). Art and literature that has been deemed "obscene," depending on the morals of the day, was also made criminal, and only a vocal few have objected. Ongoing examples are numerous. The trend in Western democracies has been to liberalize speech laws, but not without the occasional considered retreat. One example is the introduction (and successful constitutional defence) in Canada of criminal prohibitions on certain forms of "hate speech," such as the advocacy of genocide. One of Canada's landmark freedom of expression cases, *R v. Keegstra*, is examined in Box 3.2.

Similarly, religious practices have also been prohibited where they are considered to be harmful, although religious beliefs have been persistently protected. Political affiliation is no longer a ground for imprisonment, but affiliation with a criminal organization may be.

This discussion erodes the simplistic view expressed at the beginning of this section that society is a binary struggle between individual and state. We can now appreciate that laws are made in the context of a constantly changing soup of various interests, both group and individual. As a result, the struggle to define the limits of criminal law has become complex, both for legislators and courts.

BOX 3.2

The Limits of Free Expression

In *R v. Keegstra* (1990), the Supreme Court of Canada reviewed the constitutionality of criminal laws prohibiting hate speech. Section 319(2) of the *Criminal Code* states the following:

> Every one who, by communicating statements, other than in private conversation, wilfully promotes hatred against any identifiable group is guilty of
> (a) an indictable offence and is liable to imprisonment for a term not exceeding two years; or
> (b) an offence punishable on summary conviction.

This provision was used to arrest, charge, and prosecute James Keegstra, an anti-Semitic high school teacher. Keegstra taught his classes that Jewish people were responsible for depressions, anarchy, chaos, wars, and revolution. According to Keegstra, Jews "created the Holocaust to gain sympathy" and, in contrast to the open and honest Christians, were said to be deceptive, secretive, and inherently evil. Keegstra expected his students to reproduce his teachings in class and on exams, and they were given poor grades if they didn't. Keegstra argued that hate speech laws unjustifiably infringed his Charter right to freedom of expression in section 2(b), which states:

> Everyone has the following fundamental freedoms:
> (b) freedom of thought, belief, opinion and expression, including freedom of the press and other media of communication;

The government replied that the Charter protects equality, human dignity, and multiculturalism, as well as freedom of expression, and that hate speech laws are designed to protect the rights of victims as well as important public values. For those reasons, it argued, the laws are justified in a free and democratic society.

A main difficulty in setting limits on criminal law is determining when a law serves legitimate social purposes or instead is simply the handmaiden of an outdated paternalism or empty morality. For example, the criminal law against homosexual sodomy has persisted in one form or another throughout our history and arguably lingers to this day (inasmuch as the age of consent is different from that which applies to "normal" sexual acts). Some say that other criminal prohibitions relating to sexual intimacy, such as the ban on consensual adult incest or multi-party marriage (polygamy), are similarly irrational vestiges of Victorian puritanism. But weighing individual rights against the public interest is a tricky business: in a society where both prostitution and its criminalization have been held as unacceptable violations of women's dignity, what is a lawmaker or a constitutional court to do?

Not all such problems are necessarily vexing. Increasingly, courts and—perhaps more sluggishly—legislators have become attuned to historical patterns of prejudice and have begun to view criminal law, and even criminal procedure, in that light. The particular challenges faced by victims of sexual assault, for instance, led to changes in the criminal process to protect against "revictimization" of women and children in a number of ways. Lately, and belatedly, the recognition of the woeful overrepresentation of Aboriginal people in the prison system has led to extensive rethinking of sentencing, in both process and substance, among numerous other legal and social reforms.

Conclusion: The Future of Criminal Law

Criminal justice faces many challenges in the years ahead. The increasing emphasis on rights and due process has contributed to a system that many regard as cumbersome, inefficient, and overly expensive. Trials, which historically would generally last days or (in particularly complex cases) a couple of weeks now often take months or, in some cases, years. State funding of defence counsel, increasingly viewed as fundamental to a fair trial, has nevertheless become concentrated on the most serious cases, and a growing number of criminal defendants are left with little or no recourse to legal advice. In all this, judicial resources are stretched thin in an age of fiscal austerity, resulting in delays and abandoned prosecutions. Many are calling for a fundamental rethinking of the entire justice system, but the direction that this will take is far from certain.

And while criminal law has struggled to accommodate the post–Second World War "rights revolution," it now finds itself stymied in the face of the other great postwar phenomenon, globalization. In the age of international industry and commerce, easy travel, and the Internet, many criminal activities from child exploitation to securities fraud and environmental crimes are inherently **interjurisdictional**. Yet investigation and prosecution have remained firmly rooted in individual countries, provinces, states, and municipalities. Interjurisdictional cooperation in everything from policing to extradition has improved but is far from adequate; international criminal courts, where they are effective at all, concern themselves with breaches of international law such as genocide, not with "ordinary" crimes.

The prescription for the problem is far from clear. Even if a truly international criminal court were established, whose law would it apply, for instance, to Internet gambling? Surely, we cannot expect online activity to be held to the lowest common denominator, with so many countries imposing hideous restrictions on their own citizens' speech and other liberties.

interjurisdictional
Relating to crimes, legislation, or other legal issues that cross the boundaries of nations, provinces, or other jurisdictions.

At its core, criminal law is deeply entrenched, calcified, and resistant to change or sudden movement. However, at its periphery, it is constantly evolving, sometimes quickly, in response to political and social trends. Criminal law is the product of humans, and, like them, it is brilliant and inevitably deeply flawed. However one views the role of criminal law, one thing is clear: it is impossible to understand criminal law without an understanding of its historical, sociological, political, and psychological context.

SUMMARY OF KEY POINTS

- All societies have developed mechanisms for the collective enforcement of group norms in the service of what might be called a "public purpose." Unlike violations of social norms that are embodied in the law of contract or tort, criminal behaviour is addressed by state, not individual, action.

- Most of the "core" criminal prohibitions in Canada—such as murder, robbery, trespass, and assault—originate in ancient history and were inherited in more or less their modern form along with the laws of England. However, the Canadian criminal law tradition differs from the English tradition in several important ways.

- The laws that most people think of as "criminal laws," and the laws that consume virtually all of the efforts of the criminal courts and the corrections systems, are found mainly in two pieces of federal legislation: the *Criminal Code* and the *Controlled Drugs and Substances Act.*

- The concept of a "guilty mind" (*mens rea*) is central to our understanding of most criminal sanctions. Proof beyond a reasonable doubt of mental culpability is a necessary element of every serious criminal offence and most less-serious ones.

- Whether the prospect of criminal punishment actually modifies behaviour in convicted individuals (specific deterrence) or in others who learn of it (general deterrence) has been repeatedly called into question, and is the subject of ongoing debate in Canada.

- Any successful society exists in a tension between the liberty of individuals and the power of the state. Individual fulfillment requires freedom, subject to limitations in the interest of the collective good. The borderline between these two forces is the subject of ongoing legal, political, and social debate.

NOTES

The author is grateful to Neil Boyd and Micah Rankin for their thoughtful suggestions and editorial contributions, and to Graham Hudson for his assistance.

1. The territories have similar courts, but they vary somewhat from those in the provincial model. For the sake of simplicity, the territorial systems will not be addressed in this discussion.

2. The one exception to this is "criminal contempt of court," by which courts may impose penalties, including incarceration, for disrespectful or abusive behaviour that is nowhere defined in statute. Even this, though, is authorized by the *Criminal Code* (section 9).

3. Latin terms, most of which originated millennia ago in Roman law, recur frequently in the legal lexicon. In recent years, a "plain language" movement has replaced many of these terms with ordinary English terms, but a number, such as *actus reus* and *mens rea*, have survived in common use.

4. Section 8(3) of the *Criminal Code* reads:

> Every rule and principle of the common law that renders any circumstance a justification or excuse for an act or a defence to a charge continues in force and applies in respect of proceedings for an offence under this Act or any other Act of Parliament except in so far as they are altered by or are inconsistent with this Act or any other Act of Parliament.

QUESTIONS FOR CRITICAL DISCUSSION

1. How does an understanding of criminal law and its related processes affect one's understanding of criminology?
2. Is it possible to study criminology without any consideration of criminal law?
3. What are the primary purposes of criminal law?
4. Is criminal law shaped by society's values, or are our values shaped by criminal law?
5. Is it the role of criminal law to promote social changes? Or should it serve primarily to uphold established, traditional notions of justice?
6. Why has the United States, among other countries, refused to be part of the International Criminal Court?

SUGGESTED FURTHER READINGS

Brown, D.H. (1995). *The birth of a criminal code: The evolution of Canada's justice system*. Toronto: University of Toronto Press.

Cameron, J., & Stribopoulous, J. (Eds.). (2008). *The Charter and criminal justice: Twenty-five years later*. Markham, ON: LexisNexis.

Katz, H. (2011). *Inside wrongful convictions in Canada*. Toronto: Dundurn Press.

Websites

Canadian Legal Information Institute: http://www.canlii.org

Department of Justice Canada: http://www.canada.justice.gc.ca

International Criminal Court: http://www.icc-cpi.int

REFERENCES

Paternoster, R. (2010). How much do we really know about criminal deterrence? *Journal of Criminal Law and Criminology*, *100*(3), 765.

Roach, K. (2008). A Charter reality check: How relevant is the Charter to the justness of our criminal justice system? *Supreme Court Law Review*, *40*(2), 717–759.

Legislation

An Act to Further Amend the Criminal Law. (1890). 53 Vict., c. 37, s. 8.

Criminal Code. (1985). RSC 1985, c. C-46.

Regulations Prescribing Certain Firearms and Other Weapons, Components and Parts of Weapons, Accessories, Cartridge Magazines, Ammunition and Projectiles as Prohibited or Restricted. (1998). SOR/98-462.

Cases

The Canadian Federation of Agriculture v. The Attorney-General of Quebec and Others. (1950). [1950] UKPC 31, [1951] AC 179.

MacMillan Bloedel Ltd. v. Simpson. (1995). [1995] 4 SCR 725.

Mihalchan v. The King. (1945). [1945] SCR 9.

R v. Holmes. (1998). [1988] 1 SCR 914.

R v. Keegstra. (1990). [1990] 3 SCR 697.

R v. Malmo-Levine; R v. Caine. (2003). 2003 SCC 74, [2003] 3 SCR 571.

R v. Sharpe. (2001). 2001 SCC 2, [2001] 1 SCR 45.

Reference re: Assisted Human Reproduction Act. (2010). 2010 SCC 61, [2010] 3 SCR 457.

Reference re: Remuneration of Judges of the Provincial Court (P.E.I.). (1997). [1997] 3 SCR 3.

Reference re: Section 293 of the Criminal Code of Canada. (2011). 2011 BCSC 1588.

RJR-MacDonald Inc. v. Canada (Attorney General). (1995). [1995] 3 SCR 199.

Schenck v. United States. (1919). [1919] 249 US 47.

United States v. Burns. (2001). 2001 SCC 7, [2001] 1 SCR 283.

Flawed Analyses? Crime in Fort McMurray and Thunder Bay

Crime is said to be rampant in the Regional Municipality of Wood Buffalo, home to Fort McMurray and nine other rural communities in Alberta. The population of the municipality has exploded since the late 1960s, when there were only about 2,500 residents. Today, its population is over 40 times bigger, with well over 100,000 people living in the region. "Fort Mac," as it is often referred to, is the urban anchor for the Athabasca oil sands, the largest known reserve of heavy crude oil in the world, and a controversial but booming energy initiative, often criticized for its environmental impacts.

Some of the nightlife in downtown Fort McMurray, Alberta.
Source: GetStock.

Alex Hannaford wrote in the magazine *British GQ* in 2012:

> Unfortunately, just like the gold-rush towns of the 1800s, Fort McMurray—or Fort McMoney as it's now known—has become synonymous with crime, an explosion in prostitution and the tough, young, bored single men with too much money and little to do, who are fuelling the chaos.

Even *Maclean's* magazine has jumped on the bandwagon in its annual rankings of crime, typically labelling Fort McMurray as one of the more dangerous places to live in the country.

What is the truth about crime in Fort McMurray and the Regional Municipality of Wood Buffalo? Is it a municipality whose name should be synonymous with crime? Is the criticism actually fair and accurate? And why would *Maclean's* label Fort McMurray as it has, given that it relies on data from Statistics Canada?

In fact, after closer scrutiny, the crime rate in Wood Buffalo, for almost all kinds of crime, appears to be below Alberta averages, and often below Canadian norms. The rate of all forms of property crime is below national and provincial averages, and the rate of all forms of violent crime is below Alberta averages. More specifically, rates of sexual assault, robbery, and breaking and entering are well below both national and provincial rates and have seen significant declines over the past decade.

The problem for *Maclean's* and Statistics Canada is that they are not counting a daily population of about 40,000 workers who live in the camps, hotels, and homes that service the oil sands projects. Because these people have homes elsewhere in the country, the federal census does not view them as relevant to the construction of a crime rate. They are erroneously viewed as "transient," despite the fact that on any given day, they make up almost 40 percent of the municipality's population. Put differently, the municipal census, relied upon for the population of most of Alberta's cities, indicates that more than 116,000 people currently live in Wood Buffalo, substantially more than the 61,000 figure that Statistics Canada has derived from its 2011 census.

It's actually a matter of simple arithmetic. If you are trying to calculate a rate, and your denominator (in this case, the population) isn't accurate, it doesn't matter how accurate the numerator (crimes reported to the police) actually is. If you significantly underestimate the denominator—and this is what Statistics Canada has done—you significantly overestimate the crime rate.

Consider another scenario from the realm of media reports about crime rates. In December 2011, again based on *Maclean's* magazine rankings, and again derived from Statistics Canada, *CTV News* declared Thunder Bay to be the murder capital of Canada: "Thunder Bay, Ontario, in the province's rugged northwest on the north shore of Lake Superior, has now earned the macabre title as Canada's murder capital" (Johnson, 2011). But what does this mean, in practical terms? Consider the data in Table 4.1.

In both 2004 and 2008, Thunder Bay had no homicides. In those years, we can reasonably conclude that Thunder Bay could be described as the safest city in the country, at least with respect to homicide. Table 4.1 seems to demonstrate a limitation in defining safety by using year-over-year comparisons of reported homicides: small annual numbers that are highly variable. Would it be more accurate to state that between 2003 and 2012, the province of Alberta had a homicide rate that was 50 percent higher than the national average?

Finally, consider the data in Table 4.2, which compares homicide rates in 2012 with the change in homicide rates between 2003 and 2012. What does it reveal, and what are the limitations in the utility of the data in this table?

Before You Read Chapter 4

- Review the statistics included in the Table 4.1. What can we conclude from this table?
- Why are statistics valuable? What uses do you think they serve?
- Do you pay attention to crime statistics? Do they affect your opinions about crime in particular places?

Table 4.1   Homicide Rates per 100,000, 2003–2012

Jurisdiction	2003 rate	2004 rate	2005 rate	2006 rate	2007 rate	2008 rate	2009 rate	2010 rate	2011 rate	2012 rate	10-year average
Canada	1.74	1.95	2.06	1.86	1.80	1.83	1.81	1.62	1.73	1.56	1.80
Alberta*	2.11	2.80	3.39	2.93	2.62	3.20	2.70	2.13	2.99	2.26	2.71
Guelph	0.88	2.58	0.84	1.67	0.83	0.00	0.81	0.00	0.79	0.00	0.84
Kelowna	0.00	1.89	2.79	0.91	1.77	0.87	2.55	0.84	1.65	1.64	1.49
Wood Buffalo*	3.50	2.98	2.73	2.54	0.00	3.40	1.11	3.27	2.96	0.86	2.34
Sannich	0.92	1.82	0.00	0.90	0.00	0.88	0.00	0.85	0.85	0.00	0.62
Thunder Bay	0.84	0.00	2.51	1.68	1.70	0.00	5.12	4.27	3.41	5.96	2.55
Strathcona County	0.00	1.32	2.49	1.25	1.21	0.00	2.27	0.00	0.00	0.00	0.85
Red Deer*	2.75	2.63	5.06	0.00	0.00	3.42	2.22	0.00	6.53	2.18	2.48
Lethbridge*	1.38	0.00	1.30	0.00	2.45	2.38	1.17	0.00	2.28	3.37	1.43

* Asterisks represent selected municipalities within Alberta and the province as a whole.

Source: Boyd (2014, p. 7).

Table 4.2   Homicide Rates per 100,000, 2012

Jurisdiction	2012 rate	10-year % change
Canada	1.56	−10
Alberta*	2.26	7
Guelph	0.00	−100
Kelowna	1.64	n/a
Wood Buffalo*	0.86	−75
Sannich	0.00	−100
Thunder Bay	5.96	610
Strathcona County	0.00	n/a
Red Deer*	2.18	−21
Lethbridge*	3.37	145

* Asterisks represent selected municipalities within Alberta and the province as a whole.

Source: Boyd (2014, p. 7).

Measuring Crime

LEARNING OBJECTIVES

After reading this chapter, students will be able to:

- Understand the theoretical nature of crime statistics and the four perspectives (structuralist, positivist, constructionist, and integrationist) through which crime may be identified, interpreted, and counted.

- Understand how crime statistics are constructed, what they do and do not show, and the social factors that guide their production.

- Understand the process by which a behaviour that is perceived as a crime becomes an official crime statistic.

- Identify the strengths and limitations of the different data gathering measures used to collect crime data including the UCR2, victimization surveys, and the Crime Severity Index.

- Identify specific ways in which the Internet has altered existing crime and created new opportunity for crime, as well as how these crimes are discovered and measured.

Introduction

If criminology comprises the study of crime and responses to it, then it is clearly important to know how much crime takes place. Any consideration of crime—including what causes it, whom it victimizes, what its general social impacts are, and what should be done about it—requires the ability to assess how it varies from place to place and increases or decreases depending on changes to crime control policies and practices.

The kinds of crime statistics that you typically see referred to in the media and used in much criminological research are often referred to as **quantitative** data, which generally refers to data that are represented in numeric form and generated by methods that are highly structured and seek to aggregate as many cases as possible. Quantitative data are often contrasted with **qualitative** data, which tend to involve fewer cases, are more interested in people's words, and are generated by methods that emphasize interaction with research participants to find the meaning they associate with events.

Qualitative and quantitative methods should be seen as complementary, rather than rivals. Quantitative data help show overall patterns, and their consistent structure allows for comparisons to be made between groups, times, and places. Qualitative observations

quantitative
Relating to the measurement of something—its quantity—rather than its qualities.

qualitative
The study of phenomena based not on measurement but an exploration of the reasons for human behaviour and the qualities of subjective experience.

serve to strengthen statistical results and help to put them into context; when we understand the meaning that people attach to different phenomena, it can help us understand *why* the aggregate results are the way they are. While there is often much made of the differences between qualitative and quantitative research methods, the social sciences benefit far more from an approach that uses multiple methods or a convergent methodology (see Palys & Atchison, 2014). Combining methods, sometimes referred to as *triangulation* (Denzin, 1978), can give us a more comprehensive understanding of a phenomenon, and result in research that is more complete, holistic, and contextual (Jick, 1979).

This chapter is a case in point. Although "crime statistics" are typically conceived as "quantitative data," understanding the prevalence of crime, and what crime statistics can tell us, has benefited from research that involves both qualitative and quantitative traditions. This is because counting the number of criminal acts that occur is not as straightforward as counting phenomena in other areas of study; for example, a health researcher might look at death certificates to find out how many Canadians died from heart attacks last year, or a political scientist might look at voting records to determine how many Canadians voted in the last federal election. Two factors contribute to the complexity of measuring crime: (1) the inherently theoretical nature of "crime" as a construct; and (2) the practical challenge of knowing where crime occurs, what to count, and how to count it.

"Crime" as a Theoretical Construct

Once we embrace the goal of trying to measure the volume of crime, our first challenge is to agree on which acts are "criminal" and which are not. Muncie (2001) offered 11 bases on which an act can be defined as "criminal," including prohibition based in law (that which is prohibited by the state and punishable by law), violation of moral values (that which violates norms of religion and morality and is punishable by a supreme being), violation of social convention (that which violates cultural norms and customs and is punishable by the community), and an act that has behavioural consequences (that which harms others). No doubt all of these and more play a role in how what is "criminal" comes to be defined in any society. Stated another way, the concept of crime is socially defined and hence inherently intertwined with theory.

Whatever its basis, the typical starting point for any discussion of crime in Canada is the *Criminal Code*, a federal statute that first came into force July 1, 1893. Following that, an examination of the frequency and distribution of crime often involves the consideration of "crimes known to the police," which form the basis for crime statistics released periodically by Statistics Canada. We will examine below how these statistics are gathered and generated, but the inherently theoretical nature of crime requires that we first consider the meaning that proponents of different schools of thought attribute to crime statistics. It is important to do so because how crime statistics are conceived by the different schools of thought has significant implications for the kinds of research conducted, which, in turn, informs areas of concern to those who support the different schools of thought. The four general approaches we will review are the *structuralist*, *positivist*, *constructionist*, and *integrationist* approaches. Note that these crime theories are discussed in much greater detail in the chapters of Part Three in this book, but the following serves as a preview to how various theories relate to the practical question of how crime is measured.

Structuralist Perspectives

Structuralist perspectives fall within the general scope of **conflict theories**. Examples of structuralist perspectives include Marxist theories, which focus on inequities in the distribution of capital in society, and feminist theories, which focus on gender inequity in societies organized on largely patriarchal lines. Researchers who follow these and other structuralist perspectives pay particular attention to power structures and ideological influences that play out in a wide array of social contexts. They tend to view the *Criminal Code* not as a neutral social consensus about what a particular society prohibits but, rather, as a contemporary scorecard that reflects who has the power to create the laws that define what is and is not criminal. Crime statistics then become little more than a measure of the extent to which agents of social control recognize and deal with activities those with the power to do so identify as criminal.

Certainly, a good deal of evidence affirms the reasonableness of a structuralist point of view. When Aboriginal communities and corporations come into conflict over the latter's interest in a development project on traditional Aboriginal territory, why is it that the police seem to protect corporate rights and interests instead of those of the Aboriginal community? Why are the possession and consumption of intoxicants favoured by the Western European people who first colonized Canada—alcohol, in particular—legal, while the intoxicants associated with "minorities"—coca, marijuana, peyote, and opium— all illegal? Why is it that when an individual kills someone, we call it "murder" and look for a criminal charge, but when a corporation demonstrates neglect or follows a policy that results in a death, that death is considered a civil matter? Is it mere coincidence that minorities are incarcerated at higher rates than one would expect, given their proportion in the population?

With respect to gender issues, feminists have been at the forefront of various social debates and justice system challenges regarding the legality and illegality of particular acts. Feminists fought to institutionalize women's control over their own bodies in abortion debates and succeeded in making legal what was formerly illegal. They also exposed the blind eye that society had turned to wife assault and succeeded in making illegal what had formerly been tolerated.

Structuralists believe that if the *Criminal Code* is the battleground where we institutionalize a society's conception of right and wrong, then official crime statistics are not particularly relevant because they reveal more about the distribution of societal power than the distribution of societal misconduct. Research from this perspective tends to focus not on crime statistics but on the activities around the creation and implementation of laws, and/or on what happens in the absence of law that the structuralist advocate deems desirable. Those who advocate for legal reform from a structuralist perspective strive to ensure that the changes they seek do not unfairly advantage or disadvantage identifiable groups based on factors such as gender, culture, race, or socioeconomic status.

conflict theories
Theories, originating primarily with Marx, that focus on the unequal distribution of power in society—for example, due to class, race, or gender. Conflicts between classes or groups are driven to a large extent by this unequal power and unequal access to resources.

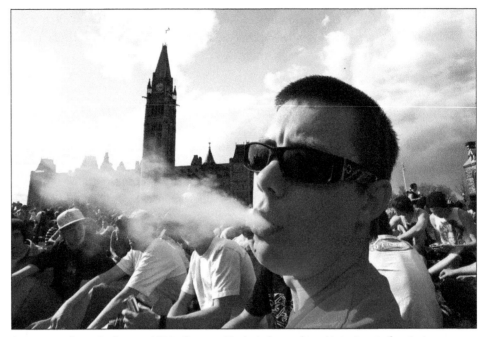

A pro-pot rally on Parliament Hill in Ottawa. Alcohol, the preferred intoxicant of mainstream Canadian culture, is legal, while another, arguably less harmful substance, cannabis, remains illegal. A *conflict* perspective would see this discrepancy in what gets counted as "crime" as evidence of ideological power structures at play in Canadian society, and connected to the association of cannabis with subcultures labelled as deviant. By contrast, a *consensus* view would consider recent shifts in public attitudes. Any consensus supporting criminality that may have once existed appears to be breaking down, as pot becomes more mainstream, with some US states (Washington and Colorado) recently legalizing it. Eventually, a new consensus over legal cannabis use in Canada may emerge.

Source: Leon T. Switzer/Front Page Media Group.

Positivist Perspectives

consensus theories
In opposition to conflict theories, consensus theories, which originate with Durkheim, hold that society functions through social bonds and collective beliefs, and is characterized by widespread acceptance of values, norms, and laws.

Positivist perspectives fall within the general scope of **consensus theories**. Unlike conflict theorists, who see the *Criminal Code* as a battleground influenced by differential access to power, positivists tend to take the *Criminal Code* as a reflection of societal consensus about what is and is not criminal. Positivists assume that the *Criminal Code* is a reflection of a society's collective social values, and therefore consider crime statistics generated by the criminal justice system and governmental agencies such as Statistics Canada unbiased measures of societal crime and criminality.

Crime statistics are gathered by most justice agencies and have been for a very long time. As John Lowman and Ted Palys (1991) note, "Such records are still the most lengthy time-series crime data available to us, having been collected in parts of Europe and North America since the early nineteenth century." It is also arguably the case that, in democratic societies at least, the *Criminal Code* really does represent something of a general societal consensus on what defines crime.

In Canada, police-recorded crime statistics have been collected and published since 1921 (Reed, 2008), although the early data were highly inconsistent due to the small number of police agencies that submitted information and the lack of consistency from year to year and place to place for crimes reported. More standardized and comprehensive practices were developed; the most significant occurred in 1962, when Canada implemented the Uniform Crime Reporting Survey (UCR) with the goal of providing police-reported crime statistics that were complete, accurate, and standardized to facilitate temporal (time-to-time) and spatial (place-to-place) comparisons (Reed, 2008). Ongoing research shows that these statistics have their imperfections—variations between police departments in how crime data were collected and counted, even when standardized, produced results that seemed to obfuscate what was "really" going on.[1] However, the process of reviewing and attempting to improve on these statistics has continued.

As well, the **dark figure of crime**—crimes that occur that are never reported to police—has always been a problem in measuring crime. It makes the collected data both erroneous *and* incomplete. Accordingly, Statistics Canada and the agencies that report to them have constantly looked for ways to create even greater standardization, resolve inconsistencies, and reduce ambiguities in crime statistics. Although positivist researchers acknowledge that the reported crime statistics are imperfect, they argue that these statistics are still useful. Paul Brantingham and Patricia Brantingham (1984), for example, compare these statistics to a miscalibrated bathroom weigh scale that always reads 10 kilograms too light. Even though the weight readings are incorrect (invalid), they can still be used to measure *changes* in weight or to compare different people, since the error is constant.

dark figure of crime
Refers to the variation between the number of crimes that occur and the number of crimes that are actually reported to the police. This figure highlights the large number of unreported crimes.

Constructionist Perspectives

Implicit in positivist approaches to measuring crime is the notion that the challenge of creating better crime statistics is primarily a *technical* problem that can be overcome by identifying sources of error and finding ways to correct them. **Constructionist** theorists do not disagree with the wisdom of trying to minimize error, but suggest that we cannot fully understand crime and its causes and consequences unless we also accept that the identification, coding, and counting of crime is a human and, thus, social process that says as much about our society and justice system as it does about the amount of "crime" that occurs. Stated another way, interpreting crime statistics is not only a technical problem but also a theoretical one.

constructionist
Constructionist perspectives emphasize the idea that life does not come with categories and labels, and that we understand and define the world on the basis of our socialization and interactions with others.

Constructionist theorists argue that crime and crime rates cannot be fully understood unless we understand the justice system response to crime, criminality, and deviance. Indeed, one of the more extreme positions in this perspective, asserted by Jason Ditton (1979), is that crime statistics have little to do with the amount of crime that really exists and are instead primarily measures of police activity. According to this view, police "produce" crime statistics by virtue of the calls for service they respond to, the proactive efforts they make to find crime, and the discretion they exercise in reporting it once they find it. Not surprisingly, those who subscribe to such a view have spent considerable time researching the police in the belief that understanding police theories of crime and criminality is integral to understanding the crime rates their behaviour generates. In this view, "profiling" is no more than institutionalized stereotyping that can create self-fulfilling prophecies by the selective attention police pay to particular groups they view as troublesome. The more attention paid to a particular group, the more members of that group will be caught in illegal activity, while similar activities of other groups will escape attention. As a result, the stereotype associated with the group is reaffirmed, which leads to even greater police attention and further entrenches the stereotype and "legitimacy" of police scrutiny. Indeed, police closely observe people they believe are "out of place" in certain settings—the black youth in a predominantly white neighbourhood; the single woman standing for an extended period on a street corner; the Aboriginal youth driving an expensive newer car (e.g., Sacks, 1972).

Integrationist Perspectives

integrationist
A combination of structuralist, positivist, and constructionist approaches in criminology facilitating the inclusion of philosophy and sociology of law, the empirical study of crime, and its interpretation by those who control and implement the law.

A fourth perspective, referred to as **integrationist** (see Lowman & Palys, 1991), sees some merit in all three perspectives. We suggest that any criminological theory that seeks to offer a complete explanation of crime and its causes and consequences should include both (1) a philosophy and sociology of law that focuses on the development and change in laws, incorporating an analysis of whose interests are served; and (2) an empirical study of crime and deviance focused on not only how the criminality revealed by crime statistics is distributed in society, but also how these categories are interpreted and managed by those who control the development and implementation of law.

This fourth perspective guides the rest of our discussion in this chapter. We continue by analyzing how crime statistics are constructed, which in turn will help us see what they do and do not show, as well as identify the social factors that guide their production.

Deconstructing the Crime Statistic

Figure 4.1, which is adapted from Wesley Skogan (1975), shows a simplified model of the events that must occur before behaviour contrary to the *Criminal Code* (a "crime") will make its way into the crime statistics reported by Statistics Canada. Of course, by adopting this model, we have bypassed the debate about whether the behaviour in question *should be* considered a crime. We leave that to others in this text and elsewhere to consider. On the left side of this figure, one can see that a number of steps occur from the time a criminal act takes place to the point that it becomes—or does not become—a statistic. This is known as a **crime funnel**. Moving through this process step by step, the number of acts that will eventually be registered as an official statistic is reduced.

crime funnel
A model indicating that the actual total quantity of crime is much higher than the decreasing proportion that is detected, reported, prosecuted, and punished.

Crimes Witnessed by the Public

The left side of the figure shows the process that must occur for a criminal event to be brought to the attention of the police by a member of the general public. The first thing that must happen is that a person must recognize an event as "criminal." Even if an event is criminal, if somehow the person does not notice it (e.g., money is stolen from a person, but that person doesn't realize it or thinks that he or she might have lost it) or does not consider the event to be "criminal" (e.g., a physical interaction is viewed as "roughhousing" rather than "an assault"), then clearly that will be the end of it.

Understanding this first step in the process also allows us to consider other human factors that might influence whether the event is dismissed or moves to the next step in the process. Certainly, one's knowledge of the criminal justice system could play a role here; however, with more than 40,000 laws on the books, it is doubtful that any of us knows all of the "crimes" that might be committed. Cultural differences could also play a role in the interpretation of events. For example, years ago one author of this chapter was involved in research that involved visiting RCMP detachments in different parts of the country (see Dutton, Boyanowsky, Palys, & Heywood, 1982). One thing that was clear was that different communities had different standards for defining "assault." In northern mining communities such as Flin Flon, Manitoba, a certain amount of "roughness" was tolerated that might well be considered "assault" in an urban centre such as Winnipeg. This finding suggests that it would be reasonable to compare the rate of assault in Flin Flon at two different points in time because the local interpretation of what constitutes "assault" is likely to be the same. However, it would be problematic to compare the rate of assault in Flin Flon and Winnipeg because the meaning of "assault" is not the same in the two communities.

FIGURE 4.1   The Processes by Which a Behaviour That Is a "Crime" According to the Criminal Code Becomes an Official "Crime Statistic"

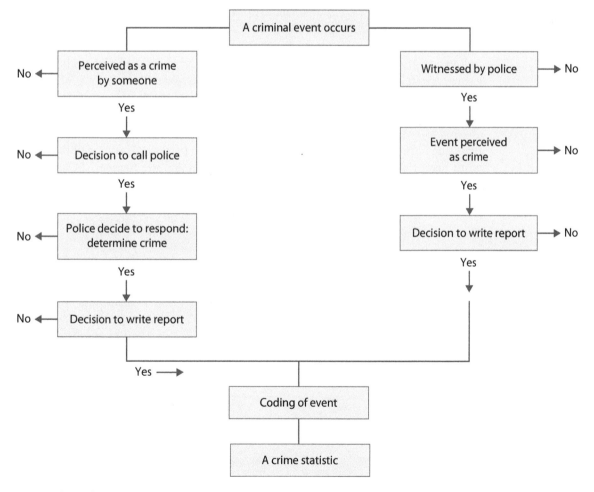

Source: Adapted from Skogan (1975, p. 21).

Even if an event *is* perceived as a crime, it will never become a statistic unless an individual who experiences or witnesses it decides to call the police. Many factors come into play here. Some individuals—such as teachers and social workers—have legal duties to report particular kinds of crimes, while others do not. One's confidence in the police and/or the extent to which one sees the police as the "appropriate" agency to contact will also play a role in the decision to report an event. For example, one author of this chapter has done research with an Aboriginal Justice Program that operates in a major Canadian city (Palys, Isaac, & Nuszdorfer, 2012). Over time, for many forms of trouble—which include acts that might well be considered "criminal"—members of the city's Aboriginal community have become more likely to call the Aboriginal Justice Program than to dial 911. They prefer the way that the program deals with offenders compared with the way the police and Canadian justice system do.

Broad social surveys, such as the General Social Survey (GSS) that is conducted by Statistics Canada every five years, help shed light on the extent to which people fail to call police and a few of the reasons why. Statistics Canada regularly finds that a large percentage of individuals fail to report criminal victimization to police. In 2004, on average, only 31 percent of those polled in the GSS had reported the crimes they experienced to the police (Perrault & Brennan, 2010). This percentage was down from 34 percent in 2004, which raises the question why an increasing percentage of Canadians decide not to report the crimes they experience.

Reporting rates are also related to the type of crime. Break-ins and motor vehicle theft were most often reported, at 54 percent and 50 percent, respectively, and sexual assaults were least likely to be reported, at 12 percent (Perreault, 2013). Reporting of other types of violent victimization ranged from 43 percent for robbery down to 34 percent for physical assault (Perrault & Brennan, 2010). Some of the most common reasons for not reporting crimes include "not important enough" (68 percent), "nothing police could do to help" (59 percent), and "dealt with situation in another manner" (42 percent)

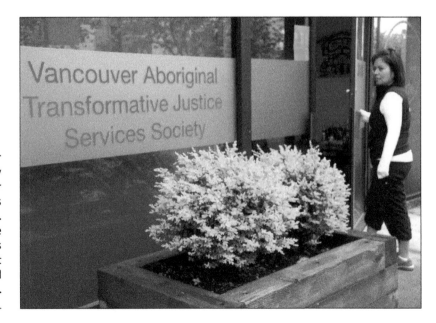

Rather than contacting a municipal or provincial police department, many Aboriginal people prefer to contact their local Aboriginal Justice Program, such as the office in Vancouver pictured here. This is one example of how the reporting of crime through various channels can have an influence on what is included in, and left out of, official government statistics.

Source: Ted Palys.

(Perrault & Brennan, 2010). (For more on this study, see Figure 5.1 in Chapter 5, Victims of Crime.) In sum, despite being recognized as a "crime," many criminal events never become crime statistics because they are never reported to police.

Citizens' expectations about the prospective outcome of their call significantly affects whether they will call the police. For example, years ago, after "Operation Identification" was first implemented—a program that encouraged individuals to engrave identifying information on precious items to make it easier to recognize them as stolen and thereby easier to potentially foil and convict thieves—crime rates *increased*. It appears that this increase had nothing to do with the actual frequency of break and enters and theft, but rather with people's belief that it was now worth calling police because the program was advertised as increasing the chance of getting stolen goods back (Lowman, 1982).

Even if the police *are* called, the first decision they make is whether to respond. This involves deciding whether the call involves a "police matter" and whether it is worthwhile for them to attend the scene. For example, years ago, Bruce Levens and Donald Dutton (1980) found that when one major Canadian police department received calls from women who had been or were being assaulted by their husbands, it sent out officers to investigate less than 50 percent of the time. More recently, many police departments have adopted mandatory attendance policies for domestic disputes. Clearly, this change in policy will affect the extent to which such events will appear in crime statistics.

If the police do respond when called, they still have considerable discretion about what to do when they get to the scene. Research by Donald Black (1970) and Donald Black and Albert Reiss (1970) has shown that a variety of factors influence whether the police decide to write a report instead of simply issue a warning, confiscate illicit goods (e.g., flushing illegal drugs down the toilet), interrupt some escalating activity (e.g., by separating combatants in a bar fight and sending them off in separate taxis), or undertake some other non-processed alternative. They found that police officers were *less* likely to write reports when the relationship between the perpetrator and the victim was close, believing that such incidents were less likely to end up in court; and they were *more* likely to write a report when the complainant was deferential or someone of high social status.

If anything, police officers these days are required to keep even more detailed records and fill out even more forms for any given incident, and we have yet to meet a police officer whose favourite part of the job is the paperwork. As this suggests, every time the police encounter an incident, they weigh the pros and cons of "making a case" or letting it go, depending on aspects of the crime (Is it serious enough? Is it clearcut enough to generate a conviction?), the offender (Is the individual known to police? Is the individual deferential and apparently a "good" person?), and the complainant or witness (Is the person a "good witness"? Is culpability clearcut, vague, or perhaps shared?).

Crimes Witnessed by the Police

The right side of Figure 4.1 shows the process the police follow when they witness a criminal event either because they have gone looking for it (e.g., they drive through areas where sex workers might ply their trade; they set up drinking-and-driving roadblocks) or because they are out and happen to be where one takes place (e.g., they pass by a bar as it empties and a fight breaks out or a shooting occurs; they turn a corner and come upon individuals consuming or dealing illicit drugs).

The proactive aspect of this side of Figure 4.1 immediately invites the methodological concern of whether some increases (or decreases) in a particular crime rate are due to increases (or decreases) in criminal behaviour or are simply indicative of greater police attention that, in turn, produces more arrests (see Cohen, 2002). In Vancouver, for example, street prostitution brought about a media frenzy in the 1980s and 1990s—both because of citizen concern about the visibility of sex worker–client exchanges and because of feminist concerns that the clients (mostly men) were being violent against vulnerable women. The result was a concentrated police campaign to "shame the johns" by arresting them for soliciting in a public place, which at that time was against the law. The result was a huge increase in the number of charges laid, not because of any change in activity, but because of the increased police attention.

As all these examples suggest, police influence on crime statistics extends beyond the level of individual patrol officers or detectives to jurisdictional differences in the way certain crime categories are addressed from one detachment to another and from one municipality to another.

Many of the factors that influence whether an act becomes a crime statistic on the right side of Figure 4.1 mirror those already mentioned on the left side of the figure. The police must witness the event, must determine that the event is "criminal," and must make a decision to intervene in some formal way that will require them to process the individual(s) involved and write a report. After these steps are taken on both sides of the figure, the event is then categorized and processed.

Categorizing and Processing the Event

We have seen how various filters may intervene between the occurrence of a criminal event and its being archived as a crime statistic, with some proportion of events passing through to the point of being officially recorded and processed. Remember that crime statistics are meant to enumerate the amount of crime that occurs in different categories. Single crimes that involve a single perpetrator and single victim are dealt with easily enough, but what happens when we have multiple crimes and/or multiple perpetrators and/or multiple victims? Under the UCR Survey rules that went into effect in 1962, the first key distinction in counting was whether the crime was a crime of violence or a crime of property. The general counting rules were as follows (Dauvergne & Turner, 2010):

1. for crimes of violence, one counts the number of victims;
2. for crimes of property, one counts the number of events; and
3. for mixed or multiple offences, only the most serious offence is recorded.

To illustrate, imagine two perpetrators enter a store, steal some candy bars, rob the proprietor and a customer, shoot a police officer who tries to apprehend them, set the store on fire, and jaywalk as they return to their getaway car. The event includes both crimes of property (theft under $5,000) and crimes of violence (armed robbery and murder), which makes it a "multiple offence." However, the UCR Survey counts only the most serious offence. Accordingly, despite the various crimes that were involved, the police would report that "one murder" was committed. As Skogan (1975) suggests, the effect of such counting rules was to enhance reliability—different police forces would all use the same rules and presumably all count in exactly the same way—but they did so at the

---

BOX 4.1

Distortions in Crime Measurements: Three Examples

United Kingdom: Jurisdictional differences affecting reported volumes of crime were presented by David Farrington and Elizabeth Dowds (1985) in a study on the disparity of officially recorded crime rates in Leicestershire, Nottinghamshire, and Staffordshire. While police-reported statistics showed Nottinghamshire to have significantly higher crime rates, victimization surveys demonstrated that they were only one-third to one-quarter the difference suggested by official statistics.

United States: New York City also experienced reporting errors after the introduction of **CompStat**, a computer-based real-time mapping system that allowed tracking of serious index crimes such as homicide and rape in New York City in the mid-1990s. Commanding officers in each of the boroughs would be called into a CompStat meeting every Friday morning and, in front of politicians and other police officers, asked to explain what CompStat showed regarding index crimes (crimes included in the FBI's annual crime index) in their area. Pay raises, promotions, as well as demotions and public shame were doled out as a result of CompStat's crime statistics. In 1994, after adopting the use of CompStat, New York police recorded a 12 percent decline in crime, a further drop of 16 percent in 1995, and another drop of 16 percent in 1996. Despite this amazing reduction in reported crime, later studies showed that patrol officers were pressured to "write down" crime—record lower-level offences rather than higher-level index crimes—and to disregard witness statements to ensure that crime dropped in their boroughs (Eterno & Silverman, 2010).

Australia: The police department in Victoria was recently exposed as having a "significant and cumulative" distortion of crime data related to underreporting crime (the department failed to disclose up to 15,000 of the 380,000 annual crimes) and over-reporting **clearance rates** (Rood, 2011). Political pressure, public outrage, and police funding all have been shown to have an effect on police activity and their reported crime statistics (MacDonald, 2002).

CompStat
COMPuter STATistics; the name given to New York City Police Department's accountability process that was introduced in the 1990s to facilitate a reduction in crime.

clearance rates
The proportion of criminal incidents solved by the police. A crime is cleared when the police believe they have found its perpetrator.

---

expense of validity. The resulting crime statistic failed in two notable respects: (1) it failed to capture the true nature of the event; and (2) because of the counting bias that favoured the reporting of violent crime, it would consistently underestimate the amount of property crime and give a distorted (inflated) picture of the relative amount of violent crime in Canada.

Other Ways to Count Crime

If there is one certainty about crime, it's that it is multi-faceted and complex. Thus, it is highly unlikely that any one measure of crime will capture its complexity. Every crime statistic has strengths as well as limitations that place some aspects of crime beyond its reach. Accordingly, researchers, statisticians, and policy-makers have sought other ways to measure crime to get a more complete picture of the crime that does exist.

Victimization Surveys

We saw from the left side of Figure 4.1 that a number of steps exist between a citizen experiencing or witnessing a criminal act and its being processed by the police in such a way as to become a crime statistic. Those steps—often referred to as a *crime funnel*—see the police gradually reduce the number of events that achieve official recognition through the application of different filters. Some of these reductions are reasonable; for example, if we want to count *Criminal Code* "crime," then it seems appropriate to ensure that non-criminal events are set aside. But other reductions are not, for example, those based on personal interest (e.g., reducing the amount of paperwork one has to deal with), pragmatic considerations regarding conviction (e.g., getting the victim to withdraw a complaint because of the low likelihood of gaining a conviction), or other policy considerations (e.g., downgrading crimes in order to intentionally reduce crime rates in the area). Another way researchers have attempted to look at crime is through social surveys in which a sample of citizens is asked to divulge information about experience with crime and the criminal justice system.

Canada produces a number of victimization surveys, including the Canadian Urban Victimization Survey, the Violence Against Women Survey, and the commonly cited General Social Survey (GSS) conducted by Statistics Canada. The GSS is used more generally to gather data on social trends to allow the government to monitor changes in living conditions and the well-being of Canadians over time. However, one portion of the survey is dedicated to victimization, and eight crime types are targeted in the survey. A sample of Canadians, aged 15 and over, is polled to gain a better understanding of how Canadians perceive crime, the justice system, and personal experiences of victimization (Statistics Canada, 2014). The GSS uses a cross-sectional design and, in 2009, surveyed approximately 19,500 households. Starting in 2014, the GSS will use Statistics Canada's new telephone sampling frame that, for the first time, will include cellphone numbers from the census and other administrative sources provided to Statistics Canada (Statistics Canada, 2014).

The GSS provides an important complement to official crime statistics by bringing to light information on crimes that individuals fail to report or police fail to discover. In addition to queries about victimization, respondents are asked questions relating to the reasons why they would not report their victimization to the police. Victimization surveys are not without their own limitations, however. Figure 4.2 shows the steps that must be taken before a criminal event becomes a "crime statistic" reported to and recorded by an interviewer as well as sources of errors that affect results.

Again, we start with a "criminal" event, something that is really a crime, and the first filter indicates that the event must involve a victim because people are unlikely, for example, to spontaneously admit to having consumed illicit drugs or to having solicited the services of a prostitute (often referred to as **victimless crimes**). A related issue identified by Skogan (1982) revolves around our often erroneous assumption that crimes are discrete, one-time events, such as a robbery or a murder. He points out that some criminal acts are ongoing and almost continuous—such as child abuse or partner abuse—which may make them less likely to be reported when or if a survey is constructed in such a way as to ask about discrete events.

Next comes the **sampling** issue. Victimization surveys typically seek a representative sample of the population—sometimes of residents of a particular urban centre—although national samples are more likely to be sought these days, as is the case with Statistics Canada's GSS and similar US and UK surveys. Given that victimization rates are actually relatively low, particularly for more serious offences, samples must be huge in order to

victimless crime
Actions (often perpetrated consensually) that are ruled illegal but do not directly violate or threaten the rights of other individuals.

sampling
In statistics, the selection of a subset of the population in such a way that will allow the results of one's research to be generalizable to the population as a whole.

FIGURE 4.2   The Construction of Crime Statistics Via Victimization Surveys

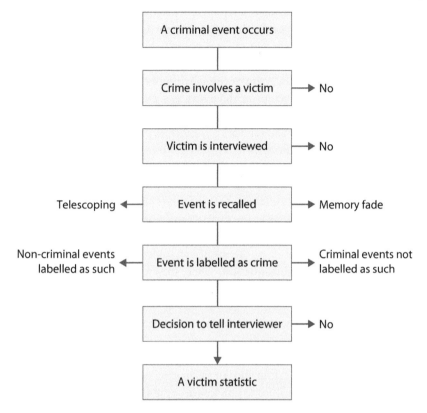

Source: Palys and Atchison (2008, p. 234).

find enough people who have actually experienced certain forms of victimization as well as to ensure subsamples of interest—for example, members of minority groups and vulnerable or marginalized populations—so that analyses based on those subsamples are both generalizable and meaningful. Yet, as Skogan (1982) points out, victimization is not equally distributed across society, and those who are the most vulnerable are often also the most difficult to access and interview.

Once the interview begins, the next issue is to determine whether the interviewee has, indeed, been victimized. Victimization surveys typically ask about victimization within a specific time frame. Sometimes that time frame is as short as six months (which is most common when the individuals being interviewed are known victims); other times it is as long as two years (which is most common in surveys of the general population, especially in countries where crime rates are very low). Three different sources of invalidity or distortion may arise. First, sometimes individuals are not aware of or able to recall the victimization. Second, there may occur **memory fade**, which happens when respondents forget about a victimization that has taken place or recall it erroneously as having taken place outside the time period addressed in the survey. Note that both of these sources of error create false negatives; that is, people who were actually victimized end up not reporting the event(s) and thereby cause an underestimation of actual victimization rates. A third source of error arises from **telescoping**. When you look through

memory fade
The phenomenon whereby a survey participant forgets about a victimization that has taken place.

telescoping
The phenomenon whereby a survey participant recalls events as having occurred more recently than is actually the case.

a telescope or binoculars, things that are far away appear much closer; in the survey realm, "telescoping" is said to occur when people recall events as having occurred more recently than was actually the case. This type of error creates false positives; that is, individuals report victimizations that did not actually occur during the study period, which inflates rates of victimization.

The next step in the process involves the labelling or categorization of the crime, which requires the victim to recognize the event as a crime, and to correctly identify the crime category to which it belongs. The evidence on this point suggests that interviewees can do this quite well; Skogan (1975) describes a study conducted in San Jose, California that found legal authorities and interview participants classified an event in the same way 88 percent of the time.

Finally, even when each of the filters above has been passed, the victim must be willing to tell the interviewer about the event. Skogan (1982) suggests that this may well be the biggest tripping point in the entire process, not only because different crimes are more likely to be reported than others, but also because there are so many ways that the recollection of the particulars of the event are subject to error: forgetting, misremembering, lying (particularly in situations where the victim bears some complicity in the event), and the differential reconstruction of events (persons unaccustomed to violence may see events as more menacing than do those who are more accustomed to violence, so that the former are more likely and the latter less likely to report the event to the interviewer).

Notwithstanding all of these prospective difficulties, victimization surveys succeed in offering a different view of crime and, in particular, help explain the how and why of people's decisions to report crimes to police. These data, in turn, help interpret official crime statistics.

Developing "Better" Crime Statistics
Uniform Crime Reporting Survey 2

The original Uniform Crime Reporting Survey (UCR) that Canada adopted in 1962 included a number of reported offences, actual offences, offences cleared by charge, and offences cleared by other means (Government of British Columbia, 2013). It did not ask police to report victim or incident characteristics, had a limited number of offence codes, and had no ability to add offence codes for new crimes (such as cybercrime) created through legislation. As new crimes came into existence—including criminal harassment, extortion, and offences against the administration of justice—they were merely categorized under "Other" (Government of British Columbia, 2013). In the late 1980s, Statistics Canada moved to adopt a more detailed reporting and collection system: UCR2. This survey was slowly adopted over the following three decades and became the standard for most police services across Canada by 2007 and has been the official police-reported crime survey nationally since 2009.

UCR2 uses a set of nationally set scoring rules, created and managed by the Canadian Centre for Justice Statistics (CCJS). It includes the same data collected under UCR—thereby ensuring some degree of comparability with the older UCR data—but adds detailed information on individual criminal incidents reported to the police, including victim, accused persons, and incident characteristics. UCR2 also allows for the entry of up to four different offences for each incident, which provides a better understanding of multiple-event occurrences, and a wider list of offence categories to better reflect the nature of criminal offences. The "violent crime" category was revised to include events such as criminal harassment, sexual offences against children, forcible confinement/ kidnapping, extortion, uttering threats, and threatening/harassing phone calls, while the "property crime" category was revised to include mischief and arson.

Other changes to UCR2 will undoubtedly alter future statistics, making it even more difficult to compare data from year to year. Robbery, which was historically counted by incident, will now be tabulated by number of victims, with each new victim counting as a new crime. Other violations, such as assault with a weapon, causing bodily harm to a peace officer, aggravated assault on a peace officer, robbery to steal a firearm, kidnapping, forcible confinement, sexual exploitation of a person with a disability, break and enter to steal a firearm, break and enter to steal a firearm from a motor vehicle, and identity theft and fraud were all added as categories of crime in the past four years. These changes will alter counts of historic crimes as Statistics Canada backdates the data to reflect these changes in policy. Similarly, future statistics will be affected, because some crimes will now be recorded under different categories. British Columbia's Ministry of Justice warns, "Police services are able to utilize the new codes as their records management systems are updated. As a result, these data should be interpreted with caution" (Government of British Columbia, 2013).

Crime Severity Index

The vast majority of crime in Canada tends to be of the non-severe type, which means that UCR2 is dominated by less serious crimes. As a result, Statistics Canada developed a Crime Severity Index (CSI), which does not distinguish the severity of crime and only counts violations of the *Criminal Code*, to complement UCR2 (Government of British Columbia, 2013). CSIs were instituted in 2009 and include "Overall CSI" (based on the total volume of police-reported federal statute offences—a measure of the relative severity of overall crime); "Violent CSI" (based on the total volume of police-reported violent federal statue offences—a measure of the relative severity of violent crime); "Non-Violent CSI" (based on the total volume of police-reported federal statute offences not considered violent in nature—a measure of the relative severity of non-violent crime); and "Youth CSI" (based on the number of youth accused of crime—a measure of the relative severity of overall youth crime). CSIs are based on the total volume of federal statute crimes (including those listed in the *Criminal Code*) and are designed to measure both year-to-year changes in crime volume as well as crime seriousness (Wallace, Turner, Matarazzo, & Babyak, 2009). Each crime is weighted according to seriousness; for example, a serious offence such as murder is weighted at a value several hundred times higher than a less-serious offence such as mischief. By weighting crimes, the CSI allows more-serious but lower-volume offences to have a greater impact on the crime rate than high-volume, less-serious offences.

While the CSI allows more-serious crimes to be weighted more heavily than other crimes, more-serious crimes are not weighted on the basis of an objective determination of their seriousness, but rather on the basis of court sentencing, thus relying on the subjectivity of the judge imposing the sentence (Dauvergne & Turner, 2010). Using sentencing to weight crime has significant limitations. One problem is that data related to time served on remand (the amount of time a person serves in jail prior to sentencing) are not collected and not included in the weighting of the CSI. While judges often factor remand time in their sentencing decisions, the CSI survey data cannot show the entire sentence length (days in jail including remand time or days in jail excluding remand time) (Wallace et al., 2009). Furthermore, repeat offenders, youth offenders, and life sentences can all skew the weightings, given that judges often take into consideration a person's prior criminal record when determining a sentence. Also, information related to recidivism is not collected for the CSI. As well, conditional sentences are viewed as non-incarceral for the purposes of the CSI weighting model. Moreover, a life sentence cannot be measured in terms of actual time but is estimated at a value of 25 years (Wallace et al., 2009). Additional limitations on the usefulness of year-to-year comparisons in the CSI arose when weights were updated in 2013 (for the first time since the introduction of this measure), reflecting court data from 2006 to 2011 and altering the prior published CSI ratings (Wallace et al., 2009).

Trying to Capture a Moving Target

In a recent *Star Trek* film, Scottie becomes the starship *Enterprise*'s chief engineer and explains the difficulty involved in transporting ("beaming") someone from a fixed location to another starship that is moving in space: "The notion of trans-warp beaming is like trying to hit a bullet with a smaller bullet, whilst wearing a blindfold, riding a horse." Statisticians, who try to improve crime statistics, face an analogous complexity. While previous research can tell us about potential sources of error and the limitations of existing statistics that have implications for how they might be improved, society itself is changing, which means that one is always trying to capture, in a fixed way, a target that is always moving.

UCR and UCR2 have focused on traditional types of crimes, including violence and property offences, despite the creation and common use of the Internet in the late 20th century. The Internet is used to commit both crimes of a traditional nature and new crimes; crime committed over the Internet or a computer network is known as **cybercrime** (Smyth, 2010). Although the Internet started to be used commercially in the 1990s and was rapidly adopted by criminals and non-criminals alike, Canada did not begin to collect statistics on cybercrime until 2005 (Griffiths, 2007).

cybercrime
Crime committed over the Internet or a computer network.

Understanding Societal Change: Crime Drop or Crime Swap?

Over the past two decades, industrialized countries worldwide have reported dramatic decreases in some police-reported crimes (FBI, 2012; Home Office, United Kingdom, 2013; Perrault, 2012). Researchers have begun to offer some explanations for these decreases. For instance, crimes such as automobile theft, at least by less-skilled thieves, may have dropped due to the installation of government-mandated disabling and anti-theft devices in all new cars. The idea that a change in the level and quality of security leads to a decrease in crime has been coined the "security hypothesis" by Graham Farrell, Nick Tilley, Andromachi Tseloni, and Jen Mailley (2011). According to the United Nations Crime Trends Survey for developed countries, worldwide levels of homicide have also fallen, whereas levels of assault have increased (Gruszczyńska & Heiskanen, 2012). While no one is quite certain why these changes have occurred, competing explanations include the following:

1. Improvements have been made in emergency medical care, which have led to an increased number of assault victims surviving their assault rather than dying as they would have 20 or 30 years ago.
2. Young adults have become less risk tolerant, which has led to safer behaviours and a reduction in potential victimization (Mishra & Lalumière, 2009).
3. The advent of commerce on the Internet led a greater number of young adults (males, particularly) to stay home playing online video games (ComScore, 2011), removing them from potential harm as a victim (they are safe at home) and offering a substitute for excitement and risky behaviour that could lead to fatal assaults.

The Effect of the Internet on Crime Measurement

The question remains: Has crime really dropped? By examining Figure 4.1, we are able to offer avenues by which to explore this issue by placing rival plausible explanations in the decision-making framework. This allows us to explore the idea that crime has not necessarily dropped but some types of traditional crime have merely been displaced by cybercrime. Although crimes such as identity theft and identity fraud have been directly linked to the growth in Internet adoption and usage, Canada is only now drafting and tabling related legislation, such as Bill C-13—the *Protecting Canadians from Online Crime Act*—which received its first reading in November 2013. With the exception of child pornography and child luring, cybercrimes have been entirely excluded from UCR2 until now. Not only are new crimes emerging due to the Internet, but also, as the RCMP report, almost any traditional crime can be perpetrated via computer (RCMP, 2014).

Recall that for crime to make its way into police-recorded statistics, it must first be noticed. Crimes in the virtual space of the Internet are often far less visible than those that happen in the face-to-face world. It is much easier to be certain that you have been mugged than to know that your bank account was hacked or your identity stolen—especially immediately after these crimes have occurred. Once a crime is noticed, the police must then be called. But how many people know to call the police for an Internet-related crime? When most people notice an error on their bank or credit card statement, they are more likely to call their bank than the police. When their computer is hacked, people are more likely to take the computer in for servicing or call the technical support number of their computer's manufacturer. For the police, handling cybercrime can be complicated. Finding a perpetrator who is anywhere on earth is much more difficult than finding a perpetrator who is somewhere in one's own town (even then, the task is a challenge). Should the perpetrator be found, where should the crime statistic be recorded? In the country of the victim? In the country of the perpetrator? Where the Internet service provider is stationed? These are all questions that law enforcement agencies are grappling with today. Historically, crime was a local phenomenon. Thinking of routine activity theory, the perpetrator met in time and space in the absence of a capable guardian. For cybercrime, how do we measure time and space? Finally, if the crime is noticed and reported, does it even exist as a crime, and how will the police respond?

Despite the numerous possible difficulties in dealing with cybercrime, according to data collected by Kapersky Labs and B2B International, a Canadian anti-virus and software company that conducted a survey of Canadian computer users in 2014, cybercrime is highly prevalent in Canada: 62 percent of respondents reported experiencing at least one attempt by cybercriminals to steal their personal financial information, and 41 percent reported that they had lost money they were unable to retrieve (Udemans, 2014).

Cybercrime includes a wide variety of offences against computer data and systems. It includes money laundering; corruption; offences against confidentiality, integrity, and availability of computer data and systems—including unauthorized entry into computers or the unauthorized use or manipulation of electronic systems—data and/or software—including illegal downloading of data and programs; as well as crimes against persons such as harassment, bullying, child luring, and child pornography. Despite the lack of police-reported statistics, regular news reports highlight the vast number and pervasiveness of these cybercrimes.

Defining, discovering, and prosecuting cybercrime (both traditional crime that takes place online and strictly Internet-related crime) pose challenges for law enforcement agencies. Issues to be determined relate to jurisdictional boundaries and domains, the application of newly tabled legislation, police practices, and the ability to process Internet-related evidence. (For more on these topics, see Chapter 18, White-Collar Crime.)

Conclusion

Measuring crime statistics involves multiple steps and processes of interpretation and understanding—with each one adding complexity and the possibility for measurement error, both deliberate and accidental. Police-generated statistics are not an objective measure of crime. Rather, they reflect the attitudes and opinions of the officers, policies, and procedures of the police; legislation passed by government, at multiple levels; and larger societal influences. The interpretation of crime statistics is equally nuanced, often reflecting the opinions and beliefs as well as the general philosophy of the researcher. Structural, positivist, constructionist, and integrationist approaches to understanding crime statistics all reflect different world views and affect not only the understanding of how crime is measured and recorded but what gets measured and why. While government and police agencies have worked over the years to improve the quality of crime statistics, inherent weaknesses remain that, at least at this time, simply cannot be fixed. Victimization surveys help fill in some of the missing information on crime, but they also have weaknesses. The current, apparent drop in crime witnessed in most industrialized countries has presented a puzzle for criminologists, not only because it appears as though human behaviour may have radically changed, but that the Internet poses challenges to measuring crime statistics that may take years to address effectively.

SUMMARY OF KEY POINTS

- The theoretical nature of crime, its identification, interpretation, and statistical enumeration are examined through four perspectives: structuralist, positivist, constructionist, and integrationist.

- Understanding the theories and perspectives through which crime statistics are constructed allows the individual to consider what they do and do not show and the social factors that guide their production.

- Understanding the process by which a behaviour is perceived to be a crime and eventually becomes a crime statistic must take into account the crime funnel—the process through which the actual quantity of crime is reduced in stages such that only a small proportion of total crime is detected, prosecuted, and punished.

- A number of data-gathering measures are used in Canada to collect crime data, including the UCR2, victimization surveys, and the Crime Severity Index. Although each measure has its own strengths and weaknesses, it is hoped that by collecting the different measures statisticians might be able to determine a more accurate count of crime in Canada.

- Changes in the way in which Canadians live, including Internet use, have vastly altered the landscape of crime and offending, creating both new opportunities for crime and new ways to commit traditional crimes. Currently, most developed countries are grappling with ways in which to discover and measure these crimes.

NOTE

1. For example, when multiple crimes occur—someone breaks into an establishment, steals various goods, and assaults three victims, one of whom dies—UCR rules required that only the most serious event would be reported; that is, the homicide in this case, with the result that violent crimes tended to be over-represented and lesser crimes underrepresented in crime statistics.

QUESTIONS FOR CRITICAL DISCUSSION

1. What is meant by the terms *structuralist*, *positivist*, *constructionist*, and *integrationist*? How do these perspectives influence the construction of crime statistics?
2. What are the strengths and weaknesses of our various measures of crime (including the UCR2, the General Social Survey, and the Crime Severity Index)?
3. Discuss how the Internet has influenced crime (both new and traditional crime) and how it has made the discovery and counting of crime much more complex than crime committed in the physical world?
4. Explain the process of the crime funnel. What are some of the factors that affect the reduction of crime at each stage?

SUGGESTED FURTHER READINGS

Adorjan, M. (2012). The lens of victim contests and youth crime stat wars. *Symbolic Interaction*, *34*(4), 552–573. doi:10.1525/si.2011.34.4.552

Cook, A.N. (2012). Tough on crime reforms: What psychology has to say about the recent and proposed justice policy. *Canadian Psychology*, *53*(3), 217–225. doi:10.1037/a0025045

Websites

BC Ministry of Justice Police Services Division: http://www.pssg.gov.bc.ca/policeservices/index.htm

Employment and Social Development Canada: http://www.esdc.gc.ca

Juristat: http://www.statcan.gc.ca/pub/85-002-x/index-eng.htm

REFERENCES

Black, D.J. (1970). Production of crime rates. *American Sociological Review, 35*, 733–748.

Black, D.J., & Reiss, A.J. (1970). Police control of juveniles. *American Sociological Review, 35*, 63–77.

Boyd, N. (2014). *Crime in the Regional Municipality of Wood Buffalo*. Wood Buffalo, AB: Regional Municipality of Wood Buffalo.

Brantingham, P.J., & Brantingham, P.L. (1984). *Patterns in crime*. New York: MacMillan.

Cohen, S. (2002). *Folk devils and moral panics* (3rd ed.). New York: Routledge.

ComScore. (2011). It's a social world: Top 10 need-to-knows about social networking and where it's headed. *ComScore*. Retrieved from http://www.comscore.com/Press_Events/ Presentations_Whitepapers/2011/it_is_a_social_world_top_10_need-to-knows_about _social_networking.

Dauvergne, M., & Turner, J. (2010). Police-reported crime statistics in Canada, 2009 (Catalogue no. 85-002-X). *Juristat, 30*(2), 1–37.

Denzin, N.K. (1978). *The research act* (2nd ed.). New York: McGraw-Hill.

Ditton, J. (1979). *Controlology: Beyond the new criminology*. London, UK: Macmillan.

Dutton, D.G., Boyanowsky, E.O., Palys, T.S., & Heywood, R. (1982). *Community policing: Preliminary results from a national study of the RCMP*. Research report prepared for the Research Division of the Solicitor General Canada.

Eterno, J.A., & Silverman, E.B. (2010). The NYPD's CompStat: Compare statistics or compose statistics? *International Journal of Police Science & Management, 12*(3), 426–449. Retrieved from http://nylawyer.nylj.com/adgifs/decisions/011311eterno_silverman.pdf.

Farrell, G., Tilley, N., Tseloni, A., & Mailley, J. (2011). The crime drop and the security hypothesis. *Journal of Research in Crime and Delinquency, 48*(2), 147–175. doi:10.1177/0022427810391539.

Farrington, D.P., & Dowds, E.A. (1985). Disentangling criminal behaviour and police reaction. In D.P. Farrington & J. Gunn (Eds.), *Reactions to crime: The public, the police, courts and prisons* (pp. 41–72). Chichester, UK: Wiley.

FBI. (2012). Crime in the United States: By volume and rate per 100,000 inhabitants, 1992–2011. Retrieved from http://www.fbi.gov/about-us/cjis/ucr/crime-in-the-u.s/2011/ crime-in-the-u.s.-2011/tables/table-1.

Government of British Columbia. (2013). Overview of crime data collection in British Columbia, 2012. Retrieved from www.pssg.gov.bc.ca/policeservices/shareddocs/ crime-data-collection.pdf.

Griffiths, C. (2007). *Canadian criminal justice: A primer* (3rd ed.). Toronto: Nelson.

Gruszczyńska, B.Z., & Heiskanen, M. (2012). Trends in police-recorded offences. *European Journal of Criminal Policy Research, 18*(1), 18–83. doi:10.1007/s10610-011-9160-0.

Hannaford, A. (2012, March). No country for young men. *British GQ*. Retrieved from http://www.gq-magazine.co.uk/comment/articles/2012-03/08/canada-oil-rush.

Home Office, United Kingdom. (2013). A summary of recorded crime data from 1898 to 2001/02 (Microsoft Excel file). Statistics: Historical crime data. Retrieved from http://www.gov.uk/government/publications/historical-crime-data.

Jick, T.D. (1979). Mixing qualitative and quantitative methods: Triangulation in action. *Administrative Science Quarterly, 24*(4), 602–611. Online: http://www.jstor.org/ stable/2392366.

Johnson, A. (2011, December 27). Thunder Bay takes murder capital title from Abbotsford. *CTV News*. Retrieved from http://www.ctvnews.ca/thunder-bay-takes-murder-capital -title-from-abbotsford-1.744233#ixzz2yQRwu5qo.

Levens, B.P., & Dutton, D.G. (1980). *The social service role of the police: Domestic crisis intervention*. Ottawa: Solicitor General of Canada.

Lowman, J. (1982). Crime, criminal justice policy and the urban environment. In D.T. Herbert & R.J. Johnston (Eds.), *Geography and the urban environment* (Vol. 5, pp. 307–341). Chichester, UK: Wiley.

Lowman, J., & Palys, T.S. (1991). Interpreting criminal justice system records of crime. In M.A. Jackson & C.T. Griffiths (Eds.), *Canadian criminology: Perspectives on crime and criminality* (pp. 349–369). Toronto: Harcourt Brace Jovanovich.

MacDonald, Z. (2002). Official crime statistics: Their use and interpretation. *The Economic Journal, 112*(477), F85–F106. doi:10.1111/1468-0297.00685

Mishra, S., & Lalumière, M. (2009). Is the crime drop of the 1990s in Canada and the USA associated with a general decline in risky and health-related behavior? *Social Science & Medicine, 68*(1), 39–48. doi:10.1016/j.socscimed.2008.09.06

Muncie, J. (2001). The construction and deconstruction of crime. In J. Muncie & E. McLaughlin (Eds.), *The problem of crime* (2nd ed., pp. 7–70). London, UK: Sage.

Palys, T., & Atchison, C. (2008). *Research decisions: Quantitative and qualitative perspectives* (4th ed.). Toronto: Thomson Nelson.

Palys, T., and Atchison, C. (2014). *Research decisions: Quantitative, qualitative and mixed methods approaches* (5th ed.). Toronto: Thomson Nelson.

Palys, T., Isaac, R., & Nuszdorfer, J. (2012). *Taking indigenous justice seriously: Fostering a mutually respectful coexistence of Aboriginal and Canadian justice*. Research report prepared for Vancouver's Downtown Community Court and Vancouver Aboriginal Transformative Justice Services. Retrieved from http://www.sfu.ca/~palys/PalysEtAl -2012-Aboriginal&CanadianJustice-final.pdf.

Perreault, S. (2012, December 4). Homicide in Canada, 2011 (Catalogue no. 85-002-x). *Juristat*. Retrieved from http://www.statcan.gc.ca/pub/85-002-x/2012001/article/11738-eng.pdf.

Perreault, S. (2013, July 25). Police-reported crime statistics in Canada, 2012 (Catalogue no. 85-002-x). *Juristat*. Retrieved from http://www.statcan.gc.ca/pub/85-002-x/2013001/ article/11854-eng.pdf.

Perreault, S., & Brennan, S. (2010). Criminal victimization in Canada, 2009 (Catalogue no. 85-002-X). *Juristat*. Retrieved from http://www.statcan.gc.ca/pub/85-002-x/2010002/ article/11340-eng.htm.

RCMP. (2014). Internet security. Retrieved from http://www.rcmp-grc.gc.ca/qc/pub/ cybercrime/cybercrime-eng.htm.

Reed, P. (2008). Statistics on crime and law enforcement (Series Z1-65). *Statistics Canada* (archive). Retrieved from http://www.statcan.gc.ca/pub/11-516-x/sectionz/4147446-eng.htm.

Rood, D. (2011, May 27). Police will outsource crime stats. *The Age* (Victoria, Australia). Retrieved from http://www.theage.com.au/victoria/police-will-outsource-crime-stats -20110526-1f6b7.html.

Sacks, H. (1972). Notes on police assessment of moral character. In D. Sudnow (Ed.), *Studies in social interaction* (pp. 280–293). New York: Free Press.

Skogan, W.G. (1975). Measurement problems in official and survey crime rates. *Journal of Criminal Justice, 3*, 17–32.

Skogan, W.G. (1982). Methodological issues in the measurement of crime. In H.J. Schneider (Ed.), *The victim in international perspective* (pp. 203–208). Berlin: DeGruyter.

Smyth, S. (2010). *Cybercrime in Canadian criminal law*. Toronto: Thomson Reuters Canada.

Statistics Canada. (2014). General Social Survey—Victimization (GSS): Definitions, data sources and methods. Retrieved from http://www23.statcan.gc.ca/imdb/p2SV.pl ?Function=getSurvey&SDDS=4504.

Udemans, C. (2014, January 27). 62% have experienced attempted cybercrime—survey. *HumanIPO*. Retrieved from http://www.humanipo.com/news/39231/62-have -experienced-attempted-cybercrime-survey.

Wallace, M., Turner, J., Matarazzo, A., & Babyak, C. (2009). *Measuring crime in Canada: Introducing the Crime Severity Index and improvements to the Uniform Crime Reporting Survey* (Catalogue no. 85-004-X). Ottawa: Statistics Canada.

Amanda Todd

In October 2012, 15-year-old Amanda Todd hanged herself at her home in Port Coquitlam, BC. One month earlier, she had posted a nine-minute YouTube video entitled "My Story: Struggling, bullying, suicide and self-harm." The video showed Amanda using a series of flash cards, without any audible commentary, to tell her story.

Students observe a moment of silence in memory of bullying victim Amanda Todd.

Source: Carlos Osorio/GetStock.com.

"I've decided to tell you about my never-ending story," she began. "In 7th grade I would go with friends on webcam ... I got called stunning, beautiful, perfect, etc. They wanted me to flash ... so I did."

About a year later, she continued, she received a message from someone on Facebook saying that "if you don't put on a show for me I will send ur boobs." The young man knew her name, address, and her friends. A short time later, Amanda received a knock on her door at 4 a.m. from the police; the photo had been sent everywhere online.

Amanda felt sick and began to suffer from anxiety, depression, and panic disorder. She moved to another school and became involved with alcohol and other drugs. The topless photo followed her to this new location, and her difficulties worsened. She did not have any friends, was called names, and concluded that the photo is "out there, forever."

Amanda started cutting herself; at school, she sat alone at lunch—and then moved schools again. Things were better for a while, although she still ate lunch alone. About a month later, she started texting with "an old guy friend" who "liked me, led me on, he had a girlfriend."

She went over to his house and had sex with him while his girlfriend was on vacation. "Big mistake," she said. A week later, she received this text: "get out of your school." A group of young teens approached her, with the support of the young man she had had sex with. One of them, a young girl, threw her to the ground, and punched her several times; a few kids filmed the event.

"I thought he really liked me," she continued in the video, "but he just wanted the sex." She lay in a nearby ditch until her father came to pick her up. "I wanted to die so bad," she wrote, "when he brought me home, I drank bleach." She thought she was going to die, but the ambulance came, brought her to hospital, and flushed the bleach from her system.

Facebook posts were unrelenting and unkind. "She deserved it," was a common theme. Amanda moved again, to another city, to be with her mother. She decided against pressing charges, just wanting to move on with her life. But the commentaries on Facebook continued—with posted photos of bleach and ditches. One comment went so far as to suggest a hope that she would actually kill herself next time.

"Life's never getting better," she said, adding, "I can't meet or be with people ... am constantly cutting. I'm really depressed." She went to counselling and was placed on anti-depressants, but nothing seemed to improve her mood. She overdosed and ended up in hospital.

"I have nobody; I need someone," her video concluded, along with a photo of her arm, revealing a series of bloody slashes. A month later she was dead.

The media response to the death of Amanda Todd was international in scope. Her YouTube video has now attracted more than 9 million viewers, and shortly after her death more than 1 million Facebook users reported that they "liked" her Facebook page. But some negative sentiments persisted. Among the mostly positive commentaries on Facebook were some continuing attacks from students claiming to be former classmates. And ABC News reported from the United States that a number of fraudulent websites had been set up, linked to the tragedy, to solicit donations on behalf of Amanda Todd.

Technology has clearly changed both the scope and nature of victimization. Social media can work to amplify harm and to distribute harmful material to literally anyone with a computer and access to the Internet. This case provides a clear example of a type of victimization that simply did not exist until the last decade.

Before You Read Chapter 5

- What can be done in law and policy and in our schools to diminish the likelihood of this kind of tragedy?
- What is it about social media that amplifies this sort of victimization?
- We may typically think of "victims of crime" as somehow different from people who commit suicide. How does the case of Amanda Todd suggest otherwise?

Victims of Crime

LEARNING OBJECTIVES

After reading this chapter, students will be able to:

- Describe the differences between criminology and the study of victims.
- Understand issues surrounding the researching of victim experience, including who we define as a victim and issues related to measuring victim experience.
- Understand common responses to victimization and victim resilience.
- Understand who is most vulnerable to victimization.
- Describe the victim-blaming process and problems with the victim precipitation model.

Introduction: Victimology in Canada

Think about the last news story you heard or read about that involved a criminal act. If you cannot think of such a story, go to your favourite news website and find one. Now think about what you know about the victim from that story. Do you know more about the victim experience or the criminal and what the criminal did to the victim? Chances are, if the story came from the media, you know significantly more about the criminal than the victim. Consider, for example, that the average Canadian has probably heard of mass murderers Paul Bernardo and Karla Homolka, Robert Pickton, Marc Lépine, and Clifford Olson, but likely cannot name any of their victims. But when we know someone who has been victimized, whether a family member, friend, or even the friend of a friend, we tend to want to know about his or her experience, not the offender's. Moreover, we tend to discuss with others what we know about the victim experience (what happened, to whom, at what time of day, what was the victim doing when it happened, how badly was the victim hurt, and so on) so that we can learn from it, and perhaps bring some understanding to our own experiences or how to avoid victimization ourselves.

It is critical for anyone studying victims of crime to recognize that without the victim's courage to report a criminal act, very few criminals would ever be apprehended. After experiencing something traumatic, victims must invoke the criminal justice system (i.e., call the police). Often, the state can only pursue charges if a victim exists and is willing to report the crime(s) against him or her. In some cases, the victim must also be prepared to testify in court about the experience. Without the victim, the criminal justice system would grind to a halt. The decision to come forward can be a very difficult one. Victims may hesitate to report a crime for many reasons. With more serious crimes, these reasons could include fear of repercussion, or concerns that many others would learn about their experience, which in turn may lead to stigmatization. In some cases, victims who have come forward have reported poor treatment by police or medical personnel. In light of all this, changes have recently been made to enhance legislation protecting future victims (see page 110).

While other chapters in this book focus on criminology (i.e., the study of crime), this chapter will focus instead on **victimology** (i.e., the study of victims). *Victimologists* study the victim experience and larger victimization trends. Table 5.1 lists some of the ways in which victimology differs from criminology. In this chapter, we will use the term "victimizer" interchangeably with "offender," which is consistent with a victim-centred approach.

victimology
The study of victims.

Table 5.1 A Comparison of Victimology and Criminology

Victimology	Criminology
• It focuses on the study of victims.	• It focuses on the study of criminals.
• It emphasizes a victim-centred approach to analyzing crime.	• It emphasizes an offender-centred approach to analyzing crime.
• It seeks to understand challenges facing victims of crime.	• It seeks to understand challenges facing criminal offenders.
• It is an emerging discipline.	• It is an established discipline.
• It emphasizes personal solutions to dealing with victims.	• It emphasizes dealing with the criminal via the criminal justice system.
• Victims initiate the criminal justice response by calling the police and deciding to report a crime.	• The police apprehend a criminal based on a victim report.
• Prior victimization has been found to increase the likelihood of subsequent victimization as well as a criminal lifestyle in some individuals.	• A criminal lifestyle has been shown to increase the risk of being victimized.
• Victims are represented by a Crown counsel at trial.	• Offenders are represented by their own personal attorney.
• Victim rehabilitation is rarely financially supported by the state.	• Criminal rehabilitation is often financially supported by the state.
• Data on victims are collected using victimization surveys. The surveys ask members of the public about victimization experiences they have had, and include both crime reported and not reported to police.	• Data on criminals are collected by police, the courts, and the corrections system and include only those crimes reported to those agencies.

Victimology as an Emerging Discipline

As you read through this chapter, keep in mind that victimology is an *emerging discipline*. In other words, this area in the study of crime is relatively new. Traditionally, crime studies, as well as theories that developed from this early research, were predominantly concerned with how people, especially males, became criminals (Naffine, 1987). Early questions centred on whether criminals were simply born bad (suggesting a biological root cause for their offending) or pushed, in some way, into a life of criminal activity. Early Chicago School theorists (such as Robert Park, Ernest Burgess, Clifford Shaw, and Henry McKay), who focused on crime in Chicago from the 1920s to the 1940s, wrote about the acts of male offenders. The victims of crime were of little interest.

Only a handful of academics engaged in studying the victim experience until the 1970s. Research on victims emerged out of human rights movements, such as the civil rights and women's movements in both Canada and the United States. Like criminology, victimology's theoretical roots are American. More recently, a growing number of universities and colleges around the globe are teaching more victim-centred courses within their criminology and criminal justice programs, including courses in victimology, domestic and/or family abuse, and understanding the importance of the role of victim. In your own studies, how many of your projects have focused on the criminal as the subject of inquiry?

Who Is a Victim?

Many people believe they have a clear idea of who a victim is. Ask any number of people to define *victim* and the answers will probably be fairly similar. According to the *Oxford English Dictionary* (n.d.), a **victim** is "a person harmed, injured, or killed as the result of a crime, accident, or other event or action." For example, an individual can be a victim of spousal violence or a fraud or hoax. As well, an individual can identify as a victim when he or she feels helpless and develops a victim mentality. Animals, too, can be victims of various types of abuse, and it is worth remembering that cruelty to animals is a criminal offence (see sections 444–447 of the *Criminal Code*).

victim
A person harmed, injured, or killed as a result of a crime, accident, or other event or action.

Former NHL player Sheldon Kennedy (left), himself a victim of childhood sexual abuse, has been an outspoken advocate for the rights of other victims. The efforts of people such as Kennedy, fellow former hockey player Theoren Fleury, and organizations such as MADD (Mothers Against Drunk Driving) have helped generate much broader awareness and public discussion of these issues in recent years.

Source: Tanya Talaga/GetStock.com.

Even with this apparently clear definition, how we come to identify a victim is complex. Let us take the example of a car accident. Imagine that one car hits another in an intersection. Each car has a driver and a passenger. Both of the drivers are seriously injured, but both of the passengers receive only minor scratches and bruises. Directly after the accident, people who witnessed the collision called for emergency services and tried to help the victims as best they could while awaiting the arrival of the first responders. The two drivers and two passengers were taken to the hospital, and the cars were towed away. Family and friends were notified about the accident and met the injured parties at the hospital.

Deciding who is and who is not a victim can be a challenge. In the example of the car accident, who were the victims? Each of the four people involved experienced some form of injury, even if the passengers' injuries were only minor. Typically, a person's status as a victim is tied to the idea of **culpability**. For example, your assessment of which driver was a victim may be affected by the knowledge that one driver was obeying the traffic signal, while the other was distracted and did not obey the traffic signal. What if one driver intentionally drove through the intersection, knowing that halfway through the light would turn red? If one driver intentionally drove through a red light, is that driver a victimizer instead of a victim? The circumstances surrounding an event are critically important to addressing victimization issues. For the purposes of this example, we will assume that no one was at fault.

In victimology, there are many levels of victimization and victimization experience. Back to our example, all drivers and passengers experienced physical injuries, which makes them **primary victims** in the accident. Primary victims are the most easily identifiable victims because they are directly affected, and often physically injured, in an event. But what about the other people who witnessed the accident and called emergency services? Anyone who has ever witnessed a car accident knows that it can be traumatizing, especially when victims are seriously injured. These witnesses are **secondary victims**, in that they did not directly experience the accident, but were present at the scene when it took place and may have been hurt psychologically by the unfolding events. Family members who were not at the scene of the accident but met the injured parties at the hospital were also probably saddened and worried about the primary victims. Moreover, some family members will have to physically and emotionally support the victims while they recover from their injuries, so their lives become disrupted as a result of the accident. These individuals are **tertiary victims**, in that they were not directly victimized and may not have witnessed the event, but will suffer negative repercussions as a result of it.

In addition, we can categorize victims based on their direct or indirect involvement with the event. Individuals who were directly involved and suffered as a result of it are called **direct victims**. Back to our example, all of the people who were in the vehicles and were hurt as a result of the accident are direct victims. Those who were not directly involved in the event, such as the witnesses and the people who showed up at the hospital to be with the victims, are called **indirect victims**. These individuals experienced negative indirect consequences as a result of the event.

We can also categorize victims based on whether they undergo the victimization themselves or feel traumatized by the victimization of others and undergo many of the same emotional experiences that the actual victims do. Individuals who directly experience an event are **actual victims**. Those who experience trauma just by being aware of an event

culpable
Deserving of blame; guilty of wrongdoing.

primary victim
A person who is directly harmed as a result of a victimizing experience.

secondary victim
A person who is not directly impacted by the harmful effects of a victimizing event, but may witness the event or have to deal with the after-effects of a victimizing event, such as supporting a victim in recovery.

tertiary victim
A person who may suffer repercussions of victimization even though they are not directly involved in or witness to the harmful event.

direct victim
A person who is present at the time of victimization and experiences harm.

indirect victim
A person who is not immediately affected by victimization, but nonetheless suffers in some way as a result of it.

actual victim
A person who is the direct target of victimization.

that has befallen others are **vicarious victims**; they can become fearful and anxious, and sometimes suffer the same symptoms as those who have had the actual experience. In our car accident example, those in the car who were injured are the actual victims. However, those who saw the accident or supported the victims after the accident would be vicarious victims if they had heightened anxiety or became fearful of driving because they felt scared that they might get into a similar accident. Applying this to crime, Figure 5.1 shows how fear and anxiety over victimization can affect people's daily behaviour.

Therefore, it is possible for individuals involved in an event to be categorized as multiple types of victims. In our example, both the drivers and the passengers can be considered to be direct, primary, and actual victims. We can draw this conclusion because no driver was at fault, and neither driver intended to hurt anyone in the accident. All four individuals in the cars witnessed the accident and witnessed other people being hurt. Both passengers and drivers, because they witnessed each other get injured, are primary victims and secondary victims in that they witnessed victimizations other than their own. Because of the many roles that victims can play in a single victimizing event, victimization can also be compounded, depending on the circumstances of the event.

Victim status is also based on the perceptions of those directly involved in a criminal act. Consider whether two people involved in a criminal act would agree on the level of harm experienced as a result of a victimization experience, or even whether one or the other was hurt. For example, imagine two people are arguing. They become angry and start shouting at each other. Others start to notice the argument. Sometimes, these events can turn violent and one person will hit the other. The physically injured person may choose to retaliate in kind and attempt to hurt the attacker in some way. The initial victim then becomes an attacker as well. Ultimately, who becomes the victim in this incident depends on the outcome of the altercation. These situations can be resolved in a number of ways. The individuals may choose to stop victimizing one another or someone (a witness) may attempt to break up the fight. Alternatively, the police might be called and may charge one or both of the victimizers with assault.

vicarious victim

A person who does not experience direct victimization but nonetheless responds as if they had been victimized directly after learning of the event.

FIGURE 5.1 Canadians Who Would Perform Various Activities If They Felt Safer from Crime, by Sex, 2009

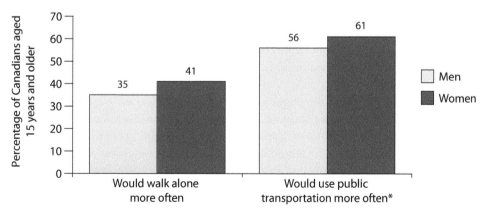

* Includes only those who had access to public transportation in their communities.

Source: Statistics Canada, General Social Survey (2009).

BOX 5.1

Victims and Offenders

As noted in Table 5.1, those who lead a criminal lifestyle face an increased risk of victimization. In other words, there is a correlation between being a victim of crime and engaging in criminal activity. Young males are both the group most likely to commit criminal offences and, as Table 5.3 confirms, the group most at risk of victimization.

Criminologists have known for many years that the risk of being a victim of crime is not randomly distributed across populations in Canada, the United States, or other Western nations. Rates of criminal victimization are somewhat like rates of offending: they tend to be at their highest among young men and in geographic areas that have a significant amount of *social disorganization* (this will be discussed in more detail in Chapter 12, Sociological Approaches). As a result, this finding has prompted the conclusion that victims of crime and offenders are often quite similar and are largely overlapping populations.

There is some logic and some empirical evidence to support this conclusion. Victims are, statistically, more likely to have a history of criminal offending and risk-taking behaviour than are non-victims. Those who are inclined toward *routine activity theory* and *self-control theories* for understanding criminality (which will be discussed in the chapters of Part Three) argue that young males who have little self-control typically engage in high-risk lifestyles and activities that expose them to the possibility of criminal involvement, both as an offender and as a victim. One recent study of particular incidents of homicide, for example, found that victims tended to look a lot like offenders: they shared similar demographic and behavioural characteristics with their victims (Lauritsen and Laub, 2007). It should also be noted that this behavioural risk is truer for men than it is for women. As Figure 1.1 clearly demonstrates (see Box 1.1, "Correlates of Crime," in Chapter 1), women are far less likely to engage in criminal activity, thereby suggesting that women are far less likely to have this risk factor.

However, victims and offenders are also far from uniformly overlapping populations. Not surprisingly, crime victims without a criminal history tend to be much less likely to resemble criminal offenders in their characteristics. And while it is important to note the overlap between victims and offenders, it is also important not to blame victims for this correlation.

Source: Lauritsen and Laub (2007).

Rainer Strobl (2010) argues that for people to be classified as victims, some agreement must exist between people's subjective view of their victim status and the interpretation of that status by others. Strobl identifies four types of victim experiences, shown in Table 5.2. To illustrate how they apply, let us use the example of a physical altercation that occurs at a bar. Two people, Jack and Alex, engage in a short fist fight, and the fight is broken up. The *actual victim* is the person who believes he or she was victimized and the person others believe was victimized. In our example, if Alex believes that he was victimized and others agree, he is the clearly identifiable actual victim. This is our most common understanding of victimization. If Jack and Alex agree that neither one was victimized and others agree that no victims exist in the altercation, Jack and Alex both become *non-victims*; perhaps the fight was rationalized as a way of releasing aggression and resolving a dispute. (This scenario is reminiscent of the discussion in Chapter 4, Measuring Crime, in which it was noted that in northern mining communities such as Flin Flon, Manitoba, a certain amount of "roughness" is tolerated, but the same behaviour might be considered assault in an urban centre such as Winnipeg.)

In some cases, others who observe an event designate a person as a victim, even when that person does not agree that he or she has been victimized. In our example, this classification might be made if Alex is too injured to continue the fight, and the fight was stopped. Alex, as the *designated victim*, may want to keep fighting, but others

Table 5.2   Strobl's Self and Other Victim Classification

	Others do regard the individual is a victim	Others do not regard the individual as a victim
Individual does regard himself or herself as victim	Actual victim	Rejected victim
Individual does not regard himself or herself as victim	Designated victim	Non-victim

Source: Strobl (2010, p. 6).

agree that a clearly larger harm exists for him than for Jack if he continues. Finally, if Jack claims that he has been hurt and is a victim, yet others do not agree, Jack becomes a *rejected victim*. When people are classified as rejected victims or designated victims, the victims and others surrounding them may end up with bitter feelings about one another after the event.

How Do We Measure Victimization?

As we saw in the previous chapter, criminologists measure crime in a number of ways. The Canadian criminal justice system collects data on many aspects of the victimizer experience. Government statistics on offenders relate to such things as the initial police call for service to arrest, court verdict, admission to a correctional facility, and some elements of the correctional experience. However, measuring victimization is more difficult because the data must come from the victims themselves. Victims are a vulnerable population, and although we may be interested in their experiences, we cannot just go up to victims and ask them how they were victimized. Doing so could be traumatic for them for many reasons, and researchers should not harm their research subjects in any way. The question is, How can we learn about the experience of victims without causing them harm? The answer is to conduct victim surveys.

The two main sources of crime data are (1) the annual Uniform Crime Reporting Survey (UCR2), which records microdata on incidents, victims, and the accused based on police reports and (2) self-reported victimization surveys. Although self-reported victimization surveys can be conducted in a number of ways, all of them entail victims reporting their victimization experiences to researchers. Although most self-reported victimization surveys are undertaken with small, non-random groups and focus on a specific victimizing experience, every five years the Canadian government carries out a large-scale victimization survey as part of the annual General Social Survey (GSS). The GSS, which began in 1985, uses a random sample of the Canadian population and asks them a number of questions about their quality of life, as well as victimization experiences and feelings of safety. The latest version of the GSS that includes a cycle on victimization experience and perceptions of safety is from 2009. The unique advantage of the GSS is that it includes data on victimizing events that were reported and *not reported* to the police. The next cycle of the GSS concerned with victimization will be conducted in 2014, and initial results will become available in September 2015 (Statistics Canada, 2014).[1]

Not all victims of crime wish to involve the police after they have been victimized. Figure 5.2 shows why people do not report victimization incidents to the police, based on data from the GSS. The most common reason cited was that the incident was not considered important enough for police involvement (68 percent) or, if the person thought about reporting the incident, he or she thought the police could not do anything about it (59 percent). A slightly lower percentage of respondents chose to deal with the matter another way (42 percent) and/or felt it was a personal matter (36 percent). Some victims also feared revenge by the offender if the police were to become involved (7 percent), while others did not report the incident because they did not want any publicity or news coverage of the incident (5 percent).

A Profile of Victimization in Canada

The GSS collects hundreds of variables on victimization, only a small portion of which we will show here. Some results from the 2009 survey are found in Table 5.3. The table shows that those who are most at risk for violent crime victimization are young adults aged 15 to 24 and single people (15–24: 284/1,000; single: 231/1,000); they are also the most at risk for theft of personal property (15–24: 200/1,000; single: 171/1,000). Other factors that put individuals at risk for violent crime are having a household income under $20,000, identifying as Aboriginal, being homosexual, or having activity limitations. According to the GSS (Perreault & Brennan, 2010), when we look at the total number of violent incidents self-reported, males are more likely to report victimization than females (males: 125/1,000; females: 112/1,000). Males are more likely to report experiencing a robbery (males: 222/1,000; females: 146/1,000) and significantly more likely to report physical assault (males: 94/1,000; females: 67/1,000), while women are

FIGURE 5.2   Reasons for Not Reporting Victimization Incidents to Police, 2009

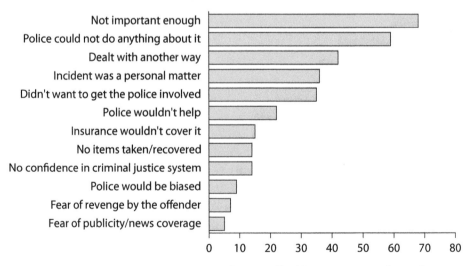

Percent of incidents not reported to police

Note: Excludes all incidents of spousal sexual and physical assault. Excludes data from the Northwest Territories, Yukon, and Nunavut.

Source: Adapted from Perreault and Brennan (2010, Chart 4, p. 16).

Table 5.3   Self-Reported Violent Victimization and Theft of Personal Property by Selected Demographic Characteristics, 2009

Characteristics	Sexual assault		Robbery		Physical assault		Total—violent incidents		Theft of personal property	
	Number (thousands)	Rate[1]	Number (thousands)	Rate[1]	Number (thousands)	Rate[1]	Number (thousands)	Rate[1]	Number (thousands)	Rate[1]
Sex										
Female†	472	34	146	10	945	67	1,563	112	1,609	115
Male	204^E	15^{E*}	222	16	1,277	94*	1,704	125	1,372	101
Age										
15 to 24†	307	69	209^E	47^E	757	169	1,273	284	898	200
25 to 34	161^E	35^{E*}	56^E	12^{E*}	545	118*	761	165*	642	139*
35 to 44	92^E	19^{E*}	43^E	9^{E*}	413	86*	548	114*	578	121*
45 to 54	96^E	18^{E*}	F	F	316	59*	444	84*	487	92*
55 to 64	F	F	F	F	118	29*	156	39*	257	63*
65 and over	F	F	F	F	73^E	17^{E*}	84^E	19^{E*}	118	27*
Marital status										
Married†	131^E	9^E	66^E	5^E	677	48	874	62	1,112	79
Common law	82^E	26^{E*}	F	F	335	105*	440	137*	442	138*
Single	385	54*	237	34*	1,011	143*	1,633	231*	1,207	171*
Widowed	F	F	F	F	F	F	F	F	26^E	19^{E*}
Separated/ divorced	74^E	40^{E*}	36^E	19^{E*}	184^E	99^{E*}	293	158*	192	103*
Household income										
Less than $20,000†	41	29^E	F	F	148	103	212	147	112	78
20 to $39,999	85^E	26^E	F	F	246	75	364	112	302	93
40 to $59,999	83^E	22^E	F	F	294	76	406	105	343	89
60 to $99,999	138^E	22^E	72^E	12^E	536	86	746	120	633	102
$100,000 or more	220^E	31^E	113^E	16^E	598	83	932	129	1,037	143*
Aboriginal identity										
Aboriginal people†	63^E	71^E	F	F	123	141^E	204	232	127	145
Non-Aboriginal people	612	23*	347	13	2,081	78*	3,039	114*	2,838	107
Immigrant status										
Immigrant†	F	F	F	F	244	43	355	62	477	84
Non-immigrant	598	27	334	15	1,977	90*	2,909	133*	2,502	114*

Characteristics	Sexual assault		Robbery		Physical assault		Total—violent incidents		Theft of personal property	
	Number (thousands)	Rate[1]	Number (thousands)	Rate[1]	Number (thousands)	Rate[1]	Number (thousands)	Rate[1]	Number (thousands)	Rate[1]
Visible minority										
Visible minority†	F	F	F	F	189[E]	51[E]	279[E]	76[E]	376	102
Non-visible minority	604	25	332	14	2,009	85*	2,945	124*	2,578	109
Sexual orientation[2]										
Heterosexual†	509	20	262	10	1,779	71	2,550	102	2,483	99
Homosexual	F	F	F	F	F	F	108[E]	405[E]*	F	F
Activity limitations										
Limited in activities†	229	27	173[E]	20[E]	832	96	1,234	143	916	106
No limitation	445	24	194	10*	1,384	73*	2,023	107*	2,060	109

* Significantly different from reference category ($p < 0.05$).

† Reference category.

E = Use with caution.

F = Too unreliable to be published.

1. Rates are calculated per 1,000 population age 15 years and older.

2. Data for those who self-identified as bisexual have been suppressed due to the unreliability of the estimates.

Note: Excludes responses of "Don't know and not stated." Excludes data from the Northwest Territories, Yukon, and Nunavut.

Source: Adapted from Perreault and Brennan (2010, Table 4, p. 22).

slightly more likely to report theft of personal property (females: 115/1,000; males: 101/1,000) and significantly more likely to self-report being sexually assaulted (females: 34/1,000; males: 15/1,000).

The study by Perreault and Brennan (2010) reveals that while women are more likely to report sexual assault at a rate that is about double that of males, the majority of these reported assaults (81 percent) involve "less serious" forms of sexual assault, such as unwanted sexual touching, grabbing, kissing, or fondling. The remainder of self-reported incidents of sexual assault (19 percent) are classified as sexual attacks, which involve threats or physical violence.

Reactions to Victimization: The Aftermath of Crime

Victims react to victimization just as people do to other traumas, as Figure 5.3 shows. Self-reported responses to criminal victimization in the GSS indicate that the most common emotional consequence is anger (34 percent), followed by being upset, confused, or frustrated (22 percent) and being annoyed (14 percent). Even though some may expect victims to have a more subdued response, such as shock, confusion, or disbelief, these responses are less common (7 percent). One of the most common reactions to victimization, whether one is a direct victim or hears about a victimizing incident, is fear (10 percent). Fear is a fairly typical reaction to a threat. Ferraro (1996) suggests

FIGURE 5.3   Emotional Consequences of Self-Reported Victimization Incidents

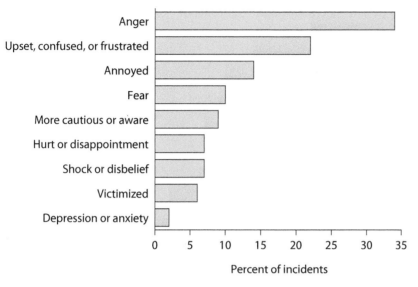

Note: Excludes all incidents of spousal sexual and physical assault. Excludes data from the Northwest Territories, Yukon, and Nunavut.

Source: Adapted from Perreault and Brennan (2010, Chart 5, p. 17).

that fearful reactions differ depending on the crime under consideration. For example, a person may feel less fear about having his or her bike stolen and more fear about violent crime, such as murder and sexual assault. When people are asked about their fear of being the victim of crime, many refer to "stranger danger," meaning that they fear being attacked by someone they do not know. However, both victimization and police data show that, in most cases, the victimizer and the victim know each other (Scott, 2003).

Another common response to victimization is stress. However, the way in which stress manifests itself differs from experience to experience and from person to person. For this reason, symptoms of stress can be difficult to identify. For example, some people may stop communicating with people when they are stressed, while others may increase their communication levels. Some people may stop eating when they are very stressed, while others may increase their consumption of food.

Sometimes the reaction to stress can be particularly severe. Some individuals who have experienced a severe traumatic event have reported symptoms that align with **post-traumatic stress disorder (PTSD)**. This condition occurs when "people experience an event which is so unexpected and so shattering that it continues to have a serious effect on them, long after any physical danger involved has passed" (Canadian Mental Health Association, n.d.). Symptoms of PTSD are often seen in those who have served in combat, been raped/sexually assaulted, survived natural disasters, lived through a homicide attempt, or survived a terrorist act.

According to the *Diagnostic and Statistical Manual of Mental Disorders* (DSM-5), symptoms of PTSD in adults can include feelings of intense fear, helplessness, or horror (American Psychiatric Association, 2013). Victims may have intense, vivid, and repeated

post-traumatic stress disorder (PTSD)

A set of symptoms that emerge as a result of the stress of experiencing severe trauma. Symptoms may include recurring nightmares, jumpiness, agitation, trouble sleeping, trouble concentrating, and social isolation.

recollections of the event; trouble sleeping and recurrent nightmares; jumpiness; agitation; feelings of detachment or estrangement from others; difficulty concentrating; and difficulty functioning. Victims may also engage in reckless and self-destructive behaviour, act aggressively, or be hypervigilant. *Acute PTSD* can last for up to three months, while *chronic PTSD* can last for longer than three months. **Rape trauma syndrome (RTS)** (Frazier & Borgida, 1992; Giannelli, 1997) is a unique set of PTSD symptoms that have been linked specifically to victims who have survived more severe experiences of sexual assault.

rape trauma syndrome (RTS)
A set of PTSD symptoms that have been linked specifically to those who have experienced severe violence in the form of sexual assault.

Victim Precipitation

In his study of 588 homicides in Philadelphia between 1948 and 1952, criminologist Marvin Wolfgang (1958) declared that in some homicides, the eventual victim was the initial aggressor. Specifically, in about one-quarter of the homicides he reviewed, the victim appeared to have engaged in actions that contributed to his or her own death. The idea that victims could somehow influence the outcome of their own victimization was termed **victim precipitation**. Wolfgang's work in this area became very well known, and the idea of victim precipitation was extended to other crimes, most notably sexual assault (Amir, 1971). Menachem Amir, in his early research on sexual assault, was one of the first researchers to assert that victims of sexual assault could behave in such a way as to bring about their own victimization—for example, by dressing provocatively, using provocative language, or engaging in risky situations. These assertions drew significant criticism from other researchers, who argued that Amir and others who followed this line of thinking were reinforcing **rape myths** as well as engaging in **victim blaming**.

victim precipitation
The problematic assumption that victims can somehow influence or bring about their own victimization by exhibiting behaviours that provoke a victimizer.

rape myths
Stories that reflect belief systems that reveal incorrect assumptions about the causes of sexual assault.

victim blaming
A process whereby a victim is found at fault for his or her own victimization, in whole or in part.

Helen Eigenberg (2003) identified five major issues with the attempt to blame victims for their own victimization. First, Eigenberg notes that victims are no different from non-victims, except for the fact that they have been victimized. Research has not been able to identify distinct characteristics of victims as compared with non-victims because they do not exist. The *process* of victimization is the factor that leads one person to become a victim and not another. The behaviours of a prospective victim only matter if that person is victimized. The reasoning behind victim precipitation, Eigenberg argues, is tautological, or circular. For example, consider the idea that it is inadvisable that we should spend time alone with strangers because this may leave us vulnerable to victimization. Now consider what happens when two people are in a dating situation: they often seek time alone to get to know one another better. If the date is successful, we would not consider that either person has engaged in actions that would precipitate victimization. If the same date involves one person harming the other, rather than blame the victim for seeking time alone with a "stranger," the question should be what *process* may have brought on this victimization. In other words, only after being victimized does one look to what the victim did to precipitate the event. If the experience was positive (i.e., it did not result in a victimizing experience), we would not be putting any of the victim's behaviours in question.

blame continuum
The range of blaming possibilities, from total guilt to total innocence, of both the victim and the victimizer.

Second, Eigenberg (2003) asserts that the notion that victims are either guilty or totally innocent is problematic. She asserts that on one end of the **blame continuum**, a totally guilty victim essentially means that there must be no victimizer, given that the victim holds total responsibility for his or her own victimization. On the other end of the continuum, a totally innocent victim does not exist because everyone, whether they have experienced direct or indirect victimization, could identify actions that could have been taken to avoid victimization had they suspected they were going to be victimized.

Third, the insinuation that victims hold blame for their victimization suggests that they have absolute control over the actions of others, which is not the case.

Fourth, if we accept the problematic premise that victims can be blamed, then Eigenberg (2003) argues we are creating culturally legitimate victims. If we consider that some individuals engage in risky behaviour and that they must accept the risk of victimization, such a view could be applied more collectively. If society accepts the existence of culturally legitimate victims, we could see the police and court systems also adopt this view. As a result, legitimate victims would become more vulnerable to victimization because they would be systematically discriminated against by the police and the law.

Fifth, if victims are to blame for their victimization, then it follows, according to Eigenberg, that victimizers are absolved of responsibility for their criminal behaviour. The idea of victim precipitation is oddly comforting, in that it supposes that people are empowered to control whether they are victimized. If we accept this idea of control, then it means that we do not have to spend time concerning ourselves with why victimizers are motivated to harm others and target individuals.

Resilience and Victimization

How people recover from victimization is important, and a key factor is the resilience of victims after a trauma. **Resilience** has several facets. According to Ann Masten and Jennifer Powell (2003), resilience involves the ability not only to resist trauma but also to cope and recover from such events successfully. This ability to recover from trauma and the stress that accompanies trauma is not as rare as once suspected (Bonanno, 2004). We now understand that traumatizing and stressful events, such as victimization, are not rare. Most, if not all, people experience some type of trauma during their lifetime, such as personal injury due to an accident, ill health, or the death of a loved one. However, most of us are unlikely to experience serious criminal victimization during our lifetime.

How we recover, or "bounce back," from traumatic events depends on our *protective mechanisms*. These protective mechanisms act as **insulators** from the victimization experience as well as from the negative effects of victimization, enhancing the recovery process. Protective mechanisms are those characteristics or resources that victims have access to that help in the victimization/trauma recovery process. These protective mechanisms can be divided into two broad categories: **personal protective factors** and **community and social support factors**. Personal protective factors are the characteristics an individual possesses to help deal with stress (Bergeman & Wallace, 1999). Personal protective factors include coping skills, the ability to handle new situations, and social skills (the ability to communicate effectively and solve problems). The basic premise is that having good coping skills, the ability to handle new situations, and good social skills can have a positive effect on how quickly and how well we recover from traumatic events (Garmezy, 1991). Anthony Ong, Cindy Bergeman, Toni Bisconti, and Kimberly Wallace (2006) found that routine daily positive emotions can enhance resilience by moderating the effects of stress. In other words, those who are more effective in recovering from traumatic events seem to have more positive thoughts and emotions throughout the day. These researchers suggest that positive emotion cognitive therapies,

resilience
The ability to successfully recover from trauma.

insulators
Social and psychological factors that protect an individual from being harmed.

personal protective factors
The characteristics an individual possesses to help deal with stress, including coping skills, the ability to handle new situations, and social skills.

community and social support factors
The people and resources that support the individual experiencing traumatic stress; that is, community members, family, and friends that serve to insulate the community and its members from traumatizing events through prevention and/or by fostering resilience.

which introduce positive emotions to those who have suffered trauma, may be an effective way of bolstering resilience in those suffering the stressful effects of victimization.

Community and social support factors include the people and resources that support the individual experiencing traumatic stress. They involve supportive acts by bystanders after the victimization has occurred, the kindness of neighbours, the emotional support of family and friends, as well as community supports that might help the individual work through the impact of the stressful event. Cynthia Rienick, Darlanne Mulmat, and Susan Pennell (1997) found that those who had strong social supports had fewer emotional problems after they had experienced violent crime. Robert Davis, Arthur Lurigio, and Wesley Skogan (1999) found that people were more likely to use these informal support networks in the initial aftermath of their victimization experience, such as talking to family members and close friends. As the victims' needs became more focused later on in the recovery process, the more likely victims were to use formal support systems, such as victim assistance programs.

Changes to Canada's Criminal Justice System Favouring Victims

In recent decades there have been several changes within Canada's criminal justice system intended to address some of the burdens victims take on as a result of their experiences. One of the most significant has been the introduction, in 1988, of the **victim impact statement (VIS)**. A VIS is a written or oral statement by the victim that gives him or her the opportunity to demonstrate the physical, financial, and emotional impacts of victimization. Victims are not allowed to introduce new evidence into the case in their statements. The statement can be introduced at various stages as the victimizer is processed through the criminal justice system. In both the Canadian and the American systems, VISs are allowed at sentencing hearings and may be allowed at other stages, such as bail and parole hearings and in plea-bargaining sessions, depending on the procedures followed in different provinces or states.

These statements have both positive and negative impacts. VISs allow the victim to be humanized, may increase the use of restitution/compensation orders, and help to demonstrate that the victim is committed to the process (Summer, 1987). Statements also allow the court to see how the victimization has affected the victim, and tend to be a factor in making sentences more appropriate (Erez & Rogers, 1999).

There is concern that VISs may make the court less objective in its decision-making process, by hearing the more "subjective" impacts of a crime as experienced by the victim. The victim may also have to defend his or her VIS to defence counsel in some jurisdictions. Furthermore, it is conceivable that if the victim does not choose to prepare a VIS, the court may see the victim as less committed to the outcome of the case (Ashworth, 1993). Learning about the process of the VIS also differs among jurisdictions. Some victims may receive a form or a pamphlet from police, while others may be referred to a Victim Services Unit. Training on how to write a VIS is also not standardized across jurisdictions, leaving some victims frustrated because they are unclear as to what may or may not be admissible in their statements.

Another significant change in the criminal justice system is the recent support for a Canadian *Victims' Bill of Rights*. Only two provinces, Ontario (1995) and Manitoba (1998), have long-standing legislation. More recently, the federal government has decided to

victim impact statement (VIS)

A written document describing the harm done to the victim as a result of victimization and may include statements about physical, emotional, or financial impact(s).

open consultations to develop similar legislation that would apply to all Canadians (Department of Justice, 2013). The goal of this legislation, like others before it, is to entrench the rights of victims into law at the federal level. A major concern with this type of legislation is ensuring that the rights of the victim do not interfere with the rights of the victimizer, which are protected under the *Canadian Charter of Rights and Freedoms.*

Conclusion

This chapter has focused on the victim rather than the victimizer (or offender). The average criminal act takes a very short time—the time it takes to grab someone's purse, wallet, or cellphone, or engage in a fight at a bar. What happens before and after the event is also of interest to those who study crime. Those students who will become more involved with criminology will probably have classes that predominantly focus on victimizers. However, it is essential to keep in mind that victims and their experiences are also important areas of concern.

SUMMARY OF KEY POINTS

- Victimology looks at crimes from a victim-centred approach, understanding the victim experience. Victims are seldom afforded the same resources to deal with the victimization experience as are the victimizers, who can have legal representation and rehabilitation efforts provided through public funds.

- Conducting research about the victim experience can be difficult because the population is vulnerable. Victims can also carry multiple statuses; they may be primary victims of an event and, if they witness others being victimized, they may be secondary victims and have other victimizing experiences. Furthermore, doing larger studies on victims is difficult, because many individuals may not want to talk about their victimizing experience. Research must be conducted carefully when trying to understand these issues.

- Responses to victimization can vary significantly from victim to victim. Surprising to many, the most common response to victimization is anger. This may conflict with our ideas of how victims should respond. Likewise, resiliency among victims is more common than we understand it to be, given that most individuals have experienced or will experience at least some form of victimization over their lifetimes.

- Vulnerability to victimization varies over one's lifetime and varies with life experiences. General trends show that those most at risk for violent victimization are young, single males, followed closely by young, single females. Those with higher incomes are also at risk for violent victimization.

- We must guard against seeking to blame the victim for their own victimization. Many problems exist with this common practice, most notably that it assumes that the victim is somehow culpable in the crimes committed against them. Victim blaming also assumes that the victim can control his or her environment and must be watchful against victimization at all times. If we blame victims, we run the risk creating culturally legitimate victims, which goes against Canadian social values of equality and fairness for all.

NOTE

1. For updates on this study and other relevant information, go to the Updates tab for this book, at www.emp.ca/CRIM.

QUESTIONS FOR CRITICAL DISCUSSION

1. When we think of people as *victims*, what other themes are associated with this word? Do we make assumptions about people when we identify them as victims? Are there both positive and negative associations with the word *victim*? Can you think of other words that could also identify this experience that would change the way we think about victims?

2. Look up the word *victim* in the thesaurus of your word-processing software. What kinds of synonyms for *victim* come up? Now look up another word that you have chosen as a better word that describes victim in the same thesaurus. Repeat this exercise, but online. Look up the word *victim* in your favourite online dictionary or thesaurus. What kinds of synonyms for victim come up? Now look up another word that you believe is a better word that describes victim in the same site. How do your word processor's thesaurus and your online source differ in their descriptions of *victim* and the synonym you chose for *victim*?

3. Identify the victim experience: In today's newspaper or an online news website, find a story in which a victim is identified. Most news stories focus on the offender. Is this story offender-focused or victim-focused? Now, try to understand what the victim experienced that day, before, during, and after the victimization experience.

4. Protective mechanisms: What protects individuals against victimization? How many insulators can you think of? Why do you think these insulators help protect individuals against victimization?

5. Blaming the victim—identifying rape myths: Rape myths are defined as untrue assertions surrounding rape and/or sexual assault. Many colleges and universities discuss these myths as part of student awareness campaigns. What are some of these myths? Why do you think these myths emerged, and how do these myths blame victims for their own assaults?

SUGGESTED FURTHER READINGS

Bonanno, G.A. (2004). Loss, trauma, and human resilience: Have we underestimated the human capacity to thrive after extremely adverse events? *American Psychologist, 59*, 20–28. doi:10.1037/0003-066X.59.1.20

Eigenberg, H. (2003). Victim blaming. In L. Moriarty (Ed.), *Controversies in victimology* (pp. 15–24). Cincinnati, OH: Anderson.

Perreault, S., & Brennan, S. (2010). Criminal victimization in Canada, 2009 (Catalogue no. 85-002-X). *Juristat*. Retrieved from http://www.statcan.gc.ca/pub/85-002-x/2010002/article/11340-eng.htm.

Scott, H. (2011). *Victimology: Canadians in context*. Don Mills, ON: Oxford University Press.

Websites

Canadian Crime Victim Foundation: http://www.ccvf.net

Canadian Resource Centre for Victims of Crime: http://crcvc.ca

Mothers Against Drunk Driving (Canada): http://www.madd.ca/madd2

Office for the Federal Ombudsman for Victims of Crime: http://www.victimsfirst.gc.ca

REFERENCES

American Psychiatric Association. (2013). *Diagnostic and statistical manual of mental disorders* (5th ed.). Washington, DC: Author.

Amir, M. (1971). *Patterns in forcible rape*. Chicago: University of Chicago Press.

Ashworth, A. (1993). Victim impact statements and sentencing. *Criminal Law Review, 7*, 498–509.

Bergeman, C.S., & Wallace, K.A. (1999). Resiliency in later life. In T.L. Whitman, T.V. Merluzzi, & R.D. White (Eds.), *Life-span perspectives on health and illness* (pp. 207–225). Mahwah, NJ: Erlbaum.

Bonanno, G.A. (2004). Loss, trauma, and human resilience: Have we underestimated the human capacity to thrive after extremely adverse events? *American Psychologist, 59*, 20–28. doi:10.1037/0003-066X.59.1.20

Canadian Mental Health Association. (n.d.). Post-traumatic stress disorder (PTSD). Retrieved from http://www.cmha.ca/mental_health/post-traumatic-stress-disorder.

Davis, R.C., Lurigio, A.J., & Skogan, W.G. (1999). Services for victims: A market research study. *International Journal of Victimology, 6*, 101–115.

Department of Justice. (2013, April 23). Government of Canada launches consultations on the Victims Bill of Rights [News release]. Retrieved from http://www.justice.gc.ca/eng/news-nouv/nr-cp/2013/doc_32876.html.

Eigenberg, H. (2003). Victim blaming. In L. Moriarty (Ed.), *Controversies in victimology* (pp. 15–24). Cincinnati, OH: Anderson.

Erez, E., & Rogers, L. (1999). Victim impact statements and sentencing outcomes and processes: The perspectives of the legal professionals. *British Journal of Criminology, 39*(2), 216–239.

Ferraro, K.F. (1996). Women's fear of victimization: Shadow of sexual assault? *Social Forces, 75*(2), 667–690. doi:10.1093/sf/75.2.667.

Frazier, P.A., & Borgida, E. (1992). Rape trauma syndrome: A review of case law and psychological research. *Law and Human Behavior, 16*, 293–311.

Garmezy, N. (1991). Resilience in children's adaptation to negative life events and stressed environments. *Pediatric Annals, 20*, 459–466.

Giannelli, P. (1997). Rape trauma syndrome. *Criminal Law Bulletin, 33*, 270–279.

Lauritsen, J.L., & Laub, J.H. (2007). Understanding the link between victimization and offending: New reflections on an old idea." In M. Hough & M. Maxfield (Eds.), *Surveying crime in the 21st century* (pp. 55–75). Monsey, NY: Criminal Justice Press/Willow Tree Press.

Manitoba. (1998). *The Victims' Bill of Rights*, CCSM, c. V55. Retrieved from http://web2.gov.mb.ca/laws/statutes/ccsm/_pdf.php?cap=v55.

Masten, A.S., & Powell, J.L. (2003). A resilience framework for research, policy, and practice. In S.S. Luthar (Ed.), *Resilience and vulnerability: Adaptation in the context of childhood adversities* (pp. 1–25). New York: Cambridge University Press.

Naffine, N. (1987). *Female crime: The construction of women in criminology*. London, UK: Allen and Unwin.

Ong, A.D., Bergeman, C.S., Bisconti, T.L., & Wallace, K.A. (2006). Psychological resilience, positive emotions, and successful adaptation to stress in later life. *Journal of Personality and Social Psychology*, *91*, 730–749. doi:10.1037/0022-3514.91.4.730

Ontario. (1995). *Victims' Bill of Rights, 1995*, SO 1995, c. 6. Retrieved from http://www.e-laws.gov.on.ca/html/statutes/english/elaws_statutes_95v06_e.htm.

Oxford Dictionaries (n.d.). Victim. Retrieved from http://www.oxforddictionaries.com/definition/english/victim.

Perreault, S., & Brennan, S. (2010). Criminal victimization in Canada, 2009 (Catalogue no. 85-002-X). *Juristat*. Ottawa: Statistics Canada, Canadian Centre for Justice Statistics. Retrieved from http://www.statcan.gc.ca/pub/85-002-x/2010002/article/11340-eng.htm.

Rienick, C., Mulmat, D.H., & Pennell S. (1997). *Meeting the needs of victims*. San Diego, CA: San Diego Association of Governments.

Scott, H. (2003). Stranger danger: Explaining women's fear of crime. *Western Journal of Criminology*, *4*, 203–214.

Statistics Canada. (2014). *General Social Survey—victimization*. Ottawa: Statistics Canada. Retrieved from http://www23.statcan.gc.ca/imdb/p2SV.pl?Function=getSurvey&SDDS=4504&lang=en&db=imdb&adm=8&dis=2.

Strobl, R. (2010). Becoming a victim. In S.G. Shoham, P. Knepper, & M. Kett (Eds.), *International handbook of victimology* (pp. 3–26). Boca Raton, FL: CRC Press.

Summer, C.J. (1987). Victim participation in the criminal justice system. *Australian and New Zealand Journal of Criminology*, *20*, 195–217.

Wolfgang, M.E. (1958). *Patterns of criminal homicide*. Philadelphia: University of Pennsylvania Press.

PART THREE
Theories of Crime

Sentencing for Manslaughter: Two Opposing Views

Osgoode Hall in Toronto, site of the Ontario Court of Appeal.

On a summer afternoon in 1996, after having lunch with his 71-year-old mother, Olive, 47-year-old Robert Turcotte went with her to the Royal Canadian Legion to drink beer. The mother and son were there from about two in the afternoon until 11 that night. Robert estimated that he drank about 16 pints of beer—when blood alcohol readings were taken later that night, he had more than 230 milligrams of alcohol in 100 millilitres of blood. Robert drove his mother back from the Legion to the apartment that they shared; his mother had also been drinking excessively, and she fell several times just walking from the car to the apartment. As he was preparing for bed, his mother confronted him with a knife (she often became aggressive after drinking).

Robert removed the knife and put it away, but shortly afterward his mother went after him with her bare hands. He does not recall anything that happened after that, until he saw his mother lying on the floor, with blood coming from her nose. He soon understood that he had strangled her with a television cable cord and a telephone cord, and he called police. After a trial for second-degree murder, Robert Turcotte was ultimately convicted of manslaughter. The Crown suggested a sentence of 10 to 12 years; the defence asked for a conditional sentence, to be served in the community.

The majority of the Ontario Court of Appeal, in determining this case, quoted approvingly from the trial judge, Mercier J (who had imposed a conditional sentence of two years less one day, to be served in the community):

> What does society stand to gain by such a sentence? Who benefits from this type of sentence? The daughters of the victim do not benefit; they have made that clear. The offender would not benefit. His rehabilitation would be greatly hindered, if not totally destroyed, by such a sentence. Society or the community gains nothing. It will end up supporting the offender while in prison and may well be faced with a person whose rehabilitation will have been seriously negatively affected when he is eventually released. (*R v. Turcotte*, 2000, para. 22)

> This offence was committed under very specific difficult conditions unlikely to ever reoccur. This offender has expressed sincere remorse for his actions. This offender has taken very extensive and positive steps towards his rehabilitation and it is most important that his treatment and counselling be continued without interruption. This offender's siblings, the surviving victims of the offence, understand the circumstances under which the offence occurred and wish him to be allowed to continue his rehabilitation. This offender presents no risk to the community. Robert Turcotte will then be permitted to serve his sentence in the community. (para. 23)

Consider, however, the view of MacPherson JA, the dissenting judge in this decision. Justice MacPherson asked: "was the sentence imposed by the trial judge, namely, a conditional sentence of two years less day, 'demonstrably unfit'?" (para. 27a). He responded to his question as follows:

With great respect for the trial judge … I have reached the reluctant conclusion that the conditional component of the sentence he imposed was demonstrably unfit. I reach this conclusion for several reasons.

First, this was a violent and terrible crime. The victim was a thoroughly drunk 71-year-old woman. The offender was her adult son. Mrs. Turcotte was completely defenceless. The son used not one, but two, cords … to strangle his mother. He tied half-knots in one of the cords. He wrapped them so tightly around his mother's neck that the police officers had trouble removing them when they arrived at the scene. The strangulation went on for several minutes and was accompanied by the mother's screams. Neighbours testified that between midnight and 12:20 a.m. they heard banging noises and a woman's cries: "help," "help me, please help me," "Bobby stop. Don't Bobby, please." (paras. 29a–30a)

Justice MacPherson noted:

Later, when he turned to considering whether he should impose a conditional sentence, the trial judge said nothing about denunciation. The focus of this later part of his reasons is almost entirely on the rehabilitation of Mr. Turcotte. (para. 31a)

Justice MacPherson quoted approvingly from a previous judgment of the Ontario Court of Appeal (*R v. Inwood*, 1989) on the matter of sentencing in the context of family violence:

This court has acted on the principle that where there is a serious offence involving violence to the person, then general and individual deterrence must be paramount considerations in sentencing in order to protect the public. In my opinion, this principle is applicable not only to violence between strangers but also to domestic violence. Domestic assaults are not private matters, and spouses are entitled to protection from violence just as strangers are. This does not mean that in every instance of domestic violence a custodial term should be imposed, but that it should be normal where significant bodily harm has been inflicted, in order to repudiate and denounce such conduct. (para. 42)

Justice MacPherson concluded by suggesting that Turcotte receive a custodial sentence of two years less a day in prison.

Before You Read Chapter 6

- Consider these sharply contrasting decisions—the majority and the dissent. How might you summarize both positions, in a sentence or two each?
- Which decision do you think most closely reflects the notion of "free will"? Which most closely reflects "determinism"?
- Keep these decisions in mind as you read Chapter 6, and then return to this case study. What theoretical approaches, or ways of analyzing crime, are represented in these decisions: Classical? Positivist? Other approaches?

Theories of Crime: A Brief Introduction

Introduction

The major theoretical perspectives of crime and deviance are based on biological, psychological, and sociological explanations. However, several criminological theories do not fall squarely within the parameters of biology, psychology, or sociology, such as critical criminology, rational choice theory, opportunity theory, and feminist theory. Indeed, many of the theories encountered in Part Three cannot be classified easily as biological, psychological, or sociological in origin. Contemporary social learning theory, for example, involves a combination of sociological, psychological, and in some instances, biological thinking (Akers & Sellers, 2009; Tremblay, 2012). Classical School theory, in contrast, is neither sociological, psychological, nor biological, but premised on 18th-century notions of free will, hedonism, and utilitarianism (Mutchnick, Martin, & Austin, 2009).

This chapter provides a general introduction to these and other key concepts as well as the main historical currents in criminological thought.[1] After reading it, you will be prepared to explore in more detail the various theories that follow in Chapters 7 through 12.

Why Do We Need Theories?

We have all heard expressions such as "theoretically speaking" or "it sounds good in theory," which imply that theory does not necessarily work in practice. That said, all of the chapters in this book—not just those in Part Three—have theoretical underpinnings, even though they may not be readily apparent at first glance. Without a theoretical foundation, we could soon find ourselves advancing ungrounded, fragmented opinions

The Canadian federal government unveiling its "tough on crime" legislation in 2011 (above). Criminologists have found that in many cases, popular solutions for reducing crime are not supported by research findings.

rather than a disciplined, scientific approach to exploring and explaining crime and deviance. And, of course, not all theories have similar methods or frameworks of analysis. Put differently, conceptions of science vary across theoretical perspectives.

If you asked your family and friends what causes crime or why certain individuals become criminals, most would be able to offer some sort of explanation, even if it was unrefined and based mostly on truisms or what they had heard in the media. They might suggest that crime is the result of poor child-rearing, that criminals suffer from mental illness, or that crime rates are high because of soft-on-crime laws and lax enforcement on the part of the criminal justice system (Lilly, Cullen, & Ball, 2011). Some might even insist that we could reduce crime by imposing lengthier sentences or by bringing back capital punishment, despite a dearth of evidence demonstrating that harsher punishments work to deter or reduce crime (Donohue & Wolfers, 2009; Piquero & Blumstein, 2007).

In a sense, explanations that state crime is caused by poor child-rearing or by mental illness are theories about crime, except that both explanations are overly simplistic and lack the critical elements required to be "good" theory (Williams & McShane, 2010). Most individuals who experience poor parental control and role modelling during their youth eventually turn out to be law-abiding adults, whereas individuals from seemingly ideal family backgrounds sometimes go on to become adult criminals (Sampson & Laub, 1992). Relatively few mentally ill individuals become criminal offenders, while any number of "sane," rational individuals may engage in crime if given a good opportunity, especially when it looks like little chance exists of being caught and punished (Clarke & Cornish, 2001). As we shall see, most well-travelled criminological theories are quite complex, even when they attempt to explain only one type of crime. For example, Chapter 13 (Violent Crime) observes that interpersonal violence typically involves a blend of biological, psychological, sociological, and personal factors.

Thinking Critically

To be good, a theory must be logical, with a valid structure—that is, it must follow the most basic rules of critical thinking and logic, such as the requirement that premises be provided that support a conclusion. It must also help us make sense of reality: a good theory should make statements or propositions about reality that can be *tested*, so that the theory can be accepted or rejected on the basis of solid evidence. Otherwise, it becomes difficult to distinguish a logical argument that supports a true theory from a simple *opinion*. Good theories should also be parsimonious. This term is a fancy way of saying that if two theories explain the same phenomenon equally effectively, scientists should prefer the one that offers the simplest and most straightforward explanation (this tenet is known as "Occam's razor"). Simpler theories are also easier to test. Those that have earned widespread acceptance have usually been tested (successfully) on many occasions and under many different circumstances. Social disorganization theory, social control theory, and social learning theory—all discussed in Part Three—have been successfully tested multiple times, in many different countries, at different periods in history.

That said, it is not always possible to adequately test a new theory when it is first proposed (Williams & McShane, 2010). For instance, if someone in the 18th century had proposed the big bang theory for the origin of the universe, that person likely would have been ridiculed. Astronomers required the type of large, sophisticated telescopes and isolated observatories not available until the 20th century in order to confirm that other galaxies existed and were moving apart from one another. While it is reasonably well accepted in astronomical circles today, some would argue that we still lack the necessary instruments to successfully measure and prove (or disprove) the big bang theory.

A parallel exists in criminology. Advances in self-report surveys and victimization surveys during the 1970s persuaded criminologists to examine new dimensions of crime—victim characteristics, immediate environmental opportunities, lifestyle choices—that went beyond the characteristics and motivations of individual offenders (Sacco & Kennedy, 2011). Routine activity theory, lifestyle exposure theory, opportunity theory, and rational choice theory all came onto the scene at this time (see Chapter 11, Crime Choice Theory). Recent developments in genetic research and brain-imaging techniques have subsequently challenged the neoclassical notions of rational choice and free will that are commonly associated with rational choice theory, routine activity theory, and lifestyle exposure theory, causing some criminologists to re-examine the degree to which free will and rational choice are actually components of offender decision making. And, as Case Study 1.1 showed, David Milgaard's 1997 exoneration was only possible once DNA testing—which did not exist at the time of Gail Miller's 1969 murder—was developed.

The Significance of Social Context

Social context is very influential when it comes to the formulation of theory, criminological or otherwise. We should bear in mind that all theories—and the theorists who propose them—are affected to one degree or another by their social, political, economic, and historical circumstances (Cullen, Jonson, Myer, & Adler, 2011). The **Positivist School** notion of criminality as an inherited (genetic) propensity was a reflection of what was going on in the mid- to late-1800s, intellectually linked to Charles Darwin's 1859 theory of evolution, Gregor Mendel's 1865 work on genetics, and then current developments in the fields of physical anthropology, medicine, and psychiatry (Wortley, 2011). The **Chicago School** view of criminality as a product of the social environment was shaped by the rapid urbanization that took place around the globe in the late 1800s and early 1900s, by the emergence of the discipline of sociology in the 1890s, and by social forces such as the Progressive movement (Lilly, Cullen, & Ball, 2011). Theories do not emerge in isolation but, rather, reflect what has gone on in the past and what is happening at the time they are being proposed.

Even theories originating in the so-called hard sciences—chemistry, physics, and biology—are influenced by the type of research universities deem "acceptable" or "desirable"; the amount of funding available from internal and external sources; and the opinions of colleagues regarding the originality, utility, and acceptability of the research. In certain circumstances, scientists can even be persuaded to discard or repudiate perfectly good theory. To illustrate, we need look no further than Galileo, who was forced

Positivist School
A school of thought that attributed criminal behaviour to biological or psychological factors; often referred to as the "Italian School."

Chicago School
The first school of sociology in the United States; contributed to social disorganization theory, cultural transmission theory, differential association theory, subcultural theory, the sociology of deviance, and symbolic interactionism.

by religious authorities (under threat of death) to recant his observation that the earth and the planets revolved around the sun because at that time, established religious doctrine held firmly to the belief that the sun and planets revolved around the earth.

As we examine criminological theories, we should always ask ourselves how certain ideas about criminals come to be regarded as self-evident or true. In other words, as mentioned above, we should remember to think critically (Young, 2002). Why are we currently hearing slogans or phrases such as "the war on drugs," "get tough on crime," "zero tolerance," "truth in sentencing," and "three strikes and you're out" (Garland, 2001)? Where did these sayings come from, when did they first appear in public discourse, and why do they seem to have struck such a resonant chord with politicians and members of the public? Why have certain criminological theories become popular in their time, only to be consigned to the dustbin of history? At one point during the infancy of criminal psychology, for example, it was widely held that most serious criminals were morally insane—that is, they were considered "psychopaths" (Rafter, 2009b). Today, while the notion of criminal **psychopathy** still exists, it is believed that most criminals are not psychopaths, and that many so-called normal people who might meet the definition of psychopathy are not necessarily criminals (Andrews & Bonta, 2010). These shifts in ways of thinking can be attributed in part to what is accepted by society as "conventional wisdom" or "knowledge" in any given period and to the accumulation of knowledge over time.

psychopathy
A personality disorder characterized by a lack of empathy and an inability to feel for others.

Criminological Theory and Public Policy

While theories may at times appear to be abstract or removed from reality—fanciful ideas conjured up by people sitting in armchairs in ivory towers—the fact remains that criminological theories have had, and continue to have, a substantial impact on public policy. **Classical School of criminology** recommendations regarding the need for due process, the use of imprisonment as a form of punishment, and limitations on the severity of punishment found their way into a number of laws and policies, including the US Constitution, the *English Penitentiary Act*, and the French criminal code (Lilly, Cullen, & Ball, 2011). Early Positivist School theorists also had a major impact on the criminal justice system. Cesare Lombroso endorsed the "medical model"—the notion that criminals were sick and in need of treatment. This idea gave rise to a number of prison reforms and a new emphasis on rehabilitation (Rafter, 2009a). *Social disorganization theory*, put forward by Chicago School theorists Clifford Shaw and Henry McKay in the early 1940s, resulted in the ongoing Chicago Area Project, which focuses on redesigning (reorganizing) socially disorganized slums through the creation of community organizations, cleaning up neighbourhoods, and reviving community pride (Williams & McShane, 2010). Current efforts by the City of Surrey to "renew" the Whalley-Newton area (examined in Chapter 12, Sociological Approaches) provide a contemporary illustration of how sociological theories of this nature continue to inform public policy.

Classical School of criminology
A body of work that emerged in Europe in the 17th and 18th centuries that argued people have the capacity to think rationally; contemporary deterrence theory is rooted in this school of thought.

Lawrence Cohen and Marcus Felson's 1979 *routine activity theory*, Michael Hindelang, Michael Gottfredson, and James Garofalo's 1978 *lifestyle exposure theory* and Derek Cornish and Ronald Clarke's 1986 **rational choice theory** have contributed to the development of a number of crime prevention programs that are currently in use around the world, such as situational crime prevention, target hardening (designing out crime) and community (or problem-oriented) policing (Felson & Clarke, 2010). Examples of

rational choice theory
A modern version of Classical School thinking originating in economics; it assumes that humans are rational and have free will, and that offenders make conscious choices to commit crime, based on a cost–benefit analysis.

such measures abound, including improved street lighting, burglar alarms, CCTV cameras, automobile immobilizers, GPS tracking, secure parking lots with barriers, boutique-style community police stations, and bike patrols by police (Clarke, 2009; Farrell, 2010). Routine activity theory, rational choice theory, pattern theory, situational crime prevention, and their influence on public policy and crime reduction strategies are described in greater detail in Chapter 11.

Many of today's successful correctional rehabilitation programs are premised, in part, on the tenets of Ronald Akers' *social learning theory*, which in turn are premised on the tenets of Edwin Sutherland's **differential association theory** (Cullen, Wright, Gendreau, & Andrews, 2003). During the early 20th century, when others were describing criminals as "psychopaths," "feeble-minded," "genetically inferior," or "evolutionary throwbacks," Chicago School theorist Edwin Sutherland (1947/1994) proclaimed, through his differential association theory, that criminal behaviour was learned, not inherited. He argued that it was learned in the same manner as other normative behaviour, for example, tying your shoes, reading, and writing—that is, by learning the necessary techniques, values, and attitudes through social interaction with family members, peers, and significant others (teachers or role models). In his social learning theory, Akers built on Sutherland's notion that criminal behaviour is learned through social interaction, adding that processes of reinforcement and punishment were critical, in accordance with the principles of B.F. Skinner's *operant conditioning* and Albert Bandura's work on imitation and *modelling behaviour*, both emanating from the field of psychology (Akers & Jensen, 2003). Social learning theory—often delivered in the form of cognitive behavioural programs targeting anti-social associations and anti-social values—has been proven to deliver results superior to other programs, notably in reducing offender recidivism (Akers & Jensen, 2006; Cullen et al., 2003).

We should remember that public policy and public opinion have also played, and continue to play, a role in shaping criminological theory. If the public and politicians believe that crime is caused by a poor social environment—as was believed to a large extent during the 1940s, 1950s and 1960s—then we can expect a wellspring of sociological theories explaining crime in those terms, buttressed by public support and public policy, and aimed at eradicating *criminogenic* (crime-causing) social conditions. On the other hand, if the crime rate is going up exponentially—as it was throughout the 1960s, 1970s, and 1980s—we can expect to see growing public support for conservative politicians such as Ronald Reagan in the United States and Margaret Thatcher in the United Kingdom. Conservative politics and public perceptions of rising crime rates can in turn lead to greater demand for rational choice theories, deterrence theories, or theories that support the incapacitation of "life-course persistent offenders." Or, to express this shift differently, theories that put the blame back on the offenders, rather than on society (Williams & McShane, 2010). If we want to know why terms like "zero tolerance" and "truth in sentencing" captured the public imagination and became political buzzwords, we need look no further than this period of increasing crime rates, the growing public hostility toward crime and criminals, and the corresponding increase in conservative, "tough on crime" politics (Garland, 2001; Skiba & Peterson, 1999).

We noted above that the Positivist School view of criminality as an inherited or genetic predisposition was influenced by developments in the mid-19th century, in fields such as evolution and genetics. In the following sections of this chapter, we will see how

differential association theory
Sutherland's theory that criminal behaviour is learned through the process of social interaction, and that the process includes the learning of criminal skills, motivations, attitudes, and rationalizations.

similar historical circumstances—social, political, scientific, or intellectual—gave rise to various theories. We will examine them in roughly chronological order, beginning over two centuries ago with the Enlightenment (or Age of Reason), which gave rise to Classical School thinking.

The Classical School of Criminology

The Classical School of criminology was not a "school" in the sense that we may think of schools today. To illustrate, the three most well-known members of the Classical School were French philosopher Baron de Montesquieu (1689–1755), Italian philosopher Cesare Beccaria (1738–1794), and widely influential English philosopher Jeremy Bentham (1748–1832). They lived at different times and in different countries. Essentially, the Classical School consisted of a group of European social philosophers who lived during the 18th-century Enlightenment (Zeitlin, 2001). Members of the Classical School were social reformers who challenged the way criminals were dealt with, criticized the absence of due process, and argued against the death penalty and the use of torture to extract confessions.

Before the Classical School

Prior to the emergence of the Classical School, it was generally believed that criminals were possessed by evil spirits, or demons. This view of crime is referred to as "demonology" or "spiritualism." Demonology was essentially a theological (religious) theory about crime. It took the position that individuals who behaved in a socially disapproved manner had succumbed to temptation, becoming evil as a result. Even the mentally ill were thought to be possessed by evil spirits (Einstadter & Henry, 2006).

Found guilty of the attempted assassination of King Louis XV of France in 1757, Robert-François Damiens was subjected to grotesque public torture. His fate influenced Cesare Beccaria's 1764 treatise *On Crimes and Punishments*, as well as Michel Foucault's 1975 book, *Discipline and Punish*.

The prescribed remedies for criminality and insanity were also of a religious nature, typically involving confession (under interrogation and torture), repentance, and then execution. The means of torture or execution often involved fire, considered an essential ingredient in the purification ritual. Accused "witches" would be burned at the stake, while the bodies of condemned criminals who had been executed by hanging and/or dismemberment would often be burned, following their execution (Pfohl, 1985).

During this "demonic" period, when spiritualistic explanations and remedies held sway, accusations, interrogations, and executions were often carried out by religious authorities. When they were not, they were carried out by the aristocracy (e.g., kings and queens) or their official delegates. Such procedures were generally not governed by written law (at least, not written law as we know it today), nor were any safeguards in place to protect the rights of the accused. It was assumed that individuals accused by the aristocracy or the religious authorities were already guilty (otherwise, they would not have been accused in the first place), that it was simply a matter of getting them to confess to their guilt through interrogation and torture, and that executing them was the most logical way to rid the earth of their presence.

The Social Context of the Classical School

Classical School thinking was very much a product of its times. The Classical School emerged during the 18th-century Enlightenment, bracketed by the English Revolution of 1689 at one end and the French Revolution of 1789 at the other, with the American Revolution of the 1770s in-between. Clearly, this era was marked by great social and political turmoil. England lost control of America, its former colony, and the French aristocracy lost their heads to the guillotine. It was also during this period that Sir Isaac Newton discovered the laws of gravity, Voltaire argued against superstition (i.e., religion), Jean-Jacques Rousseau wrote about "the social contract," and Adam Smith inquired into "the nature and causes of the wealth of nations" (Yar, 2010; Zeitlin, 2001).

Cesare Beccaria and Jeremy Bentham

While de Montesquieu, Voltaire, and English prison reformer John Howard were arguably members of the loosely defined "Classical School," the two most well-known Classical School theorists of relevance to criminology were Cesare Beccaria and Jeremy Bentham. Their works make extensive mention of **hedonism**, **utilitarianism**, **free will**, and human beings as rational, logical actors. The term hedonism refers to the view that humans will naturally seek pleasure and avoid pain. Utilitarianism suggests that the actions of governments and individuals should be measured in terms of their utility—how much pleasure they bring, and how many people benefit (derive pleasure) from those actions (DiCristina, 2012a).

In *On Crimes and Punishments*, Beccaria argued against secret accusations and the use of torture, insisting instead that accused individuals should have the right to know their accusers and the right to a fair trial. He was an opponent of the death penalty, arguing that punishment should be proportional to the crime. Consistent with the concept of the social contract, Beccaria pointed out that when people agreed to join society, they did not agree that society should be able to kill them if they misbehaved (Mutchnick, Martin, & Austin, 2009). Beccaria also argued fervently against religious

hedonism
The view that pleasure is the primary good; the pursuit of pleasure.

utilitarianism
A philosophy that suggests reasoned decisions will produce the greatest good for the greatest number.

free will
A will whose choices are not conditioned or determined by factors external to itself; also, the doctrine that free will exists.

Cesare Beccaria
(1738–1794)

Jeremy Bentham
(1748–1832)

dogma and the authority of the Church, causing his treatise on crimes and punishments to be placed on the Catholic Church's list of prohibited readings, where it remained until the mid-20th century (DiCristina, 2012a). Nevertheless, Beccaria's recommendations regarding presumed innocence, trial by jury, restraints on judicial authority, and limitations on the severity of punishment—things that we take for granted today—formed the basis for new criminal codes in the United States and France, following the American and French Revolutions (Bernard, Snipes, & Gerould, 2010; Einstadter & Henry, 2006).

Bentham is most well known for his argument that humans are rational, free-willed actors, and that their behaviour is governed by a hedonistic (pleasure–pain) calculus. Following Beccaria, Bentham argued that individuals would make a rational choice—a hedonistic calculation—about whether or not to commit crime, based on the anticipated amount of pleasure they would derive from their crime and the anticipated amount of pain they might suffer if they were caught and punished (O'Malley, 2010). According to Bentham, excessive punishment was evil in itself. Extreme and unnecessary punishment was not thought to deter crime, and might even cause the public to view the criminal justice system as tyrannical. He argued that punishment should be restricted only to the amount required to achieve **deterrence**, that the prescribed punishment should be made widely known to the public in advance, and that certainty and swiftness of punishment were more important for deterrence than the severity of the punishment (DiCristina, 2012b).

The Legacy of the Classical School

We can still find many examples of Classical School thinking in our modern criminal justice system, such as the codification of criminal offences (and a well-articulated list of possible penalties or sentences for violating the law), the presumption of innocence, the right to a fair trial, the right to know the case against you, and the right to be tried by a jury of your peers (DiCristina, 2012a). The legal concept of *mens rea* (or criminal intent; see Chapter 3, Criminal Law in Canada)—which is essential to a finding of guilt in criminal court—is linked to Classical School notions of free will, rational choice, and individual culpability (Wortley, 2011). Our contemporary prison system is also a reflection of Classical School thinking. Before the Classical School, relatively few prisons resembled those we know now; prisons were generally used to hold accused people, first, while they were being interrogated and tortured, and second, while they were awaiting execution (following their inevitable confession) (Foucault, 1979). Contemporary prisons are based more on the notion of imprisonment as a form of punishment, with prescribed limitations on the duration and severity of the punishment.

Classical School thinking has enjoyed something of a revival in recent decades, with the emergence of contemporary deterrence theory, rational choice theory, and situational crime prevention theory. All of these approaches have their roots in Classical School thinking about free-willed individuals making rational choices to engage in or refrain from crime, based on an economic calculation of the perceived pleasure (benefit or gain) if they get away with it, and the perceived pain if they are caught and punished. These topics are canvassed in detail below, in Chapter 11 (Crime Choice Theory) and Chapter 15 (Property Crime).

deterrence

A principle of sentencing or punishment intended to discourage citizens from offending or reoffending.

The Positivist School

The term *Positivist School* is often used interchangeably with *Italian School*, primarily to describe three 19th-century Italian theorists—Cesare Lombroso, Raffaele Garofalo, and Enrico Ferri—who attempted to apply what they regarded as a "scientific" method to the study of crime and deviance (DiCristina, 2012c; A. Walsh, 2012). These members of the Positivist School did not, however, invent the term **positivism**. Henri de Saint-Simon, an Enlightenment philosopher (and the forefather of sociology), is credited with first using the term *positivism*, in his call for the use of scientific method to study human society (Zeitlin, 2001). The birth of what is commonly known as the Positivist School was also preceded by August Comte, another sociologist who wrote about positivism, "positive philosophy," and "positive politics" in the mid-1800s (Mutchnick, Martin, & Austin, 2009). Basically, the term *positivism* refers to the application of the scientific method to the study of society, including the study of crime and criminals. The application of this form of method to the study of society (positivism) is not the sole domain of those in the so-called hard sciences. Most social scientists—for example, sociologists, psychologists, and criminologists—try to develop logical, scientific theories and test the validity of those theories through systematic observation and measurement (Sacco & Kennedy, 2011). In fact, of the three members of the Positivist School, only Lombroso could be described as a medical doctor or "scientist"; Garofalo was more concerned with moral and legal matters, while Ferri was trained in psychology and criminal law (Mutchnick, Martin, & Austin, 2009).

positivism
The application of the scientific method to the study of society, including the study of crime and criminals

The Social Context of the Positivist School

As we noted above, the Positivist School was influenced by Darwin's theory of evolution and Mendel's study of genetics. A number of other 19th-century fields of study contributed to Positivist School thinking, among them physiognomy, phrenology, and psychiatry. Physiognomy—which had been around for centuries but enjoyed something of a revival during the 18th and 19th centuries—proposed that facial features could reveal an individual's inner characteristics, such as cowardice, deceitfulness, or propensity to engage in violence and crime (DiCristina, 2012c). Phrenology, sometimes referred to as *craniometry*, held that abnormalities or anomalies in the shape of the skull were indicative of a person's morality and intelligence (Bradley, 2010). Psychiatry, with its increasing interest in moral insanity (psychopathology), was a precursor to the Positivist School view of habitual (incorrigible) criminals as insane, genetically unfit, or intellectually inferior (Rafter, 2009b). Essentially, the Positivist School rejected the main tenets of the Classical School, arguing that individuals did *not* exercise free will or make rational choices. Instead, members of the Positivist School claimed that behaviour was predetermined by genes, and/or by an individual's evolutionary circumstances.

Cesare Lombroso and the Atavistic Man

Cesare Lombroso has often been referred to as the father of modern criminology because he was the first to attempt to systematically apply scientific method to the study of criminality (Williams & McShane, 2010). Lombroso worked at different times as an army doctor, a psychiatrist, and as a university professor in medical jurisprudence, psychiatry, and anthropology (Mutchnick, Martin, & Austin, 2009). In the course of his duties, he measured and classified the skulls and body types of many prisoners and

Cesare Lombroso
(1835–1909)

Some specimens from Lombroso's collection of hundreds of human skulls, whose size and shape he carefully studied in his attempts to understand criminality. Though this research was badly flawed, it did represent a serious attempt to apply scientific methods to the study of crime, and also reflected the growing influence of Charles Darwin's theory of evolution at the time.

atavism

A term associated with Cesare Lombroso and the Positivist School of thought; the notion that criminals are less evolved than "normal" humans.

inmates confined to insane asylums. Lombroso concluded from his studies that criminals were **atavistic**—that they were degenerate, evolutionary throwbacks.

In his 1879 book *On Criminal Man*, he argued that criminals exhibited distinguishing features much like those of apes or Neanderthals—retreating foreheads, large ears, large jaws, and long arms—which, according to Lombroso, demonstrated their primitive evolutionary condition (DiCristina, 2012c). He also wrote about "insane criminals," such as kleptomaniacs (compulsive thieves), nymphomaniacs (sex addicts), and pederasts (older males who engaged in sexual relations with teenage males) (Mutchnick, Martin, & Austin, 2009). Lombroso went on to co-author the 1903 book *The Female Offender*, in which he and his son-in-law Gugliemo Ferrero described female offenders as "physically deformed" with "degenerative traits"—in other words, as, once again, evolutionary throwbacks, similar to their male counterparts (Akers & Sellers, 2009). While Lombroso later added social and environmental factors to his theory, he is primarily known for his characterization of criminals as being like cavemen, cavewomen, or apes (Bradley, 2010).

Enrico Ferri and Raffaele Garofalo

Enrico Ferri and Raffaele Garofalo were both trained initially in law, and later became students of Cesare Lombroso at the University of Turin in Italy (DiCristina, 2012c; Mutchnick, Martin, & Austin, 2009). Ferri was active in politics, and was at one time a Marxist and a member of the Socialist Party. Perhaps surprisingly (or perhaps not), he later became aligned with Benito Mussolini's fascist government, and was at one point invited to help redraft the Italian criminal code (Lilly, Cullen, & Ball, 2011). Although a member of the early Positivist School, Ferri employed a blend of anthropology, psychology, and biology, and wrote in the area of sociological criminology (DiCristina, 2012c). It was Ferri—not Lombroso—who first talked about "the born criminal." Nevertheless, Ferri also acknowledged the influence of age, gender, ethnicity, and social class on criminality. In particular, Ferri was known for his vehement rejection of Classical School notions of free will and rational choice, and his insistence that criminal behaviour was determined by a combination of biological, political, economic, and social factors (Lilly, Cullen, & Ball, 2011; Williams & McShane, 2010).

Garofalo was, at different times throughout his career, a prosecutor, a magistrate, and a member of the Italian Senate (DiCristina, 2012c). Consistent with his experience in law and politics, he focused on "social defence" and what he regarded as "natural crimes." For Garofalo, there were certain "natural crimes" that all societies would instantly recognize as abhorrent, such as murder or the sexual abuse of children. He believed that societies had a right to defend themselves against offenders who committed such crimes, through execution, transportation to another (distant) country, or incapacitation through imprisonment (Mutchnick, Martin, & Austin, 2009). Garofalo argued against the Classical School notion of free will, claiming that criminal thinking was inherited or "organic," and not the result of environmental factors or logical thinking. In addition, he called for the abolition of juries, claiming that judges were in a better position to weigh evidence—and avoid undue influence—than members of the general public (Mutchnick, Martin, & Austin, 2009).

Free Will Versus Determinism

Early Positivist School theorists rejected the Classical School view that individuals exercised free will and made rational choices, arguing instead that the behaviour of individuals was primarily predetermined by their inherited genetic makeup, which in turn affected the inner working of their minds. In other words, according to Positivist School thinking, criminals were born, not made. This was felt by Positivist School adherents to be the correct, "scientific" approach to understanding criminal behaviour, as it was rooted in the burgeoning disciplines of medicine, psychiatry, and biology, and based on scientific methods of observation, measurement, and classification (Pfohl, 1985). According to this "medical model," criminality was a "disease" that could best be studied, understood, and "treated" by medical doctors and scientific "experts" (Foucault, 1979; Pfohl, 1985).

This debate between free will and **determinism** has raged on for centuries. Until quite recently, those who supported the deterministic perspective (e.g., evolutionary biologists) insisted that human behaviour was predetermined by genes—that it was inherited, in the same fashion that animal behaviour was inherited. Those who traditionally favoured the free-will perspective argued, to the contrary, that humans were born without "instincts"—that human behaviour was socially constructed through interaction with the social environment (Fishbein, 1990). This debate hinged on the issue of whether "nature" or "nurture" played the largest role in the shaping of individual characteristics. In our contemporary era, evolutionary biologists are more likely to accept the existence of an interplay between genes and the environment, with both factors contributing to criminality in different ways (Anderson, 2007). Similarly, sociologists have gradually come to accept that certain characteristics—intelligence, physical abilities, and perhaps even problematic personalities—are at least partially heritable.

determinism
The doctrine that one's will is not the sole cause of choices, but that those choices are conditioned or determined by factors external to one's will.

Criticisms of the Positivist School

Members of the Positivist School were roundly criticized for their simplistic assumptions about "the born criminal," the existence of identifiable criminal body types, and their unfounded belief that "innate" anomalies such as immorality, deceitfulness, or low intelligence could be ascertained by examining a person's skull or facial features. They were also criticized for discounting the relationship between crime and social factors like poverty, lack of education, and lack of employment opportunities (Akers & Sellers, 2009). Members of the Positivist School tended to view impoverished individuals as genetically inferior, when in fact most were poor because they were born into the lower social classes and had no way to rise up through the social ranks. Positivist School theorists would also describe uneducated, illiterate people as "feeble-minded," when most simply lacked exposure to the kind of public schooling system that we have today.

More than anything, Positivist School adherents were criticized for their support for the so-called science of *eugenics*—the misguided notion that the bad genes that led to "diseases" like feeble-mindedness, homosexuality, and criminality could and should be eliminated from the human gene pool through selective breeding; that is, through sterilization, segregation, and (if necessary) extermination. People whose only crime was vagrancy (being poor and homeless) found themselves being locked up indefinitely, while those designated as feebleminded (usually the uneducated or illiterate) found themselves subjected to enforced sterilization, or castration, so that they could not breed (Lilly, Cullen, & Ball, 2011). As recently as 1976, some states in the United States still permitted involuntary sterilization of habitual criminals, epileptics, the mentally ill, and those deemed to be mentally "retarded" (Pfohl, 1985).

Note that this "scientific" approach was very much in keeping with the Social Darwinist perspective that was prevalent during the late 1800s and early 1900s, and the concomitant belief that society is a reflection of what goes on in the animal kingdom. To follow the logic of Social Darwinism, those who were on the bottom-most rungs of society—the poor, the "feeble-minded," the physically deformed—were evolutionary throwbacks. Those who were on the uppermost rungs—the wealthy, the educated, the politically powerful—were at the very pinnacle of evolution, having arrived there through the processes of "natural selection" and "survival of the fittest" (Lilly, Cullen, & Ball, 2011). It was reasoned that the rich and powerful deserved their elevated position in society due to their advanced stage of evolution, whereas the poor deserved to be poor (and even to be eliminated), because of their lower, primitive evolutionary status. This view worked well for those who were born into wealth and title, such as the aristocracy, but not so well for those who were born into poverty.[2]

The Legacy of the Early Positivist School

Despite numerous criticisms, the tradition set in motion by the early Positivist School persisted for many years. Examples of early and mid-20th-century Positivist School thinking include Earnest Hooton's "hierarchy of degeneration" and William Sheldon's **somatotyping**. In his 1939 study, Hooton examined 17,000 inmates in a variety of correctional institutions and concluded that prisoners had distinctive and inferior characteristics—lower intelligence, mixed eye colours, and sloping foreheads (Akers & Sellers, 2009; Lilly, Cullen, & Ball, 2011). He described a hierarchy of degeneration, descending from sane civilians to sane criminals, and from insane civilians to insane criminals, with decreasing intelligence, increasing insanity, and more physical "deformities" the further you went down the scale (Deutschmann, 2002). In 1949, Sheldon's somatotyping theory, premised on 19th-century biological and psychiatric thinking, described three distinct (unusual) body types: the *ectomorph*, who was skinny, frail, and prone to nervous disorders and anxiety; the *endomorph*, who was rotund (overweight), sociable, and loved to eat; and the *mesomorph*, who had a muscular, triangular

somatotyping
A research technique that links behavioural characteristics to body types, such as mesomorphy.

torso and was competitive, aggressive, and prone to violence (Bartol, 1999). Sheldon claimed that delinquents were more mesomorphic than non-delinquents, thus attempting—like Lombroso before him—to link a person's body type to their supposed propensity for criminal behaviour. Sheldon and Hooton both enthusiastically endorsed eugenics as a means to eliminate crime and criminals (Deutschmann, 2002).

As was the case with the Classical School, early Positivist School thinking has had a significant impact on criminal justice policy. If it was assumed that individuals became criminals due to circumstances beyond their control—poor genes, inbred feeble-mindedness, inferior body type—then logically, they could not be held accountable for their behaviour. Nothing would be accomplished by punishing (deterring) criminals, because their behaviour was predetermined. Instead, crime was seen as a disease, requiring treatment by medical professionals (S. Cohen, 1985; Pfohl, 1985). Greater emphasis was given to "treatment," "rehabilitation," and the use of indeterminate sentences to ensure that criminals had been cured prior to their release into society. This brings us back to the medical model—the notion that there should be "no treatment without diagnosis, and no penal sanction without expert advice" (Garland, 2001, p. 36).

We still see vestiges of this medical model in the Canadian court system today, where lawyers argue that their clients deserve special consideration because of psychological disorders, diminished mental capacity, or inability to understand the nature of their actions. Experts testify at trial as to the degree of physical or mental incapacity, and judges weigh this expert testimony prior to sentencing. The same applies to the Canadian correctional system, where transfer to a reduced security institution or release on parole routinely involves psychiatric and psychological reports, that is, "expert" opinion. The "dangerous offender" designation is intended to incapacitate "untreatable" criminals indefinitely, while the "long-term offender" designation is intended to extend and increase the level of control over chronic offenders who have not responded adequately to repeated attempts at "treatment."

FIGURE 6.1   Sheldon's Somatotypes

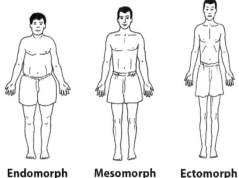

Endomorph   Mesomorph   Ectomorph

Psychology, Psychobiology, Criminology, and Positivism

During the 19th and early 20th centuries, theories of criminal behaviour proposed by psychiatrists and psychologists were similar to—and in many cases overlapped with—Positivist School thinking. Both approaches viewed (and continue to view) criminality through a medical lens—as a disease or abnormality that can be cured if diagnosed and treated properly by scientific experts. Also, both approaches applied the scientific method—observation, experimentation, measurement, classification, and explanatory (testable) theories—to the study of criminality. Sigmund Freud, the founder of psychoanalysis and a forerunner of modern-day psychiatry, typifies the 19th-century "positivist." Freud, a medical doctor specializing in neurology, was also interested in psychology, biology, and anthropology (Lemert, 1993). Freud's "psychodynamic" theory postulated that human psychology was shaped by biological processes (instincts), family dynamics, and early childhood experiences. Although Freud did not focus on criminality to a great extent in his own work, Freudian thinking presaged much of the contemporary work

Sigmund Freud
(1856–1939)

in psychological explanations of crime and deviance, such as psychopathology, social learning, and the relationship between frustration and aggression (Andrews & Bonta, 2010).

The 1950 book *Unraveling Juvenile Delinquency*, by husband and wife team Sheldon and Eleanor Glueck, is a prime example of psychobiology, or biopsychology. In their study of 500 delinquents and 500 non-delinquent boys, the Gluecks observed that delinquent boys were more mesomorphic than non-delinquent boys. This conclusion is reminiscent of William Sheldon's 1949 work on somatotyping (see above) and hearkens back to Cesare Lombroso's earlier characterization of criminals as atavistic (Lilly, Cullen, & Ball, 2011). At the same time, the Gluecks stated that delinquent boys had a greater number of psychological or temperamental problems (Glueck & Glueck, 1950/1994), implying that delinquents displayed characteristics normally associated with psychopathy.

Contemporary criminal psychology is considerably more sophisticated and is often grounded in *cohort studies* that measure the development of large birth cohorts over a period of many years. One of the most well-known of these cohort studies—*Cambridge Study in Delinquent Development [Great Britain], 1961–1981*—was spearheaded by psychologist David Farrington (Farrington et al., 2006). In his article "Criminological Psychology in the Twenty-First Century," Farrington (2004) calls for a discipline that embraces an array of explanations, including biological factors (low intelligence and cognitive disabilities), sociological factors (poverty, family conflict, delinquent peers), and psychological factors (individual differences in impulsivity, attentiveness, and learning). He even adds rational choice theory and routine activity theory to the mix (see Chapter 11, Crime Choice Theory). Contemporary work in the area of psychobiology is exemplified by Terrie Moffitt's study on *life-course-persistent (LCP)* offenders and *adolescent-limited (AL)* offenders. According to Moffitt (whose work is discussed in Chapters 7, Biological Theories, and 8, Psychological Approaches), LCP offenders and AL offenders are two entirely different groups, each warranting its own theoretical explanation. She says that LCP offending can best be explained by heritable factors, such as cognitive deficits, and by prenatal and neonatal trauma (maternal alcohol or drug abuse during pregnancy, deprivation of affection following birth). AL offending, on the other hand, can best be explained in terms of social learning—the type of peer pressure, peer approval, or peer rejection routinely experienced by teens (Moffitt, 1993).

The Schism Between Sociology and Biology

As noted above, sociologists can be just as positivist as medical specialists, biologists, and psychologists. Recall that positivists endorse the application of the scientific method to the study of society, an approach to which most social scientists would subscribe. Historically, psychology and sociology have shared a fruitful—if at times uneasy—relationship. While sociology searches for the causes of criminal behaviour in social structure, social institutions, and social interaction, psychology searches for causes of criminal behaviour in the characteristics of individual offenders. However, the two disciplines have traditionally recognized that an interplay exists between the social environment and the inner workings of the mind (Andrews & Bonta, 2010; Wortley, 2011). Akers's social learning theory and Agnew's general strain theory (see Chapter 12, Sociological Approaches) are both excellent examples of *social psychology*, a blend of sociology and psychology.

The same cannot be said for the fractious relationship between sociology and biology. French sociologist Émile Durkheim was highly critical of the early Positivist School, particularly with respect to its characterization of crime as "abnormal" or "pathological" (A. Walsh, 2002). Durkheim pointed out that all societies had crime, that crime had existed throughout history, and that crime had not been weeded out through evolutionary processes. Therefore, Durkheim concluded that a certain amount of crime must be normal (Durkheim, 1964). He objected to the Positivist School portrayal of criminality as a disease invading an otherwise healthy organism, and to the notion that human beings should be quarantined, sterilized, and even eradicated to prevent them from spreading the disease of criminality. Durkheim argued that a limited amount of crime actually served a social function by reinforcing social values and demonstrating what might happen to those who refused to play by society's rules (Erikson, 1962).

Edwin Sutherland (1883–1950)

This divide, or *schism*, between sociology and biology was widened further by Edwin Sutherland's withering attack on the 1950 work of Sheldon and Eleanor Glueck, whose thinking was in turn influenced by William Sheldon's somatotyping, and by prison psychiatrist Bernard Glueck, the older brother of Sheldon Glueck (Laub & Sampson, 1991; Rafter, 1997). William Sheldon, a supporter of eugenics, claimed that violent criminals could be identified through their mesomorphic body type. Bernard Glueck was convinced that most criminals were psychopaths and should be committed to psychiatric institutions for life (Rafter, 1997). Edwin Sutherland, a Chicago School sociologist, ridiculed such notions. He argued that criminal behaviour was learned through interaction with the social environment, and observed that crime existed in the supposedly "normal" middle and upper classes, as well as among members of the lower classes (Sutherland, 1940, 1947/1994, 1950). Between the 1920s and the 1970s, biological explanations of criminal behaviour fell into disfavour and were largely supplanted by sociological explanations, many emanating from the Chicago School (see Chapter 12, Sociological Approaches).

The Rebirth of the Positivist School

After decades of being discounted, biological and psychological explanations enjoyed something of a revival during the 1970s and 1980s, in part because society started to view the social solutions to crime as ineffective. In the 1950s, crime rates were relatively low; however, in the 1960s crime rates started to rise in the United States, Canada, and the United Kingdom. This trend continued through the next two decades, until the early 1990s. During the mid-1970s, people started to lose faith in the criminal justice system as well as the social theories that formed the basis for the penal-welfare system (Garland, 2001). In criminology, socially oriented theories, such as the labelling perspective, conflict theories, critical criminology, and Marxist theories, had come to dominate the field. Ironically, the criticisms levelled by socially-oriented critical criminologists and Marxist criminologists against traditional mainstream criminology—and its alleged focus on measuring and "treating" only those whom the state defined as "criminal"— caused many criminologists to begin to re-evaluate sociological theories of crime and deviance. Eventually, positivist contributions from biology began to re-enter criminological theorizing (Jeffery, 1978).

In 1976, Samuel Yochelson and Stanton Samenow—who worked at a forensic psychiatric institution—published *The Criminal Personality*, in which they argued that criminals were born with abnormal thought patterns that affected their ability to make normal decisions (Williams & McShane, 2010). Beginning in 1977, Sarnoff Mednick and Karl Christiansen (working with a variety of colleagues over the years) disseminated the results of a series of studies on disturbances in the autonomic nervous system and low cortical arousal in high-risk offenders, suggesting that serious criminal offending was linked to biological processes (Lilly, Cullen, & Ball, 2011). In 1985, James Wilson and Richard Herrnstein published *Crime and Human Nature*, in which they asserted that constitutional factors (such as mesomorphy) were indeed related to criminality (Paternoster & Bachman, 2001). In 1994, Richard Herrnstein and Charles Murray took this one step further, arguing in *The Bell Curve* that a relationship existed between criminality and low intelligence (Lilly, Cullen, & Ball, 2011).

During the 1990s, a number of evolutionary biologists—for example, Anthony Walsh and Lee Ellis—made a concerted effort to mend fences with sociology and restore biology to what they considered to be its rightful place in criminology (Ellis & Walsh, 1997). Emerging knowledge about DNA, neurotransmitters, the human genome, and the use of MRIs for brain imaging have added significantly to biology's contribution to the study of criminal behaviour (Beaver & Ratchford, 2009; Raine & Yaralian, 2001). Biology's stature in criminology has also been enhanced by its abandonment of eugenics, the search for a specific crime gene, and the search for an identifiable criminal body type (Lilly, Cullen, & Ball, 2011). Chapter 7 (Biological Theories) examines a number of contemporary biological explanations of criminal behaviour.

Conflict Versus Consensus: Karl Marx and Émile Durkheim

Karl Marx (1818–1883)

Émile Durkheim (1858–1917)

While neither was a criminologist, both Karl Marx and Émile Durkheim had a profound influence on the development of criminological theory. Marx was a political philosopher and economist, and although a prolific writer, did not say much about crime in his writings. To the extent that Marx touched on the topic, it was mostly in reference to crime as a byproduct of the social inequality and class struggle that he associated with the capitalist mode of production (Renzetti, Curran, & Carr, 2003; Williams & McShane, 2010). While Durkheim touched occasionally on the subject of crime—as he did in his critique of the early Positivist School—it was not his main focus (Passas, 1995). Rather, Durkheim was more concerned with articulating what he felt to be a scientific approach to the understanding of society. Nevertheless, the conflict tradition in criminology is typically associated with the thinking of Marx, whereas the consensus tradition is typically associated with Durkheim (Burtch, 2003). Most criminological theories can generally be classified as either conflict or consensus theories, although a number admittedly fall somewhere in-between.

conflict theories
Theories, originating primarily with Marx, that focus on the unequal distribution of power in society—for example, due to class, race, or gender. Conflicts between classes or groups are driven to a large extent by this unequal power and unequal access to resources.

Conflict theory posits that society and its laws and legal system are rooted in social, political, and economic conflict. Those who have wealth and power get to decide what will be against the law and who will be targeted by the legal authorities. Examples of conflict theory include *cultural criminology*, *labelling theory*, *critical constructionism*, *critical criminology*, and many branches of feminist criminology (see Chapters 2, The Media:

Shaping Our Understanding of Crime; 9, Critical Criminology; 10, Gender and Crime; and 12, Sociological Approaches). Some of these perspectives are not necessarily Marxist in origin, but most conflict-oriented theorists would agree that an ongoing struggle, albeit not necessarily explicit, exists between the rich and powerful and the poor and powerless, with the rich and powerful largely getting their own way, ultimately imposing their will over the poor and powerless (Lilly, Cullen, & Ball, 2011; Reiman, 2003). Thus, both law and the criminal justice system do not reflect widely held social values and beliefs but, rather, the attitudes, values, and beliefs of those who have the power to make and enforce laws. Instead of asking why certain individuals become criminals, conflict theorists would argue that we should question why certain individuals end up being criminalized while others do not, and who benefits most from this criminalization process.

Consensus theory, on the other hand, argues that society and its laws are rooted in the shared values and beliefs of its members. Society is viewed as a natural, organic entity that works to the benefit of all its constituents. Those who do not share the values and beliefs of society, and who behave in a socially unacceptable manner, are regarded as deviant or criminal (abnormal) and therefore legitimately subject to punishment, incapacitation, or "treatment." In other words, the role of the criminal justice system (and criminologists as well) is to protect society. Examples of consensus theory include *anomie-strain theory*, *social control theory*, and *rational choice theory*, although all three theories would acknowledge that socio-economic inequalities and social conflict are factors in criminal motivation and in social reactions to crime (Williams & McShane, 2010). Psychological and biological theories could also be regarded as consensus theories, in that they begin with the assumption that such a thing as "normal" behaviour exists, and then set about to study (and cure) what they deem to be "abnormal" behaviour (Pfohl, 1985).[3] As you read the chapters that follow in Part Three, or those in other parts of this book, try to identify which perspectives are conflict-oriented, which are consensus-oriented, and which fall somewhere in-between.

consensus theories
In opposition to conflict theories, consensus theories, which originate with Durkheim, hold that society functions through social bonds and collective beliefs, and is characterized by widespread acceptance of values, norms, and laws.

Conclusion: The Future of Criminological Theory

Given its rather chaotic past, it is difficult to predict with precision what lies ahead for criminological theory. With the rapid development of the biological sciences, it seems safe to assume that biosocial explanations of criminal behaviour will experience vibrant growth in the foreseeable future. New discoveries in genetics and evolutionary theory, accompanied by the use of new tools and technology (e.g., brain scans) will surely contribute to more research and further theoretical contributions from this area (cf. Raine, 2013). Recent developments in the field of *epigenetics*—which examines how stimuli in the immediate environment can alter the functioning of genes without changing the basic structure of DNA—have presented a challenge to those who favour more socially-oriented explanations (Beaver & Ratchford, 2009; Lilly, Cullen, & Ball, 2011). At the same time, it can be anticipated that sociologists and critical criminologists will respond to the theoretical challenges raised by biological and psychobiological criminology, attempting to provide ever stronger empirical evidence to demonstrate that society, culture, politics, and the economy play a larger role than inherited genes when it comes to the shaping of criminal behaviour (Duster, 2006).

White-collar and corporate crime are other areas that have received increasing attention from criminological theorists in recent years (see Chapter 17, Organized Crime and Gangs). The collapse of the savings and loan industry during the 1990s, the Enron scandal in the early 21st century, and the meltdown of the stock market in 2008 have generated extensive media coverage, drawing increasing public attention to the crimes of the rich and powerful. Social strain theory has traditionally been used to explain white-collar and corporate crime (Lilly, Cullen, & Ball, 2011), but labelling, differential association, social control, rational choice, and opportunity theories have also been applied to this problem (Benson & Simpson, 2009; Sutherland, 1940). While evidence exists of increased activity in these areas, white-collar and corporate crime have generally received far less attention than more traditional street crimes, such as robbery, breaking and entering, and theft. However, given the level of media attention to—and the public interest in—white-collar and corporate crime, it seems likely that they will receive more attention in the future.

The same can be said for cybercrime. The Internet has expanded exponentially over the past 20 years, arguably becoming one of the predominant social domains (Alpert & Hajaj, 2010; Netcraft, 2010). It competes for time and space with the family (household), workplace, and leisure domains that have been front and centre in earlier iterations of criminal event theory and routine activity theory (L.E. Cohen & Felson, 1979; Sacco & Kennedy, 2011). Cyberspace is a place where many people go to commit crime such as identity theft, credit card fraud, the distribution of child pornography, the luring of children for sexual purposes, and even cyberterrorism (Broadhurst, 2006; W.A. Walsh & Wolak, 2005). To date, most studies in the area of cybercrime tend to be a-theoretical, in the sense that they focus more on describing the various types of cybercrime, quantifying the costs of cybercrime, examining the laws (or lack thereof) in cyberspace, and exploring ways in which to prevent cybercrime and track down cybercriminals. However, it seems likely that socially-oriented criminology will soon devote more attention to cybercrime, given that cyberspace is socially constructed and is primarily grounded in the type of symbolic interaction first identified by members of the early Chicago School. Some of the existing sociological theories of crime and deviance that could be mobilized to explain cybercrime include anomie-strain theory, differential association theory, social learning theory, social control theory, and routine activity theory.

In the past decade, interest in theoretical integration has continued within criminology. Using ideas from several different disciplines, these *integrated theories* attempt to fuse explanations across the micro and macro levels. In many cases, these theories attempt to explain both crime rates and patterns of individual criminality by incorporating ideas from biology, psychology, sociology, ecology, and economics. Future research efforts will likely seek to specify interactions between the variables suggested by each discipline (Agnew, 2005; Robinson & Beaver, 2008), including (but not limited to) genes, cognition, social structure, the social environment, and the exercise of individual choice (free will).

In addition, we can expect to see increasing emphasis on cohort studies, which follow large birth cohorts over a period of years. Many of these cohort studies—for example, Farrington et al.'s Cambridge study and Moffitt et al.'s Dunedin study—set out to examine a range of variables proposed by different (competing) criminological theories. The Cambridge study investigated family background variables such as economic deprivation, family size, parental conflict, family disruption, poor child-rearing, the influence of educational attainment, occupational status, and low income, as well as such psychological or biological traits as intelligence and impulsivity (Farrington et al., 2006). The Dunedin study is also exploring an array of variables, including impulsivity, neuroticism, introversion or extraversion, schizophrenia, and anti-social personality disorder (all thought to be partially or largely heritable), along with social relationships, education, income, and employment (i.e., social factors) (Moffitt, Caspi, Harrington, & Milne, 2002). These cohort studies have served as testing grounds for existing criminological theories, and will no doubt serve to generate both further refinements and continuing critiques in the years to come.

SUMMARY OF KEY POINTS

- The major theoretical perspectives of crime and deviance are based on biological, psychological, and sociological explanations. However, some theories, such as rational choice theory, or opportunity theory, do not fall squarely within one of those three. Contemporary social learning theory, for example, involves a combination of sociological, psychological, and, in some instances, biological elements.

- A good theory must follow basic rules of logic, and must help us make sense of reality. A good theory can be accepted or rejected on the basis of solid evidence. Otherwise, it becomes difficult to distinguish a simple opinion from a logical argument that supports a true theory.

- All theories are affected to one degree or another by their social, political, economic, and historical circumstances. For example, the Positivist School reflected what was going on in the latter 19th century, such as Darwin's theory of evolution. The Chicago School's views were shaped by, among other things, the rapid urbanization that took place around the turn of the 20th century.

- We can still find many examples of Classical School thinking in our modern criminal justice system, such as the codification of criminal offences, the presumption of innocence, the right to a fair trial, the right to know the case against you, and the right to be tried by a jury of your peers.

- The Positivist School rejected the main tenets of the Classical School, arguing that individuals did not exercise free will or make rational choices. Instead, members of the Positivist School claimed that behaviour was predetermined by genetics and evolution.

- While sociology searches for the causes of criminal behaviour in social structures and interactions, psychology examines the characteristics of individual offenders. These two disciplines have traditionally recognized an interplay between these factors. In contrast, the relationship between sociological and biological theories has been much more contentious.

- Conflict theory posits that society and its laws and legal system are rooted in social, political, and economic conflict. It is typically associated with the thinking of Marx. Consensus theory holds that society and its laws are rooted in the shared values and beliefs of its members, and is typically associated with Durkheim. Most criminological theories can generally be classified as either conflict or consensus theories, although a number fall somewhere between the two.

NOTES

1. Note that while definitions of several key terms are provided in this chapter, a number of terms relating to specific theories are defined within their respective chapters.
2. Like many applications of evolutionary theory that emerged during this time, this line of reasoning is based on a misinterpretation of Darwin's ideas. Evolutionary theory states that organisms develop different traits that allow them to survive in their surroundings. It might be more accurate to argue that some forms of criminality (e.g., drug dealing, white-collar crime) actually provide evolutionary advantages that help criminals thrive in their environments. Further, in some cases law-abiding behaviour does not seem to be very adaptive, since it really provides no clear evolutionary advantages, especially if the likelihood of being caught and punished for committing a crime is very low.
3. Examples of "pure" conflict and consensus theories are few and far between. Even Durkheim, the forefather of consensus theory, would acknowledge that conflict exists between individual wants and aspirations, and the social institutions and regulations that restrain individual conduct. Some biologists accept the notion that the law is a product of social conflict, rather than consensus. While they might argue that biology trumps the environment in producing criminality, biologists could still be skeptical of state definitions of criminal behaviour and the moral legitimacy of state sanctions.

QUESTIONS FOR CRITICAL DISCUSSION

1. Which theories seem to have stood the test of time and continue to be influential or broadly accepted? Which ones have not?
2. How have various theories influenced one another? Provide some examples.
3. What accounts for the most heated debates among criminologists, such as sociological versus biological approaches, or consensus versus conflict approaches? Can you imagine these debates ever being resolved? What other key debates can you identify in this chapter?
4. What are the external disciplines that appear to have had the most influence on criminological theories?
5. Is it possible for any single theory to adequately explain crime?
6. What does a theory require in order to be considered useful, or valid? How does one judge the merit of a given theory?

SUGGESTED FURTHER READINGS

Agnew, R. (1985). A revised strain theory of delinquency. *Social Forces, 64*(1), 151–167.

Broadhurst, R. (2006). Developments in the global law enforcement of cyber-crime. *Policing: An International Journal of Police Strategies and Management, 29*(3), 408–433. doi:1108/13639510610684674

Burgess, R.L., & Akers, R.L. (1966). A differential association-reinforcement theory of criminal behavior. *Social Problems, 14*(2), 128–147.

Duster, T. (2006). Comparative perspectives and competing explanations: Taking on the newly configured reductionist challenge to sociology. *American Sociological Review, 71*(1), 1–15. Retrieved from http://www.jstor.org/stable/30038973

Ellis, L., & Walsh, A. (1997). Gene-based evolutionary theories in criminology. *Criminology*, *35*(2), 229. doi:10.1111/j.1745-9125.1997.tb00876.x

Farrington, D.P. (2004). Criminological psychology in the twenty-first century. *Criminal Behavior and Mental Health*, *14*(3), 152–166. doi:10.1002/cbm.583

Jeffery, C.R. (1978). Criminology as an interdisciplinary behavioral science. *Criminology*, *16*(2), 149–169.

Laub, J.H., & Sampson, R.J. (1991). The Sutherland-Glueck debate: On the sociology of criminological knowledge. *American Journal of Sociology*, *96*(6), 1402–1440.

Piquero, N.L., Tibbetts, S.G., & Blankenship, M.B. (2005). Examining the role of differential association and techniques of neutralization in explaining corporate crime. *Deviant Behavior*, *26*(2), 159–188.

Sampson, R.J., & Groves, W.B. (1989). Community structure and crime: Testing social-disorganization theory. *American Journal of Sociology*, *94*(4), 774–802.

Sutherland, E.H. (1940). White-collar criminality. *American Sociological Review*, *5*(1), 1–12.

REFERENCES

Agnew, R. (2005). *Why do criminals offend? A general theory of crime and delinquency*. New York: New York University Press.

Akers, R.L., & Jensen, G.F. (2003). *Social learning theory and the explanation of crime: A guide for the new century*. New Brunswick, NJ: Transaction.

Akers, R.L., & Jensen, G.F. (2006). The empirical status of social learning theory of crime and deviance: The past, present and future. In F.T. Cullen, J.P. Wright, & K.R. Blevins (Eds.), *Taking stock: The status of criminological theory* (pp. 37–76). New Brunswick, NJ: Transaction.

Akers, R.L., & Sellers, C.S. (2009). *Criminological theories: Introduction, evaluation, and application* (5th ed.). New York: Oxford University Press.

Alpert, J., & Hajaj, N. (2010). We knew the web was big … Retrieved from http://googleblog. blogspot.com/2008/07/we-knew-web-was-big.html.

Anderson, G. (2007). *Biological influences on criminal behavior*. Boca Raton, FL: CRC Press.

Andrews, D.A., & Bonta, J. (2010). *The psychology of criminal conduct* (5th ed.). Cincinnati, OH: Anderson.

Bartol, C.W. (1999). *Criminal behaviour: A psychosocial approach*. Upper Saddle River, NJ: Prentice Hall.

Beaver, K.M., & Ratchford, M. (2009). Evidence of genetic and environmental effects on the development of low self-control. *Criminal Justice and Behavior*, *36*(11), 1158–1172. doi:10.1177/0093854809342859

Benson, M.L., & Simpson, S.S. (2009). *White-collar crime: An opportunity perspective*. New York: Routledge.

Bernard, T.J., Snipes, J.B., & Gerould, A.L. (2010). *Vold's theoretical criminology* (6th ed.). New York: Oxford University Press.

Bradley, K. (2010). Cesare Lombroso (1835–1909). In K. Hayward, S. Maruna, & J. Mooney (Eds.), *Fifty key thinkers in criminology* (pp. 25–30). London: Routledge.

Broadhurst, R. (2006). Developments in the global law enforcement of cyber-crime. *Policing: An International Journal of Police Strategies and Management*, *29*(3), 408–433. doi:1108/13639510610684674

Burtch, B.E. (2003). *The sociology of law: Critical approaches to social control* (2nd ed.). Toronto: Nelson Thomson.

Clarke, R.V. (2009). Situational crime prevention. In B.R.E. Wright & R.B. McNeal Jr. (Eds.), *Boundaries: Readings in deviance, crime and criminal justice* (pp. 145–193). Boston: Pearson Custom.

Clarke, R.V., & Cornish, D.B. (2001). Rational choice. In R. Paternoster & R. Bachman (Eds.), *Explaining criminals and crime: Essays in contemporary criminological theory* (pp. 23–42). Los Angeles: Roxbury.

Cohen, L.E., & Felson, M. (1979). Social change and crime rate trends: A routine activity approach. *American Sociological Review, 44*(4), 588–608.

Cohen, S. (1985). *Visions of social control: Crime, punishment, and classification.* New York: Polity Press.

Cullen, F.T., Jonson, C.L., Myer, A.J., & Adler, F. (2011). Introduction: Preserving the origins of American criminology. In F.T. Cullen, C.L. Jonson, A.J. Myer, & F. Adler (Eds.), *The origins of American criminology: Advances in criminological theory* (Vol. 16, pp. 1–14). New Brunswick, NJ: Transaction.

Cullen, F.T., Wright, J.P., Gendreau, P., & Andrews, D.A. (2003). What correctional treatment can tell us about criminological theory: Implications for social learning theory. In R.L. Akers & G.F. Jensen (Eds.), *Social learning theory and the explanation of crime: A guide for the new century* (pp. 339–362). New Brunswick, NJ: Transaction.

Deutschmann, L.B. (2002). *Deviance and social control* (3rd ed.). Toronto: Nelson Thomson Learning.

DiCristina, B. (2012a). The emergence of the classical school. In B. DiCristina (Ed.), *The birth of criminology: Readings from the eighteenth and nineteenth centuries* (pp. 12–21). New York: Wolters Kluwer Law & Business.

DiCristina, B. (2012b). Jeremy Bentham. In B. DiCristina (Ed.), *The birth of criminology: Readings from the eighteenth and nineteenth centuries* (pp. 55–56). New York: Wolters Kluwer Law & Business.

DiCristina, B. (2012c). Physiognomy, phrenology and the Italian school. In B. DiCristina (Ed.), *The birth of criminology: Readings from the eighteenth and nineteenth centuries* (pp. 69–82). New York: Wolters Kluwer Law & Business.

Donohue, J.J., & Wolfers, J. (2009). Estimating the impact of the death penalty on murder. *American Law and Economics Review, 7*(2), 249–309. doi:10.1093/aler/ahp024

Durkheim, É. (1964). In G.E.G. Catlin (Ed.), *The rules of sociological method* (J.H. Mueller & S.A. Solovay, Trans.) (8th ed.). New York: The Free Press of Glencoe.

Duster, T. (2006). Comparative perspectives and competing explanations: Taking on the newly configured reductionist challenge to sociology. *American Sociological Review, 71*(1), 1–15. Retrieved from http://www.jstor.org/stable/30038973.

Einstadter, W.J., & Henry, S. (2006). *Criminological theory: An analysis of its underlying assumptions* (2nd ed.). Lanham, MD: Rowman & Littlefield.

Ellis, L., & Walsh, A. (1997). Gene-based evolutionary theories in criminology. *Criminology, 35*(2), 229. doi:10.1111/j.1745-9125.1997.tb00876.x

Erikson, K.T. (1962). Notes on the sociology of deviance. *Social Problems, 9*(4), 307–314.

Farrell, G. (2010). Situational crime prevention and its discontents: Rational choice and harm reduction versus "cultural criminology." *Social Policy & Administration, 44*(1), 40–66. doi:10.1111/j.1467-9515.2009.00699.x

Farrington, D.P. (2004). Criminological psychology in the twenty-first century. *Criminal Behavior and Mental Health, 14*(3), 152–166. doi:10.1002/cbm.583

Farrington, D.P., Coid, J.W., Harnett, L.M., Jolliffe, D., Soteriou, N., Turner, R.E., & West, D.J. (2006). *Criminal careers up to age 50 and life success up to age 48: New findings from the Cambridge Study in delinquent development* (no. 299). London, UK: Home Office Research, Development and Statistics Directorate.

Felson, M., & Clarke, R.V. (2010). Routine precautions, criminology and crime prevention. In H.D. Barlow & S.H. Decker (Eds.), *Criminology and public policy: Putting theory to work* (pp. 106–127). Philadelphia: Temple University Press.

Fishbein, D.H. (1990). Biological perspectives in criminology. *Criminology, 28*(1), 27–72.

Foucault, M. (1979). *Discipline and punish: The birth of the prison* (A. Sheridan Trans.). (Vintage books ed.). New York: Vintage Books.

Garland, D. (2001). *The culture of control: Crime and social order in contemporary society.* Chicago: University of Chicago Press.

Glueck, S., & Glueck, E. (1994). Unraveling juvenile delinquency. In J.E. Jacoby (Ed.), *Classics of criminology* (2nd ed., pp. 241–246). Prospect Heights, IL: Waveland Press. (Original work published 1950.)

Jeffery, C.R. (1978). Criminology as an interdisciplinary behavioral science. *Criminology, 16*(2), 149–169.

Laub, J.H., & Sampson, R.J. (1991). The Sutherland-Glueck debate: On the sociology of criminological knowledge. *American Journal of Sociology, 96*(6), 1402–1440.

Lemert, C.C. (1993). *Social theory: The multicultural and classic readings.* Boulder, CO: Westview Press.

Lilly, J.R., Cullen, F.T., & Ball, R.A. (2011). *Criminological theory: Context and consequences* (5th ed.). Thousand Oaks, CA: Sage.

Moffitt, T.E. (1993). Adolescence-limited and life-course-persistent antisocial behavior: A developmental taxonomy. *Psychological Review, 100*(4), 674–701.

Moffitt, T.E., Caspi, A., Harrington, H., & Milne, B.J. (2002). Males on the life-course-persistent and adolescence-limited antisocial pathways: Follow-up at age 26 years. *Development & Psychopathology, 14*(1), 179–207.

Mutchnick, R.J., Martin, R., & Austin, T.W. (2009). *Criminological thought: Pioneers past and present.* Upper Saddle River, NJ: Prentice Hall.

Netcraft. (2010). April 2010 web server survey. Retrieved from http://news.netcraft.com/archives/2010/04/15/april_2010_web_server_survey.html.

O'Malley, p. (2010). Jeremy Bentham (1748–1832). In K. Hayward, S. Maruna, & J. Mooney (Eds.), *Fifty key thinkers in criminology* (pp. 7–12). London, UK: Routledge.

Passas, N. (1995). Continuities in the anomie tradition. In F. Adler, W.S. Laufer, & R.K. Merton (Eds.), *The legacy of anomie theory* (pp. 91–112). New Brunswick, NJ: Transaction.

Paternoster, R., & Bachman, R. (2001). The positive school of criminology: Biological theories of crime. In R. Paternoster & R. Bachman (Eds.), *Explaining criminals and crime: Essays in contemporary criminological theory* (pp. 47–56). Los Angeles: Roxbury.

Pfohl, S.J. (1985). *Images of deviance and social control: A sociological history.* New York: McGraw-Hill.

Piquero, A.R., & Blumstein, A. (2007). Does incapacitation reduce crime? *Journal of Quantitative Criminology, 23*(4), 267–285. doi:10.1007/s10940-007-9030-6

Rafter, N.H. (1997). Psychopathology and the evolution of criminological knowledge. *Theoretical Criminology, 1*(2), 235–259. doi:10.1177/1362480697001002004

Rafter, N.H. (2009a). Criminal anthropology. In N.H. Rafter (Ed.), *The origins of criminology: A reader* (pp. 161–162). Oxon, UK: Routledge.

Rafter, N.H. (2009b). Introduction. In N.H. Rafter (Ed.), *The origins of criminology: A reader* (pp. xiii–xxvi). Oxon, UK: Routledge.

Raine, A. (2013). *The anatomy of violence: The biological roots of crime.* New York: Pantheon.

Raine, A., & Yaralian, P.S. (2001). Biological approaches to crime: Psychophysiology and brain dysfunction. In R. Paternoster, & R. Bachman (Eds.), *Explaining criminals and crime: Essays in contemporary criminological theory* (pp. 57–72). Los Angeles: Roxbury.

Reiman, J. (2003). The Marxian critique of criminal justice. In C.M. Renzetti, D.J. Curran, & P.J. Carr (Eds.), *Theories of crime: A reader* (pp. 179–189). Boston: Allyn and Bacon.

Renzetti, C.M., Curran, D.J., & Carr, P.J. (Eds.). (2003). *Theories of crime: A reader.* Boston: Allyn and Bacon.

Robinson, M.B., & Beaver, K.M. (2008). *Why crime? An interdisciplinary approach to explaining criminal behavior*. Durham, NC: Carolina Academic Press.

Sacco, V.F., & Kennedy, L.W. (2011). *The criminal event: An introduction to criminology in Canada* (5th ed.). Toronto: Nelson Education.

Sampson, R.J., & Laub, J.H. (1992). Crime and deviance in the life course. *Annual Review of Sociology, 18*(1), 63–84.

Skiba, R., & Peterson, R. (1999). The dark side of zero tolerance: Can punishment lead to safe schools? *Phi Delta Kappan, 80*(5), 372–382.

Sutherland, E.H. (1940). White-collar criminality. *American Sociological Review, 5*(1), 1–12.

Sutherland, E.H. (1950). The diffusion of sexual psychopath laws. *American Journal of Sociology, 56*(2), 142–148.

Sutherland, E.H. (1994). Differential association. In J.E. Jacoby (Ed.), *Classics of criminology* (2nd ed., pp. 226–227). Prospect Heights, IL: Waveland Press. (Original work published 1947.)

Tremblay, R.E. (2012). Developmental origins of aggression: From social learning to epigenetics. In R. Loeber & B.C. Welsh (Eds.), *The future of criminology* (pp. 20–29). New York: Oxford University Press.

Walsh, A. (2002). *Biosocial criminology: Introduction and integration*. Cincinnati, OH: Anderson.

Walsh, A. (2012). *Criminology: The essentials*. Thousand Oaks, CA: Sage.

Walsh, W.A., & Wolak, J. (2005). Nonforcible Internet-related sex crimes with adolescent victims: Prosecution issues and outcomes. *Child Maltreatment, 10*(3), 260–271. doi:10.1177/1077559505276505

Williams, F.P., & McShane, M.D. (2010). *Criminological theory* (5th ed.). Upper Saddle River, NJ: Pearson/Prentice Hall.

Wortley, R. (2011). *Psychological criminology: An integrative approach*. London, UK: Routledge.

Yar, M. (2010). Cesare Beccaria (1738–94). In K. Hayward, S. Maruna, & J. Mooney (Eds.), *Fifty key thinkers in criminology* (pp. 3–7). London, UK: Routledge.

Young, J. (2002). Critical criminology in the twenty-first century: Critique, irony and the always unfinished. In K. Carrington, & R. Hogg (Eds.), *Critical criminology: Issues, debates and challenges* (pp. 251–274). Cullompton, UK: Willan.

Zeitlin, I.M. (2001). *Ideology and the development of sociological theory* (7th ed.). Upper Saddle River, NJ: Prentice Hall.

Cases

R v. Inwood. (1989). 48 CCC (3d) 174 (ONCA).

R v. Turcotte. (2000). 2000 CanLII 14721 (ONCA).

CASE STUDY 7.1

Jeffrey Landrigan: Biologically Susceptible to Violent Crime?

Jeffrey Landrigan.
Source: Arizona Department of Corrections.

Jeffrey Landrigan was abandoned by his alcoholic parents as an infant and adopted in 1962 by a well-educated couple living in Oklahoma. His adoptive father was a geologist. Landrigan indicated that he felt loved by his adoptive parents, but also felt that he never really was a part of the family. By the time he was 10 years old, Landrigan had a drinking problem. As a teenager he became involved with the use of illegal drugs, and at the age of 20 he stabbed a childhood friend to death.

He was convicted of first-degree murder and sentenced to life in prison, but that conviction was overturned on appeal, and Landrigan agreed to a plea of guilty to second-degree murder, with a 20-year prison term. While in prison in Oklahoma, he stabbed another inmate, and in November 1989 he escaped from a prison work crew and headed for Arizona. Just a month later, Landrigan murdered Chester Dyer in Dyer's Phoenix apartment. Dyer had met Landrigan at a Burger King and called friends to tell them he was going back to his apartment to have sex with a man named Jeff. Dyer was found stabbed and strangled to death with an electrical cord, and he had lacerations on his face and back.

Unfortunately for Landrigan, he left a footprint on Dyer's floor, and that provided a crucial evidentiary link in the case. In 1990, Landrigan was found guilty of murder and sentenced to death by lethal injection. While on death row in Arizona, Landrigan learned that his biological father was a man named Darrel Hill, who ultimately died of natural causes on death row in Arkansas in 2005. Like Landrigan, Hill was also a drug addict with an extensive criminal history of violent crime. While on death row, Landrigan also learned that his grandfather (Hill's father) had been a career criminal, shot to death by police during a high-speed chase in 1961, after robbing a drug store.

Jeffrey Landrigan began to think that he had inherited a "killer gene" from his father. In 1999 he told the *Sunday Mirror* newspaper, "I've never met my father. But he was definitely, even without being there, a big influence in my life." Criminologist Adrian Raine has said of the Landrigan case, "This fascinating natural experiment—in which a baby with a violent heritage was transferred from a life of poverty and squalor into a loving, caring, successful family, yet still became a killer—suggests that there really is a genetic predisposition to violence" (Fuchs, 2013).

At trial, Landrigan directed his lawyer not to present mitigating evidence, but he later argued that his lawyer was ineffective and that counsel should have presented evidence to the trial court, documenting his client's fetal alcohol syndrome and the extensive history of violence within his biological family. A Ninth US Circuit Court of Appeals decision granted Landrigan a hearing on his claim that his lawyer did not do enough to present this kind of evidence—evidence that might have prevented imposition of the death penalty. However, a majority of the US Supreme Court disagreed with the Court of Appeals, and ruled in a 5–4 judgment that the Court of Appeals should have deferred to the trial court—that it was not reasonable for Landrigan to direct his lawyer not to present evidence and then claim that his lawyer was ineffective.

On October 26, 2010, Jeffrey Landrigan was executed by lethal injection in Arizona, after consuming his final meal of steak, fried okra, french fries, strawberry ice cream, and a Dr. Pepper. His final words before execution were "Well, I'd like to say thank you to my family for being here and all my friends, and Boomer Sooner" (a reference to the football team at the University of Oklahoma).

Before You Read Chapter 7

- Would you say that Jeffrey Landrigan was genetically predisposed to violence? What other explanations could you point to that might explain his behaviour?
- This chapter examines adoption and twin studies, and what they can tell us about criminal behaviour. Criminologists consider factors that arise from biology or the environment. How might these factors influence one another? Do you think there might be circumstances in which the impact of biology trumps that of environment? Or the other way around? Try to think of some examples.

Biological Approaches

Introduction

Criminologists, law enforcement, and the general public have tried to understand why people commit crime for millennia. Environmental, psychological, and sociological explanations for criminal behaviour are readily accepted, but biological explanations are considered highly controversial. This is, in part, due to a lack of understanding of biology and to the appalling atrocities that have been committed in the past by just such a lack of understanding and the abuse of biology.

Most early criminogenic theories postulated biology to be the *single* causal agent for crime. Franz Gall (1758–1828) believed that a criminal could be identified by the shape of the skull, and **phrenology** developed a massive following. In the late 1890s, pioneering Italian criminologist Cesare Lombroso studied convicted criminals and described certain physical features, or **atavisms**, of criminals. He considered people who exhibited such atavisms to be less developed, more primitive, and more violent. Today, it seems absurd that anyone would believe such unscientific theories, yet we are all inclined to judge individuals by the way they look or dress, so one can understand how people could accept such theories at the time. Thankfully, these theories fell out of favour as they had no scientific backing whatsoever.

Darwin's theory of evolution (*On the Origin of Species*, 1859) explained how certain *genetic* characteristics can lead an individual to be more or less successful, or fit, in some environments than others (a theory that influenced Lombroso's ideas). Although Darwin's work had nothing to do with crime, due to a lack of understanding of genetics at that time, contemporaries began to suggest that many *non-genetic* factors could be inherited, such as poverty, promiscuity, and crime (Niehoff, 1999). This terrifying misunderstanding led to the **eugenics** movements in North America, the racial policies of the German Third Reich (1933–1945), and the subsequent Nazi genocide of European

phrenology
The study of the shape and size of the skull as a supposed indication of character and mental abilities. This theory has been discredited.

atavism
A term associated with Cesare Lombroso and the Positivist School of thought; the notion that criminals are less evolved than "normal" humans.

eugenics
Methods to improve populations by controlling breeding to increase the occurrence of desirable heritable characteristics.

Jews during the Second World War. This frightening past has led people to forget that, at the time, scientists frequently explained that no scientific basis existed for these assumptions whatsoever; in fact, science proved the opposite. However, politicians abused the public's lack of understanding, with appalling consequences.

Nature and Nurture

Today it is important to look at the true science behind biology and crime and realize, as scientists have done before, that behaviour, whether criminal or otherwise, is not caused by one single entity but by a combination of many factors that *include* biology as part of the equation. Anyone who does not believe that biology can impact behaviour has clearly never known a newborn baby or experienced a biological change such as puberty. Any parent will tell you that their baby was not born as a total nonentity but instead immediately exhibited (often while still in the womb) a distinct personality. This personality, of course, will be greatly influenced by the environment the child grows up in, but the way a child's personality responds to that environment is based on the child's biology. Puberty, with its massive change in hormones, often results in behaviour changes and mood swings in adolescents. Past scholarly arguments have often spoken of "nature versus nurture." Biologists have recognized for years that such a phrase is incorrect and that it should be nature *and* nurture.

It is truly unfortunate that biological explanations for crime are not better understood, as they often offer much greater hope for rehabilitation than environmental explanations for crime. It is often considered that a person's DNA is his or her destiny, and that a person is "born that way" and so cannot be changed. This assertion is very far from the truth. We alter our genetic future all the time. For instance, a person who has a family history of heart disease may greatly decrease his or her own risk with diet and exercise. In the past, a disease called phenylketonuria was a leading cause of severe mental retardation. Phenylketonuria is a genetically controlled disease that results in a baby being unable to metabolize certain amino acids. As a result, by the age of five years old, such a child would be severely retarded. After the genetic basis of the disease was discovered in the 1930s, researchers eventually developed a simple way to treat it: carefully regulate the child's diet until age seven, when high levels of the amino acids in question can no longer damage the brain. Today, this disease is unheard of as babies are tested at birth, and those with the condition are treated and grow up to lead normal, healthy lives. Of course, when these same people have children, they pass on the gene, increasing the prevalence of the disease. However, the destiny of those carrying the gene has changed.

Genetic Predispositions for Criminal Behaviour

Studying human genetics for any purpose is ethically, numerically, and biologically difficult. Even in large-scale studies, such as drug trials, every person is influenced by different, biological and **environmental** (e.g., diet, lifestyle) factors. Ideally, a good experiment requires a large number of identical animals, but cloning large numbers of people for experiments is not possible or ethical. However, fortunately, clones do exist in nature in the form of twins. Two types of twins exist. Dizygotic (DZ) twins are the result of two sperm fertilizing two eggs. They are no more genetically similar than any other pair of full siblings. Monozygotic (MZ) twins, however, are the result of a single

environment
The external conditions, resources, and stimuli a person interacts with.

sperm fertilizing a single egg which then cleaves into two separate zygotes shortly after fertilization, resulting in two genetically identical babies.

Twin Studies

Full siblings and DZ twins are said to share 50 percent of their DNA. This assertion is incorrect because all humans share about 99 percent of the same DNA that controls functions such as digestion, respiration, and physical makeup (e.g., the number of arms, legs, and eyes the species exhibits). So, DZ twins share 50 percent of the approximately 1 percent of human DNA that explain variations in characteristics. However, 100 percent of the DNA of MZ twins is the same; MZ twins are natural clones. Both types of twins are considered to share 100 percent of their environment, as they are reared together and are the same age. Therefore, comparing a trait in MZ and DZ twins allows us to consider that trait in a natural, non-experimental situation. Most studies use **concordance rates** to compare the traits of MZ and DZ twins. For instance, if the concordance

concordance rate
In a random sample of pairs, the proportion of pairs that share a certain characteristic.

BOX 7.1

Twin Coincidences Explained

Tabloids occasionally announce the reunion of twins separated at birth who suddenly meet as adults and note how incredibly similar they are. For instance, Gerald Levey and Mark Newman were reunited in 1985, when they were 32 years old. Remarkably, both are firefighters in New Jersey, both wear glasses and have a moustache, both have a fondness for Chinese food and John Wayne movies, and both even hold cans of their favourite beer, Budweiser, in the same way. Such stories can give twin studies a bad name, as it is quite clear to anyone that liking Chinese food and enjoying John Wayne movies are not heritable traits. However, if you break it all down, you can begin to see how such similarities might appear.

- *The twins became firefighters.* This choice of profession could relate to both genetics and the environment. A firefighter must be strong and fit and have a personality that succeeds under pressure, which partially relate to genetics, but careers go in phases with some being very fashionable (and therefore desirable) at certain times. For instance, the proliferation of *CSI*-type television shows has meant a great leap in the number of children wanting to go into forensic science. So perhaps firefighting was very popular when the twins were kids (they are the same age, remember).

- *The twins wear glasses and have a moustache.* Glasses could relate very much to genetics, and what about the moustache? Well, it could simply be fashionable

at the time, but also, we wear our hair in a way that suits our face. The men are identical, so presumably the moustache suits both of them.

- *The twins like Chinese food and John Wayne movies.* Such preferences are not heritable, but food and movies go through fashion trends, so it is probable that both were popular as they grew up. For instance, many movies and TV shows today focus on zombies, vampires, and the supernatural; a few years ago, science fiction was very popular; and before that, there were many Western shows. Presumably the twins grew up in the era when John Wayne movies were popular.

- *The twins like Budweiser and hold beer cans in the same way.* Budweiser is a common and popular beer in America, and has been for a long time. It is only in the last few years that America has discovered micro breweries. When the twins were young men, there were few choices of beer in America, and Budweiser was popular. Like the twins, many beer drinkers of their era would have preferred Budweiser. As for the way they hold beer cans, the particular manner (with one pinkie curled) could have been a fad of the time, but it could also relate to genetics and general hand dexterity. No doubt they hold the can in a way that is comfortable to them.

Adapted from Anderson (2007, pp. 89–91).

rate for a trait in MZ twins is determined to be 85 percent, then, because they are identical, we expect both twins to have an 85 percent chance of developing the trait. If the concordance rate for the same trait is only 15 percent in DZ twins, then the trait most likely has an inherited component because the twins that are identical are more likely to exhibit it than the twins who have less genetic similarity. If, on the other hand, the concordance rate for a trait is 85 percent in both DZ and MZ twins, then it is more probable that the trait relates to the environment because the greater genetic relationship does not impact concordance rates. A scientist could then go further and look at the trait in other, unrelated people. If the trait were found to occur much less in unrelated people, that would suggest the trait has both an environmental and a genetic component or is specific to a twin environment.

A wide variety of twin studies have been conducted over the last 100 years, including research on a range of criminal activities (with some long-term studies still ongoing). Concordance rates vary in studies and by type of crime, but overall, a much greater concordance rate for criminal behaviour is seen in MZ twins than in DZ twins, which indicates a strong genetic basis for criminal behaviour. Early twin studies have been criticized as many had only small sample sizes and determined *zygosity* (whether twins were MZ or DZ) not based on blood tests but on resemblance. Siblings can look very similar, especially if they are the same age, so zygosity may have been mistaken in some studies. As well, it could be suggested that some German studies may have been politically biased because they were conducted during the Nazi era. However, a later reanalysis of a large number of early twin studies showed that those conducted in Germany were actually the most experimentally robust and resulted in some of the lowest concordance rates, which suggests that these studies were not politically influenced (Raine, 1993).

meta-analysis
A quantitative statistical analysis of several similar experiments or studies to test for statistical significance.

In his **meta-analysis** of the raw data taken from 13 twin studies, Raine (1993) removed studies with small sample sizes and possible political bias, separately analyzed data using blood to determine zygosity, and separately analyzed data for males and females. The results still showed much higher concordance rates for crime in MZ twins than in DZ twins, with some studies showing rates two or three times higher in MZ twins.

etiology
The cause of a condition.

A common question in criminology is whether juvenile and adult criminal behaviour have the same **etiology**. A reanalysis of twin studies from around the world showed that although the concordance rate for adult crime was high, almost no concordance existed for juvenile crime, indicating that although adult crime is influenced by genetics, juvenile crime is almost entirely environmentally based. An ongoing US study has been looking at twins registered in the Vietnam Era Twin Registry and includes 3,226 pairs of male twins (Lyons, 1996). This self-report study has asked respondents about early, later, and multiple arrests; felony convictions; and early and later criminal behaviour. Importantly, this study separates criminal behaviour from actual arrests. Overall, the study has found crime to be low, but although a strong influence of genetics was found in adult criminal behaviour, the environment had a much greater influence on juvenile criminal behaviour (Lyons, 1996).

Twin studies have been very valuable in showing behaviours that are not only linked to genetics but also influenced primarily by the environment, because one cannot study one without the other. Such studies have been conducted in many countries, over many years, and by a variety of researchers. So, the results can be considered robust, but some concerns remain (Anderson, 2007). We assume that the environment is the same for both DZ and MZ twins. However, as DZ twins may be of different sexes and MZ twins look identical, it is possible that pairs of MZ twins are treated more similarly than pairs of DZ twins, or, alternatively, that MZ twins deliberately try to be individually distinct, all of which would impact the assumptions related to environment. Also, MZ twins, although genetically identical, may have other biological differences due to the gestational environment or birth complications that are more common in twins. As well, some early studies did not determine true zygosity by blood and often used very small sample sizes. As crime in general is rare, it often means that very low numbers of respondents have been studied. Very few data are available for females, as female crime is rarer than male crime. Violent crime is also very rare. Thus, almost all the twin studies look only at non-violent crime in males.

Adoption Studies

Possibly the biggest concern with twin studies is the similarity of environments in which the twins live. This concern is eliminated with a more powerful natural genetic study type: an adoption study. In adoption studies, researchers compare the criminal behaviour of people who were adopted by non-family members with that of their adoptive and biological parents. This approach is much more effective in separating genetic and environmental influences and does not rely on an assumed identical environment for two people (twins). If adoptees who commit crimes have a statistically higher number of criminal biological parents, then this finding would suggest that criminal behaviour has a genetic basis. However, if adoptees who commit crimes have a statistically higher number of criminal adoptive parents, then this finding would suggest that criminal behaviour has an environmental basis. Many adoption studies have shown a higher level of anti-social or criminal behaviour in adoptees with criminal biological parents, although in almost all cases, the relationship was for non-violent crimes only (see the review in Anderson, 2007).

Is Violence Heritable?

As violent crime is rare, most studies have not been able to look specifically at the **heritability** of violence, but a Danish adoption study (see Box 7.2) was so large that a comparison could be performed between violent offenders and those that had committed only property offences (Mednick, Gabrielli, & Hutchings, 1987). In the Danish study (as in the twin studies), property crime had a very significant genetic component, but violent crime was not significantly impacted by genetics. This finding is interesting because when the public hear the words "genetics" associated with "crime," they tend to assume that the crime is violent and major (such as homicide or rape). In reality, the opposite has often been shown to be the case. The Danish study is exhaustive, and the researchers considered many possible caveats (Mednick, Gabrielli, & Hutchings, 1987). The study covered adoptions over a 43-year period (1924 to 1967) and the ongoing adult lives of those adopted. The researchers were concerned that major world events such as war, recession, or industrialization may have had an impact on results, so they repeated the analyses in five-year increments—and arrived at identical results. They looked at time from birth to adoption, as a later adoption might suggest that the child was influenced by the biological home. It was found that all of the adoptees were either immediately adopted or placed in a foster institution prior to adoption, so there was

Twin brothers Reginald and Ronald Kray, notorious London gangsters in the 1950s and 1960s.

heritability
The quality of being heritable, via genes.

What Can Adoption Studies Tell Us About Criminal Behaviour?

One of the largest adoption studies was conducted in Denmark, and examined 14,427 non-familial adoptions (Mednick, Gabrielli, & Hutchings, 1984). Denmark maintains complete records on its citizens, so researchers were able to access extensive data on adoptees and their adoptive and biological parents. Criminal convictions were used as an index of criminal behaviour, and data on the crime, the date of the crime, and the sentence were obtained. Demographic data for adoptees and adoptive and biological parents were also examined, including date and place of birth, sex, address, occupation, and size of local community. These data could be used to imply socio-economic status as well as whether the child grew up in a city or in the country. The study showed that if a male child's adoptive and birth parents had never been convicted of a crime, then only 13.5 percent of the male adoptees received a conviction. If only the adoptive parents had a criminal record, then 14.7 percent of the adopted sons had also received a conviction. However, if only the biological parents had a criminal record, then the percentage of convicted sons jumped to 20 percent. If both sets of parents had a criminal record, then the conviction rate in the sons reached 24.5 percent (Mednick, Gabrielli, & Hutchings, 1984). This shows a genetic basis for crime, but one that is influenced by the environment. Obviously, it was rarer for adoptive parents to have criminal records, as it is unusual for a couple to be allowed to adopt a child if they have a criminal background.

However, when the data were further refined to eliminate families in which an adoptive parent had a record, the relationship remained, with biological parents having a genetic influence on offspring criminality. The number of criminal convictions of adoptees with biological parents who had multiple convictions increased with the level of biological parent recidivism. In some cases, a parent gave up more than one child for adoption, which allowed a comparison of siblings and half siblings raised in different adoptive homes.

Overall, the data indicated that the chance any two randomly picked adoptees would both have a criminal record was 8.5 percent (so, this percentage was considered a baseline). Concordance rates for criminal records were 12.9 percent for half siblings, 20 percent for full siblings, and 30.8 percent if the biological father also had a criminal record—again, clearly indicating that a genetic relationship increases concordance. The number of females who had criminal records was much lower than males, but the researchers did investigate just female offenders and found that the pattern remained. Interestingly, the relationship between biological mother and female adoptee was actually statistically stronger than that between biological father and male adoptee, although the sample size available was small (Mednick, Gabrielli, & Hutchings, 1984). Adoption studies more clearly show the relationship between biology and crime, while also indicating the additive impact of the environment.

labelling
Based on labelling theory, the act of describing someone as deviant.

no environmental impact from the biological home. The researchers then reanalyzed the data to separate children adopted immediately from those who were adopted in their first year, their second year, and after age two. No effect of age of adoption was observed. Finally, they considered the effect of **labelling** the adoptee. If the biological parents had been convicted of a crime prior to the adoption, the adoptive parents were informed. However, if the conviction occurred after the adoption, the adoptive parents would not be informed. The researchers considered that if adoptive parents were aware of the biological criminal history, that information might affect how the child would be raised. In this data set, one-third of biological parents were convicted prior to adoption. Reanalysis separating the two groups showed no influence of potential labelling.

Alcoholism

More recent adoption studies have shown that adopted children are significantly more likely to be arrested multiple times and incarcerated if their biological parents had a criminal background (Beaver, 2011). Other adoption studies have looked at not only criminality but also the interrelationship between crime, alcoholism, and mental illness. A large ongoing Swedish study found a high **correlation** of both criminal behaviour and alcoholism between biological fathers and biological sons who were adopted, indicating a genetic relationship between both criminality and alcoholism (Bohman, 1996). Moreover, two forms of alcoholism have been identified: Type I is found in both males and females, begins later in life, and is influenced by both the environment and genetics. Type II is found almost always in men, begins early in life, and is almost entirely genetic (Begleiter, 1995).

Research has shown that alcoholic criminals commit repeated violent offences, whereas non-alcoholic criminals commit property offences and are more likely to have biological parents who committed petty offences only (Bohman, 1996). When only criminal behaviour was considered, if both biological and adoptive parents were not criminals, then there was less than a 3 percent risk of criminality in male offspring. When only the adoptive parents were criminals, this figure increased to 6.7 percent, and when only the biological parents were criminals, it reached 12.1 percent. However, when both biological and adoptive parents were criminals, the risk of criminality in male offspring jumped to 40 percent, which shows the interactive and additive effects of genetics and the environment (Bohman, 1996). As well, research has shown that a three-fold increase in the rate of schizophrenia occurs in both male and female adoptees of violent biological fathers. Interestingly, environment had differing effects on male and female adoptees. Long-term institutional care increased the risk of criminal behaviour in females but not males. Meanwhile, many short-term stays in homes of low socio-economic status greatly increased the risk of criminal behaviour in males but not females. Overall, low socio-economic status alone did not increase the risk of criminal behaviour in males, but unstable homes, repeated institutionalization, and having stayed in a large number of foster homes did increase the risk of alcoholism and petty criminality (Bohman, 1996). (See also the related discussion concerning fetal alcohol spectrum disorder [FASD] later in the chapter.)

Many genetic studies have shown that a good stable environment can offset a genetic predisposition for crime (Bohman, 1996; Mednick, Gabrielli, & Hutchings, 1984). As well, many genetic studies have shown a genetic basis for externalizing behaviours or "acting out" in very young children, as well as academic achievement (measured as general knowledge, mathematical knowledge, and reading ability), although shared environments (as opposed to genetics) also played a major factor (Newsome, Boisvert, & Wright, 2014). These findings could mean that a greater understanding of a specific behaviour and how environmental factors can shape it may help in allocating resources to ensure a more protective environment. As well, the link between academic outcomes and acting out suggests that improving one will improve the other (Newsome, Boisvert, & Wright, 2014).

Attention Deficit Hyperactivity Disorder and Other Personality Disorders

Anti-social behaviour in youth is sometimes a prelude to criminal behaviour later in life. Twin and adoption studies have shown that many personality disorders, such as conduct disorder (CD), **attention deficit hyperactivity disorder (ADHD)**, and borderline personality disorder (BPD) have strong genetic bases. Twin studies have shown a heritability

correlation
The finding that two measurable phenomena occur together, suggesting a relationship, but not necessarily one of direct cause and effect.

attention deficit hyperactivity disorder (ADHD)
A condition that includes a combination of behaviours, such as difficulty sustaining attention, hyperactivity and impulsive behaviour.

rate of 68 percent for CD and 63 percent for BPD (Coolidge, Thede, & Jang, 2001). Researchers using four independent sources of data on anti-social behaviour in young twins (mothers, teachers, researchers, and twins' self-reports) found that anti-social behaviour identified by all four sources was highly heritable (82 percent). However, anti-social behaviour reported by only one of the four sources ranged from 33 to 71 percent, suggesting that very clear anti-social behaviour had a strong genetic basis, but milder behaviours may relate more to the situation or environment (Arseneault et al., 2003).

Children who suffer from personality disorders do not do well in school, with over 25 percent of children with ADHD exhibiting reading disabilities. A lack of education and appropriate peer models will compound the genetic predisposition for ADHD. An analysis of almost 5,000 twins and adoptees has shown that reading success and reading disability are highly heritable (70 percent) (Kirkpatrick, Legrand, Iacono, & McGue, 2011). Studies have also identified genetic factors for ADHD on chromosomes 10, 16, and 17, and genetic factors for reading disabilities on chromosomes 2, 8, and 15 (Loo et al., 2004). The better understanding we have of the actual biological deficit, the better chance we have of treating the condition. For instance, ADHD has been linked to a variant of the **dopamine** transporter gene (Cook et al., 1995). This finding is very important, as many of the drugs found to be beneficial to children with ADHD work by inhibiting the dopamine transporter system. Preliminary research has shown that in some cases, differences in siblings' contacts with the criminal justice system can be partly explained by differences in their dopamine-processing systems (Schwartz & Beaver, 2014). Breaking down the criminal act can allow researchers to understand which specific behaviour is responsible for it and, thus, how it can be ameliorated. Genetic studies have been able to indicate not only whether some behaviours are heritable but also which disorders are heritable and which *alleles* (or variants of a gene) actually control them, allowing for specific treatments.

Although early genetic studies showed a heritable basis for petty and non-violent crimes, more recent twin and adoption studies have shown a heritable basis for aggression. This finding makes sense, as aggression was a vital part of survival for early humans, and violence is simply misplaced aggression. In a study of rhesus monkeys, female offspring were taken from aggressive mothers and placed with non-aggressive females and vice versa in an effort to determine whether female aggression was inherited or merely copied. Over a three-year period, it was clear that offspring exhibited the aggressive or non-aggressive behaviour of their biological mothers, and the behaviour of the adoptive mothers had little impact (Maestripieri, 2003). Several studies on humans have found similar results. For instance, in a large twin study in Britain and Sweden, aggressive behaviour (such as fighting and bullying) and non-aggressive behaviour (such as truancy and petty theft) were studied in both males and females. A highly heritable basis for aggressive behaviour was found in both sexes, but non-aggressive behaviour was significantly heritable in girls but less so in boys (Eley, Lichtenstein, & Stevenson, 1999). Both countries yielded similar results, which speaks to the robustness of the findings.

dopamine

A neurotransmitter that controls the reward and pleasure centres of the brain.

The Brain

When considering a biological basis for criminal behaviour, one must ask exactly what part of the behaviour is under genetic control. Clearly, one does not inherit a desire to steal cars or strike out violently. However, criminal behaviour may be controlled by various factors, such as impulsivity, an inability to understand consequences, the need for immediate gratification, lack of empathy, anxiety, depression, or reduced cognitive ability. In the twin study by Eley, Lichtenstein, and Stevenson (1999), the researchers suggested that the genetic predisposition for violent behaviour related to brain chemistry and the functionality of various **neurotransmitters**, such as serotonin, dopamine, and norepinephrine (see Figure 7.1).

neurotransmitter
A substance that carries signals from cell to cell.

Brain Chemistry

The body contains two major types of communication systems that allow us to function: the hormonal system and the nervous system. The *hormonal system* works through chemicals released into the bloodstream, and hence acts relatively slowly. In contrast, communication between nerve cells in the brain and throughout the *nervous system* is extremely rapid, occurring in nanoseconds or less. Neurochemistry is a very complex subject and is rarely discussed outside biology, but it is an area that is very important for criminology as it controls much of our behaviour. To simplify greatly, much of the communication between our nerve cells involves chemical messengers, or neurotransmitters, which are released by one nerve cell and received and acted upon by another (for a more detailed explanation, see Anderson, 2007). These neurotransmitters are the

FIGURE 7.1   Neurotransmitters

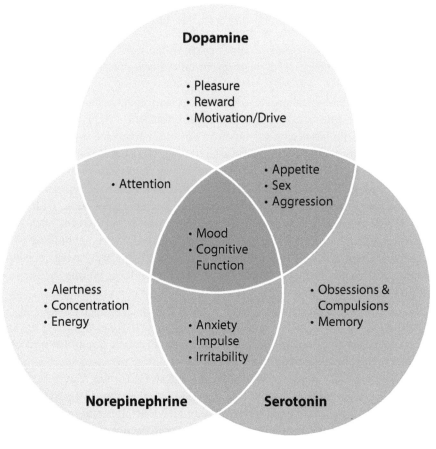

basis for behaviour. The actual neurotransmitter is made up of amino acids (or precursors), which are converted into a neurotransmitter by specific enzymes. Once its message is delivered, the neurotransmitter is broken down into specific metabolites. Therefore, researchers can measure the levels of neurotransmitters at any one of these four areas: precursor, neurotransmitter, enzyme, or metabolites. These chemicals can be measured in cerebrospinal fluid, blood, or urine, with decreasing levels of invasiveness.

Serotonin

serotonin

A neurochemical that plays an important role in depression, anxiety, and bipolar disorder. Also involved in brain development, serotonin dysfunction could lead to an increase in impulsiveness.

One of the most studied neurotransmitters is **serotonin** (5-HT or 5 hydroxytryptamine). Serotonin has been repeatedly shown to play a major role in impulsive-aggressive behaviour. It is a behavioural inhibitor, so high levels of serotonin *reduce* impulsive-aggressive behaviour. Therefore, problems occur in people who have low or irregular serotonin levels. Many studies have linked low serotonin levels to violent methods of suicide, an inability to cope with stress, aggression, anti-social personality disorder, and impulsivity.

In order for serotonin to be produced, a person must possess adequate levels of its precursor, tryptophan, which is obtained from food. The production of serotonin occurs over many stages, and a defect in any stage could result in low serotonin levels. A person may simply have an inadequate or irregular diet, and does not possess enough of the precursor to produce adequate levels of serotonin. Or they may have a condition that prevents or reduces the uptake of dietary tryptophan. Such problems can sometimes be treated with something as simple as a dietary change or, more controversially, with drugs that can increase the dietary uptake of tryptophan. In order to have an effect, neurotransmitters must bind to receptor sites in the receiving cells, and studies have shown that some people have fewer binding sites than normal, which influences the overall effect of even adequate levels of serotonin (Coccaro & Astill, 1990; Coccaro & Kavoussi, 1996).

In most cases, a biological predisposition may only impact behaviour under certain environmental conditions. The serotonin transporter gene (5-HTT) involved in the recycling of serotonin has been shown to be important in handling stress. Humans have two alleles or versions of the 5-HTT gene, a long version that helps a person handle stress and a short version that makes a person much more susceptible to stress. In a long-term study of individuals who had suffered multiple life stresses, those with the short version were much more likely to develop depression (43 percent) than those with the long version (17 percent). Of those who did develop depression, 11 percent of those with the short version attempted suicide in comparison with only 4 percent of those with the long version (Caspi et al., 2003). This finding highlights the interaction between biology and the environment. Many behaviours have a biological basis but may only show an effect under certain environments.

Dopamine

Many studies have also shown that neurotransmitters such as dopamine and norepinephrine can have adverse effects on behaviour (including increased aggression) when they are at higher-than-normal levels (Coccaro & Kavoussi, 1996; Young et al., 2002). Dopamine in particular is a "happy" neurotransmitter that creates pleasurable sensations when we eat, experience feelings of love, and have sex. It is often released by illicit drugs to produce sensations of euphoria. Some people do not get enough stimulation from natural pleasurable activities, and consequently are more likely to become addicted to drugs that increase the high. Drugs that alter the function of the dopamine transporter gene can reduce aggression in violent people. Recently, preliminary research has shown that differences in sibling criminality may relate to differences in dopamine-related alleles, with some variants being more commonly linked with anti-social behaviour and criminal outcomes (Schwartz & Beaver, 2014).

MAOA: The "Warrior Gene"

Two enzymes, monoamine oxidase A and B (MAOA and MAOB, respectively), break down several neurotransmitters. Therefore, they too impact the levels of neurotransmitters in the body. The genes that control both MAOA and MAOB are found on the X chromosome, so they are sex linked. Therefore, any variants are expressed mostly in men. Brunner, Nelen, Breakefield, Ropers, and van Oost (1993) studied a large Dutch family in which several males but no females exhibited a specific behavioural condition. The affected males, who could be identified in childhood, were slightly mentally challenged, verbally and physically aggressive, fire setters, and were responsible for committing many violent crimes. An examination of this family showed that affected males carried a variant of the normal MAOA gene, which influenced their ability to metabolize neurotransmitters (Brunner et al., 1993).

An exciting recent discovery related to MAOA helps to partially explain a major conundrum in criminology. Often, violent and dangerous men have suffered an extremely abusive childhood, and the later criminality is usually blamed on the earlier abuse. However, many boys who suffer similar abuse do not become criminals. So, the conundrum is this: Why do some abused boys become violent men and others do not? One explanation was offered in a series of studies by Caspi et al. (2002) in New Zealand. They assessed a large number of male adults who had been abused as boys to determine whether they had a normal allele of the MAOA gene or a lower-functioning variant. Eighty-five percent of the severely abused men who carried the lower-functioning allele later exhibited violent behaviour. However, those men who had the normal gene almost never exhibited any form of violence or criminal activity, even if they had suffered severe physical childhood abuse. This finding clearly shows a link between a genetic trait, a lower-functioning MAOA gene, and the environment—which, in this case, included childhood abuse (Caspi et al., 2002).

This discovery also indicates that a normal MAOA genotype (the genetic constitution of an individual) has protective effects, although some studies have shown that the normal MAOA genotype is not protective in cases of extreme childhood abuse (Weder et al., 2009). Further work has shown that the anti-social behaviour in abused children with a lower-functioning variant could be seen in children as young as seven (Kim-Cohen et al., 2006). A later study found that the presence of the lower-functioning variant greatly increased the risk of developing CD in children who were abused, but the presence of the gene had no deleterious effects in children who were not abused (Foley et al., 2004). A recent study has found interactions among serotonin control, MAOA, and childhood abuse (Reif et al., 2007). These studies pave the way to explain the interaction between genes and the environment. The genes create the basic blueprint, but the environment shapes the final outcome. People born with this genetic variant are "designed" to live normal lives, unless they experience abuse, which then changes the normal outcome.

Unfortunately, this discovery can be misused in criminal trials. Testimony regarding a defendant's MAOA (coined the "warrior gene") has been used by both the defence and prosecution in a number of cases, primarily in the United States (Bernet, Vnencak-Jones, Farahany, & Montgomery, 2007; Bozanich, 2013). Although many cases that sought to found their arguments on the defendant's genotype were not successful, some did result in a change of charge (from first-degree murder to second-degree murder or manslaughter) or affected the outcome of the penalty phase of the trial. In most cases, although the defendant was tested for the warrior gene, whether the defendant had also suffered childhood abuse was not addressed, despite the fact that scientific research shows that the allele is *only* harmful under such circumstances.

Changes in Brain Chemistry

Changes in brain chemistry can result from genetic and environmental factors, and usually through an interaction of both factors. We often relate childhood environmental conditions such as poverty and abuse to later criminal behaviour. From an understanding of basic brain chemistry, we can now see how environmental conditions interact with criminal behaviour. Poverty often leads to a poor diet, which may be low in the essential amino acids that act as precursors to building proper neurotransmitter levels. A poor diet may also contain other substances that can block the uptake of vital precursors. A poor diet during pregnancy may impact the fetus, and damage caused during pregnancy and early childhood may be permanent.

fetal alcohol spectrum disorder (FASD)
The range of disorders that can arise in a child if the child's mother drank alcohol while pregnant. It is a leading cause of preventable developmental disability in Canada.

Women who consume alcohol during pregnancy put their babies at risk of developing **fetal alcohol spectrum disorder (FASD)**. Depending on the timing of the alcohol consumption, different organs of the fetus can be damaged, with the brain being the most vulnerable. FASD children have many disabilities including reduced IQ, facial anomalies, reduced cognitive ability, inability to understand the consequences of their behaviour, and an increased response to stress. FASD results in low self-esteem, low levels of education, poor peer relationships, low job expectancy, and a desire to please people. People with FASD are disproportionally represented in the criminal justice system (Fast, Conroy, & Loock, 1999).

Imbalances in brain chemistry also impact cognitive abilities, such as reasoning and memory, so affected individuals may misinterpret a situation and react violently and impulsively when such a reaction is not warranted, or be unable to remember punishment and thus be unable to avoid repeating mistakes. The effects of imbalances in brain chemistry highlight the interaction between a person's genetic background and the environment. They clearly indicate that investing in

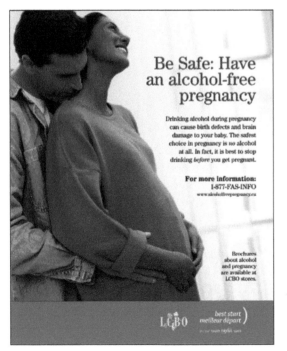

Be Safe: Have an alcohol-free pregnancy

Drinking alcohol during pregnancy can cause birth defects and brain damage to your baby. The safest choice in pregnancy is *no* alcohol at all. In fact, it is best to stop drinking *before* you get pregnant.

For more information:
1-877-FAS-INFO
www.alcoholfreepregnancy.ca

Brochures about alcohol and pregnancy are available at LCBO stores.

best start
meilleur départ

Drinking during pregnancy is a major concern due to the damage alcohol can cause to the developing brain of the fetus—damage that is known to result in potentially serious behavioural problems.
Source: Best Start Resource Centre. Used by permission.

child protection and measures to provide suitable social and health care, education, and mentorship are not just socially valuable but may have previously unconsidered benefits that reduce anti-social behaviour and crime.

Brain Injuries

All behaviours, whatever their basis, are controlled by the brain. Therefore, any damage to the brain is likely to lead to a change in behaviour. This is particularly true of a child's brain because it is still developing. Head injuries are extremely common in society and often occur in children—during play, sports, or due to child abuse—and may also occur during childbirth. We have only recently become aware of the permanent damage that can be caused by repeated mild concussions during sports. The area of the brain damaged and the timing of the injury will affect the behavioural outcome. For instance, our frontal lobe is mostly involved in internal control and is one of the latest parts of the brain to complete development. Therefore, damage to this area in childhood will have a much greater effect on social interaction, impulsivity, and innate control than it will on an adult who has already learned acceptable social behaviours. The frontal lobe is responsible for many aspects of our behaviour, such as self-control, inhibition, judgment, patience, reasoning, problem solving, self-esteem, using and understanding appropriate social skills, and the ability to comprehend the results of our actions. Thus, it is clear how damage in this area will not only impact personality and the ability to interact with others but also lead to anxiety, hostility, impulsivity, edginess, and a lack of regard for consequences, all potentially predisposing to anti-social behaviour.

Much of our behaviour and our personality is controlled in the frontal lobe, which is also an area very easily injured as it is at the front of our head (just behind our forehead), so it is most readily damaged in a fight or accident. The classic case of Phineas Gage provides a chilling description of the potential results of frontal lobe damage. In 1848, young Phineas Gage was a railroad construction crew supervisor when an accident resulted in a metal rod going through his left cheek and up through his brain, exiting the top of his head, completely pulverizing his frontal lobe. Amazingly, he survived and his memory, intelligence, and ability to do his job had not changed, but friends and family simply said he was "no longer Gage." His personality (what made him "Gage") was destroyed. He had previously been a polite and considerate man, but after the accident he lost all his social graces and became violent and irritable. Since then, many examples have been documented of similar injuries that do not destroy memory or abilities (such as the ability to do one's job) but instead destroy social abilities and personality, which is very difficult for family and friends to deal with.

Many studies have linked head injuries to later criminal behaviour. It could be argued that a person who has suffered a head injury may be predisposed

Phineas Gage was an American railroad crew supervisor who suffered a gruesome head injury in 1848. He is pictured here with the steel rod that pierced his skull. He is famous in the annals of neurology and psychology because of the effects that this injury had on his behaviour and personality.

NFL player Jovan Belcher committed a murder–suicide in December 2012. His family launched a lawsuit claiming that his violent behaviour was caused by head trauma suffered playing football (a condition known as *chronic traumatic encephalopathy*, or CTE).

computer tomography
A medical technique combining X-rays taken at many different angles and computer technology.

magnetic resonance imaging
A medical diagnostic technique that uses a powerful magnet, radiofrequency waves, and computer imaging to produce images of tissues.

positron emission tomography
A recording of body images via a radioactive isotope injected into the blood that can be followed in the body during activities. It is commonly used to study the functioning of parts of the brain.

single-photon emission computed tomography
A recording of body images via a radioactive isotope injected into the blood that provides a 3D image of tissues. It is commonly used to measure brain blood flow.

to violence and so was injured in a violent confrontation; in other words, the head injury was a result of a violent lifestyle rather than violence being a result of head injuries. However, this is not the case as most head injuries are caused by accidents or sports rather than violence. In studies of adult and juvenile death-row inmates, all inmates were found to have suffered a severe brain injury *prior* to committing their offences (Lewis et al., 1986, 1988). In Australia, 82 percent of men in prison self-identified as having received a prior head injury (Schofield et al., 2006). A meta-analysis of several studies of males who commit domestic violence showed that 53 percent suffered from traumatic brain injury (Farrer, Frost, & Hedges, 2012). We usually think of brain injury as a physical trauma, but the developing brain can be damaged in other ways, for instance, by disease (e.g., syphilis, meningitis, a tumour), stroke, emotional trauma, or a lack of appropriate nutrition. In a study on rats, separating rat pups early from their mothers resulted in damage to the hippocampus, part of the temporal lobe, suggesting that early childhood trauma may impact the developing brain (Andersen & Teicher, 2004).

In many cases, the injury may be compounded by the environment in which it occurred; for example, an environment of child abuse not only results in physical injury but also is a hostile and damaging environment. Understanding the damage is important in developing treatment programs and routines that can help people gain greater control over their behaviours. Even mild head injuries can create problems, so it is important that offenders are properly assessed (many offenders are unaware that they have received a head injury). Information on a head injury may be important in court, particularly during sentencing and in developing treatment programs.

Although we do not yet fully understand the functioning of the brain, many recent imaging techniques are helping us make great strides in understanding brain function. **Computer tomography** and **magnetic resonance imaging** allow us to see the structure of the brain in a minimally invasive manner, while **positron emission tomography** and **single-photon emission computed tomography** allow us to understand functional changes or deficits. Many studies have been conducted using these techniques and have identified differences in brain function and structure between non-criminals and a variety of offender populations. It is hopeful that once we can identify specific areas of brain deficits, we will have a much greater hope of treating or ameliorating damage.

Body Chemistry

The brain is the seat of all behaviour, so it is obvious that brain chemistry can affect behaviour. But many other chemicals, or hormones, in our body also impact our behaviour. The very word *hormone* is itself derived from a Greek word that means "to excite" or to put in motion. Hormones are released directly into the blood system or stored in glands and released in a controlled manner later. Because the blood stream reaches every cell in our body, hormones are circulated everywhere. However, only certain target cells respond to certain hormones. Hormones control many aspects of our life including growth, metabolism, development, and behaviour. Some hormones fluctuate naturally in the body, and others—antagonistic hormones—work to regulate body conditions within acceptable limits. For instance, high blood sugar is dangerous, as are wide swings in blood sugar levels, so when the blood sugar level reaches a certain high, a hormone (insulin) is released from the pancreas to bring the sugar level down. However, when the blood sugar level drops too low, an antagonistic hormone (glucagen) is released to bring the sugar level back up. The two hormones work together to keep our blood sugar level as even as possible, despite the fact that we regularly intake sudden large amounts of sugar when we eat.

Changes in a hormone itself, the cells involved in its production, the antagonistic hormone, or the target cells can all affect how the body responds; and because hormones work in very tiny quantities, even a slight shift can greatly impact behaviour and mood. The first hormone that comes to mind when we consider crime is testosterone. Innumerable studies have looked at testosterone levels in violent and non-violent offenders as well as the effects on the body of increasing and decreasing testosterone. The results have been mixed. Studies assessing testosterone levels in incarcerated populations have shown a link between testosterone levels and violent crime, rule violations, and negative parole board decisions in men (Dabbs, Frady, Carr, & Besch, 1987) and also in women (Dabbs & Hargrove, 1997). Some studies have linked testosterone levels with domestic abuse and also with alcohol use, so it is hard to determine whether the link is to alcohol, a known predisposer for crime, or directly to testosterone (Soler, Vinayak, & Quadagno, 2000). A meta-analysis of 45 separate studies showed a weak positive relationship between testosterone levels and aggression in males and females (Book, Starzyk, & Quinsey, 2001).

Testosterone levels fluctuate constantly and, interestingly, many studies have suggested that competition rather than aggression is what heightens testosterone levels (Archer, 1991). For instance, testosterone levels in male judo competitors pre- and post-fight were correlated with aggression within the fight, although the same researchers also found an earlier positive correlation between testosterone levels and vigorous exercise (Salvador, Suay, Martinez-Sanchis, Simon, & Brain, 1999). Even more intriguing is that an increase in testosterone levels also occurs in people watching a fight or even a sporting event. Testosterone levels were measured in two groups of sports fans before and after a game (Bernhardt, Dabbs, Fielden, & Lutter, 1998). The first group watched a live basketball game between rival university teams, and the second group watched a televised World Cup football match between two national teams. Dramatic differences in testosterone levels were recorded between sports fans in each group, with an increase in the testosterone levels of fans of the winning side and a decrease in the testosterone levels of fans of the losing side. The authors attributed these results to self-esteem and status, which could suggest an adaptive evolutionary response—that is, in our evolutionary past, success in a competition over resources or a mate was extremely important. In a more modern context, these results might explain the violent confrontations that frequently occur after large sporting events.

Although some studies have shown higher levels of testosterone in violent men, no proof exists that this relationship is causal. Moreover, many men with high levels of testosterone are not violent. Another way to look at the situation is to compare the activities of individuals who have had their testosterone levels deliberately increased, for instance, elderly men, those suffering from sexual dysfunction, and athletes illegally using anabolic steroids. A number of studies have shown that although sexual appetite and mental acuity may improve with a higher level of testosterone, no correlation exists between a higher level of testosterone and increased violence. Finally, and more controversially, we can look at individuals in whom testosterone has been removed, by either surgical or chemical castration, thereby removing the source of the testosterone. Studies have shown a dramatic reduction in sexual crimes after castration, but no difference in non-sexual recidivism (Wille & Beier, 1989).

Testosterone does not act in isolation, and high testosterone levels are often correlated with low serotonin levels as well as alcoholism, which individually are linked to anti-social behaviour. Testosterone certainly relates to sex drive and has been shown to have an indirect link to violence, but no direct causal relationship has been proven. It is probable that many factors interact to provide an indirect link with violence. Other gonadotrophic hormones have recently been shown to correlate more closely with self-reports of hostility than testosterone in a large population of convicted sex offenders up to 20 years post-release (Kingston et al., 2012). Although still not well understood, scientists now recognize that testosterone can regulate both anti-social and pro-social behaviours and acts in different ways (depending on the social situation) when a person faces a low or high threat (Van Honk, Terburg, & Bos, 2011).

Although most hormone studies seem to focus on testosterone, many other hormones can affect behaviour, such as those that relate to menstruation. Some work has suggested links between criminal acts and menstruation, but others have suggested the link relates instead to stress at arrest that could trigger menstruation. Stress in premenstrual women was found to result in much more aggression in those who had reduced serotonin levels, again showing the interaction between several factors. Women with higher serotonin levels were able to cope with stress much better (Bond, Wingrove, & Critchlow, 2001). As well, many other body changes occur during and just prior to menstruation, such as changes in blood sugar and neurotransmitter levels.

Cortisol, another well-studied hormone, is released during stress and is also involved in autonomic arousal. Those with low cortisol levels may respond much more negatively to stress and will not respond to the concept of punishment or cause and effect. Cortisol levels can be impacted by numerous things such as neurotransmitters, other hormones, and brain injury. Low cortisol levels have been linked in numerous studies with anti-social behaviour in children, habitually violent offenders, and girls with CD, although some studies have suggested that the link relates to clinical anxiety, alcohol, or testosterone (Raine, 1993), with cortisol moderating the relationship between testosterone and violence (Dabbs, Jurkovic, & Frady, 1991; Popma et al., 2007). A study of salivary levels of testosterone and cortisol in children hospitalized in a child psychiatric ward indicated a link between cortisol levels and number of aggressive incidents, with testosterone levels linked to the severity of the incident (Barzman et al., 2013). Finally, thyroid hormones and adrenalin also have an impact on our behaviour, and abnormal levels have been linked to anti-social behaviour as well as various clinical disorders, although, again, no direct causal link has been shown.

Hormones clearly impact our behaviour; that is one of their normal functions. But do they cause violent or anti-social behaviour? So far, no direct causal relationship has been found between hormones and violent or anti-social behaviour, but it is clear that hormones interrelate with many other factors (such as neurotransmitter levels) that are fundamentally under genetic control. Interestingly, one area in which a biological predisposition for homicide has been consistently accepted in our court system is hormonal imbalance. Infanticide, the killing of a baby under the age of one year by the biological mother, is considered by our legal system to be entirely different from the murder of the child by someone else or by the mother after the age of one, due to the acceptance that postnatal depression, caused by hormones, can affect the mother's behaviour beyond her control.

Conclusion

This chapter has sought to clarify that although biology does *not* cause a person to be criminal, it can impact behaviours that can *predispose* a person to commit a criminal act. Biology does not act in a vacuum and is greatly influenced by our experiences and environment. Our personality, behaviour, and the experiences that shape us impact the way we handle situations. Research into biological predispositions has also shown us the protective and advantageous role a stable environment can have on those who are predisposed to anti-social behaviour. For instance, researchers studying youth in Holland have shown that childhood delinquency is impacted by the interaction of gender attitudes, child abuse, parental connectedness, and socio-economic status, with children who suffer from less parental monitoring and greater parental rejection significantly more likely to engage in delinquent behaviour (Lahlah, Lens, Bogaerts, & van der Knaap, 2013). Cognitive and developmental behaviour programs are being developed (including developmental intervention and prevention strategies), beginning at the prenatal stage or age two and continuing through the school years (Rocque, Welsh, & Raine, 2012). Many behavioural changes occur due to very small shifts in biochemical balance and, when understood, might be corrected easily. Also, understanding what protective factors are most advantageous in certain situations may help guide resource allocation.

SUMMARY OF KEY POINTS

- It is important to recognize that behaviour, whether criminal or otherwise, is not caused by one single entity but by a combination of many factors that *include* biology as part of the equation.

- Studies of human genetics require a large number of identical animals, which is why twin studies have been important in this area. Two types of twins exist: dizygotic (DZ) twins (non-identical) and monozygotic (MZ) twins (identical). Concordance rates vary in studies and by type of crime, but overall, a much greater concordance rate for criminal behaviour is seen in MZ twins than in DZ twins, which indicates a strong genetic basis for criminal behaviour.

- In adoption studies, researchers compare the criminal behaviour of people who were adopted by non-family members with that of their adoptive and biological parents. This approach seeks to separate genetic and environmental influences and does not rely on an assumed identical environment for two people (twins).

- Criminal behaviour may be controlled by various factors, such as impulsivity, an inability to understand consequences, the need for immediate gratification, lack of empathy, anxiety, depression, or reduced cognitive ability. Researchers have suggested that genetic predisposition for violent behaviour could be related to brain chemistry and the functionality of various neurotransmitters, such as serotonin, dopamine, and norepinephrine.

- Damage to the brain is likely to lead to a change in behaviour. Damage to the frontal lobe will not only impact personality and the ability to interact with others but also lead to anxiety, hostility, impulsivity, edginess, and a lack of re-gard for consequences, all potentially predisposing to anti-social behaviour.

- Hormones such as testosterone and cortisol can affect behaviour. Although no direct causal relationship has been found between hormones and violent or anti-social behaviour, it is clear that hormones interrelate with many other factors (such as neurotransmitter levels) that are fundamentally under genetic control.

QUESTIONS FOR CRITICAL DISCUSSION

1. Most genetic studies show a clear genetic predisposition for certain types of crime in adults but not in adolescents. Why would adolescent crime be different?
2. Genetic studies show a predisposition for petty crime. What evolutionary value might there be for this trait?
3. Many studies are done on incarcerated volunteers. Consider the ethical and experimental issues involved with investigating such a population.
4. Why is infanticide treated differently by our criminal courts than other biologi-cally predisposed crimes, such as those predisposed by FASD?
5. Consider protective factors involved in preventing someone who is genetically predisposed to commit a crime. How might we exploit these?
6. In the past, consideration of biological bases for criminal behaviour have re-sulted in two main schools of thought that can be encapsulated as "he could not stop himself, so he should not be held responsible" and "she can never be treated, so we should lock her up and throw away the key." Envision trying to explain to people in these two camps a more rational approach based on this chapter.

SUGGESTED FURTHER READINGS

Anderson, G.S. (2007). *Biological influences on criminal behavior*. Boca Raton, FL: CRC Press.
Boyd, N. (2000). *The beast within: Why men are violent*. Vancouver: Greystone Books.
Glenn, A.L., & Raine, A. (2014). *Psychopathy: An introduction to biological findings and their implications*. New York: New York University Press.
Raine, A. (2013). *The anatomy of violence: The biological roots of crime*. New York: Pantheon Books.

Websites

Crime Times: http://www.crimetimes.org

REFERENCES

Andersen, S.L., & Teicher, M.H. (2004). Delayed effects of early childhood stress on hippocampal development. *Neuropsychopharmacology, 29*(11), 1988–1993.
Anderson, G.S. (2007). *Biological influences on criminal behavior*. Boca Raton, FL: CRC Press.
Archer, J. (1991). The influence of testosterone on human aggression. *British Journal of Psychology, 82*, 1–28.
Arseneault, L., Moffitt, T.E., Caspi, A., Taylor, A., Rijsdijk, F.V., Jaffee, S. R., ... Measelle, J.R. (2003). Strong genetic effects on cross-situational antisocial behaviour among 5-year-old

children according to mothers, teachers, examiner-observers, and twins' self-reports. *Journal of Child Psychology and Psychiatry, and Allied Disciplines, 44*(6), 832–848.

Barzman, D.H., Mossman, D., Appel, K., Blom, T.J., Strawn, J.R., Ekhator, N.N., … Geracioti, T.D. Jr. (2013). The association between salivary hormone levels and children's inpatient aggression: A pilot study. *Psychiatry Quarterly, 84*(4), 475–484. doi:10.1007/s11126-013-9260-8

Beaver, K.M. (2011). Genetic influences on being processed through the criminal justice system: Results from a sample of adoptees. *Biological Psychiatry, 69*(3), 282–287. doi:10.1016/j.biopsych.2010.09.007

Begleiter, H., Reich, T., Hesselbrock, V., Porjesz, B., Li, T.-K., Schuckit, M.A., … Rice, A.P. (1995). The collaborative study on the genetics of alcoholism. *Alcohol, Health and Research, 19*(3), 228–236.

Bernet, W., Vnencak-Jones, C.L., Farahany, N., & Montgomery, S.A. (2007). Bad nature, bad nurture, and testimony regarding MAOA and SLC6A4 genotyping at murder trials. *Journal of Forensic Sciences, 52*, 1362–1371. doi:10.1111/j.1556-4029.2007.00562.x

Bernhardt, P.C., Dabbs, J.M., Fielden, J.A., & Lutter, C.D. (1998). Testosterone changes during vicarious experiences of winning and losing among fans at sporting events. *Physiology & Behavior, 65*(1), 59–62.

Bohman, M. (1996). Predisposition to criminality: Swedish adoption studies in retrospect. *Ciba Foundation Symposium, 194*, 99–109.

Bond, A.J., Wingrove, J., & Critchlow, D.G. (2001). Tryptophan depletion increases aggression in women during the premenstrual phase. *Psychopharmacology, 156*(4), 477–480.

Book, A.S., Starzyk, K.B., & Quinsey, V.L. (2001). The relationship between testosterone and aggression—A meta-analysis. *Aggression and Violent Behavior, 6*, 579–599.

Bozanich, E. (2013). *The potential impact of the "warrior" gene on the Canadian criminal justice system* (Simon Fraser University, Burnaby, BC).

Brunner, H.G., Nelen, M., Breakefield, X.O., Ropers, H.H., & van Oost, B.A. (1993). Abnormal behavior associated with a point mutation in the structural gene for monoamine oxidase A. *Science, 262*(5133), 578–580.

Caspi, A., McClay, J., Moffitt, T.E., Mill, J., Martin, J., Craig, I.W., … Poulton, R. (2002). Role of genotype in the cycle of violence in maltreated children. *Science, 297*(5582), 851–854. doi:10.1126/science.1072290

Caspi, A., Sugden, K., Moffitt, T.E., Taylor, A., Craig, I.W., Harrington, H., … Poulton, R. (2003). Influence of life stress on depression: Moderation by a polymorphism in the 5-HTT gene. *Science, 301*(5631), 386–389.

Coccaro, E.F., & Astill, J.L. (1990). Central serotonergic system function in parasuicide. *Progressive Neuro-Psychopharmacology & Biological Psychiatry, 14*, 663–674.

Coccaro, E.F., & Kavoussi, R.J. (1996). Neurotransmitter correlates of impulse aggression. In D. Stoff & R.B. Cairns (Eds.), *Aggression and violence: Genetic, neurobiological and biosocial perspectives* (pp. 66–85). Mahwah, NJ: Erlbaum.

Cook, E.H., Stein, M.A., Krasowski, M.D., Cox, N.J., Olkon, D.M., Kieffer, J.E., & Leventhal, B.L. (1995). Association of attention-deficit disorder and the dopamine transporter gene. *The American Journal of Human Genetics, 56*(4), 993–998.

Coolidge, F.L., Thede, L.L., & Jang, K.L. (2001). Heritability of personality disorders in childhood. *Journal of Personality Disorders, 15*, 33–40.

Dabbs, J.M., Frady, R.L., Carr, T.S., & Besch, N.F. (1987). Saliva testosterone and criminal violence in young adult prison inmates. *Psychosomatic Medicine, 49*, 174–182.

Dabbs, J.M., & Hargrove, M.F. (1997). Age, testosterone and behavior among female prison inmates. *Psychosomatic Medicine, 59*(5), 477–480.

Dabbs, J.M., Jurkovic, G.J., & Frady, R.L. (1991). Saliva testosterone and cortisol among late adolescent male offenders. *Journal of Abnormal Child Psychology, 19*, 469–478.

Eley, T.C., Lichtenstein, P., & Stevenson, J. (1999). Sex differences in the etiology of aggressive and non-aggressive antisocial behavior: Results from two twin studies. *Child Development, 70*(1), 155–168.

Farrer, T.J., Frost, R.B., & Hedges, D.W. (2012). Prevalence of traumatic brain injury in intimate partner violence offenders compared to the general population: A meta-analysis. *Trauma Violence Abuse, 13*(2), 77–82. doi:10.1177/1524838012440338

Fast, D.K., Conroy, J., & Loock, C.A. (1999). Identifying fetal alcohol syndrome among youth in the criminal justice system. *Journal of Developmental and Behavioral Pediatrics, 20*(5), 370–372.

Foley, D.L., Eaves, L.J., Wormley, B., Silberg, J.L., Maes, H.H., Kuhn, J., & Riley, B. (2004). Childhood adversity, monoamine oxidase A genotype and risk for conduct disorder. *Archives of Genetic Psychiatry, 61*, 738–744.

Fuchs, A. (2013, June 4). This cold-blooded murderer could help prove there's a "killer gene." *Business Insider*. Retrieved from http://www.businessinsider.com/adrian-raines -take-on-jeffrey-landrigan-2013-6.

Gardner, D. (1999, May 30). Killer son finds lost father … on death row; "I really am a natural born killer." *Sunday Mirror.*

Kim-Cohen, J., Caspi, A., Taylor, A., Williams, B., Newcombe, R., Craig, I. W., & Moffitt, T.E. (2006). MAOA, maltreatment, and gene–environment interaction predicting children's mental health: New evidence and a meta-analysis. *Molecular Psychiatry, 11*(10), 903–913. doi:10.1038/sj.mp.4001851

Kingston, D.A., Seto, M.C., Ahmed, A.G., Fedoroff, P., Firestone, P., & Bradford, J.M. (2012). The role of central and peripheral hormones in sexual and violent recidivism in sex offenders. *Journal of the American Academy of Psychiatry and the Law, 40*, 476–485.

Kirkpatrick, R.M., Legrand, L.N., Iacono, W.G., & McGue, M. (2011). A twin and adoption study of reading achievement: Exploration of shared-environmental and gene-environment-interaction effects. *Learning and Individual Differences, 21*(4), 368–375. doi:10.1016/j.lindif.2011.04.008

Lahlah, E., Lens, K.M., Bogaerts, S., & van der Knaap, L.M. (2013). When love hurts: Assessing the intersectionality of ethnicity, socio-economic status, parental connectedness, child abuse, and gender attitudes in juvenile violent delinquency. *Child Abuse & Neglect, 37*(11), 1034–1049. doi:10.1016/j.chiabu.2013.07.001

Lewis, D.O., Pincus, J.H., Bard, B., Richardson, E., Prichep, L.S., Feldman, M., & Yeager, C. (1986). Psychiatric, neurological and psycho-educational of 15 death row inmates in the United States. *American Journal of Psychiatry, 143*(5), 838–845.

Lewis, D.O., Pincus, J.H., Bard, B., Richardson, E., Prichep, L.S., Feldman, M., & Yeager, C. (1988). Neuropsychiatric, psychoeducational, and family characteristics of 14 juveniles condemned to death in the United States. *American Journal of Psychiatry, 145*(5), 584–589.

Loo, S.K., Fisher, S.E., Francks, C., Ogdie, M.N., MacPhie, I.L., Yang, M., & Monaco, A.P. (2004). Genome-wide scan of reading ability in affected sibling pairs with attention-deficit/hyperactivity disorder: Unique and shared genetic effects. *Molecular Psychiatry, 9*(5), 485–493.

Lyons, M.J. (1996). A twin study of self reported criminal behavior. *Ciba Foundation Symposium, 194*, 61–70.

Maestripieri, D. (2003). Similarities in affiliation and aggression between cross-fostered rhesus macaque females and their biological mothers. *Developmental Psychobiology, 43*(4), 321–327.

Mednick, S.A., Gabrielli, W.F.J., & Hutchings, B. (1984). Genetic influences in criminal convictions: Evidence from an adoption cohort. *Science, 224*(4651), 891–894.

Mednick, S.A., Gabrielli, W.F.J., & Hutchings, B. (1987). Genetic factors in the etiology of criminal behavior. In S.A. Mednick, T.E. Moffitt, & S.A. Stack (Eds.), *The causes of crime: New biological approaches* (pp. 74–91). Cambridge, UK: Cambridge University Press.

Newsome, J., Boisvert, D., & Wright, J.P. (2014). Genetic and environmental influences on the co-occurrence of early academic achievement and externalizing behavior. *Journal of Criminal Justice, 42*(1), 45–53. doi:10.1016/j.jcrimjus.2013.12.002

Niehoff, D. (1999). Seeds of controversy. In D. Niehoff (Ed.), *The biology of violence: How understanding the brain, behavior and environment can break the vicious circle of aggression* (pp. 1–30). New York: Free Press.

Popma, A., Vermeiren, R., Geluk, C.A., Rinne, T., van den Brink, W., Knol, D.L., & Doreleijers, T.A. (2007). Cortisol moderates the relationship between testosterone and aggression in delinquent male adolescents. *Biological Psychiatry, 61*(3), 405–411. doi:10.1016/j.biopsych.2006.06.006

Raine, A. (1993). *The psychopathology of crime: Criminal behavior as a clinical disorder*. San Diego, CA: Academic Press, Elsevier Science.

Reif, A., Rosler, M., Freitag, C.M., Schneider, M., Eujen, A., Kissling, C., & Retz, W. (2007). Nature and nurture predispose to violent behavior: Serotonergic genes and adverse childhood environment. *Neuropsychopharmacology, 32*(11), 2375–2383. doi:10.1038/sj.npp.1301359

Rocque, M., Welsh, B.C., & Raine, A. (2012). Biosocial criminology and modern crime prevention. *Journal of Criminal Justice, 40*(4), 306–312. doi:10.1016/j.jcrimjus.2012.05.003

Salvador, A., Suay, F., Martinez-Sanchis, S., Simon, V.M., & Brain, P.F. (1999). Correlating testosterone and fighting in male participants in judo contests. *Physiology & Behavior, 68*(1–2), 205–209.

Schofield, P.W., Butler, T.G., Hollis, S.J., Smith, N.E., Lee, S.J., & Kelso, W.M. (2006). Traumatic brain injury among Australian prisoners: Rates, recurrence and sequelae. *Brain Injury, 20*(5), 499–506. doi:10.1080/02699050600664749

Schwartz, J.A., & Beaver, K.M. (2014). Exploring whether genetic differences between siblings explain sibling differences in criminal justice outcomes. *Comprehensive Psychiatry, 55*(1), 93–103. doi:10.1016/j.comppsych.2013.06.002

Soler, H., Vinayak, P., & Quadagno, D. (2000). Biosocial aspects of domestic violence. *Psychoneuroendocrinology, 25*(7), 721–739.

Van Honk, J., Terburg, D., & Bos, P.A. (2011). Further notes on testosterone as a social hormone. *Trends in Cognitive Sciences, 15*(7), 291–292. doi:10.1016/j.tics.2011.05.003

Weder, N., Yang, B.Z., Douglas-Palumberi, H., Massey, J., Krystal, J.H., Gelernter, J., & Kaufman, J. (2009). MAOA genotype, maltreatment, and aggressive behavior: The changing impact of genotype at varying levels of trauma. *Biological Psychiatry, 65*(5), 417–424. doi:10.1016/j.biopsych.2008.09.013

Wille, R., & Beier, K.M. (1989). Castration in Germany. *Annals of Sex Research, 2*, 103–134.

Young, S.E., Smolan, A., Corley, R.P., Krauter, K.S., DeFries, J.C., Crowley, T.J., & Hewitt, J.K. (2002). Dopamine transporter polymorphism associated with externalizing behavior problems in children. *American Journal of Medical Genetics, 114*(2), 144–149.

The Mask of Sanity:
Colonel Russell Williams

Colonel Russell Williams under police interrogation in Ottawa, February 7, 2010.

Colonel Russell Williams was charged in February 2010 with two counts of first-degree murder, sexual assault, forcible confinement, and breaking and entering. At the time, he was the 46-year-old commander of Canadian Forces Base Trenton, apparently happily married, and enjoying a remarkably successful military career.

However, at some point during his forties, Williams had begun breaking into homes, entering women's bedrooms, dressing in the lingerie he found there, and masturbating. He took photos of himself clad in their underwear, and these became important "trophies," which he carefully catalogued when he returned home. From that point his criminal conduct escalated. He broke into homes where women were sleeping, committing two brutal sexual assaults, and then two sexually motivated murders. After police traced tire treads from his car to tire treads near the home of the victim of his second murder, he was brought in for questioning and, during a ten-hour interview, confessed to dozens of crimes. He was convicted of two counts of first-degree murder and is currently serving a life term in a Canadian prison.

Is Russell Williams a psychopath? Dr. Brad Booth, a forensic psychiatrist based in Ottawa, has indicated that Williams might be properly classified as such, noting that psychopathy is "marked by charming behaviour and a complete disregard for the feelings of [the] victims." Anne McIlroy and Erin Anderssen, writing in the *Globe and Mail*, seem to agree:

> Though never officially diagnosed as a psychopath, Mr. Williams appears to fit the profile. The way he toyed with his victims like playthings, unable to offer mercy: "Have a heart," one pleaded, as he unflinchingly duct-taped her nose to suffocate her. The singular attention with which he catalogued photos and video of his crimes. The fleeting shows of remorse. (He feels "disappointed," he tells police in his confession, about what he's done.) All the while, he wore the mask of sanity, in place for so long and so well, that he tortured and killed, and then went to work to discuss whether the military should buy a new aircraft transport. That's also the measure of a cunning psychopath: He's often the last guy you'd ever suspect. (McIlroy & Anderssen, 2010)

And yet Timothy Appleby, in his account of the case in his book *A New Kind of Monster*, argues that Williams is not best understood as a psychopath. Appleby notes that Williams could demonstrate genuine concern and compassion for friends and colleagues and was also capable of feeling shame. Appleby suggests that Williams is best understood as a sexual deviant: he had a sexual preoccupation with non-human objects, he was focused on sexually oriented suffering and humiliation, for both himself and others; he had a sexual interest in children; and he also participated in violent sex with an unwilling partner.

How are we to make sense of the murderous conduct of Russell Williams? What explanations might we find in the realm of psychological theories of crime for this sort of behaviour? We can say, as Appleby has, that Williams has a mental disorder—an amalgamation of sexual deviance with obsessive-compulsive disorder. We can suggest, alternatively, that he is a heartless psychopath, unable to feel compassion for others, except in circumstances where such a display might work in his self-interest, to present his actions in a more positive light.

It is possible that Russell Williams is all of the above and more, a reminder that the science of mental disorder and the science of psychopathy cannot always describe and dissect individuals and events with an unerring precision.

Before You Read Chapter 8

- Does it seem improbable that someone like Williams could rise to such a position of prominence and responsibility in his career? Why or why not?
- Do you think psychological explanations of crime are sufficient for explaining this sort of behaviour?
- After reading Box 8.1 in this chapter, return to this case study and reread it. How might the definition of *psychopathy* apply to Williams, if at all?

Psychological Approaches

<table>
<tr><td>

</td><td>

</td></tr>
</table>

Introduction

Psychological theories examine a number of factors thought to contribute to criminality and criminal behaviour. The discipline of psychology is composed of several different (and often competing) perspectives including *psychoanalysis*, *behaviourism*, *social cognitivism* (or *social learning*), and *developmental psychology*. These different approaches have produced numerous psychological theories that seek to explain criminal behaviour or certain aspects of criminal behaviour. It would be a mistake to lump all of the psychological explanations of criminal behaviour together and consider them as a single theory because various psychological theories of criminal behaviour exist (Bartol & Bartol, 2011; Einstadter & Henry, 2006).

Studies linking intelligence (or **IQ**) to criminality have been a staple of psychological research on crime dating back to the early 1900s. In fact, links between low intelligence and criminality can be found all the way back to the work of Cesare Lombroso (1835–1909), an individual many consider to be "the father of modern criminology." Other more recent theories and research have also considered the importance of IQ and its relationship to criminality (Eysenck, 1964; Hirschi & Hindelang, 1977; Wilson & Herrnstein, 1985). Contemporary theories also examine various aspects of brain function, which often involves aspects of intelligence (see, e.g., Farrington, 1992; Moffitt, 1993).

Several branches of psychological theory are relevant to criminology. These include a range of explanations that examine individual differences that may result in criminality (e.g., certain personality traits like aggression, impulsivity, and low empathy) as well as theories that focus on socialization, conditioning processes, learning experiences, and psychological development. These theories have also had a considerable impact on various

IQ (intelligence quotient)
A standardized measure of intelligence used by psychologists.

practices used in modern criminal justice systems. This impact is easy to see in the area of correctional treatment and risk prediction (Andrews & Bonta, 2010; Hare, 1996).

The Intelligence–Criminality Connection

Early *positivist criminologists* (i.e., those concerned with finding objective statistical and scientific ways to understand crime) noted that there were connections between **feeble-mindedness** (or low intelligence) and criminality. A well-known example of this early line of research is Henry Goddard's (1913) longitudinal study of the Kallikaks. The Kallikaks were two families fathered by the same man. One of the wives was a Quaker woman, and the other was, in Goddard's words, a "tavern wench." Goddard found that the side of the family mothered by the Quaker woman exhibited very little criminality, while the other side exhibited a great deal of criminality. Interestingly, he did not jump to the conclusion that criminality was a result of heredity. Instead, he thought that feeble-mindedness was inherited, and suggested that less intelligent people were at greater risk for criminality.

> **feeble-mindedness**
> A term used in the 19th century to describe individuals with low intelligence or low IQ.

Approximately two decades after this research, Edwin Sutherland (1931), founder of *differential association theory* (discussed in Chapter 12, Sociological Approaches) argued that the research linking intelligence to criminality was flawed. He claimed that the tests were biased and unreliable, and that similar rates of intelligence were likely found in criminal and non-criminal populations. Because of his influence on the field of criminology, research in this area fell into disfavour for several decades, and was generally dismissed by criminologists.

Almost 50 years after Sutherland's dismissal of the connection between IQ and criminality, Travis Hirschi and Michael Hindelang (1977) resurrected interest in this area with their article "Intelligence and Delinquency: A Revisionist Review." They argued that intelligence does not have a *direct* impact on criminal behaviour; rather, it affects criminality indirectly, through poor school performance. In other words, doing poorly in school can lead to other problems, including problematic behaviour, punishment, and possibly negative labelling and weakened social bonds. In addition, opportunities for future employment are cut off, which reduces one's pro-social options later in life. According to Hirschi and Hindelang, trouble in school seems predictive of problems later in life. Figure 8.1 describes Hirschi and Hindelang's positivist view of the link between IQ and crime.

William Herrnstein and Charles Murray's (1994) theory on race, IQ, and criminality is perhaps the most controversial work in this area. Herrnstein and Murray start out by citing research that suggests a link between criminality and IQ. Next, they refer to the fact that certain racial minorities (i.e., black people) tend to test much lower on IQ tests than white and Asian people. They then state that black populations are typically overrepresented in official crime statistics. Based on this information, they argue for a racial connection to criminality by way of low IQ.

Herrnstein and Murray's (1994) line of argument raised a variety of issues. To summarize the objections: the authors disregarded numerous studies linking social class to both IQ scores and criminal opportunities. Perhaps the most damning criticism of this theory is the fact that IQs have steadily risen over time, a phenomenon known as the "Flynn effect." In the 1980s, James Flynn was able to demonstrate that IQ rates had been rising for at least 60 years, and these increases could not be attributed to changes in genetics as Herrnstein and Murray (1994) would have us believe (Bernard, Snipes, &

FIGURE 8.1   The Positivist View on IQ and Crime

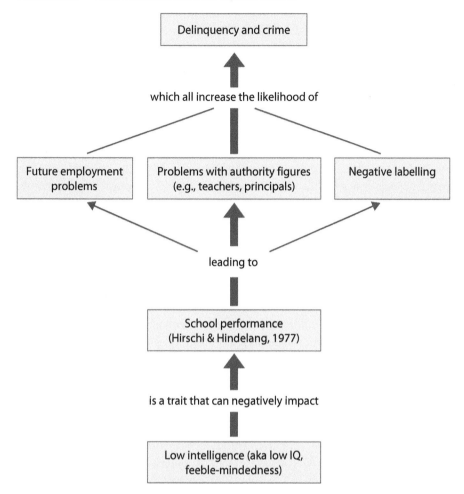

Gerould, 2010). More recent research seems to indicate that IQ is an important *correlate* of crime; however, the *causal connection* is not readily apparent. In most cases, theories that rely upon race to explain crime and/or IQ are misguided because they often fail to consider factors such as socio-economic status, criminal opportunities, and the inter- actions between biological factors and social context. For example, people living in poverty-stricken areas often face challenges accessing proper nutrition and prenatal care, and may even risk exposure to environmental toxins because of poor living condi- tions. All of this can affect early brain development, which later affects IQ (Robinson & Beaver, 2008).

Psychoanalysis and Crime: From Personality to Thought Patterns

Sigmund Freud (1856–1939) was an Austrian psychiatrist and founder of the **psycho- analytic** (or *psychodynamic*) approach. While Freud's writings are quite extensive, he had very little to say about crime and deviance specifically. However, some of his students did study crime. To understand Freudian explanations of criminality, it is necessary to be familiar with some basic psychoanalytic concepts.

psychoanalysis

A therapeutic technique in psychiatry and philosophy pioneered by Sigmund Freud.

id

An aspect of Freud's theory of personality; the impulsive part of one's personality.

pleasure principle

The notion that one should maximize pleasure and minimize pain.

superego

An aspect of Freud's theory of personality; one's moral compass, conscience, and ethical principles.

ego

An aspect of Freud's theory of personality; the aspect of personality that helps negotiate the demands of the real world.

reality principle

The notion that one should assess the demands of the real world and act accordingly.

neurotic

According to psychoanalytic theory, a condition that results from an overactive superego.

Freud (1920, 1923) claimed that personality has three components: the *id*, the *ego*, and the *superego*. The **id** is the instinctual and impulsive aspect of one's personality that embodies all of our desires, wishes, and drives (Redl & Toch, 1979). Many of these drives stem from our biological urges for aggression and sex; it should not be difficult to see how these urges relate to criminal behaviour (Andrews & Bonta, 2010). Not surprisingly, the id functions according to what Freud (1923) called the **pleasure principle**, and demands instant gratification of these urges. The **superego** develops as we mature and is similar to the idea of a moral compass or conscience; it embodies all of our values and socialization experiences. The **ego** serves as the regulator between the demands of the id and the superego. This aspect of the personality functions according to the **reality principle**, meaning that it attempts to delay gratification until it can be achieved in socially acceptable ways. The ego may also serve to stop or prohibit behaviour that is socially and/or morally unacceptable. Consequently, the ego plays a role in deterrence because it helps distinguish right from wrong (Redl & Toch, 1979).

An example might be useful to illustrate how these components of one's personality control behaviour: When confronted with studying for an exam, your id is the part of you that does not want to study. You may be tempted to watch television, play a computer game, check up on Facebook, or go out drinking with friends at the pub instead. The superego is the part of you that is pressuring you to study because you want to do well on the exam. After all, doing well on the exam will help you get a better mark and will make your parents proud of you. At this point, the ego will step in and attempt to balance out the situation. Your ego might insist that you study for three hours and then have a nice meal and relax for the rest of the evening.

In most cases, Freudian criminologists attribute criminality to problems in childhood resulting from poor parenting practices. Given their emphasis on family and early childhood development, it should come as no surprise that most Freudian criminologists (including Freud's own daughter, Anna) studied juvenile delinquency (see also Aichhorn, 1925; Alexander & Healy, 1935; Redl & Wineman, 1951).

Psychoanalytic theorists have identified a number of different paths to criminality (see Figure 8.2). First, people with an overactive superego are said to experience increased levels of guilt. These **neurotic** offenders, as they are sometimes called, commit crime to be punished in order to lessen negative feelings arising from this guilt (Freud, 1920, 1923).

FIGURE 8.2   Psychoanalytic Theories of Crime

Second, some people are thought to have a weak ego that fails to control behaviour. In these cases, the id is unregulated, and the individual has an impulsive personality and behaves hedonistically.

Third, Freudians believe that criminal behaviour could stem from deviant self-identification (Blackburn, 1990). In this case, the superego develops normally, but the person identifies with and forms a close bond to someone who is a criminal (in most cases, a parent). People who have undergone the process of deviant self-identification are sometimes referred to as *sociopaths* or *anti-social offenders* (Andrews & Bonta, 2010; Serin, Forth, Brown, Nunes, Bennell, & Pozzulo, 2011).

Fourth, the psychopathic personality results when the superego fails to develop properly. Psychopaths lack a conscience and have an inability to feel empathy for others (Andrews & Bonta, 2010). See Box 8.1 for a discussion of the modern conception of psychopathy.

BOX 8.1

Psychopathy: Misunderstandings and Misconceptions

What name comes to mind when you hear the word *psychopath*? Often, the answer is a historical figure such as Adolf Hitler, Joseph Stalin, Mao Zedong, or Saddam Hussein, or a serial killer such as Charles Manson, David Berkowitz (the "Son of Sam" killer), Ted Bundy, or Clifford Olson. Examples of movie and television characters abound: Norman Bates (*Psycho*), Hannibal Lecter (*Silence of the Lambs*), Mr. Blonde (*Reservoir Dogs*), the title character from *Dexter*, and Walter White from *Breaking Bad* (for more on psychopaths in the media, see Blair, Mitchell, & Blair, 2005; Cleckley, 1964; and Hare, 1993). It has been suggested that in the business world, people such as Bernie Madoff and Steve Jobs are psychopaths. Some have even claimed that political figures such as Margaret Thatcher, Bill Clinton, and George W. Bush resemble psychopaths based on their calculating natures and lack of empathy in certain situations. However, after learning more about the definition of *psychopathy* and the psychopathy checklist, you will realize that very few if any of these examples really fit the profile of a psychopath (Blair, Mitchell, & Blair, 2005; Dutton, 2012). One of the foremost experts on psychopathy, Robert Hare (1993) provides the following advice:

> *Psychopathic* killers ... are not mad, according to accepted legal and psychiatric standards. Their acts result not from a deranged mind but from a cold, calculating rationality combined with a chilling inability to treat others as thinking, feeling, human beings. ... As disturbing as this is, we must be careful to keep some perspective here, for the fact is that the majority of psychopaths manage to ply their trade without murdering people. By focusing too much on the most brutal and newsworthy examples of their behavior we run the risk of remaining blind to the larger picture: psychopaths who don't kill but who have a personal impact on our daily lives. We are far more likely to lose our life savings to an oily-tongued swindler than our lives to a steely-eyed killer. (p. 6)

The notion of a psychopathic personality has been around for at least a century, and it was a common theme in early psychiatric work (Rafter, 2008; Serin et al., 2011). John Johns and Herbert Quay (1962, p. 18) famously remarked that psychopaths hear the words, but not the music. This means that on an intellectual level, psychopaths can understand that people have emotions and can feel pain; however, they fail to fully comprehend empathy and have an inability "to put themselves in another person's shoes." Other key characteristics of psychopaths include glib and superficial charm, egocentricity or egotism, lack of guilt, deceitfulness, impulsiveness, and interest in risk-taking activity (Cleckley, 1964; Hare, 1993).

Psychopaths have been described as intraspecies predators that manipulate, intimidate, and sometimes use violence to control others and fulfill their own selfish goals. It is important to keep in mind that not all psychopaths are criminals; psychopaths are found in politics, the legal profession, and the business world (Babiak & Hare, 2006; Dutton, 2012, Hare, 1996). At the beginning of this section, one important misconception about psychopathy was identified: psychopaths are not all serial killers, or even violent; many work in more subtle ways. A number of other common misunderstandings exist about this phenomenon.

First, psychopathy is a *personality disorder*, not a *mental illness*. Psychopaths are not psychotic, mentally ill, or "sick" in the legal sense of the term (Hare, 1993). In contrast, *psychotics* are mentally ill and often have hallucinations and delusions that spur on their abnormal behaviours; for example, they may suffer from schizophrenia.

Second, the terms *psychopathy*, *anti-social personality disorder*, and *sociopathy* are often used interchangeably (often by criminologists who should know better), despite the fact that they refer to different (and sometimes outdated) classifications (Babiak & Hare, 2006). Psychopathy and sociopathy were once considered to be the same disorder; however, this idea changed when revisions were made to the Diagnostic and Statistical Manual of Mental Disorders (DSM-II) in 1968 (Hare & Cox, 1978). *Sociopathy* was changed to **anti-social personality disorder (APD)**. Later, psychiatrists attempted to distinguish psychopathy from APD (Hare, 1996). It should be noted that the term *sociopathic personality disorder* is no longer in use; however, the term *sociopath* is sometimes used to refer to those with APD. The main difference between individuals with APD and those with psychopathy is that APD is thought to result from one's environment, whereas true psychopaths seem to have physical and mental abnormalities (such as lower resting heart rates, less fear response, and structural brain abnormalities).

The varying prevalence of psychopathy and APD also helps set them apart. According to Hare (1996), psychopaths represent about 1 percent of the general population and may comprise as much as 25 percent of the prison population. Meanwhile, APD is seen in about 6 to 9 percent of the general population and roughly 50 to 75 percent of inmates. These figures imply that psychopaths represent a small subset of people with APD. Thus, almost all psychopaths have APD, but only a small subset of those diagnosed with APD would qualify as psychopaths (Hare, 1996).

The modern conception of the psychopath was heavily influenced by Hervey Cleckley's seminal work, *The Mask of Sanity* (1964). Hare (1970; Hare & Cox, 1978) used this research to develop his psychopathy checklist, a scale that can reportedly measure levels of psychopathy in individuals. This scale has been revised and adjusted numerous times (see, for example, Hare, 2003), and is commonly used in corrections work to estimate risk of reoffending. However, the scale has also been used in other arenas, such as university campuses.

The Psychopathy Checklist: Are You Sitting Beside a Psychopath?

Some notable attempts have been made to apply the Psychopathy Checklist-Revised (PCL-R) to groups of non-criminal and mentally normal individuals. Kevin Williams, Delroy Paulhus, and Robert Hare's (2007) research study on psychopathy in the university environment is one example. These researchers administered a version of the PCL-R to a group of undergraduate students at a large western university. The goal was to gain insights into the applicability of the psychopathy checklist to non-clinical and non-forensic populations. In other words, these researchers were seeking to develop a scale that could detect non-criminal psychopaths in university and possibly workplace settings.

Williams and colleagues (2007) claimed that self-report psychopathy measures are the most practical way of capturing information on non-clinical and non-forensic populations. This conclusion seems unusual because in his book *Without Conscience* (1993), Hare offers the following emphatic cautionary note about using the psychopathy checklist:

> The *Psychopathy Checklist* is a complex clinical tool for professional use. What follows is a general summary of the key traits and behaviours of psychopaths. Do not use these symptoms to diagnose yourself or others. A diagnosis requires explicit training and access to the formal scoring manual. (p. 34)

While self-report measures are not exactly the same as untrained assessments, the stern warning above might well apply to self-reports too. It seems at least important to acknowledge the potential for self-report research to lead to some very misleading data.

The researchers also used several questionable measures as indicators for the various factors in their model of psychopathy, especially if we consider that their sample was composed of college students. For example, the indicators of the erratic lifestyle index (e.g., breaking rules, taking risks, and drinking) all seem to capture behaviour that is quite common among college students. Moreover, the indicators of the offensive activity dimension (e.g.,

anti-social personality disorder (APD)
A personality disorder characterized by a lack of morality, impulsivity, and aggressive behaviour; individuals with APD often have a history of criminal behaviour.

listening to aggressive music, watching violent movies, and playing violent video games) seem to be highly susceptible to cultural influences. Consider the widespread popularity of gangsta rap during the mid-1990s or the current popularity of violent video games among a very large, diverse cross-section of young people.

These points might lead us to ask some important questions about this research: Does more attention need to be paid to defining typical undergraduate behaviours? Is it common for a larger percentage of people to be irresponsible during their college years? Is it reasonable to conclude that we can differentiate between psychopaths and non-psychopaths by investigating the types of music they listen to or the types of movies they watch? Is it reasonable to assume that psychopaths prefer violent and aggressive media more than other people do?

Fifth, Samuel Yochelson and Stanton Samenow's (1976) theory of the criminal personality explains criminal behaviour based, in part, on psychoanalytic thought. These theorists examined the thinking patterns and problematic cognitions apparent in criminals. The sample for their study was a group of serious offenders imprisoned in a hospital for the criminally insane. According to Yochelson and Samenow, the offenders studied were self-centred, impulsive, low in empathy, and easily angered. This description is very similar to the psychopathic personality arising from a weak superego described above. Yochelson and Samenow attempted to catalogue the traits or problematic thinking patterns that were present in criminals. This list included notions such as fear of injury and personal insult; a preference for concrete over abstract thinking; a mixture of responsibility and irresponsibility (i.e., an "inconsistent inconsistency"); a belief that they are special or unique; a susceptibility to suggestibility in group settings; lying; a lack of trust; and a super-optimistic outlook.

Some serious issues need to be raised with this research. First, the study sample that was the basis of the theory is highly questionable. It is unlikely that the patterns observed in the sample would be found in all or even most offenders, since most offenders are not criminal psychopaths. In other words, since this sample was drawn from a forensic psychiatric institution, it should come as no surprise that the sample of offenders exhibited serious psychiatric issues uncommon in other offenders. Second, these theorists seem to be proposing a theory with an internal logical contradiction: they suggest that criminality is inborn, while at the same time claiming criminals make rational choices to commit crimes (Lilly, Cullen, & Ball, 2007). The problem here is that the theorists seem to assume that criminals are *made* and not *created*, while still insisting that criminals have free will and choose to commit crimes.

Psychoanalytic theories remain influential in criminology today. For example, the impact of psychoanalytic approaches is still visible in some forms of *control theory* (e.g., Gottfredson & Hirschi, 1990; Hirschi, 1969). However, other psychological approaches have gained popularity. In the following section, we will turn to a discussion of the origins of *learning theories* in psychology, and explain how they are relevant to criminology.

Psychological Learning Theories and Criminology

Psychological learning theories have contributed a great deal of insight to theories in criminology. Specifically, *classical* and *operant conditioning*, the *frustration–aggression hypothesis*, and *social learning theory* have all informed criminology, and, in some cases, have offered fully developed explanations of why people commit crime (see Figure 8.3).

FIGURE 8.3   Psychological Learning Theories of Criminal Behaviour

Classical Conditioning

Most people are familiar with the story of Pavlov's dogs. Ivan Pavlov was a Russian physiologist who studied digestive reflexes in dogs. During his experiments, he discovered that he could induce salivation in dogs by simply ringing a bell. The dogs salivated because they had come to associate the ringing of the bell with receiving food. This process of learning is referred to as *classical conditioning*. Pavlov's (1927/1960) work was the inspiration for a number of learning theories that later emerged in psychology.

Hans Eysenck's (1964) theory of the criminal personality was greatly influenced by classical conditioning theory. Eysenck argued that three key traits define one's personality. **Extraversion (E)** focuses on a person's activity level. People who are high in extraversion are called *extraverts* and tend to be more outgoing, sociable, and action-oriented. *Introverts* are people on the other end of this continuum, and tend to be more withdrawn, isolated, and introspective. **Neuroticism (N)** refers to a person's level of excitability and emotional stability. People high in neuroticism tend to be emotionally unstable and overreact to minor situations. **Psychoticism (P)** includes attributes such as aggression, lack of empathy, and tough-mindedness. Although psychoticism has been compared to psychopathy, the connection between these two concepts is still unclear (Eysenck & Eysenck, 1978).

According to Eysenck (1964), **cortical arousal** (the level of activity in the reticular formation of the brain) is tied to one's level of extraversion. Extraverts tend to be cortically underaroused, and therefore seek out stimulation in their environment. They also condition (or respond to punishment and fear) less readily than introverts, which makes them prone to impulsive types of behaviour, including crime.

Eysenck's theory posits that people who are high in all three traits are at the greatest risk for committing crime because they condition poorly (high E), are very emotionally volatile (high N), and have little regard for others' feelings (high P). These traits lay the groundwork for a personality well suited to crime. Conversely, those low in all traits will condition most effectively, be much easier to socialize, and, therefore, be unlikely to commit crime.

extraversion (E)
A person's activity level; people high in extraversion enjoy social interaction and being around groups of people, while people low in extraversion generally prefer solitude and quiet conversations with those close to them.

neuroticism (N)
A person's excitability level and emotional stability; highly neurotic people tend to be emotionally unstable and overreact to minor situations.

psychoticism (P)
A measure of attributes such as aggression, empathy, and tough-mindedness; those who score high in psychoticism tend to be cold, callous, and manipulative.

cortical arousal
Activation of the reticular formation of the brain.

Edward Thorndike (1898), a contemporary of Pavlov, had a similar interest in animals and learning. His work also laid the foundation for conditioning theories that would come later. In his experiments, Thorndike placed cats into boxes equipped with levers that could be manipulated to open a hatch and escape. He found that as the cats gained experience working the lever, they were able to escape the box more quickly. His theory, referred to as the "law of effect," suggested that behaviour can be shaped by its consequences.

Operant Conditioning

B.F. Skinner's (1953) operant conditioning theory builds on the work of Thorndike and represents another major advancement in learning theory. Skinner's approach, also known as **behaviourism**, suggests that all behaviour can be shaped by rewards and punishments. He supported his theory with a variety of experiments done on pigeons and rats. In these experiments, he demonstrated that he could make these animals do amazing things (e.g., solve simple puzzles, play Ping-Pong) by motivating them with rewards in the form of food. Like Pavlov's (1927/1960) classical conditioning, Skinner's (1953) operant conditioning has also influenced the field of criminology, giving rise to several theories of criminal behaviour.

behaviourism
A learning theory that suggests all behaviour can be shaped by rewards and punishment.

C. Ray Jeffery (1965) proposed a theory based on Skinner's operant conditioning and Sutherland's differential association theory. The central proposition in Jeffery's theory was as follows: if the reward for crime is high and the likelihood of punishment is low, the chances of criminal behaviour increase. He also said that *non-social reinforcers* (e.g., material goods, money, and instinctual drives) are more important than *social reinforcers* (e.g., praise, status, and sense of belonging from one's intimate groups) when it comes to criminal behaviour.

James Q. Wilson and Richard Herrnstein (1985) also applied operant conditioning in their well-known book *Crime and Human Nature*, arguing that behaviour is determined by its consequences. They also argued that individual differences in biological, constitutional, and personality factors affect the learning process and an individual's likelihood of committing crime. In other words, individual differences such as low IQ, high impulsivity, and a weak conscience affect the ways in which offenders perceive and respond to rewards and punishments. The authors stated that in some cases, these differences arose from factors such as race, sex, and age, making their work controversial. Clearly, the evidence presented in support of a racial connection to crime was questionable at best (see the discussion above about Herrnstein and Murray's [1994] theory about IQ and race, and problems with this line of thought).

The Frustration–Aggression Hypothesis

John Dollard, Neal Miller, Leonard Doob, O.H. Mowrer, and Robert Sears's (1939) **frustration–aggression hypothesis** elaborates on the learning theory of Thorndike (1898) by incorporating Freudian insights. Specifically, this group of psychologists and social psychologists (sometimes referred to as "the Yale School") fused the early behaviourist approach to learning with the pleasure principle offered in psychoanalytic approaches to personality to explain how frustration can lead to aggression.

frustration–aggression hypothesis
The view that crime is a natural byproduct of aggression and can be explained as a consequence of frustration.

goal responses
Behaviours meant to achieve particular goals that provide pleasurable outcomes.

These theorists argued that various stimuli (e.g., desire for money and material goods) motivate behaviour and lead to different types of **goal responses**, or behaviours meant to achieve particular goals that provide pleasurable outcomes. Of course, crime is often committed in pursuit of these pleasurable outcomes. When a goal response (e.g., stealing to get money) is rewarded or is accompanied by little or no punishment, the learning process that takes place leads to similar behaviour in the future. *Frustration* is thought to result when a goal is inaccessible or when the individual is punished in response to seeking a particular goal. Dollard and colleagues viewed *aggression* as a normal response to frustration. However, they point out that people do not always express that aggression because most learn to suppress their aggressive impulses when properly socialized.

According to this theory, crime is a natural byproduct of aggression, and most crime can be explained as a consequence of frustration (Andrews & Bonta, 2010). Crime is also thought to be a function of a high level of frustration and a low level of anticipated punishment. In other words, if one is very frustrated and perceives a low risk of being punished, the likelihood of criminal behaviour will increase (Dollard et al., 1939).

Social Cognitivism (aka Social Learning Theory)

Albert Bandura is a well-known psychologist and is the leading proponent of social learning theory in psychology. While most refer to Bandura's work as *social learning theory*, he prefers to call it *social cognitive theory*, or *social cognitivism*. (For that reason, we will use that term in this chapter, and it will also help avoid confusion between this theory and Ronald Akers's [1998] social learning theory, examined in more detail in Chapter 12, Sociological Approaches.)

Bandura's (1959, 1965) early research focused on aggression, particularly in children and adolescents. His simple, well-known experiment involved young children observing adults physically assaulting a Bobo doll (a children's toy resembling a clown, designed to bounce back up when struck). Bandura found that children imitated aggressive, violent behaviour after observing it. Critics suggested that the doll was designed to be punched, and that the children would not have attacked an actual person after merely observing others do it. In later studies, researchers were able to demonstrate that children were also willing to attack people dressed as clowns, as long as the behaviour was modelled by adults.

Social cognitive theory includes several explanatory mechanisms, including modelling and self-efficacy, both of which are relevant to understanding criminality. According to Bandura (1963, 1977), **modelling** is an important form of learning:

> Learning would be exceedingly laborious, not to mention hazardous, if people had to rely solely on the effects of their own actions to inform them what to do. Fortunately, most human behavior is learned observationally through modeling: from observing others one forms an idea of how new behaviors are performed, and on later occasions this coded information serves as a guide for action. (Bandura, 1977, p. 22)

Modelling (also known as *observational learning* or *imitation*) refers to learning that occurs through observation of others and **vicarious reinforcement** (Bartol & Bartol, 2011). In other words, if an impressionable person sees someone perform some behaviour that's rewarded, the person will be more likely to imitate that behaviour based on the anticipation of the reward.

Bandura (1977) also claims that models vary in their ability to influence observers, and observers vary in their susceptibility to be influenced. If observers lack confidence

modelling
A form of learning that occurs through observation of others and vicarious reinforcement; also known as *observational learning* or *imitation*.

vicarious reinforcement
Reinforcement that is experienced indirectly through observing another person's behaviour being rewarded.

or self-esteem, they are generally more likely to copy the behaviour of more confident people. However, confident and well-adjusted observers will model behaviour that is demonstrated to be highly useful (e.g., a clever student doing poorly in a course will figure out how to study more effectively by observing students who are doing well). A model is more likely to be imitated by the observer if the model is held in high esteem by or has high status for the observer. Further, if the model has a close relationship with the observer (e.g., if the model is a parent, sibling, or close friend), modelling is more likely to occur.

On the basis of findings of research on modelling theory, social cognitive theorists question the effectiveness of overreliance on deterrence as crime control policy and practice (Bandura, 1977). While they do concede that observing punishment can have an inhibiting effect on criminal behaviour, they also point out that the vicarious reinforcement of crime is much more common and widespread. In other words, within one's own intimate groups it is much more common to see someone successfully commit a crime and be rewarded for it (either monetarily or with praise from one's peers) than it is to see someone apprehended and punished for a crime. This is simply because of all crime that is committed, very little is reported, let alone punished. Instead of focusing primarily on deterrence achieved though punitive tactics, social cognitive theorists suggest that crime control policies should also seek to help offenders develop pro-social alternatives to crime (Bandura, 1977).

Another key aspect of social cognitive theory is self-efficacy. Self-efficacy is an important self-regulatory mechanism, and refers to one's belief in his or her own ability to accomplish difficult tasks and deal with threatening situations. According to Bandura (1997), positive modelling and social support are ways of raising levels of self-efficacy. While self-efficacy is only marginally relevant to criminology, in the sense that it determines one's likelihood to change and possibly desist from criminal behaviour, its macro-level counterpart, collective efficacy, has received much more attention from criminologists.

Collective efficacy theory in criminology is a modern incarnation of social disorganization theory that accounts for disparities in neighbourhood crime rates. Robert Sampson (2013), the founder and main proponent of collective efficacy theory, argues that neighbourhoods with higher levels of collective efficacy are able to more effectively control crime (Sampson's work is discussed in greater detail in Chapter 12, Sociological Approaches).

The psychological learning theories discussed above have offered a more rigorous account of criminality than did earlier psychoanalytic explanations. However, these more recent theories still seemed to overlook factors and processes that many thought were important to understanding criminal behaviour. For example, how do people develop morals? This question seems relevant to understanding why people commit crime. It is also the focus of the moral development theories that will be discussed in the following section.

Moral Development and Criminality

Moral development theory has provided a significant contribution to the understanding of criminal behaviour. The origins of this theory can be found in the work of Jean Piaget (1932), who studied cognitive development in children and adolescents. To summarize,

Piaget argued that morality is not a natural state of humans, and develops in a series of stages. According to Piaget, moral development takes place alongside cognitive development. In other words, the development of one's morals is linked to the ability to reason (Palmer, 2003).

Kohlberg's Six Stages of Moral Development

Inspired by Piaget's work, Lawrence Kohlberg (1958) set out to replicate his research, and to extend the theory beyond adolescence. Kohlberg proposed that people progress through six stages of moral development, divided into three levels (see Figure 8.4).

FIGURE 8.4   Moral Development

Moral development occurs over three levels, each with two stages.

Sources: Adapted from Garz (2009, p. 40) and Kohlberg (1969).

The first level of moral development is the *pre-conventional level*, or the hedonic level. At this level, the individual makes no distinction between moral and selfish values. In stage one, known as *punishment and obedience*, the individual follows rules to avoid punishment and obeys authority figures without question. Punishment is evidence that a behaviour is wrong and should be avoided. In stage two, *instrumental purpose and exchange*, self-interest emerges, and the individual begins to justify behaviour based on his or her personal needs. Not surprisingly, this stage also involves an increased interest in rewards as a motivation for behaviour (Garz, 2009; Kohlberg, 1969).

The second level of moral development is the *conventional level*. At this level, the individual appreciates the importance of conformity and social expectations. In stage three, *interpersonal expectations, relationships, and conformity*, the individual becomes aware of the needs of others close to him or her. This stage is also called the "good child" orientation (Kohlberg, 1969). During this stage, the focus is on maintaining important relationships by demonstrating loyalty (Palmer, 2003). In stage four, *preservation of the social system*, the individual's concerns branch out to society, and he or she understands the importance of obeying laws and performing one's duties. The view here is clearly a "law and order" stance that has its basis in a respect for authority and a consideration of wider social needs.

The third level of moral development is the *post-conventional level*, or the "principled," level. It involves developing a more nuanced understanding of the relationship between individual behaviour and membership in society. In stage five, *social contract and individual rights*, the individual understands more abstract ideas such as the social contract and the notion that people sacrifice some individual freedoms in exchange for the benefits of living in society. At this stage, the individual also understands that the law is not infallible. The realization emerges that laws can be broken under some circumstances (e.g., if the laws inflict unnecessary pain on people, or if they are applied in unfair ways). During the sixth and final stage, *universal ethical principles*, the individual uses abstract moral and ethical principles to help guide behaviour. At this stage, the individual realizes that the law must always be questioned and held to higher moral standards (Kohlberg, 1969).

Although Kohlberg did not technically offer a theory of criminal behaviour, his ideas on moral development suggest that behaviours, whether law-abiding or criminal, are merely functions of one's stage of moral development and one's wider conception of justice. For example, offenders could be considered to be at a lower stage of moral development than non-offenders. Further, his ideas suggest that offenders' rationalizations and justifications for crime could be attributed to their stage of moral development. Criminals who are at a lower stage of moral development might be selfish and impulsive, and miscalculate the consequences of their behaviour (i.e., they are not concerned with how their actions affect others) and their ability to avoid punishment. According to this theory, offenders with higher levels of moral development tend to be activists, protesters, and those who believe they are violating the law in the name of a greater good.

Eventually, criminologists began to integrate ideas from many different theories to produce more robust explanations of criminal behaviour. Several examples of these theories will be discussed in the following sections.

Integrating Psychological Explanations

Psychologists have offered a variety of integrated theories of criminal behaviour. These theories are more complex than earlier theories because they attempt to fuse together ideas from a number of different areas, some originating outside of psychology. A summary of these theories is depicted in Figure 8.5.

Andrews and Bonta's Personal, Interpersonal, Community-Reinforcement Theory

D.A. Andrews and James Bonta's (2010) personal, interpersonal, community-reinforcement (PIC-R) theory is an attempt to integrate many of the psychological theories described above into one theory of criminal behaviour. According to Andrews and Bonta (2010), four key risk factors appear in almost every empirical study of criminality as the strongest predictors of criminal behaviour. They call these factors "the Big Four," which are as follows:

- anti-social attitudes;
- anti-social associates;
- a history of anti-social behaviour; and
- an anti-social personality pattern.

FIGURE 8.5   Integrated Psychological Theories

The key explanatory mechanisms in PIC-R theory are derived from various psychological theories, and Andrews and Bonta propose how these are connected to the Big Four factors. For example, they draw on psychodynamic theory, especially notions of self-control and impulsivity, to explain the development of anti-social personality patterns. They also consider cognitive processes associated with social learning theory, such as self-regulatory mechanisms (e.g., self-efficacy) and criminal thinking patterns, to explain the development of anti-social personality patterns (Andrews & Bonta, 2010).

Aspects of modelling as well as classical and operant conditioning are also used to explain behavioural outcomes, and are particularly useful to understanding why factors such as anti-social associates and anti-social attitudes consistently predict criminal behaviour. For example, if an individual is constantly around friends that are involved with crime, that individual will eventually either quit associating with them (out of fear of getting into trouble) or will adopt their anti-social attitudes. These attitudes are usually adopted because an individual sees his or her peers (i.e., models) being rewarded for their criminal behaviour in both social (e.g., praise, belonging, and status) and non-social ways (e.g., money, personal items). Further, the individual may come to feel close to these criminal models, which may further reinforce his or her law-breaking attitude.

Finally, Andrews and Bonta (2010) acknowledge that social systems and environments are important to understanding criminal behaviour. However, in their view, these social factors are important primarily because they furnish opportunities to commit crime. Developmental and life-course theories pay more attention to these social and environmental dimensions, and will be the focus of the next section.

Integration Across the Life Course: Developmental and Life-Course Criminology

Another example of integrated theory can be found in developmental and life-course criminology (DLC). DLC theories emerged during the 1990s and have become increasingly popular in criminology in recent years. These theories have three key influences.

First, they rely on insights from developmental psychology. Specifically, they focus on the development of criminal and anti-social behaviour, and the impact of life events on the course of this development (Farrington, 2003a).

Second, DLC theories rely on research on the criminal career paradigm. The criminal career paradigm emerged in a National Academy of Sciences report on the subject undertaken in 1986. Researchers found that a small number of offenders were responsible for a large number of crimes. Data obtained from this study also raised questions about the onset, maintenance, and cessation of criminal behaviour (Piquero, Farrington, & Blumstein, 2003). Building on this insight, DLC theorists sought to explain how and why people become involved in criminal behaviour, how they stay involved in it over time, and why they choose to stop committing crime (Farrington, 1992).

Third, like Andrews and Bonta (2010), DLC theorists embrace a risk factor approach. In other words, they attempt to identify key biological, psychological, and sociological variables that place certain people at greater risk to commit crime. Common risk factors include impulsivity, low empathy, low intelligence, delinquent friends, weak social bonds, economic/financial strain, and presence of criminal opportunities (Farrington, 2003a).

While DLC theories incorporate a number of different factors, both David Farrington's (1992, 2003a) integrated cognitive anti-social potential (ICAP) theory and Terrie Moffitt's (1993) developmental taxonomy have their foundations in psychology.

Farrington's Integrated Cognitive Anti-Social Potential Theory

David Farrington's (1992) integrated cognitive anti-social potential theory (ICAP) theory was proposed to explain the results of the *Cambridge Study in Delinquent Development [Great Britain], 1961–1981* (see also Farrington, 2003b). The key underlying construct in this theory is anti-social potential. Farrington (1992) argues that anti-social potential has both short-term and long-term aspects. Long-term anti-social potential focuses on the various individual differences between people that might contribute to a criminal predisposition. Key factors that determine one's long-term anti-social potential include impulsivity, low IQ, lack of empathy, weak conscience, anti-social models, delinquent peers, weak social attachments, and economic problems. People who have these risk factors will have a higher risk of engaging in criminal activity (Farrington, 1992).

Short-term anti-social potential refers to environmental and/or immediate situational factors that might lead to offending. This element of the theory emphasizes the dynamics of the crime rather than individual factors that predispose some people to crime. For example, in order for crime to take place, opportunities must be present in one's environment, and this often depends on the everyday or routine activities of the offender. The offender must also assess the situation and determine whether the crime is worth committing (i.e., there must be some sort of cognitive process involving a cost-benefit analysis). Another important situational factor is the mental state of the offender (e.g., intoxicated, angry, bored, or frustrated) that might make a person more prone to crime.

Moffitt's Developmental Taxonomy Theory

Terrie Moffitt's (1993) developmental taxonomy is another leading DLC theory. The theory has been tested by using data supplied by the Dunedin Multidisciplinary Health and Development Study, a 32-year-long longitudinal study of a birth cohort of over 1,000 New Zealanders (Moffitt, 2007). The developmental taxonomy is an attempt to further explain the relationship between age and crime, also known as the age–crime curve. The age–crime curve demonstrates that rates of offending peak sharply around the age of 17 and then decline rapidly in young adulthood, with about 85 percent of offenders completely desisting by the age of 28 (Moffitt, 1993). Moffitt (1993) argues that the age–crime curve obscures two distinct categories of offenders: life-course persistent (LCP) and adolescent-limited (AL) offenders.

LCP offenders represent a small percentage of all offenders, at about 5 percent. These people show evidence of anti-social behaviour early in childhood, and offend frequently through adolescence and into adulthood. Their anti-social behaviour is thought to stem from neuropsychological deficits occurring very early in life, often during fetal development. These deficits may be caused by a number of factors, including maternal substance abuse, poor prenatal nutrition, and exposure to toxic agents (Moffitt, 1993).

Neuropsychological deficits manifest themselves in a variety of ways, and affect both verbal and executive functions. Moffitt (1993) states that problems with verbal and executive functions are known to be associated with anti-social behaviour. Verbal deficits lead to problems in reading, writing, expressive speech, and memory, while deficits in executive functions involve impulsive behaviour and inattention. In addition to contributing to anti-social behaviour, these deficits also create problems when interacting with parents, school teachers, and other authority figures. These negative interactions promote more anti-social behaviour through attenuated social bonds and negative labelling effects. The result is a life-course trajectory that slowly limits options for pro-social change, leading the person to become entrenched in crime and other forms of anti-social behaviour. It is clear that this theory is attempting to specify how traits (i.e., neuropsychological deficits) and one's environment (i.e., negative social interactions and labelling) interact to produce criminality and anti-social behaviour.

AL offenders have little to no childhood history of anti-social behaviour and participate in crime during their adolescent years only. AL offenders represent the largest percentage of all offenders, at about 95 percent. According to Moffitt (1993), the onset of AL offending occurs in response to the maturity gap created by modernization. The maturity gap refers to societal changes that have occurred in the past century that have served to delay entry into adulthood and activities associated with being an independent adult (e.g., drinking, sex, labour force participation, getting married, and having children). At the same time, improvements in nutrition and health care have also lowered the age of biological maturity. All of these factors serve to lengthen the amount of time spent in the stage of adolescence; teenagers are forced to delay adult activities, contrary to some of the biological urges they may be experiencing.

Moffitt (1993) claims that the longer time spent in adolescence creates a role vacuum that causes some adolescents to look for ways to assert their independence. For example, AL offenders mimic LCP offenders because the older offenders appear to be adept at gaining the freedom desired by AL offenders. In short, offending is a way of expressing individualism and personal independence for AL offenders. AL offenders naturally desist from criminal activity as they age because adult responsibilities (such as having a job and family) begin to limit opportunities and motivation for delinquency.

Practical Implications: Treatment and Risk

Psychological theories have had a considerable impact on the criminal justice system, especially in the areas of correctional treatment and risk assessment. In the 1920s, the medical model made its way into correctional systems in Canada and the United States. The medical model was introduced by the Positivist School of criminology and viewed criminals as "sick" and in need of help or rehabilitation (Griffiths, 2010).

Early correctional treatment approaches in prison were implemented by people with psychiatric training, and were based primarily on a clinical approach heavily influenced by psychoanalytic thought (Cohen, 1983). In the 1950s and 1960s, the correctional treatment model shifted to a behavioural approach based on learning theories that were popular in psychology at the time (i.e., operant conditioning and social learning). Modern forms of correctional treatment focus on cognitive aspects of behaviour and criminal thinking patterns (Andrews & Bonta, 2010; Ross & Ross, 1995).

Risk assessment is another area that has been influenced by psychological theories. Correctional Services Canada and the National Parole Board use many scales and other instruments to predict the risk posed by offenders after release. Many of the characteristics included on these scales (e.g., anti-social attitudes and associates, impulsivity, and lack of empathy) are derived from psychoanalytic and learning theories, and from factors identified on the Psychopathy Checklist-Revised (PCL-R) (Hare, 2003; see Box 8.1 for a discussion of psychopathy). Instruments that are commonly used to predict risk include the General Statistical Information on Recidivism (GSIR), the Violence Risk Appraisal Guide (VRAG), and the Level of Service/Case Management Inventory-Revised (Andrews & Bonta, 2010; Pozzulo, Bennell, & Forth, 2009).

Policies that target chronic and persistent offenders are another area of risk assessment that psychological theories can contribute to. Moffitt's (1993) developmental taxonomy of LCP offenders is particularly relevant to this discussion. While Moffitt's developmental taxonomy is too recent to have influenced policy in any meaningful way, it is possible that it may lend itself to addressing problems that lead to criminal behaviour, such as neuropsychological deficits, earlier on in people's lives (Bernard, Snipes, & Gerould, 2010).

Conclusion

Psychologists have offered numerous theories that have influenced criminology. Early approaches focused primarily on explaining the intelligence–crime connection, aggression, the psychopathic personality, and aspects of social learning and moral development (Aichhorn, 1925; Bandura, 1965, 1973; Dollard et al., 1939; Freud, 1920; Goddard, 1913; Kohlberg, 1969). Later, these insights were applied more directly and used to explain general forms of criminal behaviour (Burgess & Akers, 1966; Eysenck, 1964; Jeffery, 1965). Modern incarnations of psychological theories in criminology are often integrated in nature and include Andrews and Bonta's (2010) PIC-R theory and developmental theories such as Farrington's (1992) ICAP theory and Moffitt's (1993) developmental taxonomy. Psychological explanations of criminal behaviour have also influenced the criminal justice system in a variety of areas, such as correctional treatment and risk assessment.

SUMMARY OF KEY POINTS

- The discipline of psychology is composed of several different (and often competing) perspectives including *psychoanalysis*, *behaviourism*, *social cognitivism* (or *social learning*), and *developmental psychology*. These different approaches have produced numerous psychological theories that seek to explain aspects of criminal behaviour. They should not be lumped together as a single theory.

- IQ may be an important *correlate* of crime; however, the *causal connection* is not readily apparent. In many cases, IQ may be influenced by factors such as socio-economic status or prenatal care, which undermines theories that attempt to link crime, IQ, and race, for example.

- Psychiatrist Sigmund Freud, founder of psychoanalysis, influenced many criminologists. Freud claimed that personality has three components: the *id*, the *ego*, and the *superego*. Many basic human impulses and drives stem from the id, which functions according to the pleasure principle. Biological urges for aggression and sex can instigate criminal behaviour, but they are counterbalanced by the superego; both of these aspects are regulated by the ego.

- Not all psychopaths are criminals, and many are not even violent. Many are successful in politics, law, and business. Misconceptions about psychopathy abound. It is a personality disorder, not a mental illness. *Psychopaths* are not psychotic, mentally ill, or "sick" in the legal sense of the term. In contrast, *psychotics* are mentally ill and often have hallucinations and delusions that spur on their abnormal behaviours, and may suffer from schizophrenia. Furthermore, the terms *psychopathy*, *anti-social personality disorder*, and *sociopathy* are often used interchangeably, which is incorrect.

- Psychological learning theories have contributed a great deal to the field of criminological theory. The main theories in this area (and key names associated with each) are, *classical* and *operant conditioning* (Eysenck and Skinner, respectively), the *frustration–aggression hypothesis* (Dollard et al.), and *social learning theory* (Bandura).

- Moral development theory has its origins in the work of Piaget, who studied cognitive development in children and adolescents. Piaget argued that morality is not a natural state of humans, and develops in a series of stages. Kohlberg extended the theory beyond adolescence, proposing that people progress through six stages of moral development, divided into three levels.

- Psychologists (including Andrews and Bonta) have offered a variety of *integrated theories* of criminal behaviour. These theories are more complex than earlier theories because they attempt to combine ideas from a number of different areas, some originating outside of psychology.

- Psychological theories have had a considerable impact on the criminal justice system, especially in the areas of correctional treatment and risk assessment.

QUESTIONS FOR CRITICAL DISCUSSION

1. In what ways has the field of psychology influenced criminal justice processes? How has it influenced the study of criminology?
2. What are the key differences between a psychopathic person and a psychotic person?
3. How does one's level of moral developmental affect their interpretation of the law? How does it affect the likelihood that they will break it?
4. How is IQ connected to criminality? Is it reasonable to argue that less intelligent people will be more likely to break the law?
5. Is it possible to predict crime based solely on a person's psychological characteristics?
6. Are the integrated theories an improvement over the original theories?

SUGGESTED FURTHER READINGS

Appleby, T. (2011). *A new kind of monster: The secret life and chilling crimes of Colonel Russell Williams*. Toronto: Vintage Canada.

Fowles, D.C. (1987). Psychophysiology and psychopath: A motivational approach. *Psychophysiology, 25*, 373–391.

Haney, C. (2002). Making law modern: Toward a contextual model of justice. *Psychology, Public Policy and the Law, 8*, 3–63.

Robinson, M.B., & Beaver, K.M. (2008). *Why crime? An interdisciplinary approach to explaining criminal behavior*. Durham, NC: Carolina Academic Press.

Ross, R.R., & Ross, R.D. (1995). *Thinking straight: The reasoning and rehabilitation program for delinquency prevention and offender rehabilitation*. Ottawa: Air Training.

Websites

Association for Behavior Analysis International: http://www.abainternational.org

Society for the Scientific Study of Psychopathy: http://www.psychopathysociety.org/en

"Without Conscience": Robert Hare's website devoted to the study of psychopathy: http://www.hare.org

REFERENCES

Aichhorn, A. (1925). *Wayward youth*. New York: Viking Press.

Akers, R.L. (1998). *Social structure and social learning: A general theory of crime and deviance*. Boston: Northeastern University Press.

Alexander, F., & Healy, W. (1935). *Roots of crime*. Montclair, NJ: Patterson Smith.

Andrews, D.A., & Bonta, J. (2010). *The psychology of criminal conduct*. Cincinnati, OH: Anderson.

Babiak, P., & Hare, R.D. (2006). *Snakes in suits: When psychopaths go to work*. New York: Regan, 2006.

Bandura A. (1959). *Adolescent aggression: A study of the influence of child-training practices and family interrelationships*. New York: Ronald Press.

Bandura, A. (1963). *Social learning and personality development*. New York: Holt, Rinehart, and Winston.

Bandura, A. (1965). Influence of models' reinforcement contingencies on the acquisition of imitative responses. *Journal of Personality and Social Psychology, 1*(6), 589–595.

Bandura, A. (1973). *Aggression: A social learning analysis*. Englewood Cliffs, NJ: Prentice Hall.

Bandura, A. (1977). *Social learning theory*. Englewood Cliffs, NJ: Prentice Hall.

Bandura, A. (1997). *Self-efficacy: The exercise of control*. New York: W.H. Freeman.

Bandura, A., Ross, D., & Ross, S.A. (1963). Imitation of film-mediated aggressive models. *Journal of Abnormal and Social Psychology, 66*(1), 3–11.

Bartol, C., & Bartol, A.M. (2011). *Criminal behavior: A psychosocial approach* (9th ed.). Boston: Prentice Hall.

Bernard, T.J., Snipes, J.B., & Gerould, A. (2010). *Vold's theoretical criminology*. New York: Oxford University Press.

Blackburn, R. (1990). *The psychology of criminal conduct: Theory, research, and practice*. New York: John Wiley and Sons.

Blair, R.J.R., Mitchell, D., & Blair, K. (2005). *The psychopath: Emotion and the brain*. Malden, MA: Blackwell.

Burgess, R.L., & Akers, R.L. (1966). A differential association-reinforcement theory of criminal behavior. *Social Problems, 14*, 128–146.

Cleckley, H. (1964). *The mask of sanity*. Augusta, GA: Emily S. Cleckley.

Cohen, S. (1983). Social control talk: Telling stories about correctional change. In D. Garland & P. Young (Eds.), *The power to punish: Contemporary penality and social analysis* (pp. 101–129). London, UK: Heinemann Educational.

Dollard, J., Miller, N.E., Doob, L.W., Mowrer, O.H., & Sears, R. (1939). *Frustration and aggression*. New Haven, CT: Yale University Press.

Dutton, K. (2012). *The wisdom of psychopaths: What saints, spies and serial killers can teach us about success*. Toronto: Doubleday.

Einstadter, W., & Henry, S. (2006). *Theoretical criminology: An analysis of its underlying assumptions*. Lanham, MD: Rowman and Littlefield.

Eysenck, H.J. (1964). *Crime and personality*. London, UK: Methuen.

Eysenck, S.B.G., & Eysenck, H.J. (1978). Impulsiveness and venturesomeness: Their position in a dimensional system of personality description. *Psychological Reports, 43*(3), 1247–1255.

Farrington, D.P. (1992). Explaining the beginning, progress, and ending of antisocial behavior from birth to adulthood. In J. McCord (Ed.), *Facts, frameworks, and forecasts: Advances in criminological theory* (Vol. 3, pp. 253–286). New Brunswick, NJ: Transaction.

Farrington, D.P. (2003a). Developmental and life course criminology: Key theoretical and empirical issues—The 2002 Sutherland award address. *Criminology, 41*(2), 221–255.

Farrington, D.P. (2003b). Key results from the first forty years of the Cambridge Study. In T. Thornberry & M.D. Krohn (Eds.), *Taking stock of delinquency: An overview of findings from contemporary longitudinal studies* (pp. 137–174). New York: Kluwer Academic/Plenum.

Freud, S. (1920). *A general introduction to psychoanalysis*. New York: Boney and Liveright.

Freud, S. (1923). *The ego and the id*. New York: W.W. Norton.

Garz, D. (2009). *Lawrence Kohlberg: An introduction*. Leverkusen Opladen, Germany: Barbara Budrich.

Goddard, H.H. (1913). *The Kallikak family*. New York: Macmillan.

Gottfredson, M.R., & Hirschi, T. (1990). *A general theory of crime*. Stanford, CA: Stanford University Press.

Griffiths, C.T. (2010). *Canadian corrections* (3rd ed.). Toronto: Nelson.

Hare, R.D. (1970). *Psychopathy: Theory and practice*. New York: Wiley.

Hare, R.D. (1993). *Without conscience: The disturbing world of the psychopaths among us*. New York: Pocket Books.

Hare, R.D. (1996). Psychopathy: A clinical construct whose time has come. *Criminal Justice and Behavior, 23*, 25–54.

Hare, R.D. (2003). *Manual for revised psychopathy checklist revised* (2nd ed.). Toronto: Multi-Health Systems.

Hare R.D, & Cox, D.N. (1978). Clinical and empirical conceptions of psychopathy, and the selection of subjects for research. In R.D. Hare & D. Schalling (Eds.), *Psychopathic behavior: Approaches to research* (pp. 107–144). Chichester, UK: Wiley.

Herrnstein, W., & Murray, C. (1994). *The bell curve*. New York: Free Press.

Hirschi, T. (1969). *Causes of delinquency*. Berkeley, CA: University of California Press.

Hirschi, T., & Hindelang, M. (1977). Intelligence and delinquency: A revisionist review. *American Sociological Review, 42*, 571–587.

Jeffery, C.R. (1965). Criminal behavior and learning theory. *The Journal of Criminal Law, Criminology and Police Science, 56*, 294–300.

Johns, J.H., & Quay, H.C. (1962). The effect of social reward on verbal conditioning in psychopathic and neurotic military offenders. *Journal of Consulting and Clinical Psychology, 26*, 217–220.

Kohlberg, L. (1958). *The development of modes of thinking and choices in years 10 to 16* (Doctoral dissertation). Chicago: University of Chicago.

Kohlberg, L. (1969). Stage and sequence: The cognitive-developmental approach. In D.A. Goslin (Ed.), *Handbook of socialization theory and research* (pp. 347–480). Chicago: Rand McNally.

Lilly, R.J., Cullen, F.T., & Ball, R.A. (2007). *Criminological theory: Context and consequences* (4th ed.). Thousand Oaks, CA: Sage.

McIlroy, A., & Anderssen, E. (2010, October 22). How a psychopath is made. *Globe and Mail.* Retrieved from http://www.theglobeandmail.com/life/health-and-fitness/health/conditions/how-a-psychopath-is-made/article4268124/?page=all

Moffitt, T. (1993). Adolescence-limited and life-course-persistent antisocial behaviour: A developmental taxonomy. *Psychological Review, 100,* 674–701.

Moffitt, T.E. (2007). A review of the research on the taxonomy of life-course persistent versus adolescence-limited antisocial behavior. In F.T. Cullen, J.P. Wright, & K.R. Blevins (Eds.), *Taking stock: The status of criminological theory* (pp. 277–312). New Brunswick, NJ: Transaction.

Palmer, E.J. (2003). *Offending behavior: Moral reasoning, criminal conduct, and the rehabilitation of offenders.* Cullumpton, UK: Willan.

Pavlov, I. (1960). *Conditioned reflexes: An investigation of the physiological activity of the cerebral cortex.* New York: Dover. (Original work published 1927.)

Piaget, J. (1932). *The moral judgement of the child.* London, UK: Routledge and Kegan Paul.

Piquero, A.R., Farrington, D.P., & Blumstein, A. (2003). The criminal career paradigm. *Crime and Justice, 30,* 359–506.

Pozzulo, J., Bennell, C., & Forth, A. (2009). *Forensic psychology* (2nd ed.). Toronto: Pearson.

Rafter, N. (2008). *The criminal brain: Understanding biological theories of crime.* New York: New York University Press.

Redl, F., & Toch, H. (1979). Psychoanalytic perspective. In H. Toch (Ed.), *Psychology of crime and criminal justice* (pp. 183–197). New York: Holt, Rinehart, and Winston.

Redl, F., & Wineman, D. (1951). *Children who hate: The disorganization and breakdown of behavior controls.* New York: Free Press.

Robinson, M.B., & Beaver, K.M. (2008). *Why crime? An interdisciplinary approach to explaining criminal behavior.* Durham, NC: Carolina Academic Press.

Ross, R.R., & Ross, R.D. (1995). *Thinking straight: The reasoning and rehabilitation program for delinquency prevention and offender rehabilitation.* Ottawa: Air Training.

Sampson, R.J. (2013). *Great American city.* Chicago: University of Chicago Press.

Serin, R., Forth, A., Brown, S., Nunes, K., Bennell, C., & Pozzulo, J. (2011). *Psychology of criminal behavior.* Toronto: Pearson.

Skinner, B.F. (1953). *Science and human behavior.* New York: Macmillan.

Sutherland, E. (1931). Mental deficiency and crime. In K. Young (Ed.), *Social attitudes* (pp. 357–375). New York: Henry Holt.

Thorndike, E. (1898). *Animal intelligence: An experimental study of the associative processes in animals.* New York: London: Macmillan.

Williams, K.M., Paulhus, D.L., & Hare, R.D. (2007). Capturing the four-factor structure of psychopathy in college students via self-report. *Journal of Personality Assessment, 88,* 205–219.

Wilson, J.Q., & Herrnstein, R. (1985). *Crime and human nature.* New York: Simon and Schuster.

Yochelson, S., & Samenow, S. (1976). *The criminal personality.* New York: Jason Aronson.

Racial Profiling: A "Watershed Experience" in Rawle Maynard's Life

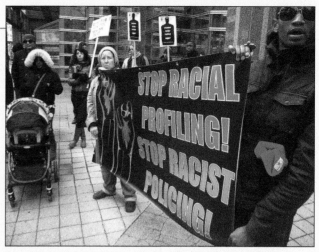

People protesting against racial profiling in front of police headquarters in Toronto.

On a Saturday morning in late November 2005, Rawle Maynard left his Toronto office and headed to his parents' home in Scarborough. He was driving a two-door black BMW, licensed to his father. At a little after 11:15 a.m., he noticed that a police car had taken a U-turn and was now following him. He drove carefully, monitoring his speed, given that a police officer was driving right behind him.

He was not sure that the patrol car, driven by Police Officer Ryan Baker, was following him, however, until he made a final turn onto his parents' street and the police car stayed with him. He pulled into his parents' driveway and parked the car next to the garage. The police officer pulled up to the edge of the driveway and stopped.

Maynard was on his cellphone, talking to a wedding planner, and telling her that he was going to get out of the car and see what the officer wanted. Maynard had, according to his later testimony, "no apprehension about approaching Officer Baker because he had nothing but positive interactions with police officers in the past."

He asked the officer if there was a problem, and if he was being followed. The officer responded aggressively, asking Maynard where he was coming from. He replied that he did not have to tell the officer anything without first having an explanation as to why this information was needed. After repeated refusals to tell the officer where he was coming from, Officer Baker drew his firearm and pointed it at Maynard.

Maynard quickly became very frightened, afraid that he would be shot. He continued to talk on his cellphone, telling the wedding planner to call his parents, and then he hung up. An additional three police vehicles pulled up to the house and police officers ran from their cars; Maynard now had four guns pointed at him. He was asked to walk backward and to drop to his knees, which he did. He was then put in the back of a police car.

Within minutes police received a call that the suspect they were looking for had been seen on foot, wearing red—clearly not Maynard. The officers spoke among themselves, and then let Maynard out of the police cruiser and returned his keys to him. "Sorry, man," Officer Baker said, putting his hand out to Maynard, "we're looking for someone who fits your description, 6 feet, black and slim."

"The only part that I fit was I was black," Maynard responded.

Officer Baker had followed Maynard that morning after receiving a call that a black man with a gun had been at the Malvern Town Centre, driving a black sports car.

After the incident, Maynard launched an action with the Ontario Human Rights Commission, alleging discrimination on the basis of colour, ethnic origin, and race, in respect of policing services. In June 2012, the Ontario Human Rights Tribunal handed down its decision regarding Maynard's claim. Vice-Chair Leslie Reaume wrote:

> The problem is that Officer Baker cast his investigative net so wide that Mr. Maynard's race was the predominant factor that put him at risk of being investigated that day. I do not believe that if the suspect had been a Caucasian man in the same circumstances, with no other defining characteristics, particularly age, and with as little information available about the car and direction of travel, that Officer Baker would have chosen to investigate the first Caucasian man he saw driving the same car at the same intersection. It is consistent with a finding of racial profiling that all black men or all black men of a certain age, driving alone in the area in a black car, were possible suspects at the moment that Officer Baker decided to commence his investigation of Mr. Maynard.
>
> In my view, having commenced an investigation in whole or in part on the basis of racial bias, the events that ensued at [Maynard's parents' home] cannot be disentangled from that initial act. (*Maynard v. Toronto Police Services Board*, 2012, paras. 176–177)

The tribunal awarded Rawle Maynard $40,000 for "injury to dignity, feelings, and self-respect." Maynard had testified that this was a watershed experience in his life, humiliating him in front of his friends and neighbours, and leaving him with a continuing sense of anxiety and fear whenever he sees a police officer.

Before You Read Chapter 9

- Does this case study seem to you like an isolated incident? Or do you think it is representative of a larger problem?
- What does this case study suggest about police attitudes toward visible minorities?
- What broader social issues does an incident such as this bring to the foreground?
- Can you think of other situations in which racial profiling occurs?

Understanding Critical Criminology

<table>
<tr>
<td>

LEARNING OBJECTIVES

After reading this chapter, students will be able to:

- Explain how critical criminology relates to more traditional forms of criminology.
- Understand what "critical" means in the context of criminology.
- Describe the various streams or schools of thought within the field of critical criminology.
- Identify the key thinkers and theories that have influenced critical criminology.
- Define the "punitive turn" and identify the explanations that are offered for it by critical criminologists.

</td>
<td>

CHAPTER OUTLINE

</td>
</tr>
</table>

Introduction

By 2012, 1 in 35 American adults—almost 7 million people—were living under some form of correctional supervision[1] (Glaze & Herberman, 2013). Of these, more than 2.2 million individuals were incarcerated in local jails or in state or federal prisons. To place this figure in perspective, there are almost as many people incarcerated in the United States as the entire population of Canada's largest city, Toronto.

The US Bureau of Justice Statistics (BJS) announced in 2012 that the number of adults being supervised by local, state, or federal correctional systems had actually declined slightly over the previous two years (Glaze & Herberman, 2013). This decline is remarkable, given that in recent decades US incarceration rates have been rising steadily, largely as a result of a series of state and federal laws that promised to "get tough on crime." Many observers would take these declining custody rates as a welcome sign. Politicians, judges, and ordinary citizens have grown tired of policies that do little more than generate an ever-expanding prison system that increases social, economic, and other burdens. However, it might be premature to see this small reversal in a long-term trend as cause for optimism.

Various explanations have been put forward as to why so many people have been locked up in the United States, when crime rates have been consistently declining (Federal Bureau of Investigation, 2011). Although their views may differ in some respects, as we will see shortly, one group of academic scholars—loosely known as "critical criminologists"—have generally attributed the rise in prison populations in the United States to a shift in public attitudes. This shift has been termed the **punitive turn**, in that it represents a move toward punishing offenders simply for the sake of punishment, rather than dealing with them through lesser sanctions and rehabilitation efforts (Garland, 2001; Simon, 2007; Wacquant, 2009; Young, 1999). Some have suggested that this shift can be explained in part as a result of media coverage of horrendous crimes (Tonry,

punitive turn
The move from criminal justice policies and programs aimed at rehabilitating offenders toward those that simply offer punishment for its own sake. This shift occurred despite declining crime rates and evidence that punishment is not always effective.

2004), while others point to the formation of victims' rights groups and their increasing presence in the public debate on crime issues (Caplow & Simon, 1999). Still others point out that incarceration in the United States has become a private multi-billion dollar industry, with profitability tied to keeping prison beds full and costs low (Christie, 2002). One thing most critical criminologists agree upon, however, is that many American and Canadian politicians have seized on crime as a public policy issue that holds great appeal for voters (Simon, 2007). In recent decades, many elected officials have been trying to outdo one another on the question of who is "tougher on crime."

Beginning in the early 2000s, criminologists who had been studying the punitive turn in the United States started to look at other nations and their penal policies. Several researchers noted something unusual: Canada, right next door to the United States, had maintained adult imprisonment rates that were not only relatively stable but also relatively low (Christie, 2004; Meyer & O'Malley, 2005). This phenomenon caused noted criminologist Nils Christie (2004, p. 59) to ask: "What is so peculiar to Canada?" It also caused some Canadian criminologists to worry that perhaps we were not immune to the mass incarceration that had been happening in the United States and that, in time, it could also happen here (Meyer & O'Malley, 2005). Fast-forward to the current decade and, despite steadily declining crime rates over the past 20 years (Brennan, 2012), Canadians are experiencing their own version of the punitive turn. This change after a decades-long period of relatively cautious penal policies has come courtesy of a Conservative government that—seeing how popular "tough on crime" stances are in the United States—has adopted a similar agenda for Canada. With Stephen Harper's election in 2006 and subsequent re-elections, Canadians began to see many changes: an increase in mandatory minimum sentences for drug and other offences; restrictions on the use of conditional sentences; the creation of a new section of the *Criminal Code* that deals specifically with motor vehicle theft;[2] harsher sentences for sex offenders; a *Truth in Sentencing Act* (which prohibits judges from giving offenders a "2 for 1" credit for time served pretrial); the repeal of the "faint hope clause" that allowed individuals convicted of first-degree murder to apply for parole eligibility at 15 years instead of 25 years; and a *Tackling Violent Crime Act*, which, among other things, contains a "three strikes" provision that makes it easier for individuals to be labelled dangerous offenders and receive indeterminate sentences. The Harper government signalled its willingness to end statutory release for inmates and to give police new surveillance powers over Internet traffic and subscriber data. The offender population in Canada has increased by 7.1 percent over the past five years, with much of this increase coming from marginalized groups such as Aboriginal people and black people (Correctional Investigator Canada, 2013).

As critical criminologists have been at the forefront in exploring the rise of punitive policies in Canada and elsewhere, examining the punitive turn from various perspectives within the field will provide a better understanding of critical criminology. This chapter will draw upon insights from the six main areas of the field of critical criminology in Canada today. In doing so, we will also examine the work of several Canadian criminologists who focus on this area. First, however, it is useful to explain the nature and scope of critical criminology.

What Is Critical Criminology?

Critical criminology encompasses a broad range of criminological theories and perspectives that share one key element: a desire to challenge inequality, whether it is inequality linked to how crimes are created, defined, or applied to certain groups or individuals, or oppressive treatment or practices found within the criminal justice system. The starting point for critical criminology is the assumption that power is unequally distributed throughout society and that this is also true when it comes to crime and criminal justice. A critical criminologist's task is not simply to find and call attention to oppression, but to actively oppose it. Opposition can come in many forms: issuing calls for change, raising public awareness, participating in public debate and policy-making, and, for some practitioners, even engaging in protest.

The origins of critical criminology lie in the turbulent 1960s, a time of significant social upheaval. Criminologists were immersed in the radical politics of the day—civil rights, women's liberation, the anti-war movement, and, beginning in the early 1970s, queer rights issues. They increasingly found that mainstream criminology, with its focus on the pathology of individual offenders, ran counter to their beliefs and practices. They rejected the idea of the so-called criminal mind, and instead turned their attention to how criminals are created, not by birth, but through social processes. To better understand this process, critical criminologists use as their fundamental theoretical and empirical building blocks the concepts of class, race and ethnicity, gender and sexuality, and other social categories that have been employed to maintain oppressive relations between groups.

Many of the earliest critical criminologists shared a world view based on **Marxism**—that is, they were interested primarily in class relations and how the structure of capitalism produces inequalities linked to crime and criminal justice. Over the years,

critical criminology
A school of thought with multiple subfields, but largely concerned with social justice and inequality, promoting active opposition to the status quo, and favouring larger-scale societal transformations rather than minor policy changes.

Marxism
A school of thought developed by Karl Marx (1818–1883) arguing that society must be understood in terms of social conflict, class relations, and the inequalities caused by capitalism; Marxists promote revolution by the working class.

FIGURE 9.1

Source: Steve Sack, Minneapolis Star Tribune. Courtesy of Cagel Cartoons. Reprinted by permission.

however, critical criminology developed lines of academic research and thought, most of which are distinctly different from its early Marxist roots (e.g., Quinney, 1977; Taylor, Walton, & Young, 1975). *Neo-Marxist* scholars continue to explore the intersection of capitalism and oppression, but they are now joined under the critical criminology umbrella by *feminist* scholars, who look at gender issues within criminal justice; *critical race/post-colonial* scholars, who explore the intersection of race and criminal justice; *left realist* scholars, who explore the deep social causes of crime in order to develop practical solutions; *post-structuralist* scholars, who seek to untangle the many ways in which power and inequality can manifest within and across social institutions; and *peace-making* scholars, who challenge conventional responses to crime that are considered not merely retributive but violent and counterproductive to the goal of community safety (Milovanovic, 2002).

Prominent Streams Within Critical Criminology

Neo-Marxism

Neo-Marxists take many of their cues from the work of 19th-century thinkers Karl Marx and Friedrich Engels, who condemned the social, political, and material inequalities produced within capitalist systems. Neo-Marxist criminologists focus on how the state uses the criminal justice system to legitimize unequal social arrangements through laws that cater to elite groups while oppressing the working class, the poor, and other marginalized groups. According to this perspective, crime is not a neutral, value-free concept, but a deeply political issue over which differently situated social groups struggle to maintain or overthrow oppression. Because of this view, neo-Marxists are typically referred to as **conflict theorists**[3]—they hold that society is not built on consensus but, rather, on class conflict (Chambliss & Seidman, 1971).

You may wonder why this group is called *neo-Marxist* and not simply *Marxist*. The name shift can be traced to Ian Taylor, Paul Walton, and Jock Young's book *The New Criminology* (1973), which included three key ideas derived from traditional Marxism:

1. In a capitalist system, the economy dictates the structure and functioning of society (including crime).
2. Capitalism is directly to blame for crime because it creates the conditions of inequality that lead to crime.
3. The only way to eliminate crime is to eliminate the conditions that create it—that is, eliminate capitalism.

Taylor, Walton, and Young's modern (or *neo*) approach differed from traditional Marxism because it also incorporated some aspects of the **interactionist perspective**, in particular the concept of "labelling" derived from labelling theory. (For more on labelling theory, see Chapter 12, Sociological Approaches.) An excellent example of how labelling theory helps flesh out Marxist ideas can be found in Hall, Critcher, Jefferson, Clarke, and Roberts's *Policing the Crisis* (1978). This book demonstrates how a **moral panic** over mugging incidents in the United Kingdom created new fears (the term *mugging* was reportedly not even a part of British vocabulary prior to the moral panic), demonized black males, and united the public against this perceived threat. Notably, this "crisis" had the effect of diverting public attention away from the fact that the United Kingdom was in the midst of a serious economic decline.

conflict theories
Theories, originating primarily with Marx, that focus on the unequal distribution of power in society—for example, due to class, race, or gender. Conflicts between classes or groups are driven to a large extent by this unequal power and unequal access to resources.

interactionist perspective
A theoretical approach that focuses on relatively small-scale social interactions among individuals or small social groups, as well as the conscious acts of individuals and their interpretation of others' behaviour.

moral panic
Phenomena—socially constructed by the media, politicians, and "moral entrepreneurs"—in which certain people or groups are labelled or stigmatized as the cause of a perceived social problem, resulting in widespread public alarm.

Private security guards patrol a public thoroughfare in Toronto's Chinatown, having been hired to deal with loiterers, beggars, or other people considered "undesirables" by local businesses. The increasing presence of private security in many public spheres can blur the lines between public and private space. It also alters one's concept of "policing" the public realm. Instead of fulfilling its commonly understood role—to "serve and protect" the public and the public good—this form of policing instead tends to emphasize the protection of certain privileged interests.

Source: Toronto Star/GetStock.com.

A number of notable neo-Marxist criminologists are writing today. They include Colin Sumner in Ireland, Michael Welch in the United States, and George Rigakos in Canada. Rigakos draws on the Marxist tradition and infuses it with theoretical strands drawn from other perspectives. He has written extensively on the rise of private security and the role that this "commodity"[4] plays in facilitating social control of those seen as "dangerous." In a recent article, George Rigakos and Aysegul Ergul (2011) argue that policing—both public and now increasingly private—has historically served the interests of capital in a variety of ways, including supporting the retention and accumulation of private property (such as shopping malls and business complexes), cutting worker costs by replacing paid police officers with private security staff, and assisting in monitoring and regulating potential threats to capital from dissatisfied workers or citizens (e.g., striking labourers or public protestors). Rigakos's overall objective is to create a "Marxist political economy of policing" (Rigakos & Ergul, 2011). His work often explores the ways in which public and private policing intersect in the service of capitalist enterprise. For instance, he has explored the use of bouncers at nightclubs and the leasing of public police services to the private sector.

The Creation of a Criminalized Class

A now classic text in neo-Marxist criminology is Jeffrey Reiman's *The Rich Get Richer and the Poor Get Prison* (1979/2004). An excerpt appears in Box 9.1. Reiman's work offers a quintessential neo-Marxist view that can be used to explain the punitive turn. In it, Reiman argues that the goal of the US criminal justice system is not to fight crime, but to maintain existing class relations through the creation of a criminalized class among the poor. Those who might represent a potential challenge to the political, social, and economic elites are neutralized behind bars. The state does this by creating and policing crimes that are most typically associated with poverty and harshly sentencing offenders. If the goal of the criminal justice system is actually to fight crime, Reiman says, the state would attempt to address the root causes of street crime by eliminating the conditions that give rise to them, and focus instead on the predatory crimes of the wealthy and powerful that affect everyone (such as white-collar and environmental crimes).

BOX 9.1

"The Rich Get Richer and the Poor Get Prison"

A key work in the field of critical criminology is Jeffrey Reiman's *The Rich Get Richer and the Poor Get Prison*. Reiman's approach is summarized in the following excerpt, which also touches on the theme of white-collar crime (discussed in more detail in Chapter 18 of this text).

> Though crime rates have recently declined around the United States, the truth is that the criminal justice system is still failing. While politicians and police chiefs rush to claim credit for the declines, most independent observers credit most of the decline to factors such as the stabilization of the drug trade (which has led to reduced drug-gang violence) and the (until recently) improving economy, which offers idle young men better things to do than look for trouble. What's more, the decline is measured from the abnormally high crime rates of recent years. Crime and criminal violence are still extremely prevalent in the United States, as a look at any daily newspaper or TV news program will confirm. Now, instead of crime rates being *very, very* high, they have come down to only *very* high! Our crime rates are still higher by far than those of other modern nations, and we lead the world in the percentage of our children who are murdered.
>
> So, the criminal justice system is still failing to protect us, even if the crime rates sometimes go down. But the failure is not random. It has a pattern. We have, over the last two decades, been on an imprisonment binge that has made us the country with the highest percentage of citizens behind bars. The vast majority of those locked up are poor inner-city men—many for drug dealing and non-violent offenses—insuring that there will be more children without fathers around, and more men with prison records unable to find decent jobs. On the other hand, still only a fraction of those responsible for Saving and Loan frauds are being made to face criminal prosecution, and, though there has been tough talk about the new crop of Enron and Enron-like corporate cheats, criminal prosecutions to date have been rare. So, while we throw more and more poor people into prison for non-violent offenses, high-class crooks continue to be treated leniently. But this is only the most visible bias against the poor. It applies to people found guilty of acts defined in law as crimes. The subtlest bias against the poor happens earlier, at the very point at which the powers that be decide which acts to define as crimes in the first place. Many of the ways in which the well-off harm their fellows (deadly pollution, unsafe working conditions, and the like) are not even defined as crimes *though they do more damage to life and limb than the acts that are treated as crimes*.

Source: Excerpted from the preface of Reiman, J. (1979/2004). *The rich get richer and the poor get prison: Ideology, class, and criminal justice*, 7th ed. Boston, MA: Allyn and Bacon/Pearson, p. xiii.

Feminist Criminology

Spurred by the political struggles of the women's liberation movement in the 1960s and 1970s, feminist criminology emerged as a reaction to the biases that dominated the field of mainstream criminology. In the larger movement, feminists have been concerned with gender inequality, particularly within social institutions that create and/or sustain male privilege and female oppression (note that these themes will be discussed in more depth in Chapter 10, Gender and Crime). In surveying the landscape of mainstream criminology, feminist criminologists noted that much of this work was **patriarchal** in nature, which resulted in one of two significant problems:

patriarchy
An elitist form of social structure, in which men dominate politics, economics, and other aspects of society, and perpetuate that domination by limiting opportunities for women to exercise power.

1. androcentrism, with males routinely referenced as the de facto standard for criminological research (i.e., treating men and women the same despite their very different socialization, social problems, and social statuses) (Daly & Chesney-Lind, 1988; Griffin, 2010) and;
2. disregard for women's issues altogether, particularly where they might represent a challenge to male dominance.

When women were represented in mainstream criminology works, they were depicted either as passive victims whom men sought to protect or, because they transgressed gender norms, as offenders who must be psychologically disturbed ("mad") or otherwise inherently pathological ("bad"). Feminist criminologists seek to challenge gender norms and assumptions, as well as uncover systemic biases, in order to equalize treatment of women within law, the criminal justice system, and the larger society. Increasingly, feminist criminologists have turned their attention to the unequal treatment of males who are poor and persons of colour as well as non-biological females in society—those who are clearly less privileged than their white, heterosexual, wealthy male counterparts.

Although some overlap exists among them, the four major forms of feminist criminology are *liberal*, *Marxist*, *socialist*, and *radical* (Daly & Chesney-Lind, 1988):

- Liberal feminists typically focus on the legal system and the role that it and other social institutions play in generating inequality; they seek change by working within existing social, legal, and political structures.
- Marxist feminists focus on the unequal class and gender relations fostered by the capitalist mode of production.
- Socialist feminists apply a combination of Marxist and socialist ideas, locating the problem of inequality in class and gender conflict associated with the capitalist system, and advocating for sweeping (socialist) changes to the capitalist system, as well as an end to patriarchy.
- Radical feminists see patriarchy as present in all social relations, which requires nothing less than a radical overhaul of society and an equalizing of relations (Burgess-Proctor, 2006; Flavin, 2001).

BOX 9.2

Feminism and the War on Drugs

In recent decades, many North American governments and law enforcement agencies have pursued a "war on drugs," a multi-billion dollar effort to find, arrest, and severely punish offenders, but which has proven a failure in limiting the actual availability and consumption of drugs. However, the war on drugs has been cited as a principal contributor to harsher North American sentencing laws and increasing prison numbers. Meda Chesney-Lind (n.d.) examined the impact of the punitive turn on women when these policies began to be implemented. She noted that after 1980, female incarceration rates in the United States quintupled as a result of "gender blind, get tough policies on drugs." The "national zeal for imprisoning women," as she described it, had a particularly negative impact on women of colour: between 1986 and 1991, rates of female African-American imprisonment for drug offences rose by 828 percent, followed by 328 percent among Hispanic women and 241 percent among white women. At the same time, state budgets experienced cuts to spending on education and social assistance programs. As Chesney-Lind observed:

> What we are seeing is a mindless and massive transfer away from education and welfare into prisons. This means that monies that once went to support low-income women and their children in the community, as well as the dollars to provide her with educational opportunities, are being cut back dramatically at the same time that monies to arrest, detain, and incarcerate women and men on the economic margins are being increased. (n.d.)

More recently, similar phenomena have emerged in Canada, as female incarceration rates increased by 60 percent over the ten-year period between 2003 and 2013, and with marginalized Aboriginal and black females again being disproportionately represented in the Canadian prison population. The majority of black women are incarcerated for drug offences, including trafficking, which many of them pursued, according to interviews with these inmates, in an effort to rise above poverty (Correctional Investigator Canada, 2013).

Feminist criminologists are well represented in the field of critical criminology. They include Meda Chesney-Lind, Nicole Rafter, and James Messerschmidt in the United States, and Pat Carlen, Loraine Gelsthorpe, and Frances Heidensohn in England. Notable Canadians working in this field include Karlene Faith, Gillian Balfour, and Elizabeth Comack. Since the 1990s, Comack has contributed substantially to our understanding of women's involvement with the criminal justice system. Much of her early work centred on women's imprisonment and the means by which women became "offenders." Through this research, which revealed significant patterns of physical and sexual abuse in the histories of female offenders, she became involved in projects aimed at understanding the "standpoint" of women in trouble with the law. That is, Comack was interested in representing how female study participants saw and understood the world and their experiences within it. She also became one of the first feminist criminologists in Canada to draw attention to the concept of the "battered woman's syndrome" and the potential pitfalls surrounding its use as a legal defence (Comack, 1996).

Critical Race Theory and Post-Colonial Theory

critical race theory
A theory that examines the ways in which race and racial power are constructed by law and society, and that sees the law and criminal justice system not as solutions but as part of the problem.

post-colonial theory
The wide-ranging academic study of the social, political, and cultural legacy of colonial rule and its effects on individual and group identities and social power relations. It also examines the domination of other cultures through a discourse of "otherness."

systemic racism
The belief that racism does not occur only in isolated instances, but is entrenched in and perpetuated by our criminal justice system and other institutions.

Although they share different beginnings, critical race theory and post-colonial theory overlap in their common goal: to fight racist oppression that is built into social structures and the very fabric of society. **Critical race theory** emerged in the 1970s, becoming in the 1990s an umbrella term for a variety of theories and practices developed by African-American, Latino, and Asian-American scholars who were actively engaged in anti-racist scholarship and activism. Its roots are deeper, however, and can be found in the work of intellectuals such as 19th-century social reformer Frederick Douglass and early 20th-century sociologist and activist W.E.B. Du Bois. Critical race scholars have been instrumental in taking apart "essentialist" ideas of race that consider it as a biological category. Rather, for these scholars, race is a social category or "construct"—a meaning created by society that is placed upon a person, significantly affecting his or her opportunities in life. Opportunities are open or closed to people not simply because other individuals carry prejudiced ideas around in their heads, but because racism exists within social relations, practices, and institutions. By contrast, **post-colonial theory** was developed largely from the struggles for political freedom among many former colonies of Britain, France, and other European powers. Frantz Fanon's *Black Skin, White Masks* (1952/2008) is a key anti-colonial text that documents the terrible effects of colonialism on the psyches of individuals. Post-colonial theory helps us understand how racialized relations play out across the globe and influence how we view and thus treat "the other."

Much of the work conducted by critical criminologists using these perspectives focuses on two important issues. One of these is the problem of **systemic racism** in the criminal justice system and its effects on people of colour. A significant early essay that tackled this issue was Robert Staples's *White Racism, Black Crime, and American Justice* (1975). Staples used Fanon's ideas on colonialism to explain "the American pattern of racial dominance and subjugation" evidenced in the overpolicing of black communities and the ill-treatment of black citizens by police and the larger justice system (Staples, 1975, p. 14). Such maltreatment, he noted, is often justified by references to higher rates of violent offences within black communities ("black on black" crime), a social fact that Staples acknowledges and explains. Violence within colonized groups, he argues, is not unusual in that the colonized have absorbed the aggressiveness of the dominant community that has attempted to impose its cultural values upon them. The result is displaced aggression. A further significant contribution of critical criminologists in this area has been their critiques of the discipline of criminology itself and the means by which criminologists contribute to forms of oppression at home and abroad. One such example is the work of Tamari Kitossa (2012), who notes that critical race theory challenges mainstream criminology by uncovering its underlying racialized assumptions.

A number of criminologists draw inspiration from these theories, including Coretta Phillips in England and Elijah Anderson in the United States. In Canada, Renisa Mawani uses post-colonial theories to better understand how legal rules are used and applied in the social world. Using historical case studies, Mawani (2009) shows how racialized fears of "the other" by white Canadian colonists led to various forms of social control targeting Aboriginal peoples and non-European migrants. What Mawani reveals is how the history of race relations—in particular white anxieties—led to the creation of racist forms of law. Mawani's work is more than just a look back at some long-forgotten time. For example, the racist stereotypes associated with First Nations peoples and alcohol originated in the belief that Aboriginal drinking was a product of their purported lack of civilization. It was feared that through alcohol consumption, they would become even more "barbaric." Thus, the development of strict liquor restrictions aimed at controlling who could sell and buy alcohol continues today. Mawani argues that whenever we discuss multiculturalism and the pluralist society that Canada has supposedly become, we are always doing so within the context of a colonialist history that was far from benign.

BOX 9.3

Racial Profiling

Although much of the discussion in this chapter has focused on incarceration rates (i.e., sentencing), policing policies also play a significant role in this phenomenon. Ben Bowling, for example, has explored how policing systems unfairly target black and other minority communities. (The tendency for law enforcement officers to make assumptions about someone's potential involvement in criminal activity based on the colour of their skin or their ethnicity is known as **racial profiling**; see Case Study 9.1 preceding this chapter.) Bowling's review of claims by the New York police that "zero tolerance" policing reduced that city's homicide rate reveals how aggressive crackdowns against people of colour (often for very minor offences, such as subway turnstile jumping) had little effect on the violent crime rate, which was already in decline. Looking at the British context, Bowling and Coretta Phillips (2002) have drawn attention to the overrepresentation of ethnic minorities among deaths in police custody and to the police practice of "stop and frisk," which entails conducting random spot searches of "suspect" minority youth, some as young as ten years old.

racial profiling
The act or tendency of law enforcement officers and others to consider people suspicious or more likely to commit crime because of the colour of their skin or their ethnicity.

Left Realism

In response to what is often termed the "left idealist" view of neo-Marxism, a number of critical criminologists began in the 1980s to advocate for a socially progressive form of criminology that was tempered by an awareness of the realities of crime. Where neo-Marxist scholars had focused largely on white-collar crime and other crimes of the elite, the "left realist" branch of criminology, as it came to be known, explored crime and criminality more broadly. Left realist scholars started from the position that crime is a serious issue rooted in social conditions, the dynamics of which needed to be better understood and addressed in order to offer practical solutions. To help in this process, they expanded upon the basic crime triangle—the offender, the victim, and the state— by introducing the "square of crime," which includes a fourth element: informal social controls within civil society.

Aside from widening the criminological lens, left realists have drawn attention to what are seen as three important and interrelated concepts for understanding the nature of crime within Western societies.

The first of these concepts is *relative deprivation*. Building upon Robert Merton's earlier work on anomie-strain theory (described in Chapter 12, Sociological Approaches), relative deprivation, and reference group theory, left realists have argued that crime is more likely in situations where members of a particular group experience discontent as a result of being deprived of things to which other groups have access (Lea & Young, 1984; Young, 1999). For example, a number of years ago a young man walking at night through a park in Vancouver was assaulted in what police described as a "swarming incident." A group of youths had surrounded him for the sole purpose of taking his running shoes. The idea of attacking someone for his or her running shoes might seem like odd, random violence. However, this incident makes better sense when one considers that at the time, Air Jordans were highly desirable, and many of the young people within this community were not able to afford them.

A second important concept for left realists is *subculture*. A subculture is a segment of society that forms in response to a shared problem, and which possesses its own distinctive patterns of beliefs, values, mores, and expressions. Historically, much of the earlier Chicago School work on subculture formation focused on marginalized youth (see Chapter 12, Sociological Approaches, for more on the Chicago School). Left realism has expanded this focus to include the formation of subcultures among middle-class youth and the forces that drive them to offend.

The third concept is *marginalization*, which refers to the social and economic processes that lead some groups to be excluded from opportunities available to others. The result is that group members find themselves as social outcasts on the borders of society, looking in at those who are in the privileged position of being able to achieve the desired fame, fortune, and/or social standing. Returning to the example of the running shoes, we can begin to see how being exposed to socially desirable goals and objects when one is locked out of legitimate means of acquiring them can lead frustrations to boil over.

Although originating in England with key thinkers such as Jock Young, John Lea, Richard Kinsey, and Roger Matthews, left realism has had a wide influence in North America and elsewhere. For example, in the United States, left realism is commonly associated with the work of Elliott Currie and Martin Schwartz. In Canada, the left realist perspective has been exemplified by the work of Walter DeKeseredy. In recent decades, DeKeseredy and colleagues have explored the social, economic, and political forces that result in violence against women. For example, in a recent study, DeKeseredy and Schwartz (2010) examined how marginalized male youth, increasingly excluded from the formal economy due to the economic crisis, come into contact with others to form subcultures leading to criminal behaviour. DeKeseredy has also turned his left realist scope to the issue of violence against women, notably exploring how the relationship between the North American masculine ideal—the economically successful male—and the reality of increasing economic disenfranchisement leads men within certain subcultures and communities to attempt to reassert masculinity through violence against women (DeKeseredy, Alvi, & Schwartz, 2006).

"The Exclusive Society"

In relation to the punitive turn, a key text is Jock Young's *The Exclusive Society* (1999). In it, Young argues that the punitive turn is linked to economic changes that are making life increasingly precarious, not only for the poor and working class but also for middle-class families who fear poverty and overt symbols of poverty. As Young explains, relative deprivation is not just about the poor and working classes looking upward; it is also about the middle classes looking down the social hierarchy to reassure themselves that there *are* people below them. In a time of increasing economic and social instability, looking downward produces fear, because it reminds the middle classes of the often precarious state of their economic existence. This fear, Young suggests, underlies increased intolerance of marginalized groups and support for harsher treatment of offenders and other "deviant" groups.

BOX 9.4

A Case of "Affluenza"

In June 2013, news emerged of an affluent Texas teenager, Ethan Couch, who had killed four people while driving drunk. What made this all-too-common tragedy particularly newsworthy was the startling fact that he was able to avoid severe punishment because his defence team had successfully argued that he suffered from what has been dubbed "affluenza." Some believe that people with this condition, which is seen as an outgrowth of increasing social inequality, suffer from a form of mental illness and acute social alienation due to their extreme wealth, which effectively renders them unable to properly understand the consequences of their actions.

Not surprisingly, the case generated extensive debate about sentencing practices, as well as whether this was even a legitimate psychological condition. Boyce Watkins drew on the title of Jeffrey Reiman's famous book (see Box 9.1) in writing his response to the case, entitled "Rich, White Kids Have 'Affluenza,' Poor, Black Kids Go to Prison":

> The very idea that this kid's wealth was turned into a convenient liability lies in contradiction to the fact that his wealth has always been a tremendous asset. It's allowed him to get whatever he wants, whenever he wants. But when the spoiled rich kid's actions finally catch up with him, the very thing that's given him an advantage is suddenly considered to be a huge disadvantage. … This case is even more sickening when one considers how often serious psychological problems are not taken into consideration when the cases involve poor, Black or brown people. How often do our kids commit crimes after being victims of years of abuse, neglect, hunger, miseducation and dire poverty? When my deceased uncle … was sent to prison, I never once heard a judge consider the fact that he suffered from severe mental illness all throughout his life. In fact, going to prison only served to worsen his mental illness, not make it better.

In what ways might this case be considered an example of "the exclusive society" described by Jock Young?

Source: http://newpittsburghcourieronline.com/2013/12/15/rich-white-kids-have-affluenza-poor-black-kids-go-to-prison/.

Post-Structuralism

post-structuralism

A theoretical perspective concerned with how power operates between and among individuals, groups, and social institutions (as opposed to belonging to the state or power elites alone). Post-structuralists look for differences in power in areas such as language use and social practices.

Post-structuralist[5] criminology also developed as a reaction against prevailing ways of looking at crime: Marxism and structural functionalism. Despite their fundamental differences, Marxism (conflict theory) and structural functionalism (consensus theory) are perspectives that share two common features: first, they both focus on the structure of societies and how the operation of the various parts of society support the state; and second, they both assume that individuals can stand outside of a social system in order to critique it. Post-structuralists counter that power and prospects for oppression permeate all levels of society. To illustrate, just consider how different and yet similarly unequal relations could be between a parent and a child, a teacher and a student, two lovers, or a boss and a worker.

Post-structuralists also argue that one can never stand outside of a social system as an objective, neutral observer. They point out that our understanding of social and natural "realities" is dependent upon language, and that the acts of naming, describing, and understanding phenomena vary across time and culture; therefore, it necessarily follows that interpretations of social reality will always be based on our subjective point of view. In fact, they argue that language wholly shapes our understanding of the world and what constitutes "knowledge," and thus guides our actions, often in unthinking ways. Drawing on the work of Michel Foucault, the term post-structuralists employ to describe this phenomenon is **discourse**. As an example, groups within criminology and criminal justice use discourse to communicate shared meanings with other group members. Police talk about "bad guys," corrections officers might refer to someone as a "DO" (dangerous offender), and criminologists might call themselves "quants" (quantitative researchers) or be interested in "RJ" (restorative justice).

discourses

Refers to forms of language, representation, and practices and how meaning is created and shared. Discourses take place within specific cultural and historical contexts.

Foucault's work on historical changes in the nature of social control within a variety of social contexts provided a foundation for post-structuralism during the 1990s. Foucault (1979) described how different societies in different epochs dealt with punishment, sexuality, and the treatment of insanity and criminality. Indeed, after reading Foucault's work, as well as the writings of other prominent post-structuralist theorists (such as Jacques Derrida and Gilles Deleuze), a number of criminologists began to adopt post-structuralist theories, concepts, and methodological techniques.

In the United Kingdom, a group of Foucauldian scholars emerged in the 1990s, including criminologist Nikolas Rose. Other key post-structuralist criminologists include Pat O'Malley in Australia and David Garland in the United States, as well as legal scholar Jonathan Simon (also in the United States). Canadian criminologists have also drawn on post-structuralist theory and methodology to explain crime and criminal justice. Among them is Stéphane Leman-Langlois, who has conducted extensive research on human rights and post-conflict efforts in addressing human rights violations. His approach to these issues is to examine the discourses that structure both our understanding of what has taken place and how we develop modes of moving forward. For example, looking at the South African Truth and Reconciliation Commission (TRC), established in the mid-1990s after the fall of apartheid in that country, Leman-Langlois (2000) points to the creation of a language (or "discourse") that sought to legitimize the commission in the eyes of victims of human rights abuses and the larger society, at the same time excluding the possibility of offenders being punished or forced to provide compensation to victims. Similarly, Leman-Langlois has employed a post-structuralist framework to explore other ways in which "human rights" language operates as discourse, as well as aspects of how we think, speak, and act about issues such as surveillance and terrorism.

BOX 9.5

A "Culture of Control"

Among notable post-structuralist scholars who have explored the punitive turn is David Garland. In his 2001 book, *Culture of Control*, Garland draws on his **Foucauldian** roots to argue that punishment and other forms of social control are tied to social forces that can often be understood only in hindsight. The turn to more punitive forms of social control, which Garland traces to the 1970s, is an example of this phenomenon. The 1960s were turbulent times, in which all levels of society underwent significant economic, social, and demographic changes. The resulting uncertainty led people to become increasingly anxious for themselves and their families, and their anxieties consequently began to centre on what were considered "criminal threats." In criminal justice circles, an influential study on offender rehabilitation argued that "nothing works" (Martinson, 1974). Politicians, the public, and some criminologists and criminal justice officials latched onto the idea that "nothing works." The outcome was a shift in the discourse on how prisons and offenders were viewed, which resulted in major cutbacks to prison rehabilitation programs and lengthier offender sentences. As Garland notes, in the United States, little to no focus has been placed on rehabilitating the offender. Instead, "the prison is used today as a kind of reservation, a quarantine zone in which purportedly dangerous individuals are segregated in the name of public safety" (2001, p. 78).

Foucauldian
Relating to the works of influential French thinker Michel Foucault.

Peace-Making Criminology

Peace-making criminology is a theoretical perspective that favours a **social justice** approach to preventing and responding to crime. The ultimate goal of peace-making criminologists is the eradication of crime through policies and programs that end the suffering they believe causes crime—poverty, racism, sexism, family violence, and social alienation. Adapting a slogan from the 1960s to help state their case ("make peace, not war"), peace-making criminologists oppose oppressive criminal justice measures such as the "war on drugs." Instead, they favour empathetic approaches to social problems, treating offenders as human beings who, despite their past behaviour, still need and deserve understanding, empathy, and kindness.

While peace-making criminologists express some interest in the causes of crime, their focus is more typically on the treatment of offenders by the state. In keeping with their adoption of **restorative justice** models that seek to foster understanding and reconciliation between the offender, victim, and community, they are opposed to any form of violence enacted against offenders by the state. This opposition can be seen in their attitudes toward capital punishment, which peace-making criminologists wish to see abolished wherever it is still practised. Peace-making criminologists differ somewhat

social justice
Movement promoting the need for equality, tolerance, and fairness for all members of society, particularly with regard to different classes and the less privileged.

restorative justice
An approach to justice and sentencing, often influenced by Aboriginal culture, that emphasizes the healing and reconciliation of victims, perpetrators, and their communities, and promotes positive social engagement instead of social control.

in their attitudes toward imprisonment, however, and these differences say much about the diverse strands of thought—existentialism, Buddhism, Quakerism, Aboriginal cultural beliefs, feminism, anarchism, and neo-Marxism, among others—that underlie "peace-making criminology" (Quinney, 1995). For example, some within this group seek to reduce the use of imprisonment through the use of social justice–oriented programs (*minimalists*), whereas others oppose the use of imprisonment altogether (*abolitionists*).

Notable individuals working within the framework of the peace-making perspective include Australian restorative justice proponent John Braithwaite and Americans Hal Pepinsky, Richard Quinney, Howard Zehr, and Jeff Ferrell. A number of Canadian critical criminologists with very different theoretical approaches are also working within peace-making criminology, including Kevin Walby (who can be considered an *anarcho-abolitionist*).

A prominent advocate of restorative justice is Andrew Woolford. In various books and articles, Woolford has examined both the politics of restorative justice and its potential to engender social transformation along class, gender, race, and other lines. Recently, Woolford (2009) has explored the political nature of restorative justice, and how such programs develop (or not) within social and political environments in which different sets of actors and social forces work to support or constrain its use. He argues that while restorative justice is still a tool of governance—meaning that it is used by the state to regulate individual and group behaviours—it is also a social movement that can transform the social and political landscape of societies by eradicating social injustices. Among other projects, Woolford has also been a strong proponent for a criminology of **genocide**, an approach that explores the phenomenon of genocide from a purely criminological standpoint in order to help minimize future group conflicts.

genocide
The deliberate and systematic attempt to exterminate an entire population or subpopulation that shares a racial, religious, national, or cultural identity.

Fostering a More Humane Society

One of the first critical criminologists to tackle the problem of rising incarceration rates across the Western world was Norwegian Nils Christie. In *Limits to Pain* (1981/2007), Christie took the radical position that our current practice of criminal justice is essentially a pain delivery system that is more about a given society's willingness to inflict pain on its citizens than a perceived need to respond to acts labelled as criminal. Christie expanded upon this idea in *Crime Control as Industry* (1993/2002), wherein he demonstrated the extent to which criminal justice systems operate akin to private industries, which have continual growth as their ultimate objective. He further elaborated upon this theme in *A Suitable Amount of Crime* (2004). Long before anyone was discussing the "punitive turn," Christie drew on statistical and observational data to highlight the alarming extent to which the United States, Britain, and other Western states were expanding their penal systems through the creation of an increasing array of crimes, coupled with harsher penalties against offenders. For Christie, the **prison industrial complex** benefits only those who are employed by it or benefit from its profitability. Rather than treating individuals as "criminals" and punishing them with harsher sanctions that fail to prevent future criminal acts, he believes that we should treat the majority of offenders as individuals requiring therapeutic interventions aimed at helping them to reconcile with both their victims and the larger society. A minimalist approach to the delivery of pain, Christie suggests, would help foster a more humane society, one that will lessen the conditions that create and sustain anti-social behaviours.

prison industrial complex
Adapted from "military industrial complex"; a term used to attribute increases in incarceration rates to the efforts of private for-profit corporations that build and maintain prisons with the active legislative and financial support of their political allies.

BOX 9.6

Is There "A Suitable Amount of Crime"?

In his book *A Suitable Amount of Crime*, Norwegian criminologist Nils Christie poses many provocative questions about the role, and severity, of punishment in Western societies:

> How large can we let the penal system grow, or conversely, how small can we have it, if we need it at all? Is it possible to establish upper, and eventually lower, limits to the amount of punishment that ought to be applied in a modern society? And lastly, for those of us working close to this field, is it possible to influence what happens? ... Is it possible to establish *some sort of criteria* for what might be seen as the suitable amount of punishment in a society? ... Turned into questions of the evaluation of the volume and of the life conditions of prisoners in modern times, when is enough, enough? And when is it more than enough? Where is the limit in modern societies? When has a prison population in a country reached a level when at least our intuition says that this is wrong, completely wrong, unacceptable! And when are life conditions below dignity? We have some intuitive answers. ... But is it possible to anchor views from the heart to some sort of reasoning? Let me attempt to do so by the discussion of three cases of *IF*.
>
> 1. IF we believe in the values of kindness and forgiving—then we ought to keep the institution of penal law a small one ...
> 2. IF we believe in the values of keeping civil societies civil—then we have to keep the institution of penal law a small one ...
> 3. IF we believe in the value of living in cohesive, integrated societies—then we must retard the growth of the institution of penal law ...

An essential question for us in the Nordic countries, and also in Western Europe and Canada, is whether the developments in the US are inevitable. Are they a consequence of their economic system? And will welfare states also gradually face consequences similar to the US model, consequences that will lead to increased class differentiation as well as to increased uncertainty among the population at large? We observe how the criminal policies of a number of industrial nations are becoming a central arena for presentation by politicians. ... Uncertainties are muffled by political promises about severe measures to be taken against *offenders*, a term that gradually has become a euphemism for *the lower-lower classes*, a term that may become a euphemism for *the dangerous classes* or in certain countries people of the wrong colour.

Source: Excerpted from Nils Christie, *A Suitable Amount of Crime* (pp. 101–107). London: Routledge, 2004.

Conclusion

Although considerable overlap exists among the various branches of critical criminology, each branch has a distinct approach to theory and policy. Some critical criminologists call for a minimalist approach to state intervention, whereas others are outright abolitionists and call for the total abolition of imprisonment and capital punishment. Some come from a neo-Marxist perspective, while others come from a Foucauldian (or post-structuralist) perspective. The left realists have turned away from the neo-Marxist perspective that dominated much of critical criminology in the 1970s and focus instead on what can be done to ameliorate what they regard to be the criminogenic (crime-causing) conditions associated with capitalism (Young, 2002). Despite the diverse approaches, critical criminologists have by and large emerged from the conflict perspective in criminology. In other words, they consider that society and its laws are based on social conflict, not social consensus. Critical criminologists are united in challenging our basic assumptions about the existing social order and the purpose of law, arguing that the law primarily serves the interests of the power elite, not the interests of the marginalized, oppressed classes in society. They are typically unconcerned about "criminal motivation" (a preoccupation of most mainstream criminologists), because they start with the assumption that crime is the result of economic and political inequality. Putting people in prison or executing them does not resolve long-standing social problems like poverty, unemployment, and marginalization.

In many respects, critical criminology has acted as "the conscience" of mainstream (or orthodox) criminology, asking why criminologists traditionally spend so much of their time studying only those who are defined by the state as deviant, and/or obsessively measuring the criminalization of the lower classes. It also questions why "suite crime" (white-collar crime) is often regarded as a civil violation or simply as a shrewd business practice, whereas "street crime" is usually met with the full force of the criminal justice system. As Jock Young argues in *Critical Criminology in the Twenty-First Century: Critique, Irony, and the Always Unfinished* (2002), all criminology should be "critical." Criminologists should reflect on what they are doing, asking themselves who they are doing it for, and why.

SUMMARY OF KEY POINTS

- *Critical criminology* encompasses a broad range of criminological theories and perspectives, all of which share a desire to challenge inequality. This approach is applied not only to any oppressive treatment or practices found within the criminal justice system, but also to discussions about how crime is defined, and extends to discussions about the goals of criminology itself.

- The starting point for critical criminology is the assumption that *power* is unequally distributed throughout society and that this is also true when it comes to crime and criminal justice. A critical criminologist's task is not simply to find and call attention to oppression, but to actively oppose it.

- A shift in criminal justice policies and programs from those aimed at rehabilitating offenders toward those that simply offer punishment for its own sake is referred to by critical criminologists as *the punitive turn*.

- *Neo-Marxist* criminologists focus on how the state uses the criminal justice system to legitimize unequal social arrangements through laws that cater to elite groups while oppressing the working class, the poor, and other marginalized groups. Neo-Marxists are typically referred to as *conflict theorists*, because they hold that society is not built on consensus but, rather, on class conflict.

- *Feminist criminologists*—of which there are many streams—generally seek to challenge gender norms and assumptions, as well as uncover systemic biases, in order to equalize treatment of women within law, the criminal justice system, and the larger society.

- *Critical race theory* and *post-colonial theory* overlap in their goal to fight racist oppression that is built into social structures and the very fabric of society. A key area of focus is the view that criminal justice institutions—the police, the courts, and so on—are inherently racist—that is, they are an example of *systemic racism*.

- *Left realist* criminology explores crime and criminality more broadly, starting from the position that crime is a serious issue rooted in social conditions, the dynamics of which need to be better understood and addressed in order to offer practical solutions. They expand upon the basic crime triangle—the offender, the victim, and the state—by introducing the "square of crime," which includes a fourth element: informal social controls within civil society.

- *Post-structuralism* is a theoretical perspective that has been applied to criminology, which is concerned with how power operates between and among individuals, groups, and social institutions, as opposed to belonging to the state or power elites alone. Post-structuralists examine power in relation to, in particular, language and social practices.

NOTES

The author wishes to thank Barry Cartwright for his assistance on this chapter.

1. Correctional supervision encompasses not only incarceration (local jails, and state and federal prisons) but also community corrections (probation and parole).
2. This offence was previously dealt with under general *Criminal Code* provisions for "theft," or "taking motor-vehicle … without consent."
3. It should be noted that conflict theory is not necessarily the sole domain of critical criminology. Notable conflict theorists who came onto the scene prior to the advent of critical criminology include Thorsten Sellin and Austin Turk.
4. "Commodity" in this sense refers to the fact that private security is a contract service; thus, it represents something that can be bought and sold.
5. In critical criminology literature, *post-structuralism* is often confused or conflated with *postmodernism*, likely because both of these relatively recent philosophies focus on language as a key component to understanding how we view the world.

QUESTIONS FOR CRITICAL DISCUSSION

1. Consider the ways in which critical criminologists examine the practice of criminal justice in Canada, and elsewhere. In what ways do their critiques raise questions about economics or politics? To what extent do you think problems of crime are the result of economic factors?
2. How does the use of the term *critical* in this differ from its more common usage?
3. How can critical criminology be applied in concrete ways to the study of criminology and criminal justice? Provide examples.
4. What critiques do you imagine other criminologists make of critical criminology? Give reasons and examples for your answers.
5. Review the excerpt in Box 9.1. How applicable to Canada are Jeffrey Reiman's observations about the US criminal justice system?
6. Compare critical criminology to the other schools of criminological theory that are presented in the other chapters of Part 3. Where do you see overlaps or similarities? In which other school(s) of thought might you find thinkers who are most at odds with the tenets of critical criminology?

SUGGESTED FURTHER READINGS

Bowling, B., & Phillips, C. (2002). *Racism, crime and justice*. London, UK: Longman.

Christie, N. (2004). *A suitable amount of crime*. London, UK: Routledge.

Comack, E. (1996). Women in trouble: Connecting women's law violations to their histories of abuse. Halifax: Fernwood.

Fanon, F. (1952/2008). *Black skin, white masks*. New York: Grove.

Foucault, M. (1979). *Discipline and punish: The birth of the prison* (A. Sheridan, Trans.). New York: Vintage.

Reiman, J. (1979/2004). *The rich get richer and the poor get prison: Ideology, class, and criminal justice* (7th ed.). Boston: Allyn and Bacon/Pearson.

Websites

Critical Criminology Information and Resources: http://www.critcrim.org

Critical Criminology: An International Journal: http://critcrim.org/journal

Critical Criminology Working Group (Kwantlen University) and Radical Criminology (an open journal): http://radicalcriminology.org

Ontario Human Rights Commission eLearning: Information on human rights issues, including racial profiling: http://www.ohrc.on.ca/en/learning

Michel Foucault, History Learning Site: Information on Foucault's views on crime and deviance: http://www.historylearningsite.co.uk/michel_foucault.htm

Restorative Justice (Correctional Service Canada): http://www.csc-scc.gc.ca/restorative-justice/index-eng.shtml

REFERENCES

Bowling, B., & Phillips, C. (2002). *Racism, crime and justice*. London, UK: Longman.

Brennan, S. (2012). *Police-reported crime statistics in Canada, 2011*. Ottawa: Statistics Canada.

Burgess-Proctor, A. (2006). Intersections of race, class, gender and crime: Future directions for feminist criminology. *Feminist Criminology, 1*(1), 27–47.

Caplow, T., & Simon, J. (1999). Understanding prison policy and population trends. In M. Tonry & J. Petersilia (Eds.), *Prisons* (pp. 63–120). Chicago: University of Chicago Press.

Chambliss, W., & Seidman, R. (1971). *Law, order, and power*. Reading, MA: Addison-Wesley.

Chesney-Lind, M. (n.d.). Feminism and critical criminology: Toward a feminist praxis. *Critical Criminology*. Retrieved from http://critcrim.org/critpapers/chesney-lind1.htm.

Christie, N. (1981/2007). *Limits to pain: The role of punishment in penal policy*. London: Wipf & Stock.

Christie, N. (1993/2002). *Crime control as industry*. London, UK: Routledge.

Christie, N. (2004). *A suitable amount of crime*. London, UK: Routledge.

Comack, E. (1996). *Women in trouble: Connecting women's law violations to their histories of abuse*. Halifax: Fernwood.

Correctional Investigator Canada (2013). *Annual report of the Office of the Correctional Investigator, 2012–2013*. Ottawa: Government of Canada.

Daly, K., & Chesney-Lind, M. (1988). Feminism and criminology. *Justice Quarterly, 5*(4), 497–538.

DeKeseredy, W., Alvi, S., & Schwartz, M. (2006). Curbing woman abuse and poverty: Is "Wedfare" the cure? *Critical Criminology, 14*(1), 23–41.

DeKeseredy, W., & Schwartz, M. (2010). Friedman economic policies, social exclusion, and crime: Toward a gendered left realist subcultural theory. *Crime, Law and Social Change, 54*(2), 159–170.

Fanon, F. (1952/2008). *Black skin, white masks*. New York: Grove Press.

Federal Bureau of Investigation (FBI). (2011). FBI releases 2011 crime statistics. *FBI*. Retrieved from http://www.fbi.gov/about-us/cjis/ucr/crime-in-the-u.s/2011/crime-in-the-u.s.-2011/fbi-releases-2011-crime-statistics

Flavin, J. (2001). Feminism for the mainstream criminologist: An invitation. *Journal of Criminal Justice, 29*(4), 271–285.

Foucault, M. (1979). *Discipline and punish: The birth of the prison* (A. Sheridan, Trans.). New York: Vintage.

Garland, D. (2001). *The culture of control: Crime and social order in contemporary society*. Chicago: University of Chicago Press.

Glaze, L.E., & Herberman, E.J. (2013, December 19). *Correctional populations in the United States, 2012*. Washington, DC: Bureau of Justice Statistics (BJS). Retrieved from http://www.bjs.gov/content/pub/pdf/cpus12.pdf.

Griffin, M. (2010). Feminist criminology: Beyond the slaying of dragons. In H.D. Barlow & S.H. Decker (Eds.), *Criminology and public policy: Putting theory to work* (pp. 215–232). Philadelphia: Temple University Press.

Hall, S., Critcher, C., Jefferson, T., Clarke, J., & Roberts, B. (1978). *Policing the crisis: Mugging, the state and law and order*. London, UK: Palgrave Macmillan.

Kitossa, T. (2012). Criminology and colonialism: Counter colonial criminology and the Canadian context. *The Journal of Pan African Studies, 4*(10), 204–226.

Lea, J., & Young, J. (1984). *What is to be done about: law and order?* Harmondsworth, UK: Penguin.

Leman-Langlois, S. (2000). Mobilizing victimization: The construction of a victim-centred approach in the South African Truth and Reconciliation Commission. *Criminologie, 33*(1), 145–166.

Martinson, R. (1974). What works? Questions and answers about prison reform. *The Public Interest, 35*, 22–54.

Mawani, R. (2009). *Colonial perspectives: Crossracial encounters and juridical truths in British Columbia, 1871–1921*. Vancouver: UBC Press.

Maynard v. Toronto Police Services Board. (2012). 2012 HRTO 1220.

Meyer, J., & O'Malley, P. (2005). Missing the punitive turn? Canadian criminal justice, "balance," and penal modernism. In J. Pratt, D. Brown, M. Brown, S. Hallsworth, & W. Morrison (Eds.), *The new punitiveness: Trends, theories, perspectives* (pp. 201–217). Cullompton, UK: Willan.

Milovanovic, D. (2002). *Critical criminology at the edge: Postmodern perspectives, integration and applications*. Westport, CT: Praeger.

Quinney, R. (1977). *Class, state and crime: On the theories and practices of criminal justice*. New York: David McKay.

Quinney, R. (1995). Socialist humanism and the problem of crime: Thinking about Erich Fromm in the development of critical/peacemaking criminology. *Crime, Law & Social Change, 23*(2), 147–156.

Reiman, J. (1979/2004). *The rich get richer and the poor get prison: Ideology, class, and criminal justice* (7th ed.). Boston: Allyn and Bacon/Pearson.

Rigakos, G., & Ergul, A. (2011). Policing the industrial reserve army: An international study. *Crime, Law and Social Change, 56*(4), 329–371.

Simon, J. (2007). *Governing through crime: How the war on crime transformed American democracy and created a culture of fear*. New York: Oxford University Press.

Staples, R. (1975). White racism, Black crime, and American justice: An application of the colonial model to explain crime and race. *Phylon, 36*(1), 14–22.

Taylor, I., Walton, P., & Young, J. (1973). *The new criminology: For a social theory of deviance.* London, UK: Routledge.

Taylor, I., Walton, P., & Young, J. (1975). Critical criminology in Britain: Review and prospects. In I. Taylor, P. Walton, & J. Young (Eds.), *Critical criminology* (pp. 6–62). London, UK: Routledge and Kegan Paul.

Tonry, M. (2004). *Thinking about crime: Sense and sensibility in American penal culture.* New York: Oxford University Press.

Wacquant, L. (2009). *Punishing the poor: The Neoliberal government of social insecurity.* Durham, NC: Duke University Press.

Woolford, A. (2009). *The politics of restorative justice: A critical introduction.* Halifax: Fernwood.

Young, J. (1999). *The exclusive society.* London, UK: Sage.

Young, J. (2002). Critical criminology in the twenty-first century: Critique, irony, and the always unfinished. In K Carrington, R. Hogg, & D. Cullompton (Eds.), *Critical criminology: Issues, debates and challenges* (pp. 63–94). Devon, UK: Willan.

Mark Chahal's "Revenge": Gendered Violence

A woman lays a rose and a candle at the memorial to the nine people murdered in Vernon, British Columbia.

Source: Daniel Hayduk/Castanet.

In April 1996, 30-year-old accountant Mark Chahal left his apartment in the Lower Mainland of Vancouver to drive to Vernon, British Columbia. Chahal had been separated from his wife Rajwar Gakhal for about a year. He was carrying a shotgun and two handguns in his red Nissan. Chahal knew that Gakhal's family was gathering that weekend in Vernon to celebrate the marriage of her younger sister.

Chahal's marriage to Gakhal had been short-lived. She had left Chahal after only a few months, moving into her parents' home, and citing physical abuse as the reason for the end of their relationship. Chahal had continued to threaten his estranged wife and Gakhal had gone to police for assistance on several occasions.

Chahal arrived at the Vernon home at about 10:30 on the Friday morning before the wedding. He was carrying two handguns as he walked up the driveway. "One in each hand, just like the old western-style shooters," said a neighbour. Chahal first encountered his father-in-law, washing one of the family's cars. He shot him in the face; he died instantly. Amidst the sounds of screams, Chahal walked into the house and continued firing, killing his ex-wife, her mother, her sisters, her brother and brother-in-law, and her grandmother. He then left through the back door of the house and drove away.

When police arrived a short time later, they found six people dead; three more found at the scene died later in hospital. After leaving the house, Chahal returned to his rented motel room in Vernon and shot himself, dying instantly. He had written a note, apologizing for what he had done and asking the police to call his family to tell them of his death.

"The motive that we're pursuing," RCMP Sergeant Doug Hartl said the day following the killings, "is that he chose to take revenge on the entire family" ("Gunman 'took revenge' on family," 1996).

In the aftermath of the murders, a number of different explanations, both competing and complementary, were put forward for the violence. Some commentators focused on the fact that Mark Chahal had obtained his handguns and other firearms legally, despite the fact that the police knew that complaints of violence had been lodged by his estranged wife.

Others noted that the marriage of Chahal and Gakhal was an arranged marriage. It was suggested that although this fact could neither fully explain nor justify what happened, there would necessarily be conflicting expectations between traditional, conservative Sikh culture and liberal Western culture in which marriage is typically based on freely chosen romantic and emotional commitments.

Domestic violence is a cause for serious concern. In Canada, women who die at the hands of their estranged spouse or common law partner represent 10 percent of total solved homicides (Sinh, 2012, p. 20). A close friend of the Gakhal family said, "I think all women in abusive situations should be aware of the reality that this can happen" (Talreja, 1996).

And then there is the issue of imagining whether this kind of killing could have been perpetrated by a woman, estranged from her husband. Is it difficult to construct a scenario in which a woman, rejected by her husband, might seek the kind of revenge perpetrated by Mark Chahal? Was the seething anger of Chahal essentially a patriarchal sentiment, unlikely to find expression in a woman who might find herself separated from her husband?

Communications professor Yasmin Jiwani (2006) of Concordia University has written of Chahal and noted that after the murders took place, the manager of the rifle club to which Chahal belonged said, "Guys go bonkers ... If a guy goes nuts, he goes nuts" (p. 99). Jiwani observed:

> Here, the murders are explained away in the language of common sense—as normalized responses to the breakup of a relationship and as expressions of rage. That it is normal to express such rage through gendered violence remains unexamined. (p. 99)

Before You Read Chapter 10

- Is Yasmin Jiwani correct? Is this male rage being "explained away" or "justified" in some way?
- Is male violence fundamentally different in form and character from female violence?
- What might this case and others like it suggest to us about the gendered nature of violence?

Gender and Crime

<table>
<tr>
<td>

LEARNING OBJECTIVES

After reading this chapter, students will be able to

- Identify key gender differences in patterns of criminal offending and victimization.
- Understand the nature of the narrowing gender gap in arrests for violent crime that has taken place in recent decades.
- Describe how criminological theories explain differences in male and female offending patterns.
- Understand the rudiments of social learning and gender role theories, control perspectives, general strain theory, and feminist perspectives on crime.
- Explain some of the reasons youths join urban street gangs and how girls and boys differ in their motivations.
- Identify risk factors associated with femicide and homicide.

</td>
<td>

CHAPTER OUTLINE

</td>
</tr>
</table>

Introduction

Gender is a powerful correlate of criminal behaviour. A multitude of data sources, including police official arrest data, criminal court records, victimization surveys, and self-report surveys, reveal that men far exceed women in their rates of participation in an array of criminal behaviours. Yet, until recently, little research compared women and men in their motivations for and participation in crime; even less work directed attention to the nature and context of female criminality. The last 30 years has seen significant growth in the literature on gender and crime. This chapter explores this literature, addressing several key questions: How do women and men differ in terms of the types of crime they commit? Do women and men experience different motivations, prior victimizations, and social relationships that encourage their involvement in crime? What explanations have been offered to address the **gender gap** (the "gender ratio" problem) in crime? Is it possible to explain female criminality with mainstream theories of crime that were originally developed to explain male criminality (the **generalization problem**)?[1] What is a feminist theory of crime? Is gender central to understanding definitions of crime and responses to crime?

This chapter aims to achieve three goals: (1) to provide an overview of gender differences in criminal offending and victimization; (2) to offer an introduction to contemporary theories of the gender gap in crime; and (3) to highlight research studies that examine gender differences and similarities in criminal offending and victimization, including gangs and urban crime, intimate partner violence, and homicide and femicide.

gender gap
The difference between men and women in areas such as social, political, and economic attainment; a persistent finding in criminology is that men commit more crime than women.

generalization problem
The question of whether it is possible to explain female criminality with mainstream theories of crime that were originally developed to explain male criminality.

Trends in the Gender Gap in Criminal Offending

This section outlines some of the main gender differences in criminal offending in Canada. Where do we see the greatest contrast and similarity between men and women?

At first glance, official data suggest a high level of similarity between the criminal behaviour of women and men. In Canada, the Uniform Crime Reporting Survey (UCR) data, compiled by the Canadian Centre for Justice Statistics, demonstrate that men and women tend to engage in similar crimes. These data show that theft under $5,000 topped the list for women and was second for men. Assault—level 1 (an offence that does not involve a weapon or serious bodily harm) ranked second for women and first for men (Mahony, 2011, p. 20). The dramatic difference in male and female offending is not so much in the types of crime, but the volume of criminal offending.

Many more men are arrested each year than women. In fact, more than three times as many men as women were arrested in 2009 in Canada (Mahony, 2011, p. 20). In 2009 the total arrest rate for *Criminal Code* violations by adult men was 1,460 (per 100,000 men in the population); for women, the rate was 372. The differences in arrest rates are particularly pronounced for serious violent offences. Men vastly outnumbered women in the serious violent crimes of homicide (seven times the rate of women), attempted murder (six times the rate of women), sexual assault, assault, robbery, arson, break and enter, motor vehicle theft, and forcible confinement, kidnapping, or abduction. The smallest gender gaps in offending were for relatively less serious property crimes such as theft under $5,000, fraud, and possession of stolen goods (Mahony, 2011, p. 20).[2]

Patterns among youths largely parallel those among adults. In Canada, the Canadian Centre for Justice Statistics reported that the top arrest categories in 2009 for girls (12 to 17 years of age) were as follows:

1. theft of $5,000 or under,
2. assault—level 1,
3. mischief, and
4. uttering threats.

For boys (12 to 17 years of age), the top arrest categories in 2009 were as follows:

1. theft under $5,000 or under,
2. mischief,
3. assault—level 1, and
4. break and enter (Mahony, 2011, p. 20).

Although there are similarities in the rank order of criminal arrests for boys and girls, boys far outpace girls in their sheer volume of arrests. Male youths have twice the arrest rate of female youths (2,582 compared with 1,066 per 100,000) for violent *Criminal Code* violations (Mahony, 2011, p. 20). In sum, arrest data reveal similarities across gender (youths and adults) in the types of crime committed, with the most impressive difference in the sheer volume of male offending, a gender difference that is particularly pronounced for violent crimes.

A Narrowing of the Gender Gap in Crime over Time

The bigger question is whether this gender gap in crime has persisted or changed over time. Canadian crime data are displayed in Figure 10.1. This figure presents women as a percentage of adults charged with *Criminal Code* offences from 1979 to 2009. At first glance, it appears that women's involvement in violent crime has been on a steady rise since the late 1980s, and certainly women's share of property crime appears to have increased during the late 1980s and again since 2003. However, the figure represents only women as a percentage of adults charged with *Criminal Code* offences. Perhaps men are committing fewer crimes and, therefore, a constant rate of female offending (or a less dramatic decline in female offending) might mean that women make up a greater share of the total offending. Perhaps both men and women are participating more in crime, but women's crime rates are increasing at a faster rate, making up a greater share of the total. Focusing on the percentage increases in women's offences alone is not particularly helpful either, because the very low base numbers lead us to see dramatic percentage increases. So, what do the rising percentages in Figure 10.1 tell us about women's rates of offending? Are women becoming more violent? Are women engaged in more property offences and crime generally? Is there more to this crime story?

The background to these questions, which evolved into a debate, started in the mid-1970s with the publishing of two influential books: *Women and Crime* (Simon, 1975) and *Sisters in Crime: The Rise of the New Female Criminal* (Adler, 1975). Freda Adler and Rita Simon each reported that women's rates of crime and violence were increasing at a faster rate than those of men. The result was a narrowing of the gender gap in offending.

FIGURE 10.1   Women as a Percentage of Adults Charged with Criminal Code Offences, 1979-2009

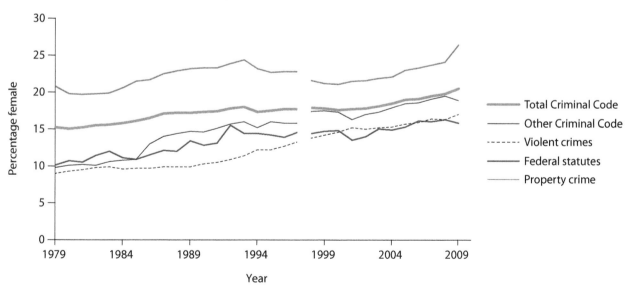

Note: Due to the introduction of revised offence category definitions to better reflect those used by the policing community, there is a break in the series in 1998. Data excludes traffic violations.

Source: Mahony (2011, Chart 7).

These two books spurred research into the gender gap in crime across crimes, context, and time. Subsequent research, examining annual data on the gender gap in arrest rates from the 1960s to 2000, provided evidence that some significant narrowing occurred in the gender gap in arrests for property and violent crimes during this period (Heimer, Lauritsen, & Lynch, 2009; Steffensmeier, Zhong, Ackerman, Schwartz, & Agha, 2006).

But what does it *mean* that the gender gap in arrests for violent crime is narrowing? One possibility is that a narrowing gap represents a real change in female behaviour in recent decades. The *liberation hypothesis* (Adler, 1975; Simon, 1975) asserts that as women gain social power and freedoms, they are subject to fewer informal controls and should have more opportunities to commit crime and violence. The *economic marginalization hypothesis* contends that the economic circumstances of poor, uneducated women have worsened in comparison with those of male counterparts in recent decades (Heimer, 2000; Heimer, Wittrock, & Ünal, 2006). The result is linked to greater increases in women's than in men's offending rates during periods of rising crime and smaller declines in women's rates during the recent crime bust (decline). A third hypothesis is that of *changing criminal justice practices*. This hypothesis suggests that strides toward gender equality, combined with the public's reduced tolerance for violence, have led police to see female offending as a growing problem. Police are more inclined to charge women as accomplices to crime, and "charge up" offences that might have earlier been treated as lesser offences when committed by women. As well, domestic violence, once viewed as a private matter, increasingly receives intervention by the police, leading to greater arrests of women. Therefore, a narrowing of the gender gap in arrests could be the product of changing criminal justice practices (Steffensmeier & Schwartz, 2004; Steffensmeier, Schwartz, Zhong, & Ackerman, 2005; Steffensmeier et al., 2006).

These three explanations for changes in the gender gap in crime have been examined by Janet Lauritsen, Karen Heimer, and James Lynch (2009) using US UCR arrest data and victim reports from the National Crime Victimization Survey (NCVS). These scholars refute the claim that a "new violent female offender" has emerged. Their study shows that female rates of violent offending have in fact declined over time. Lauritsen, Heimer, and Lynch (2009) also argue that the narrowing of the gender gap in violent crime is not simply the outcome of changing police practices; at least some of this narrowing of the gender gap reflects changes in the behaviours of male and female offenders. Most important, their analysis of victim reports suggests that the closing of the gender gap in violent offending was driven primarily by larger decreases in male offending and not by remarkable increases in female offending.

The patterns observed by Lauritsen, Heimer, and Lynch (2009) cast doubt on the liberation hypothesis. The liberation hypothesis would predict less substantial drops in female relative to male offending in the "crime drop" period of the 1990s and a more impressive and earlier impact of the feminist movement on women's opportunities for crime. The data are more consistent with the economic marginalization hypothesis (see also Heimer et al., 2006). Lauritsen, Heimer, and Lynch (2009) argue that women did not gain as much income as men during the late 1990s, and consequently women's offending rates did not drop as much as those of men. It was during this period that the US government introduced substantial cutbacks to welfare assistance to marginalized women, which eroded an important buffer against poverty (Lauritsen, Heimer, & Lynch, 2009).

Explaining the Gender Gap in Crime

Explaining the gender gap in crime raises important questions. Can existing criminological theories be applied or elaborated to encompass women's involvement in crime? Are the causes of women's crime better understood through gender-specific theories of crime? In response to these questions, three approaches have emerged. One approach is simply to add women to samples that examine criminal offending. Keep in mind that many of the early studies of crime used samples of boys and men, excluding girls and women from analyses. The inclusion of girls and women in social survey samples is often termed the "add and stir" approach. A second approach is to explore how current theories may be developed further to help us understand differences in the types of crime women engage in, women's roles in collaborative offending, and the lesser volume of female offending. Finally, a third approach is to propose a new and gender-specific theory that treats female criminality as distinct from that of male criminality. In the next section, we explore several different theories, each born from one of these three general approaches to the study of gender and crime.

Social Learning as the Catalyst of Crime

Early studies emphasized biological factors and sexual problems as the roots of gender differences in crime (see Lombroso & Ferrero, 1895/1958; Pollak, 1950; Thomas, 1923/1969; Vedder & Somerville, 1975). A break from a biological emphasis came with social learning theories. For example, Edwin Sutherland (1947) argued that the higher rate of crime for boys can be explained by the differences in care and supervision of boys and girls. He maintained that girls are supervised more carefully and taught social codes with greater care and consistency than are boys. From infancy, girls are taught that they must be nice, while boys are taught that they must be tough. Furthermore, he argued that parents' fear that their daughters might become pregnant was a driving concern in the supervision of girls. As Sutherland noted, "The difference in care and supervision presumably rested originally on the fact that the female sex is the one which becomes pregnant. The personal and familial consequences of illicit pregnancy lead to special protection of the girl not only in respect to sex behaviour but in reference to social codes in general" (Sutherland, 1947, pp. 100–101). Ruth Morris (1964) further developed the idea that female delinquency was deeply influenced by **socialization** patterns. Morris speculated that women experience both reduced access to illegitimate means to reach success goals (e.g., criminal opportunities) and greater social disapproval of delinquent acts than do their male counterparts. She also observed that girls are expected to abide by stricter moral standards, and deviant behaviour by girls is likely to result in greater guilt and disapproval by others. By contrast, more subcultural support exists for misbehaviour by boys (Morris, 1964).

socialization

The process through which children learn language, culture, roles, expectations, and beliefs. It is facilitated by parents, siblings, and relatives, and later by friends and within schools and community organizations.

More recent research has examined how gender roles are learned and influence youth delinquency and criminal offending (Akers & Jensen, 2003; Kreager, 2007; Mullins, Wright & Jacobs, 2004; Steffensmeier & Allan, 1996). Darrell Steffensmeier and Emilie Allan (1996) argued that the adoption of masculine gender norms, which emphasize physicality, aggressiveness, and risk taking, is more conducive to delinquency. In contrast, stereotypes of femininity, including "weakness, submission, domestication, nurturance, and 'ladylike' behavior) are basically incompatible with qualities valued in the criminal world" (Steffensmeier & Allan, 1996, p. 476). Gender norms also result in greater supervision of girls and women in society, limited opportunities to engage in crime, and condemnation of women who engage in serious predatory crime (Steffensmeier & Allan, 1996). Recent studies have explored social learning and gender roles in the contexts of male adolescent violence in connection with school contact sports teams (Kreager, 2007), substance abuse by boys and girls (Whaley, Hayes-Smith, & Hayes-Smith, 2010), gangster subculture (Bengtsson, 2012), and fear of crime itself (Rader & Haynes, 2011).

gendered
The notion that processes (e.g., learning roles) and behaviours (e.g., participation in crime) are gender-based.

A *social learning perspective* emphasizes not simply the processes through which women engage in less crime, or less violent crime, than men, but also the context and forms of deviant behaviour by each gender. For example, Christopher Mullins, Richard Wright, and Bruce Jacobs (2004) interviewed 40 men and 12 women, recruited from the streets of St. Louis, Missouri. They found that retaliatory violence is **gendered**, and perceptions of appropriate and inappropriate behaviour for men and women are learned through interactions with others on the street. In their study, men viewed violent retaliation as a key street survival tactic, deeply rooted in their identities as men. In this context, a reputation for violence (being a "bad ass") or enacting the "code of the street" enhanced their chances of survival on the streets and success at crime (see Connell, 2002). Mullins, Wright, and Jacobs (2004) found that women, compared with men, resorted to violence less frequently, with less severity, and were more likely to seek non-violent methods of retaliation. Although most retaliatory disputes among men and women typically involved reputation (e.g., disrespect, challenge), women were more likely than men to get involved in disputes over domestic matters (e.g., intimate relationships, family). Despite gender stereotypes that generally call for shielding women from violence, several men interviewed stated that when a woman "acts like a man" on the streets, she risks getting treated like one. As Mullins, Wright, and Jacobs (2004, p. 936) note:

> Men get locked into retaliatory cycles not only as an inevitable by-product of their criminal embeddedness, but also due to the demands of actualizing a street masculinity identity. Women moving within the same criminal networks also find themselves ensnared by these broader rules of violent engagement, both as targets and as transgressors.

Control Perspectives on Gender and Crime

Another perspective focuses on dimensions of control in shaping gender differences in crime. Early work by Travis Hirschi, in his book *Causes of Delinquency* (1969), examined the importance of bonds to society and conformity that are instructed through the family, schools, religious institutions, and the law. Michael Gottfredon and Travis Hirschi, in a *General Theory of Crime* (1990), focused on the concept of *self-control* rather than societal control, emphasizing how some individuals may become crime-prone through individual behaviours and attitudes, such as an urge to gratify desires immediately; a lack of diligence and persistence in a course of action; a lack of skills and planning; a lack of commitment to a job, marriage, and children; and a tendency to drink excessively, use illegal drugs, or gamble. A further development in control research is a *life-course-developmental theory* of informal social control (Laub & Sampson, 2003; Sampson & Laub, 1993). A life-course perspective stresses the importance of informal social ties at all ages, but differentiates the roles played by important institutions in informal social control on the basis of age or life span. Therefore, family, school, and peer groups are dominant forces of informal social control in childhood and adolescence, while in adulthood, dominant social control institutions are marriage, children, and employment (Giordano, Deines, & Cernkovich, 2006; King, Massoglia, & Macmillan, 2007; Massoglia & Uggen, 2010).

For theories of social control, including bonds, self-control, and life-course theories of informal control, a key issue is how people develop "control." One control theory that has focused special attention on gender differences is **power-control theory**. Originally formulated by John Hagan, A.R. Gillis, and John Simpson (1985), power-control theory explores how males and females differ in emotional reactions and behavioural responses, with close attention paid to the role of family socialization. According to this theory, parents with greater workplace authority and autonomy eschew rigid disciplinary practices at home to foster entrepreneurial, risk-taking orientations in their children. Freedom and control in the workplace are therefore reproduced in the family. Hagan and colleagues also contend that parental control of children is stratified by gender. They describe this as a fundamental instrument-object relationship (Hagan, Gillis, & Simpson, 1985). The two sides of this relationship are that mothers more than fathers are the instruments of familial controls, and daughters more than sons are the objects of familial controls. Female adolescents are taught to avoid risks generally and the risk of legal sanctions specifically.

Power control theory also has a class element. Power control theory argues that in all classes males are freer to be delinquent than females. However, males are most free to be delinquent in the most powerful classes. Hagan and colleagues' early work examined common forms of youth delinquency, such as smoking cigarettes, drinking alcohol, fighting, stealing, illegal copying of software and music, and vandalism (Hagan, Gillis, & Simpson, 1985; Hagan & Kay, 1990). Later research extended power-control theory to analyze attitudes toward risk that are central to a range of risk-taking behaviours among adults (Grasmick, Hagan, Blackwell, & Arenklev, 1996). A further formulation of the theory described gendered schemas embedded in parenting styles. These gendered schemas create behavioural disparities when mothers and fathers use different parenting styles for sons and daughters (Hagan, McCarthy, & Foster, 2002; McCarthy, Hagan, & Woodward, 1999).

Research on power-control theory has produced mixed results. Some studies found evidence to support the theory and elaborated the theory to consider the influence of peer relations and group risk (Singer & Levine, 1988) and perceived threats of **informal sanctions** (e.g., shame and embarrassment) (Blackwell, 2000). Other studies developed the concept of parental support and specified the types of controls exercised on girls and boys (Hill & Atkinson, 1988). Meanwhile, some scholars criticized the theory on the basis of class-related predictions (Jensen & Thompson, 1990) and for its treatment of single-parent households as egalitarian families (Leiber & Wacker, 1997). Feminist scholars, in particular, have criticized the theory for its emphasis on the role of mothers in socializing and regulating their children: they question the idea that women who defy traditional femininity and work outside the home in the paid-labour market risk increasing the chance that their daughters will become delinquent (Chesney-Lind, 1989). Other feminists argue that the theory casts daughters as merely the object of their mothers' instrumental control to be compliant, whereas conforming boys appear

power-control theory
A theory of crime that emphasizes the socialization by parents in the development of different levels of risk taking and the perceived sanctions among boys and girls.

informal sanctions
The actions taken by others, such as a verbal reprimand, punishment, withdrawal of privileges, and suspension of activities. These actions may lead to shame and embarrassment and may deter individuals from participating in crime.

formal sanctions
Punishments or corrections undertaken by official organizations such as schools, the police, and the courts.

intelligent and rational (Naffine, 1997). In an interesting twist, Christopher Uggen (2000), analyzing data from a youth development survey in St. Paul, Minnesota, uncovered a brighter side to power-control theory: girls whose mothers hold workplace authority are likely to engage in a constellation of risk-taking behaviours that include pro-social and anti-social behaviours. He found these daughters were likely to pursue athletic competition, non-traditional employment, and entrepreneurial business and financial activity.

So far, we have discussed control theories including self-control, life-course theories of control, and power control. These theories emphasize a quality of control that is both internal (one's self-control) and external (bonds or attachment to others, including job, family, spouse, and children). Some recent work suggests that control might be innate and not entirely developed through one's social context. Guang Guo, Michael Roettger, and Tianji Cai (2008) found that genetic factors (specifically, variants in specific genes) were significant predictors of serious and violent delinquency. The authors observed that the expression of genes depends heavily on environmental context. Specifically, they argued that the stronger social control influences of family, school, and friendship networks reduce the delinquency-increasing effects of a genetic variant, whereas weaker social control influences in these realms amplify the delinquency-increasing effect of a genetic variant (Guo, Roettger, & Cai, 2008, p. 561). Guo, Roettger, and Cai (2008, p. 549) proposed that these effects likely differ by sex. Recent research suggests that genetic factors may play a greater role in behavioural outcomes among males (Beaver et al., 2011). However, research on gender differences with regard to genetics and crime remains in its infancy (Barnes, Beaver, & Boutwell, 2011; DeLisi, 2012; Guo, 2006; Wright & Beaver, 2005). For a more detailed discussion of biological explanations of crime, see Chapter 7, Biological Approaches.

General Strain Theory Perspectives on Gender and Crime

General strain theory (GST) has been used to explore our understanding of gender differences in criminal offending. Robert Agnew (1985) proposed GST as a way of expanding on and generalizing the concept of strain, developed by Robert Merton (1938), at the social psychological level. The theory examines how individuals cope with strain emotionally and behaviourally. It broadens the concept of strain to include a variety of negative relations with others, and it assesses strain in term of several criteria. When these criteria are elevated, crime is more likely (for a detailed discussion of GST, see Agnew, 2006; Agnew, Bresina, Wright, & Cullen, 2002).

Lisa Broidy and Robert Agnew (1997) extended and applied GST to the study of gender differences in crime. Together, Broidy and Agnew addressed two questions: (1) How can we explain the higher rate of crime among males? and (2) How can we explain why females engage in crime? With respect to the first question, the authors suggested that gender differences in types of strain and the reaction to strain help explain the gender gap in criminal behaviour. With respect to the second question, they argued that several types of strain may lead to female crime under the right circumstances. Broidy and Agnew contended that GST cannot explain the higher rate of male crime by simply claiming that males experience more strain. They argued that males and females experience strain in qualitatively distinct ways. Broidy and Agnew outlined three important differences: (1) males and females experience different types of strain;

(2) males and females differ in their emotional response to strain; and (3) males and females experience strain under different sorts of circumstances.

The first argument is that males and females experience different types of strain, with male strains being more conducive to serious violent and property crimes. For example, males more often report financial problems and are more upset when they experience financial or work-related problems. The greater emphasis on material considerations and greater financial stress may explain males' higher rates of property crimes. In addition, males are also more likely to be victims of most types of crime and targets of others' aggression and anger. Interpersonal conflicts and criminal victimization are more often experienced by males, which may explain their higher rates of violent crime. In contrast, females' strains, often connected to family violence, lead to escape behaviour such as running away and to more self-directed forms of control, such as drug use. Women also are more likely to report gender-based discrimination, low prestige in work and family roles, excessive demands from family members, and restrictions on their behaviours (Broidy & Agnew, 1997).

Second, Broidy and Agnew (1997) argued that males and females differ in their emotional response to strain. Although females and males may both respond to strain with anger, there may be gender differences in the way that anger is experienced (Agnew, 2006). The anger females experience is more likely to be accompanied by depression, guilt, anxiety, and related states as a result of cultural socialization. These emotional states reduce the likelihood of confrontational crimes and increase the likelihood of self-destructive offences. In comparison, males externalize their anger and react with "moral outrage." The angry male's moral righteousness may lead to serious violent and property offending. Nevertheless, Broidy and Agnew (1997) acknowledge that some females may react to strain with the same anger that males do, helping to explain the serious female offending that does take place.

Third, Broidy and Agnew (1997) maintained that males and females experience strain under different sorts of circumstances. That is to say, males may be more likely than females to respond to a given level of strain or anger with serious property and violent crime because of differences in *moderating factors*. Societal proscriptions against crime for females reduce the likelihood that females will respond to strain with crime. Moreover, females may have lower levels of self-esteem and self-efficacy, which may decrease the likelihood of their decision to commit a crime. Furthermore, gender differences in social support may affect how males and females respond to strain. Females tend to be more immersed in intimate networks, which lend them emotional social support that can reduce stress. Differences also exist in opportunities for crime and social control. Males may be granted more opportunities by others to join in criminal activities, and males may be less supervised and controlled by authority figures (Broidy & Agnew, 1997).

Broidy and Agnew's initial work was theoretical, with hypotheses drawn from a larger review of the existing empirical literature on gender differences. What do empirical tests of GST tell us? Nicole Piquero and Miriam Sealock (2004) tested this elaborated GST using a sample of delinquent youths in the United States to examine gender differences in interpersonal and property offending. Their results offer some support for a gendered GST. Broidy and Agnew (1997) suggested there would be no difference in the amount of strain experienced by males and females. Piquero and Sealock (2004) also found no significant differences in the amount of strain experienced by both genders. However, Piquero and Sealock found that females reported higher levels of depression (as predicted by the theory) and higher levels of anger (GST predicted males would have higher anger levels). GST proposed that negative emotions would be significantly associated with crime. Here, Piquero and Sealock's results were mixed. They found that anger in males directly predicted property crime, but depression in males was unrelated to property offences. On the other hand, they found that anger was positively related to interpersonal aggression for both males and females, even when controlling for strain. Piquero and Sealock found that for males, the availability of social coping resources actually exacerbated, rather than deterred, crime. This finding suggests that males appear to turn to a social network that encourages criminal behaviour or provides opportunities for crime. The availability or use of coping mechanisms suggested by GST may be qualitatively different for both genders.

Overall, Piquero and Sealock (2004) found support for Broidy and Agnew's hypotheses about GST and gender, although their study points to the need for more research on qualitative differences in the types of strain, emotions, and copying styles of both genders. Recent research provides evidence that the experience of strain, both emotionally and behaviourally, is gendered (Cheung & Cheung, 2010; Piquero, Fox, Piquero, Capowich, & Mazerolle, 2010; Sigfusdottir, Farkas, & Silver, 2004).

conditioning factors
Factors that shape the impact of a certain cause or correlate of crime.

Recent work exploring the role of **conditioning factors** has also contributed to a gendered theory of GST. Wesley Jennings, Nicole Piquero, Angela Gover, and Deanna Pérez (2009) extended GST to explain interpersonal aggression and property offending among southwestern Mexican American adolescents. Their study provides partial support for GST-related processes and highlights the importance of conditioning factors such as peer social support, spiritual coping resources, and physical coping resources (e.g., involvement in music) in crime prevention. Stephen Baron's (2007) analysis of high-risk homeless street youths in Canada revealed how socio-economic strain in the forms of homelessness, monetary dissatisfaction, and feelings of relative deprivation are linked to property and violent crime. Although Baron found few gender differences in the main effects of strain on crime, his research revealed gender differences in the effect of conditioning factors on certain strains and crime. For example, financial strains affected both males and females, but the effect on female violent crime was stronger when females had deviant peers and developed attitudes favourable to violent crime; and the sense of relative deprivation (feeling one's situation is unfair when compared with that of others) had a stronger effect on males' property offending when males attributed their struggles to others (external attributions for strain). These findings suggest that conditioning factors (or interactions of emotional responses, peer networks, and attitudes) are different depending on the types of strain experienced and one's gender (Baron, 2007).

Research has also explored strain, emotional responses, and youth delinquency in relation to offences other than property and violent crime. Joanne Kaufman (2009) analyzed gender differences in the experience of the strain caused by suicide attempts of family and friends and violent victimization, as well as the impact of associated emotions on the deviant outcomes of suicidal thoughts, weekly drinking, running away from home, and violence. Kaufman found that for females, depressive symptoms were positively predictive of all four deviant outcomes. However, for males, depressive symptoms were positively predictive for only two deviant outcomes: suicidal thoughts and running away. Meanwhile, anger (bad temper) had no effect on either suicidal thoughts or running away for either gender.

A Break from Tradition: Feminist Explanations

Feminist critiques have argued that traditional theories of crime tend to overlook female offending. Many of the early studies of crime and delinquency used samples of males, and theories were developed with male youth and adult offenders in mind. Therefore, most of criminology has been a male-centred enterprise. The rationale for the focus on males is based on women's small numbers relative to men in criminal offending, particularly in violent crime. As a result, until recently, women were not of interest and deemed less relevant to the study of crime. Studies that began to include women and girls generally adopted an "add women and stir" approach, assuming that similar underlying processes generate male and female criminality. A further critique of these early works was that women lawbreakers were often portrayed as morally corrupt, hysterical, manipulative, and devious (Chesney-Lind, 2006). Feminist scholars argued that in attempting to understand criminality, researchers needed to pay greater attention to female voices (as victims and offenders) and revise interpretations by the inclusion of women's experiences. Feminists have claimed that past work has failed to interrogate the nature of maleness and femaleness (masculinity and femininity) or the historically grounded relationship between them. Feminist criminology represents a radical break from traditional theories (Smart, 1977).

Common to feminist inquiries into crime is a focus on the forces that shape women's lives and experiences in order to explain female criminality (Miller & Mullins, 2006a). Some of this work emphasizes how physical and sexual victimization of girls and women can be underlying causes of women's criminal behaviour (Chesney-Lind, 1992; McDaniels-Wilson & Belknap, 2008; Owen & Bloom, 1995). A considerable body of feminist scholarship has critiqued methodological strategies in criminology that rely on social surveys and statistical analyses, claiming that objectivist, value-neutral science overlooks the lived experiences of women (Harding, 1990; Naffine, 1997) and prevents more social activist and transformative research from taking place (Chesney-Lind, 2006). Therefore, the majority, although not all (see Heimer & De Coster, 1999; Simpson & Gibbs, 2006) of feminist criminology embraces qualitative methods of interviewing that seek to build theory inductively.

Within feminist criminology, various theories exist (for example, liberal, radical, and intersectional feminism), although the differences are generally a matter of emphasis (e.g., political economy, equality through law, connections with race) rather than a paradigm shift. For example, *liberal feminists* emphasize comparisons of sameness and difference in criminal behaviour and treatment. This approach pays close attention to the impact of gender role socialization and women's reduced opportunities to engage in criminal networks in shaping women's lower offending rate (Burgess-Proctor, 2006). *Radical feminism* emphasizes dominance, or patriarchy, as the root cause of women's oppression. Radical feminist criminologists have examined male dominance and privilege through such crimes against women as domestic violence, sexual harassment, rape, and pornography. Radical feminists have also advanced law reform to improve the treatment of criminalized women (MacKinnon, 1991), revealed evidence of women's unequal treatment in sentencing (Daly & Tonry, 1997; Gaarder & Belknap, 2002), and formulated a critique of women's prisons and parole (Chesney-Lind, 2004; Hannah-Moffat & Yule, 2011). Recently, *intersectional feminism*, informed by multi-racial feminism, explores multiple interlocking inequalities (it is sometimes called the "race-class-gender" approach) (Daly, 1997; Sokoloff, Price, & Flavin, 2004; Thompson, 2002). The intersectional feminist approach recognizes that race, class, gender, sexuality, and other social positions of inequality influence one another (Lynch, 1996). These differences are grounded in historical contexts and operate at the level of individual day-to-day interactions and at the more macro level of law and governance (Burgess-Proctor, 2006). Contemporary feminist criminology has examined the intersection of gender and race with reference to drug treatment programs and imprisonment (McCorkel, 2013), women's victimization in partner violence (Sokoloff & Dupont, 2005a, 2005b; Sokoloff & Pearce, 2011), women's violence on the street (Althoff, 2013), and hate-motivated violence (Meyer, 2010).

In Sum: Contrasting Theories of Gender and Crime

Contemporary theories that seek to explain the relationship between gender and crime are diverse. Scholars build on past and current theoretical arguments, often importing research findings, concepts, and arguments from other theories. This dialogue of critique, infusion of ideas, and elaboration reminds us that each of these theories offers insight into different dimensions of gender and crime.

Contemporary Research on Gender and Crime

Three areas of contemporary research on gender and crime will be explored next: (1) gender, gangs, and urban crime; (2) domestic violence; and (3) femicide and homicide. Several other chapters in this book explore other areas of crime relevant to gender, including Chapter 5 (Victims of Crime), Chapter 13 (Violent Crime), Chapter 14 (Sexual Offences and Problematic Sexual Interests), and Chapter 16 (Crimes of Morality).

Gender, Gangs, and Urban Crime

Considerable research in the urban context has focused on gender and gang membership. Three common themes emerge in the literature on why males join gangs: (1) neighbourhood disadvantage; (2) gang-involved family members or friends; and (3) problems within the family (e.g., neglect, lack of supervision, and drug and alcohol addiction) (Chesney-Lind & Shelden, 2004; Kolb & Palys, 2012; Miller & Mullins, 2006b). Jody Miller's (2008) research in St. Louis, Missouri found females' neighbourhood contexts provided exposure to gangs. Serious family problems of drug abuse and violence led girls to avoid home and join gangs in an attempt to meet social and emotional needs. Karen Joe and Meda Chesney-Lind (1995) found in their study of gangs that the vast majority of female gang members reported a family member, usually a sibling, in a gang. Their research also documented extensive physical and sexual victimization in females' lives. Finn-Aage Esbensen, Elizabeth Deschenes, and L. Thomas Winfree (1999) found similarities between males and females, who both reported joining gangs primarily for protection. Differences also exist. For example, Anne Campbell (1990, 1995) found that female gang members came from more disadvantaged backgrounds than male gang members. Specifically, Campbell (1995) found that female gang members were more likely than male gang members to come from broken, unemployed homes with family violence, including parental drug abuse. Numerous studies argued that girls join gangs because they have few options in severely disadvantaged neighbourhoods and because they are in search of a "familial" peer group and emotional support that they do not find in their own families (Bell, 2009; Fleisher, 1998). Recent research provides insight into girls in gangs and their involvement in prostitution (Dorais & Corriveau, 2009) and the abuse and violence girls are exposed to within gangs (Haymos & Gatti, 2010). Other work has examined group-based offences, although not necessarily gang-related (see Box 10.1).

Although many studies highlight gender differences in urban crime, some work suggests the importance of underlying factors common to men's and women's involvement in crime. In a landmark study of urban crime, Darrell Steffensmeier and Dana Haynie (2000) analyzed data from 178 US cities using data from the Bureau of Census publications, the UCR Survey, and FBI city arrest data. They found that despite an enormous difference in mean rates of offending between females and males, structural disadvantage variables (e.g., poverty, income inequality, joblessness, female-headed single households) had significant effects on female rates of homicide and robbery, as well as moderate effects on female rates of aggravated assault, burglary, and larceny. Steffensmeier and Haynie (2000) also noted a difference in the strength of effects: the indicators of structural disadvantage were more robustly associated with male than with female rates of offending. The researchers uncovered other parallels: structural variables

BOX 10.1

Case Study: Gender and Burglary

Research has shown that women's motives for entering into criminal behaviour, such as burglary, and ceasing it can be quite different from those of men.

In a fascinating study, Christopher Mullins and Richard Wright (2003) examined the ways in which gender affects participation in residential burglary, a quintessentially group-based offence. They explored how gender influences initiation into, participation in, and potential desistance from burglary. Their study revealed how males control both entry to burglary crews and access to networks for disposing of goods. In their study, men were initiated into burglary crews from a broad array of associates, including male relatives and friends. In contrast, females were most often drawn into male-dominated burglary crews by their boyfriends. Moreover, while men typically held marginal roles early in their careers (e.g., lookout and get-away driver), men began undertaking more central and profitable roles as they gained experience. In contrast, women's roles were often limited to an accomplice role. Mullins and Wright (2003) also uncovered a striking gender difference in desistance from crime. When men were asked to explain why they had ceased burglaries, they cited the influence of a stable relationship with a woman as the main reason. For women, the situation was the opposite. Just as relationships with criminally involved men opened the door for women's initiation to burglary, the end of that romantic relationship also brought an end to women's offending.

of residential instability, structural density, and population size also had similar effects on rates of male and female offending. A key conclusion of this study was that macro-level causes of female crime are not fundamentally different than those of male crime. This finding suggests that the quest to identify gender differences in the causes of crime may focus too much on differences rather than on similarities.

Domestic Violence

One of the most significant contributions to the burgeoning body of literature on gender and crime has been the growth in research on criminal victimization. Violence against women has been identified as a major public health and human rights issue (Ellsberg, Jansen, Heise, Watts, & García-Moreno, 2008) and as a crime that has reached epidemic proportions in many societies (Alhabib, Nur, & Jones, 2010). Scholarship has shed light on previously understudied areas of violence against women, such as sexual assault, sexual harassment in the workplace, intimate partner violence, and **femicide** (the killing of women). We highlight research on intimate partner violence next.

femicide
The act of killing a woman.

Numerous studies have examined the prevalence of different patterns of violent victimization among family members. Early research using the US National Survey of Family Violence (Stets & Straus, 1989) found that in households where there was violence between spouses, the most common situation was both spouses attacking each other. This early work also found that the percentage of children attacking their siblings increased as the rate of parent-to-child violence increased, and spouses' verbal abuse of their partners was strongly associated with the use of physical violence against their partners. Recent research builds on this work. Using the US National Crime Victimization Survey, Wendi Goodlin and Christopher Dunn (2010) found that one-time victimization of a family member by others in the family occurred in about 80 percent of instances of family violence in households. Much lower rates of repeated victimization of the same victim took place—these occurred in close to 15 percent of the family violence in households. In addition, Goodlin and Dunn (2010) found that the co-occurrence of violence among different family members (e.g., spouse, parental, sibling and other family relationships) was about 5 percent of the family violence in households. The study also revealed that victims with less than a high school education (compared with victims with a high school education) had much higher odds of living in a co-occurrence household compared with a repeat victimization household.

Other research has focused on spousal violence, with the aim of understanding how socio-economic stresses impact families. Ross Macmillan and Rosemary Gartner (1999), for example, focused on spousal violence using a national survey of Canadian women. Their analysis revealed little evidence that employment as a measure of economic resources affects the risk of spousal violence. Instead, Macmillan and Gartner (1999) found that women's labour force participation lowers the risk of spousal abuse when male partners are also employed; however, women's labour force participation substantially increases the risk of spousal abuse when male partners are unemployed. In contrast, direct measures of socio-economic resources, such as personal and household income, had little impact on the risk of spousal abuse. Therefore, it is not the case that economic deprivation, which leads to stress and frustration, causes domestic violence. Instead, the symbolic aspects of who has employment in the household are important: when women hold jobs and their male partners are unemployed, the risk of spousal violence

BOX 10.2

"Enough Is Enough"

The following is an excerpt from an Ontario Court of Appeal decision in a case of a homicide that took place after a woman had been subjected to long-term, non-violent spousal abuse.

> In the early morning of March 31, 2006, the appellant, a middle-aged woman, who is by all accounts a decent person and a good mother, put a pillow over her husband's face as he was lying asleep in a drunken stupor on the couch. A few minutes later, the appellant took a large butcher knife from the kitchen and stabbed her husband four times in the chest. She then left the RV in which they were living and ran to a neighbour's house. The deceased was still alive when the appellant left, but died of blood loss a short time later.
>
> The appellant went directly to her neighbour's house. She told them that she had killed her husband, and asked them to call 911. The appellant spoke to the 911 operator, again admitted killing her husband, and said, "I'm sick of my life ... everything is wrong."
>
> After her arrest, the appellant gave lengthy video-taped statements to the police in which she acknowledged stabbing her husband to death. When asked by the officer to explain why she had done so, the appellant said, "enough is enough." The appellant's explanation that "enough is enough" can only be understood in the context of her relationship with the deceased. ...
>
> On the evidence, the appellant fit the description of a battered wife. She was trapped in a relationship that belittled and dehumanized her to the point where she suffered a serious and ongoing mental disorder rendering her unable to perceive the obvious consequences of her actions. We are satisfied that the effect that the long-term abuse had on this appellant should have been treated as a substantial mitigating factor on sentence. The trial judge erred in principle in diminishing that mitigating impact because the abuse did not involve serious physical abuse or sexual abuse. ...
>
> Having regard to the entirety of the circumstances, and despite the powerful mitigating features, we are satisfied that incarceration was necessary in this case. This was a brutal homicide. As the trial judge observed, the sentence imposed must reflect the value that our society places on all human life. The appellant must bear responsibility for what she did, despite the mitigating features of this case.
>
> The appellant has served about three years (two and a half years plus five months' pre-sentence custody). We are satisfied that a sentence of three years in custody certainly fully meets the needs of deterrence and denunciation in the circumstances. There is no need for any further incarceration.
>
> As indicated at the end of oral argument, the conviction appeal is dismissed, the sentence appeal is allowed and the sentence is varied to time served.
>
> Ontario Court of Appeal, case heard January 27, 2011, judgment released February 24, 2011.

What do you think should be considered as "mitigating factors" in homicide? In what ways does the appellant in this case fit (or not fit) the description of a "battered wife"? What are your thoughts on the court of appeal's decision to uphold the conviction while shortening the sentence (to time already served)?

Source: *R v. Craig*, 2011 ONCA 142, paras. 4–6, 60, 64–65.

is greater (Macmillan & Gartner, 1999). Recent research suggests that employed women's risk of victimization appears partly contingent on the race of the victim. Ráchael Powers and Catherine Kaukinen (2012) found that for white women, employment heightened the risk of victimization, whereas for non-white women, the effects of employment were less clear, although regardless of employment status, non-white women were overall at greater risk of victimization.

A sizable body of research on family violence assesses policing strategies and legal interventions. Since the 1980s, law enforcement, prosecution, and criminal and civil courts developed a variety of new policies for responding to the victimization of women by intimates. Although considerable research has examined these new policies and practices, little consensus exists on which interventions are most effective. Results from the Minneapolis field experiment, which involved a study of police responses to domestic

Supporters chant during the release of a report by the Missing Women Commission of Inquiry in Vancouver in December 2012. The inquiry examined the years of inaction by police in investigating the disappearances of dozens of missing women, many of them poor Aboriginals working as prostitutes in Vancouver's Downtown Eastside. Many of the disappeared women were victims of mass murderer Robert Pickton.

Source: Carmine Marinelli/Vancouver 24hrs/QMI Agency.

violence from 1981 to 1982, were heralded as scientific evidence that arrest was the most appropriate and effective response to domestic violence (Sherman & Berk, 1984). However, a subsequent spousal abuse program that adopted this strategy and was implemented in six other US cities failed to reproduce results supporting the superiority of arrest in reducing domestic violence (Sherman, Schmidt, Rogan, Cohn, Cohn, Collins, & Bacich, 1992). Other interventions have also been examined. For example, where hotlines are prevalent, abuse victims are more likely to reach help and access targeted domestic violence resources, including legal advocacy, police, and prosecutorial services (Dugan, Nagin, & Rosenfeld, 2003). Legal advocacy has been found to provide women with assistance in obtaining protection orders (called "restraining orders" in the United States and "no contact orders" in Canada). Moreover, as women seek legal remedies to domestic violence, they are less inclined to resort to lethal remedies (Dugan, Nagin, & Rosenfeld, 2003). The effectiveness of criminal justice responses to domestic violence also depends on local prosecutorial policy, including the willingness to grant protection orders (Basile, 2005; Muller, Desmarais, & Hamel, 2009) and to prosecute violators (Dugan, Nagin, & Rosenfeld, 2003). Specialized domestic violence courts and community services and networks have also been found to be effective in addressing domestic violence (Akoensi, Koehler, Losel, & Humphreys, 2013; Auchter & Backes, 2013).

Femicide and Homicide

The killing of women (femicide) appears to be quite different from the killing of men (homicide). Among those who study homicide, it is well known that women and men are killed in different numbers, by different types of people, and in different circumstances.

Women are less likely to be victims of homicide than men in virtually all societies. Women are also more likely than men to be killed by someone of the opposite sex. Women are more likely to be killed by persons with whom they are intimately involved. In contrast, men are more likely to be killed by acquaintances and strangers. Women are more likely to be killed in their own house than in any other place, while men are more likely to be killed in public places (Eke, Hilton, Harris, Rice, & Houghton, 2011; Gartner, 1990; Gartner & McCarthy, 1991).

In a study of intimate femicide (including spouses, ex-spouses, legal common law spouses, and current and former boyfriends) in Ontario, Rosemary Gartner, Myrna Dawson, and Maria Crawford (1999) identified several risk markers. They found that estrangement and common-law status were associated with a higher risk of spousal killings of women. Compared with couples in registered marriages, common law partners were more likely to be poor, young, unemployed, and childless—all factors associated with higher homicide rates. Compared with co-residing couples, estranged couples were more likely to have a history of domestic violence. In addition, Gartner, Dawson, and Crawford (1999) found that Aboriginal women's rates of spousal homicide were between five and ten times higher than those of non-Aboriginal women. Furthermore, men's unemployment was a risk factor for wife assaults and was also associated with elevated risks of spousal homicide. They also found men who killed their intimate partners were more likely to be unemployed and to have a history of criminal violence. Perhaps the most disturbing element of Gartner, Dawson, and Crawford's study is that one of the distinguishing features of intimate femicide is the extent and nature of the violence done to the victim. Unlike killings by women of their intimate partners, intimate femicides often involve multiple methods or far more violence than is necessary to kill the victim. Moreover, compared with killings of men by intimate female partners, intimate femicides are more likely to involve extreme and sexualized violence, to be motivated by anger over separation, to be followed by the suicide of the offender, and to involve the killing of additional victims. These features highlight the gender specificity of intimate partner killings (Gartner, Dawson, & Crawford, 1999).

Other research provides international comparisons on homicide. Gary LaFree and Gwen Hunnicutt (2006) documented female and male homicide victimization trends in 35 countries from 1950 to 2001. A widely held assumption in criminology is that homicide rates are higher for men than women. However, LaFree and Hunnicutt (2006) found that female rates exceeded male rates for at least part of the time period assessed in 11 countries (about one-third of their sample). The countries in which female rates were higher than male rates were clearly patterned. Female homicide victimization rates were greater than male rates in Western European democracies (Denmark, Switzerland, Sweden, Austria, Belgium, Norway, and Ireland) or countries with strong links to Western democracies (Israel, New Zealand, and Hong Kong). These patterns are consistent with research by Gartner (1990), suggesting that the gap in homicide victimization for women and men is smaller in nations with less **gender stratification**. In addition, LaFree and Hunnicutt (2006) found little evidence of convergence in the victimization rates of women and men during the second half of the 20th century (1950–2000). In fact, they found slightly more evidence of a female–male divergence in homicide victimization rates. For most countries in their sample, the gender gap in homicide victimization either remained constant or widened during the 50-year span (LaFree & Hunnicutt, 2006, p. 223).

gender stratification
A society's unequal distribution of wealth, power and privilege between men and women.

Conclusion

This chapter set out to trace gender differences in criminal offending, to outline explanations for the involvement of men and women in crime, and to explore areas of research relevant to gender and crime. Available crime data show that the dramatic difference in male and female offending is in the quantity of criminal offending, rather than the types of crime committed. Research also suggests that in recent years a significant narrowing of the gender gap in crime has occurred, particularly for property and violent crimes. Theoretical explanations for women's and men's criminal offending are richly diverse. Some theories attempt to understand gender differences in crime through socialization processes and gendered roles. Some focus on control, including processes of parental control, the cultivation of self-control, and the role of genetic influences on self-control and crime. Another approach extends general strain theory to include gendered emotional responses and coping mechanisms that in turn shape deviance and criminal outcomes. Finally, feminist theories break from traditional theories by placing girls and women at the centre of inquiry and providing a critique of criminal justice system responses to the treatment of women. The final section of this chapter examined three areas of contemporary research on gender and crime, including gangs, intimate partner violence, and homicide and femicide. This overview demonstrates how contemporary studies seek to document important differences and underlying similarities in male and female criminal involvement and to create effective intervention strategies.

SUMMARY OF KEY POINTS

- Available police arrest data reveal that men and women are arrested for similar crimes, including theft, assaults, and substance-related crimes.

- The dramatic difference between male and female offending relates to the quantity of criminal offending rather than the types of crime committed. In Canada, more than three times as many men as women are arrested for criminal violations. The differences are most pronounced for serious violent crimes, where men vastly outnumber women in homicide, sexual assault, assault, robbery, arson, break and enter, and motor vehicle theft.

- Research suggests that in recent years a significant narrowing of the gender gap in crime has occurred, particularly for property and violent crimes. The most persuasive explanations lie with the economic marginalization hypothesis and changing criminal justice practices rather than the liberation hypothesis or an increase in violent female offenders.

- Scholars have attempted to explain gender differences in crime through conventional theories (social learning, control), by extending traditional theories (general strain theory), and with theories tailored to women's unique circumstances (feminist theories).

- Feminist theories break from traditional theories by placing girls and women at the centre of inquiry, challenging assumptions embedded in law, and calling for extensive reform of the criminal justice system's treatment of women.

- Research on gangs reveals that family problems with drug abuse and violence lead girls to avoid home and join gangs in an effort to meet social and emotional needs.

- Violence against women has been identified as a major public health and human rights issue and is a crime that has reached epidemic proportions in many countries.
- Women and men are killed in different contexts. Women are more likely to be killed by persons with whom they are intimately involved, while men are more likely to be killed by acquaintances and strangers. Women are more likely to be killed in their own home than in any other place, while men are more likely to be killed in public places.
- Studies identify risk factors for interpersonal violence escalating to killing, revealing that femicide is not an unpredictable crime of passion.

NOTES

1. These two problems, gender ratio and generalization of theories, have been central to inquiry on gender and crime (see Kaufman, 2009, p. 411; Miller & Mullins, 2006a, pp. 226–227).
2. A notable reversal of this gender pattern exists in the United States, where women consistently outnumber men in prostitution and as runaways (a juvenile offence in the United States). For both of these crimes, women and girls represent about 60 percent of those arrested (Britton, 2011, p. 27). In contrast, in Canada the *Criminal Code* does not criminalize prostitution but rather communication for the purpose of prostitution in a public place (Lowman & Louie, 2012), and as a result the arrest rates are similar for men and women (12/100,000 for men and 10/100,000 for women) (Mahony, 2011, p. 20); the youth status-type offence of running away is absent from Canada's *Youth Criminal Justice Act* (Sprott, 2012).

QUESTIONS FOR CRITICAL DISCUSSION

1. What are the *gender ratio problem* and the *generalization problem*? How are these two problems different from each other?
2. Which approach to the study of gender and crime seems most persuasive (i.e., apply existing theories to samples of men and women, extend current theories to specify gender differences, or break from traditional theories to develop a separate theory of female criminality)? Why?
3. Which theories of male and female criminality do you find to be the most convincing? Are some theories better suited to particular types of deviance, delinquency, and crime?
4. How do men and women differ in terms of the types of crime in which they engage? Are there noteworthy differences between adult and youth offending and between Canadian and American crime statistics?
5. Are the rates of women's and men's offending converging, diverging, or remaining parallel? Are women becoming more violent? What are some of the possible reasons for the changing patterns observed in male and female criminal behaviour?

6. Studies of burglary, street gangs, intimate partner violence, and homicide/femicide reveal gendered processes in terms of motivations, entry to criminal networks, roles in co-offending crimes, levels of violence used, and reasons for ending criminal behaviour. Discuss any two of these crimes in terms of the gender differences and similarities that you find most intriguing.

7. Explore the economic marginalization hypothesis. What does it suggest are the causes of women's changing crime rates? For what types of crime would we expect to see more female participation? During which economic and political periods might we expect to see an increase in female crime?

8. Thinking about causes of crime, what factors best explain how male and female youths enter into crime and delinquency? Do similar processes generate male and female criminality? What differences exist? Do differences require a separate theory of crime for each gender? What are your thoughts?

SUGGESTED FURTHER READINGS

Boyce, J., & Cotter, A. 2013. *Homicide in Canada, 2012*. Ottawa: Statistics Canada. Retrieved from http://www.statcan.gc.ca/pub/85-002-x/2013001/article/11882-eng.pdf.

Brennan, S. (2012). *Police-reported crime statistics in Canada, 2011*. Ottawa: Statistics Canada. Retrieved from http://www.statcan.gc.ca/pub/85-002-x/2012001/article/11692-eng.pdf.

Britton, D.M. (2011). *The gender of crime*. Plymouth, UK: Rowman and Littlefield.

Chesney-Lind, M., & Shelden, R.G. (2014). *Girls, delinquency, and juvenile justice* (4th ed.). Chichester, UK: John Wiley and Sons.

Heimer, K., & Kruttschnitt, C. (Eds.). (2006). *Gender and crime: Patterns in victimization and offending*. New York: New York University Press.

Mahony, T.H. (2011). *Women and the criminal justice system*. Ottawa: Statistics Canada. Retrieved from http://www.statcan.gc.ca/pub/89-503-x/2010001/article/11416-eng.pdf.

McCorkel, J.A. (2013) *Breaking women: Gender, race and the new politics of imprisonment*. New York: New York University Press.

Perreault, S. (2013). *Police-reported crime statistics in Canada, 2012*. Ottawa: Statistics Canada. Retrieved from http://www.statcan.gc.ca/pub/85-002-x/2013001/article/11854-eng.pdf.

Sinha, M. (2013). *Family violence in Canada: A statistical profile, 2011*. Ottawa: Statistics Canada. Retrieved from http://www.statcan.gc.ca/pub/85-002-x/2013001/article/11805-eng.pdf.

Sinha, M. (2013). *Measuring violence against women: Statistical trends*. Ottawa: Statistics Canada. Retrieved from http://www.statcan.gc.ca/pub/85-002-x/2013001/article/11766-eng.pdf.

Vaillancourt, R. (2010). *Gender differences in police-reported violent crime in Canada, 2008*. Ottawa: Statistics Canada. Retrieved from http://www.statcan.gc.ca/pub/85f0033m/85f0033m2010024-eng.pdf.

Websites

Canadian Criminal Justice Statistics (Juristat): http://www5.statcan.gc.ca/olc-cel/olc.action?ObjId=85-002-X&ObjType=2&lang=en&limit=0

FBI: Crime in the United States, 2012: http://www.fbi.gov/about-us/cjis/ucr/crime-in-the-u.s/2012/crime-in-the-u.s.-2012

FBI: Uniform Crime Reports publications: http://www.fbi.gov/about-us/cjis/ucr/ucr-publications

REFERENCES

Adler, F. (1975). *Sisters in crime: The rise of the new female criminal*. New York: McGraw-Hill.

Agnew, R. (1985). A revised strain theory of delinquency. *Social Forces*, 64(1), 151–167.

Agnew, R. (2006). *Pressured into crime: An overview to general strain theory*. Los Angeles: Roxbury.

Agnew, R, Bresina, T., Wright, J.P., & Cullen, F.T. (2002). Strain, personality traits, and delinquency: Extending general strain theory. *Criminology*, 40, 43–72.

Akers, R.L., & Jensen, G.F. (2003). *Social learning theory and the explanation of crime: A guide for the new century*. New Brunswick, NJ: Transaction.

Akoensi, T.D., Koehler, J.A., Losel, F., & Humphreys, D.K. (2013). Domestic violence perpetrator programs in Europe, Part III: A systematic review of the state of evidence. *International Journal of Offender Therapy and Comparative Criminology*, 57, 1206–1225.

Alhabib, D., Nur, U., & Jones, R. (2010). Domestic violence against women: Systematic Review of prevalence studies. *Journal of Family Violence*, 25, 369–383.

Althoff, M. (2013). Multiple identities and crime: A study of Antillean women and girls in the Netherlands. *European Journal of Criminology*, 10(4), 394–407.

Auchter, B., & Backes, B.L. (2013). NIJ's program of domestic violence research: Collaborative efforts to build knowledge guided by safety for victims and accountability of perpetrators. *Violence Against Women*, 19(6), 713–736.

Barnes, J.C., Beaver, K.M., & Boutwell, B.B. (2011). Examining the genetic underpinnings to Moffitt's developmental taxonomy: A behavioral genetic analysis. *Criminology*, 49(4), 923–954.

Baron, S.W. (2007). Street youth, gender, financial strain, and crime: Exploring Broidy and Agnew's extension to general strain theory. *Deviant Behavior*, 28, 273–302.

Basile, S. (2005). A measure of court response to requests for protection. *Journal of Family Violence*, 20, 171–179.

Beaver, K.M., Rowland, M.W., Schwartz, J.A., & Nedelec, J.L. (2011). The genetic origins of psychopathic personality traits in adult males and females: Results from an adoption-based study. *Journal of Criminal Justice*, 39, 426–432.

Bell, K.E. (2009). Gender and gangs: A quantitative comparison. *Crime & Delinquency*, 55(3), 363–387.

Bengtsson, T.T. (2012). Learning to become "gangster." *Journal of Youth Studies*, 15(6), 677–692.

Blackwell, B.S. (2000). Perceived sanction threats, gender, and crime: A test and elaboration of power-control theory. *Criminology*, 38(2), 439–488.

Britton, D.M. (2011). *The gender of crime*. Plymouth, UK: Rowman and Littlefield.

Broidy, L., & Agnew, R. (1997). Gender and crime: A general strain perspective. *Journal of Research in Crime and Delinquency*, 34(3), 275–306.

Burgess-Proctor, A. (2006). Intersections of race, class, gender, and crime: Future directions for feminist criminology. *Feminist Criminology*, 1(1), 27–47.

Campbell, A. (1990). On the invisibility of the female delinquent peer group. *Women and Criminal Justice*, 2(1), 41–62.

Campbell, A. (1995). Girls, gangs, women and drugs. *Women and Criminal Justice*, 7(1), 107–110.

Chesney-Lind, M. (1989). Capitalism, patriarchy, and crime: Toward a socialist feminist criminology. *Gender & Society*, 3(1), 132–134.

Chesney-Lind, M. (1992). Partial justice: Women, prisons, and social control. *Women and Criminal Justice*, 4(1), 177–181.

Chesney-Lind, M. (2004). Beyond bad girls: Feminist perspectives on female offending. In C. Sumner (Ed.), *The Blackwell companion to criminology* (pp. 255–267). Malden, MA: Blackwell.

Chesney-Lind, M. (2006). Patriarchy, crime, and justice: Feminist criminology in an era of backlash. *Feminist Criminology, 1*(1), 6–26.

Chesney-Lind, M., & Shelden, R.G. (2004). *Girls, delinquency and juvenile justice.* Toronto: Nelson.

Cheung, N.W.T., & Cheung, Y.W. (2010). Strain, self-control, and gender differences in delinquency among Chinese adolescents: Extending general strain theory. *Sociological Perspectives, 53*(3), 321–345.

Connell, R.W. (2002). On hegemonic masculinity and violence. *Theoretical Criminology, 6*(1), 89–99.

Daly, K. (1997). Different ways of conceptualizing sex/gender in feminist theory and their implications for criminology. *Theoretical Criminology, 1*(1), 25–51.

Daly, K., & Tonry, M. (1997). Gender, race, and sentencing. In M. Tonry (Ed.), *Crime and justice: An annual review of research* (Vol. 22, pp. 201–252). Chicago: University of Chicago.

DeLisi, M. (2012). Genetics: L'enfant terrible of criminology. *Journal of Criminal Justice, 40,* 515–516.

Dorais, M., & Corriveau, p. (2009). *Gangs and girls, understanding juvenile prostitution.* Montreal: McGill-Queen's University Press.

Dugan, L., Nagin, D.S., & Rosenfeld, R. (2003). Exposure reduction or retaliation? The effects of domestic violence resources on intimate-partner homicide. *Law & Society Review, 37*(1), 169–198.

Eke, A.W., Hilton, Z.N., Harris, G.T., Rice, M.E., & Houghton, R.E. (2011). Intimate partner homicide: Risk assessment and prospects for prediction. *Journal of Family Violence, 26*(3), 211–216.

Ellsberg, M., Jansen, H., Heise, L., Watts, C., & García-Moreno, C. (2008). Intimate partner violence and women's physical and mental health in the WHO multi-country study on women's health and domestic violence: An observational study. *Lancet, 371,* 1165–1172.

Esbensen, F.-A., Deschenes, E.P., & Winfree, L.T. (1999). Differences between gang girls and gang boys: Results from a multisite survey. *Youth and Society, 31*(1), 27–53.

Fleisher, M.S. (1998). *Dead end kids: Gang girls and the boys they know.* Madison, WI: University of Wisconsin Press.

Gaarder, E., & Belknap, J. (2002). Tenuous borders: Girls transferred to adult court. *Criminology, 40,* 481–518.

Gartner, R. (1990). The victims of homicide: A temporal and cross-national comparison. *American Sociological Review, 55*(1), 92–106.

Gartner, R., Dawson, M., & Crawford, M. (1999). Women killing: Intimate femicide in Ontario, 1974–1994. *Resources for Feminist Research, 26,* 151–173.

Gartner, R., & McCarthy, B. (1991). The social distribution of femicide in urban Canada, 1921–1988. *Law & Society Review, 25*(2), 287–311.

Giordano, P.C., Deines, J.A., & Cernkovich, S.A. (2006). In and out of crime: A life course perspective on girls' delinquency. In K. Heimer & C. Kruttschnitt (Eds.), *Gender and crime: Patterns of victimization and offending* (pp. 17–40). New York: New York University Press.

Goodlin, W.E., & Dunn, C.S. (2010). Three patterns of domestic violence in households: Single victimization, repeat victimization and co-occurring victimization. *Journal of Family Violence, 25,* 107–122.

Gottfredson, M.R., & Hirschi, T. (1990). *A general theory of crime.* Stanford, CA: Stanford University Press.

Grasmick, H.G., Hagan, J., Blackwell, B., & Arenklev, B. (1996). Risk preferences and patriarchy: Extending power-control theory. *Social Forces, 75*(1), 177–199.

Gunman "took revenge" on family. (1996, April 8). *The Independent.* Retrieved from http://archive.today/EsKh.

Guo, G. (2006). The linking of sociology and biology. *Social Forces, 85*(1), 145–149.

Guo, G., Roettger, M., & Cai, T. (2008). The integration of genetic propensities into social-control models of delinquency and violence among male youths. *American Sociological Review, 73*, 543–568.

Hagan, J., Gillis, A.R., & Simpson, J. (1985). Class in the household: A power-control theory of gender and delinquency. *American Journal of Sociology, 92*, 788–816.

Hagan, J., & Kay, F. (1990). Gender and delinquency in white-collar families: A power-control perspective. *Crime and Delinquency, 36*(3), 391–407.

Hagan, J., McCarthy, B., & Foster, H. (2002). A gendered theory of delinquency and despair in the life course. *Acta Sociologica, 45*, 37–46.

Hannah-Moffat, K., & Yule, C. (2011). Gaining insight, changing attitudes and managing "risk": Parole release decisions for women convicted of violent crimes. *Punishment & Society, 13*(2), 149–175.

Harding, S. (1990). Feminism, science, and the anti-enlightenment critiques. In L.J. Nicholson (Ed.), *Feminist/postmodernism* (pp. 83–106). New York: Routledge.

Haymos, S., & Gatti, U. (2010). Girl members of deviant youth groups, offending behaviour and victimisation: Results from the ISRD2 in Italy and Switzerland. *European Journal on Criminal Policy and Research* (September), 167–182.

Heimer, K. (2000). Changes in the gender gap in crime and women's economic marginalization. *Criminal Justice, 1*, 427–483.

Heimer, K., & De Coster, S. (1999). The gendering of violent delinquency. *Criminology, 37*(2), 277–318.

Heimer, K., Lauritsen, J.L., & Lynch, J.P. (2009). The national crime victimization survey and the gender gap in offending: Redux. *Criminology, 47*(2), 427–438.

Heimer, K., Wittrock, S., & Ünal, H. (2006). The crimes of poverty: Economic marginalization and the gender gap in crime. In K. Heimer & C. Kruttschnitt (Eds.), *Gender and crime: Patterns of victimization and offending* (pp. 115–136). New York: New York University Press.

Hill, G.D., & Atkinson, M.P. (1988). Gender, familial control and delinquency. *Criminology, 26*(1), 127–150.

Hirschi, T. (1969). *Causes of delinquency*. Berkeley, CA: University of California Press.

Jennings, W.G., Piquero, N.L., Gover, A.R., & Pérez, D.M. (2009). Gender and general strain theory: A replication and exploration of Broidy and Agnew's gender/strain hypothesis among a sample of southwestern Mexican American adolescents. *Journal of Criminal Justice, 37*, 404–417.

Jensen, G.F., & Thompson, K. (1990). What's class got to do with it? A further examination of power-control theory. *American Journal of Sociology, 95*(4), 1009–1023.

Jiwani, Yasmin. (2006). *Discourses of denial: Mediations of race, gender, and violence*. Vancouver: University of British Columbia Press.

Joe, K.A., & Chesney-Lind, M. (1995). "Just every mother's angel": An analysis of gender and ethnic variations in youth gang membership. *Gender & Society, 9*(4), 408–431.

Kaufman, J.M. (2009). Gendered responses to serious strain: The argument for a general strain theory of deviance. *Justice Quarterly, 26*(3), 410–444.

King, R.D., Massoglia, M., & Macmillan, R. (2007). The context of marriage and crime: Gender, the propensity to marry, and offending in early adulthood. *Criminology, 45*(1), 33–65.

Kolb, A., & Palys, T. 2012. Are you down? Power relations and gender reconstruction among Latina gang members in Los Angeles. *Journal of Gang Research, 20*(1), 19–32.

Kreager, D. (2007). Unnecessary roughness? School sports, peer networks, and male adolescent violence. *American Sociological Review, 72*, 705–724.

LaFree, G., & Hunnicutt, G. (2006). Female and male homicide trends: A cross-national context. In K. Heimer & C. Kruttschnitt (Eds.), *Gender and crime: Patterns of victimization and offending* (pp. 195–229). New York: New York University Press.

Laub, J.H., & Sampson, R.J. (2003). *Shared beginnings, divergent lives: Delinquent boys to age 70.* Cambridge, MA: Harvard University Press.

Lauritsen, J.L., Heimer, K., & Lynch, J.P. (2009). Trends in the gender gap in violent offending: New evidence from the national crime victimization surveys. *Criminology, 47*, 361–399.

Leiber, M.J., & Wacker, M.E.E. (1997). A theoretical and empirical assessment of power-control theory and single-mother families. *Youth & Society, 28*(3), 317–350.

Lombroso, C., & Ferrero, W. (1958). *Female offender.* New York: Philosophical Press. (Original work published 1895.)

Lowman, J., & Louie, C. (2012). Public opinion on prostitution law reform in Canada. *Canadian Journal of Criminology and Criminal Justice, 54*(2), 245–261.

Lynch, M.J. (1996). Class, race, gender and criminology: Structured choices and the life course. In M.D. Schwartz and D. Milovanovic (Eds.), *Race, gender, and class in criminology: The intersection* (pp. 3–38). New York: Garland.

MacKinnon, C.A. (1991). Difference and dominance: On sex discrimination. In K.T. Bartlett and R. Kennedy (Eds.), *Feminist legal theory* (pp. 81–94). Boulder, CO: Westview.

Macmillan, R.I., & Gartner, R. (1999). When she brings home the bacon: Labour force participation and spousal violence against women. *Journal of Marriage and the Family, 61*, 947–958.

Mahony, T.H. (2011). *Women and the criminal justice system.* Ottawa: Statistics Canada. Retrieved from http://www.statcan.gc.ca/pub/89-503-x/2010001/article/11416-eng.pdf.

Massoglia, M., & Uggen, C. (2010). Settling down and aging out: Toward an interactionist theory of desistance and the transition to adulthood. *American Journal of Sociology, 116*, 543–582.

McCarthy, B., Hagan, J., & Woodward, T.S. (1999). In the company of women: Structure and agency in a revised power-control theory of gender and delinquency. *Criminology, 37*(4), 761–788.

McCorkel, J.A. (2013). *Breaking women: Gender, race, and the new politics of imprisonment.* New York: New York University Press.

McDaniels-Wilson, C., & Belknap, J. (2008). The extensive sexual violation and sexual abuse histories of incarcerated women. *Violence Against Women, 14*, 1090–1127.

Merton, R. (1938). Social structure and anomie. *American Sociological Review, 3*, 672–682.

Meyer, D. (2010). Evaluating the severity of hate-motivated violence: Intersectional differences among LGBT hate crime victims. *Sociology, 44*(5), 980–995.

Miller, J. (2008). *Getting played: African American girls, urban inequality, and gendered violence.* New York: New York University Press.

Miller, J., & Mullins, C.W. (2006a). The status of feminist theories in criminology. In F.T. Cullen, J.P. Wring, & K.R. Blevins (Eds.), *Taking stock: The status of criminological theory: Advances in criminological theory* (Vol. 15, pp. 217–250). New Brunswick, NJ: Transaction.

Miller, J., & Mullins, C.W. (2006b). Stuck up, telling lies, and talking too much: The gendered context of women's violence. In K. Heimer & C. Kurttschnitt (Eds.), *Gender and crime: Patterns of victimization and offending* (pp. 41–66). New York: New York University Press.

Morris, R.R. (1964). Female delinquency and relational problems. *Social Forces, 43*(1), 82–89.

Muller, H.J., Desmarais, S.L., & Hamel, J.M. (2009). Do judicial responses to restraining order requests discriminate against male victims of domestic violence. *Journal of Family Violence, 24*, 625–637.

Mullins, C.W., & Wright, R. (2003). Gender, social networks, and residential burglary. *Criminology, 41*(3), 813–840.

Mullins, C.W., Wright, R., & Jacobs, B.A. (2004). Gender, streetlife and criminal retaliation. *Criminology, 42*(4), 911–940.

Naffine, N. (1997). *Feminism and criminology*. Cambridge, MA: Polity Press.

Owen, B., & Bloom, B. (1995). Profiling women prisoners: Findings from national surveys and a California sample. *Prison Journal, 75*(2), 165–185.

Piquero, N.L., Fox, K., Piquero, A.R., Capowich, G., & Mazerolle, P. (2010). Gender, general strain theory, negative emotions, and disordered eating. *Journal of Youth and Adolescence, 39*(4), 380–392.

Piquero, N.L., & Sealock, M.D. (2004). Gender and general strain theory: A preliminary test of Broidy and Agnew's gender/GST hypotheses. *Justice Quarterly, 21*(1), 125–158.

Pollak, O. (1950). *The criminality of women*. Philadelphia: University of Pennsylvania Press.

Powers, R.A., & Kaukinen, C.E. (2012). Trends in intimate partner violence: 1980–2008. *Journal of Interpersonal Violence, 27*(15), 2072–3090.

Rader, N.E., & Haynes, S.H. (2011). Gendered fear of crime socialization: An extension of Akers's social learning theory. *Feminist Criminology, 6*(4), 291–307.

Sampson, R.J., & Laub, J.H. (1993). *Crime in the making: Pathways and turning points through life*. Cambridge, MA: Harvard University Press.

Sherman, L.W., & Berk, R.A. (1984). The specific deterrent effects of arrest for domestic violence. *American Sociological Review, 49*, 261–272.

Sherman, L.W., Schmidt, J.D., Rogan, D.P., Cohn, P.R., Cohn, E.G., Collins, D., & Bacich, A.R. (1992). From initial deterrence to long-term escalation: Short-custody arrest for poverty ghetto domestic violence. *Criminology, 29*(4), 821–850.

Sigfusdottir, I.-D., Farkas, G., & Silver, E. (2004). The role of depressed mood and anger in the relationship between family conflict and delinquent behavior. *Journal of Youth and Adolescence, 33*(6), 509–522.

Simon, R.J. (1975). *Women and crime*. Lexington, MA: Lexington Books.

Simpson, S.S., & Gibbs, C. (2006). Making sense of intersections. In K. Heimer & C. Kruttschnitt (Eds.), *Gender and crime: Patterns of victimization and offending* (pp. 269–302). New York: New York University Press.

Singer, S.I., & Levine, M. (1988). Power-control theory, gender, and delinquency: A partial replication with additional evidence on the effects of peers. *Criminology, 26*(4), 627–648.

Sinh, M. (2012, May 22). *Family violence in Canada: A statistical profile, 2010*. Ottawa: Statistics Canada. Retrieved from http://www.statcan.gc.ca/pub/85-002-x/2012001/article/11643-eng.pdf.

Smart, C. (1977). *Women, crime, and criminology*. London, UK: Routledge.

Sokoloff, N.J., & Dupont, I. (2005a). *Domestic violence at the intersections of race, class, gender, and culture*. New Brunswick, NJ: Rutgers University Press.

Sokoloff, N.J., & Dupont, I. (2005b). Domestic violence at the intersections of race, class, and gender: Challenges and contributions to understanding violence against marginalized women in diverse communities. *Violence Against Women, 11*(1), 38–64.

Sokoloff, N.J., & Pearce, S.C. (2011). Intersections, immigration, and partner violence: A view from a new gateway—Baltimore, Maryland. *Women & Criminal Justice, 21*, 250–266.

Sokoloff, N.J., Price, B.R., & Flavin, J. (2004). The criminal law and women. In B.R. Price & N.J. Sokoloff (Eds.), *The criminal justice system and women: Offenders, prisoners, victims and workers* (3rd ed., pp. 11–29). New York: McGraw-Hill.

Sprott, J.B. (2012). The persistence of status offences in the youth justice system. *Canadian Journal of Criminology and Criminal Justice, 55*(2), 279–292.

Steffensmeier, D., & Allan, E. (1996). Gender and crime: Toward a gendered theory of female offending. *Annual Review of Sociology, 22*, 459–487.

Steffensmeier, D., & Haynie, D. (2000). Gender, structural disadvantage, and urban crime: Do macrosocial variables also explain female offending rates? *Criminology, 38*, 403–438.

Steffensmeier, D., & Schwartz, J. (2004). Trends in female criminality: Is crime still a man's world? In B.R. Price & N.J. Sokoloff (Eds.), *The criminal justice system and women: Offenders, prisoners, victims and workers* (3rd ed., pp. 95–111). New York: McGraw-Hill.

Steffensmeier, D., Schwartz, J., Zhong, H., & Ackerman, J. (2005). An assessment of recent trends in girls' violence using diverse longitudinal sources: Is the gender gap closing? *Criminology, 43*(2), 355–406.

Steffensmeier, D., Zhong, H., Ackerman, J., Schwartz, J., & Agha, S. (2006). Gender gap trends for violent crimes, 1980 to 2003. *Feminist Criminology, 1*(1), 72–98.

Stets, J.E., & Straus, M.A. (1989). The marriage license as a hitting license: A comparison of assaults in dating, cohabitating, and married couples. *Journal of Family Issues, 4*(2), 161–180.

Sutherland, E. (1947). *Principles of criminology*. Philadelphia: J.P. Lippincott.

Talreja, S. (1996, April 24). Massacre in Vernon. *Outlook*. Retrieved from http://www.outlookindia.com/article.aspx?201229.

Thomas, W.I. (1969). *The unadjusted girl: With cases and standpoint for behavioral analysis*. Montclair, NJ: Patterson Smith. (Original work published 1923.)

Thompson, B. (2002). Multiracial feminism: Recasting the chronology of second wave feminism. *Feminist Studies, 28*, 337–360.

Uggen, C. (2000). Work as a turning point in the life course of criminals: A duration model of age, employment and recidivism. *American Sociological Review, 65*(4), 529–546.

Vedder, C.B., & Somerville, D.B. (1975). *The delinquent girl* (2nd ed.). Springfield, IL: Thomas.

Whaley, R.B., Hayes-Smith, J., & Hayes-Smith, R. (2010). Gendered pathways? Gender, mediating factors, and the gap in boys' and girls' substance use. *Crime & Delinquency, 59*(5), 651–669.

Wright, J.P., & Beaver, K.M. (2005). Do Parents matter in creating self-control in their children? A genetically informed test of Gottfredson and Hirschi's theory of low self-control. *Criminology, 43*(4), 1169–1202.

Cases

R v. Craig. (2011). 2011 ONCA 142.

Rational Choice Theory in Action

In their 1986 work *The Reasoning Criminal*, Derek Cornish and Ronald Clarke set out a "rational choice theory" framework that, they argued, could be used to diminish the extent of crime within communities. Specifically, in relation to the example that follows, they urged policy-makers to increase the effort needed to commit crime, increase the risk of getting caught, reduce the rewards that might flow from crime, and remove the excuses that could justify crime.

A visible presence within a community and good communications with local stakeholders are just two strategies police use to prevent crime.
Source: David Cooper/GetStock.com.

A recent study in the United Kingdom, led by criminologist Stuart Kirby, imposed a rational choice theory framework to counter the activities of an organized crime group (Kirby & Nailer, 2013). The study's researchers interviewed police officers about the group's actions within the village and surrounding area, asking about its impact on the community, the effectiveness of various policing interventions to date, the effectiveness of current preventive strategies, and the approach police were using to measure their successes in dealing with the group. The researchers also asked key community stakeholders about their knowledge of the organized crime group, what actions they might want to take to reduce crimes committed by this group, their evaluation of current police efforts, and the value of current communications between police and the community. Then, the researchers created profiles of the members of the organized crime group, noting their ages, the number of offences they were reported to have committed, and the number of criminal convictions attained.

What emerged from these consultations and research were a number of initiatives to tackle the group's criminal activities, all flowing from rational choice theory. Specifically, police took the following measures to increase the effort required to commit crime:

- traffic-calming activities to reduce speeding along the main street;
- increased police visibility in the area of the residences of those in the criminal network to challenge even low-level criminal behaviour; and
- communication with legitimate businesses to inform them that their products were being used to facilitate crime.

Furthermore, the police took the following measures to increase the risk to criminals of being caught:

- using automatic number plate recognition to identify all organized crime vehicles and their movement within the village;
- monitoring mobile phones, bank accounts, and travel documents of all members of the organized crime group;
- using closed circuit television throughout the village;
- implementing a zero-tolerance response to traffic violation by group members;
- gathering more intelligence on potential crimes committed by group members;

- patrolling specific areas by plain-clothed officers; and
- supplying photos and information regarding members to partner agencies.

The police and prosecutors also took the following measures to reduce the potential rewards that might flow from crimes committed by those within the group:

- using the *Proceeds of Crime Act 2002* to seize and confiscate any moneys obtained from crime by group members;
- enforcing planning regulations to prevent group members from developing houses; and
- taking legal action (including demolition) against unlawfully built houses owned by group members.

Finally, police removed excuses that could justify crime with the following measures:

- instituting traffic-calming measures, as noted above;
- sending out notices to all residents of the village regarding anti-social conduct; and
- documenting the importance of noise bylaws and the need to take action against nuisance.

Two years after these initiatives were put in place, the police assessed their impact on the organized crime group. They found that the numbers within the group had declined, in part because some were now in prison, but also because some had simply ceased their involvement in criminal activity. The capacity of the group to commit crime had diminished, and, perhaps most noteworthy, all of those interviewed two years later—both community members and police—felt that the criminality of the organized crime group had significantly diminished.

This example demonstrates how the application of principles of choice can serve to reduce criminal activity, particularly with a group that has organized itself to commit crime as an occupation.

Before You Read Chapter 11

- Could you contemplate similar successes with responses to other crimes, such as domestic violence? Or is the principle of choice less applicable in such circumstances?
- How might one increase the effort needed to commit a crime such as, for instance, domestic violence, and increase the risk of getting caught, reduce potential rewards for the offender, and remove any excuses that might justify the crime?
- Do you think that the rational choice approach is more potent when applied to some kinds of crime and less potent when applied to others?

CHAPTER 11 / GRAHAM FARRELL AND TARAH HODGKINSON
Crime Choice Theory

<table>
<tr><td>

LEARNING OBJECTIVES

After reading this chapter, students will be able to:

- Explain how choices are made, whether related to crime or not.
- Identify the range of costs and benefits involved in choices.
- Understand the key role of non-monetary (e.g., psychological) costs and benefits in decisions.
- Understand the link between choice theory and policy efforts to design-out crime.
- Critically assess how plentiful crime opportunities, due to changed routine activities, make crime a rational choice.
- Specify how reduced crime opportunities are likely to have been a key driver of choices to reduce offending in recent years.

</td><td>

CHAPTER OUTLINE

</td></tr>
</table>

Introduction

"Choose life. Choose a job. Choose a career. Choose a family … But why would I want to do a thing like that? I chose *not* to choose life: I chose something else. And the reasons? There are no reasons. Who needs reasons when you've got heroin?" (from the film *Trainspotting* [MacDonald & Boyle, 1996])

"[A] useful theory of criminal behavior can dispense with special theories of anomie, psychological inadequacies, or inheritance of special traits and simply extend the economist's usual analysis of choice." (Nobel Prize–winning economist Gary Becker, 1968, p. 170)

"We are our choices." (Jean-Paul Sartre, n.d.)

One morning you are running late. You skip breakfast and run for the bus. The next morning you have more time. You choose oatmeal because it is tasty, good for you, and keeps you full longer.

Let's consider those early morning decisions again, but in terms of choices: When you were running late, you needed to save time. You placed a greater value on your time than on eating, so you chose to skip breakfast. On the day you chose oatmeal, you decided that the nutrition it provides (minus the "cost" of the time and effort to prepare it) was more valuable than the benefit from the alternatives (perhaps toast or sugary cereal). On this day you had already decided that time for breakfast was time well spent.

In both scenarios, you made a routine decision. Most of us are experts in such every-day choices, making them so easily and quickly that we rarely think twice about them. The consequences of a wrong decision in our daily lives are usually minor, though there are exceptions such as choosing when to cross the road.

Yet, if we look more closely, we can see that our easy, everyday decisions often involve the implicit weighing of a variety of costs and benefits. In our breakfast scenario, the main costs of having oatmeal are the money to buy it, the travel time and expense of going to the store (even if you have done that beforehand), as well as the time, effort, and resources of cooking it—a pot, a stove, some electricity or gas, a bowl, milk or water, and perhaps ten minutes or more. Then there is the time, effort, and materials needed for cleaning. Toast is cheaper, quicker, and requires fewer resources. The main benefits of having oatmeal are its nutritional value and the fact that it is satisfying. So, this simple everyday decision, made in a second or two, really involves weighing a lot of factors, even though we rarely spell them out.

We can take this further: you may want to spend your time checking your email rather than cooking oatmeal and scrubbing the pot. Or you may simply have different tastes in food from other people. Hence, your personal preferences also influence your decisions. Preferences vary between people for a lot of reasons, and they are important in explaining why two people make different decisions in circumstances that are other-wise the same. Other factors influencing our individual preferences are our abilities and experiences. For instance, a fitter person might be more likely to run for the bus than a less-fit person, and a health-conscious person might be more likely to choose a nutri-tious breakfast than a person who is less health-conscious.

Some other decisions are life changing. Deciding whether to go to university or col-lege is one example. The "costs" may include not only tuition fees but also living expenses, relocating, and perhaps the emotional cost of leaving family and friends. Studying full-time also means missing out on the wages from a full-time job. But most students are prepared to accept these costs because of the potential benefits, and expect to earn more in the long term with a degree. Students also benefit from the many life experiences of higher education, such as making new friends and enjoying new opportunities, new freedoms, and the personal gain of being better educated. Some uncertainties must also be considered: students are not guaranteed that they will enjoy university or college, get the grades they want, or land the job they desire afterward.

Big decisions in life—buying a car or a home, deciding on marriage or children—involve a more explicit weighing of costs and benefits. We try to gather good informa-tion to make a more informed choice, reducing our risks of a poor decision. But even then we can make the wrong decision, particularly if we had incorrect information. This works both ways, though, and decisions can turn out to be better than expected.

In essence, criminal decisions are made through exactly the same process as any other decisions. This chapter will introduce this area of criminological theory and ex-amine its links to real-world changes in crime and crime policy.

A Note About Terminology

Note that in this chapter we use the term **choice theory**, although a lot of the academic literature refers to **rational choice theory**. Choice theory is simpler and sidesteps com-mon misunderstandings related to the term *rational* (the term is used differently in the

choice theory
The framework for understanding how decisions are made by indi-viduals by weighing the perceived costs and benefits of an action.

rational choice theory
A modern version of Classical School thinking originating in economics; it assumes that humans are rational and have free will, and that offend-ers make conscious choices to commit crime, based on a cost–benefit analysis.

theory as compared with everyday conversation). By definition, the term has to be used differently, of course, because most crimes do not appear rational to most people! Moreover, studies show that intuition is an important part of decisions alongside reason and rationality. Because criminology has developed its own set of frameworks and concepts relating to choice theory, we refer to the overall explanation as *crime choice theory*.

Crime: Everybody Does It!

Let's begin by considering laws that nearly everyone breaks. Speeding while driving is an obvious one—virtually anyone who drives a car does it, at least sometimes. Particularly if one is running late, the perceived benefit from speeding is great, while the risk of being caught is small. Often, if you are not driving above the speed limit, other drivers are probably tailgating or honking. Or you may enjoy the thrill of speeding. And so you drive a little over the limit. So what? Everybody does it. If you are unlucky enough to be stopped by the police, you will simply pay a fine and probably keep your licence. Weighing all of this, speeding appears to be a rational choice for most of us (and we tend to discount the relatively low risk of causing death or injury to others).

In his book *Everybody Does It!* (1994), Thomas Gabor says committing crime is like the common cold: nobody is immune, but we are not all equally susceptible. We differ mainly in the frequency, seriousness, and persistence with which we commit crime. Beyond speeding, consider petty crimes that many people commit, such as taking office supplies from the workplace (perhaps justified in one's mind as a "perk of the job") or avoiding paying taxes. Anyone can commit an assault if sufficiently provoked, for example, an otherwise mild-mannered mother who feels it necessary to protect her child.

BOX 11.1

A Very Rational Bank Robber

Willie Sutton, an infamous bank robber in the 1920s and 1930s, was asked why he robbed banks. He is said to have replied: "Because that's where the money is!"

This is a humorous anecdote, but it illustrates some relevant points:

1. Banks are tempting targets because they contain a lot of money.

2. Back when Sutton was robbing banks, they were not as secure as they are now.

3. Robbing banks seemed fairly easy and highly rewarding to Sutton because he got cash quickly and easily, and probably also "benefited" from the thrill of the experience.

Willie Sutton, photographed on the day he attempted to escape Eastern State Penitentiary in Philadelphia, April 3, 1945.

Even though most people do not consider robbing banks to be a rational choice, from Sutton's perspective it was. Of course, nowadays it is far more difficult to rob banks because of the vastly improved security (the important role of security in nudging offenders away from crime is discussed later in this chapter).

The Costs and Benefits of Crime

"People think it's all about misery and desperation and death and all that shite, which is not to be ignored. But what they forget is the pleasure of it. Otherwise we wouldn't do it."
(A character in *Trainspotting*)

An individual commits a crime when its perceived benefits outweigh its perceived costs, as was the case for the infamous bank robber presented in Box 11.1. This is the basic formula for crime choice theory, and its concepts can be shown to underlie all criminal decisions. That is, crime occurs when

$$\text{perceived benefits} > \text{perceived costs}$$

This simple formula is very flexible and can easily apply to very complex decisions. The definitions of costs and benefits are broad and include the emotional aspects of crime as well as money. Likewise, the role of perceptions is important—note that the formula comprises *perceived* benefits and *perceived* costs—because it is how benefits and costs are perceived by the offender that is important. Those perceptions may be wrong, especially if the decision is skewed by factors such as emotion, alcohol, or drugs.

One of the most commonly misunderstood areas of crime choice theory is costs and benefits. It can be difficult to grasp that costs and benefits include emotions and other psychological aspects. Crime is not just about money. Other perceived benefits might be the thrill of committing crime or the psychological reward of the praise from peers (or kudos). While it is easy for us to think of the perceived benefits of a burglary or a theft in terms of money or valuables, it is not as easy (until you dig deeper) to think of the rewards of a sexual assault. The rewards to the offender from a sexual assault can include the "benefit" of the feeling of power and control gained from the crime as well as the sexual gratification. Beauregard, Proulx, Rossmo, Leclerc, and Allaire (2007) have produced excellent work on the application of choice theory to the decisions of serial sex offenders.

A summary of the different types of costs and benefits is shown in Table 11.1. Non-monetary costs and benefits are sometimes called *intangible* costs and benefits because emotions and other psychological aspects are not as easy to measure. That said, a lot of research now shows that we can, however crudely, develop estimates of the equivalent monetary costs of the impact of some crimes on victims. This area of research is still evolving, but it is important because otherwise a crime such as rape—which has a very high psychological impact on victims—appears to be less serious than a burglary if one considers only monetary aspects. In addition, the psychological aspects of committing crime—the thrill and kudos in particular—are important in understanding how the choice theory framework can be applied to all types of crime, not just property crime.

Poor Decisions

bounded rationality (limited rationality)
Decisions are often made imperfectly as best guesses given available information and time constraints. Decisions are "bounded" by the limits of our knowledge and circumstances, and so our rationality is bounded.

Choice theorists use the terms **bounded rationality** and **limited rationality** to refer to decisions that are made in imperfect circumstances. In economics these terms usually refer to the decisions of companies and investors (Simon, 1957). But the work of Gary Becker (1968) changed all of this. Becker introduced the economic approach to the study of crime in a more formal way than had been done before. He argued that a theory of offending could be developed that was based on the concept of choice as it is used

Table 11.1   The Costs and Benefits of Crime

	Monetary	Non-monetary
Benefits	• Cash from crime—from theft, robbery, etc. • Stolen consumer goods (e.g., jewellery, phone, cars) that can be resold for money • Stolen goods that can be used by offenders—e.g., phones, cars • Stolen information and personal data	• Time and energy saved by cutting corners • Excitement/thrill • Feeling of power/control over others and over own acts • Any boost to self-esteem • Kudos—peers' and others' esteem • Any other positive emotions or feelings
Costs	• Expenditure on tools used to commit crime (e.g., crowbar) • Cost of travel to offence site • Possible opportunity cost of time (including learning skills, search time, committing crime and escaping, selling stolen goods)	• Physical effort/energy • Psychological and emotional effort/energy • Shame, remorse, or guilt—peer, family, and other condemnation • Worry/concern about punishment • Any other negative emotions or feelings

Source: Adapted from Farrell (2010).

in economics (Becker won the Nobel Prize in Economic Sciences mainly for this insight because he applied it to many areas of life, including crime). He argued that our decisions relating to marriage and many other areas involve choices based on **utility maximization** (i.e., making a choice where the perceived benefits outweigh the perceived costs).

Many studies in recent years have examined how decisions—not just those relating to offending—are often not as rational as we believe them to be. Sometimes we make errors of judgment or have systematic biases in our decisions that arise, for example, from the immediate situation or recent experience. Other times, we make decisions based on imperfect information where we guess or use a rule of thumb (known as *heuristics*). Most of the studies on decision making look at decisions that do not relate to crime, but it is clear that the issues are incorporated within the crime choice theory framework. Hence, while "the intuitive criminal" might be a useful term for studies that more closely examine the systematic way that offenders make mistakes, we view intuition as compatible with most of the literature on "rational" offending.

When it comes to crime, decisions often appear to be even less rational than they do in other walks of life. Here the concept of *limited rationality* is useful. It refers to decisions that are limited by a lack of information or decisions made in circumstances where the costs and benefits were not properly assessed. When it comes to crime, decision making can be impulsive, made with a lack of information about the risks involved, or made when the person's judgment is impaired by alcohol or drugs. In fact, a large proportion of crime involves alcohol or drugs, as is clear by the rise in assaults and other street crimes that occur on weekends and during public holidays and celebrations. A summary of poor choices involving limited rationality is shown in Table 11.2.

utility maximization
Choices are made based on what one perceives will provide the greatest rewards for the lowest costs.

Table 11.2 Poor Choices

Type	Description
Impulsive decisions	They are made too quickly, without thinking: "It seemed like a good idea at the time!"; "I wasn't thinking"; "I regret it now"; "It was spur-of-the-moment"
Imperfect decisions	They are based on poor or wrong information: "I didn't know they had a dog/silent alarm/CCTV"; "At the time, I didn't see the consequences"
Impaired decisions	They are impaired by emotion, alcohol, or drugs: "I wasn't thinking straight"; "It was the alcohol/drugs not me!"; "It was my uncontrollable teenage angst/contempt for society"; "She was chatting up my boyfriend"

Source: Adapted from Farrell (2010).

Box 11.2 shows how joyriding is a "rational" choice by offenders who want the benefit of the excitement and kudos. It also gives a preview of the connection between choice theory and crime control policy that is described later, because it is clear that joyriding has been largely eliminated in recent years by greatly improved vehicle security.

BOX 11.2

Making Joyriding a Harder Choice

Joyriding is the informal name given to car thefts committed for pleasure, usually by thrill-seeking teenagers. The "joy" in joyriding is the excitement of the car ride and breaking the law, and the prestige among peers and passengers—this "joy" is the perceived benefit in the choice to commit the crime. Hence, for some people, stealing a car is a fairly rational way of gaining prestige and satisfying a need for excitement.

It used to be very easy—and hence very rational—to steal most cars. Sometimes, only a coat hanger was required to break the lock, and a screwdriver could be used to start the engine, or thieves could "hotwire" the car by connecting wires in the steering column.

Recognizing joyriding as a choice is important because it then becomes easier to determine how to stop it; that is, by reducing the joy involved or by increasing the effort or skill needed to steal a car. For example, speed bumps and other traffic-calming measures make it less enjoyable to drive a car fast. Better door locks and central locking doors make it harder to break into a car. Electronic immobilizer systems may not block a thief from entering a car, but they make it very difficult to start the engine. In addition, parking lots can be designed and managed in many ways to make it harder to steal cars, for example, by improving barriers, having attendants, and installing closed-circuit television (CCTV).

As a result of better security, car theft in Canada (and most other industrialized countries) has fallen dramatically in the last decade. It is now less easy to choose to steal a car, and less rational to do so.

For further reading on the decline in joyriding, see Brown (2004), Farrell, Tseloni, and Tilley (2011), and Kriven and Ziersch (2007).

A Brief History of Choice Theory

Having examined the basic framework and concepts for understanding choice theory and its implications, let's step back and take stock of the origins of choice theory as it relates to crime.

Crime choice theory is said to have its origins in the 1764 essay "Of Crimes and Punishments" by Cesare Beccaria. This famous work was described by criminologist Marvin Wolfgang as "the most significant essay on crime and punishment in Western civilization" (1996, p. xi). Beccaria was Italian, but his work is said to have influenced Thomas Jefferson and others involved in writing the Constitution of the United States, along with a great many 18th- and 19th-century policy-makers across Europe and Asia, including areas not directly related to crime policy (Wolfgang, 1996). Box 11.3 presents leading scholars in choice theory. In choosing only six theorists, we offer only the starting lineup of our all-star ice hockey team, while acknowledging the many others who have done excellent work in this area.

The specifics of crime choice theory have evolved since Beccaria, but the theory has largely stood the test of time; in scientific terms, this means the theory is extremely robust, in a way comparable to Charles Darwin's theory of evolution through natural

---

BOX 11.3

Leading Choice Theorists

The work of the following six scholars, past and present, has been tremendously influential on crime choice theory.

Cesare Beccaria (1738–1794): The 18th-century Italian scholar paved the way to study crimes as rational choices in his famous 1764 essay "On Crimes and Punishments." Beccaria realized that people made choices that involved calculating what was in their best interest. He termed this the **hedonistic calculus**. It outlines the basic principles of choice theory that still apply today.

Jeremy Bentham (1748–1832): Bentham's theory of utilitarianism—the doctrine that one should choose to act in a way to maximize utility (i.e., the well-being, including happiness and pleasure, of individuals or the well-being of society as a goal of public policy)—is hugely influential in the world of philosophy and is also a cornerstone of choice theory. Crime, like all behaviour, is committed to maximize the perceived utility.

Gary Becker (1930–): This Nobel Prize–winning economist's landmark 1968 study examined crime using an economic approach. Becker said, "a useful theory of criminal behavior can dispense with special theories of anomie, psycho-logical inadequacies, or inheritance of special traits and simply extend the economist's usual analysis of choice" (1968, p. 170).

Daniel Kahneman (1934–): Kahneman—a psychologist who won the Nobel Memorial Prize in Economics—has focused on intuitive choices: the errors, biases, and rules of thumb by which decisions are less than rational. While crime is not Kahneman's focus, his work is the basis for "nudge theory" that is influential in public policy (Thaler & Sunstein, 2008) and closely related to situational crime prevention and designing-out crime.

Derek Cornish (1939–): Cornish is a greatly underrated criminologist who pioneered much of the rational choice way of thinking, from the study of gambling and crime displacement to the development of scripts that show the many stages and decisions involved in criminal events. He co-authored landmark studies on criminological choice theory with Ronald V. Clarke.

Ronald V. Clarke (1942–): Clarke is widely recognized as criminology's leading scholar on rational choice and situational crime prevention. His work has focused on these areas for over 40 years. He coined the term *situational crime prevention* and showed how choice theory directly informs crime control policy. He co-authored many key studies of choice with Derek Cornish.

selection (Darwin, 1859). Like Darwin's work, Beccaria's theory continues to gather support and evidence, and is likely to continue to do so.

In the study of human behaviour, choice theory has had widespread acceptance, influence, and longevity similar to Darwin's work in the natural sciences. Choice theory is tremendously influential, not only in criminology but also in economics, psychology, law, sociology, and elsewhere. Harvard University professors James Q. Wilson and Richard Herrnstein (1985) describe it as probably the most widely used theory in the behavioural sciences (the study of human behaviour).

Choosing a Criminal Career

The collaboration of Cornish and Clarke, mentioned in Box 11.3, has produced key theoretical advances. For example, they identified four broad stages of decisions in a criminal career, shown in Table 11.3.

Within each stage, key choices are made, and a variety of factors influence decisions. Many teenagers will commit a crime of some sort. Most of them do not decide to continue to commit more crimes for various reasons: perhaps they did not enjoy it, or they were caught, or when they were sober they realized their mistake. Hence, while offending rates increase in the late teenage years, particularly as individuals gain their independence of movement, most people do not escalate to more serious crimes. The likelihood that a teenager will continue to offend or begin frequently offending is still relatively small. Even among the small proportion of people who go on to offend more frequently, most of them "age out" of offending over time. This is largely because, as we get older, our perceptions of the costs and benefits of committing crime change. We get a job, build relationships, and may start a family, which leaves much less time and energy to go out and break into cars (or we simply buy our own car). The potential personal cost (including to the family) of arrest and punishment also increases. Hence, only a very small proportion of the population, usually males, go on to an extended criminal career (Moffitt, 1993). And even then, as some studies have shown, drug dependency involves the choice to continue to take drugs. For example, Trevor Bennett's (1986) classic study of heroin users found that they often choose not to take drugs when they do not have the money or when they need to be able to do something where they prefer not to be under the influence.

Table 11.3   Key Decision Stages in a Criminal Career

Stage	Action	Decision
1	Initial involvement	The initial decision to commit a crime
2	The criminal event	Decisions relating to the crime itself (see scripts, discussed in Box 11.4)
3	Continuing involvement	The decision to continue and perhaps escalate to serious crime
4	Desistence	The decision to quit crime

Source: Based on Clarke and Cornish's (1985) models.

Crime Event "Scripts"

Breaking down particular crime types into the sequence of actions involved, or a **script**, allows us to examine the many steps in decision making and action. The concept of scripts, introduced to criminology by Cornish (1994), shows how many aspects of life can be viewed in terms of a script. Box 11.4 presents the scripts for a restaurant visit and two criminal events.

script
The steps in decision making and the sequence of actions for a particular criminal event.

BOX 11.4

Examples of Scripts

Script 1: A Restaurant Visit

1. Enter the restaurant.
2. Wait to be seated.
3. Get the menu.
4. Order.
5. Be served.
6. Eat.
7. Get the bill.
8. Pay.
9. Exit the restaurant. (Tompson, 2011)

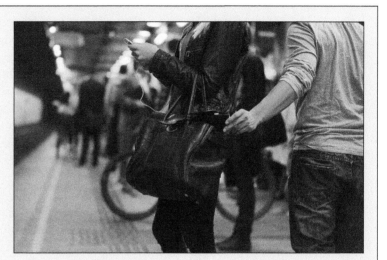

Script 2: A Snatch Theft or Robbery in a Subway System

1. Meet co-offenders and agree on hunting ground.
2. Enter the subway system.
3. Travel to hunting ground (the chosen station).
4. Wait/circulate at hunting ground.
5. Select victim and circumstance.
6. Close in/prepare.
7. **Press home attack.**
8. **Take money, jewellery, etc.**
9. Escape from the scene.
10. Exit from the system.
11. Fence the stolen goods. (Adapted from Leddo & Abelson, 1986; Ekblom, 1991)

Script 3: A Sexual Assault in a Residential Institution (e.g., Children's Home, Elderly Care Home)

1. Development of sexual fantasies, offending strategies, and inducements
2. Selection of victim-rich setting
3. Preconditions: legitimate role (job), absence of managers, disorganized setting
4. Identification of suitable victims
5. Initiation: non-threatening approach, initiation of interaction, preliminary grooming
6. Actualization: isolation from others, removal to un-supervised area
7. **Commission of sexual assault of the victim**
8. Successful disengagement
9. Disposal of evidence (adapted from Cornish, 1994; see also Beauregard et al., 2007)

Script 2 is a generic script for a snatch theft or robbery on the subway system. It involves 11 decision steps and actions. Many of these are the various stages of preparation—meeting co-offenders, travelling to the selected site, searching for a suitable victim, and closing in on the victim in suitable circumstances (where there is no *guardianship*, or someone who watches over or protects). The criminal act itself (set off in bold type) may be relatively quick. To the victim, these crimes can appear opportunistic or spur-of-the-moment, but the script shows they are not. After the offence is committed, the offenders need to escape. But even after escaping, most offenders still need to go through further decision making, including selling the stolen goods. Fencing goods is itself a multi-stage process and depends on whether the offenders know a good fence or choose to sell the goods via another route such as the Internet (which entails time, skill, computer resources, and some risks). It is clear that what seems to be an opportunistic snatch theft or robbery is, in fact, often a far more deliberately planned set of "rational" actions.

Script 3 shows a breakdown of decisions and actions for a sexual assault conducted in a residential institution, such as a children's home or an elderly care home. It is included here because sexual assault is often thought of as either impulsive or motivated by feelings beyond the control of the offender. The script shows how it is typically deliberate and often involves many decision stages and actions. When considered in this way, it clarifies how sexual offences often involve elements of rational decision making by offenders during the many stages of preparation for the crime, undertaking the crime, escaping, hiding the evidence, and making sure the victim does not report the crime. Note that the sexual assault itself takes place at step 7 of the script.

Scripts 2 and 3 are provided as fairly broad examples to show that all crime types can be broken down in this way, with some variation in the specifics for different types of crime. Though most sexual victimization is by families and known persons, the robbery script above gives a clear indication of how even sexual assaults by strangers will involve many steps of planning and "rational" decisions.

Organized crime, terrorism, and gang activity (see Chapter 17, Organized Crime and Gangs) may have so many different stages for planning and committing the crime that they have a long script that is embedded into a larger script of many crimes (Hancock & Laycock, 2010). Even bar fights have been shown to have a decision-making script, despite the fact that they may take place rapidly. The persons involved may have chosen to go to a particular bar where they know the chances of a fight are greater. The precise interaction that triggers a fight may be something relatively innocuous such as drinks spilled by bumping into another person. Even then, decisions are made that vary by a person's assessment of his or her opponent and whether the person will lose face with friends if he or she backs down. The presence of bouncers or the likelihood that someone may video a fight on a smart phone may also influence the decision to commit a crime.

Scripts are increasingly used to inform crime prevention interventions. This is because the decision steps identified by script analysis are potential intervention points. This link to scripts should become clearer when we consider situational crime prevention (below).

Routine Activity Theory

routine activity theory
Felson's theory that every-day routines and legitimate activities are key determinants of crime opportunities.

While the emphasis in this chapter is on choice theory, it should be noted that choice theory and **routine activity theory** are complementary and interlocking rather than competing. Marcus Felson is the main routine activity theorist, and his primary focus is the development of theory, concepts, and evidence in this area. Felson and Rachel Boba are the co-authors of one of the seminal works in this area, *Crime and Everyday Life* (2010).

Like the simple formula that underlies choice theory, routine activity theory can be stated very simply, as it was in the 1979 study that launched it: "Most criminal acts require convergence in space and time of *likely offenders, suitable targets* and the *absence of capable guardians* against crime" (Cohen & Felson, 1979, p. 588).

Note that it lists three basic elements that are needed for a criminal event: a potential offender, a suitable target, and the *absence* of a capable guardian. While seemingly simple, this theory is also remarkably flexible and robust and can be applied to any criminal event. The three elements are defined broadly. We prefer the term *potential offender* to *likely offender* because it captures the notion described earlier: that everyone is a potential offender. When the situation is right, almost anyone can be tempted or provoked into choosing to commit crime (note that the word *choosing* is very important here, as it links routine activity theory to rational choice theory). Thus, the definition of *potential offender* could include all of us (if there is a wallet with cash left unattended) or certain individuals who might be more experienced and more actively searching for crime opportunities. A *suitable target* might be a person in the street who could be robbed or have his or her bag snatched, to a house or car that could be broken into, to a computer terminal or network that could be hacked. Likewise, the term *capable guardian* is broad and includes any passerby who might intervene or call the police, a receptionist in an office who screens who comes and goes, and a bus driver who in addition to taking fares and driving also provides some implicit guardianship for the bus. Because many of them exist, these everyday types of guardianship are often far more important than the more formal types, such as police and security guards.

The three elements of a criminal event can be broken down further. A suitable target can be broken into "suitable" and "target" so that it refers to the number of potential targets (such as the number of cars on the road or the number of smart phones in the population) and their suitability. For example, although many target cars are on the road, more recent models are far less suitable to steal because of improvements in vehicle security.

The seemingly simple three-element framework of routine activity theory clarifies the importance of target suitability and capable guardianship. In fact, whole areas of theory have now developed relating to those concepts that are, at least in part, inspired by routine activity theory. "Target suitability" has led to studies of the characteristics of frequently stolen products, for example. Highly suitable targets are "CRAVED"—a useful mnemonic, or memory tool, developed by Ronald Clarke to identify desirable, frequently stolen objects such as smart phones and tablets (see Table 11.4).

Table 11.4 Frequently Stolen "Suitable Targets" Are CRAVED

Concealable	They are often small and easily hidden when stolen.
Removable	They are portable and not a permanent fixture.
Available	They are not locked away (unlike gold in Fort Knox) and can be accessed.
Valuable	They usually have a monetary value.
Enjoyable	They are enjoyed by offenders (e.g., smart phones) if not stolen for money.
Disposable	They can be disposed of—that is, easily fenced or sold.

Source: Clarke (1999).

The Connection Between Crime Choice Theory and Routine Activity Theory

These theories are connected via the fact that target suitability and the capability of guardians are huge influences on the decisions—the choices—of potential offenders. Simply put, if fewer or less suitable targets exist, offenders choose to commit less crime. Likewise, if more guardians exist because, say, sightlines across a residential area or office (or other place) are clearer, then offenders choose to commit less crime because it is not as easy.

Routine activity theory was originally proposed to explain why crime rates in most industrialized countries increased dramatically for much of the second half of the 20th century. Most criminological theory had tended to assert that crime would *decrease* as living standards improved, as people became wealthier and as education, health, and welfare improved. Yet—and this is the major paradox that routine activity theory addressed—while almost all social problems had lessened significantly as economies boomed in the second half of the 20th century, crime rates soared.

Routine activity theory showed how the tremendous increases in crime (Figure 11.2, later in the chapter, shows Canada's crime trends) were, in fact, caused by society being better off. The theory provided a two-pronged explanation for this phenomenon. First, because people were better off, more valuable consumer goods were available to steal— more cars on the road and more consumer goods in homes. As a result, more crime opportunities made it "rational" to choose to commit crime. Second, modern lifestyles had changed in ways that increased some crime opportunities. The fact that more women were going to work rather than staying at home meant that households were left unguarded during the daytime (which in turn meant that working women were also more routinely exposed to crimes such as theft and sexual victimization in the workplace). Routine activity theory is also closely linked to **crime pattern theory**, which offers a set of concepts for studying and understanding variations in crime patterns and trends (see Table 11.5).

crime pattern theory
A theory that helps explain how crime patterns arise; it asserts that crime is not random. Its concepts (e.g., nodes, paths, and edges) describe how offenders move in the urban environment.

Table 11.5   Key Concepts of Crime Pattern Theory

Concept	Detail
Paths	The routes (roads, train routes, walkways) along which we, including potential offenders, travel between nodes
Nodes	The main places we travel to and from—home, workplace, leisure and entertainment locations, and transportation hubs
Edges	The area between land uses of different types where crime is more likely—for example, along the road where a high- and low-income housing area meet
Ridges	The areas where crime often groups, along roads or transport routes, that form a pattern that appears as a crime "ridge"
Attractors	Places that attract offenders because they have a reputation as good places to commit crime
Generators	Places such as train stations and entertainment districts where crime is generated by the interaction of high volumes of suitable targets and potential offenders in places with low guardianship

Source: Brantingham and Brantingham (1993).

Long before routine activity theory had been proposed, Leslie Wilkins had made the connection between increased crime opportunities and increased crime. In 1964, Wilkins noted the direct relationship between increases in the number of cars and increases in the number of car crimes (see Figure 11.1). His work was ahead of its time, and his influence can be traced to the work of choice theorists such as Ronald Clarke (Gott-fredson & Clarke, 1990).

Crime opportunity theory, based on the classic study "Crime as Opportunity" (May-hew, Clarke, Sturman, & Hough, 1976), is not particularly hard to grasp, and perhaps that is why some criminologists did not take to it easily. It offers clear implications for crime control policy and suggests that convoluted social theories of crime and social inequality were largely incorrect. Bear in mind that Marxist and other "critical" theories were still influential in the 1960s.

crime opportunity theory
An umbrella term for the set of theories and concepts that are underpinned by the notion that the level of crime opportunities is the main cause of crime.

Cars played a major role in the increase in crime from the 1960s and into the 1990s because of the multiple roles they played. They were excellent targets for different crime types (car theft, car vandalism, theft of items from cars), and they played a direct role in facilitating many other types of crime. Cars made it easier to drive to an illicit drug market, to reach destinations where crime could be committed (e.g., suburban burglary became far easier), to transport stolen goods, and as getaway vehicles for store and bank robberies. So, before the 1990s, cars directly contributed to crime's more general increase. By contrast, more secure cars have likely influenced the decrease in crime over the last two decades. Figure 11.1 shows the relationship between the volume of crime opportunities (cars) and crime (car crimes), as found in one classic study.

FIGURE 11.1   The Relationship Between Opportunities to Commit Crime and the Incidence of Crime (England and Wales)

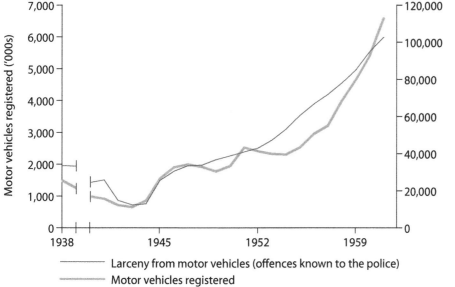

Source: Adapted from Wilkins (1964, pp. 54–55).

Crime Prevention Policy

"[U]nless a theory leads to clear and practical preventive policy, it should be regarded as suspect." (Clarke & Felson, 2011)

This section briefly introduces the link between choice theory and other key criminological theories as well as crime policy.

The notions of free will and rationality underpin the Canadian and many other legal systems. Adults are responsible for their own behaviour and decisions. That is why they are liable if they break the law.

dispositional theories
Theories that seek to explain variations between individuals in their tendency or disposition to commit crime. Explanations are usually biological or psychological.

The key connection between choice theory and **dispositional theories** of crime (those that look at individual "dispositions" or tendencies to commit crime) is the notion of individual tastes or preferences. Dispositional theories attempt to provide biological or psychological explanations of why particular people engage in crime. However, from a policy perspective it is extremely difficult to influence the "hearts and minds" of offenders. The reason choice theory is particularly useful is because it offers many practical approaches to crime control policy. The most important of these approaches is situational crime prevention, which takes a variety of different forms that will be introduced here.

Choices are determined by the balance of perceived costs and benefits. Therefore, changes to those costs and benefits, or the way they are perceived, can alter the decision to commit crime. Some factors increase the perceived benefits of committing crime, and so crime increases. This is the case when new, valuable, easy-to-steal consumer goods such as smart phones and computer tablets become widely available. Yet it also means that efforts can be made to alter the balance of costs and benefits in ways that tip the scales away from offending. Those efforts fall within the realm of situational crime prevention.

Situational Crime Prevention

situational crime prevention (SCP)
Measures taken to reduce crime opportunities. SCP takes into account the nature of the crime, the environmental factors that allow for the crime, and the risks and rewards associated with crime.

Situational crime prevention (SCP) seeks to alter the costs and benefits involved in crime choices. It does so by **designing-out** crime from products, systems, and the built environment. SCP proposes five broad categories of actions to prevent crime:

1. Increase the effort needed to commit a crime.
2. Increase the risks of crime.
3. Reduce the rewards.
4. Reduce provocations.
5. Remove excuses. (Cornish & Clarke, 2003)

designing-out
The concept that crime prevention can start at the design process so that products and places are designed with potential criminal threats or opportunities in mind.

These same categories appear in Table 11.6 and offer options for tackling crime other than trying to influence the hearts and minds of offenders—a very difficult task at best. SCP has grown to become one of the more important areas of crime control policy.

SCP was first developed in the 1980s as a description of four broad categories of approach. Ronald Clarke, for whom SCP is a core focus, proposed a set of 12 techniques of situational crime prevention in 1992. Five years later, Ronald V. Clarke and Ross Homel (1997) extended the number of techniques to 16, and then six years later, Cornish and Clarke (2003) produced 25 techniques. The 25 techniques are a set of theoretical mechanisms for preventing crime. Note that the gradual building of SCP over time is characteristic of a robust theory and, as implied, SCP has become increasingly used and

Table 11.6   The 25 Techniques of Situational Crime Prevention

Increase the effort	Increase the risks	Reduce the rewards	Reduce provocations	Remove excuses
1. **Target hardening:** • Steering column locks • Anti-robbery screens • Tamper-proof packaging	6. **Extend guardianship:** • Take routine precautions: go out in groups at night, leave signs of occupancy, carry phone • "Cocoon" neighbourhood watch	11. **Conceal targets:** • Off-street parking • Gender-neutral phone directories • Unmarked bullion trucks	16. **Reduce frustrations and stress:** • Efficient queues and polite service • Expanded seating • Soothing music/ muted lights	21. **Set rules:** • Rental agreements • Harassment codes • Hotel registration
2. **Control access to facilities:** • Entry phones • Electronic card access • Baggage screening	7. **Assist natural surveillance:** • Improved street lighting • Defensible space design • Support whistleblowers	12. **Remove targets:** • Removable car radios • Women's refuges • Prepaid cards for pay phones	17. **Avoid disputes:** • Separate enclosures for rival soccer fans • Reduce crowding in pubs • Fixed cab fares	22. **Post instructions:** • "No parking" • "Private property" • "Extinguish camp fires"
3. **Screen exits:** • Ticket needed for exit • Export documents • Electronic merchandise tags	8. **Reduce anonymity:** • Taxi driver IDs • "How's my driving?" decals • School uniforms	13. **Identify property:** • Property marking • Vehicle licensing and parts marking • Cattle branding	18. **Reduce emotional arousal:** • Controls on violent pornography • Enforce good behaviour on soccer field • Prohibit racial slurs	23. **Alert conscience:** • Roadside speed display boards • Signatures for customs declarations • "Shoplifting is stealing"
4. **Deflect offenders:** • Street closures • Separate bathrooms for women • Disperse pubs	9. **Utilize place managers:** • CCTV for double-deck buses • Two clerks for convenience stores • Reward vigilance	14. **Disrupt markets:** • Monitor pawn shops • Controls on classified ads • License street vendors	19. **Neutralize peer pressure:** • "Idiots drink and drive" • "It's OK to say no" • Disperse trouble-makers at school	24. **Assist compliance:** • Easy library checkout • Public lavatories • Litter bins
5. **Control tools/ weapons:** • "Smart" guns • Disabling stolen cellphones • Restrict spray pain sales to juveniles	10. **Strengthen formal surveillance:** • Red light cameras • Burglar alarms • Security guards	15. **Deny benefits:** • Ink merchandise tags • Graffiti cleaning • Speed humps	20. **Discourage imitation:** • Rapid repair of vandalism • V-chips in TVs • Censor details of modus operandi	25. **Control drugs and alcohol:** • Breathalyzers in pubs • Server intervention • Alcohol-free events

Source: From *Theory for Practice in Situational Crime Prevention*, edited by Martha J. Smith and Derek Cornish. Copyright © 2003 by Lynne Rienner Publishers, Inc. Used with permission of the publisher.

influential. For anyone studying crime prevention, it is particularly useful because it forces clarity of thinking about preventive mechanisms and illustrates the rich variety of ways in which crime can be designed-out of products, systems, and the environment.

In your daily routine, take notice of how things around you (other than the obvious locks and bolts) may have been designed in order to prevent or sidestep crime, and try to identify the technique that has been employed.

Everyone routinely uses many of the techniques of SCP, even though they may not realize it. Consider the *routine precautions* that we all take every day to avoid, deter, or prevent crime. Locking the front door behind us, locking our car, and keeping our money in our pocket in certain places rather than waving it around are everyday routine precautions. Many such actions we take are so mundane that we do not even recognize them. Similarly, many aspects of everyday life are so common and accepted that we barely recognize their crime prevention role. A good example of this mundanity is same-sex washrooms in public places such as universities. The reason for same-sex washrooms is, to use the terminology of the 25 SCP techniques, to deflect offenders (technique 4) and to assist compliance (technique 24). In particular, same-sex washrooms are a simple way of reducing the sexual victimization of women by men.

Public washrooms are so mundane that they are useful for illustrating other aspects of crime prevention. Some design changes are so ordinary that we take them for granted: since illicit drug dealing and drug use can take place in public washrooms, cubicle doors are often designed to have a gap at the bottom so that it is clear if multiple people are in a stall (the techniques of assisting natural surveillance and strengthening formal surveillance). In some public washrooms known to be sites of intravenous drug injection, blue lights have been fitted to reduce the ease with which veins can be identified by those involved.

Designing-out crime has been critical to the security advancements of the chip-and-pin credit and debit cards we use every day. Chip-and-pin cards were introduced to reduce credit card fraud. It was very easy to choose to commit fraud with a stolen card when only a signature was needed. The need for a four-digit personal identification number (PIN) has caused a dramatic decline in this crime. Some credit card fraud still occurs, and the PINs are now sometimes targeted by hackers who try to gain them from bank computer systems, but this is beyond the reach of most of us and can also be prevented by adequate computer software security and practices.

SCP is linked to a range of research and practice through the notion of designing-out crime. Influential thinkers include Jane Jacobs and C. Ray Jeffery, whose ideas launched the field of crime prevention through environmental design (CPTED). Influenced by C. Ray Jeffery (his colleague at the Florida State University), Paul Brantingham, with Patricia Brantingham, adopted Jeffery's term **environmental criminology** (Brantingham & Brantingham, 1980). The set of overlapping and conceptually related policy areas are shown in Box 11.5.

environmental criminology
A term coined by C. Ray Jeffery; it focuses on the environment (including targets, guardians, and places) as a key area of interest in understanding how and why crime occurs.

Many studies show that SCP can be effective in reducing many different types of crime. In Canada, SCP gains little policy attention at the national level, and seems to be largely excluded from the National Crime Prevention Strategy led by Public Safety Canada. However, SCP is commonplace in several other countries, and the United Nations Office on Drugs and Crime (2002) includes SCP in its methods through which countries should prevent crime. In Australia, CPTED is now required in urban planning,

---

BOX 11.5

Crime Prevention Policy Areas Related to Crime Choice Theory

Many of the following policy areas are linked via the notion of designing-out crime or situational crime prevention (altering the situation). However, this is a large field; some would argue that it is a separate discipline (see "Crime Science" below) and that different topics require different theories and frameworks.

Crime Prevention Through Environmental Design (CPTED)

Much of the local environment—from road layout, to building layout, to the "furniture" of the environment, such as bushes and fences—can be designed or modified in ways that discourage crime. This may be through denoting private property, or how things such as trimming hedges can increase natural and formal surveillance (Fennelly & Crowe, 2013; Jacobs, 1961; Jeffery, 1971).

Crime Prevention Through Housing Design (CPTHD)

Housing and residential areas can be designed in ways that discourage and prevent crime. Rachel Armitage examined the difference in crime rates between housing built to design-out crime and that which was not. In a pioneering study, she looked at them again ten years later and found that crime rates in the well-designed residential areas remained lower. Her recent book *Crime Prevention through Housing Design: Policy and Practice* sets the standard (Armitage, 2013).

Crime Prevention Through Product Design (CPTPD)

Andrew Lester (2001) seems to have coined this term and identified the process by which products might be designed to avoid crime. Paul Ekblom is a leading scholar in this area. His recent book *Crime Prevention, Security and Community Safety Using the 5Is Framework* (Ekblom, 2011) represents the state of the art. Many products, from cars to smart phones and computer tablets, can be designed in ways that reduce crime opportunities (see also Ekblom, 2012).

Problem-Oriented Policing (POP)

The term *problem-oriented policing* was coined by Herman Goldstein in a 1979 study and developed in his 1990 book of the same name. POP uses a problem-solving approach and situational prevention techniques to address crime and disorder problems (where problems are clusters of crime against certain people, places, at certain times, etc.).

Design Against Crime (and Designing-Out Crime)

This term is largely synonymous with situational crime prevention. In London, England, the Design Against Crime Centre is located at Central St. Martins College of Art and Design (www.designagainstcrime.com) and is one of the leaders in this field, having developed many projects and studies.

Crime Science

Crime science is pursued as a separate discipline to criminology, with its own academic journal and several dedicated university departments, institutes, and centres. Its relation to the sociology of deviance is analogous to how medicine is related to the sociology of medicine. Crime science focuses on crime prevention and incorporates the physical science disciplines as well as social science (e.g., engineering-out crime).

---

and a crime reduction checklist exists for urban planners (Knepper, 2012). Denmark, Sweden, Finland, and Norway have all included SCP in their national strategies since the 1970s and 1980s (Knepper, 2012). SCP helps address specific crime issues, and while it offers no single "silver bullet" solution to crime, when done correctly it reduces opportunities for crime in general (Clarke, 1997).

One of the criticisms sometimes raised against SCP is that it may lead crime to "displace" or just move around the corner. In fact, many studies now show that displacement often does not occur. This finding makes sense. One target is chosen over another for a reason—perhaps because it is easier to access, easier to break into, or offers a larger reward that could be easily fenced. If this target becomes harder to victimize, it is not necessarily obvious where to find another target that is equally attractive (otherwise, that target would have been chosen in the first place). The possibility of displacement is now viewed very positively for a few reasons. First, if crime can be displaced, then it can be prevented, which means we need to strategically displace it to somewhere less damaging. Second, literature reviews that draw together the evidence of many studies show that often displacement does not occur. Third, when displacement does occur, it is usually less than 100 percent, so a net gain in terms of crime reduction is the outcome (see Guerette, 2009; Guerette & Bowers, 2009). See Box 11.6 for a classic case study on SCP and displacement.

BOX 11.6

Case Study: An Unexpected Drop in Suicides

A means of committing suicide in Britain before the 1960s was to turn on the gas stove and put your head in the oven. The gas was poisonous carbon monoxide. American poet Sylvia Plath lived in Britain and committed suicide this way. When the source of the gas was changed for economic reasons, the new natural gas was not poisonous. As a result, the suicide rate fell unexpectedly. It was because people no longer had a simple, clean, and readily available way of committing suicide. Many lives were saved, even though this was not a deliberate effort to tackle suicide.

Why did the rate of suicide decline? Two main explanations have been offered. The first is that other ways of committing suicide were not as easy, available, or attractive: they tended to be more difficult and often messier. People do not like to leave a mutilated or un-recognizable corpse for their relatives, friends, or others to find. The other explanation is that making it more difficult to commit suicide gave people more of a chance to pause and think about what they were doing and change their minds. The motivation to commit suicide appears to often be fleeting, and if the act can be stalled, then it may not be committed.

The gas suicide story provides three key lessons: First, even seemingly highly motivated acts such as suicide involve elements of rationality. Second, the rational element means that such acts can be blocked and prevented. Third, preventing one way of committing a crime does not just "displace" it to other means.

Sources and further reading: Clarke and Lester (1987); Clarke and Mayhew (1989).

The *diffusion of preventive benefits* is the term given to the fact that SCP can generate positive side effects. That is, studies now suggest that SCP can reduce crime beyond the scope of what was originally intended (Clarke & Weisburd, 1994; Weisburd & Telep, 2012).

The "Crime Drop" in Canada and Elsewhere

This section links crime choice theory to recent major trends in crime. Following nearly three decades of increasing crime, street crime in Canada has declined dramatically in the past two decades. Figure 11.2 shows trends in recorded crime rates in Canada from 1886 to 2010. The data were compiled by Paul Brantingham from police recorded crime and conviction data. Figure 11.3 shows the trends in police recorded crime for a variety of crime types since 1991 based on the Uniform Crime Reports data collated annually by Statistics Canada. In this figure, all crime types start at 100 percent in 1991, and the relative change is indicated. So, between 1991 and 2010, break and enter in Canada

FIGURE 11.2   Crime Trends in Canada, 1886–2010

Source: Uniform Crime Reports from 1962; before 1962, estimates extrapolated from conviction data (personal communication by Paul Brantingham).

FIGURE 11.3   Reported Crime Trends in Canada, 1991–2010

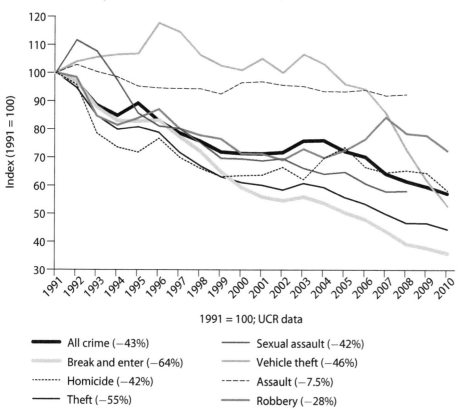

1991 = 100; UCR data

━━━ All crime (−43%)   ──── Sexual assault (−42%)

▭▭▭ Break and enter (−64%)   ──── Vehicle theft (−46%)

········ Homicide (−42%)   ‑ ‑ ‑ Assault (−7.5%)

──── Theft (−55%)   ──── Robbery (−28%)

Source: Uniform Crime Reports (see, e.g., Perreault, 2013).

declined by 64 percent and homicide declined by 42 percent. Meanwhile, car theft continued at similar levels, then started to fall dramatically from around 2003, and has continued to plummet.

An important question criminologists have sought to answer in recent years is this: Why has crime in Canada decreased so rapidly? In fact, Canada is not a special case. This "crime drop" has been experienced in most industrialized countries, including the United States, Australia, New Zealand, the United Kingdom, and most of Europe (see van Dijk, Tseloni, & Farrell, 2012).

Many criminologists have tried to explain why crime has declined, generating considerable innovative research. Some commentators attributed the crime drop to an expansion of policing or imprisonment or both (for a review of explanations, see Knepper, 2012). Others attributed the crime drop to an improvement in security. They found that better home and vehicle security reduced the opportunities for crime, specifically property crime (which exhibited the largest decrease) (Tseloni, Mailley, Farrell, & Tilley, 2010; van Dijk, 2008). The expanded use of policing and prisons, primarily a feature of crime policy in the United States, certainly cannot explain the decline in crime internationally. What is clear, however, is that the major drop in auto theft in many countries is directly attributable to improvements in vehicle security. Research provides strong evidence that it was security that reduced car theft in Australia, England, Wales, the Netherlands, and the United States, where car theft fell at different times but always consistently with the introduction of more and better security (Farrell, Tseloni, & Tilley, 2011; Fujita & Maxfield, 2012; van Ours & Vollaard, 2013).

In Canada, car theft fell dramatically since 2003, which seems to fit with the adoption of electronic vehicle immobilizers. Although the Canadian government made electronic vehicle immobilizers mandatory only in 2007, the earlier decline suggests a degree of anticipation by manufacturers as well as earlier adoption in certain provinces. In Winnipeg, for instance, long Canada's car theft capital, electronic vehicle immobilizers were introduced in 2005 as part of a comprehensive auto-theft strategy that included giving car owners financial incentives to improve vehicle security (Linden & Chaturvedi, 2005).

Other recent research suggests that the decline in residential burglary in England and Wales is linked partly to more security but largely to improvements in the quality of security achieved via the widespread introduction of double-glazing for windows (Tilley & Farrell, 2013). In essence, these studies suggest that offenders *chose* to commit less crime because fewer crime opportunities were readily available. Box 11.7 links improved security to offender choices and suggests how bank robbery is likely to have declined for reasons similar to the decline in residential burglary.

Mounting evidence suggests that the set of crime opportunity theories discussed in this chapter—choice theory, routine activities theory, and situational crime prevention—are those best able to explain major trends in crime in Canada and elsewhere.

Crime Choice Theory and the Internet

While many types of street crime have decreased since the 1990s, other types of crime are on the rise. In particular, Internet-related crime has gone up dramatically in the last decade now that broadband access and knowledge of how to use the Internet is widespread. Yet this, too, fits well with crime choice theory. Simply put, new crime opportunities (such as fraud and cyberbullying) have arisen in relation to the Internet.

BOX 11.7

Changing Offender Choices Through Improved Security

Recall Box 11.1, about prolific bank robber Willie Sutton. Nowadays, with greatly improved security, it is far less rational to rob banks. Even in Sutton's time, banks had safes that were meant to be secure, and other forms of security. Nowadays the security is multi-layered and can include timed safes that are secured underground, bandit screens at the counter, CCTV, and security guards. All of these measures increase the effort required to commit a bank robbery. Banks are alarmed or have hidden alarms that can be activated by staff, all of which increase the risk for offenders. Even if the robbery and getaway are successful, cash can often be traced by serial numbers, or packs of money may contain exploding dye that make the money worthless. These many layers of security, working via different SCP techniques (e.g., some making robbery more difficult, others lessening the rewards), all

reduce the likelihood that any one of us will rob a bank. Similar advances in security seem likely to have played an important role in explaining why many other types of crime have declined in recent years.

Because those crime opportunities are relatively easy to commit, more offenders have chosen to pursue them. The same is true in relation to the theft of smart phones. Smart phones are highly valuable and easy to steal, so they are a "rational" choice as a target for would-be offenders. However, since the rise of the Internet (and social networking) occurred after the crime drop began, we can be fairly certain it was not the reason for the drop in other types of crime like homicide and car theft.

Conclusion

Choice theory provides an immensely flexible framework and set of concepts that can be applied to all types of human behaviour and decisions, including criminal decisions. The criminological version of choice theory focuses on immediate situations relating to crime and provides insights on how to design-out crime. When combined with routine activity theory as a broader set of crime opportunity theories, choice theory is vital to understanding the major trends and patterns in crime, both past and present. Since it informs efforts to design-out crime, it is also linked to some of the most practical crime control work undertaken by police and simultaneously promoted by government and the private sector. It is, in short, a tremendously important area of criminological theory.

The media's stereotypical distinction between "us" (non-criminals) and "them" (criminals) and their depiction of criminals (particularly the genius super-criminal and the heinous-monster criminal) is often misleading. Most offenders are teenage males, and most outgrow the desire to commit crime fairly quickly; most choose not to commit crime because they get caught, crime proves unattractive or difficult, or their circumstances and preferences change. The few that go on to criminal careers can choose not to, but their increasing expertise makes it easier to continue to choose crime. However, recent large-scale reductions in crime show that even the more hardened criminals can be prevented from committing crimes or deflected to less harmful activities.

SUMMARY OF KEY POINTS

- Criminal decisions are made by the same process as all other decisions.
- When the perceived benefits outweigh the perceived costs, a crime is committed.
- Most people have the capacity to commit crime (e.g., speeding) or can be tempted or provoked into crime, depending on the circumstances.
- All crimes require an opportunity that can be taken. Fewer opportunities = fewer crimes.
- Designing-out crime opportunities is an attractive (non-punitive) way to nudge decisions away from crime.
- The large rise in crime from the 1960s to the 1990s in most industrialized countries occurred because easy crime opportunities became plentiful.
- The rapid decline in crime since the 1990s in many industrialized countries occurred because easy crime opportunities were removed, making crime less easy to choose.

QUESTIONS FOR CRITICAL DISCUSSION

1. Why would anyone choose to commit a bank robbery?
2. Why would two people make a different decision in the same circumstances?
3. If changes in the levels of crime opportunities (how easy it is to commit crime) make such a big difference to the crime rate, what does this say about offender motivation?
4. Do you think that crime opportunities or an offender's disposition to commit crime can be more easily addressed by crime policy?
5. Why has the crime rate in Canada and elsewhere fallen so much since the 1990s?
6. Based on choice theory, what policy options might be most efficient in addressing crime?

SUGGESTED FURTHER READINGS

Many good sources exist on choice theory and related areas. Almost everything written by Ronald V. Clarke is about rational choice theory and situational crime prevention—and his work is always clear, brilliant, and highly recommended. A good starting point:

Felson, M., & Clarke, R.V. (1998). *Opportunity makes the thief: Practical theory for crime prevention*. London, UK: Home Office.

The following textbook is a fine introduction for undergraduate students to many of the issues addressed in this chapter:

Felson, M., & Boba, R. (2010). *Crime and everyday life* (4th ed.). Thousand Oaks, CA: Sage.

For an excellent edited collection of academic scholarship, see the following:

Piquero, A.R., & Tibbetts, S.G. (Eds.). (2002). *Rational choice and criminal behaviour*. New York: Routledge.

Websites

Center for Problem-Oriented Policing, or POP Center: http://www.popcenter.org

REFERENCES

Armitage, R. (2013). Crime prevention through environmental design. *Encyclopedia of Criminology and Criminal Justice*. London, UK: Springer.

Beauregard, E., Proulx, J., Rossmo, K., Leclerc, B., & Allaire, J.F. (2007). Script analysis of the hunting process of serial sex offenders. *Criminal Justice and Behavior, 34*(8), 1069–1084.

Becker, G. (1968). Crime and punishment: An economic approach. *Journal of Political Economy, 76*, 169–217.

Bennett, T. (1986). A decision making approach to opioid addiction. In D. Cornish & R. Clarke (Eds.), *The reasoning criminal: Rational choice perspectives on offending*. New York: Springer-Verlag.

Brantingham, P.L., & Brantingham, P.J. (1980). *Environmental criminology*. Beverly Hills, CA: Sage.

Brantingham, P.L., & Brantingham, P.J. (1993). Nodes, paths and edges: Considerations on the complexity of crime and the physical environment. *Journal of Environmental Psychology, 13*(1), 3–28.

Brown, R. (2004). The effectiveness of electronic immobilisation: Changing patterns of temporary and permanent vehicle theft. In M.G. Maxfield & R.V. Clarke (Eds.), *Crime Prevention Studies* (Vol. 17, pp. 101–119). New York: Criminal Justice Press.

Clarke, R.V. (1997). *Situational crime prevention: Successful case studies* (2nd ed.). Guilderland, NY: Criminal Justice Press.

Clarke, R.V. (1999). Hot products: Understanding, anticipating and reducing demand for stolen goods. *Police Research Series, Paper 112*. London, UK: Home Office.

Clarke, R.V., & Cornish, D.B. (1985). Modeling offenders' decisions: A framework for research and policy. *Crime and Justice, 6*, 147–185.

Clarke, R.V., & Felson, M. (2011). The origins of the routine activity approach and situational crime prevention. In F.T. Cullen, C.L. Jonson, A.J. Myer, & F. Adler (Eds.), *The origins of American criminology* (Vol. 16, pp. 245–260). New Brunswick, NJ: Transaction.

Clarke, R. V., & Homel, R. (1997). A revised classification of situational crime prevention techniques. In S. Lab (Ed.), *Crime prevention at the crossroads* (pp. 17–30). Cincinnati, OH: Criminal Justice Press.

Clarke, R.V., & Lester, D. (1987). Toxicity of car exhausts and opportunity for suicide: A comparison between Britain and the United States. *Journal of Epidemiology and Community Health, 41*(2), 114–120.

Clarke, R.V., & Mayhew, P. (1989). Crime as opportunity: A note on domestic gas suicide in Britain and the Netherlands. *The British Journal of Criminology, 29*(1), 35–46.

Clarke, R.V., & Weisburd, D. (1994). Diffusion of crime control benefits: Observations on the reverse of displacement. In R.V. Clarke (Ed.), *Crime Prevention Studies* (Vol. 2, pp. 165–182). Monsey, NY: Criminal Justice Press.

Cohen, L.E., & Felson, M. (1979). Social change and crime rate trends: A routine activities approach. *American Sociological Review, 44*(4), 588–608.

Cornish, D., & Clarke, R. (Eds.). (1986). *The reasoning criminal: Rational choice perspectives on offending*. New York: Springer-Verlag.

Cornish, D.B. (1994). The procedural analysis of offending and its relevance for situational prevention. In R.V. Clarke (Ed.), *Crime prevention studies* (Vol. 3, pp. 91–107). Monsey, NY: Criminal Justice Press.

Cornish, D.B., & Clarke, R.V. (2003). Opportunities, precipitators and criminal decisions: A reply to Wortley's critique of situational crime prevention. In M.J. Smith and D.B. Cornish (Eds.), *Theory and practice in situational crime prevention* (Vol. 16, pp. 41–96). Monsey, NY: Criminal Justice Press.

Darwin, C. (1859). *On the origin of species*. London, UK: John Murray.

Ekblom, P. (1991). Talking to offenders: Practical lessons for local crime prevention. In O. Nello (Ed.), *Urban crime: Statistical approaches and analyses* (pp. 29–43). Barcelona, Spain: Institut d'Estudis Metropolitans de Barcelona.

Ekblom, P. (2011). Crime prevention, security and community safety using the 5Is framework. New York: Palgrave Macmillan.

Ekblom, P. (2012). The private sector and designing products against crime. In B.C. Welsh & D.P. Farrington (Eds.), *Oxford handbook of crime prevention*. New York: Oxford University Press.

Farrell, G. (2010). Situational crime prevention and its discontents: Rational choice and harm reduction versus "cultural criminology." *Social Policy and Administration, 44*(1), 40–66.

Farrell, G., Tseloni, A., & Tilley, N. (2011). The effectiveness of car security devices and their role in the crime drop. *Criminology and Criminal Justice, 11*(1), 21–35.

Felson, M., & Boba, R. (2010). *Crime and everyday life*. Los Angeles: Sage.

Fennelly, L., & Crowe, T. (2013). *Crime prevention through environmental design*. Oxford, UK: Butterworth Heinemann.

Fujita, S., & Maxfield, M. (2012). Security and the drop in car theft in the United States. In J.J.M. van Dijk, A. Tseloni, & G. Farrell (Eds.), *The international crime drop: New directions in research*. London, UK: Palgrave Macmillan.

Gabor, T. (1994). *Everybody does it*. Toronto: University of Toronto Press.

Goldstein, H. (1990). *Problem-oriented policing*. New York: McGraw-Hill.

Gottfredson, D.M., & Clarke, R.V. (1990). *Policy and theory in criminal justice: Essays in honour of Leslie T. Wilkins*. Brookfield, VT: Gower.

Guerette, R.T. (2009). *Analyzing crime displacement and diffusion*. Washington, DC: US Department of Justice, Office of Community Oriented Policing Services.

Guerette, R.T., & Bowers, K.J. (2009). Assessing the extent of crime displacement and the diffusion of benefits: A review of situational crime prevention evaluations. *Criminology, 47*(4), 1331–1368.

Hancock, G., & G. Laycock. 2010. Organised crime and crime scripts: Prospects for disruption. In K. Bullock, R.V. Clarke, & N. Tilley (Eds.), *Situational prevention of organised crime* (pp. 172–192). Cullompton, UK and Portland, OR: Willan.

Jacobs, J. (1961). *Death and life of great American cities*. New York: Vintage Books.

Jeffery, C.R. (1971). *Crime prevention through environmental design*. Beverly Hills, CA: Sage.

Kirby, S., & Nailer, L. (2013). Reducing the offending of a UK organized crime group using an opportunity reducing framework: A three year case study. *Trends in Organized Crime, 16*(4), 397–412.

Knepper, P. (2012). An international crime decline: Lessons for social welfare crime policy. *Social Policy and Administration, 46*(4), 359–376.

Kriven, S., & Ziersch, E. (2007). New car security and shifting vehicle theft patterns in Australia. *Security Journal, 20*(2), 111–122.

Leddo, J., & Abelson, R.P. (1986). The nature of explanations. In J.A. Galambos, R.P. Abelson, & J.B. Black (Eds.), *Knowledge structures* (pp. 103–122). Hillsdale, NJ: Erlbaum.

Lester, A. (2001). Crime reduction through issues product design. *Trends and Issues in Crime and Criminal Justice, 206*, 1–6.

Linden, R., & Chaturvedi, R. (2005). The need for comprehensive crime prevention planning: The case of motor vehicle theft. *Canadian Journal of Criminology and Criminal Justice, 47*(2), 251–270.

MacDonald, A. (Producer), & Boyle, D. (Director). (1996). *Trainspotting* [Motion picture]. London, UK: Channel Four Films.

Mayhew, P.M., Clarke, R.V.G, Sturman, A., & Hough, J.M. (1976). *Crime as opportunity* (Home Office Research Study No. 34). London, UK: Her Majesty's Stationery Office.

Moffitt, T.E. (1993). Adolescence-limited and life-course persistent anti-social behavior: A developmental taxonomy. *Psychological Review, 100*(4), 674–701.

Perreault, S. (2013). *Police reported crime statistics in Canada 2012.* Ottawa: Statistics Canada.

Sartre, Jean-Paul. (n.d.). Jean-Paul Sartre. Retrieved from http://www.sartre.org/quotes2.htm.

Simon, H. (1957). *Models of man: Mathematical models on rational human behaviour in a social setting.* New York: John Wiley.

Thaler, R., & Sunstein, C. (2008). *Nudge: Improving decisions about health, wealth, and happiness.* New Haven, CT: Yale University Press.

Tilley, N., & Farrell, G. (2013). *The reasoning criminologist: Essays in honour of Ronald V. Clarke.* New York: Routledge.

Tompson, L. (2011). Crime script analysis [PowerPoint presentation]. International Crime and Intelligence Analysis Conference. Retrieved from http://www.ucl.ac.uk/jdi/events/int-CIA-conf/ICIAC11_Slides/ICIAC11_5D_LTompson.

Tseloni, A., Mailley, J., Farrell, G., & Tilley, N. (2010). Exploring the international decline in crime rates. *European Journal of Criminology, 7*, 375–394.

United Nations Office on Drugs and Crime. (2002). Action to promote effective crime prevention. Retrieved from https://www.un.org/en/ecosoc/docs/2002/resolution%202002-13.pdf.

Van Dijk, J. (2008). *The world of crime.* London, UK: Sage.

Van Dijk, J., Tseloni, A., & Farrell, G. (2012). *The international crime drop: New directions in research.* Basingstoke, UK: Palgrave and McMillan.

Van Ours, J.C., & Vollaard, B. (2013). The engine immobilizer: A non-starter for car thieves (Working Paper No. 4092). Retrieved from http://www.econstor.eu/bitstream/10419/69576/1/735723133.pdf.

Weisburd, D., & Telep, C.W. (2012). Spatial displacement and diffusion of crime control benefits revisited. New evidence on why crime doesn't just move around the corner. In N. Tilley & G. Farrell (Eds.), *The reasoning criminologist* (pp. 142–159). New York: Routledge.

Wilkins, L.T. (1964). *Social policy, action, and research: Studies in social deviance.* London, UK: Tavistock.

Wilson, J.Q., & Herrnstein, R.J. (1985). *Crime and human nature.* New York: Simon and Schuster.

Wolfgang, M. (1996). Introduction. In C. Beccaria, *Of crimes and punishments.* New York: Marsilio.

CASE STUDY 12.1

Is Sociological Theory Reflected in Criminal Justice Practice?

An RCMP officer inspecting the body of Nasir Khokhar, in Merritt, BC.
Source: CBC.ca.

In September 2009, 28-year-old Nasir Khokhar was found dead in a park in Merritt, British Columbia. He had been stabbed 34 times; he had 16 knife wounds in his back and side, 10 in his chest, and 8 in his neck, one of which had severed his jugular vein. He had been drinking in the park that day with Kleon Pop and Pop's brother, a juvenile offender, both of whom were charged with second-degree murder, but who ultimately pleaded guilty to manslaughter.

At the time of the killing, all three men were very drunk. The blood alcohol level of the victim was 272 milligrams of alcohol per 100 millilitres of blood (or three times the legal limit for driving a car), and it was conceded at trial that the blood alcohol levels of all participants were quite similar. Pop could not recall much of the incident that led to the death of Khokhar.

At the time of the offence, Pop, an Aboriginal man, was 21 years old; his father is a member of the Soda Creek Indian Band and his mother is from the Canoe Creek Indian Band, both of which are near Williams Lake, British Columbia. Both of Pop's parents are alcoholics; his father left his mother when Pop was a small child, and his mother has had six children with four different fathers. Pop experienced physical abuse from both his father and his various stepfathers. Additionally, his mother and one of his stepfathers would often leave the house for days to pursue drinking binges, leaving the children to look after themselves, often without any food. In short, the Pop family has a long, multi-generational history of both alcoholism and child abuse.

Initially, Pop was effectively sentenced to five years' imprisonment. At the point of this sentencing, he was given credit for three years' imprisonment before trial and sentencing, and then sentenced to a further term of two years less a day, with this detention to be followed by a three-year probation order.

In April 2013, the British Columbia Court of Appeal concluded that the length of the sentence did not give sufficient weight to the social circumstances of Pop's upbringing, and to his unique status as an Aboriginal offender. The Court of Appeal quoted approvingly from the Supreme Court of Canada's 2012 judgment in the case of *R v. Ipeelee*:

> Canadian criminal law is based on the premise that criminal liability only follows from voluntary conduct. Many Aboriginal offenders find themselves in situations of social and economic deprivation with a lack of opportunities and limited options for positive development. While this rarely—if ever—attains a level where one could properly say that their actions were not *voluntary* and therefore not deserving of criminal sanction, the reality is that their constrained circumstances may diminish their moral culpability.

As a consequence of this logic—taking account of the diminished degree of moral responsibility for this Aboriginal offender—the Court of Appeal reduced Pop's sentence to one year from two years less a day, bringing total time to be spent in custody down from five years to four.

Madam Justice Bennett, writing for a unanimous three-member Court of Appeal bench, concluded:

> While the circumstances of the offence involved the infliction of multiple stab wounds, the level of moral blameworthiness was significantly reduced because of the circumstances of Mr. Pop, including his degree of intoxication, his background and circumstances, as well as the fact, acknowledged by the Crown at sentencing, that Mr. Khokhar appeared to be the aggressor and there were elements of self-defence and provocation. None of the factors amounted to a justification of his conduct, but are circumstances relevant to assessing Mr. Pop's moral blameworthiness. (*R v. Pop*, 2013, para. 28)

Before You Read Chapter 12

- Do you agree with the courts' opinions quoted above? Why or why not?
- To what extent should one's social background and upbringing be a consideration when assessing his or her "moral blameworthiness"? What other factors should courts consider instead of or in addition to social background and upbringing?
- Imagine that you're a dissenting judge on this Court of Appeal bench. What might your argument be?
- Make your own assessment of what Kleon Pop's sentence should be. Then, after reading this chapter, return to this case study. How has your perspective changed? Do you propose a more severe or a more lenient sentence than you did initially?
- After reading this chapter, consider the various sociological theories described. Are any reflected in the practice of criminal justice presented in this case study? If yes, which ones?

Sociological Approaches

<table>
<tr><td>

LEARNING OBJECTIVES

After reading this chapter, students will be able to:

- Distinguish between sociological, psychological, and biological approaches to explaining criminal and deviant behaviour.

- Define the concept of social disorganization and explain how social disorganization can contribute to high crime rates.

- Discuss the "sociology of deviance," its contribution to labelling theory, and its position on social problems, moral entrepreneurship, and moral panics.

- Trace the development of anomie-strain theory through Émile Durkheim, Robert Merton, Robert Agnew, and Steven Messner and Richard Rosenfeld.

- Explain the relationship between differential association theory, techniques of neutralization, and social learning theory.

- Trace the development of social control theory, from Émile Durkheim to Travis Hirschi to the recent life-course-developmental theories.

</td><td>

CHAPTER OUTLINE

</td></tr>
</table>

Introduction

Despite claims by some biologists and psychologists that sociological explanations of crime and deviance are inadequate or lacking in strong empirical support (e.g., Beaver, Ratchford, & Ferguson, 2010; Jeffery, 1978; Walsh, 2002), the fact remains that sociological approaches have been and continue to be the most prevalent and widely accepted of all criminological theories. Whether you take a larger sample of the 50 key thinkers in criminology or a smaller sample of 15 past and present pioneers in criminological thought (cf. Hayward, Maruna, & Mooney, 2010; Mutchnick, Martin, & Austin, 2009), between 60 and 75 percent of the theorizing can be attributed to the field of sociology alone. Even in areas of criminological theory covered in other chapters in this book, where the relationship might not be so readily apparent—such as feminist criminology and critical criminology—the majority of prominent thinkers come from a sociological background (Hayward, Maruna, & Mooney, 2010; Renzetti, 2013; Young, 2002).

The long-standing and durable relationship between sociology and criminology can be traced back to Émile Durkheim, the founder of academic sociology in France in the late 1800s, and to the sociology department at the University of Chicago (often referred to as the **Chicago School**). Durkheim was the originator of anomie theory and social control theory, both of which remain widely accepted today (Cullen, Wright, & Blevins, 2004). The Chicago School gave rise to social disorganization theory, differential association theory, the sociology of deviance, and labelling theory—all of which are very

Chicago School
The first school of sociology in the United States; contributed to social disorganization theory, cultural transmission theory, differential association theory, subcultural theory, the sociology of deviance, and symbolic interactionism.

much a part of mainstream criminological thinking (Lilly, Cullen, & Ball, 2011; Williams & McShane, 2010).

Edwin Sutherland, a member of the Chicago School, and arguably the most prominent criminologist of the 20th century, played a key role in establishing sociology's dominance in the field of criminology (Laub & Sampson, 1991). The interrelationship between sociology and criminology can also be explained by the fact that, until recently, the discipline of criminology was often subsumed under the auspices of sociology departments (Sacco & Kennedy, 2011). It was not until about 40 years ago that independent criminology departments began to spring up around North America (Ratner, 2006).

Sociological explanations tend to view crime and deviance as normal, or at least semi-normal—as socially or culturally learned responses to social circumstances (Clinard & Meier, 2004; L.E. Cohen & Machalek, 1994). Rather than focusing on the biological or psychological deficiencies of individuals, sociological explanations place more emphasis on the effects of social structure, social institutions, social organization, social class, social roles, social norms, and social learning in the shaping of criminal or deviant behaviour (Giddens, 1987). Biological explanations, on the other hand, investigate inherited biogenetic deficits or abnormalities that predispose certain individuals to engage in criminal or deviant activities (e.g., Beaver, Ratchford, & Ferguson, 2010; Ellis & Walsh, 1997). Psychological explanations examine individual differences in personality, memory, perception, learning, and cognition, and how such differences can lead to abnormal behaviour or character disorders (Andrews & Bonta, 2010; Gelles, 1993).

Sociologists might ask why some societies deem marijuana use, prostitution, or polygamy (having multiple wives) to be abnormal or criminal, whereas other societies do not, or why members of certain social classes seem more likely to be criminalized than members of other social classes. Biologists and psychologists, by contrast, might ask why certain individuals are more likely to behave in an abnormal or criminal manner, and then search for clues within that individual's genetic makeup or personality.

That said, considerable overlap exists between sociological, psychological, and biological explanations of crime and deviance. Ronald Akers's social learning theory (Akers, 2001; Burgess & Akers, 1966) combines Edwin Sutherland's differential association theory (a sociological theory) with B.F. Skinner's work on operant conditioning and Albert Bandura's work on imitation and modelling behaviour (both psychological approaches). Robert Agnew's general strain theory (1992) combines Robert Merton's anomie-strain theory (again, a sociological theory) with psychological and physiological variables, such as the "frustration–aggression hypothesis" and "pain-avoidance behaviour." Similarly, a number of recent psychological explanations have turned to a more integrative or "psychosocial" approach (involving sociological as well as individual variables) (Bartol, 1999; Wortley, 2011), while some biologists have actively been calling for what is referred to as "biosocial criminology," or a biologically informed sociology (Walsh, 2002).

Durkheim's Influence

Émile Durkheim's influence on sociological approaches to crime and deviance cannot be overstated. Durkheim contributed to the "consensus perspective" in sociology and criminology, to what is now known as "structural functionalism" (the view that society is "natural" or "organic"), and to the notion that society requires both integration and regulation in order to be effective or "cohesive" (Burtch, 2003; Williams & McShane, 2010). His work underpins Merton's anomie-strain theory, Agnew's general strain theory, Erikson's sociology of deviance, Messner and Rosenfeld's institutional-anomie theory, Hirschi's social bond theory, Thornberry's interactional theory, and Sampson and Laub's life-course-developmental theory (all discussed later in this chapter).

To fully appreciate the work of Émile Durkheim, it is important to understand the historical circumstances that gave rise to his thinking. Durkheim was influenced by the French thinkers who preceded him: by Baron de Montesquieu, who is credited with laying the groundwork for what later became known as the "sociology of law" and the "sociology of knowledge"; by Henri de Saint-Simon, who called for a "human science" that would apply scientific principles to the study of society; and by August Comte, who first coined the terms *sociology* and *positivism* (Mutchnick, Martin, & Austin, 2009; Zeitlin, 2001). Durkheim's work was also affected by the political turmoil of the 17th and 18th centuries, marked by the English Revolution, where the British monarchy was replaced by parliamentary democracy; the American Revolution, which threw off the yoke of the British monarchy; and the French Revolution, which led to the guillotining of the French monarchy, the rise of Napoleon Bonaparte, and a century of political instability in France (Lilly, Cullen, & Ball, 2011; Zeitlin, 2001). In addition, Durkheim's writings were a reaction to the work of 19th-century German philosopher and economist Karl Marx, who advocated the overthrow of capitalism, and to the work of the Positivist School of criminology, which attempted to explain criminality in terms of inherited genetic defects such as "feeble-mindedness," and argued—consistent with the social Darwinism that was rampant in those times—that criminals were degenerative, evolutionary throwbacks (Williams & McShane, 2010).

In "The Normal and the Pathological," Durkheim (1895/1970) rejected the "disease" analogy put forward by the Positivist School—the notion that criminality was an inherited trait, or that it was "abnormal" or "pathological" (L.E. Cohen & Machalek, 1994; Durkheim, 1964). Instead, he observed that crime had existed throughout history, and that it was present in all types of societies. He pointed out—applying the same scientific approach that early members of the Positivist School claimed to apply themselves—that abnormal, pathological, or morbid phenomena would not survive over time (i.e., they would be screened out through the evolutionary process of natural selection). Thus, Durkheim concluded that a certain amount of crime must be "normal," or at least, that crime must serve some sort of social function. He proposed that crime defined the moral boundaries of the community (i.e., crime helped to set social standards), and that crime contributed to the development of social cohesion or social solidarity (by creating a "them versus us" mentality or a "good guys" versus "bad guys" distinction) (Durkheim, 1964; Greenberg, 2010).

Unlike Marx, who saw society as rooted in social conflict and postulated that capitalism would eventually be overthrown and replaced with socialism, Durkheim argued that society was based upon consensus (shared norms, values, and beliefs) and was comparable to a natural, functioning organism that does what it has to do to survive (Durkheim, 1965; Zeitlin, 2001). Durkheim talked about the "forces of integration" and the "forces of regulation," both necessary to the cohesiveness and smooth functioning of society. The forces of integration were the social bonds and shared (collective) beliefs that drew people together and held them together. The forces of regulation were the laws and the social institutions that helped ensure compliance with social norms, values, and beliefs (Lilly, Cullen, & Ball, 2011). We will see Durkheim's notion of social bonds and collective beliefs again, when we come to Hirschi's social bond theory, Thornberry's interactional theory, and Sampson and Laub's life-course-developmental theory. We will also see the forces of integration and regulation again, when we come to Merton's anomie-strain theory and Messner and Rosenfeld's institutional-anomie theory.

anomie
A term coined by Durkheim to describe periods of law-lessness, normlessness, and unrestrained choice, or a breakdown in social solidarity.

Durkheim is perhaps best known for his work on **anomie**, which he described as a state of lawlessness, normlessness, or unrestrained ambition, which if left unchecked could lead to a breakdown in social solidarity (Clinard, 1964; Durkheim, 1965). While Durkheim did not specifically relate anomie to crime, he saw periods of anomie as an impediment to the development of social relationships, and as a contributing factor to periodic increases in suicide rates (Cartwright, 2011; Clinard & Meier, 2004; Durkheim, 1951). Durkheim's anomie theory will be revisited when we discuss Merton's anomie-strain theory, Albert Cohen's work on "delinquent boys and the culture of the gang," Cloward and Ohlin's "illegitimate opportunity structures," and Messner and Rosenfeld's institutional-anomie theory.

The Chicago School

The Chicago School, established in 1892, was the first school of sociology in the United States (Lilly, Cullen, & Ball, 2011; Williams & McShane, 2010). Chicago School thinking was shaped by a number of factors, including the rapid growth of the city of Chicago, the relatively new science of ecology, and a growing interest in the type of ethnographic work associated with cultural anthropology (Williams & McShane, 2010). The Chicago School is renowned for its urban sociology, its life histories, and its focus on community-level analysis (Sampson, 2002). Like Durkheim before them, members of the Chicago School rejected the social Darwinist notion that the poor were poor because of their degenerative evolutionary condition, and challenged the then popular notion that most criminals were either criminal psychopaths or feeble-minded (of low intelligence) (Laub & Sampson, 1991; Lilly, Cullen, & Ball, 2011; Rafter, 1997). Rather, members of the Chicago School concluded that it was "the nature of the neighbourhood," not "the nature of the individual," that was the primary cause of criminality (Lilly, Cullen, & Ball, 2011). The Chicago School brought us many well-known criminological theories, including social disorganization theory, cultural transmission theory, cultural conflict theory, differential association theory, the sociology of deviance, labelling theory, and environmental or ecological criminology.

Social Disorganization Theory

In the 100-year period between 1830 and 1930, Chicago increased in size from approximately 4,000 residents to 3 million residents (Lilly, Cullen, & Ball, 2011). Most of this population growth came through mass immigration from other countries (e.g., Germans trying to escape the political instability and constant warring in Europe, Polish people leaving various countries in Europe just prior to the First World War, etc.), as well as waves of migrants from other parts of the United States (e.g., African-Americans fleeing the American South after the Civil War, and farm workers and displaced farmers leaving the American countryside in hope of finding work in the recently industrialized urban centres) (Williams & McShane, 2010).

Park and Burgess's Concentric Zone Model

Robert Park and Ernest Burgess, two of the earlier Chicago School theorists, observed that Chicago had grown in a series of five concentric rings or zones, and each zone had its own distinctive land usage and population (Park & Burgess, 1967). Zone 1, the Loop (or Central Business District), was situated on the waterfront on Lake Michigan, and was the main rail and water transportation hub. Zone 2, the Zone in Transition (or Interstitial Zone), was immediately adjacent to the Loop, or Central Business District. Zone 3, the Zone of Workingmen's Homes, was between the Zone in Transition and the Residential Zone (Zone 4). Zone 5 was the Commuters Zone, and is now commonly referred to as "the suburbs" (see Figure 12.1).

In keeping with the ecological and **functionalist** thinking that was prevalent in the early 20th century, Park and Burgess saw the city as a functioning organism—as a natural human environment. They regarded the formation of these concentric rings or zones as part of the natural evolutionary process of "invasion, dominance and succession" (Bernard, Snipes, & Gerould, 2010), much like what might happen in the Animal Kingdom, when a new and more successful species invades a territory and gradually

functionalism

In sociology, the idea that society is comparable to a functioning organism with interrelated parts and structures to ensure that the parts work together; functionalists believe that society is based on consensus (shared values, beliefs), not conflict.

FIGURE 12.1   Park and Burgess's Concentric Zone Model

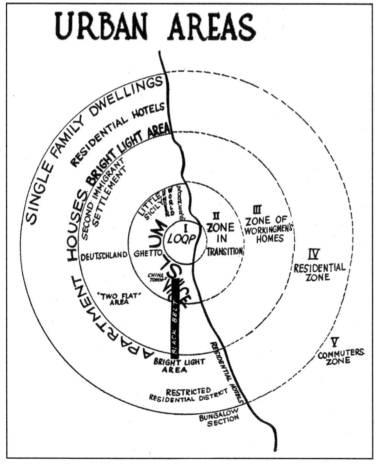

Source: Burgess (1925/1967, p. 55).

pushes the original—less successful or less adaptable—inhabitants to the periphery, or to extinction (Traub & Little, 1985; Williams & McShane, 2010). As the Loop (or Central Business District) grew and expanded outward, it put pressure on the Zone in Transition, which became a rundown urban slum, or ghetto. Those who had the ability to leave or avoid the Zone in Transition moved to the Zone of Workingmen's Homes, the Residential Zone, or the Commuters Zone.

The socially disorganized Zone in Transition was populated primarily by recently arrived immigrants, transient workers, and others who could not afford to live in one of the more affluent zones of the city. The attraction for recently arrived immigrants or transient workers (or for people who were just plain "poor") was that the rents were cheaper in the transitional zone, because the buildings were old and rundown. Park and Burgess did not, however, attempt to explore the relationship between crime and the social disorganization found in the Zone in Transition. Rather, they regarded themselves more as urban geographers, ethnographers, or ecologists, mapping out the city and trying to understand how the urban landscape had evolved over time (Lilly, Cullen, & Ball, 2011; Mutchnick, Martin, & Austin, 2009).

Shaw and McKay's Study of Social Disorganization in Chicago

social disorganization theory
The theory that a breakdown of the networks, norms, and trust that facilitate coordination and cooperation among residents of neighbourhoods can lead to greater crime and violence.

Although they did not invent the concentric zone model or come up with the concept of **social disorganization**, Clifford Shaw and Henry McKay's study of social disorganization remains a landmark in sociological explanations for why crime rates tend to be higher in urban centres. While they were not faculty members in the Chicago School, Shaw and McKay both did their graduate studies in sociology at the University of Chicago, and both were active in working with—and conducting research studies on—delinquents in the Chicago area (Snodgrass, 2011). Using the concentric zone model created by Park and Burgess, Shaw and McKay (1969) set out in the 1930s and 1940s to demonstrate that juvenile delinquency rates were indeed related to the type of social disorganization found in the Zone in Transition (Kornhauser, 1978). In order to accomplish this, Shaw and McKay used official delinquency rates and official census data for Chicago.

Shaw and McKay identified five main characteristics associated with socially disorganized areas: poverty, overcrowding, ethnic and cultural heterogeneity, residential instability, and broken homes (Lilly, Cullen, & Ball, 2011; Williams & McShane, 2010). They found that juvenile delinquency rates were highest in the Zone in Transition, and that those rates tailed off dramatically as you moved away from the centre of the city; they were lower in the Zone of Workingmen's Homes, lower still in the Residential Zone, and lowest in the Commuters Zone. Shaw and McKay also observed that social disorganization led to a breakdown in informal social controls—the type of controls exercised over children and teens by family members, adult neighbours, school teachers, religious leaders, and community organizations (Kornhauser, 1978). This breakdown in informal social controls in turn led to the formation of juvenile gangs or criminal subcultures, the development of criminal values, and the transmission of those criminal values from gang member to gang member and from one generation to the next (Bernard, Snipes, & Gerould, 2010; Cullen, Wright, & Blevins, 2004). Shaw and McKay's observations can be regarded as a prelude to cultural transmission theory, subcultural theory, and social control theory (Cartwright, 2011). More will be said about these other theories later in this chapter.

Sampson and Groves's Replication of Shaw and McKay's Study

In 1989, Robert Sampson and W. Byron Groves completed their replication of Shaw and McKay's earlier study of social disorganization and delinquency. However, Sampson and Groves (1989) conducted their replication study in England and Wales rather than Chicago. Avoiding some of the problems associated with using official crime statistics (e.g., policing activities tend to be concentrated in poorer, socially disorganized areas), Sampson and Groves used the results from the British Crime Survey, in which community members were asked to report their own victimization experiences. Moreover, data from the British Crime Survey—gathered at the community level rather than from aggregated census data—permitted them to drill down and examine what was happening within a particular community (or neighbourhood). Sampson and Groves also added three new intervening variables to their model—"sparse local friendship networks," "unsupervised teenage peer groups," and "low organizational participation" (see Figure 12.2)—which they said mediated between the five characteristics of social disorganization described by Shaw and McKay (residential density, poverty, ethnic and cultural heterogeneity, residential mobility, and family disruption) and the end product of "crime and delinquency" (Sampson & Groves, 1989).

The study by Sampson and Groves provides solid support for Shaw and McKay's earlier study of social disorganization in Chicago. The results are compelling, given that the Sampson and Groves study was conducted in an entirely different country on the other side of the Atlantic Ocean, using an entirely different data set, some 50 years after the Shaw and McKay study. Sampson and Groves found that one or more of the five main characteristics of socially disorganized areas identified by Shaw and McKay—in combination with one or more of the three intervening variables introduced by Sampson and Groves—predicted 61 percent of muggings and street robberies, 61 percent of burglaries, 42 percent of vandalism, and 42 percent of overall victimization (Sampson & Groves, 1989). The findings of the Sampson and Groves study were reconfirmed in a subsequent study by Christopher Lowenkamp, Francis Cullen, and Travis Pratt (2003) using more recent data from the British Crime Survey. The study by Lowenkamp et al. "revealed a high level of support for social disorganization theory" (p. 377).

FIGURE 12.2   Community Structure and Crime

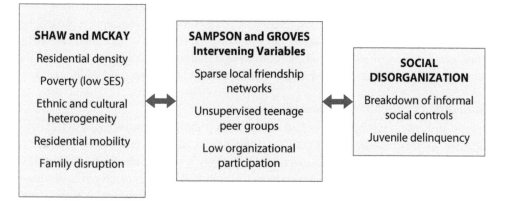

Source: Adapted from Sampson and Groves (1989, p. 783).

BOX 12.1

Transforming a Community

The rundown and socially disorganized Whalley-Newton neighbourhood is currently in the process of being transformed by large new redevelopments, such as the one in the renamed "Surrey City Centre."

While the Chicago School concept of social disorganization is not specifically mentioned in the City of Surrey's mission statement, there may be no better example of an official attempt to address the problem of social disorganization than the city's recent initiatives to transform the socially disorganized Whalley-Newton area into a socially organized or socially cohesive community (City of Surrey, 2010, 2012). The Whalley-Newton area of British Columbia has one of the highest crime rates in Canada (Munro, 1998; Skelton, 2004; Zytaruk, 2009). It also exhibits many of the characteristics of social disorganization and social disorder that were identified by the Chicago School, such as residential mobility (transience), poverty, broken homes, ethnic and cultural heterogeneity, and cheap and rundown rental accommodations (with landlords unwilling to maintain the properties because they're expecting the buildings to be knocked down as the land is purchased at a high price for real estate development/urban renewal projects) (Munro, 1998; O'Brian, 2003). The city has renamed Whalley as "Surrey City Centre" (Lamb, 1992) and built a

Surrey, old and new: A rundown section of the city is contrasted with recent redevelopments in the new city centre, seen in the distance.
Source: Victor Andre.

new civic centre, community plaza, recreational centre, centre for the performing arts, and regional library, as well as many new residential developments. In essence, the City of Surrey is attempting to tackle criminogenic (crime-causing) social conditions such as poverty, unemployment, rundown housing, and general urban decay (social disorganization) by totally reorganizing the social environment and creating a sense of social cohesion and social identity.

The studies by Shaw and McKay, Sampson and Groves, and Lowenkamp et al. involved urbanized areas because social disorganization is generally considered to be a byproduct of urbanization (large population movements and overcrowding). Nonetheless, Wayne Osgood and Jeff Chambers (2000)—using census data and official arrest rates, like earlier Chicago School researchers—found that one or more of the social disorganization variables of residential instability, ethnic heterogeneity, and broken homes (family disruption) had a strong effect on juvenile arrest rates for robbery, rape, and aggravated assault in rural areas of the United States. Thus, it can be said that social disorganization theory is a well-travelled, well-established sociological explanation of crime and delinquency.

Sutherland's Differential Association Theory

differential association theory
Sutherland's theory that criminal behaviour is learned through the process of social interaction, and that the process includes the learning of criminal skills, motivations, attitudes, and rationalizations.

Edwin Sutherland has been described as "the most important criminologist of the 20th century" (Akers & Sellers, 2009, p. 85) and the individual most responsible for making sociology "the centerpiece ... of American criminology" (Akers & Matsueda, 1989, p. 24). Sutherland did his Ph.D. at the University of Chicago, and was a research professor there from 1929 until 1935 (Cullen & Messner, 2011). Apart from his **differential association theory**, he is known for his 1937 book *The Professional Thief*, which—consistent with the Chicago School predilection for ethnographies and life histories—recounted the life story told to Sutherland by "professional thief" Chic Conwell. Sutherland (1940) is also known for his article on white-collar criminality, published when virtually every other scholar was talking about delinquency among the lower classes. In his subsequent 1949 book, *White Collar Crime*, he elaborated on his claim that white-collar crime was as prevalent as street crime, and that it actually did more damage and cost society more than street crime (Mutchnick, Martin, & Austin, 2009).

Sutherland is best known for his differential association theory. Although he set out nine separate principles or propositions of differential association, the most important are as follows:

- "Criminal behaviour is learned."
- Criminal behaviour is "learned in a process of interaction with other persons" through communication (including words and gestures).
- Learning criminal behaviour "includes techniques of committing the crime" plus the "motives, drives, rationalizations and attitudes" that go along with being a criminal (Sutherland, 1947/1994, pp. 225–227).

In essence, Sutherland asserted that criminal behaviour is not the result of genetic defects, criminal psychopathy, or feeble-mindedness. Instead, he argued that people learn criminal behaviour, just like they learn other types of human behaviour, such as how to tie their shoes, or how to read and write (Lilly, Cullen, & Ball, 2011). Here, Sutherland was drawing upon the Chicago School concept of **symbolic interactionism**—the notion that meaning and reality are socially constructed through gestures used to show emotion or demonstrate how to do something, through symbols such as monetary instruments or university degrees, or through words, which are themselves socially created symbols that convey socially agreed-upon meanings (Bernard, Snipes, & Gerould, 2010). According to Sutherland (1947/1994), individuals will learn criminal behaviour to a different degree, depending upon the frequency, duration, and intensity of their exposure to delinquent peers and delinquent values.

Sutherland helped expand the dominance of sociological explanations over biological and psychological explanations of criminality during the 1940s and 1950s by way of his vociferous (and largely successful) critique of the works of William Sheldon and the husband and wife team of Sheldon and Eleanor Glueck (the Gluecks) (Laub & Sampson, 1991). William Sheldon was engaged in somatotyping, in which he used physical constitution or body type (i.e., ectomorphy, endomorphy, or mesomorphy) to predict an individual's propensity to engage in criminal behaviour (Bartol, 1999). Sheldon argued that the mesomorph—with a hard, muscular body type and a competitive or risk-taking temperament—would be most inclined to engage in violent behaviour. In their 1950 book *Unraveling Juvenile Delinquency*, the Gluecks concluded that delinquent boys were indeed more mesomorphic than non-delinquent boys, and that delinquent boys exhibited more temperamental problems (thought to be hereditary) (Glueck & Glueck, 1950/1994). For Sutherland, these ideas hearkened back to the earlier days of Positivist School thinking regarding the criminal body type, and to the concomitant development of "eugenics criminology"—the notion that criminals as well as feeble-minded and mentally ill individuals should be prevented from reproducing (passing along their

symbolic interactionism
The Chicago School notion that meaning and reality are socially constructed through the use or sharing of gestures, symbols, or words, which are themselves socially-created symbols that convey socially agreed-upon meanings.

defective genes) through enforced incapacitation, sterilization, and, if necessary, extermination (cf. Lilly, Cullen, & Ball, 2011; Rafter, 1997).

Sykes and Matza's Techniques of Neutralization

In 1957, Gresham Sykes and David Matza expanded upon Sutherland's statement that criminal behaviour is learned, asserting that this learning includes the rationalizations, motivations and attitudes that go along with being a criminal. According to Sykes and Matza (1957), criminals actually know that committing crime is wrong and experience feelings of guilt as a consequence. Thus, Sykes and Matza set out to enumerate the various rationalizations that criminals learn and use to neutralize their guilt and/or justify their criminal behaviour. They identified five techniques of **neutralization**:

neutralization
An extension of Sutherland's differential association theory; the notion that criminals learn motivations and rationalizations to justify their criminal behaviour.

1. denial of responsibility ("I didn't do it");
2. denial of injury ("Nobody was hurt");
3. denial of the victim ("He had it coming to him");
4. condemnation of the condemners ("The police and the politicians commit crimes themselves"); and
5. appeal to higher loyalties ("I did it to protect my gang's reputation") (Sykes & Matza, 1957).

Various research studies have provided support for Sykes and Matza's techniques of neutralization. For example, a study of 114 convicted rapists found that rapists excused or justified their behaviour by saying that their female victims were "seductresses," that "nice girls don't get raped," that the victims actually meant "yes" when they said "no," and that they (the rapists) were actually "nice guys" whose poor choice of behaviour was attributable to emotional problems or being under the influence of alcohol at the time of the offence (Scully & Marolla, 2003). Another study found that differential association theory and techniques of neutralization were helpful in explaining white collar and corporate crime. The 113 MBA students who were asked what they would do if they knew that a product was potentially dangerous indicated that they would continue to sell the product, justifying or excusing their behaviour by saying that the government typically exaggerated the danger of such products, that strict government regulations impeded business activity, that the profitability of the business was more important than complying with regulations, or that it was the consumer's responsibility to decide whether or not the product was safe (Piquero, Tibbetts, & Blankenship, 2005). Another study, this time involving an online survey of 420 university students, demonstrated that a number of students excused or justified academic dishonesty by saying that the teaching was of a poor quality, the class (or the test) was too difficult, they had no choice unless they wanted to fail the course, or they only cheated to help out a close friend or family member (Brent & Atkisson, 2011).

Burgess and Akers's Differential Association-Reinforcement Theory

As the name suggests, Robert Burgess and Ronald Akers's (1966) differential association-reinforcement theory is another elaboration on Sutherland's differential association theory. Starting from Sutherland's contention that criminal behaviour is learned in the same manner that non-criminal behaviour is learned, Burgess and Akers set out to specify the mechanisms that were involved in the learning process. To this end, they added elements of B.F. Skinner's behaviour modification (operant conditioning) plus Albert Bandura's observations on imitation and modelling behaviour. Rather than simply say, as Sutherland had, that "criminal behaviour is learned … in a process of interaction with other persons," Burgess and Akers stated that criminal behaviour is learned in accordance with the principles of operant conditioning (i.e., through re-inforcement and punishment), and that it can also be learned in non-social situations (consistent with imitation and modelling). As behaviour modification and imitation and modelling behaviour both emerged from the field of psychology, it can be said that Burgess and Akers's differential association-reinforcement theory is a form of social psychology. Akers subsequently took ownership of differential association-reinforce-ment theory, which he went on to describe as "social learning theory" (Akers, 2011; Akers & Sellers, 2009). As social learning theory is a major theoretical perspective in its own right, it will be dealt with in significantly greater detail, later in this chapter.

The Sociology of Deviance and Labelling Theory

Kai Erikson and Howard Becker, widely recognized as two of the most prominent think-ers in the sociology of deviance and labelling theory, were both products of the Chicago School (Matsueda, 2001; Plummer, 1979). Erikson did his PhD in sociology at the University of Chicago, where he was influenced by a number of the Chicago School symbolic interactionists, including George Mead, Charles Cooley, and Erving Goffman (cf. Erikson, 1962; Erikson, 1964). Becker was born in Chicago, lived in Chicago, did his PhD in sociology at the University of Chicago, and even taught at the famed Chicago School for several years (Mutchnick, Martin, & Austin, 2009; Snyder, 2010).

The sociology of deviance takes the position that deviance is "relative"—what is con-sidered "normal" behaviour by some societies may be considered "abnormal" or even "criminal" behaviour by other societies (Clinard & Meier, 2004; Curra, 2011). To illustrate, polygamy is illegal in Canada, but legal in some countries. By contrast, adultery is legal (although frowned upon) in Canada, yet is punishable by death in certain societies or cultures. Two American states (Colorado and Washington) have now legalized marijuana, whereas other American states have not. To express it differently, deviance is "in the eye of the beholder" and thus is socially constructed. Those who are deemed by society to be deviant are often stigmatized or labelled as such, and treated as social outcasts (Becker, 1963; Erikson, 1964; Erikson, 2005). Once an individual is labelled as deviant or criminal, that label becomes his or her new social identity (or master status), which then becomes a self-fulfilling prophecy (Lilly, Cullen, & Ball, 2011; Pfohl, 1985; Williams & McShane, 2010).

Erikson's Sociology of Deviance

At the beginning of this chapter, we explored Durkheim's work on "The Normal and the Pathological." Durkheim (1964) argued that even a "society of saints" would seek out some unusual behaviour within the community and declare it to be deviant to establish the moral boundaries of the community. Erikson's **sociology of deviance** is a blend of Chicago School symbolic interactionism and Durkheimian thinking about how crime and deviance function to maintain social cohesion. In *Wayward Puritans: A Study in the Sociology of Deviance*, Erikson described how the Puritans—a group of Christians

sociology of deviance
Blends Chicago School symbolic interactionism with views on how crime and deviance are used to maintain social bound-aries and/or social control; it examines how certain groups or behaviours come to be viewed as "social problems."

who migrated to Massachusetts in the 1600s in search of religious freedom—suddenly discovered heretics and witches in the midst of their "society of saints" (Erikson, 2005). These "deviant" members of the religious community were banished, and in some cases (the Salem Witch trials), they were even hung. According to Erikson, this persecution of imaginary witches was evidence of the need that all societies have for a certain amount of deviance, to draw a "symbolic set of parentheses" around what is believed to be *socially* acceptable behaviour (Erikson, 1962; Erikson, 2005).

Building upon the work of Goffman, a Chicago School symbolic interactionist, Erikson also talked about the stigmatization (labelling) that takes place at "status degradation ceremonies" such as trials, insanity hearings, and courts martial, which are generally dramatic and staged to maximize public visibility (Erikson, 1962; Garfinkel, 1956; Goffman, 2005). A stigma (or label) is affixed at the end of the ceremony (e.g., guilty, mentally ill, etc.), and once affixed, becomes difficult to remove, because there are no status restoration ceremonies. If individuals are stigmatized permanently, they may develop a deviant self-image, come to believe that they're no longer a part of the so-called normal community, and thus feel compelled to continue with the disapproved behaviour.

Becker's Labelling Theory

labelling theory
The theory that the stigma (or label) affixed through the criminalization process may lead individuals to develop a deviant self-image and feel separate from the "normal" community, and thus continue with deviant behaviour.

Although Howard Becker never described himself as a labelling theorist, his name is most commonly associated with **labelling theory** (Deutschmann, 2002; Matsueda, 2001). Becker talked about how certain groups or behaviours come to be viewed as "social problems," not because they are necessarily deviant or criminal but because of the social reaction to these groups or behaviours (Matsueda, 2001; Mutchnick, Martin, & Austin, 2009). If these groups or behaviours were simply ignored by society, then they would not come to be regarded as deviant or criminal. According to Becker (1963), social groups actually create deviance by making up rules that turn other individuals—or entire groups—into outlaws or "outsiders."

Becker also described the role of "moral entrepreneurs" or "moral crusaders" in rule making. Moral entrepreneurs generally come from the upper classes, have money and power, and feel that it is their duty to stomp out evil and impose their own moral standards on minority groups and/or the lower classes (Becker, 1963). Once their mission is accomplished (e.g., a new law is implemented prohibiting public servants from wearing visible religious symbols at work), they move on to find other causes that seem worthy of their attention. The rule enforcers (the police, corrections officials, etc.) need to demonstrate that their enforcement activities are successful, yet at the same time, have to maintain the public perception that more work still needs to be done (Becker, 1963). Otherwise, they could soon find themselves out of a job.

Social Problems, Moral Panics, and Critical Constructionism

moral panic
Phenomena—socially constructed by the media, politicians, and "moral entrepreneurs"—in which certain people or groups are labelled or stigmatized as the cause of a perceived social problem, resulting in widespread public alarm.

The sociology of deviance and the labelling perspective gave rise to critical constructionism, a field that examines how social problems and **moral panics** are socially constructed by the media, politicians, and special interest groups (Burns & Crawford, 1999; S. Cohen, 1987). Work in this area continues to this day, as evidenced by Timothy Brezina and Herbert Phipps's (2010) study on "false news reports" and "the role of public officials" in stirring up moral panic in the aftermath of Hurricane Katrina. Police and public officials—unprepared for the disaster and unable to organize rescue efforts—

started blaming the powerless, low-status hurricane refugees, who (with vilification by the media) came to be viewed as the very personification of evil. Closer to home, Adorjan's (2011) discourse analysis of Canadian newspapers demonstrates the propensity of some journalists to exaggerate and sensationalize youth crime, focusing on the most serious of the offenders and portraying young offenders in general as significantly more sinister, calculating, and dangerous than they are in reality.

Critical criminology was in large part an outgrowth of the sociology of deviance, labelling theory, and critical constructionism. Critical criminologists subsequently criticized labelling theorists for what was seen as their "inadequate" analysis of the socio-economic inequalities of capitalism and the role of the rich and powerful in defining crime in their own interests (Taylor, Walton, & Young, 1973). That said, labelling theorists laid the groundwork for critical criminology by starting to examine the process through which certain individuals or groups came to be defined as deviant or criminal, and by asking who makes the rules and why. William Chambliss and Richard Quinney—two sociologists who eventually went on to become "critical criminologists"—began their careers as critical constructionists (or conflict theorists), talking about how laws and social reality were socially constructed (Lilly, Cullen, & Ball, 2011; Williams & McShane, 2010). Jock Young, co-author of *The New Criminology* (Taylor, Walton, & Young, 1973) (which roundly criticized labelling theory) and co-editor of *Critical Criminology* (Taylor, Walton, & Young, 1975) was also co-editor of *The Manufacture of News: Social Problems, Deviance and the Mass Media* (Cohen & Young, 1973), which focused on the role of the media in manufacturing deviance and social problems. For further information on conflict and critical criminology, see Chapter 9, Understanding Critical Criminology.

Anomie-Strain Theory

As noted earlier, Durkheim's work on anomie underpins Merton's **anomie-strain theory**, Agnew's general strain theory and Messner and Rosenfeld's institutional-anomie theory. Recall that Durkheim described *anomie* as a state of lawlessness, normlessness, or unrestrained ambition, which if left unchecked could lead to a breakdown in social solidarity (Clinard, 1964; Durkheim, 1965). Durkheim said that a state of anomie would arise when the "forces of integration" (social bonds and collective beliefs) and the "forces of regulation" (laws and social institutions) were out of balance, and therefore not functioning properly (Lilly, Cullen, & Ball, 2011). While Durkheim discussed the function of crime and punishment in maintaining social solidarity, he did not specifically link anomie to crime. This task was left to American sociologist Robert Merton.

Merton's Anomie-Strain Theory

Robert Merton's (1938) article "Social Structure and Anomie" has become one of the most widely cited works in the social sciences. In his article, Merton employed Durkheim's notion of anomie to explain high crime rates in American society. Using a functionalist approach, Merton argued that a dysfunction (a disjunction or imbalance) existed between the cultural goals of American society (e.g., accumulation of wealth and social advancement) and access to the institutional means through which to achieve those cultural goals (e.g., education and good employment opportunities). This dysfunction created a sense of strain or anomie—Americans believed that they were supposed to pursue the cultural goals but felt that their opportunity to do so was blocked (Bernard, 1995).

anomie-strain theory
Merton's theory describing the state of anomie in American society caused by the disjunction (or dysfunction or strain) between the cultural goals of the "American dream" and the institutional means to achieve those goals.

In other words, social institutions—education, the economy, and the government—were unable to adequately integrate and regulate the cultural goals and the institutional means (Agnew, 1997).

Merton (1938) observed that individuals in society dealt with this sense of anomie or strain through five possible modes of adaptation: conformity, innovation, ritualism, retreatism, and rebellion. The mode of adaptation would depend upon whether the individual accepted or rejected the cultural goals of American (capitalist) society and the institutional means through which to achieve those goals (see Table 12.1). If the individual accepted the cultural goals and also accepted the institutional (legitimate) means through which to achieve those goals, as indicated by a "+" sign in Table 12.1, then he or she would be more likely to adapt through conformity. If the individual accepted the cultural goals (e.g., accumulation of wealth and social advancement) but rejected the means, as indicated by a "−" sign in Table 12.1 (i.e., they did not feel that they had adequate access to a good education or a good job), then they would be more likely to adapt through innovation. In this case, innovation refers to finding different or novel ways to attain the cultural goals of society, such as theft or fraud. Retreatists, who rejected the cultural goals and the institutionalized means through which to achieve them, might drop out of society and become alcoholics, drug addicts, or street people. Those who chose the rebellion mode would reject the cultural goals and institutionalized means of the society, attempt to overthrow society, and try to replace the existing goals and means with new ones. While the behaviour of retreatists and rebels might be regarded as deviant and even criminal, Merton argued that the innovators were most likely to typify criminals that came to the attention of the criminal justice system (Williams & McShane, 2010).

cultural transmission theory
The Chicago School notion that criminal subcultures develop their own subcultural (criminal) values or norms, which are then transmitted from gang member to gang member, and from generation to generation.

Subcultural Theories

Many of the subcultural theories that emerged in the 1950s and 1960s were premised upon a combination of Merton's anomie-strain theory and Sutherland's differential association theory. These theories were also grounded in **cultural transmission theory**, the Chicago School notion that criminal subcultures (usually found in socially disorganized areas) develop their own subcultural (criminal) values, which are transmitted from

Table 12.1 Robert Merton's Five Modes of Adaptation

Mode of adaptation	Cultural goals	Institutional means	Criminal?
Conformity	+ (Accepts)	+ (Accepts)	No
Innovation	+ (Accepts)	− (Rejects)	Yes
Ritualism	− (Rejects)	+ (Accepts)	No
Retreatism	− (Rejects)	− (Rejects)	Yes
Rebellion	± (Rejects—tries to replace)	± (Rejects—tries to replace)	Yes

Source: Adapted from Merton (1938, p. 676).

member to member within these subcultures (Williams & McShane, 2010). The argument that these subcultural values would be in conflict with the conventional values of regular society gave rise to cultural conflict theory (Bernard, 1995; Clinard & Meier, 2004).

The Culture of the Gang

In *Delinquent Boys: The Culture of the Gang*, Albert Cohen (1955/1964) set out to explain how delinquent subcultures formed, how they developed their new subcultural values, and how these values were transmitted within the subculture. Cohen argued that lower-class males had similar aspirations to middle- and upper-class males, but found that they were unable to compete successfully for social status in the school environment. Thus, lower-class males developed what Cohen (1955/1964) referred to as a sense of "status deprivation," which could be compared to a type of anomie or strain (Mutchnick, Martin, & Austin, 2009). They dropped out of school (a "reaction formation") and formed delinquent gangs (a "collective solution"), wherein they created a new set of "normative" values, and proceeded to redefine the meaning of social status in terms of those new values. For instance, members could achieve status within the gang by demonstrating their "toughness" or their willingness to violate conventional norms by committing acts of vandalism or theft (A.K. Cohen, 1955/1964). In other words, they rejected the unattainable goals of typical middle-class teens (e.g., being popular, dressing in the latest fashion, doing well at school) and replaced them with unconventional goals that they could attain.

Illegitimate Opportunity Structures

Richard Cloward and Lloyd Ohlin's (1960) *Delinquency and Opportunity* built on Merton's notion that lower-class individuals lacked access to legitimate opportunity structures (e.g., a good education or a high-paying, high-prestige job). Drawing on life histories written by members of the Chicago School (such as *The Jack-Roller* by Shaw and *The Professional Thief* by Sutherland), Cloward and Ohlin elaborated on the notion that criminal skills were learned through cultural transmission (Lilly, Cullen, & Ball, 2011). Cloward and Ohlin also identified three types of illegitimate opportunity structures— the criminal subculture, the conflict subculture, and the retreatist subculture—through which lower-class youth could cope with their sense of strain, or "status frustration." However, they said that access to these subcultures would be differentially available, depending upon where the individual lived, and the degree of social organization (or disorganization) in that particular neighbourhood (Williams & McShane, 2010).

According to Cloward and Ohlin, criminal subcultures existed primarily in organized slums, where they already had networks of "professional" criminals who could take prospective gang members under their wing and teach them the tricks of the trade. Conflict subcultures existed in disorganized slums, where there was little organized criminal activity and, therefore, limited opportunity to learn criminal skills. Instead, conflict subcultures in socially disorganized slums placed an emphasis on toughness and a willingness to engage in physical violence (Cloward & Ohlin, 1960). Retreatist subcultures existed in both organized and socially disorganized slums, and these subcultures focused primarily on the buying and selling of illegal drugs, which individuals used to escape (or retreat) from a sense of status frustration, or anomie-strain (Williams & McShane, 2010).

Agnew's General Strain Theory

Earlier versions of anomie theory were criticized for placing too much emphasis on the type of strain supposedly experienced by the lower classes in society (Agnew, 1995). Critics said that anomie-strain theory failed to offer an explanation for crime committed by the upper classes (e.g., white collar and corporate crime) and for delinquent acts committed by teens from relatively affluent family backgrounds (Winfree & Abadinsky, 2010). Thus, Robert Agnew (1985) introduced his **general strain theory**, which was intended to rectify some of the oversights of original anomie-strain theory.

Agnew (1985, 1992) pointed out that teens do not have the same concerns as adults: teens are not worried about accumulation of wealth or social advancement, or even about getting a good job or a good education. Rather, teens have more immediate concerns or sources of strain, such as physical appearance, being popular (or unpopular) with peers, parental discipline, doing poorly at school, and pressure from peers to join gangs and participate in delinquent behaviour. Unlike adults, however, teens cannot escape from their stressful circumstances by moving to a new neighbourhood or a different town, changing jobs, or quitting or changing schools, because they are financially dependent and still subject to parental (and school) control (Hoffman, 2010). Agnew described the sources of strain experienced by teens as "the presentation of negative stimuli" (e.g., parental punishment) and "the removal of positively valued stimuli" (e.g., being kicked off the high school football team), arguing that these strains or stressors could lead to frustration, anger, and, in some cases, juvenile delinquency.

Agnew's general strain theory represents a combination of sociological theory (e.g., Durkheim's anomie theory and Merton's anomie-strain theory) and psychological theory (e.g., differences in personality, negative affect, the frustration–aggression hypothesis, cognitive and behavioural coping mechanisms) (Agnew, 1995; Inderbitzen, Bates, & Gainey, 2013). As such, it is part of a newer trend toward theoretical integration. General strain theory has been highly researched and is one of the more well-supported theories in criminology (Cullen, Wright, & Blevins, 2004; Hoffman, 2010).

general strain theory
Explains delinquent acts by teens from relatively affluent families; teens have more immediate strains than adults, such as physical appearance, popularity, parental discipline, academic performance, and peer pressure to join gangs and participate in delinquent behaviour.

Messner and Rosenfeld's Institutional-Anomie Theory

In *Crime and the American Dream*, Steven Messner and Richard Rosenfeld (1994/2007) revisited Durkheim's forces of integration and regulation and Merton's anomie-strain theory, arguing that most criminological theories are overly focused on micro-level inquiry (the individual level), rather than on macro-level inquiry (the level of social structure or social organization) (Rosenfeld & Messner, 1995). Following Merton's 1938 theoretical statement about the relationship between social structure and anomie, Messner and Rosenfeld pointed to the cultural goals of capitalist society and the failure of social institutions—the political system, education, the family, and the economy—to properly integrate and regulate the pursuit of those goals (Messner & Rosenfeld, 1994/2007). If the social institutions were functioning properly, then the political system, educational system, and the family would act as restraints on the unfettered demands of the economy and on the unrestrained behaviour of individuals who were in hot pursuit of financial rewards. Essentially, they noted the existence of an institutional imbalance (institutional-anomie) in which the economy dominates the political system, the educational system, and the family, leading to an amoral "ends justifies the means" attitude in society (Merton, 1938; Messner & Rosenfeld, 1994/2007).

We are surrounded by evidence of the explanatory power of **institutional-anomie theory**. We need look no further than the economic meltdown of 2007 and 2008, when the selling of "subprime mortgages" brought financial institutions, homeowners, and entire economies around the world to the brink of disaster. The public sector failed to provide adequate regulation and oversight, permitting financial institutions to issue mortgages to countless high-risk borrowers, and to borrow recklessly to back up those mortgages (Immergluck, 2011; Thompson, 2012). Rather than punishing bankers who had recklessly lent out vast amounts of money, secured by basically worthless "derivatives," governments around the world stepped in and bailed them out, using trillions of dollars of taxpayers' money. This is a clear-cut example of how the economy has come to dominate other social institutions, and how an "ends-justifies-the-means" attitude has come to permeate society.

institutional-anomie theory
Messner and Rosenfeld's theory that institutional-anomie (institutional imbalance) is caused by the cultural goals of capitalist society and the failure of social institutions to properly integrate and regulate the pursuit of those goals.

Social Learning Theory

Social learning theory has its roots in the Chicago School's symbolic interactionism and Sutherland's differential association theory (Akers & Sellers, 2009). Starting with Sutherland's contention that criminal behaviour is learned, Burgess and Akers set out in their 1966 differential association-reinforcement theory to specify the mechanisms involved in the learning process, adding elements of B.F. Skinner's operant conditioning and Albert Bandura's observations on imitation and modelling behaviour (Burgess & Akers, 1966). Akers (1998) has continued to refine his earlier statements regarding social learning theory, clarifying the main concepts and propositions.

social learning theory
Definitions (values about acceptable and unacceptable behaviour) favourable to criminal behaviour are learned through differential reinforcement; criminal behaviour depends on reward or punishment for past behaviour and anticipated consequences of persistence.

As was the case with Sutherland's differential association theory, social learning theory posits that individuals learn definitions that are favourable or unfavourable to committing crime. According to Akers and Sellers (2009), individuals learn both positive and neutralizing definitions. Positive definitions might include the attitude held by certain subcultures that carrying a weapon and being prepared to use it is socially acceptable behaviour (cf. Wolfgang & Ferracuti, 1967). Neutralizing definitions—as described originally in Sykes and Matza's (1957) techniques of neutralization—include rationalizations or justifications for engaging in criminal behaviour (e.g., being drunk at the time or being the victim of a poor upbringing). These definitions are learned through a process of differential reinforcement. Individuals are more or less likely to engage in criminal behaviour depending upon whether their behaviour has been reinforced (rewarded) or punished in the past, and the sort of consequences they anticipate if they continue (Akers, 1998). Social rewards are largely symbolic and can range from acquiring money or material goods to gaining social acceptance or prestige.

Today, Akers's social learning theory is regarded as one of the most well established and well researched of all criminological theories (Cullen, Wright, & Blevins, 2004). A recent meta-analysis of research studies on Gottfredson and Hirschi's low self-control theory (see the next section) found that social learning theory offered as good an explanation for criminality as low self-control theory (Pratt & Cullen, 2000). Another meta-analysis of studies conducted specifically on correctional treatment programs found that programs based on the principles of social learning theory had the greatest impact when it came to reducing recidivism (i.e., reducing the likelihood of offenders committing new crimes following their release from prison) (Cullen, Wright, Gendreau, & Andrews, 2003). A more recent meta-analysis indicated that stronger empirical support exists for social learning theory than for rational choice or deterrence theories (Pratt et al., 2010). (See Chapter 11, Crime Choice Theory.)

Social Control Theory

social control theory
Rooted in Durkheim's forces of integration, the Chicago School's concern with the breakdown in informal social controls; holds that social bonds and informal social controls act as restraints on teen delinquency.

As is the case with many of the other sociological theories discussed in this chapter, the roots of **social control theory** can be traced back to Durkheim and to his view that individuals would behave immorally if left to their own devices. Durkheim stressed the role of social bonds and collective beliefs (forces of integration) and the law and social institutions (forces of regulation) in restraining individual wants and aspirations (Durkheim, 1951, 1964; Paternoster & Bachman, 2001).

The origins of social control theory can also be traced back to the Chicago School's social disorganization theory, and the notion that social disorganization contributes to the breakdown of informal social controls usually exercised by parents, adult neighbours, school teachers, and community leaders (Cullen, Wright, & Blevins, 2004; Sampson & Groves, 1989). Some of the earliest forays into social control theory were led by Chicago School theorists, such as Albert Reiss, who wrote in 1951 about "delinquency as a failure of personal and social controls," and Walter Reckless, who in 1967 introduced containment theory, which included inner containments (a good self-concept, ability to tolerate frustration) and outer containments (institutional reinforcement, good family values) as sources of social control (Lilly, Cullen, & Ball, 2011; Williams & McShane, 2010).

Hirschi's Social Bond Theory

social bond theory
Social control theory by Hirschi (based on Durkheim's concept of the social bond); the four elements of the social bond include attachment, commitment, involvement, and belief.

Travis Hirschi's 1969 **social bond theory** is unquestionably the most well known of all the earlier social control theories. At one time, if somebody mentioned social control theory, it was automatically assumed that they were talking about social bond theory (Winfree & Abadinsky, 2010). Social bond theory was clearly rooted in Durkheimian notions about social bonds and collective beliefs, and Hirschi openly acknowledged as much. He also acknowledged the influence of Chicago School theorists Reiss and Reckless. Essentially, Hirschi's social bond theory can be broken down into four main elements or components:

1. attachment (to parents, school teachers and significant others);
2. commitment (to doing well at school, keeping a good reputation);
3. involvement (in organized sports, doing homework); and
4. belief (in the law, and in conventional norms and values) (Hirschi, 1969).

Hirschi argued that if the four components of the social bond were working as they should, then an individual would be disinclined to engage in criminal or deviant behaviour. Hirschi's social bond theory underpins a number of more recent social control theories, including Thornberry's interactional theory and Sampson and Laub's life-course-developmental theory.

In 1990, Gottfredson and Hirschi went on to co-author *A General Theory of Crime*. According to Gottfredson and Hirschi's general theory of crime, all crime is caused by low self-control, which is itself caused by poor parenting, usually provided—or not provided, as the case may be—by parents who are themselves lacking in self-control (Gottfredson & Hirschi, 1990). Some observers have argued that the general theory of crime is a sociological (social process) theory, in that it talks about the socialization process, and what happens within the social institution of the family (Beaver, Ratchford, & Ferguson, 2010; Walsh, 2012). Others have observed that Gottfredson and Hirschi's theory more closely resembles a bio-psychological (neo-Freudian) theory, in that it focuses on a number of characteristics—personality traits, temperament, impulsivity—that are thought to be inherited or, if not, then at least inculcated in very early childhood (Andrews & Bonta, 2010; Pratt & Cullen, 2000).

Thornberry's Interactional Theory

Terrence Thornberry's **interactional theory** is another type of social control theory, which combines elements of Hirschi's social bond theory with elements of Akers's social learning theory (Thornberry, 1987; Thornberry & Krohn, 2005). Thornberry observes that social bond theory and social learning theory are both unidirectional. Social bond theory assumes that if the social bond is weakened, individuals will be less constrained, and therefore more likely to engage in crime. Social learning theory assumes that if individuals learn definitions that are favourable to committing crime and have their deviant or criminal behaviour reinforced, then that may encourage involvement in crime (Cartwright, 2011). Thornberry argues that the interaction between social bonds and social learning is actually a two-way street, which can go in either direction, or even go back and forth (Akers & Sellers, 2009; Lilly, Cullen, & Ball, 2011). According to Thornberry, weakened social bonds can lead to exposure to delinquent peers and to the learning of delinquent values; at the same time, exposure to delinquent peers and the learning of delinquent values can lead to further weakening of social bonds. Therefore, he says that we need both theories in order to provide an adequate explanation of crime and delinquency.

Thornberry also points out in his interactional theory that social bonds are not static; they change over the life course. Preschool children are primarily attached to (bonded with) their parents and close family members. Elementary school children are still attached to their parents and family members, but may develop bonds with teachers and friends. Teenagers are more likely to be concerned with impressing their teen peers than they are about pleasing their parents or their schoolteachers. Adults develop social bonds with their spouses, employers, and fellow employees, and may forget entirely about any bonds that they had with schoolteachers and teen peers (Thornberry, 1987; Thornberry & Krohn, 2005). In many respects, Thornberry's interactional theory is similar to Sampson and Laub's life-course-developmental theory.

interactional theory
Thornberry's theory that both social bond theory and social learning theory are needed to explain criminal behaviour, because weakening of the social bond and the social learning of criminal values is interactional or reciprocal (not unidirectional).

Sampson and Laub's Life-Course-Developmental Theory

Robert Sampson and John Laub's **life-course-developmental theory** is a more recent extension of Hirschi's social bond theory. However, Sampson and Laub redefine the attachment and commitment elements of the social bond as "social capital," which they say is acquired as individuals reach adulthood and start to gain a stake in society by obtaining a high school or college diploma, finding a good job, getting married, and having children (Laub & Sampson, 1993; Laub, Sampson, & Allen, 2001; Sampson & Laub, 1992). They say that while some individuals might appear to be on an inevitable "trajectory" (or pathway) toward a criminal career, they can still be deflected off of this trajectory when they come to "turning points" through which they might transition out and actually desist from committing crime (Laub, Nagin, & Sampson, 1998; Laub &

life-course-developmental theory
Sampson and Laub's theory that individuals can be deflected off of the trajectory toward a criminal career by life events ("turning points") that can lead them to transition out of criminal behaviour.

Sampson, 1993). Indeed, they argue that desistance is by far the most common outcome of juvenile delinquency. Once individuals acquire social capital, or a stake in society, they are not willing to risk it because of the potential attachment and commitment costs involved (e.g., loss of a job, loss of a spouse, loss of reputation). Considerable evidence supports Sampson and Laub's contention that the quality and quantity of social bonds vary over the life course, and that the propensity to engage in criminal activity varies over time, with most individuals aging out of crime when they reach adulthood (Akers & Sellers, 2009; Farrington et al., 2006; Lilly, Cullen, & Ball, 2011).

Conclusion

This has been a brief tour of sociological approaches to crime and deviance. Out of necessity, a number of sociological theories or perspectives have been left out, including (but by no means limited to) the following:

- Thorsten Sellin's (1938/1994) work on conflict theory and cultural conflict
- Marvin Wolfgang and Franco Ferracuti's (1967) "subcultures of violence," premised on Sutherland's differential association theory and the notion that individuals in these subcultures learn norms that are favourable to carrying weapons and using them when provoked
- Stanley Cohen's (1987) renowned work on folk devils and moral panics, which underpins many present-day endeavours in the field of critical constructionism
- John Hagan's 1985 power-control theory, which seeks to explain why males commit more crimes than females, by examining the structure of the "patriarchal" family in capitalist society (Hagan, Gillis, & Simpson, 1985)
- Jock Young's (1975, 2002) work on "left realism," an expansion on earlier efforts in the field of critical criminology
- James Messerschmidt's (1993, 2005) "sociology of masculinity," which examines how males construct masculinity differently, depending upon their race and position in the class structure
- David Garland's (2001) sociological analysis of why control theories and rational choice theories have gained traction over the past 30 years, due to observable economic, social, and political changes

Apart from comprising the lion's share of criminological theories, sociological approaches have been the driving force behind many past and present public policies aimed at reducing crime. Most public policies attempt to tackle criminogenic (crime-causing) social conditions, such as poverty, unemployment, lack of education, poor parenting, and poor housing (or homelessness) (Lilly, Cullen, & Ball, 2011). Urban renewal projects (including that of the Whalley-Newton community profiled in Box 12.1), social support centres, and parent-training programs aimed at improving social bonding with children are all examples of such initiatives (Agnew, 2010). In the Canadian criminal justice system, judges may impose a more lenient sentence on an offender who comes from a "disadvantaged background" (Schmalleger, MacAlister, & McKenna, 2004). Parole certificates may include a non-association condition, aimed at preventing a released offender from hanging out with and being influenced by delinquent peers. All of these actions come back to the Chicago School notion that "the nature of the neighbourhood" rather than "the nature of the individual" is the cause of crime (Lilly, Cullen, & Ball, 2011).

SUMMARY OF KEY POINTS

- While there are many theoretical approaches to studying crime, sociological approaches continue to be the most widely accepted. Several areas covered in other chapters in this book, such as feminist criminology and critical criminology, are strongly influenced by sociological theorists.

- Rather than focusing on the biological or psychological deficiencies of individuals, sociological explanations of criminal or deviant behaviour place more emphasis on the effects of social structures and institutions, social organization and class, and roles, norms, and social learning.

- Émile Durkheim contributed to the *consensus perspective* (which contrasts with *conflict theories* rooted in Marx) and to the notion that society is essentially organic (*structural functionalism*). His work underpins Merton's anomie-strain theory, Agnew's general strain theory, and several others.

- Durkheim observed that crime had existed throughout history and was present in all types of societies. He concluded that a certain amount of crime must be "normal," or at least that crime must serve some sort of social function. He proposed that crime defined the moral boundaries of the community.

- Members of the Chicago School rejected social Darwinist notions and challenged the notion that most criminals were either criminal psychopaths or feebleminded. Rather, members of the Chicago School concluded that it was "the nature of the neighbourhood," not "the nature of the individual," that was the primary cause of criminality. The Chicago School brought us many well-known criminological theories, including social disorganization theory, the sociology of deviance, and labelling theory.

- Edwin Sutherland, one of the leading criminologists of the 20th century, is best known for examining white-collar crime and for his *differential association theory*. It states that criminal behaviour is learned through the process of social interaction.

- The sociology of deviance takes the position that deviance is *relative*—what is considered "normal" behaviour by some societies may be considered "abnormal" or "criminal" by other societies. Those deemed by society to be deviant are often stigmatized or labelled as deviant.

- Robert Merton used Durkheim's notion of *anomie* to explain high crime rates. His *anomie-strain theory* argued that the distance between the cultural goals of American society, and the means for most to achieve those goals, created strain or anomie.

- Critics said that anomie-strain theory failed to offer an explanation for crime committed by the upper classes (e.g., white-collar and corporate crime) or affluent teens. Robert Agnew introduced his *general strain theory*, which was intended to rectify this.

- *Social learning theory* holds that definitions favourable to criminal behaviour are learned through differential reinforcement; criminal behaviour depends on reward or punishment for past behaviour and anticipated consequences of persistence. Burgess and Akers's *differential association-reinforcement theory* aimed to specify the mechanisms involved in the learning process, adding elements of B.F. Skinner's operant conditioning and Albert Bandura's observations on imitation and modelling behaviour.

- *Social control theory* is rooted in Durkheim's forces of integration and the Chicago School concern with the breakdown in informal social controls. It holds that social bonds and informal social controls act as restraints on teen delinquency.
- Hirschi's *social bond theory* was based in Durkheimian notions about social bonds and collective beliefs. It can be broken down into four main elements: attachment, commitment, involvement, and belief.
- Sampson and Laub's *life-course-developmental theory* is a more recent extension of Hirschi's social bond theory. Sampson and Laub redefine the attachment and commitment elements of the social bond as "social capital," acquired as individuals reach adulthood and complete their education, find a job, get married, and have children.

QUESTIONS FOR CRITICAL DISCUSSION

1. How do sociological explanations of crime and deviance differ from psychological and biological explanations?
2. Why have sociological explanations tended to dominate the discipline of criminology?
3. What are the major criminological theories that can be traced back to the 19th-century French sociologist Émile Durkheim?
4. What major contributions did the Chicago School make to the study of criminology?
5. What (recent) evidence exists to validate earlier Chicago School notions of the relationship between social disorganization and crime rates?
6. What is the relationship (connection) between differential association theory, techniques of neutralization, and social learning theory?
7. What are the main principles of differential association theory?
8. What is the "sociology of deviance," and how is it related to labelling theory, to moral entrepreneurship, and to the concept of moral panics?
9. What are the four main components of Travis Hirschi's social bond theory?
10. Why would Terrence Thornberry's interactional theory and Robert Sampson and John Laub's life-course-developmental theory be considered contemporary extensions of (or elaborations on) Travis Hirschi's social bond theory?

SUGGESTED FURTHER READINGS

Agnew, R. (1985). A revised strain theory of delinquency. *Social Forces, 64*(1), 151–167.

Brezina, T., & Phipps, H.E. (2010). False news reports, folk devils, and the role of public officials: Notes on the social construction of law and order in the aftermath of Hurricane Katrina. *Deviant Behavior, 31*(1), 97–134. doi:10.1080/01639620902854803

Burgess, R.L., & Akers, R.L. (1966). A differential association-reinforcement theory of criminal behavior. *Social Problems, 14*(2), 128–147.

Erikson, K.T. (1962). Notes on the sociology of deviance. *Social Problems, 9*(4), 307–314.

Laub, J.H., & Sampson, R.J. (1993). Turning points in the life course: Why change matters to the study of crime. *Criminology, 31*(3), 301–325.

Merton, R.K. (1938). Social structure and anomie. *American Sociological Review, 3*(5), 672–682.

Piquero, N.L., Tibbetts, S.G., & Blankenship, M.B. (2005). Examining the role of differential association and techniques of neutralization in explaining corporate crime. *Deviant Behavior, 26*(2), 159–188.

Sampson, R.J., & Groves, W.B. (1989). Community structure and crime: Testing social-disorganization theory. *American Journal of Sociology, 94*(4), 774–802.

Sutherland, E.H. (1940). White-collar criminality. *American Sociological Review, 5*(1), 1–12.

Sykes, G.M., & Matza, D. (1957). Techniques of neutralization: A theory of delinquency. *American Sociological Review, 22*(6), 664–670.

REFERENCES

Adorjan, M.C. (2011). Emotions contests and reflexivity in the news: Examining discourse on youth crime in Canada. *Journal of Contemporary Ethnography, 40*(2), 169–198. doi:10.1177/0891241610385456

Agnew, R. (1985). A revised strain theory of delinquency. *Social Forces, 64*(1), 151–167.

Agnew, R. (1992). Foundation for a general strain theory of crime and delinquency. *Criminology, 30*(1), 47–87.

Agnew, R. (1995). The contribution of social-psychological strain theory to the explanation of crime and delinquency. In F. Adler, W.S. Laufer, & R.K. Merton (Eds.), *The legacy of anomie theory* (pp. 113–137). New Brunswick, NJ: Transaction.

Agnew, R. (1997). The nature and determinants of strain: Another look at Durkheim and Merton. In N. Passas & R. Agnew (Eds.), *The future of anomie theory* (pp. 27–51). Boston: Northeastern University Press.

Agnew, R. (2010). Controlling crime: Recommendations from general strain theory. In H.D. Barlow & S.H. Decker (Eds.), *Criminology and public policy: Putting theory to work* (pp. 25–44). Philadelphia: Temple University Press.

Akers, R.L. (1998). *Social learning and social structure: A general theory of crime and deviance.* Boston: Northeastern University Press.

Akers, R.L. (2001). Social learning theory. In R. Paternoster & R. Bachman (Eds.), *Explaining criminals and crime: Essays in contemporary criminological theory* (pp. 192–210). Los Angeles: Roxbury.

Akers, R.L. (2011). The origins of me and social learning theory: Personal and professional recollections and reflections. In F.T. Cullen, C.L. Jonson, A.J. Myer, & F. Adler (Eds.), *The origins of American criminology: Advances in criminological theory* (Vol. 16, pp. 347–366). New Brunswick, NJ: Transaction.

Akers, R.L., & Matsueda, R.L. (1989). Donald R. Cressey: An intellectual portrait of a criminologist. *Sociological Inquiry, 59*(4), 423–438.

Akers, R.L., & Sellers, C.S. (2009). *Criminological theories: Introduction, evaluation, and application* (5th ed.). New York: Oxford University Press.

Andrews, D.A., & Bonta, J. (2010). *The psychology of criminal conduct* (5th ed.). Cincinnati, OH: Anderson.

Bartol, C.W. (1999). *Criminal behaviour: A psychosocial approach.* Upper Saddle River, NJ: Prentice Hall.

Beaver, K.M., Ratchford, M., & Ferguson, C.J. (2010). Evidence of genetic and environmental effects on the development of low self-control. *Criminal Justice and Behavior, 36*(11), 1158–1172.

Becker, H.S. (1963). *Outsiders: Studies in the sociology of deviance.* London, UK: Free Press of Glencoe.

Bernard, T.J. (1995). Merton versus Hirschi: Who is faithful to Durkheim's heritage? In F. Adler, W.S. Laufer, & R.K. Merton (Eds.), *The legacy of anomie theory* (pp. 81–90). New Brunswick, NJ: Transaction.

Bernard, T.J., Snipes, J.B., & Gerould, A.L. (2010). *Vold's theoretical criminology* (6th ed.). New York: Oxford University Press.

Brent, E., & Atkisson, C. (2011). Accounting for cheating: An evolving theory and emergent themes. *Research in Higher Education, 52*(6), 640–658. doi:10.1007/s11162-010-9212-1

Brezina, T., & Phipps, H.E. (2010). False news reports, folk devils, and the role of public officials: Notes on the social construction of law and order in the aftermath of Hurricane Katrina. *Deviant Behavior, 31*(1), 97–134. doi:10.1080/01639620902854803

Burgess, E.W. (1967). The growth of the city: An introduction to a research project. In R.E. Park, E.W. Burgess, & R.D. McKenzie (Eds.), *The city* (pp. 47–62). Chicago: University of Chicago Press. (Original work published 1900.)

Burgess, R.L., & Akers, R.L. (1966). A differential association-reinforcement theory of criminal behavior. *Social Problems, 14*(2), 128–147.

Burns, R., & Crawford, C. (1999). School shootings, the media and public fear: Ingredients for a moral panic. *Crime, Law and Social Change, 32*(2), 147–168.

Burtch, B.E. (2003). *The sociology of law: Critical approaches to social control* (2nd ed.). Toronto: Nelson Thomson.

Cartwright, B. (Ed.). (2011). *Sociological explanations of crime and deviance*. Boston: Pearson Learning Solutions.

City of Surrey. (2010). *Surrey city centre: The future lives here*. Surrey, BC: City of Surrey.

City of Surrey. (2012). *Sustainability charter: A commitment to sustainability*. Surrey, BC: City of Surrey.

Clinard, M.B. (1964). The theoretical implications of anomie and deviant behavior. In M.B. Clinard (Ed.), *Anomie and deviant behavior: A discussion and critique* (pp. 1–56). New York: Free Press of Glencoe.

Clinard, M.B., & Meier, R.F. (2004). *Sociology of deviant behaviour* (12th ed.). Belmont, CA: Thomson Wadsworth.

Cloward, R.A., & Ohlin, L.E. (1960). *Delinquency and opportunity: A theory of delinquent gangs*. New York: Free Press.

Cohen, A.K. (1964). *Delinquent boys: The culture of the gang*. Glencoe, IL: Free Press of Glencoe. (Original work published 1955.)

Cohen, L.E., & Machalek, R. (1994). The normalcy of crime: From Durkheim to evolutionary ecology. *Rationality and Society, 6*(2), 286–308. doi:10.1177/1043463194006002007

Cohen, S. (1987). *Folk devils & moral panics: The creation of the mods and rockers*. Oxford, UK: Basil Blackwell.

Cohen, S., & Young, J. (Eds.). (1973). *The manufacture of news: Social problems, deviance and the mass media*. London, UK: Constable.

Cullen, F.T., & Messner, S.F. (2011). The making of criminology revisited: An oral history of Merton's anomie paradigm. In F.T. Cullen, C.L. Jonson, A.J. Myer, & F. Adler (Eds.), *The origins of American criminology: Advances in criminological theory* (Vol. 16, pp. 89–119). New Brunswick, NJ: Transaction.

Cullen, F.T., Wright, J.P., & Blevins, K.R. (Eds.). (2004). *Taking stock: The status of criminological theory*. New Brunswick, NJ: Transaction.

Cullen, F.T., Wright, J.P., Gendreau, P., & Andrews, D.A. (2003). What correctional treatment can tell us about criminological theory: Implications for social learning theory. In R.L. Akers & G.F. Jensen (Eds.), *Social learning theory and the explanation of crime: A guide for the new century* (pp. 339–362). New Brunswick, NJ: Transaction.

Curra, J. (2011). *The relativity of deviance* (2nd ed.). Thousand Oaks, CA: Sage.

Deutschmann, L.B. (2002). *Deviance and social control* (3rd ed.). Toronto: Nelson Thomson Learning.

Durkheim, É. (1951). *Suicide: A study in sociology* (J.A. Spaulding & G. Simpson, Trans.). Glencoe, IL: Free Press.

Durkheim, É. (1964). In G.E.G. Catlin (Ed.), *The rules of sociological method* (J.H. Mueller & S.A. Solovay, Trans.) (8th ed.). New York: Free Press of Glencoe.

Durkheim, É. (1965). *The division of labor in society* (G. Simpson, Trans.). New York: Free Press.

Durkheim, É. (1970). The normal and the pathological. In M. Wolfgang, L. Savitz, & N. Johnstone (Eds.), *The sociology of crime and delinquency*. London, UK: Wiley. (Original work published 1895.)

Ellis, L., & Walsh, A. (1997). Gene-based evolutionary theories in criminology. *Criminology*, *35*(2), 229. doi:10.1111/j.1745-9125.1997.tb00876.x

Erikson, K.T. (1962). Notes on the sociology of deviance. *Social Problems*, *9*(4), 307–314.

Erikson, K.T. (1964). Notes on the sociology of deviance. In H.S. Becker (Ed.), *The other side: Perspectives on deviance* (pp. 9–21). New York: Free Press of Glencoe.

Erikson, K.T. (2005). *Wayward puritans: A study in the sociology of deviance*. Boston: Allyn and Bacon.

Farrington, D.P., Coid, J.W., Harnett, L.M., Jolliffe, D., Soteriou, N., Turner, R.E., & West, D.J. (2006). *Criminal careers up to age 50 and life success up to age 48: New findings from the Cambridge study in delinquent development*. (No. 299). London, UK: Home Office Research, Development and Statistics Directorate.

Garfinkel, H. (1956). Conditions of successful degradation ceremonies. *American Journal of Sociology*, *61*(5), 420–424.

Garland, D. (2001). *The culture of control: Crime and social order in contemporary society*. Chicago: University of Chicago Press.

Gelles, R.J. (1993). Through a sociological lens: Social structure and family violence. In R.J. Gelles & D. Loseke (Eds.), *Current controversies on family violence* (pp. 31–46). Thousand Oaks, CA: Sage.

Giddens, A. (1987). *Social theory and modern sociology*. Stanford, CA: Stanford University Press.

Glueck, S., & Glueck, E. (1994). Unraveling juvenile delinquency. In J.E. Jacoby (Ed.), *Classics of criminology* (2nd ed., pp. 241–246). Prospect Heights, IL: Waveland Press. (Original work published 1950.)

Goffman, E. (2005). Stigma and social identity. In H.N. Pontell (Ed.), *Social deviance: Readings in theory and research* (5th ed., pp. 77–96). Upper Saddle River, NJ: Pearson Prentice Hall.

Gottfredson, M.R., & Hirschi, T. (1990). *A general theory of crime*. Stanford, CA: Stanford University Press.

Greenberg, D.F. (2010). *Building modern criminology: Forays and skirmishes*. Surrey, UK: Ashgate.

Hagan, J.A., Gillis, A.R., & Simpson, J. (1985). The class structure of gender and delinquency: Toward a power-control theory of common delinquent behavior. *American Journal of Sociology*, *90*(6), 1151–1178.

Hayward, K., Maruna, S., & Mooney, J. (Eds.). (2010). *Fifty key thinkers in criminology*. London, UK: Routledge.

Hirschi, T. (1969). *Causes of delinquency*. Berkeley, CA: University of California Press.

Hoffman, J.P. (2010). Contemporary retrospective on general strain theory: The status of general strain theory. In H. Copes & V. Topalli (Eds.), *Criminological theory: Readings and retrospectives* (pp. 156–168). New York: McGraw-Hill.

Immergluck, D. (2011). The local wreckage of global capital: The subprime crisis, federal policy, and high-foreclosure neighborhoods in the US. *International Journal of Urban and Regional Research*, *35*(1), 130–146. doi:10.1111/j.1468-2427.2010.00991.x

Inderbitzen, M., Bates, K., & Gainey, R. (2013). *Deviance and social control: A sociological perspective.* Thousand Oaks, CA: Sage.

Jeffery, C.R. (1978). Criminology as an interdisciplinary behavioral science. *Criminology, 16*(2), 149–169.

Kornhauser, R.R. (1978). *Social sources of delinquency: An appraisal of analytic models.* Chicago: University of Chicago Press.

Lamb, J. (1992, October 29). Living in Whalley now means having to say you're Surrey. *Vancouver Sun,* p. B1.

Laub, J.H., Nagin, D.S., & Sampson, R.J. (1998). Trajectories of change in criminal offending: Good marriages and the desistance process. *American Sociological Review, 63*(2), 225–238.

Laub, J.H., & Sampson, R.J. (1991). The Sutherland-Glueck debate: On the sociology of criminological knowledge. *American Journal of Sociology, 96*(6), 1402–1440.

Laub, J.H., & Sampson, R.J. (1993). Turning points in the life course: Why change matters to the study of crime. *Criminology, 31*(3), 301–325.

Laub, J.H., Sampson, R.L., & Allen, L.C. (2001). Explaining crime over the life course: Toward a theory of age-graded informal social control. In R. Paternoster & R. Bachman (Eds.), *Explaining criminals and crime: Essays in contemporary criminological theory* (pp. 97–112). Los Angeles: Roxbury.

Lilly, J.R., Cullen, F.T., & Ball, R.A. (2011). *Criminological theory: Context and consequences* (5th ed.). Thousand Oaks, CA: Sage.

Lowenkamp, C.T., Cullen, F.T., & Pratt, T.C. (2003). Replicating Sampson and Groves's test of social disorganization theory: Revisiting a criminological classic. *Journal of Research in Crime and Delinquency, 40*(4), 351–373.

Matsueda, R.L. (2001). Labeling theory: Historical roots, implications, and recent developments. In R. Paternoster & R. Bachman (Eds.), *Explaining criminals and crime: Essays in contemporary criminological theory* (pp. 223–241). Los Angeles: Roxbury.

Merton, R.K. (1938). Social structure and anomie. *American Sociological Review, 3*(5), 672–682.

Messerschmidt, J.W. (1993). *Masculinities and crime: Critique and reconceptualization of theory.* Lanham, MD: Rowman & Littlefield.

Messerschmidt, J.W. (2005). Men, masculinities and crime. In M.S. Kimmel, J. Hearn, & R.W. Connell (Eds.), *Handbook of studies on men and masculinities* (pp. 196–212). Thousand Oaks, CA: Sage.

Messner, S.F., & Rosenfeld, R. (2007). *Crime and the American dream* (4th ed.). Belmont, CA: Thomson Wadsworth. (Original work published 1994.)

Munro, H. (1998, February 3). Recapturing Whalley: This poor, crime-ridden section of Surrey has a tough reputation inside the RCMP. *Vancouver Sun,* p. B1.

Mutchnick, R.J., Martin, R., & Austin, T.W. (2009). *Criminological thought: Pioneers past and present.* Upper Saddle River, NJ: Prentice Hall.

O'Brian, A. (2003, January 25). Surrey's get-tough plan has backers: A-team will hit Whalley streets block by block. *Vancouver Sun,* p. B1.

Osgood, D.W., & Chambers, J.M. (2000). Social disorganization outside the metropolis: An analysis of rural youth violence. *Criminology, 38*(1), 81–115.

Park, R.E., & Burgess, E.W. (1967). *The city.* Chicago: University of Chicago Press.

Paternoster, R., & Bachman, R. (2001). Control theories of crime. In R. Paternoster & R. Bachman (Eds.), *Explaining criminals and crime: Essays in contemporary criminological theory* (pp. 80–191). Los Angeles: Roxbury.

Pfohl, S.J. (1985). *Images of deviance and social control: A sociological history.* New York: McGraw-Hill.

Piquero, N.L., Tibbetts, S.G., & Blankenship, M.B. (2005). Examining the role of differential association and techniques of neutralization in explaining corporate crime. *Deviant Behavior*, *26*(2), 159–188.

Plummer, K. (1979). Misunderstanding labelling perspectives. In D.M. Downes & P.E. Rock (Eds.), *Deviant interpretations* (pp. 85–121). Oxford, UK: Martin Robertson.

Pratt, T.C., & Cullen, F.T. (2000). The empirical status of Gottfredson and Hirschi's general theory of crime: A meta-analysis. *Criminology*, *38*(3), 931–964. doi:10.1111/j.1745-9125.2000.tb00911.x

Pratt, T.C., Cullen, F.T., Sellers, C.S., Winfree, L.T., Madensen, T.D., Daigle, L.E., & Gau, J.M. (2010). The empirical status of social learning theory: A meta-analysis. *Justice Quarterly*, *27*(6), 765–802.

Rafter, N.H. (1997). Psychopathology and the evolution of criminological knowledge. *Theoretical Criminology*, *1*(2), 235–259. doi:10.1177/1362480697001002004

Ratner, R. (2006). Pioneering critical criminology in Canada. *Canadian Journal of Criminology and Criminal Justice*, *48*(5), 647–662. doi:10.1353/ccj.2006.0055

Renzetti, C.M. (2013). *Feminist criminology*. London, UK: Routledge.

Rosenfeld, R., & Messner, S.F. (1995). Crime and the American dream: An institutional analysis. In F. Adler, W.S. Laufer, & R.K. Merton (Eds.), *The legacy of anomie theory* (pp. 159–181). New Brunswick, NJ: Transaction.

Sacco, V.F., & Kennedy, L.W. (2011). *The criminal event: An introduction to criminology in Canada* (5th ed.). Toronto: Nelson Education.

Sampson, R.J. (2002). Transcending tradition: New directions in community research, Chicago style. *Criminology*, *4*(2), 213–230. doi:10.1111/j.1745-9125.2002.tb00955.x

Sampson, R.J., & Groves, W.B. (1989). Community structure and crime: Testing social-disorganization theory. *American Journal of Sociology*, *94*(4), 774–802.

Sampson, R.J., & Laub, J.H. (1992). Crime and deviance in the life course. *Annual Review of Sociology*, *18*(1), 63–84.

Schmalleger, F., MacAlister, D., & McKenna, P.F. (2004). *Canadian criminal justice today* (2nd ed.). Toronto: Pearson Prentice Hall.

Scully, D., & Marolla, J. (2003). Convicted rapists' vocabulary of motive. In P. Adler & P. Adler (Eds.), *Constructions of deviance: Social power, context and interaction* (4th ed., pp. 247–271). Belmont, CA: Thomson Wadsworth.

Sellin, T. (1994). Culture conflict and crime. In J.E. Jacoby (Ed.), *Classics of criminology* (2nd ed., pp. 188–192). Prospect Heights, IL: Waveland Press. (Original work published 1938.)

Shaw, C.R., & McKay, H.D. (1969). *Juvenile delinquency and urban areas: A study of rates of delinquency in relation to differential characteristics of local communities in American cities* (Rev. ed.). Chicago: University of Chicago Press.

Skelton, C. (2004, February 6). Surrey's auto theft rate worst in English-speaking world: Mayor pledges tough new measures. *Vancouver Sun*.

Snodgrass, J. (2011). Clifford R. Shaw and Henry D. McKay: Chicago criminologists. In F.T. Cullen, C.L. Jonson, A.J. Myer, & F. Adler (Eds.), *The origins of American criminology: Advances in criminological theory* (Vol. 16, pp. 17–35). New Brunswick, NJ: Transaction.

Snyder, G.J. (2010). Howard Becker. In K. Hayward, S. Maruna, & J. Mooney (Eds.), *Fifty key thinkers in criminology* (pp. 163–168). London, UK: Routledge.

Sutherland, E.H. (1940). White-collar criminality. *American Sociological Review*, *5*(1), 1–12.

Sutherland, E.H. (1994). Differential association. In J.E. Jacoby (Ed.), *Classics of criminology* (2nd ed., pp. 226–227). Prospect Heights, IL: Waveland Press. (Original work published 1947.)

Sykes, G.M., & Matza, D. (1957). Techniques of neutralization: A theory of delinquency. *American Sociological Review, 22*(6), 664–670.

Taylor, I., Walton, P., & Young, J. (1973). *The new criminology: For a social theory of deviance.* London, UK: Routledge & Kegan Paul.

Taylor, I., Walton, P., & Young, J. (Eds.). (1975). *Critical criminology.* London, UK: Routledge & Kegan Paul.

Thompson, H. (2012). The limits of blaming neo-liberalism: Fannie Mae and Freddie Mac, the American state and the financial crisis. *New Political Economy, 17*(4), 399–419. doi:10.1080/13563467.2011.595481

Thornberry, T. (1987). Toward an interactional theory of delinquency. *Criminology, 25*(4), 863–891.

Thornberry, T.P., & Krohn, M.D. (2005). Applying interactional theory to the explanation of continuity and change in antisocial behavior. In D.P. Farrington (Ed.), *Integrated developmental & life-course theories of offending* (pp. 183–209). New Brunswick, NJ: Transaction.

Traub, S.H., & Little, C.B. (1985). *Theories of deviance* (3rd ed.). Itasca, IL: F.E. Peacock.

Walsh, A. (2002). *Biosocial criminology: Introduction and integration.* Cincinnati, OH: Anderson.

Walsh, A. (2012). *Criminology: The essentials.* Thousand Oaks, CA: Sage.

Williams, F.P., & McShane, M.D. (2010). *Criminological theory* (5th ed.). Upper Saddle River, NJ: Pearson Prentice Hall.

Winfree, L.T., & Abadinsky, H. (2010). *Understanding crime: Essentials of criminological theory* (3rd ed.). Belmont, CA: Wadsworth, Cengage Learning.

Wolfgang, M.E., & Ferracuti, F. (1967). *The subculture of violence: Towards an integrated theory in criminology.* London, UK: Tavistock.

Wortley, R. (2011). *Psychological criminology: An integrative approach.* London, UK: Routledge.

Young, J. (1975). Working class criminology. In I. Taylor, P. Walton, & J. Young (Eds.), *Critical criminology* (pp. 63–94). London, UK: Routledge & Kegan Paul.

Young, J. (2002). Critical criminology in the twenty-first century: Critique, irony and the always unfinished. In K. Carrington & R. Hogg (Eds.), *Critical criminology: Issues, debates and challenges* (pp. 251–274). Cullompton, UK: Willan.

Zeitlin, I.M. (2001). *Ideology and the development of sociological theory* (7th ed.). Upper Saddle River, NJ: Prentice Hall.

Zytaruk, T. (2009, February 20). "Time to stop the carnage": politicians and police gather at Surrey city hall in search of gang violence fix. *Now,* 1.

Cases

R v. Ipeelee. (2012). 2012 SCC 13, [2012] 1 SCR 433.

R v. Pop. (2013). 2013 BCCA 160.

PART FOUR
Types of Crime

A Trilogy of Violent Crimes

In the summer of 1960, a young woman named Kathleen Chouinor went for a ride with Mickey Feener, an unemployed labourer, in what he said was his new red sports car. He confided to Kathleen during the drive that he had killed another woman, and she encouraged him to turn himself in. Instead, however, he panicked, and hit her on the head with his metal flashlight until she passed out. He then stabbed her in the throat and drove her well outside the town of Timmins, Ontario, where he dumped her body.

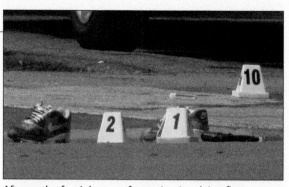

Aftermath of a violent confrontation involving fists, a gun, and knives.

Feener was arrested a few days later and confessed to the crime. Police learned that he had been married during the 1950s and that his wife reported a history of physical abuse. Feener himself had a childhood characterized by abuse and neglect; both parents deserted him, and he was institutionalized at an early age. A psychiatrist who examined him when he was 12 determined that he had an IQ of 64 (suggesting at least a mild intellectual disability), and a history of both assaulting his younger brother and being victimized by others.

A few hours before he was to hang for his crime in June 1961, Feener confessed to police that he had murdered another woman. He believed that he was going to "roast in hell" and wanted to die with a clear conscience. He also asked that his eyes be given to an eye bank, saying, "I hope the poor devil who gets them trains himself to look at something besides skirts." Feener was hanged in the provincial jail in Haileybury, Ontario, one of the last men to be executed in Canada.

Consider, alternatively, the case of a middle-class woman we'll call Jenny Buchanan, who lived in Nova Scotia with her husband Rob. Both of them were drinkers. When they drank heavily, they would sometimes argue. On one occasion, Rob hit Jenny to the point where she had bruises all over her body. "I couldn't go anywhere 'cause people would have seen the bruises. I couldn't use my arm the next day. The nerves in my elbow had been smashed."

Jenny decided that the drinking had to stop. She made arrangements to go into detox and had her husband drive her there. A few days later, he begged her to come home and she agreed. On the way to the house, she picked up a bottle of hard liquor and some sleeping pills. She knew that neither she nor her husband really wanted to stop drinking.

Five days later, after a lot more heavy drinking, Jenny shot her husband. She remembered only bits and pieces of the evening. She said that he was yelling and screaming and that she was also somewhat angry, drunk, and afraid. She went to get the family shotgun and sat in a chair downstairs. When he came downstairs, she pulled the trigger, and he fell to the ground, dead. She called the police and told them that she had shot her husband. Blood alcohol tests revealed that he had almost four times the legal limit of alcohol in his system; her reading was similar—almost three times the impaired driving threshold. Although her lawyer assured her that the likely charge and conviction would be for manslaughter, she was convicted of second-degree murder and sentenced to ten years' imprisonment.

"It was the damn booze," she said later during an interview. Her husband was described in court by her daughters as her best friend. "It's now two years and a bit since my husband died," she added, "and my deepest wish is that I could do whatever time I have to do and we could be together again. I wish we had a chance to make up on the mistakes because there was just so damn much good between us."

Finally, consider the case of a man we'll call Danny Harrigan, a member of a biker gang that dealt in illegal drugs. A problem had arisen with a local speed dealer, and Harrigan and his friend Jake Blenheim decided that they should go over to the dealer's house and try to sort out the problem. After smoking a few joints, sniffing a little PCP (phencyclidine, a dissociative drug), and drinking a few beers, they drove over to the dealer's house. As soon as they came through the front door, the dealer and his accomplice reached for their guns; a young woman, a friend of the dealer, was also in the house. There would be no negotiated resolution of their differences. The dealer was, in Harrigan's words, "a bad dude." He was wanted for murder, and was on parole for attempted murder.

Harrigan's friend Blenheim took the first shot, and the dealer was killed instantly. It was a horrifying scene. Harrigan then shot the other man four times, and he was also dead at the scene. The female friend of the two was stabbed repeatedly; Harrigan and Blenheim left the house, awash in blood, with three people dead.

"Two people were dead because the speed dealer pulled a gun and we shot him," Harrigan said, "then we've got to kill everybody and get the hell out of there—get rid of this. I had no intention of going there and killing anybody. Neither of us did. But it just happened like that. It just erupted. We went back home and we were pretty shaken up. We washed everything and smoked a few joints, trying to calm down. But it was hard—what we did was terrible."

Harrigan and Blenheim were convicted of first-degree murder and sentenced to life imprisonment.

Before You Read Chapter 13

- Consider the nature of each of these violent episodes in terms of the characteristics of the victims, the offenders, their relationship, and of the violent incident itself. In what ways are they similar to one another? In what ways are they different?
- Can you say that one of these crimes is in any way "worse" than the others? If so, in what way?
- What do you believe are the primary causes of violent crime in our society?
- Throughout history, violence has been a part of most cultures. Is it simply an intrinsic element of human beings? Or, is it possible that we in modern Western society are becoming less violent overall? Provide reasons for your answer.

Violent Crime

LEARNING OBJECTIVES

After reading this chapter, students will be able to:

- Describe the various definitions of *violence* and how they differ from one another.
- Understand how and why criminologists attempt to measure violent crime at a particular time and place.
- Describe trends in violent crime in Canada over time.
- Identify "risk markers" that increase the likelihood that someone will offend violently or be a victim of violence.
- Describe criminological theory and research on current issues related to urban violence, including the role masculinity plays in boys' and men's decision to use violence to deal with conflict; "no snitching" codes; urban gun culture; and hot spots of violent crime.
- Identify the strategies used to respond to violent crime, and which ones the research suggests may be most effective in preventing or reducing violent crime.

Introduction

- A teenage mother smothers her newborn child in an attempt to conceal the birth.
- A young male gang member is shot by a rival gang member in front of a neighbourhood community centre.
- A husband stabs his wife to death after she tells him she is leaving him because of a history of physical violence in the relationship.
- A gay man is attacked by two straight young men in a "gay-bashing" incident.
- A man is hit with a broken beer bottle in a bar fight with another patron.

The incidents described above are examples of various forms of **interpersonal violence**, violence that is most commonly inflicted by one individual against another, or by a small group of individuals against another. One of the first questions that people tend to ask when they hear of crimes such as these is *why?* Unfortunately, typically there is no easy answer because human behaviour, including the perpetration of violence, is complicated—and it is complicated because no single answer explains why people do what they do.

Someone who engages in violence does so for a variety of reasons. The weight of the available evidence suggests that no single factor causes violence; instead, it is the end result of multiple factors that converge to play important and interactive roles (Collins & Messerschmidt, 1993; White & Gorman, 2000). These factors include biology, psychology, personal history and experiences, socialization, community, and culture, which are discussed in detail in the various chapters in Part Three, Theories of Crime. To further

interpersonal violence
Violence that is most commonly inflicted by one individual against another, or by a small group of individuals against another.

multi-causal
The notion that an event occurs as a result of more than one factor.

complicate matters, the factors that converge to produce a violent act also vary from person to person. Given the *heterogeneous* and **multi-causal** nature of interpersonal violence, it should come as no surprise that no single theoretical perspective can explain all violence.

Defining Violence

A quick Internet search of the term *violence* produces a long list of different behaviours that occur in a wide range of contexts. Violence is indeed a multi-faceted phenomenon, and considerable disagreement exists over just how the term should be defined, prompting one scholar to describe violence as an "essentially contested concept" (de Haan, 2008). In the academic literature, definitions of *violence* range in scope from restrictive (narrow) to inclusive (broad). These definitions differ from one another in terms of the kinds of harm that qualify as violence. For example, some definitions restrict *violence* to behaviours that threaten or inflict physical harm, while other definitions include a host of other "injurious acts" (Jackman, 2002) such as psychological, emotional, verbal, and/or social harms. Still others argue that violence can not only be committed by an individual, but also by collectivities (e.g., genocide committed by one ethnic group against another), by agents of the state (e.g., violence perpetrated by the police and/or armed forces), and by corporate entities (e.g., when corporations ignore health and safety measures, thereby putting employees at risk of harm). Despite these important differences, the definitions are bound by a common understanding that interpersonal violence is harmful, destructive behaviour. Examples of definitions of *violence* currently in use by those who study crime appear below.

Measuring Violence

Is gun violence increasing in Canadian cities? What are the risk markers for violent victimization and offending? Which city experiences the highest levels of gun violence, and why?

Answering these and other questions about the nature and extent of violent crime in Canada requires the collection and analysis of relevant data. These data are also important for gauging the effectiveness of public policy responses. As is the case with research on crime more generally, estimates of interpersonal violence are usually based on two key data sources: official reports, such as the Uniform Crime Reporting Survey (UCR), and surveys of the general population, such as the General Social Survey (GSS). While both surveys measure crime, important differences exist between them in terms of how they do so. As such, direct comparisons of the data findings from the two surveys are not recommended (Perreault, 2013). It is important to view data from the UCR survey and the GSS as complementary because, taken together, they enable researchers to gain a more complete picture of violent crime in Canada than could be gleaned from either source on its own. (For more details on these surveys, see Chapter 4, Measuring Crime.)

The Uniform Crime Reporting Survey

The most common source of official data on violent crime in Canada is the Uniform Crime Reporting Survey (UCR), compiled by the Canadian Centre for Justice Statistics (CCJS), a division of Statistics Canada. The UCR, as with most official sources of data on violent crime, relies on a narrow, restrictive definition of *violence* that emphasizes intended threatened or actual use of physical force against a person:

Violent crimes or offences/crimes against the person
Crimes against the person involve the use or threatened use of violence against a person, including homicide, attempted murder, assault, sexual assault and robbery. Robbery is considered a crime against the person because unlike other theft offences it involves the use, or threat of, violence. (Statistics Canada, n.d.)

Highlights of the findings of the 2012 UCR survey are presented in Box 13.1.

BOX 13.1

Highlights from the 2012 Uniform Crime Reporting Survey

- The police-reported violent crime rate declined in 2012, down 3 percent from 2011 to 1,190 incidents per 100,000 population. Canadian police services reported about 415,000 violent incidents, about 9,000 fewer than in 2011. The police-reported violent crime rate was at its lowest level since 1987.

- Among the provinces, Saskatchewan had the highest violent crime rate in 2012, despite reporting the largest decrease from 2011. Ontario had the lowest rate. All provinces and territories except Prince Edward Island, Newfoundland and Labrador, Quebec, and Nunavut recorded declines in their police-reported violent crime rates.

- Canada recorded its lowest homicide rate in more than 40 years: Police reported 543 homicides in 2012, 55 fewer than in 2011. As a result, the homicide rate fell 10 percent, to 1.56 per 100,000 population, its lowest level since 1966.

- The decrease in the number of homicides was more pronounced in Western Canada. Together, Alberta (−24), British Columbia (−16), and Saskatchewan (−9) were responsible for most of the decline in 2012. Nevertheless, homicide rates remained lower in Eastern Canada. Every province east of Manitoba, except Nova Scotia, recorded a homicide rate that was below the national average.

- About 21,900 sexual assaults were reported to police in 2012, about 60 fewer than in the previous year. This relatively modest decline is primarily due to a decrease in major sexual assaults (levels 2 and 3). However, the number of sexual assaults reported by police likely understates the actual number of sexual assaults that occurred in Canada in 2012. According to 2009 victim-ization data from the General Social Survey, the vast majority of sexual assaults are never reported to police.

- For the second consecutive year, the number of sexual offences against children increased slightly (+3 percent). These crimes include violations specific to children, such as sexual interference, invitation to sexual touching, sexual exploitation, and luring a child via a computer. Police reported nearly 4,000 such offences in 2012.

- Major assaults declined in 2012 yet remained higher than a decade ago. In 2012, police reported more than 223,000 level 1, 2, and 3 assaults, about 10,600 assaults against a peace officer, and nearly 3,000 other types of assaults (e.g., criminal negligence causing bodily harm).

- All types of assault were down in 2012 compared with the previous year. The largest decrease was in the rate of assaults against a peace officer (−8 percent). Despite these decreases, the rates of major assault (levels 2 and 3) and assault against a peace officer remained higher than ten years ago. However, the rate of level 1 assault, which is less serious but much more frequent, was nearly 20 percent lower than it was ten years earlier.

- Robbery, one of the most serious and most frequent types of violent crime, also fell in 2012 and reached its lowest level in more than 30 years. The decrease was driven by large drops in Quebec (−15 percent) and Alberta (−11 percent), and, more specifically, in Montreal (−18 percent) and Calgary (−23 percent).

Source: Perreault (2013).

The General Social Survey

As discussed in Chapter 4, because official data sources reflect the number of violent crime reported to the police, they *undercount* the true incidence of violence in any given time and place. As such, victimization surveys, such as the General Social Survey (GSS), can help to uncover the **dark figure of crime**.

The GSS aims to estimate the amount of criminal victimization that exists in Canada among persons aged 15 and older; it seeks to measure victims' experiences, regardless of whether those experiences were reported to the police. The GSS includes three measures of violent victimization: **assault**, **sexual assault**, and **robbery**.

In addition to quantifying the amount of violent victimization in Canada, the GSS asks a series of questions to examine risk factors associated with victimization; to understand the reasons people do or do not report their victimization to the police; to evaluate fear of crime; and to gauge public perceptions of the criminal justice system. As such, and in addition to its value in uncovering the dark figure of violent crime, the GSS allows for a more nuanced understanding of violent crime and its effects than do official data sources.

Since 1999, the GSS has also included a separate set of questions about **spousal violence** in Canada. Like the UCR survey, GSS estimates of violent victimization in general are based on a narrow definition of *violence* that is limited to physical force and injury. However, GSS questions about spousal violence adopt a much broader understanding of violence that recognizes a variety of harms that victims (who are disproportionately women) typically suffer at the hands of violent spouses. Box 13.2 indicates how spousal violence is measured in the GSS and presents Figure 13.1, data from the GSS on self-reported financial and emotional abuse in 2009.

Trends over Time

Overall levels of violent crime in Canada have been declining for over a decade. Figure 13.2 shows the violent crime rate in Canada between 1998 and 2011. In this period, the national rate of violent crime rose from 1,345 incidents per 100,000 people in 1998, peaked at 1,494 incidents per 100,000 people in 2000, then subsequently dropped to a low of 1,231 incidents per 100,000 people in 2011. Examining national rates, however, obscures important regional differences in rates of violent crime.

Figure 13.3 shows violent crime rates in Canada's provinces and territories in 2011. In this year, the rates were highest in Nunavut (9,887 incidents per 100,000 people), the Northwest Territories (8,499 per 100,000 people), and Yukon (4,226 per 100,000 people). In the remaining regions, violent crime rates tend to be higher in the West and lower in the East. Only three regions experienced rates of violent crime that were lower than the national average of 1,231 incidents per 100,000 people: Ontario (950 incidents per 100,000 people), Quebec (1,045 per 100,000 people), and Prince Edward Island (1,137 per 100,000 people).

Correlates of Violent Crime

As social scientists, criminologists that study violence look to identify social factors that increase the likelihood, or the risk, of violent victimization and offending. A large body of criminological research has identified a consistent set of **correlates**, or factors that are associated with or related to violent crime. These risk factors cannot be said to be

dark figure of crime
Refers to the variation between the number of crimes that occur and the number of crimes that are actually reported to the police. This figure highlights the large number of unreported crimes.

assault
Applying force on a person, attempting to or threatening to apply force on a person, or using a weapon (or imitation of a weapon) to accost or impede a person.

sexual assault
Unwanted sexual activity, including sexual attacks and sexual touching.

robbery
Stealing property from someone, with or without using violence, threats of violence, or a weapon (or imitation of a weapon).

spousal violence
Acts including common assault, assault with a weapon, sexual assault, homicide, forcible confinement, uttering threats, criminal harassment, failure to provide the necessities of life, psychological abuse, and financial abuse.

correlates
In criminology, factors that are associated with or related to crime.

BOX 13.2

GSS Measurement of Spousal Violence and Data on Emotional and Financial Abuse

In the GSS, spousal violence is measured by a series of questions that indicate a broad understanding of violence:

> The questions measure both physical and sexual violence, as defined by the *Criminal Code*, that could be acted upon by the police. This includes acts such as being threatened with violence, being pushed, grabbed, shoved, slapped, kicked, bit, hit, beaten, choked, threatened with a gun or knife or forced into sexual activity.
>
> Respondents are also asked about emotional and financial abuse that they had experienced at the hands of a current or ex-partner within the previous five years. While incidents of emotional and financial abuse are not used to calculate the overall proportion of spousal violence victims, information about these other forms of abuse help to create a better understanding of the context in which physical or sexual violence may occur. (Statistics Canada, 2011, p. 8)

FIGURE 13.1   Victims of Self-Reported Emotional and Financial Abuse, by Sex and Type of Abuse, 2009

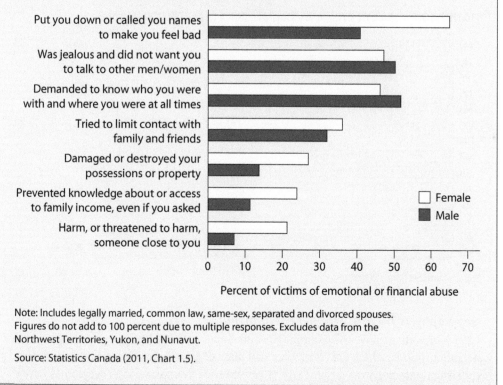

Percent of victims of emotional or financial abuse

Note: Includes legally married, common law, same-sex, separated and divorced spouses.
Figures do not add to 100 percent due to multiple responses. Excludes data from the Northwest Territories, Yukon, and Nunavut.

Source: Statistics Canada (2011, Chart 1.5).

causes of violence; rather, they are factors that can help identify the context within which violence occurs. Identifying risk factors is important, not only to recognize those most vulnerable to violence, but also to develop crime prevention initiatives and interventions to help reduce violent victimization and offending.

FIGURE 13.2 Violent Crimes, Canada, 1999–2012 (per 100,000 People)

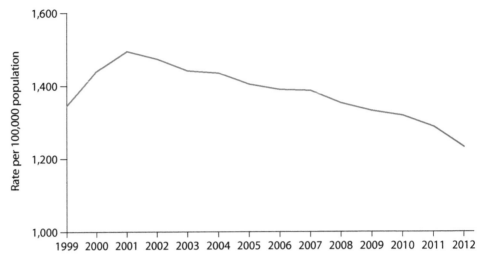

Source: Statistics Canada (2012).

FIGURE 13.3 Violent Crimes by Region, 2011 (per 100,000 People)

Source: Statistics Canada (2012).

Geography: Is There a "Frontier Phenomenon"?

Later in this chapter, we will examine the differences in the risk of violence across urban neighbourhoods, which are relatively small units of geography. However, research also consistently demonstrates that there is variation in the risk of violence across larger geographies, such as at the provincial/territorial level. For example, rates of homicide, and of violent crime in general, rise as one moves northward and westward from central Canada (see Figure 13.3, above). The reasons for this variation are not yet well understood, though some have suggested that it may be due to variations in criminal justice policies, policing practices, or the legacy of a historical "culture of violence" that may have existed during the settlement of Canada's northern and western frontiers.

The rest of this section provides an overview of some of the most consistent *individual-level correlates* of violent victimization and offending that have been identified in the criminological literature. Although these correlates are examined separately, it is important to understand that they never exist in isolation. When we look at the relationship between sex and violence, for example, we do so with the understanding that "men" and "women" are not homogeneous groups that share common experiences with violence on the basis of their sex. Instead, the experience of being male or female varies depending on age, race/ethnicity, social class, etc. And these characteristics intersect and interact with one another to produce a particular context within which violent victimization and offending occur.

Age and Violence

In the criminological literature, the relationship between age and violence has robust empirical findings. Studies indicate that a disproportionately large share of violent offending involves those in the age range between mid-adolescence and young adulthood (Farrington, 1986; Farrington, Piquero, & Jennings, 2013; Piquero, Farrington, & Blumstein, 2007). For example, in 2011, rates of police-reported violent offending increased among those aged 12 to 17, peaked among those aged 18, and then declined with increasing age (Brennan, 2012).

Why does the likelihood of violent offending accelerate in adolescence and peak in early adulthood? Many theories have been offered to account for this pattern. Some explanations point to biological and psychological factors, such as fluctuating hormones and lower levels of maturity (Cruise et al., 2008). Others highlight socialization processes, such as conformity to peer group behavioural norms and expectations, risk-taking behaviours, and attitudes that defy authority—all of which may promote violent behaviour (Henry, Tolan, & Gorman-Smith, 2001). Other explanations point to lifestyles that may expose young adults to situations where violence is possible, particularly if alcohol use is also involved (such as drinking in bars and clubs). Adolescence and early adulthood are also periods that typically have fewer work- and family-related responsibilities that tend to make people consider the potential consequences of their actions.

Why does the likelihood of violent offending decline with age? Explanations in the literature are many and remain open to continuous debate among scholars. For example, some research on deceleration points to a variety of "co-occurring developmental changes" that take place in early adulthood and are thought to drive declines in violent offending (Sweeten, Piquero, & Steinberg, 2013). These include "salient life events" (Loeber & LeBlanc, 1990; Sampson & Laub, 1990, 1993) such as completing one's education, entering the labour market, getting married, and becoming a parent—all of which could be jeopardized by continuing to engage in criminal behaviour.

Sex and Violence

Sex also very strongly correlates with violent victimization and offending, and while some similarities exist in the levels of certain types of violence experienced by males and females, important differences appear when it comes to more serious forms of violent victimization. Further, marked differences exist in the nature of violence that is typically experienced by males and females. The following discussion provides an overview of key trends in this area.

sub-lethal violent victimization

Violent victimization that does not cause death.

situational characteristics

Factors associated with an incident; in the case of a violent act, location, weapon type, motive, and the victim–offender relationship are situational characteristics.

lethal violence

Violent victimization that causes death.

Sex and Violent Victimization

Overall, the levels of **sub-lethal violent victimization** (i.e., violent victimization that does not cause death) show relative symmetry/parity between males and females, meaning that men and women experience similar rates of this type of violence. For example, as Table 13.1 shows, in 2009, police-reported data show that 197,354 incidents involving male victims were reported to police, compared with 201,614 incidents for females (Mahony, 2011), and these levels have remained more or less stable over the last five years (Vaillancourt, 2010). Self-reported violent victimization data from the GSS provide similar estimates; in 2009, approximately 1.6 million violent crimes (most of which were property-related crimes) were reported by female victims, compared with 1.7 million by male victims (Mahony, 2011).

Despite similarities in the *quantity*, or amount, of sub-lethal violent victimization experienced by males and females, important differences exist in the *quality*, or the nature, of this victimization. For example, as Table 13.1 shows, males were more likely to be victims of attempted murder, aggravated and other physical assault, and robbery, whereas females were more likely to be victims of common assault and sexual assault (Mahony, 2011). Other police-reported offences that disproportionately involved female victims include forcible confinement, kidnapping, or abduction, and criminal harassment.

The **situational characteristics** of men's and women's violent victimization also differ in important respects. Situational characteristics refer to factors associated with the violent incident such as location, weapon type, motive, and the victim–offender relationship. Both police and self-reported victimization data show that men's victimization is more likely to involve a weapon (16 percent of incidents against men, compared with 8 percent of incidents against women), occur in public spaces (streets, parks, parking lots, places of leisure, etc.), and involve offenders who are acquaintances or strangers (Mahony, 2011; Perreault & Brennan, 2010). Female victimization, on the other hand, is more likely to occur in the home and be perpetrated by a former or current intimate partner (e.g., legally married, separated, divorced, common law, dating [current and previous], or other intimate partner).

In contrast to relative parity across the sexes in the quantity of sub-lethal violent victimization, research consistently shows marked sex differences in the amount of **lethal violence** experienced by males and females. For example, in 2011, 422 of the 598 (71 percent) homicide victims in Canada were male (Perreault, 2012). Homicide victimization in Canada, as elsewhere, is therefore a male-dominated phenomenon. As we will see below, so, too, is homicide offending.

As with sub-lethal violent victimization, key sex differences exist in the nature of homicide. For example, female homicide victims are most often killed by a current or former intimate partner as a result of anger, despair, jealousy, or sexual violence (Vaillancourt, 2010). Male homicide victims, on the other hand, are more likely to be killed by friends/acquaintances or strangers, in public places (streets, parking lots, stores, bars, common areas of buildings), and with a firearm (Vaillancourt, 2010). Gang-related homicides are also more prevalent among male victims.

Sex and Violence: Offending

When compared with men, women commit a much smaller amount of violent crime; women are charged with violent offences generally about one-fifth of the rate for males

Table 13.1   Victims of Police-Reported Violent Crimes, by Type of Crime, 2009

Type of violent crime	Female victim		Male victim		% female victims
	Number	%	Number	%	
Homicide	158	0.1	442	0.2	26.3
Attempted murder	182	0.1	556	0.3	24.7
Other violations causing death	32	0.0	61	0.0	34.4
Sexual assaults—all levels	17,719	8.8	2,587	1.3	87.3
Other sexual violations[a]	2,727	1.4	682	0.3	80.0
Assault—level 3—aggravated	848	0.4	2,612	1.3	24.5
Assault—level 2—weapon or bodily harm	17,846	8.9	34,018	17.2	34.4
Assault—level 1—common assault	93,279	46.3	82,136	41.6	53.2
Other assaults[b]	2,410	1.2	9,518	4.8	20.2
Forcible confinement, kidnapping, or abduction[c]	3,832	1.9	1,187	0.6	76.3
Robbery	8,651	4.3	20,298	10.3	29.9
Extortion	442	0.2	682	0.3	39.3
Criminal harassment	14,350	7.1	4,617	2.3	75.7
Threatening or harassing phone calls	11,161	5.5	5,310	2.7	67.8
Uttering threats	26,850	13.3	30,973	15.7	46.4
Other violent *Criminal Code* violations[d]	1,127	0.6	1,675	0.8	40.2
Total	201,614	100.0	197,354	100.0	50.5

Note: One incident may involve multiple violations. Counts are based upon the most serious violation against the victim. Incidents where the sex of the victim is unknown were excluded.

[a] Other sexual violations primarily include sexual offences against children as well as other sexual offences involving adults.

[b] Includes assaults against peace officers, unlawfully causing bodily harm, criminal negligence causing bodily harm, and other assaults.

[c] Includes forcible confinement, kidnapping; abduction under 14, not parent/guardian; abduction under 16; removal of children from Canada; abduction under 14 contravening a custody order; abduction under 14, by parent/guardian.

[d] Excludes other sexual violations involving adults and includes firearm violations.

Source: Mahony (2011, Table 1)

(Kong & AuCoin, 2008). For the ways in which scholars have hypothesized men's and women's violent offending, along with women's lesser involvement in violent offending, see Chapter 10, Gender and Crime.

Despite these differences in levels of violent offending by sex, women and men have some commonalities in the types of *Criminal Code* violent offences they are most likely to commit. Table 13.2 shows the number and rate of males and females accused of violent

Table 13.2   Number and Rate of Youth and Adults Accused of Violent Crime by Police, by Sex and Type of Crime, 2009

Criminal Code violations	Total accused	Female accused				Male accused			
		Total	Total	Youth	Adult	Total	Total	Youth	Adult
	number	number	rate per 100,000			number	rate per 100,000		
Total *Criminal Code* violations (including traffic)	1,008,615	233,074	1,580.3	4,010.8	1,360.3	775,541	5,403.1	9,700.4	4,981.4
Violent *Criminal Code* violations	287,362	63,314	429.3	1,065.7	371.7	224,048	1,560.9	2,581.6	1,460.8
Homicide	530	55	0.4	0.4	0.4	475	3.3	5.6	3.1
Attempted murder	564	79	0.5	1.2	0.5	485	3.4	4.1	3.3
Other violations causing death	65	11	0.1	0.0	0.1	54	0.4	0.2	0.4
Sexual assaults—all levels	10,695	253	1.7	5.4	1.4	10,442	72.7	146.7	65.5
Other sexual violations[a]	1,729	72	0.5	2.5	0.3	1,657	11.5	24.2	10.3
Assault—level 3—aggravated	3,132	496	3.4	5.1	3.2	2,636	18.4	28.7	17.4
Assault—level 2—weapon or bodily harm	37,301	8,140	55.2	107.7	50.4	29,161	203.2	391.4	184.7
Assault—level 1—common assault	131,144	32,788	222.3	579.3	190.0	98,356	685.2	996.3	654.7
Other assaults[b]	11,852	2,956	20.0	45.3	17.8	8,896	62.0	74.8	60.7
Forcible confinement, kidnapping, or abduction[c]	4,446	403	2.7	3.9	2.6	4,043	28.2	20.7	28.9
Robbery	14,500	1,742	11.8	49.5	8.4	12,758	88.9	305.4	67.6
Extortion	869	130	0.9	1.3	0.8	739	5.1	11.3	4.5
Criminal harassment	13,414	2,965	20.1	38.8	18.4	10,449	72.8	64.7	73.6
Threatening or harassing phone calls	9,125	3,650	24.7	31.8	24.1	5,475	38.1	50.0	37.0
Uttering threats	45,474	9,195	62.3	185.5	51.2	36,279	252.7	417.1	236.6
Other violent *Criminal Code* violations[d]	2,522	379	2.6	8.0	2.1	2,143	14.9	40.3	12.4

Note: One incident may involve multiple violations. Counts are based upon the most serious violation in the incident. Incidents where the age or sex of the victim is unknown were excluded.

[a] Other sexual violations primarily include sexual offences against children as well as other sexual offences involving adults.

[b] Includes assaults against peace officers, unlawfully causing bodily harm, criminal negligence causing bodily harm, and other assaults.

[c] Includes forcible confinement, kidnapping; abduction under 14, not parent/guardian; abduction under 16; removal of children from Canada; abduction under 14 contravening a custody order; abduction under 14, by parent/guardian.

[d] Includes firearm violations. Excludes other sexual violations involving adults.

Source: Mahony (2011, Table 7).

crime in 2009. Common assault (level 1) is the most prevalent violent offence committed by both men and women. For both sexes, level 2 assaults (assault with a weapon or causing bodily harm) and uttering threats were the next most prevalent violent offences, although the rate at which women were accused of each of these offences was approximately one-quarter of the rate for males accused (Mahony, 2011). Overall, however, as the severity of violence increases, female participation declines. The greatest sex differences emerge when it comes to sexual offences (all levels); in 2009, females were charged with a tiny proportion of these offences.

Although the gap between males and females in criminal offending is substantial, evidence suggests that it is becoming smaller, or converging, over time. For example, the last several decades have seen an increase in the number of women charged with violent offences; since 1991, the rate of females charged with violent crime has increased 34 percent. It is important to note that official crime data on trends in female offending over time may reflect changes in the criminal justice response to female offending as much as or more than to actual changes in offending rates. Indeed, some scholars have suggested that in the past, agents of the criminal justice system demonstrated "chivalry" or "paternalism" toward female offenders—and that these tendencies meant that women were not viewed as fully responsible/culpable for their offending, resulting in a lesser likelihood of charges. More recently, however, girls and women have been more likely to be viewed as responsible actors, and as such may be held increasingly responsible for their violent offending. These and other possible explanations for the convergence in men's and women's rates are reviewed in depth in Chapter 10, Gender and Crime.

Poverty and Violence

Socio-economic disadvantage, typically measured using indicators of poverty or income inequality, has generally been found to be highly correlated with violent crime (Blau & Blau, 1982; Fajnzylber, Lederman, & Loayza, 2002; Hannon, 2005). However, considerable debate exists among researchers with respect to the mechanisms through which economic disadvantage may lead to violence, which has prompted the development of a number of theoretical perspectives that aim to explain this relationship. For example, the concepts of strain, absolute deprivation, and relative deprivation suggest that as poverty and income inequality rise, so too does the risk of violent interpersonal conduct. According to classical **strain theories** (discussed in Chapter 12, Sociological Approaches), the contradiction between culturally ascribed goals of achieving status and wealth and the unequal distribution of opportunities to achieve those goals can lead to feelings of frustration, resentment, and injustice among those who perceive themselves to be unfairly disadvantaged over others in a purportedly egalitarian society (Merton, 1938). As feelings of resentment grow, so too does the potential for crime and violence.

Some studies suggest that **absolute deprivation** (low income or poverty in and of itself) increases the risk of violence (Huff-Corzine, Corzine, & Moore, 1986; Williams & Flewelling, 1988). Under conditions of absolute deprivation, violence may be perceived as one of the few options available to those of limited economic means. That is, criminal activities designed to fulfill instrumental goals, such as the acquisition of money or other forms of calculable personal gain, may require or result in violence. Yet absolute deprivation may also give rise to expressive forms of violence, which may be the consequence of the dehumanizing effects of extreme poverty along with the "brutal

strain theories

Theories that state certain societal stressors (e.g., unequal opportunities to achieve success) increase the likelihood of crime.

absolute deprivation

Low income or poverty in and of itself.

and demoralizing" treatment suffered by the poor (Lynch & Groves, 1989, p. 63; Parker, 1989). The likeliest victims of this violence are those in close proximity to the absolutely deprived.

relative deprivation

The perception of unfair disparity between one's situation and that of others.

Other scholars argue that the concept of **relative deprivation** (the perception of unfair disparity between one's situation and that of others) is more relevant to an explanation of the poverty/violence relationship (Bailey, 1984; Messner, 1989). Relative deprivation may encourage violent crime because it generates a sense of injustice; perceived deprivation relative to others may create such feelings due to the disjunction between widely held cultural success goals and the distribution of opportunities to achieve them. People who experience relative deprivation may evaluate their socio-economic position relative to others (in their neighbourhoods and in the larger population) by the cultural success goals disseminated by the mass media. Robert Merton (1938) argued that inequality of opportunity creates situations in which some individuals engage in crime in order to achieve the social and economic goods that others possess. As with the conditions of absolute deprivation, the resulting frustration could manifest as expressive violence (acts that release anger or rage) or instrumental violence (attempts to acquire material goods that some individuals are unable to attain by legitimate means).

A variety of indicators of economic distress have also been linked to the risk of intimate partner violence. For example, financial problems can lead to feelings of stress and frustration that may find violent expression, most notably against female intimates (Macmillan & Gartner, 1999). Further, unemployed males or males earning low wages may be particularly likely to become violent during confrontations with their female partners. The reasons for this reaction may be twofold. First, violence may serve as a substitute for "socio-economic leverage" (Benson, Fox, DeMaris, & Wan Wyk, 2003, p. 212), a means for men to establish their dominance and authority in the home (Macmillan & Gartner, 1999). The second reason has to do with opportunity: compared with their employed counterparts, unemployed males may commit more violence in the home as a function of the amount of time they spend there (Cohen & Felson, 1979).

Race and Violence

US-based criminological research has shown that race is highly correlated with violence (Tonry, 1995). However, less is known about the relationship between race and crime in the Canadian context. Although Canadian criminal justice agencies routinely collect information about the race of offenders that are processed through the system, they do not make this information public. There is, however, one exception: Aboriginal identity data are collected and disseminated by many criminal justice agencies in Canada (Roberts & Doob, 1997; Thompson, 2013).

Aboriginal identity data show that in 2006, Aboriginal people experienced violent victimization at a rate that was nearly three times that of non-Aboriginal Canadians (Brzozowski, Taylor-Butts, & Johnson, 2006). The risk of violent victimization varies according to victim sex: the average violent victimization rate for Aboriginal males was 292 per 1,000 population, compared with a rate of 343 per 1,000 population for Aboriginal females. These figures highlight the intersecting nature of race and sex.

Levels of spousal violence are also higher among Aboriginal than non-Aboriginal people. For example, the 2004 GSS found that 21 percent of Aboriginal people reported having experienced physical or sexual violence at the hands of a spouse over the past five years (i.e., the five years that preceded the 2004 survey), a figure 3.5 times greater than the proportion of non-Aboriginal people (6 percent) who experienced spousal violence over the same period. Aboriginal victims—particularly Aboriginal women—were also much more likely to suffer the most serious forms of spousal violence, such as being beaten, choked, threatened or assaulted with a weapon, and sexually assaulted (Brzozowski et al., 2006).

Figure 13.4 shows that Aboriginal victimization rates are especially pronounced compared with non-Aboriginal people when it comes to lethal violence. Between 1997 and 2000, Aboriginal people experienced homicide victimization rates that were nearly seven times the rate for non-Aboriginal people (8.8 versus 1.3 per 100,000). The risk of this violence also shows sex differences; male Aboriginal people were killed at more than double the rate of their female counterparts (12.2 versus 5.4 per 100,000).

The rate at which Aboriginal people are accused of homicide is also disproportionately high, particularly among Aboriginal males, who were charged with murder at almost nine times the rate for non-Aboriginal males (17.9 versus 2.0 per 100,000 population). This finding is not surprising given the large body of research that demonstrates that homicide tends to be an **intra-racial** phenomenon (Silverman & Kennedy, 2004). That is, if Aboriginal people are at a greater risk of homicide victimization, given the intra-racial nature of homicide more generally, they are also more likely to perpetrate homicides involving Aboriginal victims.

intra-racial
Within the same race of people.

What might account for these higher levels of violent victimization and offending among Aboriginal people in Canada? Many explanations point to the role of colonialism, racial discrimination (past and present), sexism, social and economic inequality, and the material conditions within which many Aboriginal people live (La Prairie, 2002; Zimmerman, 1992).

Some evidence also suggests that black Canadians are vulnerable to high levels of homicide. Using unofficial data to examine homicide in Toronto over the last several

FIGURE 13.4   Rates of Homicide Much Higher for Aboriginal Victims, 1997–2000

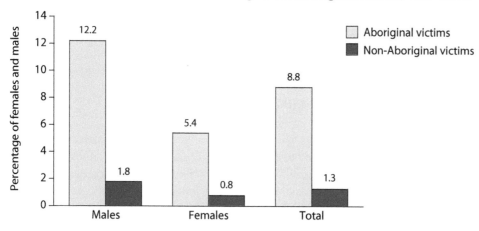

Note: Rates are calculated per 100,000 population and are based on the average number of homicides per year, between 1997 and 2000. They exclude homicides where the Aboriginal status of the victim was unknown. Population estimates were derived from 2001 post-censal estimates and 1996 census counts, provided by Statistics Canada, Census and Demographic Statistics, Demography Division.

decades, Rosemary Gartner and Sara Thompson (2004) and Thompson (2009, 2013) found that blacks and, in particular, young black males, were disproportionately represented as homicide victims and offenders since at least the late-1980s. For example, since at least 1991, the risk of homicide victimization for Toronto's black population has been substantially higher than the overall risk of homicide in Toronto. Even when excluding 1991, which had an unusually high number of black homicides, the homicide rate per 100,000 blacks in Toronto averaged 10.1 between 1992 and 2003. This figure was almost five times greater than the average overall homicide rate of 2.4 per 100,000 population (Gartner & Thompson, 2004).

The issue of black disproportionality in violent victimization and offending has received considerable research attention in the United States, but comparatively little academic consideration in Canada. This limited research is due, in large part, to the suppression of race-based criminal justice data for groups other than Aboriginal people. Yet it is likely that many of the factors that are thought to contribute to high levels of Aboriginal victimization and offending—and that have been identified in American research in the relationship between race and violence—may also be at play for some segments of the black community in Canada. These factors include high levels of poverty, economic inequality, segregation, and social isolation (Sampson & Wilson, 1995; Stewart & Simons, 2006; Wilson, 1987).

racialized
The process of marginalizing a group of people based on perceived physical and socio-cultural differences.

Research suggests that high rates of violent crime among some **racialized** populations may be the result of the relative deprivation and associated frustrations experienced by these groups. For example, the social injustices generated by income inequality lead to a state of **anomie**, which in turn leads to the expression of hostility in the form of violent crime (Blau & Blau, 1982). Feelings of relative deprivation may be especially pronounced in members of those racial groups that experience the highest levels of social and economic disadvantage (Stolzenberg, Eitle, & D'Alessio, 2006).

anomie
A term coined by Durkheim to describe periods of lawlessness, normlessness, and unrestrained choice, or a breakdown in social solidarity.

Studies show that Aboriginal and black Canadians are disproportionately likely to experience chronic and acute levels of poverty (Fong & Shibuya, 2000). This issue has been called the *racialization of poverty*, and it may go some way toward understanding the high levels of violent victimization and offending discussed above. That is, black Canadians may experience higher levels of violence because they are also more likely to experience high levels of poverty and income inequality (Messner & Tardiff, 1985; Sampson, 1995), which, as we saw in the discussion of poverty and violence, are themselves associated with high levels of violent victimization and offending.

Current Issues in Criminological Research on Violence
Masculinity and Violence

Thus far we have seen that males, particularly young, economically disadvantaged, and racialized males, are more likely to be the victims and perpetrators of violent crime, and that although females experience high levels of victimization, they are, overall, underrepresented as perpetrators of violent crime. In addition to the theoretical perspectives on criminal and violent offending discussed above and elsewhere in this text, the concept of gender may be useful in making sense of these consistent sex differences in trends and patterns of violent victimization and offending. Indeed, since at least the early 1990s, interest in research that examines the relationship between *masculinity* and violence has grown.

The concept of **hegemonic masculinity** refers to the idealized form of masculinity at a particular time and in a particular place. Connell (1987, 2002) points out that in contemporary North American society, mainstream hegemonic masculinity emphasizes normative heterosexuality, autonomy, and success (Connell, 1987; Mullins & Mullins, 2006). For middle- and upper-class males, hegemonic masculinity is typically demonstrated through workplace success, which generates "masculine capital"—such as social and political clout, and various material accoutrements (designer clothing, a large home, a high-end car, and other forms of "bling") that communicate their power to others (Mullins & Mullins, 2006). But such resources and material displays are only available as symbols of masculinity for a small proportion of men. As such, less affluent men strive to enact some version of hegemonic masculinity in varying ways and using whatever resources are at their disposal to demonstrate their masculinity to others (Mullins & Mullins, 2006). For some men, a violent presentation of self is a key way of performing masculinity and generating masculine capital.

The work of Elijah Anderson (1999) highlights the link between social inequality, economic disadvantage, and the construction of violent masculinities among some men. Anderson argues that in some disadvantaged neighbourhoods and among some residents, a set of informal rules emerges that govern interpersonal public behaviour and define masculine identity for those who abide by them. Toughness, dominance, and the willingness to resort to violence to resolve interpersonal conflicts are central dictates of this "street code."

When navigating the streets, many residents, whether decent or street, "go for bad"—adopting a "tough guy" pose that is intended to prevent violent attacks against them. Ironically, however, this posturing may invite violence rather than deter it. Adhering to the street code may actually increase the likelihood of a violent encounter due to the perception that others (who are also abiding by the dictates of the code) will use violence against them. In this sense, the use of violence becomes a pre-emptive strike of sorts, in that "it's either him or me."

The street code also provides a means by which to acquire respect, or "juice," and avoid humiliating situations of status degradation, or disrespect. For example, if one young man is assaulted by another, the code dictates that he must salvage his self-respect and the respect of his "running buddies" by avenging himself, or else risk being labelled "soft" and targeted for violent attack by others. Further, the proliferation of guns on the streets of some urban neighbourhoods has implications for the degree of violence that is ultimately meted out: guns provide a quick and sometimes final resolution to a dispute, transforming a minor dispute over a "diss" into a deadly act (Chapter 17, Organized Crime and Gangs, examines this street code in further detail).

Another key aspect of the street code and the particular form of masculinity it generates involves "no-snitch codes," or the vilification of those who cooperate with formal authorities. Snitching is viewed as a violation of masculinity because a real man is expected to "act hard" and resolve interpersonal conflicts without the help of outsiders (Woldoff & Weiss, 2010). In the end, however, no-snitch codes may actually lead to additional violence, via the meting out of "street justice" to deal with interpersonal disputes. See Box 13.3.

In sum, then, Anderson's work highlights the ways in which some young men in poor urban neighbourhoods prove their manhood by conforming to a code that prescribes

hegemonic masculinity
A culturally idealized form of masculinity; in contemporary Western societies, for example, hegemonic masculinity involves displays of autonomy, aggressive individualism, a lack of emotion, normative heterosexuality, and the capacity for violence.

BOX 13.3

"Stop Snitching": From Street Code to Slogan

It was not the first time prosecutor Lisa Pellegrini had been enraged by the sight of the T-shirt with the traffic-sign message: STOP SNITCHING. But this guy was about to wear one into court, with matching baseball cap. Worse, he was a witness—her witness—and the intended victim in an attempted murder case that had brought him, her and the defendants to court that day last fall.

This was Rayco "War" Saunders—ex-con, pro boxer and walking billboard for a street movement that has sparked a coast-to-coast beef involving everyone from professors to rappers. Pellegrini, thinking "witness intimidation," told Saunders to lose the hat and reverse the shirt. Saunders, crying "First Amendment," refused. He left the courthouse, shirt in place. Case dismissed. "In almost every one of my homicides, this happens: 'I don't know nothin' about nothin,'" the prosecutor says. "There is that attitude, 'Don't be a snitch.' And it's condoned by the community."

Omerta, the Mafia's blood oath of silence, has been broken by turncoat after turncoat. But the call to stop snitching—on other folks in the 'hood—is getting louder.

Is it an attempt by drug dealers and gangsters to intimidate witnesses?

Is it a legitimate protest against law enforcers' over-reliance on self-serving criminal informers?

Or is it bigger than that?

Take the case of Busta Rhymes.

The hip-hop star has refused to cooperate with police investigating the slaying of his bodyguard outside a Brooklyn studio where Rhymes was recording a video with performers such as Missy Elliott and Mary J. Blige. Police say that although Rhymes and as many as 50 others may have seen the shooting, no one came forward—an echo of the silence that followed the unsolved murders of rappers Tupac Shakur, the Notorious B.I.G. and Run-DMC's Jam Master Jay.

It's the code of the street: To be a credible rapper, you have to know when to shut up.

"Under pressure, I lie for ya, die for ya," Lil' Kim once rapped. Now she's in a federal jail in Philadelphia for failing to tell a grand jury what she knew about some friends involved in a shooting. ...

The stigma against snitching is an old one, but the Mafia never took out newspaper ads to promote omerta. So why is an unwritten rule printed on thousands of T-shirts?

Start with the war on drugs. Over the past two decades, law enforcers have made more drug arrests and turned more defendants into informers than ever before. According to the U.S. Sentencing Commission, the agency that establishes federal court sentencing practices, about one-third of drug trafficking prosecutions involve informers' "substantial assistance." That makes them eligible for reduced sentences under otherwise inflexible federal sentencing guidelines.

Informers are a necessary evil, says Cmdr. Maurita Bryant, a 29-year veteran of the Pittsburgh Police Department. "We have to deal with who we have to deal with. ... If a dealer needs to make a deal, he'll tell on his mother. It may not be right, but it's all we have."...

According to a study by the Northwestern University Law School's Center on Wrongful Convictions, 51 of the 111 wrongful death penalty convictions since the 1970s were based in whole or in part on the testimony of witnesses who had an incentive to lie. ...

Alexandra Natapoff, a professor at Loyola Law School in Los Angeles, ... says informers strain the social fabric of poor minority neighborhoods, where as many as half the young men have been arrested. "Every family gathering, every party, every backyard barbecue probably has someone who's secretly working as an informer."

This is the world Rayco Saunders inhabits. It's filled, as he puts it, with "guys doin' all this crime and not doin' no time, because they're telling on the next man."

Hence a backlash—"stop snitching." The slogan appeared in Baltimore about two years ago as the title of an underground DVD featuring threatening, gun-wielding drug dealers and a brief appearance by NBA star and Baltimore native Carmelo Anthony. Anthony, who later said he didn't know the video's theme, told ESPN The Magazine that the dealer-turned-informer excoriated in the DVD "ran our neighborhood. Now he's working with the state and the feds. You can't do that. He turned his back on the 'hood." ...

The black community is divided. Rapper Chuck D of Public Enemy has blasted the Stop Snitching campaign on the hip-hop group's website: "The term 'snitch' was best applied to those that ratted revolutionaries like Huey P. Newton, Bobby Seale, Che Guevara. ... Let's not let stupid cats use hip-hop to again twist this meaning for the sake of some 'innerganghood' violent drug thug crime dogs, who've sacrificed the black community's women and children."

Source: Excerpted from Hampson, R. (2009, March 29). Anti-snitch campaign riles police, prosecutors. *USA Today*. Retrieved from http://usatoday30 .usatoday.com/news/nation/2006-03-28-stop-snitching_x.htm. Reprinted by permission.

norms of minding one's own business and taking care of matters without outside assistance. Respect based on one's reputation as a "tough guy" and for keeping one's mouth shut is a form of masculine capital in such environments—which may lead to the amplification of violence in affected communities.

Gun Violence

In 2011, 26 percent (158 of 598 killings) of homicides in Canada were committed with a firearm, and handguns accounted for approximately two-thirds of all firearms used to commit homicide that year (Perreault, 2012). The risk of gun violence is higher in urban areas, and research shows that, in Toronto, guns have figured more prominently in the city's homicides over time (Gartner & Thompson, 2004). During the 1970s and 1980s, for example, 25 percent of homicides in Toronto were committed with guns, a figure that increased to 32 percent by the 1990s. And since 2000, at least half of all homicides in Toronto were committed with guns. The trend for Canada as a whole is quite different, with gun homicide rates declining over time.

Thompson's (2009) research on gun homicide in Toronto between 1988 and 2003 shows that the *social distribution of gun homicide* (or the segments of the population most vulnerable to this violence) is heavily influenced by age, sex, and race. Over this period, the majority of victims of gun homicide were young (38 percent were under the age of 24, and 39 percent were in the 25 to 34 age range), male (87 percent), and black (54 percent). Further, just as the risk of gun violence is not evenly distributed across social groups, it is also not evenly distributed across the cityscape. Instead, and consistent with the research on the geography of violence, discussed below, high levels of gun homicide tend to cluster in a small number of disadvantaged neighbourhoods. This begs the question why.

The concept of *a local gun culture* may help to understand why high levels of gun homicide are concentrated in particular urban neighbourhoods. Building on Anderson's (1999) concept of "the code of the streets," Jeffrey Fagan & Deanna Wilkinson (1998) argued that guns are part of the *ecology*, or the social environment, of inner-city neighbourhoods, and have become the ultimate social tool used to attain status and respect. One of the young men they interviewed for this research explains the role of guns in creating the right "rep" on the streets: "If you got a gun you the man (laughing). Ain't no more manhood, it's gunhood" (p. 81). Fagan and Wilkinson also identify self-defence as the primary reason for carrying a firearm; all of their subjects spoke of either the "protection" or "defence" of self, family, and/or friends, and felt that safety in their neighbourhoods was uncertain, at best. One subject even deemed his gun "my visa" for navigating the streets of his neighbourhood in safety (p. 83).

Gun possession was also common among young men involved in the drug trade, burglaries, and hustling, but firearms' instrumental value existed in concert with their value as symbols of social status, self-worth, and personal power. Fagan and Wilkinson concluded that gun use has become a central part of status and identity formation within the "street-oriented" world of some inner-city US neighbourhoods. Further, the presence of firearms has changed the "scripts" for how interpersonal conflict is handled on the street. Boys in particular learn that guns are part of day-to-day life in some inner-city neighbourhoods, and that gun violence is one of the few options available for resolving interpersonal disputes.

In sum, then, gun possession, which is often associated with high levels of drug- and gang-related activity (Cohen, Cork, Engberg, & Tita, 1998), increases the risk of violent death in some inner-city neighbourhoods. However, these risks are not limited to drug dealers and gang-involved individuals; for reasons of status and personal protection, gun-related violence has also spread to other residents—namely young males—in affected communities (Blumstein, 1995; Grogger & Willis, 1998).

The Geography of Urban Violence

Thus far, we have seen that the risk of violent victimization and offending is not randomly distributed across the population. Rather, the *social distribution of risk*, or the segments of the population at greatest risk of violent victimization and offending, is heavily influenced by age, sex, race, and socio-economic status.

Research on the *geography of violence* shows that violence is also not evenly distributed across urban neighbourhoods. Instead, a disproportionate amount of violent crime is concentrated in a small number of neighbourhoods that are characterized by multiple forms of social and economic disadvantage (Messner & Zimmerman, 2012; Sampson, 1995). These patterns of **spatial inequality** were first identified by researchers in Chicago in the 1940s, and since then, a large amount of research in the United States, and an emerging body of related work in Canada, has examined violence "hot spots" in some urban neighbourhoods. This research consistently shows that neighbourhoods that experience the highest levels of violent crime are also characterized by high and concentrated levels of poverty, racial segregation, population turnover, joblessness, low educational attainment, and large numbers of young people and single-parent families (Charron, 2009; Messner & Zimmerman, 2012; Thompson & Gartner, 2014). Data maps, such as the one shown in Figure 13.5, are used to track hot spots of crime over time.

To some extent, the concentration of violence in poor neighbourhoods is to be expected, given that, as discussed above, the risk of violence is disproportionately high for socially and economically disadvantaged people. This effect is called a **compositional effect**—meaning that larger numbers of poor people living in certain neighbourhoods would necessarily mean that these neighbourhoods would also experience higher levels of violent crime.

Yet neighbourhoods also experience **contextual effects**—meaning that levels of violent crime stem from neighbourhood social context. For example, **social disorganization theory** views the geography of violence as a function of the differing degrees to which neighbourhoods can informally control the nature and amount of local illegal activity. According to this view, the prevalence and density of social networks and the level of participation in community-based organizations generate solidarity and mutual trust, or *social cohesion*, among neighbourhood residents. In turn, social cohesion promotes the neighbourhood's capacity to monitor and manage criminogenic situations. Cohesive neighbourhoods that can effectively mobilize to regulate the behaviour within their boundaries are said to have high levels of **collective efficacy** (Sampson, Raudenbush, & Earls, 1997). So-called disorganized neighbourhoods, on the other hand, are theorized to lack the networks, norms, and trust that facilitate coordination and cooperation for mutual benefit among residents. The end results, according to this perspective, are higher levels of crime and violence in the neighbourhood.

spatial inequality
The unequal distribution of resources and services from one area to another.

compositional effect
The combination of parts that make up something. In neighbourhoods, a compositional effect refers to the aggregate characteristics of individual residents.

contextual effect
The influence of environmental factors on human behaviours.

social disorganization theory
The theory that a breakdown of the networks, norms, and trust that facilitate coordination and cooperation among residents of neighbourhoods can lead to greater crime and violence.

collective efficacy
A group's shared belief that it can come together and achieve desired goals.

FIGURE 13.5   Winnipeg Hot Spots for Violent Crime, 2009–10

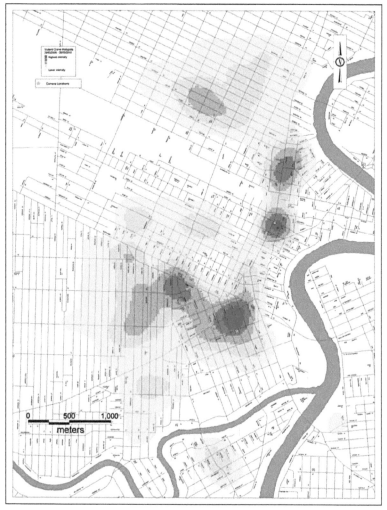

Source: Winnipeg Police Service.

Research has identified a series of neighbourhood characteristics that are thought to be indicative of social disorganizatiovn. These include poverty, high population turnover, the concentration and segregation of racialized groups, and large numbers of young males and single-parent families (Sampson, 1995). These characteristics are thought to impede the formation and maintenance of social networks, cohesion, and collective efficacy in varying ways. For example, large numbers of young male residents in neighbourhoods characterized by various forms of structural disadvantage may render that neighbourhood more susceptible to the development of local "street codes" that privilege violence as a means of status attainment and/or conflict resolution (Anderson, 1999). Further, if the population of a neighbourhood is constantly in flux (due to high population turnover), it becomes difficult for residents to get to know one another and to establish mutual trust and expectations that form the basis of collective efficacy. It is important to note, however, that disadvantaged neighbourhoods are not *necessarily* socially disorganized; research has demonstrated that some extremely socially and economically disadvantaged neighbourhoods are instead characterized by strong social ties and networks and/or high levels of collective efficacy (Patillo-McCoy, 1999; Thompson & Bucerius, 2013; Villarreal & Silva, 2006).

Responding to Urban Violence

The preceding sections discussed research that shows that the risk of violent victimization and offending is shaped by social and spatial inequalities. That is, the risk of violence depends not only on who one is, in terms of socio-economic and demographic characteristics, but also on where one lives and/or spends his or her time. This section will discuss Safer Cities initiatives, a crime-and-violence prevention model that, proponents argue, is designed to address social and spatial inequalities in urban neighbourhoods (Wekerle & Whitzman, 1995).

Safer Cities initiatives gained popularity in the United Kingdom, France, Germany, the Netherlands, and Australia in the 1980s, and have also guided crime prevention initiatives in many Canadian cities. The model stresses a *collaborative approach*—that is, partnerships among federal, provincial, and municipal governments, along with neighbourhood agencies and residents themselves. The participation of neighbourhood agencies and residents is seen as key to the model's success because both are viewed as "experts" in the issues that affect their neighbourhoods.

Using this collaborative, or partnership approach, the Safer Cities model aims to address crime by both attending to the root causes of crime and violence, and addressing issues with the neighbourhood's built environment that may be facilitating crime and violence. As such, the model rests on the "twin pillars" of crime prevention through social development (CPSD) and crime prevention through environmental design (CPTED). These approaches are discussed in Box 13.4.

In addition to CPSD and CPTED, a role also exists for law enforcement in crime prevention, although the Safer Cities model downplays the importance of so-called law-and-order approaches. Nevertheless, it would appear that law enforcement often has a significant role in applying the Safer Cities model, so much so that some scholars have suggested the model really ought to be described as a three-pronged model that includes CPSD, CPTED *and* enforcement-based initiatives (Thompson & Gartner, 2007).

What is known about the *efficacy* of the "twin pillars" of crime prevention? Research shows that CPTED strategies may be effective in reducing crime and fear of crime in urban neighbourhoods (Casteel & Peek-Asa, 2000; Cozens, Saville, & Hillier, 2005), particularly if the strategies are implemented in tandem with psycho-social initiatives, such as those that fall under the umbrella of CPSD (Saville, 1998). Indeed, a large body of research demonstrates that programs and initiatives that address the root causes of crime and violence hold the greatest promise for reducing crime and violence in urban neighbourhoods (Doob, 2004; Howell & Hawkins, 1998; Smith, Lizotte, & Thornberry, 1995; Tremblay & Japel, 2003).

Finally, as discussed above, a common intervention in high-crime neighbourhoods involves intensive, "targeted" law enforcement strategies. Research, however, suggests that while these interventions may sometimes have positive short-term effects, they generally do not reduce crime and violence in the long term (Cohen, Gorr, & Singh,

BOX 13.4

Crime Prevention Approaches

Crime Prevention Through Social Development

| BEFORE | AFTER |

A property, before and after the application of CPTED design principles.
Source: Peel Police.

Crime prevention through social development (CPSD) involves long-term, integrated actions that deal with the root causes of crime. Its aim is to reduce risk factors that start people, particularly children and youth, on the road to crime, and to build protective factors that may mitigate those risks. The risk factors associated with criminal involvement are also related to many other social problems, such as child abuse and neglect, drug and alcohol misuse, school failure, teenage pregnancy, and unemployment. So when people and organizations work to prevent crime they are also working to make our communities healthy, safe and sustainable in many respects. ...

CPSD works at making people healthy, responsible and resilient. In a free society, there will always be opportunities and temptations to do wrong—to take advantage of another person or a situation for our own benefit. CPSD promotes community values about nonviolence and respect for other people and their property, and helps young people resist peer pressure and make good decisions.

CPSD programming can occur at three levels:

1. At the primary level, crime prevention refers to universal, population-based programs such as public education and healthcare.

2. At the secondary level, crime prevention refers to programs that target those at higher risk for criminal activity. This level would include programs for youth at risk of leaving school and parenting programs for high-risk parents.

3. At the tertiary level, crime prevention refers to rehabilitative and supervision programs for offenders to reduce re-offending.

Crime Prevention Through Environmental Design

Crime prevention through environmental design (CPTED) is about the places and things, the "built environment," which can be either targets of criminal activity or the location where crime takes place. The proper design, effective use and maintenance of the built environment can lead to a reduction in the incidence and fear of crime, and an improvement in quality of life.

CPTED is complementary to, and inter-related with, CPSD strategies as people live in the built environment and the built environment influences how people behave.

CPTED is based on the premise that much crime is opportunistic and contextual. Inadvertently, nuisance and criminal behaviour can be facilitated by poorly planned and designed space, leading to actual opportunities for crime, as well as increased levels of fear.

Through the effective use of CPTED principles, crime, nuisance behaviour and the fear of crime can be reduced. Application of CPTED principles to new developments prevents future problems; and using CPTED enhances problem-solving capability for existing developments.

There are four key CPTED design principles:

1. Natural access control—design that directs and influences the flow of people to naturally maximize control and surveillance (e.g., exterior and interior design of a building, landscaping, lighting, and traffic calming).

2. Natural surveillance—design to maximize visibility and ensure legitimate users can observe and monitor activities around them in a formal or casual manner (e.g., office or apartment windows with unimpeded sightlines to parking areas or other areas where crime is likely to occur).

3. Territoriality—design of the physical environment to extend a perceived sense of influence or territory.

People taking ownership of their surroundings makes it more difficult for offenders to carry out crimes or disorder.

4. Maintenance—enhancement, maintenance and management of the built environment encourages the users of the area to respect their surroundings (e.g., removing graffiti and litter, avoiding overgrowth of hedges, fixing inoperative lighting, installing good locks).

Source: Excerpted from Law Courts Education Society. (n.d.). The community crime prevention guide. Retrieved from http://www.criminaljusticereform.gov.bc.ca/en/what_you_can_do/crime_prevention. Copyright © Province of British Columbia. All rights reserved. Reproduced with permission of the Province of British Columbia.

2003; Ludwig, 2005; Rosenfeld, Forango, & Baumer, 2005). Given that police crackdowns and related tactics are unlikely to have beneficial long-term effects, it would appear that these activities take a back seat to the "twin pillars" of CPTED and CPSD, as the Safer Cities model indicates.

Conclusion

As this chapter has demonstrated, violence is a multi-faceted phenomenon that occurs in a wide range of contexts and for a variety of reasons. Moreover, the likelihood that a person will commit a violent crime is associated with a number of factors, including age, sex, poverty, race, and where one lives and spends time. Criminological theory and research make important contributions to our understanding of patterns, trends, correlates, and consequences of different forms of violence. They are also fundamental to the development of crime prevention through social development (CPSD), crime prevention through environmental design (CPTED), and collective efficacy—initiatives that seek to reduce and prevent violent victimization and offending more generally.

SUMMARY OF KEY POINTS

- The weight of the available evidence suggests that no single factor causes violence; instead, it is the end result of multiple factors that converge to play important and interactive roles.

- Criminological research has identified a consistent set of individual-level correlates of violent victimization and offending. These include age, sex, socio-economic class, and race. A variety of theoretical perspectives seek to account for these relationships.

- The concept of masculinity may be helpful in explaining the overrepresentation of males as victims and offenders of violent crime. Research highlights the ways in which some young men in poor urban neighbourhoods prove their manhood by conforming to a code that prescribes norms of minding one's own business and taking care of matters without outside assistance. Respect based on one's reputation as a "tough guy" and keeping one's mouth shut is a form of masculine capital in such environments—which may lead to the amplification of violence in affected communities.

- Gun violence is an increasingly urban problem in Canada, and some segments of the population—in particular, young, racialized males—are especially vulnerable to this violence. The concept of a local gun culture may be helpful in understanding the *social* and *geographic distribution* of gun violence. According to this perspective, guns are part of day-to-day life in some urban neighbourhoods, and gun violence is viewed by some to be one of the few options available for resolving interpersonal disputes.

- Research on the geography of violence shows that violence is also not evenly distributed across urban neighbourhoods. Instead, a disproportionate amount of violent crime is concentrated in a small number of neighbourhoods (sometimes referred to as violence *hot spots*) that are characterized by multiple forms of social and economic disadvantage. The concepts of compositional and contextual effects can assist in understanding the ways in which violent crime "maps" across urban neighbourhoods.

- High levels of violent crime in urban neighbourhoods are usually addressed using one or a combination of the following approaches: Crime prevention through environmental design (CPTED), Crime prevention through social development (CPSD), and law enforcement-based strategies and initiatives. Research consistently demonstrates that CPSD approaches, which aim to address the root causes of violent crime, hold the greatest promise for reducing violent crime in urban neighbourhoods over the long term.

QUESTIONS FOR CRITICAL DISCUSSION

1. Consider the different sides of the debate over the use of police informants, or "snitching." Whose argument do you believe is most valid? Should the communities described in Box 13.3 be more cooperative with police in the name of reducing crime, or do they have reason to be wary of police tactics?

2. How might boys and men challenge and reconstruct the notion of a violent masculinity. Is it possible to develop alternative ways of demonstrating that one is "a real man"?

3. Why are law enforcement approaches commonly used to tackle high levels of violence when research consistently demonstrates that they generally do not work and come with serious consequences for police–community relationships?

4. In Canada, criminal justice agencies routinely collect race-based data (i.e., information on the racial/ethnic background of people who come into contact with the system as victims, offenders, etc.), but they do not publicly release these data. Why do you think that is? If these data were released to the public, what positive consequences might there be? What negative consequences might there be?

5. Residents of urban neighbourhoods that are identified as "hot spots" for violent crime sometimes argue that mapping the geography of violence in this way stigmatizes the neighbourhood and its residents in the public imagination. Why might they feel this way?

6. In what ways is the "blue code of silence" among police officers similar to, or different from "no snitch codes" that exist in some poor, urban neighbourhoods?

SUGGESTED FURTHER READINGS

Anderson, E. (1999). *The code of the street: Decency, violence and the moral life of the inner city*. New York: W.W. Norton.

Fagan, J., & Wilkinson, D. (1998). Guns, youth violence, and social identity in inner cities. In M. Tonry & M. Moore (Eds.), *Crime and justice* (Vol. 24, pp.105–188). Chicago: University of Chicago Press.

Pinker, S. (2011). *The better angels of our nature: Why violence has declined*. New York: Viking.

Thompson, S.K. (2013). Case study: Black homicide victimization in Toronto, Ontario, Canada. In S. Bucerius & M. Tonry (Eds.), *The Oxford handbook of ethnicity, crime and immigration* (pp. 450–453). New York: Oxford University Press.

Websites

Children and Youth—Crime Prevention through Social Development: http://www.ccsd.ca/cpsd/ccsd

CPTED Ontario: http://www.cptedontario.ca

Toronto crime by neighbourhood, 2004–11: http://www.cbc.ca/toronto/features/crimemap

REFERENCES

Anderson, E. (1999). *The code of the street: Decency, violence and the moral life of the inner city*. New York: W.W. Norton.

Bailey, W.C. (1984). Poverty, inequality, and city homicide rates: Some not so unexpected findings. *Criminology, 22,* 1–25.

Benson, M.L., Fox, G.L., DeMaris, A., & Wan Wyk, J. (2003). Neighbourhood disadvantage, individual economic distress, and violence against women in intimate relationships. *Journal of Quantitative Criminology, 19*(3), 207–235.

Blau, J.R., & Blau, P.M. (1982). The cost of inequality: Metropolitan structure and violent crime. *American Sociological Review, 47*(1), 114–129.

Blumstein, A. (1995). Violence by young people: Why the deadly nexus? *National Institute of Justice Journal, 229,* 2–9.

Brennan, S. (2012, July 24). Police-reported crime statistics in Canada, 2011 (Catalogue no. 85-002-X). *Juristat*. Retrieved from http://www.statcan.gc.ca/pub/85-002-x/2012001/article/11692-eng.pdf.

Brzozowski, J., Taylor-Butts, A., & Johnson, S. (2006). Victimization and offending among Aboriginal people of Canada. *Juristat, 26*(3), 1–31. Retrieved from http://publications.gc.ca/Collection-R/Statcan/85-002-XIE/85-002-XIE2006003.pdf.

Casteel, C., & Peek-Asa, C. (2000). Effectiveness of crime prevention through environmental design (CPTED) in reducing robberies. *American Journal of Preventative Medicine, 18*(4), 99–115.

Charron, M. (2009). *Neighbourhood characteristics and the distribution of police-reported crime in the City of Toronto* (Catalogue no. 85-561-M, no. 18). Ottawa: Statistics Canada.

Cohen, A.K., & Felson, M. (1979). Social change and crime rate trends: A routine activity approach. *American Sociological Review, 44*(4), 588–608.

Cohen, J., Cork, D., Engberg, J., & Tita, G. (1998). The role of drug markets and gangs in local homicide rates. *Homicide Studies, 2*(3), 241–262.

Cohen, J., Gorr, W., & Singh, P. (2003). Estimating intervention effects in varying risk settings: Do police raids reduce illegal drug dealing at nuisance bars? *Criminology, 41*(2), 257–292.

Collins, J.J., & Messerschmidt, P.M. (1993). Epidemiology of alcohol-related violence. *Alcohol Health and Research World, 17*, 93–100.

Connell, R.W. (1987). *Gender and power: Society, the person and sexual politics.* Stanford, CA: Stanford University Press.

Connell, R.W. (2002). *Gender.* Cambridge, UK: Polity Press.

Cozens, P., Saville, G., & Hillier, D. (2005). Crime prevention through environmental design (CPTED): A review and modern bibliography. *Property Management, 23*(5), 328–356.

Cruise, K., Fernandez, K., McCoy, W., Guy, L., Colwell, L., & Douglas, T. (2008). The influence of psychosocial maturity on adolescent offenders' delinquent behaviour. *Youth Violence and Juvenile Justice, 6*(2), 178–194.

de Haan, W. (2008). Violence as an essentially contested concept. In S. Body-Gendrot & P. Spierenburg (Eds.), *Violence in Europe: Historical and contemporary perspectives* (pp. 27–40). New York: Springer.

Doob, A. (2004). Preventing violent offending in youth. In B. Kidd & J. Phillips (Eds.), *From enforcement and prevention to civic engagement: Research on community safety* (pp. 81–95). Toronto: Centre of Criminology.

Fagan, J., & Wilkinson, D. (1998). Guns, youth violence, and social identity in inner cities. In M. Tonry & M. Moore (Eds.), *Crime and justice* (Vol. 24, pp. 105–188). Chicago: University of Chicago Press.

Fajnzylber, P., Lederman, D., & Loayza, N. (2002). What causes violent crime? *European Economic Review, 46*, 1323–1357.

Farrington, D.P. (1986). Age and crime. In M. Tonry & N. Morris (Eds.), *Crime and justice* (Vol. 7, pp. 189–250). Chicago: University of Chicago Press.

Farrington, D.P., Piquero, A.R., & Jennings, W.G. (2013). *Offending from childhood to late middle age: Recent results from the Cambridge Study in Delinquent Development.* New York: Springer.

Fong, E., & Shibuya, K. (2000). The spatial separation of the poor in Canadian cities. *Demography, 37*(4), 449–459.

Gartner, R., & Thompson, S.K. (2004). Trends in homicide in Toronto. In B. Kidd & J. Phillips (Eds.), *From enforcement and prevention to civic engagement: Research on community safety* (pp. 28–39). Toronto: Centre of Criminology.

Grogger, J., & Willis, M. (1998). *The introduction of crack cocaine and the rise in urban crime rates* (NBER Working Paper no. 6353). Cambridge, MA: National Bureau of Economic Research.

Hampson, R. (2009, March 29). Anti-snitch campaign riles police, prosecutors. *USA Today.* Retrieved from http://usatoday30.usatoday.com/news/nation/2006-03-28-stop-snitching_x.htm.

Hannon, L.E. (2005). Extremely poor neighbourhoods and homicide. *Social Science Quarterly, 86*(5), 1418–1434.

Henry, D.B., Tolan, P.H., & Gorman-Smith, D. (2001). Longitudinal family and peer group effects on violence and non-violent delinquency. *Journal of Clinical Child Psychology, 30*(2), 172–186.

Howell, J.C., & Hawkins, J.D. (1998). Prevention of youth violence. In M. Tonry & M. Moore (Eds.), *Youth violence: Crime and justice, a review of the research* (Vol. 24, pp. 263–315). Chicago: University of Chicago Press.

Huff-Corzine, L., Corzine, J., & Moore, D.C. (1986). Southern exposure: Deciphering the South's influence on homicide rates. *Social Forces, 64*, 906–924.

Jackman, M. (2002). Violence in social life. *Annual Review of Sociology, 28,* 387–415.

Kong, R., & AuCoin, K. (2008). Female offenders in Canada. *Juristat, 28*(1). Retrieved from http://www.statcan.gc.ca/pub/85-002-x/85-002-x2008001-eng.pdf.

La Prairie, C. (2002). Aboriginal over-representation in the criminal justice system: A tale of nine cities. *Canadian Journal of Criminology, 44*(2), 181–208.

Law Courts Education Society. (n.d.). The community crime prevention guide. Retrieved from http://www.criminaljusticereform.gov.bc.ca/en/what_you_can_do/crime_prevention.

Loeber, R., & LeBlanc, M. (1990). Toward a developmental criminology. In M. Tonry & N. Morris (Eds.), *Crime and justice* (Vol. 12, pp. 375–437). Chicago: University of Chicago Press.

Ludwig, J. (2005). Better gun enforcement, less crime. *Criminology & Public Policy, 4*(4), 677–716.

Lynch, M.J., & Groves, W.B. (1989). *A primer in radical criminology* (2nd ed.). New York: Harrow and Heston.

Macmillan, R., & Gartner, R. (1999). When she brings home the bacon: Labor force participation and the risk of spousal violence against women. *Journal of Marriage and the Family, 61*(4), 947–958.

Mahony, T. (2011). Women and the criminal justice system. In Statistics Canada (Ed.), *Women in Canada: A gender-based statistical report* (Catalogue no. 89-503-X) (pp. 169–203). Ottawa: Statistics Canada. Retrieved from http://www.statcan.gc.ca/pub/89-503-x/2010001/article/11416-eng.htm.

Merton, R. (1938). Social structure and anomie. *American Sociological Review, 3*(5), 672–682.

Messner, S. (1989). Economic discrimination and societal homicide rates: Further evidence on the cost of inequality. *American Sociological Review, 54,* 597–611.

Messner, S., & Tardiff, K. (1985). The social ecology of urban homicide: An application of the "routine activities" approach. *Criminology, 23*(2), 241–268.

Messner, S., & Zimmerman, G. (2012). Community-level influences on crime and offending. In B.C. Welsh & D.P. Farrington (Eds.), *The Oxford handbook of crime prevention* (pp. 155–171). New York: Oxford University Press.

Mullins, C.W., & Cardwell-Mullins, R. (2006). Bad ass or punk ass: The contours of street masculinity. *Universitas, 2*(2), 1–17.

Parker, R.N. (1989). Poverty, subculture of violence, and type of homicide. *Social Forces, 67*(4), 983–1007.

Patillo-McCoy, M. (1999). *Black picket fences: Privilege and peril among the black middle class.* Chicago: University of Chicago Press.

Perreault, S. (2012, December 4). *Homicide in Canada, 2011* (Catalogue no. 85-002-x). *Juristat.* Retrieved from http://www.statcan.gc.ca/pub/85-002-x/2012001/article/11738-eng.pdf.

Perreault, S. (2013, July 25). *Police-reported crime statistics in Canada, 2012* (Catalogue no. 85-002-x). *Juristat.* Retrieved from http://www.statcan.gc.ca/pub/85-002-x/2013001/article/11854-eng.pdf.

Perreault, S., & Brennan, S. (2010). *Criminal victimization in Canada, 2009* (Catalogue no. 85-002-X). *Juristat.* Retrieved from http://www.statcan.gc.ca/pub/85-002-x/2010002/article/11340-eng.htm.

Piquero, A.R., Farrington, D.P., & Blumstein, A. (2007). *Key issues in criminal careers research: New analysis from the Cambridge Study in Delinquent Development.* Cambridge, MA: Cambridge University Press.

Roberts, J., & Doob, A. (1997). Race, ethnicity and criminal justice in Canada. *Crime and Justice, 21,* 469–522.

Rosenfeld, R., Fornango, R., & Baumer, E. (2005). Did Ceasefire, Compstat, and Exile reduce homicide? *Criminology and Public Policy, 4*(3), 419–450.

Sampson, R.J. (1995). The community. In J.Q. Wilson & J. Petersilia (Eds.), *Crime* (pp. 193–216). San Francisco: ICS Press.

Sampson, R.J., & Laub, J.H. (1990). Crime and deviance over the life course: The salience of adult social bonds. *American Sociological Review, 55*(5), 609–627.

Sampson, R.J., & Laub, J.H. (1993). *Crime in the making: Pathways and turning points through life*. Cambridge, MA: Harvard University Press.

Sampson, R.J., Raudenbush, S.W., & Earls, F. (1997). Neighbourhoods and violent crime: A multilevel study of collective efficacy. *Science, 277*, 918–924.

Sampson, R.J., & Wilson, W.J. (1995). Toward a theory of race, crime and urban inequality. In J. Hagan & R.D. Peterson (Eds.), *Crime and inequality* (pp. 37–54). Stanford, CA: Stanford University Press.

Saville, G. (1998). New tools to eradicate crime places and crime niches. Retrieved from http://www.aic.gov.au/media_library/conferences/urban/saville.pdf.

Silverman, R., & Kennedy, L. (2004). *Deadly deeds: Murder in Canada*. Toronto: Nelson.

Smith, C., Lizotte, A.J., & Thornberry, T.P. (1995). Resilient youth: Identifying factors that prevent high-risk youth from engaging in delinquency and drug use. *Current Perspectives on Aging and the Life Cycle, 4*, 217–247.

Statistics Canada. (n.d.). Violent crimes or offences/crimes against the person. Retrieved from http://www.statcan.gc.ca/pub/85-002-x/2010002/definitions-eng.htm.

Statistics Canada. (2011). *Family violence in Canada: A statistical profile* (Catalogue no. 85-224-X). Ottawa: Statistics Canada, Canadian Centre for Justice Statistics. Retrieved from http://www.statcan.gc.ca/pub/85-224-x/85-224-x2010000-eng.pdf.

Statistics Canada. (2012). *Incident-based crime statistics, by detailed violations, annual* (CANSIM Table 252-0051). Ottawa: Statistics Canada. Retrieved from http://www4.hrsdc.gc.ca/.3ndic.1t.4r@-eng.jsp?iid=57.

Stewart, E., & Simons, R. (2006). Structure and culture in African-American adolescent violence: A partial test of the code of the street thesis. *Justice Quarterly, 23*, 1–33.

Stolzenberg, L., Eitle, D., & D'Alessio, S. (2006). Race, economic inequality, and violent crime. *Journal of Criminal Justice, 34*, 303–316.

Sweeten, G., Piquero, A.R., & Steinberg, L. (2013). Age and the explanation of crime, revisited. *Journal of Youth and Adolescents, 42*(6), 921–938.

Thompson, S.K. (2009). *The social ecology and spatial distribution of lethal violence in Toronto, 1988–2003* (Doctoral dissertation). Centre of Criminology, University of Toronto.

Thompson, S.K. (2013). Case study: Black homicide victimization in Toronto, Ontario, Canada. In S. Bucerius & M. Tonry (Eds.), *The Oxford handbook of ethnicity, crime and immigration* (pp. 450–453). New York: Oxford University Press.

Thompson, S.K., & Bucerius, S. (2013). Unintended consequences of neighbourhood restructuring: Uncertainty, disrupted social networks and increased fear of violent victimization among young adults. *British Journal of Criminology, 53*(5), 924–941.

Thompson, S.K., & Gartner, R. (2007). *Urban crime: The case of Toronto, Canada*. Case study prepared for *Enhancing urban safety and security: Global report on human settlements 2007*. London, UK: UN Habitat, Earthscan.

Thompson, S.K., & Gartner, R. (2014). The spatial distribution and social context of homicide in Toronto's neighbourhoods, 1988–2003. *Journal of Research in Crime and Delinquency, 51*(1), 88–118.

Tonry, M. (1995). *Malign neglect: Race, crime and punishment in America*. New York: Oxford University Press.

Tremblay, R., & Japel, C. (2003). Prevention during pregnancy, infancy, and the preschool years. In D.P. Farrington & J.W. Coid (Eds.), *Early prevention of adult antisocial behaviour* (pp. 202 –242). New York: Cambridge University Press.

Vaillancourt, R. (2010). *Gender differences in police-reported violent crime in Canada, 2008* (Catalogue no. 85F0033M, no. 24). Ottawa: Statistics Canada. Retrieved from http://www.statcan.gc.ca/pub/85f0033m/85f0033m2010024-eng.htm.

Villarreal, A., & Silva, B. (2006). Social cohesion, criminal victimization and the perceived risk of crime in Brazilian neighbourhoods. *Social Forces, 84*(3), 1725–1753.

Wekerle, G., & Whitzman, C. (1995). *Safe cities: Guidelines for planning, design and management*. New York: Van Nostrand Reinhold.

White, H., & Gorman, D. (2000). Dynamics of the drug-crime relationship. In G. LaFree (Ed.), *The nature of crime: Continuity and change* (pp. 151–218). Washington, DC: Department of Justice.

Williams, K.R., & Flewelling, R.L. (1988). The social production of criminal homicide: A comparative study of disaggregated rates in American cities. *American Sociological Review, 53*(3), 421–431.

Wilson, W.J. (1987). *The truly disadvantaged: The inner city, the underclass, and public policy*. Chicago: University of Chicago Press.

Woldoff, R., & Weiss, K. (2010). "Stop snitchin": Exploring definitions of the snitch and implications for urban black communities. *Journal of Criminal Justice and Popular Culture, 17*(1), 184–223.

Zimmerman, S. (1992). The revolving door of despair: Aboriginal involvement in the criminal justice system. *UBC Law Review, 26*, 367–427.

The Berlin café where Luka Magnotta was apprehended.

CASE STUDY 14.1

Luka Magnotta: Sexualized Crime and the Role of the Internet

In July 1910, when Dr. Hawley Crippen arrived by ocean liner in Quebec City, he was arrested for the murder of his wife.[1] The emerging technology of the wireless telegraph was responsible for his demise. The good doctor was the first person to be caught in such a manner: he had fled the United Kingdom with his lover, but the wireless telegraph (precursor to the telephone) allowed British authorities to send a message to police in Canada.

Much has changed since 1910. Today we have communication technologies that would have seemed unthinkable even 20 years ago. The arrest of Luka Magnotta is a telling illustration of the power of the Internet, which has, in a relatively short period of time, become closely intertwined with sexualized crime.

As the sordid saga of Magnotta reveals, the Internet can be both lauded and reviled. The global release of photos, videos, and stories about the "Canadian psycho" who gruesomely murdered and dismembered Jun Lin in Montreal in May 2012 left Magnotta with no place to hide; he was detected, appropriately enough, in an Internet café in Berlin a few weeks later, surfing for both pornography and news about himself.

But it was also the Internet that provided a platform for Magnotta, giving him the opportunity to broadcast repulsive videos of sadistic cruelty. And these videos, once released into cyberspace, are now almost impossible to recall, despite the efforts of authorities. (In 2013, Edmonton police charged website owner Mark Marek with the rare obscenity charge of "corrupting morals" for posting Magnotta's horrific video of the crime. For his part, Marek claims he posted the video as "a public service," in order to help track down the perpetrator [Parrish, 2013].)

And so we can see that while the Internet makes possible the wide distribution of such materials, it is that very same online visibility that served to facilitate Magnotta's capture. Put differently, every critique of the Internet's porous lack of accountability can be met with the observation that online exposure also shines a light into the darkest recesses of human behaviour, most particularly the realm of sexual deviance.

Journalism plays an important role in shining that light; however, in the digital age—when website "hits" are the main goal—sensational stories take precedence, and facts often get lost amid online gossip and opinion. We have yet to discover the extent of the crimes Luka Magnotta apparently committed (he pleaded not guilty to the murder of Jun Lin and, at the time of writing, was awaiting trial),[2] but the sensational nature of his case is also a depressingly familiar reminder of how most of us come to understand the reality of crime. Only the most horrific and sexualized allegations of homicide are reported with any detail in the mainstream press or online. The barbaric sex crimes of

331

notorious Canadian criminals Robert Pickton, Paul Bernardo, and Clifford Olson are well known. But much more typical forms of sexual crime—such as incest or inappropriate groping by a friend or an acquaintance—receive little or no attention. We learn of the rarest and most predatory of criminal acts in the media, not of the staples of crime that occupy our police officers, courts, and correctional centres.

The problem with this selective reporting ("if it bleeds, it leads"), based on the understandable journalistic principle that the most horrific acts make for more readers, is that extensive coverage of these crimes skews our perceptions of sex crime and criminals. The media tend to overemphasize the predatory offender, relative to the norm of sexual offences. We rarely hear, for example, of the reality that 35 percent of the 13,300 inmates in federal penitentiaries have significant mental health impairments and are in need of treatment (Makin, 2011).

The case of Luka Magnotta is a reminder of our collective myopia with regard to this issue, and of the media's imperatives. News organizations are selling a product, one that often verges on entertainment and spectacle; education of the public is neither critical nor necessary for this task. And so we have another riveting tale of horror: the haunting and disturbing face of Luka Magnotta on the front pages of almost every major newspaper. Unfortunately, this reliance on sexualized sensationalism is a feature of crime reporting that seems unlikely to disappear.

Before You Read Chapter 14

- What is your impression of the prevalence of sexual crime in Canada, or in your own community, based on the media coverage you have seen? What might explain the media (and the public) interest in sensational sexual crime stories?
- How has media reporting affected the public's perception of sexual offences—from high-profile sex cases (such as Magnotta's) to the more common forms of sexual offences (such as sex assault and inappropriate touching)?
- How realistic is it to expect authorities to be able to track down and prosecute a significant percentage of Internet-facilitated sexual offences?
- How could media coverage affect the trial of an alleged sex offender?

Sexual Offences and Problematic Sexual Interests

<table>
<tr>
<td valign="top">

LEARNING OBJECTIVES

After reading this chapter, students will be able to:

- Understand the difference between risk and dangerousness in sex offenders.
- Describe how sexual offenders have been dealt with by the criminal justice system over time.
- Understand the difference between sexual offences and deviant sexual interests.
- Define forms of deviant sexual interests and behaviours.
- Know factors associated with increased risk of sexual recidivism.
- Understand Canadian criminal justice approaches used in managing the risk of sex offenders.

</td>
<td valign="top">

CHAPTER OUTLINE

</td>
</tr>
</table>

Introduction

Sexual behaviours in societies throughout the world are influenced by varying moral codes, cultural and social expectations, myths, religious principles, and often unscientific beliefs. Historically, criminal sexual offences and other problematic sexual behaviours have been a concern (Bartol & Bartol, 2008). However, within the past 30 years, criminologic issues involving sexual offending have risen to prominence in academic, social, political, and clinical realms. Sexual offending, especially against children, is universally viewed as a serious problem, but what is considered deviant and/or criminal, the reasons why, and the appropriate responses vary by perspective, location, and time period.

In North America, the goal of the criminal justice system is to deter, punish, rehabilitate, and manage the risk posed by sex offenders. While doing so, the justice system must maintain a balance between public safety and protection of the individual rights of the accused. Attempts to maintain this balance can be especially difficult when dealing with sex offenders, a subgroup of offenders who are viewed by society as highly dangerous and "morally tainted." Even within the prison population, sex offenders, especially those whose crime was against children, are stigmatized.

Despite widespread coverage of sexual crimes in the media that often leads the general public to believe that sexual offending is at an all-time high, sexual offences against both adults and children have been steadily decreasing on a global scale since the 1980s (Bartol & Bartol, 2008; Bureau of Justice Statistics, 2006; Perreault, 2013). The only exceptions to this trend are child pornography offences, which have been on the rise (Seto, 2013). Highly publicized incidents of a relatively small number of child abductions and sexual assaults throughout Canada and the United States during the 1980s and early 1990s elicited widespread shock and anger. These cases catalyzed new criminal justice attempts to manage sex offenders both during incarceration and once they are released into the community (Murphy, Brodsky, et al., 2009; Petrunik, Murphy, & Fedoroff, 2008).

Individuals who have committed a sexual offence are often classified as a homogeneous group. However, wide variation exists in offender characteristics (such as gender, age, socio-economic background, personality, intelligence, attitude, and social skills). Offence characteristics and subsequent risk of recidivism vary widely. Victim characteristics can vary in terms of the age, gender, number of victims, offence history, relationship history, medical history, psychiatric history, offender–victim relationship, and many other significant variables. Offences also differ in terms of degree of planning, motivation, and the level of violence.

Perpetrators of sexual offences are typically characterized as "all the same": extremely dangerous, anonymous, unstable, and mobile (McAlinden, 2007; Murphy, Brodsky, et al., 2009). Although this singular conceptualization is not supported by research, it has been perpetuated by media portrayals that claim society needs to defend itself from "predatory pedophiles" and "rapists" who are all men, strangers, and increasingly prevalent, thereby creating an imminent high risk to the safety of all women and children. In fact, reports have found that as many as 80 to 98 percent of known sexual acts against children are committed by someone well known to the victim. Rates are similar for adult victims (Freeman-Longo, 1996; Greenfield, 1997). These facts highlight the inaccurate portrayal by the media that facilitates the concept of "stranger danger."

This chapter provides an overview of how sexual offences and responses to sex crimes have been conceptualized by criminal justice officials over time; the characteristics of sex offenders and associated levels of recidivism; the difference between clinical and legal understandings of sexual interests and behaviours; and approaches to managing sex offenders once they are released into the community.

The Concepts of Dangerousness and Risk

dangerousness
The capacity of a person to physically, psychologically, or morally harm oneself or others. It includes an estimation of both the severity and likelihood of harm.

risk
The probability that a person will commit future harmful acts.

recidivism
Also referred to as *reoffending*, when an offender goes on to commit another crime; general recidivism refers to any new offence, and sexual recidivism refers to another sexual offence.

When referring to sex offenders from criminal justice perspectives over time, two concepts are important to understand. The concepts of dangerousness and risk have a long history in civil and criminal legislation and correctional and psychiatric practice. **Dangerousness** refers to the capacity of a person to harm self or others. It includes an estimation of the severity, imminence, predictability, and likelihood of harm. The term **risk** typically refers only to the probability of a person committing future harmful acts (Petrunik, 2003, 2005; Thomas, 2005).

One assumption about the dangerousness of high-risk sex offenders is that the motivation behind their crimes is due to overly strong sexual desires and uncontrolled sexual impulses. The belief that people who commit sexual offences cannot be changed has led to a focus on incapacitation (preventing an offender from being able to commit another offence through incarceration or other means of management) to enhance public safety. An offender's past criminal behaviour is often used to appraise the risk of recidivism, but it is not the only significant variable. **Recidivism** refers to when an offender goes on to commit another crime; general recidivism refers to any new offence, and sexual recidivism refers to another sexual offence (Bartol & Bartol, 2008; Perreault, 2013).

An individual who has a **paraphilia** (sexual interest in an activity that does not include mutual consent with another person) or a personality disorder may commit a number of non-violent sexual offences against children (e.g., exposing him/herself to children in a park or asking a child to sexually touch him/her). From a criminal justice perspective, this individual may be viewed as more dangerous than an individual who commits a non-sexual murder. The murderer typically receives a sentence designed to incapacitate and punish. The sex offender not only receives a sentence designed to incapacitate and punish but also typically faces conditions intended to continue surveillance once released back into the community. Unfortunately, increasingly the trend is to withhold treatment.

paraphilia
Sexual interest in an activity other than masturbation that does not include mutual consent with another person.

Criminal Justice Responses to Sexual Offences over Time

In the early 1800s throughout North America, criminality, including sexual offending, was considered to be endemic within the "dangerous classes," where crime was associated with immoral populations (groups of people who were economically marginalized and socially stigmatized, and seemed to live by a different set of moral standards than the rest of society). Such individuals included prostitutes, vagrants, the mentally ill, and, sometimes, predatory criminals. During this time it was believed that immorality and criminality were closely intertwined, with "immorality" often acting as a precursor to criminal acts. Offenders were held accountable for their crimes within a system that emphasized "proportionate sentencing" and "due process" (Petrunik, 2003, 2005; Thomas, 2005).

Forensic-Clinical Model

Beginning in the late 19th century, proponents of a *forensic-clinical model* of dangerousness were less concerned with concepts of due process and proportionate sentencing, and lobbied for indeterminate confinement. This model developed in response to the perceived shortcomings of classical criminology (see Chapter 6, Theories of Crime: An Overview). Supporters of the forensic-clinical model considered requirements for due process and proportionate sentencing as a hindrance to the process of effective treatment. These proponents contended that offenders could not be sufficiently deterred by a fixed term of punishment due to mental or personality disorders that made them prone to criminal activity. Sentences needed to be indeterminate, since one could not specify in advance how long it would take for treatment to decrease the offender's level of dangerousness (Connelly & Williamson, 2000; Petrunik, 1982).

Justice Model

The *justice model* became popular during the 1970s and was based on the principles of due process and proportionate sentencing. Themes seen during the classical period of criminology began to resurface, with a penal shift back to determinate sentences that were proportionate to the gravity of the offence. Societal challenges emerged from a revolution in mental health legislation and criminal law reform in which due process was extended to include individuals suffering from mental illness. Some social scientists questioned the ability of forensic mental health workers to assess the risk posed by offenders, and to diagnose and treat disorders effectively (Petrunik, 2003). Greater safeguards were put in place against commitment to asylums for indeterminate periods of time, and against involuntary treatment. With few exceptions, offenders with mental illness also retained the right to refuse treatment.

Community Protection Approach

The emergence of a *community protection approach* during the late 1980s and early 1990s resulted from concerns that previous models had not given enough attention to overall public safety and the rights of victims. The primary focus of this new approach was not on the treatment or rehabilitation of the individual offender but on the overall safety of the community. This approach was guided by the concerns of victims' rights groups, crime prevention advocates, and the general public (Murphy, Brodsky, et al., 2009; Petrunik, 2003; Petrunik, Murphy, & Fedoroff, 2008). Proponents called for governments to actively address perceived increases in society's fears due to a series of highly publicized sexual crimes, and to give increased attention to the rights of victims and their families (Kemshall & Wood, 2007; Petrunik, 2003; see also Chapter 5, Victims of Crime).

One factor that contributed to the shift toward the community protection approach was the media's inaccurate construction of "stranger danger" and the stereotype of a sex offender as a "predator lurking in the bushes," who is driven by an uncontrollable impulse to victimize unsuspecting children. This sensational portrayal of the typical sex offender is false. The majority of sexual offences are committed by someone who is well known to the victim (Murphy, Brodsky, et al., 2009). In fact, most child abductions are committed by a parent estranged from his or her spouse and involved in a custody dispute.

The community protection approach justifies the preventive restriction of liberty of the offender based on the perceived risk of that person committing offences in the future, rather than solely on retribution for acts committed in the past. This approach suggests that the best way to deal with the dangerousness of high-risk sex offenders is through a combination of social controls (surveillance, monitoring, and restriction of liberties) both during incarceration and after release into the community (Petrunik, Murphy, & Fedoroff, 2008). Mechanisms of risk management for sex offenders include the following: longer and full sentences; intensive community supervision with orders restricting freedom of movement and association; notification of release into the community; sex offender registries (SORs); and civil and/or criminal incarceration, allowing for indeterminate confinement based on a designation of extreme dangerousness and severe mental illness (Kemshall & Wood, 2007; Murphy, Brodsky, et al., 2009; Petrunik, 2003). The intended goal is to manage the risk posed by this population in order to prevent the recurrence of crime and to reduce the probability or magnitude of the predicted harm.

Community Protection Approach in American and Canadian Legislation

The crucial event that sparked the emergence of the community protection approach within the United States was the 1989 abduction and sexual assault of a seven-year-old boy in Washington state by Earl Shriner. This incident became a catalyst for rapid legislative reform throughout the United States. Washington state passed the 1990 *Community Protection Act* (CPA) that called for a state-wide **sex offender registry (SOR)**, a system of community notification of release of sex offenders and post-sentence completion of

sex offender registry (SOR)
A searchable database with information on convicted sexual offenders.

civil commitment of offenders who meet the criteria of a sexually violent predator (SVP). In response to political pressure by victims' rights organizations across the country, the *Jacob Wetterling Crimes Against Children and Sexually Violent Offender Registration Act* (JWA) of 1994 required all states to establish a functioning SOR (Murphy, Brodsky, et al., 2009; Petrunik, 2002, 2003). All states in the United States now have their own SOR as well as a national SOR.

The sexual assault and murder of New Jersey's Megan Kanka by her neighbour, who had been convicted for sexual offences twice before, led to the 1994 creation of New Jersey's *Megan's Law. Megan's Law* permits the public release of specific information (such as the offender's name, photo, and address). The potential for widespread notification increased when Indiana introduced *Zachary's Law* in 1994. This legislation mandated the creation of a publicly accessible state website that listed pertinent information about known sex offenders (Jenkins, 2001). In the years to follow, public notification under *Megan's Law*, including databases publicly accessible via the Internet, became federal legislation. More recently, the 2006 *Adam Walsh Child Protection and Safety Act* replaced the Wetterling Act and resulted in amendments to mechanisms of community-based sex offender management, notably changes in registration and notification requirements (Murphy, Brodsky, et al., 2009; Petrunik, 2002, 2003).

Compared with the rapid development of policies for the management of sex offenders within the United States, legislation by the Canadian government developed in a significantly slower and more cautious manner. In 1988, one year before Shriner's crime in Washington, Joseph Fredericks abducted, sexually assaulted, and murdered a boy, Christopher Stephenson, in Ontario. Fredericks had spent his life in and out of high-security psychiatric hospitals and had left federal prison only a few months before the murder. Canadian citizens responded to the sensational media coverage of Christopher's murder with shock and outrage. Despite the clear parallels between the Shriner and Fredericks cases, it took the Ontario government 12 years to create a provincial SOR under *Christopher's Law* (Murphy, Fedoroff, & Martineau, 2009; Petrunik, Murphy, & Fedoroff, 2008).

After the creation of the Ontario SOR, community members and victims' rights advocates demanded the creation of a national SOR (NSOR). Even then, plans for an NSOR were not announced until after the provincial governments threatened to create an independent system of interlinking SORs across Canada. The *Sex Offender Information Registration Act* (SOIRA) of 2004 was finally implemented to manage registrants throughout the country. Both registries are still functioning and have undergone reviews and amendments to improve their effectiveness and functionality (Murphy & Fedoroff, 2013; Murphy, Fedoroff, & Martineau, 2009). Fortunately, to date, routine public notification has not been implemented in Canada. The fact that convicted sex offenders are not publicly disclosed means they can obtain housing, employment, and attend treatment more easily.

Base Rates and Survival Curves in Sex Offender Recidivism

Before estimating the risk posed by any population, it is critical to examine the population's recidivism base rate. The base rate is the proportion of offenders who will recidivate (go on to commit another offence) over a given period of time, known as the *follow-up period*. Base rates have been established by recidivism studies completed around the

civil commitment

Also known as *involuntary commitment,* the legal process by which a person is detained after serving a sentence due to concerns that he or she will commit further crimes.

world on a variety of samples of sex offenders. Rates of sexual recidivism can be plotted on *survival curves*. A survival curve measures the time at which released sex offenders commit a reoffence. The survival curve begins at 100 percent, which indicates that no released sex offenders in the study population have recidivated. As time goes on, if a sex offender recidivates, the curve begins to form. At the end of the follow-up period, the number left is the number not known to have recidivated, meaning those who have "survived" (Webster & Hucker, 2003). For example, if 25 out of 100 sex offenders were reconvicted for new sexual offences over a given time period, the recidivism base rate for that time period would be 25 percent and the rate of survival would be 75 percent. Survival rates are sometimes used to estimate recidivism rates over time (Hanson, Morton, & Harris, 2003). While the overall survival rate decreases with time, it is now established that the longer a sex offender does not recidivate, the less likely it is that he or she ever will (Hanson, Harris, Helmus, & Thorton, in press).

The outcome of risk prediction falls into one of four categories: true positive, true negative, false positive, and false negative. See Table 14.1 for a breakdown of the possible risk prediction outcomes.

Accurate risk prediction maximizes *true positives* (correctly identifying people who are truly high risk) and minimizes *false negatives* (miscategorizing high-risk people as low risk) while simultaneously minimizing *false positives* (incorrectly labelling innocent individuals) and maximizing *true negatives* (correctly identifying innocent individuals). The ideal outcome for risk prediction is a true negative whenever an offender is correctly predicted to not recidivate. The problematic nature of a false negative is heightened when the political and social climate becomes intensely preoccupied with issues surrounding sexual offending. False positives, on the other hand, raise ethical concerns because inaccurate predictions unjustly impinge on the rights and liberty of the former offender (Craissati, 2004). They can be due to the inadequacy of the risk-assessment instrument, but they are more often due to a misunderstanding of risk assessment. Actuarial risk-assessment estimates compare the individual being assessed with others who have similar characteristics, but they can never provide specific estimates for the individual, especially if treatment and other interventions are not taken into account.

Data sources on the prevalence of sexual offending (both first-time offences and recidivism) include official statistics (such as police-reported numbers of charges or convictions), victim surveys, clinical reports, and research studies. Since sexual offences can be unreported, the use of official statistics can be problematic because they may underestimate the prevalence of sexual offending. Of the sexual offences reported to the police, a small number lead to arrest, and an even smaller number result in official convictions. Using victim surveys and clinical reports helps provide a more comprehensive estimate. However, even these sources do not represent all incidences of sexual

Table 14.1   Outcomes of Risk Prediction

	Predict reoffence	**Predict no reoffence**
Do reoffend	True positive	False negative
Do not reoffend	False positive	True negative

offending. The unknown rates are referred to as the **dark figure of crime**. One estimate of the true rate of sexual offending is at least 10 to 15 percent higher than the official rate (Hanson, Morton, & Harris, 2003). Despite this "dark figure," the number of reported sexual assaults has been decreasing since the early 1980s (Bartol & Bartol, 2008; Bureau of Justice Statistics, 2006; Perreault, 2013).

dark figure of crime
Refers to the variation between the number of crimes that occur and the number of crimes that are actually reported to the police. This figure highlights the large number of unreported crimes.

Predictors of Sex Offender Recidivism

A common misconception is that all sex offenders have a high frequency of recidivism. Official statistics and research studies do not support this assumption. Most sex offenders recidivate significantly less often than other types of violent and non-violent offenders. Study results can vary greatly, depending on how recidivism is defined. For example, rates vary depending on whether the authors include arrests, charges, and/or convictions as a measure of recidivism. Another important variable is the length of the follow-up period. As the earlier discussion about the survival curve makes clear, the longer a person lives within the community, the more opportunity the study group has to recidivate. Commonly, follow-up periods in recidivism studies range from 5 to 15 years.

The common assumption is that sex offenders in the community are "ticking time bombs" who become increasingly dangerous the longer they are in the community. However, Harris and Hanson (2004) conducted a meta-analysis on relative recidivism rates among categories of sex offenders, and the survival curves for follow-up periods of 5 years, 10 years, and 15 years. This meta-analysis measured recidivism by a combination of arrests and convictions. Results showed that recidivism rates among sex offenders decreased in frequency over time. The authors stated that

> without exception, the longer offenders remain offence-free in the community the less likely they are to sexually recidivate ... the highest risk period is in the first few years after release. (p. 7)

No peer-reviewed papers refute this claim. See Table 14.2 for recidivism rates over time broken down by offender type.

Three types of risk factors have been associated with reoffences. **Static factors** are characteristics that cannot change (such as age at first offence and offence history). These factors can be used to determine an overall risk level but are not targets for change in therapy. **Dynamic factors** are amenable to change and are, therefore, targets for

static factors
Individual characteristics associated with the risk of reoffending that are immutable to external influences (e.g., age at first offence and offence history). They can be used to determine an overall risk level but are not targets for change.

dynamic factors
Individual characteristics associated with the risk of reoffending that are amenable to change and are targets for treatment (e.g., attitudes tolerant to criminal behaviour and criminal associates). A reduction in dynamic factors is associated with a decreased risk for recidivism.

Table 14.2   Sexual Recidivism Rates by Offender Type and Time

	5 years	10 years	15 years
Rapists	14%	21%	24%
Homosexual extrafamilial offenders	23%	28%	35%
Heterosexual extrafamilial offenders	9%	13%	16%
Heterosexual incest offenders	6%	9%	13%

Source: Harris and Hanson (2004, p. 23).

treatment. These are often referred to as criminogenic needs and include characteristics such as attitudes tolerant of criminal behaviour and criminal associates. A reduction in dynamic factors is associated with a decreased risk for recidivism and subsequently plays a larger role in identifying targets for assessment and intervention. **Acute dynamic factors** are ones that change rapidly, such as intoxication and mood (Hanson & Harris, 1998; Hanson, Morton, & Harris, 2003).

Three variables have been found to be associated with an increased risk of sexual recidivism: prior sexual offences, having committed offences against male victims, and having committed offences against extrafamilial victims. Among the population of child molesters, heterosexual intrafamilial (incest) offenders with no other victim types exhibit the lowest rates of recidivism. Same-sex extrafamilial child molesters have the highest rate of recidivism, especially when they have more than one victim (Quinsey, Harris, Rice, & Cormier, 1998).

Results from a comprehensive meta-analysis by Hanson and Bussière (1996, 1998) of 28,972 sex offenders, with an average follow-up of four to five years, identified several variables associated with an increased risk of sexual recidivism. Developmental variables included juvenile delinquency, a negative relationship with mother, and family problems (such as abuse or family disruptions). Demographic variables included a negative correlation with age (being young at the time of the offence increases risk) and being unmarried. Concerning general criminality, offence history and the victim type and relationship also played significant roles. No one variable alone predicted recidivism; however, a "deviant" sexual preference for children as measured by penile tumescence was found to have the highest correlation with sexual recidivism. This finding did not hold for a deviant preference profile for sexual assault of adult women (Quinsey et al., 1998). It is important to note that the identified factors were associations and not proven causes of the sexual offences or paraphilias.

Risk-Need-Responsivity Model

The **risk-need-responsivity (RNR) model** has been used to assess and manage the risk factors for recidivism, and is based on three principles. The *risk principle* states that in the context of limited resources, it is best to turn maximum attention to offenders with the greatest risk of reoffending. Therefore, it suggests that the likelihood of recidivism decreases when the intensity of the treatment provided to the offender is proportional to the offender's risk to reoffend. The *need principle* calls for an individualized approach to matching the needs of the person being treated to the proposed treatment. The *responsivity principle* requires that intervention be tailored to the learning style, motivation, abilities, and strengths of the offender. These principles have been associated with more positive treatment outcomes for sex offenders treated in custody (Andrews & Bonta, 1998).

Clinical Interpretation of Deviant Sexual Behaviours

The clinical term *paraphilia* is defined in the Diagnostic and Statistical Manual of Mental Disorders (DSM-5) as "any intense and persistent sexual interest other than sexual interest in genital stimulation and preparatory fondling with phenotypically normal, physiologically mature, consenting human partners" (APA, 2013, p. 685). This definition has been criticized (Fedoroff, Di Gioacchino, & Murphy, 2013).

acute dynamic factors
Individual characteristics associated with risk of reoffending that are rapidly changing and include factors such as intoxication and mood.

risk-need-responsivity (RNR) model
An assessment and rehabilitation theory that suggests it is possible to accurately predict the likelihood that someone will reoffend and provides principles on how to effectively intervene to reduce the risk.

Sex offender is a legal term denoting someone who has committed a sexual offence as determined by the *Criminal Code*, whether or not that person has been convicted. Most sex offenders do not have paraphilic disorders. However, some paraphilias, if acted upon, could be considered a sexual offence due to the non-consenting nature of the sexual interests. Many more paraphilias than are listed in the DSM-5 have been described (see Fedoroff, 2010; Murphy, Bradford, & Fedoroff, in press).

Paraphilias Associated with Criminal Activity

Pedophilia

The true prevalence of *pedophilia* is unknown, since estimates are based mainly on law enforcement statistics or clinical records. Estimates from law enforcement likely do not provide an accurate estimate, since not all individuals who commit sexual offences against a child are pedophilic, not everyone with pedophilia commits sexual offences, and of those that do act on their interests, not all are arrested (Aggrawal, 2009). Nevertheless, pedophilia is the most common paraphilia leading to arrest. The DSM-5 (APA, 2013) diagnostic criteria for pedophilia are based on persistent sexual fantasies or desires involving sex with a prepubescent child, typically under the age of 13.

Most studies on pedophilia have involved people with pedophilia who have acted on their interests and were arrested. That focus has led to confusion over the distinction between persons with pedophilia and persons that commit a sexual crime against a child for non-sexually-motivated reasons. Not all individuals who sexually abuse a child meet the DSM-5 criteria for pedophilia. Conversely, not all individuals with a sexual interest in children go on to commit child sexual abuse (Bradford & Meston, 2011; Fedoroff, 2008, 2010). Some individuals with pedophilia control their urges and never commit a hands-on offence against a child, whereas some child molesters may sexually abuse a child out of convenience and do not have a particular interest in children as compared with consenting adults. Many child molesters commit a single, situational sexual offence that is not part of any broader pattern of offending. Individuals with pedophilia who have never committed a contact sexual offence against a child highlight the important difference between paraphilic sexual interests and acting on those sexual interests. An individual should not be charged for problematic sexual interests or thoughts alone.

The persistent rise in child pornography offences since the creation of the Internet has led some criminologists and law enforcement officers to question whether it represents a new type of offence for people with the same problematic interests in children or the emergence of a truly new type of offender. Child pornography existed long before the Internet. However, with the increased popularity of personal computers and online communications, clinicians and criminal justice officials have seen a rise in the creation of, access to, and trade of child pornography that is difficult to police (see Box 14.1). In Canada, the legal age of consent for sexual activity is 16. However, the age of consent to participate in the production of pornography is 18.

Sexual Sadism

Clinically, the diagnosis of *sexual sadism disorder* applies to individuals who derive sexual pleasure from non-consensual domination and infliction of harm on another person. For people with sexual sadism disorder, the infliction of pain is a means to elicit submission,

---

BOX 14.1

Policing Online Child Pornography

The Internet has been a versatile medium for individuals to create, possess, and distribute child pornography (CP) from the comfort of their own homes. While the Internet provides access to illegal materials such as CP, it also provides a method for police to identify and arrest people that access such materials, and arrests related to these offences have increased (Wolak, Finkelhor, & Mitchell, 2011).

Given the international scope of the Internet, criminal justice officials around the world are faced with a number of challenges in policing CP offences. These challenges are based on the nature of the materials and actions depicted, and variation in legislation from one international jurisdiction to the next. Despite universal social condemnation of material depicting child sexual abuse, legislative responses vary significantly.

One area of dispute is the definition of a "child." In some cultures, the differentiation between child and adult is not marked by chronological age but by rituals that signify a "rite of passage." For some, these rituals may be marked by puberty, marriage, or death of the head of the family. Other cultures rely on a legal concept of adulthood as determined in jurisdictional legislature, usually on the basis of age (Murphy, Ranger, & Fedoroff, in press; Sinclair & Sugar, 2005).

Since it is not always known how old a person in a pornographic image is, and, more important, because it is possible to make an adult model look younger, most jurisdictions use legislation that is based on the "apparent age" of the child depicted in images as opposed to the actual age.

Even when the age cut-off for CP is clearly defined, issues arise in accurately determining the age of the individual depicted in confiscated material, since many victims in CP are never identified. Within the material itself, it is easier for investigators to identify prepubescent children compared with postpubescent children due to their physical maturity. Accurate age estimation is further aggravated by the fact that children of different ethnic backgrounds develop at different rates (Murphy, Ranger, & Fedoroff, in press; Sinclair & Sugar, 2005).

Another area of dispute between jurisdictions and countries is the threshold for determining what constitutes CP. Given the cross-jurisdictional variation in defining CP, policing issues arise when an offender is found possessing CP in one country and the images were created by an unknown offender in another country with a different legal definition of CP. A common variation in legislation relates to the legal status of the type of behaviour being depicted. Some jurisdictions have broad definitions of illegality (e.g., any erotic material depicting children) and others have more narrow definitions of illegality (e.g., material depicting children engaged in explicit sexual acts). Another variation in legislation relates to the depiction of real or pseudo children engaged in explicit sexual acts. Some jurisdictions consider the following material illegal: computer-simulated children and animated children or real children that have been digitally altered to be nude or in sexual scenarios (Murphy, Ranger, & Fedoroff, in press). Despite such challenges to law enforcement, online CP arrests have led people to seek treatment earlier than in cases where CP offenders are never detected.

---

obedience, fear, and/or humiliation. The key DSM-5 features of sexual sadism are that the individual experiences sexual arousal from the physical or psychological suffering of another person. It is important to highlight that this diagnosis does not include general sexual assault of adult women. There is no psychiatric diagnosis for sexual assault (less commonly referred to as "rape"), as this is a legal term and not a clinical term. Some individuals who sexually assault women, however, may meet the clinical criteria for sexual sadism (Fedoroff, 2008; Murphy, Bradford, & Fedoroff, in press).

Although the age of onset for non-consensual sexual sadism can vary, it typically occurs in early adulthood and is usually chronic. In a small sample of women referred to treatment for paraphilic disorders, 29 percent met the criteria for sexual sadism.

While these findings cannot be generalized to the general population, they do illustrate that females also have sexually sadistic interests and associated paraphilias (Fedoroff, Fishell, & Fedoroff, 1999).

Exhibitionism

The motivation behind the offence of exposing oneself in public can be divided into three categories. *DSM-5–defined exhibitionists* include people who derive sexual arousal from exposing their genitals to unsuspecting victims in public. They are sexually aroused by the shock and surprise of the victim. This subcategory of offender is typically not aroused by going to a nude beach, where consensual nudity is the norm. *Public masturbators* masturbate in public while attempting to remain hidden from an unsuspecting victim or group of victims. These individuals do not step out of their hiding place because they are aroused by the risk of sexual pleasure in public without actually being detected. *Exhibitionists for sex* expose themselves in public with the hope that an unsuspecting stranger will see them and become so aroused that sexual relations with that person will result.

Exhibitionism is one of the most commonly reported paraphilias and comprises about one-third of reported sexual offences, although many incidents of exhibitionism are never reported to the police. Exhibitionists, along with voyeurs, have the highest rates of sexual recidivism. However, unless they have coexisting paraphilias, exhibitionists rarely deteriorate to more serious sexual offences. Studies have identified a bimodal pattern for the age of onset, ranging from 11 to 15 and then 21 to 25, with a mean age of first arrest at 25 (Aggrawal, 2009). Few official reports are made of females exposing themselves, although they do exist (Fedoroff, Fishell, & Fedoroff, 1999).

Exhibitionism is reported to co-occur with voyeurism and frotteurism approximately 80 percent and 70 percent of the time, respectively. The prevalence of these disorders occurring together, in addition to a preference for non-consensual intercourse, have been coined "courtship disorder" based on the apparent absence of the typical progression of sexual relationships from sight, to touch, to disrobing, and finally to sexual intercourse (Freund & Blanchard, 1986). Courtship disorder is not a DSM diagnosis and is not universally accepted. Some have argued that all paraphilias are courtship disorders.

Voyeurism

Voyeurism is characterized by sexual urges or fantasies of observing unsuspecting and non-consenting persons in various stages of undress or sexual activity. It is important to distinguish between true voyeurism and normal arousal from observing nudity or sexual activity. In interviews with adult heterosexual men, 54.3 percent reported sexual fantasies of secretly witnessing sexual intercourse of others, while 40.4 percent also reported a sexual interest in being unknowingly watched during intercourse. In most instances, these men would not meet the clinical criteria for voyeurism (or exhibitionism) (Aggrawal, 2009).

People with voyeurism are typically aroused as soon as they leave their apartment at night in search of strangers to spy on. In contrast, people without voyeurism might become aroused if by accident they saw a naked person through a window; their arousal is due to the nudity and not from the non-consensual nature of the situation. True voyeurs typically are not sexually aroused by attending a strip bar or a "peep-show" because they know the dancers know they are being watched. While women can be diagnosed with voyeurism, almost all arrests for voyeurism involve male offenders. Some research has indicated that at the time of arrest, the typical voyeur is a married man in his late twenties with a long history of offending (generally and sexually), beginning in adolescence (Aggrawal, 2009).

Frotteurism

Also referred to as toucherism, *frotteurism* is characterized by sexual urges or fantasies of touching or rubbing one's genitals against an unsuspecting person. The intention is to become more sexually aroused. Typically, people with frotteurism seek out crowded places, such as crowded subways or concerts.

Some claim that approximately 85 percent of people diagnosed with frotteurism also have another courtship disorder paraphilia (Aggrawal, 2009). Most frotteurs are between the ages of 15 and 25; but there is also a subgroup of older men, often with social inhibitions, who engage in frotteuristic activities. Many incidents of frotteurism have been reported in Japan. Overcrowding on mass transit and public awareness of the problem in Japan may account for this. One survey found that 58.4 percent of adult women in Japan disclosed being touched sexually by an unknown person in public (Aggrawal, 2009).

Management of Sex Offenders Within the Community
Criminal Justice Approaches

After a sex offender is convicted and serves his or her sentence, that person is released into the community. In Canada, the majority of people charged with sexual offences are also subject to a range of other community supervision orders while on bail, during pretrial, and after release from prison (e.g., a conditional sentence, probation, parole, or long-term supervision orders). When offenders are released at their statutory release date (two-thirds of their sentence), probation and parole supervision occurs. For sex offenders who are deemed to be a high risk for committing another sexual offence or serious personal injury crime, the option exists to keep such individuals incarcerated until the very end of their sentence, known as the **warrant expiry date (WED)**. The rationale for using this option is to keep the offender incapacitated for as long as possible due to his or her high risk to recidivate. One significant drawback of holding offenders until their WED is that they are released into the community without any criminal justice control because they have served their full sentence (Rice, Murphy, & Fedoroff, 2011). This lack of criminal justice follow-up is perplexing since these high-risk individuals are the ones most in need of criminal justice sanctions to help them successfully reintegrate into the community.

In response to this shortcoming, a community policing peace bond known as the **810.1 order** was created. This is a prohibition order for sex offenders who are deemed to be a high risk to commit another sexual offence or a serious personal injury crime. This recognizance order, as well as probation or parole orders, includes a list of conditions designed to help monitor and limit the person's movement, accommodations, and social interactions. The order also includes specific requirements of the person under supervision, such as frequent meetings with a supervising officer (a probation, parole,

warrant expiry date (WED)
A correctional option to detain a sexual offender until the very end of his or her sentence. Those who are detained under a WED have been deemed to be a high risk for committing another sexual offence or serious personal injury offence until the very end of their sentence.

810.1 order
A community prohibition order for sexual offenders deemed to be a high risk that includes conditions designed to monitor and limit the person's movement, accommodations, and social interactions.

or bail officer), and attendance in specific treatment programs. The intended objectives of the order are to provide a structured release of the offender that results in maximum public protection and management of risk for sexual recidivism. Other stated objectives of this order include monitoring former offenders' whereabouts and limiting behaviours associated with their previous offence (such as consuming alcohol or using the Internet). An 810.1 order expires automatically after two years, but it can be renewed (*Criminal Code*, 1985; Rice, Murphy, & Fedoroff, 2011).

Under provincial community safety legislation, public notification about the release of high-risk sex offenders and other violent offenders is permitted. The rationale is to improve public protection through the release of information on high-risk offenders. Public notification can take the form of (1) notification of only local law enforcement; (2) notification of local law enforcement and relevant community organizations, such as schools and recreational facilities; or (3) broad notification within a certain radius through the use of media and/or flyers. Decisions on whether to undertake public notification and the appropriate level of notification are made by the police and a high-risk offender committee. However, public notification is rarely used, and when it is, it is supposed to happen only after all available alternatives have been considered (Murphy, Fedoroff, & Martineau, 2009).

When an offender who has been convicted of a designated sexual offence is released into the community, he or she is required to report to a local law enforcement agency to register on the Ontario and/or National SOR. The registrant is required to report for a designated period of time (e.g., 10 years, 20 years, or life). This database contains information such as the registrant's name, address, date of birth, photo, and sexual offence history. Unlike SORs in the United States, which are publicly accessible via the Internet, Canada's SORs are private and are not linked to the system of public notification. Critics of SORs in the United States have suggested that a system of open registries goes beyond public protection and focuses more on public shaming and branding (Murphy, Brodsky, et al., 2009). See Box 14.2 for a discussion of the ethical issues surrounding the use of SORs and public notification.

From a policing perspective, SORs are meant to be used as an investigative tool. This perspective is based on the rationale that having current and reliable information on convicted sex offenders will be useful in the investigation of new child abductions or sexual crimes, enabling police to identify or rule out suspects more efficiently. Criminologists have also suggested that SORs may provide a deterrent effect, because it is assumed that being on the registry may make offenders more reluctant to commit a new sexual offence. Additionally, SORs may be a general deterrent effect for potential first-time offenders. To date, research has yet to conclusively support such a rationale (Murphy, Fedoroff, & Martineau, 2009).

Some high-risk sex offenders and other violent offenders in Canada can be considered for a dangerous offender (DO) or long-term offender (LTO) designation. These designations are the result of a sentencing hearing and only occur following the offence that the offender was most recently convicted for (known as the *predicate offence*). Unlike SVP legislation in the United States, DOs in Canada are designated as such at the time of their criminal sentence and are not civilly committed at the end of their criminal sentence, as is the case for SVPs in the United States. The following criteria must be met for the Crown attorney (prosecution) to raise the question of a DO or LTO designation:

BOX 14.2

Ethical Issues with Public Notification and the Registration of Sex Offenders

Sex offender registration and public notification are controversial issues and have been subject to considerable ethical criticism and litigation throughout North America. Opponents have drawn attention to a number of fundamental human rights issues, such as imposing additional measures on sex offenders that do not apply to non-sex offenders. This argument suggests that since those with higher recidivism rates (e.g., break-and-enter offenders, drunk drivers) or those causing serious personal injury (e.g., murderers) are not subject to such scrutiny, sex offenders should not be either. Another argument against SORs is the fact that registries and public notification may create a false sense of security, since the majority of sex offenders are not repeat offenders (Murphy, 2013).

Similarly, critics argue that it is unfair to impose additional measures on sex offenders because they have already paid their debt to society upon completing their sentence. From a research perspective, the rationale for public notification and registration is not to add punishment but to manage risk of recidivism. This perspective can be challenged on several grounds because sex offenders as a group do not pose a higher risk to recidivate than many other offender types. Even within the sex offender population, great variation in risk exists between different sex offender types. However, this variation is not identified in public SORs, such as those found in the United States. As a result, a male convicted of sexual assault for slapping the buttocks of an unknown female after a night of drinking would appear on the registry alongside someone with a long history of violent sexual assaults against strangers. When the public accesses this registry in the United States, they will see no differentiation between these offender types.

Giving the public unrestricted access to SORs without educating them on how to deal with this information has been found to heighten general community fear. Although open SORs are intended to provide a sense of awareness for the public while the former offender reintegrates into the community, they often elicit feelings of anger and increase the danger of vigilante actions. Numerous incidents of unintended consequences and **vigilantism** have been cited across the United States, leading to ostracism of registrants by family, loss of stable jobs or housing, dropping out of therapy, destruction of personal property, and, in some cases, violence so severe it resulted in death (Murphy, 2013; Murphy, Brodsky, et al., 2009).

Research has shown that when SORs are open to the public (as is the case in the United States), the result is significantly lower rates of registrant compliance as compared with SORs that are accessible to law enforcement only (as is the case in Canada). In Canada, rates of SOR compliance are typically around 95 percent, whereas in some American states, compliance rates range between 40 percent and 60 percent (Murphy, Brodsky, et al., 2009). These findings are problematic because offenders who choose to become non-compliant and "go underground" lose access to a more stable lifestyle with social support and treatment options. Registrants who become non-compliant are at a much higher risk for recidivism (Murphy, 2013; Murphy & Fedoroff, 2013). SORs might be justified if the effectiveness of public notification and registration was supported by research. However, to date that has not been the case.

vigilantism

When a person or group of people take the law into their own hands, typically in a violent manner, in an attempt to effect justice according to their understanding of what is right and wrong.

- commission of a serious personal injury offence;
- a pattern of persistent, aggressive, and repetitive behaviour;
- failure of the offender to restrain his or her actions;
- indifference to consequences of his or her behaviour;
- index offence so brutal it is unlikely inhibited by normal standards; and
- when there is a history of sexual offences, failure to control his or her sexual impulses (Fedoroff, Ranger, & Murphy, 2013; Petrunik, Murphy, & Fedoroff, 2008).

The primary difference between a DO and an LTO is that the DO is deemed to be such a high risk that he or she cannot reasonably be managed within the community. A DO can be given either an indeterminate or determinate sentence. With an LTO, although the person meets all of the requirements above, it is determined that with appropriate interventions that are currently available, a reasonable prospect exists that the person can be managed within the community. The LTO is given a determinate sentence with up to ten years of community supervision. Judges must consider the LTO designation before they consider a DO designation (Fedoroff, Ranger, & Murphy, 2013; Petrunik, Murphy, Fedoroff, 2008).

Treatment and Prevention

Contemporary treatments of sex offenders typically combine different psychological and psychopharmalogical approaches. Three psychological therapeutic treatments commonly used during the past three decades target cognitions and behaviour. *Cognitive-behavioural therapy* (CBT) gained popularity during the 1980s and remains one of the most frequently cited approaches for the treatment of paraphilias and sexual offending. The goal of CBT in this population is to increase control over problematic sexual interests and behaviours and to equip patients with the skills and attitudes necessary to achieve their goals in healthy and prosocial ways. CBT is commonly used in combination with other treatment approaches.

Relapse prevention (RP) techniques, commonly used with CBT, work to identify behavioural chains and triggers that increase the likelihood of relapse or recidivism. The intention of RP is to assist the patient to identify, anticipate, and cope with triggers that may lead to a potential relapse or reoffence. In addition to cognitive and behavioural measures, RP uses educational and skill-developing approaches. RP therapy for sex offenders received a setback when a large randomized controlled study failed to show that it significantly improved outcomes. Explanations for this unexpected result are discussed in Fedoroff and Marshall (2010).

Emerging from criticisms of RP, which focuses on avoidance, the *Good Lives Model* (GLM) has risen in prominence to become the most commonly used psychological treatment approach in Canadian prisons and community-based treatment programs. The GLM focuses on ways to maximize human potential and individual strengths rather than focusing on psychological deficits (as is often the case in CBT and RP). This model is based on a strength-based framework and uses an individualized rehabilitative approach to interests, abilities, and aspirations. Concerning paraphilias and sexual offending, the model suggests that people exhibit deviant sexual interests or behaviours because they lack the internal and external resources necessary to satisfy sexual needs in less harmful ways. The attainment of happiness and well-being includes healthy living through physical satisfaction, inner peace through emotional regulation, and relatedness through intimacy. The GLM seeks to help individuals identify any obstacles that prevent them from living the a "good life." GLM therapy not only identifies the resources the patient is missing but also provides the patient with tools useful to live in a more fulfilling, pro-social, and law-abiding manner (Murphy, Bradford, & Fedoroff, in press).

Several psychopharmacological approaches can also be used to treat paraphilias and sex offenders. Common medications used include those that target neurotransmitters in the brain (such as selective serotonin reuptake inhibitors [SSRIs]) and hormones (such as anti-androgens that decrease circulating testosterone levels). Modulation of SSRIs has been found to decrease problematic sexual interests and behaviours; for some, a re-emergence of healthy sexual interests and behaviours occurs as a result. When the desired goal of treatment is the reduction of overall sex drive, the use of anti-androgens (sometimes called "chemical castration") has been identified as the gold standard. The suppression of sexual arousal can help patients focus on aspects of treatment designed to correct previous social skills deficits (Murphy, Bradford, & Federoff, in press). That is, the use of anti-androgens can eliminate the persistent sexual thoughts that many individuals with paraphilias report. This medication allows them to focus on treatment of the underlying issues that led to the development of their deviant sexual interest or behaviours in the first place. Once their lives are normalized, it is possible in many cases to taper or stop the medication, which results in the return of sex drive, but this time within a prosocial relationship. This approach makes the idea of trying medication much more acceptable to patients, who should always be allowed to provide informed, revocable consent to treatment.

Effectiveness of Treatment

Marshall and colleagues (2008) reviewed the effectiveness of the sex offender treatment program used in a Canadian federal prison system over the past 15 years. The program uses elements of CBT, the GLM, and RNR. The sample included 534 sex offenders (352 child molesters and 182 rapists) who had been living in the community for an average of 5.42 years. Based on the averaged risk levels, the expected recidivism rate for the group was 40 percent for general recidivism and 16.8 percent for sexual recidivism. The reported sexual recidivism rate after treatment was significantly below the rate expected: 3.2 percent for sexual recidivism (1.6 percent for rapists and 4.0 percent for child molesters) and 13.6 percent for general recidivism.

Although the majority of studies on sex offender treatment focuses on recidivism, interest has increased in preventive approaches that seek to provide treatment for individuals with problematic sexual interests before they go on to commit an offence. For example, the German initiative Prevention Project Dunkelfeld treats people who have a sexual interest in children but have never been identified by law enforcement. The initiative's media campaign has included advertisements on local buses that ask the question "Do you like kids too much?" and provides a number to call for assessment and treatment. The treatment program is located in Berlin, and the project has seen a self-referral rate of 15 to 20 individuals monthly from all over Europe. Approximately half of the self-referrals are people who had committed an offence in the past but remained undetected, and the rest are people who have never acted on their interests. Such proactive and preventive approaches not only get pedophilic men and women involved in treatment before they create a victim but also provide treatment to sex offenders who have never been detected by the criminal justice system. The positive effects of such programs are immeasurable.

Circles of Support and Accountability (CoSA) is another initiative that has been receiving increased attention for its positive work with sex offenders who have been released to the community. CoSA is an innovative, non-profit, community reintegration program designed to address the unique needs of convicted sex offenders in the process of reintegrating into the community. Sex offenders assisted by the program are at a high risk to recidivate and, as a result, have been detained by the criminal justice system until their WED. Since these offenders are detained until their WED, they are released into the community without any criminal justice supports to assist with the reintegration process. The CoSA program aims to prevent future sexual victimization by introducing offenders to trained volunteers who support the reintegration of released sex offenders into the community. The unique goals of this program are underlined by its twin mottos: "no more victims" and "no one is disposable."

A study on the recidivism rates of former sex offenders involved with CoSA in Canada showed very encouraging results. In the study, recidivism was defined as any new charges or convictions. A group of 44 former offenders in CoSA were matched with a group of similar offenders not involved in the program. Results over a three-year follow-up period found that the CoSA group had significantly lower levels of all types of recidivism. Sexual recidivism for the CoSA group was 2.27 percent as compared with 13.67 percent in the control group. Violent recidivism was 9.09 percent for the CoSA group and 34.09 percent for the control group. Any type of recidivism at all, including breaches of correctional conditions, occurred at a rate of 11.36 percent for the CoSA group and 38.64 percent for the control group (Wilson, Cortoni, & McWhinnie, 2009).

Conclusion

Sexual offending, especially against children, is a serious problem. Many factors can impact the nature of criminal sexual behaviours over time and place. The goals of the criminal justice system in Canada and the United States are to provide general deterrence, incapacitation, punishment, rehabilitation, and management of the risk posed by sex offenders. It is crucial for the justice system to maintain a balance between public safety and protection of the individual rights of victims and the accused. Sexual offences against both adults and children have been steadily decreasing on a global scale since the 1980s.

Large variations exist within sex offender populations, and it is important to examine the characteristics, risk levels, and recidivism rates of each subgroup separately. A number of developmental, demographic, and offence-related characteristics are associated with increased risk of sexual recidivism. Although Canada's sex offender legislation has developed at a much slower pace than that of the United States, no evidence indicates that recidivism rates are lower in the United States.

It is important to distinguish clinical and legal conceptualizations of sexual offences from unconventional sexual interests. Various treatment approaches and community-based initiatives have shown promise in reducing sexual recidivism. More research needs to be conducted on ways to manage the limited risk posed by sex offenders and on treatment options to prevent sexual crimes and further reduce sexual recidivism.

SUMMARY OF KEY POINTS

- While working to deter, punish, rehabilitate, and manage the risk posed by sex offenders, the justice system must also maintain a balance between public safety and protection of the individual rights of the accused. Attempts to maintain this balance can be especially difficult when dealing with sex offenders, a subgroup of offenders who are viewed by society as highly dangerous and "morally tainted."

- Individuals who have committed a sexual offence are often classified as a homogeneous group. However, there are wide variations in offender characteristics (such as gender, age, socio-economic background, personality, intelligence, attitude, and social skills). Offence characteristics and subsequent risk of recidivism vary widely.

- Two important concepts in this area are *dangerousness* and *risk*. They have a long history in civil and criminal legislation and correctional and psychiatric practice. *Dangerousness* refers to the capacity of a person to harm oneself or others. It includes an estimation of the severity, imminence, predictability, and likelihood of harm. *Risk* typically refers only to the probability that a person will commit future harmful acts.

- The emergence of a community protection approach during the late 1980s and early 1990s resulted from concerns that previous models had not given enough attention to overall public safety and the rights of victims. The primary focus of this new approach was not on the treatment or rehabilitation of the individual offender but on the overall safety of the community.

- A common misconception is that all sex offenders have a high frequency of recidivism. Official statistics and research studies do not support this assumption.

- Large variations exist within sex offender populations, and it is important to examine the characteristics, risk levels, and recidivism rates of each subgroup separately.

- It is important to distinguish clinical and legal conceptualizations of sexual offences from unconventional sexual interests.

- Various treatment approaches and community-based initiatives have shown promise in reducing sexual recidivism.

NOTES

1. Adapted from Boyd (2012).
2. For updates on this and other cases and issues, go to the Updates tab on the book's website, www.emp.ca/CRIM.

QUESTIONS FOR CRITICAL DISCUSSION

1. In what ways have the media perpetuated the myth of "stranger danger"?
2. When looking at studies on recidivism, what factors are important to take into account?

3. Why is it important to examine sex offenders by their offence type instead of as a singular type of offender?

4. Why is it important to differentiate between paraphilias and sexual offences?

5. What are the pros and cons of public sex offender registries and private sex offender registries?

SUGGESTED FURTHER READINGS

Aggrawal, A. (2009). *Forensic and medico-legal aspects of sexual crimes and unusual sexual practices*. Boca Raton, FL: CRC Press.

Bartol, C., & Bartol, A. (2008). *Criminal behaviour: A psychosocial approach* (8th ed.). Englewood Cliffs, NJ: Prentice Hall.

McAlinden, A.M. (2007). *The shaming of sex offenders: Risk, retribution and reintegration*. Portland, OR: Hart.

Petrunik, M. (2003). The hare and the tortoise: Dangerous and sex offender policy in the United States and Canada. *The Canadian Journal of Criminology and Criminal Justice*, *45*(4), 43–72.

Saleh, F.M., Grudzinskas, A.J., Bradford, J.M., & Brodsky, D.J. (2009). *Sex offenders: Identification, risk assessment, treatment, and legal issues*. New York: Oxford University Press.

Websites

American Psychiatric Association DSM-5 Development: http://www.dsm5.org

Circles of Support and Accountability (CoSA): http://www.cosacanada.com

Prevention Project Dunkelfeld (PPD): https://www.dont-offend.org

Sex Offender Information Registration Act (Government of Canada): http://laws.justice.gc.ca/eng/acts/S-8.7/

REFERENCES

Aggrawal, A. (2009). *Forensic and medico-legal aspects of sexual crimes and unusual sexual practices*. Boca Raton, FL: CRC Press.

American Psychiatric Association. (2013). *Diagnostic and statistical manual of mental disorders* (5th ed.). Washington, DC: American Psychiatric Association.

Andrews, D., & Bonta, J. (1998). *The psychology of criminal conduct*. Cincinnati, OH: Anderson.

Bartol, C., & Bartol, A. (2008). *Criminal behaviour: A psychosocial approach* (8th ed.). Englewood Cliffs, NJ: Prentice Hall.

Boyd, N. (2012, June 7). Magnotta arrest telling illustration of power of Internet. *Globe and Mail*. Retrieved from http://www.theglobeandmail.com/globe-debate/magnotta-arrest-telling-illustration-of-power-of-internet/article4237414/.

Bradford, A., & Meston, C. (2011). Sex and gender disorders. In H. Barlow (Ed.), *The Oxford handbook of clinical psychology* (pp. 446–468). New York: Oxford University Press.

Bureau of Justice Statistics. (2006). *Rape rates have been stable in recent years*. The National Crime Victimization Survey. U.S. Department of Justice. Retrieved from http://www.ojp.gov/bjs/glance/rape.htm.

Connelly, C., & Williamson, S. (2000). Review of the research literature on serious violent and sexual offenders. *Crime and Criminal Justice Research Findings*, *46*, 1–121. Edinburgh, Scottish Executive Central Research Unit.

Craissati, J. (2004). Managing high risk sex offenders in the community: A psychological approach. New York: Brunner-Routledge.

Fedoroff, J.P. (2008). Treatment of paraphilic sexual disorders. In D. Rowland & L. Incrocci (Eds.), *Handbook of sexual and gender identity disorders* (pp. 563–586). Hoboken, NJ: John Wiley and Sons.

Fedoroff, J.P. (2010). Paraphilic worlds. In S.D. Levine, C.B. Risen, & S.E. Althof (Eds.), *The handbook of clinical sexuality for mental health professionals* (2nd ed., pp. 401–424). New York: Routledge.

Fedoroff, J.P., Di Gioacchino, L., & Murphy, L. (2013). Diagnostic dilemmas for the paraphilias. *Current Psychiatry Reports*, *15*(363), 1–6.

Fedoroff, J.P., Fishell, A., & Fedoroff, B. (1999). A case series of women evaluated for paraphilic sexual disorders. *The Canadian Journal of Human Sexuality*, *8*(2), 127–140.

Fedoroff, J.P., & Marshall, W.L. (2010). Paraphilias. In D. McKay, J.S. Abramowitz, & S. Taylor (Eds.), *Cognitive behavioural therapy for refractory cases*. Washington, DC: American Psychological Association.

Fedoroff, J.P., Ranger, R., & Murphy, L. (2013). *Sexually violent predator programs: Who gets released?* Paper presented at the annual meeting of American Academy of Psychiatry and the Law (AAPL), San Diego, CA.

Freeman-Longo, R. (1996). Feel good legislation: Prevention or calamity. *Journal of Child Abuse & Neglect*, *20*(2), 95–101.

Freund, K., & Blanchard, R. (1986). The concept of courtship disorder. *Journal of Sex & Marital Therapy*, *12*(2), 79–92.

Greenfield, L. (1997). *Sex offences and offenders: An analysis of data on rape and sexual assault*. Washington, DC: US Department of Justice, Bureau of Justice Statistics.

Hanson, R.K., & Bussière, M.T. (1996). *Predictors of sexual offender recidivism: A meta-analysis* (user report 96-04). Ottawa: Department of the Solicitor General of Canada.

Hanson, R.K., & Bussière, M.T. (1998). Predicting relapse: A meta-analysis of sexual offender recidivism studies. *Journal of Consulting and Clinical Psychology*, *66*(2), 348–362.

Hanson, R.K., & Harris, A. (1998). *Dynamic predictors of sexual recidivism*. Ottawa: Public Works and Government Services Canada, Department of the Solicitor General of Canada.

Hanson, R.K., Harris, A., Helmus, L., & Thorton, D. (in press). High risk sex offenders may not be high risk forever. *Journal of Interpersonal Violence*.

Hanson, R.K., Morton, K., & Harris, A. (2003). Sexual offender recidivism: What we know and what we need to know. In R. Prentky, E. Janus, & M. Seto (Eds.), *Sexually coercive behaviour: Understanding and management*. New York: New York Academy of Sciences.

Harris, A., & Hanson, K. (2004). *Sex offender recidivism: A simple question*. Ottawa: Public Safety and Emergency Preparedness.

Jenkins, P. (2001). *Beyond tolerance: Child pornography on the Internet*. New York: New York University Press.

Kemshall, H., & Wood, J. (2007). Beyond public protection: An examination of community protection and public health approaches to high risk offenders. *Criminology and Criminal Justice*, *7*(3), 203–222.

Makin, K. (2011, January 21). Why Canada's prisons can't cope with flood of mentally ill inmates. *Globe and Mail*. Retrieved from http://www.theglobeandmail.com/news/national/why -canadas-prisons-cant-cope-with-flood-of-mentally-ill-inmates/article563604/?page=all.

Marshall, W.L., Marshall, L., & Fernandez, Y. (2008). The Rockwood Preparatory Program for sexual offenders: Description and preliminary appraisal. *Sex Abuse*, *20*(1), 25–42.

McAlinden, A.M. (2007). *The shaming of sex offenders: Risk, retribution and reintegration*. Portland, OR: Hart.

Murphy, L. (2013). *Ethics of sex offender management: Is there a right answer?* Paper presented at the annual meeting of American Academy of Psychiatry and the Law (AAPL), San Diego, CA.

Murphy, L., Bradford, J., & Fedoroff, J.P. (in press). Treatment of paraphilias and paraphilic disorders. In G. Gabbard (Ed.), *Gabbard's treatment of psychiatric disorders* (5th ed.). New York: Oxford University Press.

Murphy, L., Brodsky, D., Brackel, J., Petrunik, M., Fedoroff, P., & Grudzinskas, A. (2009). Community-based management of sex offenders: An examination of sex offender registries and community notification in the United States and Canada. In F.M., Saleh, A.J. Grudzinskas, J.M. Bradford, & D.J. Brodsky (Eds.), *Sex offenders: Identification, risk assessment, treatment, and legal issues* (pp. 412–424). New York: Oxford University Press.

Murphy, L., & Fedoroff, J.P. (2013). Sexual offenders' views of Canadian sex offender registries: A survey of a clinical sample. *Canadian Journal of Behavioural Sciences* (Sex crime edition), *45*(3), 238–249.

Murphy, L., Fedoroff, P., & Martineau, M. (2009). Canada's sex offender registries: Background, implementation, and social policy considerations. *Canadian Journal of Human Sexuality*, *18*(1–2), 61–72.

Murphy, L., Ranger, R., & Fedoroff, J.P. (in press). Legal and clinical issues in interpreting child pornography on the Internet. In *Adolescent sex offenders in the digital world*. New York: Oxford University Press.

Parrish, J. (2013, August 2). Marek says posting grisly video was a public service, claims he's being persecuted. *CTVNews.ca*. Retrieved from http://edmonton.ctvnews.ca/marek-says -posting-grisly-video-was-a-public-service-claims-he-s-being-persecuted-1.1396322.

Perreault, S. (2013). Police-reported crime statistics in Canada, 2012. *Juristat*. Catalogue no. 85-002-X. Ottawa: Minister of Industry.

Petrunik, M. (1982). The politics of dangerousness. *International Journal of Law and Psychiatry*, *5*, 225–253.

Petrunik, M. (2002). Managing unacceptable risk: Sex offenders, community response, and social policy in the United States. *International Journal of Offender Therapy and Comparative Criminology*, *46*(4), 483–511.

Petrunik, M. (2003). The hare and the tortoise: Dangerous and sex offender policy in the United States and Canada. *The Canadian Journal of Criminology and Criminal Justice*, *45*(4), 43–72.

Petrunik, M. (2005). Dangerousness and its discontents: A discourse on the socio-politics of dangerousness. In S. Burns (Ed.), *Ethnographies of law and social control: The sociology of law, deviance and social control* (Vol. 6, pp. 49–74). New York: Elsevier, JAI.

Petrunik, M., & Deutschmann, L. (2008). The exclusion-inclusion spectrum in state and community responses to sex offenders in Anglo-American and European jurisdictions. *International Journal of Offender Therapy and Comparative Criminology*, *52*(5), 499–519.

Petrunik, M., Murphy, L., & Fedoroff, P. (2008). American and Canadian approaches to sex offenders: A study of the politics of dangerousness. *Federal Sentencing Reporter*, *21*(2), 111–123.

Quinsey, V., Harris, G., Rice, M., & Cormier, C. (1998). *Violent offenders: Appraising and managing risk*. Washington, DC: American Psychology Association.

Rice, S., Murphy, L., & Fedoroff, J.P. (2011). *Community correctional conditions imposed on sex offenders in Canada: Is more always better?* Paper presented at the annual meeting of American Academy of Psychiatry and the Law (AAPL), Boston.

Seto, M. (2013). *Internet sex offenders*. Washington, DC: American Psychological Association.

Sinclair, R.L., & Sugar, D. 2005. *Internet-based child sexual exploitation environmental scan.* Ottawa: Royal Canadian Mounted Police.

Thomas, T. (2005). *Sex crime: Sex offending and society.* Devon, UK: Willan.

Webster, C., & Hucker, S. (2003). *Release decision making.* Hamilton, ON: St. Joseph's Healthcare.

Wilson, R., Cortoni, F., & McWhinnie, A. (2009). Circles of support and accountability: A Canadian national replication of outcome findings. *Sexual Abuse: A Journal of Research and Treatment, 21*(4), 412–430.

Wolak, J., Finkelhor, D., & Mitchell, K. (2011). Child pornography possessors: Trends in offender and case characteristics. *Sexual Abuse: A Journal of Research and Treatment, 23*(1), 22-42.

Legislation

Criminal Code. (1985). RSC 1985, c. C-46.

CASE STUDY 15.1

Profile of a Property Crime Offender

The following passage provides an example of the sort of context in which property crime often occurs. It also offers a glimpse into the life circumstances commonly faced by homeless youth who commit property crime, and all too often engage in knowingly self-destructive behaviours. It is a personal account of the experiences of a young girl in New Brunswick we shall call Laura. She describes the process of becoming homeless, resorting to stealing food to survive, considering suicide, and enduring abusive relationships with both parents and peers.

A young homeless woman panhandling on the street.

It all started when I was living with my father. My dad, my younger brother, and me were living with my grandfather in Fredericton. My father physically abused me and my brother so I left. My little brother stayed because he was only 8 and I felt bad about that. I went to go live with my cousin's family. I lived there for a couple months. After, I went to go live with my mom, but she kicked me out after a few weeks. She left me with some clothes, that's about it. I was 13 years old and it was the first time I had ever felt alone. I had no contact with my mom because I had no phone number from her and no contact with my dad because he moved to Newfoundland for work.

So I was living with some of my friends that had their own place. It was the worst place I had ever lived in. A lot of kids around my age might think I would be living the life, not having to go to school and hanging out with my friends all day and partying all night. And I was for awhile. It was fun for about two months, but the house was always dirty and it stunk. There were animal feces everywhere. I slept on the floor. There was barely any food in the house, and when there was, nobody was allowed to eat it. There were always people moving in and out. Sometimes there were 20 or more people staying here. There was no hot water, ever! There was always conflict between everyone.

Finally, after so long, I moved out with another friend that lived next door to my other friends. He was 20 and I was now 14. It seemed great then. But when I think about it now, what we were doing was wrong; we were having sex. But as the stupid 14-year-old I was, I thought it was okay at the time, even though my best friend told me it wasn't and that the guy could get arrested and go to jail. I just knew that it was a way to survive. I lived with him for about three weeks until we got into a fight and I got kicked out.

For about five months, I would spend the night here and there. I would steal food, collect bottles, panhandle … anything I could do to survive. At this point I felt like I had nothing. I felt suicidal and thought I had nothing to live for, but then I would think about my little brother and stay strong. The sad part about all of this is that my family wouldn't help me at all. When I was not allowed to stay at a friend's house anymore, I had to resort to the outside, sleeping on park benches and slides at the park.

In June I went to my aunt's to see if she knew either my mom's or my dad's number, and it so happened she did. I called and they both sent me a total of about $200 for my birthday. Stupid me, I spent a lot of it on booze, but I bought food and clothes with the rest of the money. I did some panhandling for food when I ran out but I got arrested and got a $140 fine. For about four months that was how my life was, lonely and worthless. I felt there was no point to it at all until I met a family that I will never forget.

They helped me with everything. I still felt lonely, but I felt that there was something to live for. I got into contact with my mom again. She came from Nova Scotia where she had moved to be with a new boyfriend. They had broken up so she wanted to start again too.

My mom and me stayed at a friend's house for about a week. I didn't feel as alone anymore, 'cause I had someone with me. My mom and me went to the Salvation Army and they told us about a family emergency shelter, so my mom's friend drove us to Moncton. We stayed till the beginning of February.

It wasn't that bad, considering I had a bed to sleep in, food in my stomach, people to talk to and money that they gave us every week. The only thing I didn't like was everyone had a problem with someone else that stayed there and some people were there only because they were lazy. Living in a shelter showed me a lot, like there are more people than just me who understand the things that I have been through. There are also people for everything. Someone to help us find a place, meet new people and someone to help us once we move into the community.

I am fifteen now, and that all happened in two years. Wow. I am happy now. I am no longer living with my mother. I was removed by the Children's Aid Society as she became abusive too. I am staying in a foster home, and my little brother is here too. I am as happy as I have been for a long time.

Source: Adapted with permission from The Homeless Hub. http://www.homelesshub.ca.

Before You Read Chapter 15

- This case study mentions an instance in which someone must steal food to simply survive. What other sorts of motivations come to mind when you think of someone committing "property crime"?

- Have you ever been the victim of property crime (e.g., had your home broken into or vehicle stolen)? What did you learn from that experience?

- After reading this chapter, return to this case study. Consider the significant factors that correlate with property crime in the study discussed later on in this chapter. How many of those factors can you identify in the case study above?

Property Crime

Introduction: A Brief History of Property Crime Laws

As we saw in Chapter 3 (Criminal Law in Canada), Canadian criminal laws, including laws governing property, came directly from English common law. Jerome Hall (1952), an internationally recognized scholar for his research on criminal law and jurisprudence, traced the growth of property and theft laws to the rise of commerce and industrialization in 18th-century England. He noted that, with the beginning of business and trade, a new economic class of traders and industrialists emerged who needed protection for their property and other business interests. These laws included what today would be called **embezzlement** laws and laws governing stolen property and **obtaining goods under false pretenses** (Vago, 1997, p. 56).

Generally, two theoretical perspectives are used to understand the emergence of such laws and their enforcement: **structural functionalism** and **conflict theory**. According to structural functionalists, crime, including property crime, is inevitable in all societies. Moreover, they consider property crime laws to be based on a shared belief system in which customs, over time, become codified into legal statutes believed to promote solidarity and stability in society. This sociological perspective was originally proposed by Émile Durkheim (1933) in France in the late 19th century, and was prominent until the 1960s (see also Chapter 12, Sociological Approaches).

In the 1970s and early 1980s, however, **Marxist**-inspired scholars (e.g., Chambliss & Seidman, 1982; Quinney, 1975; Reasons & Rich, 1978) began to interpret research such as Hall's by arguing that theft laws were created to primarily protect the interests of the capitalist class. As such, since law making and enforcement were put into place by the state to protect the interests of the propertied class,

embezzlement
To take money or misappropriate funds that belong to someone else.

obtaining goods under false pretenses
Misrepresenting the truth to obtain goods that belong to someone else.

structural functionalism
A sociological theory that explains how society functions according to the structure of a system of interrelated parts.

conflict theories
Theories, originating primarily with Marx, that focus on the unequal distribution of power in society—for example, due to class, race, or gender.

Marxism
A school of thought developed by Karl Marx (1818–1883) arguing that society must be understood in terms of social conflict, class relations, and the inequalities caused by capitalism; Marxists promote revolution by the working class.

the working class was viewed to bear the brunt of this one-sided legal system. For Marxist conflict theorists, property crimes committed by those from the working class are subject to criminalization, while the illegal activities of the elites are considered to be largely immune from legal censure.

In more recent years, the conflict viewpoint has been judged to be a rather simplistic and instrumental interpretation of the origins of property law. Law making, including the making and amending of property laws, is now considered to be a more complex and dynamic process than what the conflict interpretation would suggest. For instance, if property laws existed simply as a means to protect the property of the rich from the thieving poor, why is it that a great deal of property crime victims are from the working class? Research has shown that a majority of street crime, including that related to property, is **intra-class crime**. That is, it takes place between people with similar social class backgrounds (Tunnell, 2006). Also, in recent years, particularly in the United States, a number of high-profile property crime cases have involved offenders from privileged backgrounds who have been sentenced to lengthy prison terms. For example, in 2009, Bernie Madoff, a New York millionaire, was given a 150-year prison sentence for defrauding investors of over $60 billion dollars. And in Canada, in 2009, Garth Drabinski and Myron Gottlieb, founders and executives of Livent (an entertainment company), were found guilty of defrauding investors of $500 million and were sent to prison for seven and six years, respectively (Canadian Press, 2012; O'Grady, 2011).

Regardless of the various interpretations of the origins of property laws and whose interests they may or may not support in society, what is clear is that the vast majority of property offenders who come before the courts, unlike Drabinski and Gottlieb, are people who do not have a great amount of power and prestige in society. Many are young, have relatively low levels of formal education, and are poor. Indeed, this profile will be returned to later in the chapter when the analysis shifts to an empirical study of a group of socially excluded property crime offenders.

Defining, Measuring, and Penalizing Property Crime in Canada

Property crime involves the taking of money or property, and unlike robbery, does not involve force or threat of force against a victim. The main types of property crime listed in the Canadian *Criminal Code* are as follows:

- theft (theft under and theft over $5,000)
- break and enter
- mischief (vandalism)
- possession of stolen property
- arson
- motor vehicle theft
- fraud

According to Figure 15.1, since 1962 rates of police-reported property crimes have consistently been greater than rates of all other forms of police-reported crimes in Canada, including violent crime. In 2012, property and other *Criminal Code* non-violent offences accounted for about four-fifths of police-reported *Criminal Code* incidents in Canada (excluding traffic offences). The trend lines in Figure 15.1 clearly show that

intra-class crime
Crime in which the victim and offender are from the same social group (e.g., an ethnic or racial group); by contrast, inter-class crime takes place between different social groups.

FIGURE 15.1   Police-Reported Crime Rates, Canada, 1962–2012

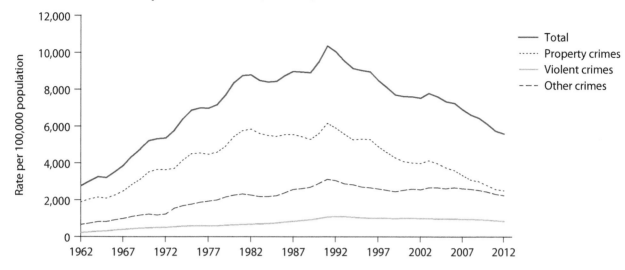

Note: Information presented in this chart represents data from the UCR Aggregate (UCR1) Survey, and permits historical comparisons back to 1962. New definitions of crime categories were introduced in 2009 and are only available in the new format back to 1998. As a result, numbers in this chart will not match data released in the new UCR2 format. Specifically, the definition of violent crime has been expanded. In addition, UCR1 includes some different offences in the "Other" crimes category.

Source: Perrault (2013, Chart 1).

rates of police-reported property offences have been declining since the early 1990s. In 2012, the rate of property offences was about half what it was in the early 1990s.

Break and enter and **motor vehicle theft** are two of the most common police-reported property crime offences. Every year in Canada, on average about one break-in happens every three minutes and one motor vehicle theft happens every seven minutes (Perreault, 2013). A key reason these property crimes are most often reported to the police is that insurance companies require police reports before home or vehicle owner claims can be processed. For this reason, criminologists tend to treat these crimes as reasonably reliable measures of property crime compared with property crimes that do not normally involve insurance companies, such as the possession of stolen property.

However, as Figure 15.2 illustrates, the number of motor vehicle theft and break and enter crimes have been declining in recent years. This trend continued in 2012, with about 5,500 fewer break-ins and 4,500 fewer motor vehicle thefts than were reported to the police in 2011. In 2012, the rate of break and enter was 43 percent lower than ten years earlier, and the rate of motor vehicle theft was 57 percent lower than ten years earlier.

Why have the rates of break and enter and motor vehicle theft been declining in Canada since the early 1990s? While criminologists are not in agreement in terms of what accounts for these particular shifts in property crime, there is good reason to believe that advances in home security systems and technological advances in motor vehicle anti-theft systems account, at least to some degree, for these decreases. However, as Figure 15.1 indicates, most other types of crime (including violent crime) in Canada have also been falling over this same time period. So it is possible that what accounts for the drop in property crime may also explain the decline in violent crime.

break and enter

A type of property crime where the accused trespasses on private property with intent to commit a crime.

motor vehicle theft

The act of stealing or attempting to steal a motor vehicle.

FIGURE 15.2   Break and Enter and Motor Vehicle Theft, Police-Reported Rates, Canada, 1982–2012

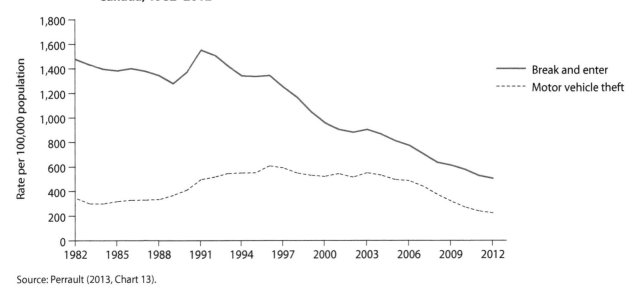

Source: Perrault (2013, Chart 13).

Even though aggregate rates of property crime have declined in Canada in recent years (particularly break and enter and motor vehicle theft), one form of property crime increased from 2009 to 2012: credit card fraud. According to data collected by the Canadian Bankers Association (n.d.), losses due to credit card fraud increased on a year-by-year basis over this four-year period. A detailed breakdown of these losses appears in Table 15.1.

In relation to credit card fraud, **counterfeiting** involves using computer devices to read and copy data encoded on a credit card's magnetic stripe, and then transferring that data to a counterfeit or blank card. The enhanced security of chip and pin technology has forced those engaged in this type of fraud to change their methods of operation. This could explain the recent increase in **card not present fraud**, which refers to fraud committed online, by phone, or by mail in a transaction for which the presence of a credit card is not necessary.

Unlike other property crimes (such as break and enter and motor vehicle theft), the police typically are not involved in investigating credit (or debit) card fraud. The major banks and financial institutions in Canada have their own security divisions that monitor and try to control this form of fraud. However, they also often work in conjunction with fraud specialists (e.g., forensic accountants from the RCMP) for credit card fraud that is committed against them. While Canadian data exist on most property crimes that could be described as "street crimes," data are lacking on the number of cases of credit card fraud that are solved as well as the nature of the penalties issued by the courts for those found guilty of this type of fraud.

The penalties for property crime vary considerably, according to the *Criminal Code*. The information in Table 15.2 displays this variation. Interestingly, maximum penalties for arson and break and enter are life in prison—the same maximum for first-degree murder.

counterfeiting

Producing imitation currency without legal sanction of the government; it is a form of fraud.

card not present fraud

A form of fraud usually carried out over the telephone or the Internet when a stolen or forged credit card is used to purchase a good or to acquire a service.

Table 15.1 Credit Card Fraud Statistics for Canadian-Issued Cards, 2009–2012

Category of credit card fraud	2009 Loss in Cdn$	2010 Loss in Cdn$	2011 Loss in Cdn$	2012 Loss in Cdn$
Lost	$13,599,382	$12,957,262	$10,757,451	$8,663,910
Stolen	$27,208,823	$22,823,193	$21,692,185	$18,322,777
Non-receipt	$6,088,948	$5,635,525	$4,736,900	$3,628,009
Fraudulent applications	$4,707,088	$4,262,498	$6,075,704	$8,552,715
Counterfeit	$158,809,947	$135,725,233	$120,166,543	$118,109,538
Card not present (fraudulent e-commerce, telephone, and mail purchases)	$140,443,893	$176,115,080	$259,498,535	$268,573,473
Account take overs/other	$140,443,893	$8,198,153	$13,661,440	$13,543,195
Total	$358,361,292	$365,916,944	$436,588,757	$439,363,617

Sources: Canadian Bankers Association (n.d.); Royal Canadian Mounted Police (n.d.).

BOX 15.1

Credit Card Fraud in Canada

An Ipsos Reid survey has found that 20 per cent of Canadians have found unauthorized charges on their credit cards as a result of accepting an offer online or on the phone.

Consumers need to read their credit card statements carefully to check for deceptive charges, experts say.

The survey also found that 78 per cent of Canadians are aware of the existence of deceptive or fraudulent marketing practices, but many fail to act on that knowledge.

The survey was commissioned by the credit card company, Visa.

"Deceptive marketing practices come in many forms," said Gord Jamieson, the head of payment system risk for Visa.

"Consumers need to be conscious that there may be fraudsters out there and they should think twice before accepting an offer that sounds too good to be true."

Unscrupulous marketers deceive consumers

A recent investigation by the U.S. Federal Trade Commission underscores how easily consumers can be bilked.

Central Coast Nutraceuticals was shut down by authorities after bilking consumers of more than $100 million through several deceptive tactics used to sell an acai berry supplement and colon cleanser.

The company used false endorsements from TV personalities Rachael Ray and Oprah Winfrey to give its website credibility, and a so-called free offer to lure consumers into ordering products. The company gained credit card numbers by telling consumers they would have to pay shipping on the free products.

However, what most consumers didn't notice was that by taking the free sample, they were signing up for monthly delivery of products and subsequent monthly credit card bills.

Credit card fraud: a growing problem in Canada.

"Customers can protect themselves by learning to recognize fraud and familiarizing themselves with some simple tips," said Staff Sgt. Paul Proulx of the Canadian Anti-Fraud Call Centre.

"Simple steps like reading and understanding the merchant terms and conditions and carefully reviewing your credit card statement each month can guard consumers from deceptive marketing scams," Proulx said.

Visa says it has enhanced its monitoring program to help spot deceptive marketers.

The survey of 1,013 Canadians was conducted by Ipsos Reid between July 8 and July 15. The margin of error is plus or minus 3.1 percentage points, 19 times out of 20.

Source: Excerpted from Credit card fraud hits 20% of Canadians. (2010, September 15). *CBC News*. Retrieved from http://www.cbc.ca/news/credit-card-fraud-hits-20-of-canadians-1.900025. Reprinted by permission.

Table 15.2 Penalties for Property Crime in Canada

Theft-Related Offences			
Offence	**Code section**	**Maximum (summary)**	**Maximum (indictable)**
Theft over $5,000	334(a)	n/a	10 years of jail
Theft under $5,000	334(b)	6 months of jail or $5,000 fine	2 years of jail
Possession of stolen property over $5,000	355(a)	n/a	10 years of jail
Possession of stolen property. under $5,000	335(b)	6 months of jail or $5,000 fine	2 years of jail
Fraud over $5,000	380(1)(a)	n/a	14 years of jail
Fraud under $5,000	380(1)(b)	6 months of jail or $5,000 fine	2 years of jail

Property Damage Offences			
Offence	**Code section**	**Maximum (summary)**	**Maximum (indictable)**
Mischief over $5,000	430(3)	6 months of jail or $5,000 fine	10 years of jail
Mischief under $5,000	430(4)	6 months of jail or $5,000 fine	2 years of jail
Arson (disregard for human life)	433	n/a	life
Arson (damage to property)	434/434.1	n/a	14 years of jail
Arson (fraudulent purpose)	435	n/a	10 years of jail
Arson (negligence)	436(1)	n/a	5 years of jail
Possession of incendiary materials	436.1	n/a	5 years of jail

Breaking and Entering			
Offence	**Code section**	**Maximum (summary)**	**Maximum (indictable)**
Breaking and entering with intent (dwelling)	348	n/a	life
Breaking and entering with intent (not dwelling)	348	6 months of jail or $5,000 fine	10 years of jail
Being unlawfully in a dwelling-house	349	6 months of jail or $5,000 fine	10 years of jail
Possession of break-in instruments	351	n/a	10 years of jail

Source: *Criminal Code* (1985).

Why Do People Commit Property Crime?

Conventional explanations of property crime tend to be based on a logic rooted in the **Classical School of criminology**. And most explanations normally deal with property crime that can be defined as "street crime," such as theft and breaking and entering into businesses and residences, and do not apply so easily to Internet crimes such as e-commerce fraud.

The origins of the Classical School can be found in the writing of Jeremy Bentham (1780/1973) and Cesare Beccaria (1764/1995) in the 18th century, which is based on the **utilitarian** belief that society is comprised of rational, free-willed decision-makers. Based on this proposition, people engage in property crime if they feel the benefits of stealing something outweigh the costs of getting caught. Conversely, based on a similar rational calculation, if people believe that the costs associated with stealing outweigh the benefits, then the crime will not be committed. In fact, Canada's sentencing laws are in keeping with deterrence-based logic because what are deemed to be more serious forms of property crime are associated with more severe penalties.

Punishment is supposed to have a deterrent effect, both on the lawbreaker (individual deterrence) and on potential criminals (general deterrence). Delving into **deterrence theory** a bit further, the effectiveness of punishment is considered to be conditioned by three factors:

1. the severity of the punishment for committing the crime;
2. the certainly that the punishment will be applied—in addition to the certainty of being apprehended in the first place; and
3. the swiftness with which the punishment will be applied.

Supporters of deterrence theory (which typically include conservative political parties) endorse policies such as longer prison sentences, increased penalty severity (e.g., a mandatory minimum sentence), and the hiring of more police officers. Together, these policies are considered to control and reduce the reoffending of convicted offenders and curb potential lawbreakers from becoming involved in crime in the future. However, little evidence confirms the effectiveness of this approach. Since the late 1960s, criminologists have been putting the deterrence hypothesis to the empirical test. In 1969, for example, Charles Tittle's often-cited study on deterrence found some support for deterrence theory and concluded that the *certainty* of imprisonment deters some crime, but that *severity* can only deter crime when the certainty of punishment is reasonably guaranteed. Little research has shown that the rapidity of punishment deters crime, and some research has shown that increasing penalty severity may actually increase the possibility of reoffending by released offenders (Tonry, 2011).

Because of the limitations of deterrence theory–based explanations of crime, including property crime, criminologists have developed other theories to explain offending. While it is beyond the scope of this chapter to provide a detailed review of these explanations (e.g., strain theory, control theory, differential association theory, routine activity theory, and the general theory of crime, which are explored in Part Three, Theories of Crime), the proceeding analysis will demonstrate that property crime needs to be understood within the social context in which it takes place. Although stealing a loaf of bread from a supermarket may be considered to be a simple matter of free-willed

Classical School of criminology

A body of work that emerged in Europe in the 17th and 18th centuries that argued people have the capacity to think rationally; contemporary deterrence theory is rooted in this school of thought.

utilitarianism

A philosophy that suggests reasoned decisions will produce the greatest good for the greatest number.

deterrence theory

A theory based on the idea that for punishment to be effective, it must be swift, sure, and certain.

decision making, criminologists consider crimes (including property crimes) not so much as *individual events* but as *social events* (Kennedy & Sacco, 1996). This distinction suggests that the backgrounds and current situational adversity of offenders need to be taken into account in addition to the actions of lawmakers, the police, the courts, the correctional system, the public, victims, and the mass media. We must not lose sight of the social character of crime. Indeed, more advanced courses in criminology and criminal justice typically go well beyond studying the simple act of crime commission and focus on the broader social context in which crime and crime control take place.

Case Study: An Analysis of Property Crime Among Homeless Youth in Toronto

Informed by a line of thinking that incorporates the social context of crime, what follows is a case study analysis of self-reported property crime based on original research carried out with a group of homeless youth in Toronto. For the purposes of this chapter, this analysis will only focus on the background and situational adversity of property crime offenders to show that decisions that people make to commit property crimes are predominantly shaped by **social forces**. While there is no denying that some degree of decision making is involved during the commission of a property crime, this analysis will point out that levels of property crime within the sample are related to the backgrounds of these youth and the situational adversity they face.

social forces

In sociology, the perspective that elements of society have the capability of causing cultural change or influencing human behaviour.

homelessness

A range of physical living conditions that can include living on the streets or in the open, staying in emergency shelters, or being provisionally housed (couch surfing with friends or relatives).

Before we turn to an analysis of data collected from 360 street-involved youth in Toronto, we will briefly review the nature of youth **homelessness** in Canada. Approximately 150,000 youth in Canada are homeless on any given night. The number of youth using Toronto shelter services where this study was undertaken increased by 16.2 percent between 2006 and 2009 (Lem, Coe, Haley, Stone, & O'Grady, 2013). Accurate homeless counts are difficult to achieve, as youth commonly "couch surf" (move from place to place), squat (stay in abandoned or unoccupied buildings), sleep rough (i.e., outdoors), engage in prostitution or other activities in exchange for shelter, or use other forms of transient or marginal housing. Research also shows that compared with Canadian youth who have stable housing, homeless youth partake in more illegal activity (Baron, 2013; Hagan & McCarthy, 1997).

Canadian youth become street involved for a number of reasons. While each youth has his or her own specific story and set of circumstances, the main causes of youth homelessness are as follows:

- *Individual/relational factors:* Between 60 and 70 percent of homeless youth left family environments where they experienced interpersonal violence, including physical, sexual, and/or emotional abuse.
- *Structural factors:* Broader systemic factors, including poverty, lack of food, inadequate housing, and discrimination, can lead to homelessness.
- *Institutional and system factors:* The failure of systems of care and support, including child protection, health, mental health care, and corrections, can lead to homelessness (Gaetz, O'Grady, Buccieri, Karabanow, & Marsolais, 2013).

Before you begin reading this case study, you may find it useful to refer back to the overview of crime statistics that appeared in Chapter 4, Measuring Crime. Note also that some of the tables in this case study include "*p* values": $p < 0.05$ means that the relationship is statistically significant and that we are 95 percent confident that the findings are not due to chance; $p < 0.01$ means that the relationship is statistically significant and that we are 99 percent confident that the findings are not due to chance; and $p < 0.001$ means that the relationship is statistically significant and that we are 99.9 percent confident that the findings are not due to chance.

As Table 15.3 shows, approximately two-thirds of the sample is male and one-third is female. This gender ratio is consistent with other Canadian research that has studied street youth (e.g., Hagan & McCarthy, 1997). The average age of the sample is 21, also in keeping with other research that has focused on this population. It is important to note that the age range that researchers normally use in Canadian research on homeless youth is 16 to 24. The reason why 16 tends to be the floor of this age range is that youth who are under the age of 16 are not legally permitted to stay in youth shelters, because young people under the age of 16 in Canada must be in the care of an adult guardian. Twenty-four years of age is the ceiling, since individuals 25 years of age and older who are in need of emergency shelter must use the adult system. In terms of the sexual orientation of the sample, 30 percent self-reported that they did not self-identify as being heterosexual. Many LGBT (lesbian, gay, bisexual, transgendered/sexual) youth in Canada have experiences with street involvement, as do youth who have spent time in foster homes and/or have experiences with Children's Aid Societies. Slightly more than one-half of the sample grew up in Toronto, and just under one-half did not finish high school, with the average level of schooling being grade 11. Many youth that were interviewed for the study reported that they have been street involved for prolonged periods of time. For example, just over 36 percent said that they have been on the streets for seven years or longer.

Table 15.3   Characteristics of the Toronto Homeless Youth Sample

Characteristic	Percentage
Gender	Male: 64% Female: 36%
Mean age	21
Sexual orientation	Straight: 70% Lesbian: 2% Gay: 5% Bi-sexual: 14% Other: 9%
Grew up in Toronto	Yes: 53% No: 47%
Completed high school	Yes: 43% No: 57%
Length of time street involved	< 1 year: 9% 2–3 years: 18% 4–6 years: 36% 7+: 37%
Lived in foster/group home	43%
Current housing status	Own place: 22% Shelter: 62% Street: 15% Squat: 1%

$n = 360$.

Source: Gaetz, O'Grady, & Vaillancourt (1999).

The Effects of a Selected Number of Variables on Property Crime

Through statistical analysis, we will now explore the effects that a selected number of variables have on three forms of property crime: break and enter/theft, scamming, and selling stolen goods. The case study sample was asked to self-report whether (within the past year) they had stolen something or committed a break and enter; been involved in scamming or conning (a common "short con" involves asking someone to change an amount of money, and exchanging coins or bills back and forth to confuse and ultimately shortchange the person); or sold stolen goods.

The data collected demonstrate that gender, housing status, and level of drug use are all strong predictors of engaging in property crime for this sample of Toronto homeless youth. After describing these predictors and their association with property crime, we will then discuss why a solid understanding of the nature of property crime requires that we look beyond explanations that focus merely on rational actors who weigh the costs and benefits of whether it is in their interest to commit crime.

In the field of criminology, gender is widely recognized as a key predictor of crime, including property crime, and research shows that crime is highly correlated with gender (Messerschmidt, 2006). With the exception of fraud (e.g., writing bad cheques) and shoplifting, males generally commit more property crime than females. It is beyond the scope of this chapter to review the wide range of explanations on why males outnumber females in the commission of crime (see Chapter 10, Gender and Crime, for more information on this topic). The literature on gender and crime provide scant evidence that would suggest females operate with a different mindset than males when it comes to weighing the costs and benefits of crimes such as stealing. Instead, gender differences have mainly been linked to unequal gender relations in society and differences in socialization patterns and opportunity structures. Not surprisingly, the data in Table 15.4 show that male homeless youth are more likely than female homeless youth to steal, scam, and sell stolen goods.

A second factor that links homeless youth to property crime is housing status. Three levels of housing quality were measured in the study. The first category, "own place," refers to youth who reported having a place of their own, which generally meant that they were provisionally housed. This category includes people who have temporary rental arrangements, such as staying in a motel, a hostel, or a rooming house. It also includes those who are couch surfers, or the hidden homeless. The "hidden homeless" are people who stay with friends, extended family, or even strangers. The second category, "shelter," refers to youth who reported sleeping in the emergency shelter system. These shelters typically have minimal eligibility criteria, offer shared sleeping facilities and amenities, and often expect clients to leave in the morning. They may or may not offer food, clothing, or other services. Some emergency shelters allow people to stay on an ongoing basis, while others are short term and are set up to respond to special circumstances, such as extreme weather (Canadian Homelessness Research Network, 2012). The final category, "street/squat," refers to youth who reported living on the street or staying in a squat. This category includes public spaces such as sidewalks, squares, parks, transit shelters, wooded areas, and spots under bridges, as well as rooftops and vacant/abandoned buildings.

Table 15.4 Property Crime of Homeless Youth in the Past Year, by Gender

	Break and enter/theft[a]	Scamming[b]	Selling stolen goods[c]
Males	Yes: 45% No: 55%	Yes: 42% No: 58%	Yes: 41% No: 59%
Females	Yes: 33% No: 67%	Yes: 33% No: 67%	Yes: 22% No: 78%

[a] $n = 284, p < 0.05$.
[b] $n = 279, p < 0.01$.
[c] $n = 278, p < 0.001$.

Source: O'Grady (n.d.).

According the data in Table 15.5, housing status is clearly related to property crime. Youth in the most precarious housing situations were most likely to engage in all three forms of property crime. For example, 23.1 percent of youth who were staying in their own place were involved in theft/breaking and entering, compared with 42.1 percent who were staying in shelters and 75.0 percent who were unsheltered. These statistics clearly illustrate the strong relationship between the quality of housing and the commission of property crime. This finding shows that situational adversity is linked to criminal behaviour among street youth, which echoes earlier research on the topic by John Hagan and Bill McCarthy (1997). In their study of homeless youth, they argued that the presence of strain and the absence of social controls lead to street crime, particularly theft of food. The **absolute deprivation** that leads to living in places that are not intended for human habitation causes stress and makes daily survival extremely difficult. The idea that theft is significantly influenced by people's immediate desperate circumstances has a long pedigree in criminology. For example, early European criminologists such as Willem Bonger (1916) argued that the poor commit crime out of need or out of a sense of injustice. It would not be a stretch to apply this logic to youth who are desperate and sleep under bridges or in abandoned, derelict buildings and steal in order to survive.

absolute deprivation
Low income or poverty in and of itself.

While not all homeless youth use drugs and alcohol, research has consistently shown that a substantial number do, at least on occasion (Buccieri, 2013). The Public Health Agency of Canada (PHAC) (2006) found that in 2003, 26.9 percent of the Canadian street youth surveyed reported drinking alcohol more than once per week, and 36 percent reported alcohol intoxication in the previous three months. Additionally, more than 95 percent reported injection and/or non-injection drug use in their lifetime (PHAC, 2006).

According to a research report from the British Home Office, a statistically significant relationship exists between opiate and cocaine use and the amount of reported annual illegal income. Almost half (46 percent) of a sample of arrestees in England who reported using drugs in the last 12 months believed that their drug use and property crime were linked. Not surprisingly, the most common connection cited was the need for money to buy drugs (Bennet & Holloway, 2004).

Table 15.5   Property Crime of Homeless Youth in the Past Year, by Housing Status

	Break and enter/theft[a]	Scamming[b]	Selling stolen goods[c]
Own place	23.1%	28.8%	21.6%
Shelter	42.1%	37.0%	34.4%
Street/squat	75.0%	70.4%	61.5%

[a] $n = 258, p < 0.001.$
[b] $n = 255, p < 0.001.$
[c] $n = 251, p < 0.01.$

Source: O'Grady (n.d.).

The data from the Toronto street youth study show that involvement in property crime is also closely linked to levels of illegal drug use. In Table 15.6, we see that engaging in break and enter/theft, scamming, and selling stolen goods is associated with elevated levels of drug use. Specifically, for those who used drugs more than once a week, 53 percent committed break and enter/theft, 51 percent scammed, and 47 percent sold stolen goods. For those who used drugs less than once a week, 18 percent committed break and enter/theft, 17 percent scammed, and 11 percent sold stolen goods. Interestingly, when levels of these three forms of property crime are measured only for males who live on the streets/squats and are regular drug users, the percentages rise to 78 percent for break and enter/theft, 77 percent for scamming, and 82 percent for selling stolen goods.

Overall, these data show that youth, particularly males, who live in the most precarious living conditions and use drugs more than once a week are the most likely to engage in property crime. Thus, while all street youth ultimately make decisions to steal, scam, or try to sell stolen property, it is clear from these data that such decision making takes place within different contexts and constraints.

Conclusion

This chapter began with a discussion on the emergence of property crime laws. The origins of such laws were traced to the rise of capitalism in England, and Canadian criminal laws are largely based on English common law. We examined how property crime is defined in Canada and how property crime statistics have been changing over time. While some forms of property crime (e.g., break and enter and motor vehicle theft) have been declining in recent years, other types of property crime (e.g., credit card fraud) appear to be on the increase. One of the main reasons for the increase of credit card fraud is the growth in online e-commerce. Although different criminological explanations of property crime exist, criminologists consider property crimes not so much as *individual events* but as *social events*. The original case study analysis of self-reported property crime by a group of homeless youth (the demographic group most commonly involved in committing property crime offences) in Toronto showed that

Table 15.6   Property Crime of Homeless Youth in the Past Year, by Level of Drug Use

	Break and enter/theft[b]	Scamming[c]	Selling stolen goods[d]
Drug use > 1 week[a]	Yes: 53% No: 47%	Yes: 51% No: 49%	Yes: 47% No: 53%
Drug use < 1 week	Yes: 18% No: 82%	Yes: 17% No: 83%	Yes: 11% No: 89%

[a] Those in category "Drug use > 1 week" (drugs = crack/cocaine/crystal meth/marijuana) use more than once a week. Those in "Drug use < 1 week" (drugs = crack/cocaine/crystal meth/marijuana) use less than once a week.
[b] $n = 274, p < 0.001$.
[c] $n = 268, p < 0.001$.
[d] $n = 267, p < 0.001$.

Source: O'Grady (n.d.).

the commission of property crimes is very much socially patterned, and that the situational adversity that these youth face needs to be considered in an attempt to explain why street youth steal, scam, and sell stolen property.

SUMMARY OF KEY POINTS

- According to *structural functionalists*, crime, including property crime, is inevitable in all societies. Moreover, they consider property crime laws to be based on a shared belief system in which customs, over time, become codified into legal statutes believed to promote solidarity and stability in society. For Marxist *conflict theorists*, property crimes committed by those from the working class are subject to criminalization, while the illegal activities of the elites are considered to be largely immune from legal censure.

- Regarding conflict theories, however, it should be noted that research has shown that a majority of street crime, including that related to property, is intra-class crime.

- The vast majority of property offenders who come before the courts are young, have relatively low levels of formal education, and are poor.

- Property crime involves the taking of money or property and, unlike robbery, does not involve force or threat of force against a victim. The main types of property crime listed in the *Criminal Code* are theft, break and enter, mischief (vandalism), possession of stolen property, arson, motor vehicle theft, and fraud.

- Most (Classical School) explanations deal with property crime that can be defined as "street crime," such as theft and breaking and entering into businesses and residences, and do not apply so easily to Internet crimes, such as e-commerce fraud.

- Supporters of *deterrence theory* endorse policies such as longer prison sentences, increased penalty severity, and the hiring of more police officers. However, little evidence confirms the effectiveness of this approach.

- Research, such as that done on Toronto homeless youth, demonstrates that gender, housing status, and level of drug use are all strong predictors of engaging in property crime.

- Gender is widely recognized as a key predictor of crime, including property crime. With the exception of fraud and shoplifting, males generally commit more property crime than females.

- While some forms of property crime have been declining in recent years, other types of property crime (e.g., credit card fraud) appear to be on the increase.

- Although there are different criminological explanations of property crime, criminologists consider property crimes not so much as *individual* events but as *social* events.

QUESTIONS FOR CRITICAL DISCUSSION

1. Discuss how structural functionalist and conflict explanations account for the emergence of property crime laws.
2. How have levels of police-reported property crime changed in Canada from 1962 to 2012?
3. How does deterrence theory explain property crime?
4. Why do gender, housing status, and levels of drug use predict differing levels of property crime for homeless youth?

SUGGESTED FURTHER READINGS

Brand, R. (2007). *My booky wook*. London, UK: Hodder and Stoughton.

Gibson, K. (2011). *Street kids: Homeless youth, outreach, and policing New York's streets*. New York: New York University Press.

Reynolds, B. (2000). *An autobiography of a thief: The man behind the great train robbery* (2nd ed.). London, UK: Virgin Books.

Websites

The Homeless Hub: http://www.homelesshub.ca

Victims of Property Crime: http://www4.hrsdc.gc.ca/.3ndic.1t.4r@-eng.jsp?iid=60

REFERENCES

Baron, S. (2013). Why street youth get involved in crime. In S. Gaetz, B. O'Grady, K. Buccieri, J. Karabanow, & A. Marsolais (Eds.), *Youth homelessness in Canada: Implications for policy and practice* (pp. 353–368). Toronto: Canadian Homelessness Research Network Press.

Beccaria, C. (1995). *Essays on crime and punishment and other essays*. New York: Cambridge University Press. (Original work published 1764.)

Bennet, T., & Holloway, K. (2004). *Drug use and offending: Summary results of the first two years of the NEW-ADAM programme* (British Home Office report 179). London, UK: British Home Office.

Bentham, J. (1973). *An introduction to the principals of morals and legislation*. Garden City, NY: Anchor Press Doubleday. (Original work published 1780.)

Bonger, W. (1916). *Criminology and economic conditions*. Boston: Little, Brown.

Buccieri, K. (2013). Back to the future for Canada's national anti-drug strategy: Homeless youth and the need for harm reduction. In S. Gaetz, B. O'Grady, K. Buccieri, J. Karabanow, & A. Marsolais (Eds.), *Youth homelessness in Canada: Implications for policy and practice* (pp. 199–216). Toronto: Canadian Homelessness Research Network Press.

Canadian Bankers Association. (n.d.). Credit card fraud and Interac debit card fraud statistics—Canadian issued cards. Retrieved from http://www.cba.ca/contents/files/statistics/stat_creditcardfraud_en.pdf.

Canadian Homelessness Research Network. (2012). *Canadian definition of homelessness*. Toronto: The Homeless Hub. Retrieved from http://www.homelesshub.ca/CHRNhomelessdefinition/.

Canadian Press. (2012, July 20). Livent co-founder Myron Gottlieb granted day parole. *CBCnews.ca*. Retrieved from http://www.cbc.ca/news/arts/livent-co-founder-myron-gottlieb-granted-day-parole-1.1167832.

Chambliss, W., & Seidman, R. (1982). *Law, order and power* (2nd ed.). Reading, MA: Addison-Wesley.

Credit card fraud hits 20% of Canadians. (2010, September 15). *CBC News*. Retrieved from http://www.cbc.ca/news/credit-card-fraud-hits-20-of-canadians-1.900025.

Durkheim, É. (1933). *The division of labor in society*. New York: Free Press.

Gaetz, S., O'Grady, B., Buccieri, K., Karabanow, J., & Marsolais, A. (Eds.). (2013). *Youth homelessness in Canada: Implications for policy and practice*. Toronto: Canadian Homelessness Research Network Press.

Gaetz, S., O'Grady, B., & Vaillancourt, B. (1999). *Making money: The Shout Clinic report on homeless youth and employment*. Toronto: Central Toronto Community Health Centres. Retrieved from http://www.homelesshub.ca/ResourceFiles/Making_Money.pdf.

Hagan, J., & McCarthy, B. (1997). *Mean streets: Youth crime and homelessness*. Cambridge, UK: Cambridge University Press.

Hall, J. (1952). *Theft, law and society*. Indianapolis, IN: Bobbs-Merrill.

Kennedy, L., & Sacco, V. (1996). *Crime counts: A criminal event analysis*. Toronto: Nelson.

Lem, M., Coe, J.B., Haley, D.B., Stone, E., & O'Grady, W. (2013). Effects of companion animal ownership among Canadian street-involved youth: A qualitative analysis. *Journal of Sociology and Social Welfare*, *15*(4), 285–304.

Messerschmidt, J. (2006). *Criminology* (4th ed.). Los Angeles: Roxbury.

O'Grady, B. (n.d.). [An analysis of property crime among homeless youth in Toronto]. Unpublished raw data.

O'Grady, W. (2011). *Crime in Canadian context: Debates and controversies* (2nd ed.). Toronto: Oxford University Press.

Perreault, S. (2013). *Police-reported crime statistics in Canada, 2012*. Ottawa: Canadian Centre for Justice Statistics, Statistics Canada.

Public Health Agency of Canada. (2006). Street youth in Canada: Findings from enhanced surveillance of Canadian street youth, 1999–2003. Retrieved from http://www.phac-aspc.gc.ca/std-mts/reports_06/pdf/street_youth_e.pdf.

Quinney, R. (1975). *Criminology: Analysis and critique of crime in America*. Boston: Little, Brown.

RCMP. (n.d.). Credit card fraud. Retrieved from http://www.rcmp-grc.gc.ca/scams-fraudes/cc-fraud-fraude-eng.htm.

Reasons, C., & Rich, R. (Eds.). (1978). *The sociology of law: A conflict perspective*. Toronto: Butterworths.

Tittle, C. (1969). Crime rates and legal sanctions. *Social Problems*, *16*, 409–423.

Tonry, M. (2011). Less imprisonment is no doubt a good thing: More policing is not. *Criminology and Public Policy*, *10*(1), 137–152.

Tunnell, K. (2006). *Living off crime* (2nd ed.). Lanham, MD: Rowman and Littlefield.

Vago, S. (1997). *Law and society* (5th ed.). Upper Saddle River, NJ: Prentice Hall.

Legislation

Criminal Code. (1985). RSC 1985, c. C-46.

Rethinking Canada's Prostitution Laws: The Bedford Case

Dominatrix Terri-Jean Bedford speaking to the media, flanked by lawyer Alan Young and prostitutes' rights activist Valerie Scott.

Source: Colin McConnell/GetStock.com.

In June 2013, the Supreme Court of Canada listened to arguments about the circumstances in which men and women might be allowed to legally buy and sell sex. The justices of the Supreme Court were considering the arguments made by the lawyer for dominatrix Terri-Jean Bedford, former prostitute Valerie Scott (both from Ontario), and Vancouver sex worker Amy Lebovitch.

The heart of the argument made by counsel Alan Young was that the law, as it is written, has the practical consequence of endangering the lives of women in the sex trade, particularly those women who work the street—women who might best be described as "survival sex workers," often drug-addicted and frequently subjected to violence at the hands of some of their customers. Women who work in massage parlours or for escort agencies also experience risks, but these risks are significantly diminished by the protections offered by each of these businesses—the tracking of clients through credit cards and other means, and an agreed-upon location for the sexual transaction, known to those operating the business.

The trial court in *Canada (Attorney General) v. Bedford* (2013) had heard from 12 women who worked in the sex trade; they all told the court that street prostitution is less safe than indoor work, and the conclusions of these 12 women were based on interviews they themselves had conducted with approximately 800 sex trade workers. They also heard evidence from academics who have studied the safety of work in the sex trade; street-level prostitutes were, in all of these studies, found to be much more likely to be assaulted, kidnapped, or killed than those working indoors.

The two *Criminal Code* provisions that directly affect prostitution are the prohibition against anyone who "keeps a common bawdy-house" (section 210) and the prohibition against communication for the purpose of soliciting "illicit sexual intercourse with another person" (section 212). But, as the court heard in *Bedford*, the bawdy-house provisions are rarely enforced; they are not generally the subject of public complaints, and, more important, police investigations of suspected bawdy houses are time-consuming and expensive. In contrast, the prosecution of street prostitutes is much less difficult, and these prosecutions now form the bulk of all cases that are heard in Canadian courts.

The federal government's response to these claims and concerns noted that even indoor sex work in bawdy houses has not eliminated violence against prostitutes. Crown lawyer Michael H. Morris argued that criminal prohibition exists to prevent the harmful effects of prostitution, and the personal interests and choices of those who engage in this economy should not trump the goal of preventing harm.

In December 2013 the Supreme Court, in a unanimous decision, declared the laws governing prostitution in Canada to be invalid for one year. The judgment of the court was delivered by Chief Justice Beverley McLachlin, who wrote in the final paragraphs in *Bedford*:

How prostitution is regulated is a matter of great public concern, and few countries leave it entirely unregulated. Whether immediate invalidity would pose a danger to the public or imperil the rule of law (the factors for suspension referred to in *Schachter v. Canada*, [1992] 2 S.C.R. 679) may be subject to debate. However, it is clear that moving abruptly from a situation where prostitution is regulated to a situation where it is entirely unregulated would be a matter of great concern to many Canadians.

On the other hand, leaving the prohibitions against bawdy-houses, living on the avails of prostitution and public communication for purposes of prostitution in place in their present form leaves prostitutes at increased risk for the time of the suspension—risks which violate their constitutional right to security of the person.

The choice between suspending the declaration of invalidity and allowing it to take immediate effect is not an easy one. Neither alternative is without difficulty. However, considering all the interests at stake, I conclude that the declaration of invalidity should be suspended for one year. (paras. 167–169)

How might prostitution be regulated? To what extent *should* it be regulated? The debates continue over the role of the criminal law in relation to current provisions against bawdy houses, living on the avails of prostitution, and soliciting. Some would like to see the law amended to target only the male customers of prostitutes. Others believe that this approach would not be a step forward and that it would only serve to entrench the harms that street prostitutes currently experience by ensuring that such transactions would increasingly take place away from public view, and further reduce any potential protection for these vulnerable women.

Before You Read Chapter 16

- Should the work of those in the sex trade be considered, in law, to be any different from work in other morally contested realms—serving drinks in a bar, selling cannabis to willing consumers, or operating a casino that includes slot machines and roulette wheels?
- Do critical differences exist across morally contested activities, and if so, what are they?

Crimes of Morality

LEARNING OBJECTIVES

After reading this chapter, students will be able to:

- Explain the characteristics of crimes of morality and how they differ from consensus crimes.
- Identify the classical arguments concerning the proper role of law in regulating moral conduct.
- Explain the tenets of the harm principle and opposing arguments on the role of government and law.
- Understand opposing views on prostitution and their implications for its treatment under law.
- Understand the history of existing drug laws and identify competing policy perspectives.

Introduction

Universal agreement exists in society that crimes such as murder, rape, and assault deserve strict punishment. The seriousness of these crimes is beyond dispute. In other words, the consensus is that committing these crimes is wrongful in itself. *Consensus crimes* (such as murder, rape, and assault) inflict real harm on persons and society, and thus require a matching societal response. However, certain crimes are more ambiguous, divisive, or subject to dispute—these crimes are the focus of this chapter.

Unlike consensus crimes, **crimes of morality** are subject to widespread disagreement and considerable debate. Laws that prohibit gambling, certain types of drug use, and the exchange of sex for money are all relevant examples. Sometimes known as "victimless" or "vice-related" crimes, crimes of morality are not crimes because they cause direct harm to society or persons but because they are seen as threatening to societal **morals**.

Crimes of morality do not necessarily cause harm or have a victim. Commonly, such crime involves an offender who has "offended" in the sense of having broken an existing norm. Crimes of morality reflect the current moral standards of a society. As moral standards change, the laws that define them are also subject to change. Whether laws evolve in step with moral standards or stay stagnant and reflect standards and opinions of an earlier era, crimes of morality are subject to debate.

Considerable disagreement exists among policy observers and lay people about the role of government in legislating morals. Canadian experience in this area offers ample illustrations of both the flexibility of law and societal resistance. Gambling has evolved in recent decades into a regulated industry and a legitimate source of revenue for governments (and charities), which reap enormous profits from casinos and Canadians

crimes of morality
Illegal activities that are against the law because they are regarded as threatening to values.

morals
The normative standards, codes, and beliefs governing judgments and values concerning right and wrong action, justice, and fairness.

Customers line up to buy lottery tickets at a variety story. In recent decades, gambling has gone from a socially unacceptable and closely policed "vice" to a government-sanctioned activity that funnels huge amounts of money into public coffers through casinos, lotteries, and sports betting. Other than the financial rewards to governments, what other reasons might account for this change in attitude toward gambling and lotteries?

who try their luck in lotteries each week. At the same time, federal government–sponsored advertisements cautioning those who gamble of the risks involved in playing games of chance have become commonplace.

The laws that govern prostitution represent moral legislation that has shifted toward a more pragmatic stance. Canada's drug laws, by comparison, have proven more resistant. With few exceptions, drug laws continue to reflect a moral standpoint that has more to do with history and dominant group interests than concern for persons who use substances per se. These observations are supported by discrepancies between the treatment of accepted drugs (such as alcohol) and others (such as marijuana) whose users are deemed criminal. To further illustrate, this chapter takes a closer look at drug use and prostitution as examples of crimes against morality. We begin with an overview of classic arguments presented by philosophers and legal scholars before examining these topics further.

What Is the Role of Law in Regulating Moral Conduct?

We are social animals whose very existence depends on those around us to fulfill our basic needs. Moreover, our survival as a species and our quality of life are dependent on the social interactions that maintain them. The benefits acquired from interaction and dependence on others in our social group, however, have a price. The cost of the fulfillment of human beings' social nature is our agreement to abide by certain rules and regulations that serve to limit freedom and immediate gratification.

Whereas presumably in our "natural state" we are free to do as we desire, as social beings we put limits on these freedoms to ensure the survival of the group. As philosophers and legal scholars (including Sigmund Freud) have long argued, the rule of law is an instrument that ensures our happiness and is our greatest source of unhappiness as well (Fisher, 1982; Freud, 2002; Gay, 1989).

The civilizing process and development of law demands conformity and the repression of our most basic instincts; these include the desire for freedom from constraint. Society's demands for conformity, however, are far from absolute. Within the realm of regulation, some room for individual freedom, and even deviance, exists. Not all deviant behaviour is universally condemned. Some varieties of deviance, even criminal behaviours, are recognized as tolerable differences that pose little risk of harm to society or to persons that commit the crime and those around them (Hagan, 1991; Hathaway, 1997; Schur, 1984; Stebbins, 1996).

Tolerable deviance includes legitimate, non-criminal, and criminal activities. In North American society, for example, considerable scope exists for freedom of religion, speech, and thought. In addition to these legally protected activities, other practices or lifestyles may violate standard norms of conduct in the general population but not legal statutes or the "letter of the law."

Of particular concern are those varieties of tolerable deviance that are technically illegal but recognized as neither particularly threatening nor harmful to society. Prostitution and the use of certain drugs are examples of criminal tolerable deviance that are often debated among scholars and others who are critical of **overcriminalization** (Richards, 1982).

overcriminalization
The intrusion of the law into consensual activities which are relatively harmless to the actor(s) and society.

The legislation and enforcement of morality through law, without either a victim or a complainant, is not only difficult but also a waste of resources. It is also arguably a threat to social order and to the legitimacy of the rule of law. In democratic, multicultural societies such as Canada and other Western nations, the legislation of morality raises important questions about the proper role of government and whose morality or justice ought to be enforced. Before continuing, this chapter will revisit some classic philosophical positions and debates on the question of morality enforcement by the state.

The Pursuit of Happiness and Law

According to the classic utilitarian perspective, the purpose of law is to make people happy. This philosophical position was developed by Jeremy Bentham (1748–1832), who built on the ideas of highly influential Enlightenment-era philosopher Immanuel Kant. (Note that some of the early philosophical influences on the development of criminology, and some related terminology, are discussed in more detail in Chapter 6, Theories of Crime: A Brief Introduction.) Bentham sought to ascertain the nature of morality. While Kant believed that morality is determined by intentions, which lead to actions that are *inherently* good or bad, Bentham believed that the morality of an action is determined by its *consequences* (Kelly, 2006; F. Rosen, 2003).

Thus, for Bentham, an action was deemed morally justified, or good, if the action produced a desirable result. This *consequentialist* perspective on morality is generally consistent with the modern view of law, which holds that its function is to maximize "the good" for the majority (Bentham, 1781/2007). This utilitarian approach to law is hedonistic in that it seeks to increase happiness, or pleasure, while reducing pain for the greatest number—that is, it serves the common good.

Bentham sought to quantify the benefits and costs that determine the utility of any given law. His calculus, based on the pleasure principle, consisted of a formula for calculating the morality of actions through the measurement of their circumstances. His equation for determining morality included the elements of intensity, duration, certainty, and the extent of influence of an action's costs and benefits in relation to the law.

Bentham's student, renowned 19th-century thinker John Stuart Mill, was more pragmatic in his recognition that the principles of law cannot be so easily reduced to mathematical equations that determine the utility of actions. Mill's primary concern was the problem of preserving individual freedoms and the rights of the minority in a democratic system of government concerned with seeking to maximize the common good.

Mill's (1859/2002) utilitarian perspective on the proper function of the state enacted through the rule of law emphasized the value of protecting individuals from the imposition of the will of the majority. The "tyranny of the majority," he argued, must be countered by limiting the authority of governments. In particular, he rejected the legislation or enforcement of morality. The only purpose for which power should be exercised, Mill asserted, is to prevent harm to other persons.

Since all persons are deemed sovereign over their minds and bodies, Mill argued, the state is never justified to interfere with actions of an individual for his or her "own good." Put otherwise, we have the right to do as we please, as long as our actions do no harm to others. Mill's utilitarian perspective was concerned with the realization of the common good through the cultivation of personal autonomy. His view of human nature likened us to trees that should be free to flourish and develop on all sides—rather than machines built from some preordained design.

The Harm Principle

Mill's (1859/2002) view suggests that that legal sanctions must be limited to actions that inflict real harm on assignable persons as opposed to actions to which others take offence. Those who are merely offended by an action or opinion have ready access to the remedy of seeking other company. Thus, formal intervention by the state in such situations is unnecessary.

Mill maintained a liberal position on morality. He viewed morality as a trait to be acquired through education, whose business it was to cultivate the propensity to act in the best interests of society. He believed that although the state is justified in seeking to prevent harm, legislators must be mindful of the circumstances of the action justifying enforcement of the law. While excessive drinking may be harmful, for example, moderate use of alcohol is not. Therefore, an outright ban is not permissible. However, restrictions may be warranted to regulate consumption and help consumers mitigate known risks.

harm principle
A central tenet in the writing of John Stuart Mill, often regarded as the father of moral liberalism. The harm principle holds that the actions of individuals should only be limited to prevent harm to other individuals.

Mill's articulation of the **harm principle** is well known for its elegant simplicity. His point of view was unequivocal. He made very few exceptions, other than for children and the mentally disabled, who arguably are lacking the capacity to exercise their right to full autonomy—thereby allowing greater scope for protection by parental figures and/or the state.

He also believed that extending the coercive power of government to limiting the personal autonomy of adults was both unnecessary and a travesty of justice impeding the realization of the common good. In Mill's own words:

> A state which dwarfs its men, in order that they may be more docile instruments in its hand even for beneficial purposes will find that with small men no great thing can really be accomplished; and that the perfection of machinery to which it has sacrificed everything will in the end avail it nothing. (1859/2002, p. 161)

Opposing Arguments

The classic Millsian perspective on the function of the state has been challenged by observers with less liberal positions on the propriety of enforcing morality through law. The most well-known propositions in the literature adopt a more conservative or moderate perspective which, in practice, tend to be reflected in legal policy provisions in Canada and many other jurisdictions around the world.

The case for the legislation of morality, in direct contradiction of Mill's position on the matter, was famously made by Lord Devlin in 1950s Britain. According to Devlin, legislating morals was precisely what the role of the government should be. Devlin (1965) firmly believed in **moral absolutism**, based on the consensus of reasonable people, that ought to be safeguarded through law enforcement. Homosexuality and prostitution are examples of activities that Devlin saw as threatening to conventional standards of morality, thereby justifying interference by the state to preserve the common good. (In contrast, **moral relativism** holds that what is considered moral behaviour can and does change over time and from culture to culture.)

A more moderate or middle-ground position between Devlin's (conservative) and Mill's (liberal) view of the function of law was taken up by legal scholar Herbert Lionel Adolphus Hart (1963). According to Hart, government is obligated to fulfill the role of parent for its citizens in order to protect them from the harm that they are liable to inflict on themselves when lacking proper guidance and moral regulation. Although his position is less punitive than Devlin's, it is also less liberal than Mill's—who would no doubt be offended by the notion that some freedom must be sacrificed by adults to protect us from ourselves "for our own good."

As an evolving system of rules and regulations, criminal law in Canada is probably best characterized as a tool reflecting all of these concerns. The principles put forward by Mill are clearly evident in section 1 of the *Canadian Charter of Rights and Freedoms*. The limitations clause states that our rights and freedoms are "subject only to such reasonable limits prescribed by law as can be demonstrably justified in a free and democratic society." This clause puts the onus on government to justify prohibiting an action. It also further establishes that the prohibition must be minimally intrusive, rational, and proportionate to the harm inflicted by the action. This clause is, of course, subject to interpretation that, necessarily, can never be conclusive. The debates and legal challenges surrounding this clause are meant to be ongoing.

The foregoing discussion was provided as a background for considering the appropriate role of law in democratic constitutional societies such as Canada. We now turn to a discussion of prominent areas of contention and continual debate in the legislation of morality: prostitution and drug use.

moral absolutism
A philosophical perspective which holds that certain actions are absolutely right or wrong, regardless of other circumstances such as their consequences or the intentions behind them.

moral relativism
A perspective on the nature of morality asserting that norms or standards of behaviour are not fixed or absolute.

Gloria Taylor, who suffered from ALS, was the first Canadian to win the right to a physician-assisted suicide (from the BC Supreme Court, but which the federal government appealed), but died of natural causes. What should the state's role be in such cases? What is the "crime" and who is harmed if a person chooses to end his or her own suffering?

Source: Darryl Dyck/The Canadian Press.

In many Canadian cities, thinly veiled ads for prostitution can be found in newspapers and online, using terms such as "massage" or "escort services." This tacit acceptance of prostitution, particularly when it is less "open" and not on highly visible street corners, suggests that Canadians' attitudes on this issue are changing.

Prostitution

In Canada, the average number of arrests for prostitution-related offences is approximately 3,500 per year. While the act of prostitution, or exchanging sex for money, is not technically illegal in this country, communication for the purposes of prostitution is a criminal offence according to section 213 of the *Criminal Code*. Although arrest rates have been dropping for about a decade, this decline is probably due to a reduction in enforcement rather than a reduction in the rates of prostitution.

Since female prostitution is more prevalent, and male clients far outnumber the females who provide the service, males are theoretically more likely to be arrested for communicating for purposes of prostitution. In reality, however, arrests for prostitution are equally distributed by gender. Prostitution charges have a high clearance rate. About three-quarters of those charged receive fines or probation (Antweiler, 2002; Siegel & McCormick, 2012).

Opinion polls suggest that approximately three-quarters of Canadians believe that prostitution should be legalized (Angus Reid Public Opinion, 2011). This majority support for law reform was recently considered among the arguments presented in a Supreme Court challenge of prostitution laws. Before examining this challenge and the related implications of proposed changes to the laws, we will put these policy discussions in perspective with particular reference to theoretical debates.

Types of Prostitution

Although policy discussions tend to refer to prostitution as a singular activity, it comprises different types of sex work with distinctive characteristics. The stereotypical depiction of prostitutes is probably closest to those known as "hookers" or "street walkers" (Clinard & Meier, 1998; Janus & Janus, 1993). The women fitting this description often come from lower-class backgrounds, use heavily addicting drugs, and are typically most visible in run-down areas of inner cities. Of all sex workers, they are often the most vulnerable and victimized, the most frequently arrested, and the most abused by clients—with many working for a "pimp" who controls their activities.

Less visible to most people are those who work in bars or hotel lounges waiting to be propositioned. Although often freelance workers who are not controlled by pimps, "bar girls" sometimes have arrangements with a bartender, who may be compensated for compliance by having clients buy them "drinks" (which are often just coloured water, thus providing generous tips).

Other kinds of sex workers set up shop in brothels, where a portion of the money earned goes to the proprietor. Although brothels are legal in some jurisdictions in other parts of the world, in Canada sex services of this kind have been limited—until recently—to those provided in "massage parlours," which disguise their services for those not "in the know."

Sex workers receive clear advantages from working in secure environments where clients are controlled and monitored by others who administrate the service in exchange

BOX 16.1

Supreme Court Strikes Down Canada's Prostitution Laws

The sections of the *Criminal Code* that criminalize sex work were recently struck down by the Supreme Court of Canada. The ruling overturned provisions against keeping a common bawdy house (section 210), living on the avails of prostitution (sections 211 and 212), and communication for the purpose of prostitution (section 213). These sections of the *Criminal Code* were ruled as violating the *Canadian Charter of Rights and Freedom*'s rights to freedom of expression and security of the person. In particular, the law was criticized for forcing prostitutes to work in dangerous circumstances.

> The Supreme Court of Canada has struck down the country's major prostitution laws, saying that bans on street soliciting, brothels and people living off the avails of prostitution create severe dangers for vulnerable women and therefore violate Canadians' basic values.
>
> Chief Justice Beverley McLachlin, writing for a unanimous court, stressed that the ruling is not about whether prostitution should be legal or not, but about whether Parliament's means of controlling it infringe the constitutional rights of prostitutes.
>
> "Parliament has the power to regulate against nuisances, but not at the cost of the health, safety and lives of prostitutes," she wrote. "The prohibitions not merely impose conditions on how prostitutes operate. They go a critical step further, by imposing dangerous conditions on prostitution; they prevent people engaged in a risky—but legal—activity from taking steps to protect themselves from the risks."
>
> [The Conservative government's Justice Minister] Peter MacKay suggested in a statement that the government will continue to look at prohibiting prostitution in some fashion. The government is "exploring all possible options to ensure the criminal law continues to address the significant harms that flow from prostitution to communities, those engaged in prostitution, and vulnerable persons," he said.
>
> The court suggested Parliament has wide options for continuing to criminalize prostitution-related activities, even perhaps maintaining aspects of the existing laws. It said the prohibitions on street soliciting, brothels and living off the avails are all intertwined and have an impact on one another.
>
> "Greater latitude in one measure—for example, permitting prostitutes to obtain the assistance of security personnel—might impact on the constitutionality of another measure—for example, forbidding the nuisances associated with keeping a bawdy-house. The regulation of prostitution is a complex and delicate matter. It will be for Parliament, should it choose to do so, to devise a new approach, reflecting different elements of the existing regime."

Source: *The Globe and Mail*, December 20, 2013. Reprinted by permission.

for rent or a cut of their profits. While this model has existed in a variety of forms throughout human history and throughout the world, its benefits are particularly evident where regulations ensure protections for sex workers and their clients in a setting that is legitimate, hygienic, and secure.

A hierarchy exists in sex work in which the most well-paid prostitutes are known as *escorts* or "call girls." Catering to wealthy clients, these women occupy the other end of the continuum of sex work from "street walkers," sometimes earning thousands of dollars a night. Often well-educated, from the middle and upper classes, call girls work independently or for an escort agency, meeting clients in hotel rooms, or their own or clients' homes. Typically, they provide more than sex to clients; they are often hired for companionship as well.

Although escorts are well paid for their services, and often have regular clients they come to know well, they face risks similar to those faced by other sex workers, and must take precautions to protect themselves. These safeguards include travelling with a personal driver (or trusted cab driver) who knows their whereabouts while on the job. Other precautions include taking business cards and requiring contact information from new clients (for those not working through an agency that can collect this information).

In summary, it seems that stereotypical portrayals of prostitution represent an over-simplification of the nature of the business of sex work. It is ordinarily assumed that women enter prostitution out of desperation—due to poverty, addiction, lack of self-esteem, abuse, or other circumstances—as victims who are forced into a lifestyle that degrades them. Undoubtedly, depictions of this nature are an accurate characterization of a segment of the population of sex workers (Cavan, 1970).

More generally, however, research shows that many prostitutes do not see themselves as victims. On the contrary, sex workers often view their occupation as fulfilling a valued function in society, in terms similar to those employed throughout the service industry. These opposing points of view on prostitution largely coincide with contradictory arguments presented in academic literature and policy perspectives. Oversimplifying these discussions is not conducive to the development of well-informed opinions and debates. Accordingly, our next task is to consider important theoretical contributions that inform discussions on the role of law in the regulation of sex work.

A Subcultural Perspective

Although financial need is an important motivation for many women who enter into prostitution, it is rarely a sufficient explanation in itself. Social learning is required to obtain the special knowledge that is ordinarily needed to succeed. Since prostitution is a highly stigmatized profession, existing on the fringes of conventional society, introduction and acceptance in the subculture of sex work is often necessary to become a prostitute.

Since ancient times, sex workers have regarded the profession as a way of gaining independence as women in societies where men have dominated wealth and power. Indeed, historically financially independent women were often prostitutes who were, by definition, women not beholden to or possessed by men. This traditional perspective on the roles of men and women is still dominant within the subculture of sex work (Dalla, 2000; Mars, 1982; Roberts, 1992).

Many prostitutes perceive themselves as equal or superior to women who marry for financial security. Sex work is often viewed as a superior alternative to low-paying jobs where women are exploited and commonly subjected to sexual harassment. In particular, female escorts who work independently see real advantages in working for themselves with no interference from male managers or bosses (Perkins, 1991; Ross, 2000).

Social learning in the prostitution subculture, moreover, promotes a view of sex work as a service that fulfills an important function in society. This outlook has been echoed and developed systematically in what is widely known as the *functionalist* approach.

Social Functions of Sex Work

A functionalist interpretation of "deviant behaviour" rejects the pathological perspective, wherein deviance is likened to a disease of the body or an activity that is necessarily harmful to society. Instead, deviance is understood as having positive functions for society, which may not be intended but nonetheless fulfill a beneficial role (Merton, 1957, 1973; Parsons, 1951).

Famous sociologist Émile Durkheim (1933, 1938) once observed that deviance and crime are universal, having always existed in society in one form or another. He argued that one could even find them in a society of saints. Even the purest of the pure of human groups, in other words, require examples of wrongdoing to maintain their moral boundaries. To understand what God is, we also need the Devil. Without the Dark, one cannot truly see the Light. Deviant behaviour serves to designate an out-group, or common enemy, whose very existence serves to strengthen social solidarity among the law-abiding. Among its other functions, social deviance facilitates greater harmony and clarifies existing moral standards in society (Erikson, 1966). It provides a scapegoat for the problems of society, enabling the righteous to feel good about themselves.

In addition to providing jobs in law and law enforcement, social work, corrections (and other jobs sought-after by criminology graduates), deviant behaviour sometimes offers an example of a society's capacity for change. Just like the first women who dared to dream of voting in Canada a century ago, prostitutes are outlaws whose behaviour may be deviant but need not necessarily be considered as such (Cohen, 1966).

Apart from its potential to initiate reform by challenging social attitudes about the role of women, prostitution arguably serves two specific functions. Historically, sex work has enabled a small segment of the female population to meet the sexual needs of men (K. Davis, 1937, 1971, 1976). Accordingly, it functions as a "safety valve" for men seeking sex outside the bonds of marriage or those who might otherwise resort to raping women (N.J. Davis, 1980). By enabling an exchange of sex for money, prostitution reduces the sex act to an impersonal transaction that avoids the kind of emotional entanglements that threaten the stability of domestic family life (Davis, 1980). This functionalist perspective on the role of prostitution, however, has been challenged by observers who dispute the chauvinistic assumptions underlying this approach (Matza, 1969; Polsky, 1985).

Feminist Perspectives

Whereas the "safety valve" interpretation may suit men, feminists argue that it also represents a double standard based on gender inequality that needs to be addressed. Male promiscuity is often celebrated. Bedding women is depicted as a mark of manhood and virility in our culture. While men with many notches in their bedposts are celebrated as successful "players," studs, and modern-day Don Juans, the same behaviour among women typically gets one labelled as a *slut*.

While it is reasonable to argue that social attitudes are changing, it is also fair to say they have not changed that much. The age-old double standard (known as the "Madonna/whore" complex) holds that men want a mate who has saintly virtue *and* the ability to meet their sexual desires. As reasonable as this idea may seem from a male perspective, it points to contradictions in our culture on the role and expectations of women, which historically have been defined in terms of men's needs.

Classic and contemporary feminist perspectives are generally consistent in their emphasis on seeking gender equality by promoting women's rights. Interestingly, however, there is considerable disagreement regarding prostitution and the nature of sex work within feminism. Nineteenth-century feminists, such as Elizabeth Cady Stanton and Susan B. Anthony, viewed prostitution as a threat to social order and stability. Sexual promiscuity, they argued, was the cause of all kinds of social ills, including prostitution. Eradicating prostitution was their primary objective, as a means to reclaim the purity and virtue of these wayward women and society at large (Jenness, 1993; Pleck, 1987).

By contrast, other feminists viewed prostitution as a legitimate expression of female sexuality outside the bonds of marriage. Repression of sexuality by criminalizing prostitution, argued Victoria Woodhall, is a goal exceeding the limits of state power. She rejected criminalizing prostitution on the grounds that such measures deny women control over their sexuality. From her perspective, sexuality is an empowering tool for women (R. Rosen, 1982). Woodhall contended that unlike married women at the time, who lacked the legal power to deny sex to their husbands, prostitutes were free to choose the men who used their bodies. Whereas the prostitute may be forced to sell her body "on piecework as a wageworker," said Engels (1884/1942), the married women "sells it once and for all into slavery" to one man. From this standpoint, prostitution represented the potential for female liberation from sexual domination by men and the male desire to control a woman's body (Meil-Hobson, 1987; Tong, 1984).

Contemporary Feminism

While early feminist perspectives put emphasis on moral purity and chastity as female characteristics, over time that emphasis shifted toward sexual liberation as a tool for challenging gender inequality. The last century has seen important social changes, which have helped facilitate these aims. Marriage laws have changed to the extent that women can legally divorce and are no longer legally defined as property belonging to their husbands (or their fathers).

Female participation in the workforce has expanded over recent decades, which has meant that women have greater independence and are not dependent on marriage for financial security. Gender inequality is still apparent in the workplace, and women tend to occupy positions of less status in many occupations as compared with men. There are signs, however, that the "gender gap" is narrowing, and that social attitudes are changing. Female representation in higher education has dramatically expanded. Moreover, the opportunities for gaining both financial and sexual independence are greater for many women than they once were.

While modern feminists agree that these changes are no cause for complacency and that important work remains to be done, the role of prostitution is especially contentious and divisive in the feminist movement. For many feminists, prostitution is a symbol of women's continued exploitation and subordination in a society that is still controlled by men. They assert that prostitution represents the socio-economic disempowerment of women, and thus threatens the security and well-being of every girl and woman. From this perspective, "prostitution thrives in a society which values women more for their sexuality than for their skilled labour, and which puts women, particularly young, poorly educated women who have limited employment records at a disadvantage" (Johnson & Rogers, 1993, p. 101).

Feminists remain divided on the role of prostitution with respect to gender inequality and choice. Without free choice, some argue, there cannot be true equality. Others note that without gender equality, choice is nothing more than an illusion for sex workers (Bell, 1987; Jenness, 1993; Roberts, 1992; Schur, 1984).

Equality First

From an equality first standpoint, women's liberation can never be fully realized in a society where men view women as sexual objects. Those who subscribe to this point of view see prostitutes as victims of male domination over women in society. From a radical perspective, heterosexual sex itself is viewed as a form of sexual slavery in which women are subjected to male power and exploitation. Although not all radical feminists believe that heterosexual sex is necessarily oppressive and demeaning, it is generally agreed that prostitution (and pornography) are obvious representations of female subordination that must be done away with for women to be free (Dworkin, 1989; Miller, 1991; Overall, 1992; Tübinger Projektgruppe, 1989).

Free Choice First

Some feminists take a more liberal perspective on the role of prostitution. They see prostitutes as workers who should have the freedom to choose what they do for a living. The basis of women's liberation, from this standpoint, is empowering women to exercise free choice. Controlling the activities of women is regarded as degrading to their status as free members of society. For example, this view considers that attempts by well-intentioned individuals to deter women from sex work "for their own good" only disempowers them (Chapkis, 1997; Schur, 1984; Walkowitz, 1982).

Criminalizing prostitution is seen as a form of interference that only perpetuates gender inequality. From this perspective, prostitutes are free agents who resist oppressive moral and social norms. Arguably, they also hold the dominant position and power to choose to whom they sell their bodies. It is the man paying for sex who occupies the subordinate position in the sex-for-money interaction. Male promiscuity is thus seen as a form of weakness to be exploited by a woman, whose service must be paid for and cannot be had for free (Coles & Hallowell Coles, 1978; Kipnis, 1996). The sex worker's promiscuity, from this point of view, is neither good nor bad, but rather an expression of individual freedom to employ her body for financial gain. Each sexual encounter between consenting adults, whether money changes hands or not, should be understood on its own terms—as opposed to the manifestation of gender inequality or other social problems (Alexander, 1987; MacKinnon & Dworkin, 1998).

In summary, feminist perspectives lead to different versions of the nature of the sex trade and different policy perspectives on regulating prostitution. The free choice first perspective favours legalizing sex work, and reflects a Millsian point of view. It is also evident in the pending changes to Canada's official response to prostitution. As suggested by the arguments presented in Box 16.1, prostitution laws in Canada are changing in response to legal claims about the rights of workers and the role of government to ensure their health and safety, rather than enforcing moral norms.

Illegal Drugs

The long history of substance use and the various efforts by the state to control it are probably best described as an ambivalent relationship in the sense that drugs are both sought after and condemned. Psychoactive drugs have been taken by people for millennia to alter consciousness or mental states, to cope with hardship, and to bring people closer to their gods. Since ancient times as well, cultural and religious taboos have existed against the use of certain drugs. Like the current ban on prostitution, the prohibition of psychoactive substances has typically been justified on the grounds that drug use is immoral and laws against it are necessary measures to protect the common good.

Whereas the use of drugs such as alcohol and tobacco are subject to control through regulation, the use of other drugs has been outlawed altogether. Our social history suggests that the legal status of a substance is connected more to the characteristics of the user and less to chemical properties or evidence of harm. In other words, it is apparent that morality is closely related to perceptions about the drugs "bad" people use. The drugs used by bad people, social outcasts, or outsiders have often been outlawed as a method of controlling people or putting undesirable people "in their place."

The history of drug laws in Canada date back about a century, when smoking opium was banned (see Boyd, 1991; Giffen, Endicott, & Lambert, 1991). Soon after, cocaine and then cannabis were outlawed. In each instance, the outlawed drug was linked, as will be explored below, to certain ethnic groups and argued to cause insanity, indecency, and sexual promiscuity on the part of ethnic men who victimized white women. Outlandish and exaggerated claims—such as the claim that using cannabis causes heroin addiction, or using LSD causes genetic abnormalities—have been a fixture of many commentaries regarding Canadian drug laws ever since.

The last half-century has seen increasing efforts to incorporate medical and scientific knowledge into policy perspectives that determine the response to use of drugs. These efforts include classifying drug addiction, for example, as a "disease" for which the addict requires treatment rather than a jail term or other form of punishment. While this point of view appears increasingly accepted, and has expanded the jurisdiction of the medical profession, the punitive response to substance use is ever-present.

People who use certain types of drugs are still considered by some to be morally deficient and deserving of punishment, in accordance with existing moral norms and legal codes. Evidence that rates of substance use are on the rise is considered proof of yet another "epidemic" to be met with calls for stricter laws, police activity, and measures to protect our kids from drugs.

In reality, the greatest harm from substance use is caused by alcohol, tobacco, and prescription medications—including OxyContin, tranquilizers, "sleeping pills," and other addictive narcotics that have become a scourge in many Canadian communities—which are regulated to reduce their harm. By comparison, illegal drugs are used by a small fraction of the Canadian population. The only exception is marijuana. Surveys suggest that nearly half of Canadians have tried it. However, only a small fraction have used it more than once, and even fewer regularly or more than once a month (Adlaf, Begin, & Sawka, 2005).

Despite the great disparity in prevalence of use, policy discussions of the "drug problem" are typically focused on the topic of illicit substance use. Accordingly, this section is devoted to examining social factors that explain why people use illicit drugs and why these drugs have been criminalized. We will conclude with a discussion of social policy positions on illicit substance use in relation to the classic debates on use of law in the enforcement of morality.

Social Learning and Subcultural Perspectives

Social learning and subcultural perspectives on the use of illicit drugs rely on the assumption that drug users learn the behaviour from peers and role models within their social group. The social learning model is supported by research evidence suggesting that the use of drugs is higher among youth whose parents, older siblings, and peers use drugs as well (Simon, Conger, & Whitbeck, 1988). Social learning typically refers to early childhood (or primary) socialization. Subcultural perspectives prioritize learning processes (or secondary socialization) occurring later among youth.

The higher rates of drug use among disadvantaged groups is also understood as a result of learning processes that take place within a deviant subculture of peers. Frustration due to lack of opportunity among social groups with lower socio-economic status provides a structural explanation for the prevalence of crime involvement and illicit drug use among the lower classes. Another observation is that neighbourhoods with a higher prevalence of substance use are socially disorganized, resulting in the absence of parental and community controls that serve to prevent criminal behaviour.

Despite the compelling logic of the subcultural perspective and the support provided by official crime statistics, the association between social class and drug use is partly a reflection of policing practices. Illegal drug use is more visible in certain disadvantaged communities, which has led police to focus more so on and gather more evidence of drug use in those communities. However, the police's greater focus on certain communities rather than others does not necessarily reflect the actual prevalence of substance use behaviour.

However, the evidence suggests that substance use is no less common among non-disadvantaged social groups, but for different reasons. Surveys of the general population show that the prevalence of drugs such as marijuana, ecstasy, and cocaine is generally consistent, if not higher, among persons in the middle and upper classes (Parker, Williams, & Aldridge, 2002). This population of drug users, rather than reacting to social deprivation or frustration stemming from a lack of opportunity, considers that some experimentation with illicit drugs is "normal."

For those who view drug use as a rational response to the demands of daily life—motivated by desire for relaxation, stimulation, altered consciousness, or merely socializing with one's peers—the fact that drug use is considered to take place within a "deviant subculture" only reflects its status under law (Mostaghim & Hathaway, 2013). Clearly, substance use can be harmful. Any drug can be abused. Substance use is rewarding and addictive for the user, and can result in adverse consequences for families, health, relationships, and careers, as well as death. On the other hand, drug laws do nothing to address these problems, and, many would argue, only contribute to the harms of substance use.

Prohibition creates the very conditions that make using outlawed substances more dangerous than substance use itself. This conclusion was drawn indisputably nearly a century ago when alcohol was banned in the United States (from 1920 to 1933, a time known as *the prohibition era*). The result was an unregulated product of unknown potency and content—among other dangerous practices by drinkers and suppliers, that included violent criminals who were willing to take risks to keep up with demand. The lessons learned were soon forgotten, or never thought to be applicable, to other outlawed substances in North America and elsewhere.

prohibition
A law forbidding a specific act.

In Canada, the notion that drug laws present a problem more serious than substance use emerged in the 1960s—an era marked by an increase in youth experimentation with illicit drugs. A new class of criminal had been created, to whom the anti-drug laws had not applied before. Before proceeding to discuss opposing policy positions arising from debates about the problems with these laws, we examine functional and critical perspectives on the ban on certain kinds of drugs.

Drug Law Functions

Like the laws that target prostitution, prohibitions against possessing psychoactive drugs support an underground economy involving persons willing to risk arrest and punishment to provide this service. In addition to the jobs created for those willing to break the law to reap black market profits, prohibitions create opportunities for legitimate employment in the criminal justice system and beyond.

A large segment of the law enforcement budget is devoted to enforcing prohibition laws. Charges for the possession and supply of outlawed drugs account for a significant proportion of public spending for police, corrections, prosecution, and rehabilitation (for those sentenced to mandatory treatment).

Other vested interests in the prohibition industry include those who deal in legal drugs such as alcohol, tobacco, and prescription medications. They include the corporations that directly profit from the sale of regulated drugs and a wide variety of peripheral parties—such as pharmacists, physicians, and the proprietors of bars, restaurants, and others in the hospitality industry.

Little indication exists that the vast array of interested parties in the present system of drug control want to see the system changed. The system has distinguished "good" drugs from "bad" drugs, and those who deal in bad drugs go to jail. Despite declining rates of crime, federal spending on prisons nearly doubled between 2006 and 2012—from $1.6 billion to $2.98 billion (J. Davis, 2011). Considering the investment, it is not remotely likely that the present government is planning to reduce the pool of eligible inmates by legalizing outlawed drugs.

A Critical Perspective

The origin of drug laws in Canada and elsewhere can be traced to class and racial conflict. Drug use by the powerful is seldom subject to the same scrutiny or legislative action as that by the non-powerful. Consider the social history of Canadian laws related to opium: in the *Opium Act, 1908*, the manufacture of opium for smoking (an activity engaged in mainly by Chinese immigrants) was banned, while its use in medications that were widely used by white Canadians at the time was not.

The same pattern of discriminatory legislation and enforcement was repeated with cocaine, then marijuana, and (decades later) synthetic drugs such as LSD and ecstasy. In all instances, the common theme over the last century has been the prohibition of a substance used (primarily) originally by persons perceived to be a threat to moral standards.

The *Opium Act, 1908*, the first drug law in Canada, served to target Chinese immigrants who presumably preferred smoking opium to drinking alcohol. This preference per se was not a problem. However, it became a problem with the emerging tide of racist sentiment in Canada. When industrious immigrants became prosperous, their presence was resented and perceived as threatening to white Canadian values.

Canada's early narcotics laws reflected a complex blend of moral–racial and financial interests. Once this formula had been established, it became a simpler legislative matter to add foreign drugs to the growing schedule of banned substances. Cocaine and cannabis, like opium, were not widely used or even known to most Canadians. This mattered little. Enough was known by citizens exposed to anti-drug hysteria to understand that these drugs presented a grave threat.

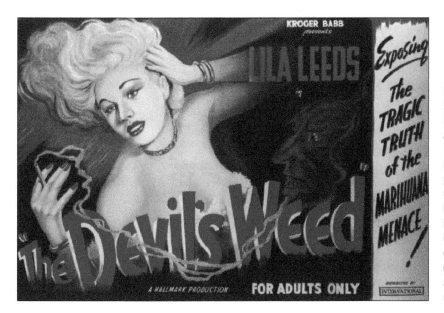

Long known simply as "cannabis," the Spanish term *marijuana* (or *marihuana*) became widely used by US legal authorities beginning in the 1920s and 1930s. By closely tying the term to the increasing Mexican immigrant populations in the US south who often used the drug, it became easier for lawmakers to target "outsiders" and implement bans on "the devil's weed." Hollywood films, whose content was closely regulated by the US government, played a major role in stigmatizing cannabis, as this 1940s movie poster attests.

It was believed that cocaine was being used by black men to lure white women into sinful interracial unions. Once under the drug's intoxicating spell, the female addict was enslaved and helpless to resist. Like the imagery associated with opium smoking, that of cocaine use was wickedness, contagion, and the invasion of a foreign substance used by outsiders who were unwelcome guests.

The ban on cannabis in Canada in 1923 (through the *Opium and Drug Act*) played on much the same themes. No debate took place in Parliament to refute the wildly exaggerated claims of its use and effects. Moreover, it became clear, despite the ease with which the ban passed, that it served a function more symbolic than instrumental in responding to a manufactured threat. The first arrests and seizures of the drug did not occur for more than a decade after the law was passed. This delay suggests that no one in the country at the time the ban was instituted was using marijuana. Important questions come to mind about the function served by the introduction of "a law without a problem" (Giffen, Endicott, & Lambert, 1991). The symbolic function of the war on certain drugs is arguably to criminalize rather than protect those who use them. The main criteria for banning drugs are devised on the basis of the characteristics of their primary consumers, as opposed to evidence of harm.

Those perceived as threatening to the established social order are ordinarily the primary targets of the law. Since targeting social groups or persons is widely recognized as a discriminatory practice in constitutional democracies, the government's focus is on substances. Enforcement of the law against those who use banned substances is thus considered equally applicable to all. The groups targeted by default via the substances they use include cultural outsiders (especially non-whites), members of the lower classes, youth, and others who use drugs for reasons other than improving productivity—that is, reasons considered to threaten the moral order.

The disparity in sentencing for cocaine users based on class and racial characteristics is a prominent example of the symbolic function of the war on drugs. In the United

States, for example, prison terms for crack cocaine users are disproportionately higher than those for powder cocaine users (Tony, 1995).

The crack scare in America in 1986 resulted in the passing of the US *Anti-Drug Abuse Act*. The Act imposed a mandatory minimum sentence of five years' imprisonment for possessing 5 grams of crack cocaine. The same prison term was mandated for possessing 500 grams of cocaine powder at the time. Although the addictive properties of "rock," or crack cocaine, presumably would justify discrepancies in sentencing, it was widely recognized that the large disparity had more to do with where, and by whom, the drug was used. While the primary consumers of crack were known to be poor and black, residing in inner-city slums, the primary consumers of powder cocaine were associated more with white, well-to-do professionals who used the drug to party. The disparity resulting from this legislation stood for a quarter-century. In 2010, the sentencing disparity between offences for crack and powder cocaine were reduced under the *Fair Sentencing Act* from 100:1 to 18:1 (Office of Research and Data, 2011).

The discrepancy in the regulatory measures used to control drugs based on race and class distinctions indicates that a hierarchy of social disapproval and punishment exists for those who use illicit drugs. This discrepancy also appears in the regulatory measures for controlling legal psychoactive drugs with properties or chemical effects similar to illegal drugs. The regulation applied to legal drugs does not guarantee no harm to users and society. But neither does the ban on outlawed drugs. Put otherwise:

> The indirect harms and costs of illicit drugs by far outweigh direct harms and are disproportionate to their level of use and are the result of drug policy and legislation, not the drugs per se. The most direct harms occur in high-risk populations such as injecting drug users, street youth, the inner-city poor and Natives. (Riley, 1998, p. 2)

Alternatives to Criminalizing Drugs

In light of the indirect harms and questionable cost-effectiveness of drug laws, the alternatives of **legalization** and **decriminalization** have been seriously discussed among drug policy observers. The legalization option has parallels with regulated substances such as alcohol, tobacco, prescription medications, and over-the-counter drugs. While some restrictions—such as age, point of sale, and driving after using—may apply, these different regulatory models generally allow for legal use of a product licensed by the government for sale.

Marijuana has been partially legalized in Canada for those who qualify for access due to chronic health conditions. Some observers recommend a regulatory system that would allow for wider legal access to the drug (see Senate Special Committee on Illegal Drugs, 2002). The prospect of legalizing marijuana and other outlawed drugs, however, remains highly controversial and unlikely in Canada (for the time being at least). Shifting boundaries of morally acceptable behaviour are evident in law reform in the United States. In 2012, at the state level, marijuana legalization initiatives (allowing sale to adults) were passed in Washington and Colorado.

Many policy observers who acknowledge the shortcomings of drug prohibition favour decriminalization. This more moderate reform option is, once again, more likely in the case of marijuana than other outlawed drugs. Indeed, this model is already followed to a certain extent in Canadian jurisdictions where arrests for small amounts of marijuana

legalization
The removal of an existing prohibition against something that is currently unlawful. In the case of drugs and prostitution, the term often implies a regulated system of supply or licensing of services provided.

decriminalization
The removal of criminal penalties, though fines may still apply.

result in fines instead of jail terms. This pragmatic option is preferred by those who argue that decriminalizing drug possession will alleviate the harm to users of acquiring a permanent criminal record—while maintaining the deterrent impact of the law and the message that the state does not condone the use of (some) drugs.

Another policy option frequently discussed by critics of the war on drugs is more oriented to the aims of public health. The harm-reduction model, as the term suggests, seeks to reduce the harm to people who use illicit drugs. The function of the state, from this perspective, is not to moralize or punish substance users (Hathaway, 2001).

In spite of stringent efforts to prevent it, there have always been (and will always be) people who use drugs. Recognizing this reality, the most pragmatic policy is to provide the services and information needed to help them use these substances more safely.

Examples of harm-reduction measures are numerous—from distributing free needles to injection drug users to using shatterproof glass in bars to prevent bloodshed. Despite the cost-effectiveness and logic of such measures, from a public health perspective on the use of state resources, the case of InSite in Vancouver is a prominent example of the controversy surrounding **harm reduction** (see Box 16.2).

harm reduction
A public health–oriented policy or program designed to reduce the harmful consequences of behaviours with known risks, which are often illegal, such as prostitution and recreational drug use.

Vancouver's InSite Drug Injection Clinic Will Stay Open: Top Court Rules on Clinic's Exemption from Federal Drug Laws

In 2011, the Supreme Court of Canada ruled that a Vancouver safe injection facility could remain open. In a unanimous decision, the court argued that its services improved the health and safety of drug addicts, thereby warranting an exemption from the federal drug laws.

Vancouver's controversial InSite clinic can stay open, the Supreme Court said Friday in a landmark ruling.

In a unanimous decision, the court ruled that not allowing the clinic to operate under an exemption from drug laws would be a violation of the Charter of Rights and Freedoms.

The court ordered the federal minister of health to grant an immediate exemption to allow InSite to operate.

"InSite saves lives. Its benefits have been proven. There has been no discernible negative impact on the public safety and health objectives of Canada during its eight years of operation," the ruling said, written by Chief Justice Beverley McLachlin.

If InSite wasn't allowed to operate it would prevent injection drug users from accessing the health services offered at the facility, threatening their health and their lives, the ruling said. Withdrawing the exemption would even undermine the purpose of the federal drug law, which includes public health and safety, the court said.

The Supreme Court said that if the health minister, currently Leona Aglukkaq, receives applications for more exemptions, she must continue to exercise her discretion and aim to strike a balance between charter rights and protecting public health and safety.

Where there is no evidence that a supervised injection site would have a negative impact on public safety, the minister "should generally grant an exemption," the court said.

The Conservative government is opposed to the InSite operation, and when it came to power it dropped harm reduction from the national anti-drug strategy. Aglukkaq said Friday the government's investments are targeted at prevention and treatment.

"Although we are disappointed with the Supreme Court of Canada's decision today, we will comply," Aglukkaq said in question period. "We believe that the system should be focused on preventing people from becoming drug addicts."

Aglukkaq said the government planned on reviewing the decision.

Source: CBC.ca/news, September 30, 2011. Reprinted by permission. http://www.cbc.ca/news/canada/british-columbia/vancouver-s-InSite-drug-injection-clinic-will-stay-open-1.1005044.

Conclusion

Notwithstanding opposition from the federal government, the foregoing policy alternatives to criminalizing drugs are arguably more consistent with the spirit of the Charter—which puts the onus on the state to justify intrusion into the affairs of individuals. Drug policy reforms need not be mutually exclusive. A multi-layered perspective on the function of the state recognizes the complexity of mitigating harm from a behaviour through criminal law. Decriminalizing the possession of small amounts of drugs, for example, need not preclude stepped-up enforcement of laws that target organized crime and large-scale trafficking. Similarly, "red light districts" that allow prostitution facilitate containment of the trade and redirect criminal justice resources to enforcing laws that target sexual slavery and prostituting children.

As noted in Box 16.1, in its unanimous decision, Canada's Supreme Court supports the role of government to "regulate against nuisances, but not at the cost of the health, safety and lives of prostitutes" (Fine, 2013). In so doing, it struck down the prohibition against earning a living on the avails of prostitution. To ensure the safety of sex workers, the Supreme Court recognized the role of drivers, managers, and bodyguards, whose services do not necessarily amount to exploitation. It was also ruled that the provision in the law prohibiting communication prevented prostitutes "from screening potential clients for intoxication and propensity to violence." The provision was accordingly deemed "grossly disproportionate … to the possibility of nuisance caused by street prostitution" (*Canada (Attorney General) v. Bedford*, 2013). At the time of writing, the Supreme Court's ruling is still pending, awaiting a response from the federal government to come up with alternatives that mitigate the risks imposed by the existing law. Whatever the outcome, it is increasingly apparent that the spirit of the Charter's constitutional protections are functioning to shape interpretation of the law.

Similarly, our drug laws are presently in limbo, and continuously in flux. Whatever the perspective of the reader, it is hoped that this chapter has provided some direction to continue to develop your position on the appropriate role of the law in these and other social policy debates.

SUMMARY OF KEY POINTS

- Unlike consensus crimes (such as murder, rape, and assault), crimes of morality are subject to widespread disagreement and considerable debate.
- In democratic, multicultural societies such as Canada and other Western nations, the legislation of morality raises important questions about the proper role of government and whose morality or justice ought to be enforced.
- Section 1 of the Charter puts the onus on government to justify prohibiting an action. It also further establishes that the prohibition must be minimally intrusive, rational, and proportionate to the harm inflicted by the action.
- Historically, sex work has enabled a small segment of the female population to meet the sexual needs of men and provide a "safety valve" for men seeking sex. Earlier and contemporary feminist perspectives (e.g., the equality first and free choice first perspectives) lead to different versions of the nature of the sex trade and different policy perspectives on regulating prostitution.

- The long history of substance use and the various efforts by the state to control it are probably best described as an ambivalent relationship in the sense that drugs are both sought after and condemned. Our social history suggests that the legal status of a substance is connected more to the characteristics of the user and less to chemical properties or evidence of harm. The origin of drug laws in Canada and elsewhere can be traced to class and racial conflict. Drug use by the powerful is seldom subject to the same scrutiny or legislative action as that by the non-powerful. Decriminalization and harm-reduction measures, however cost-effective and logical, remain sources of controversy.

QUESTIONS FOR CRITICAL DISCUSSION

1. What is your perspective on the enforcement of morality? Do you agree with Mill, Hart, Devlin? Or do you have a different point of view?
2. Can you think of other crimes of morality that might be argued to represent examples of overcriminalization?
3. Do you think that prostitution should be legalized, decriminalized, or remain illegal? Which of the feminist perspectives on sex work makes sense to you?
4. Should illegal drugs be legalized, decriminalized, or neither? If you support changes in the law, does your perspective apply to all illegal drugs or only some—and why?
5. Can you think of other examples of harm reduction—as applied to drugs or prostitution, or any other activities involving certain risks?

SUGGESTED FURTHER READINGS

Boyd, N. (1991). *High society: Legal and illegal drugs in Canada*. Toronto: Key Porter.

Hathaway, A.D. (2001). Charter rights of Canadian drug users: A constitutional assessment of the Clay trial and ruling. *Canadian Journal of Law and Society*, *16*(1), 29–43.

Phoenix, J. (2001). *Making sense of prostitution*. London, UK: Palgrave Macmillan.

Richards, D.A.J. (1982). *Sex, drugs, death and the law: An essay on human rights and overcriminalization*. Totawa, NJ: Rowman & Littlefield.

Websites

Drugs—Canadian Foundation for Drug Policy: http://www.cfdp.ca

Drugs—EROWID: Documenting the Complex Relationship between Humans and Psychoactives: http://www.erowid.org

Gambling—Alberta Gambling Institute (which researches various aspects of gambling): http://www.abgamblinginstitute.ualberta.ca/LibraryResources/Bibliographies.aspx

Prostitution—Sextrade Public Awareness and Education: http://www.sextrade101.com

Prostitution (Historica Canada): http://www.thecanadianencyclopedia.com/en/article/prostitution/

REFERENCES

Adlaf, E., Begin, P., & Sawka, E. (Eds.). (2005). *Canadian Addiction Survey (CAS): A national survey of Canadians' use of alcohol and other drugs: Prevalence of use and related harms—Detailed report.* Ottawa: Canadian Centre on Substance Abuse.

Alexander, P. (1987). Prostitution: A difficult issue for feminists. In F. Delacoste and P. Alexander (Eds.), *Sex work writing by women in the sex industry* (pp. 184–214). Pittsburgh: Cleis Press.

Angus Reid Public Opinion. (2011). Canadians remain divided on how to deal with prostitution. Vancouver: Angus Reid Global.

Antweiler, W. (2002). *Canadian crime statistics: Selected time trends and interprovincial comparisons.* Vancouver: University of British Columbia.

Bell, L. (1987). *Good girls/bad girls.* Seattle, WA: Seal Press.

Bentham, J. (2007). *An introduction to the principles of morals and legislation.* Mineola, NY: Dover Philosophical Classics. (Original work published 1781.)

Boyd, N. (1991). *High society: Legal and illegal drugs in Canada.* Toronto: Key Porter.

Cavan, S. (1970). B-girls and prostitutes. In J. Douglas (Ed.), *Observation of deviance* (pp. 55–63). New York: Random House.

Chapkis, W. (1997). *Live sex acts: Women performing erotic labor.* New York: Routledge.

Clinard, M., & Meier, R. (1998). *Sociology of deviant behavior* (10th ed.). Fort Worth, TX: Harcourt Brace.

Cohen, A.K. (1966). *Deviance and control.* Englewood Cliffs, NJ: Prentice Hall.

Coles, R., & Hallowell Coles, J. (1978). *Women of crisis.* New York: Dell.

Dalla, R. (2000). Exposing the "Pretty Woman" myth: A qualitative examination of the lives of streetwalking prostitutes. *The Journal of Sex Research, 37*(4), 344–354.

Davis, J. (2011, July 18). Prison costs soar 86% in past five years: Report. *National Post.* Retrieved from http://news.nationalpost.com/2011/07/18/prison-costs-soar-86-in-past-five-years.

Davis, K. (1937). The sociology of prostitution. *American Sociological Review, 2*(5), 744–755.

Davis, K. (1971). Prostitution. In R.K. Merton & R. Nisbet (Eds.), *Contemporary social problems* (3rd ed.) (pp. 341–351). New York: Harcourt Brace Jovanovich.

Davis, K. (1976). Sexual behavior. In R.K. Merton & R. Nisbet (Eds.), *Contemporary social problems* (4th ed.) (pp. 219–261). New York: Harcourt Brace Jovanovich.

Davis, N.J. (1980). *Sociological constructions of deviance: Perspectives and issues in the field* (2nd ed.). Dubuque, IA: William C. Brown.

Devlin, P. (1965). *The enforcement of morals.* London, UK: Oxford University Press.

Durkheim, É. (1933). *The division of labor in society* (George Simpson, Trans.). New York: Macmillan.

Durkheim, É. (1938). *The rules of sociological method* (S.A. Solovay & J.H. Mueller, Trans.). Chicago: University of Chicago Press.

Dworkin, A. (1989). *Pornography.* New York: Dutton.

Engels, F. (1942). *The origin of the family, private property, and the state.* New York: International. (Original work published 1884)

Erikson, K.T. (1966). *Wayward puritans: A study in the sociology of deviance.* New York: John Wiley & Sons.

Fine, S. (2013, December 20). Supreme Court strikes down Canada's prostitution laws. *Globe and Mail.* Retrieved from http://www.theglobeandmail.com/news/national/supreme-court-rules-on-prostitution-laws/article16067485.

Fisher, D.J. (1982). Reading Freud's *Civilization and its discontents. Journal Council for the Advancement of Psychoanalytic Education, 2*(2), 31–42.

Freud, S. (2002). *Civilization and its discontents*. London, UK: Penguin.

Gay, P. (Ed.). (1989). *The Freud reader*. New York: Norton & Company.

Giffen, P.J., Endicott, S.J., & Lambert, S. (1991). *Panic and indifference: The politics of Canada's drug laws*. Ottawa: Canadian Centre on Substance Abuse.

Hagan, J. (1991). *The disreputable pleasures: Crime and deviance in Canada* (3rd ed.). Toronto: McGraw-Hill Ryerson.

Hart, H.L.A. (1963). *Law, liberty and morality*. Stanford, CA: Stanford University Press.

Hathaway, A.D. (1997). Marijuana and lifestyle: Exploring tolerable deviance. *Deviant Behavior*, *18*(3), 213–232.

Hathaway, A.D. (2001). Shortcomings of harm reduction: Toward a morally invested drug reform strategy. *International Journal of Drug Policy*, *12*(2), 125–137.

Janus, S.S., & Janus, C.L. (1993). *The Janus report on sexual behavior*. New York: John Wiley and Sons.

Jenness, V. (1993). *Making it work: The prostitutes' rights movement in perspective*. New York: de Gruyter.

Johnson, H., & Rogers, K. (1993). A statistical overview of women in crime in Canada. In E. Adelberg & C. Currie (Eds.), *In conflict with the law: Women and the Canadian justice system* (pp. 95–116). Vancouver: Press Gang.

Kelly, P.J. (2006). Liberalism and epistemic diversity: Mill's sceptical legacy. *Episteme*, *3*(3), 248–265.

Kipnis, L. (1996). *Bound and gagged: Pornography and the politics of fantasy in America*. New York: Grove Press.

MacKinnon, C.A., & Dworkin, A. (Eds.). (1998). *In harm's way: The pornography civil rights hearing*. Cambridge, MA: Harvard University Press.

Mars, G. (1982). *Cheats at work: An anthropology of workplace crime*. London, UK: Unwin.

Matza, D. (1969). *Becoming deviant*. Englewood Cliffs, NJ: Prentice Hall.

Meil-Hobson, B. (1987). *Uneasy virtue*. New York: Basic Books.

Merton, R.K. (1957). *Social theory and social structure* (Rev. ed.). New York: Free Press.

Merton, R.K. (1973). *The sociology of science*. Chicago: University of Chicago Press.

Mill, J.S. (2002). *On liberty*. Mineola, NY: Dover Philosophical Classics. (Original work published 1859.)

Miller, J.L. (1991). Prostitution in contemporary American society. In E. Grauerholz & M.A. Koralewski (Eds.), *Sexual coercion* (pp. 45–57). Lexington, MA: Lexington Books.

Mostaghim, A., & Hathaway, A.D. (2013). Identity formation, marijuana and "the self": A study of cannabis normalization among university students. *Frontiers in Psychiatry*, *4*(160), 1–7.

Office of Research and Data. (2011). *Memorandum to the chair of the United States Sentencing Commission*. Washington, DC: United States Sentencing Commission.

Overall, C. (1992). What's wrong with prostitution? Evaluating sex work. *Signs*, *17*, 705–724.

Parker, H., Williams, L., & Aldridge, J. (2002). The normalization of "sensible" recreational drug use: Further evidence from the North West England Longitudinal Study. *Sociology*, *36*(4), 941–964.

Parsons, T. (1951). *The social system*. New York: Free Press.

Perkins, R. (1991). *Working girls: Prostitutes, their life and social control*. Canberra, Australia: Australian Institute of Criminology.

Pleck, E. (1987). *Domestic tyranny*. New York: Oxford University Press.

Polsky, N. (1985). *Hustlers, beats and others*. Chicago: University of Chicago Press.

Richards, D.A.J. (1982). *Sex, drugs, death and the law: An essay on human rights and overcriminalization*. Totawa, NJ: Rowman & Littlefield.

Riley, D. (1998). *Drugs and drug policy in Canada: A brief review and commentary*. Ottawa: Report prepared for the Senate of Canada.

Roberts, N. (1992). *Whores in history: Prostitution in Western society*. London, UK: HarperCollins.

Rosen, F. (2003). *Classical utilitarianism from Hume to Mill*. London, UK: Routledge.

Rosen, R. (1982). *The lost sisterhood: Prostitution in America, 1900–1918*. Baltimore: John Hopkins University Press.

Ross, J.I. (2000). *Making news of police violence: A comparative study of Toronto and New York City*. Westport, CT: Praeger.

Schur, E.M. (1984). *Labeling women deviant: Gender, stigma, and social control*. Philadelphia: Temple University Press.

Senate Special Committee on Illegal Drugs. (2002). *Cannabis: Our position for a Canadian public policy*. Ottawa: Information Canada.

Siegel, L.J., & McCormick, C. (2012). *Criminology in Canada: Theories, patterns, and typologies* (5th ed.). Toronto: Nelson.

Simon, R.L., Conger, R.D., & Whitbeck, L.B. (1988). A multistage social learning model of the influences of family and peers upon adolescent substance abuse. *Journal of Drug Issues*, *18*(3), 293–315.

Stebbins, R.A. (1996). *Tolerable differences: Living with deviance*. Whitby, ON: McGraw-Hill Ryerson.

Tong, R. (1984). *Women, sex and the law*. Savage, MD: Rowman & Littlefield.

Tony, M. (1995). *Malign neglect: Race, crime and punishment in America*. London, UK: Oxford University Press.

Tübinger Projektgruppe, F. (1989). *Frauenhandel in Deutschland*. Bonn, Germany: J.H.W. Dietz.

Walkowitz, J. (1982). Male vice and feminist virtue: Feminism and the politics of prostitution in nineteenth century Britain. *History Workshop*, *13*, 79–83.

Legislation

Canadian Charter of Rights and Freedoms, s. 1, Part I of the *Constitution Act, 1982*, being Schedule B to the *Canada Act 1982* (UK), 1982, c. 11.

Criminal Code. (1985). RSC 1985, c. C-46.

Cases

Canada (Attorney General) v. Bedford. (2013). 2013 SCC 72.

Carter v. Canada (Attorney General). (2012). 2012 BCSC 886 (the Gloria Taylor "death with dignity" case).

Gang Warfare on Vancouver Streets

The Bacon Brothers are well-known British Columbia gangsters. Eldest brother Jonathan was killed in a brutal targeted slaying in August 2011. Jarrod is currently serving a 12-year sentence for drug trafficking. Jamie is standing trial in Vancouver for allegedly playing a central role in the October 19, 2007 massacre in Surrey, BC that took the lives of four rival gang members and two innocent bystanders. These victims are often referred to as "the Surrey Six." If there are convictions in this case, it will officially be the worst gangland slaying in British Columbia's history.

The body of one of the shooting victims in the Surrey Six murders is removed from the crime scene.

Source: Jonathan Hayward/The Canadian Press.

These and other bloody incidents were the culmination of rivalries and power plays among a number of gangs competing for pre-eminence in the lucrative Vancouver drug trade. The tension among these gangs rose noticeably in the spring of 2007, several months before the Surrey Six slayings, when Jamie Bacon—wearing a bulletproof vest—was ambushed by gunmen in the driveway of a rented luxury home in Surrey, narrowly missing death. He said at the time he had been awaiting delivery of a special armoured SUV from Ontario. Clearly, he knew very well that there were people who wanted to see him dead.

The attempted hit was a clear warning to the Bacon Brothers, and it was believed by some to be an attempt by the United Nations gang to intimidate the Brothers from further pursuing their increasingly close relationship with a gang known as the Red Scorpions. Whatever the case, six months later, the same cycle of violence, retribution, and turf warfare would result in six people killed in a Surrey condominium complex. They were all shot in the back of the head, execution-style.

Jamie Bacon and three other gang members were charged. On the first day of the trial, lead prosecutor Mark Levitz stated that one of the victims, Corey Lal, was the primary target of Bacon and his associates, and that the other five had been killed so that there would be no witnesses (all four accused entered pleas of not guilty). It was alleged that the accused were members of the Red Scorpions gang, headed by Jamie Bacon and Michael Le, and that a short time before the murders, Bacon warned Lal, a young drug trafficker, that he would have to pay a $100,000 "tax" to Bacon and the Red Scorpions because he was selling drugs on Scorpion turf. When Lal refused, according to Levitz's statement, the Scorpions hatched their plot to kill Lal, leading to the bloody incident in a 15th-floor apartment of the Balmoral Towers in Surrey.

One particularly interesting aspect of the Bacon Brothers' gangland lifestyle is the fact that they, unlike most gang members, were not the products of a disadvantaged upbringing, nor were they surrounded by street crime from an early age. On the contrary, they enjoyed a privileged upbringing (as did United Nations gang co-founder Clayton Roueche). In short, they were not born into a criminal lifestyle, and did not have it foisted upon them at an early age; they chose it willingly, and, for a time, they enjoyed the fast cars, the women, the drugs, and the notoriety that this lifestyle brought them. Eventually, however, a series of conflicts of the sort commonly seen in the world of gangs and drug trafficking appear to have brought that lifestyle to an end.

Another notable observation about the Bacon Brothers and some other Vancouver-area gangs, such as the United Nations, is the fact that their memberships and close associates were not made up of homogeneous ethnic groups; rather, these were multi-ethnic gangs—an unusual phenomenon, and one that may represent the future of organized crime in Canada. We shall see in the years ahead.

Before You Read Chapter 17

- What effects do you think incidents such as the Surrey Six slayings and other high-profile gang activity have on a community?
- What specific measures do you think could be taken by police, the community at large, or even the federal government to quell this sort of gang activity? For instance, to what extent might this violence stem from the fact that drugs are illegal and, there-fore, unregulated? Could the legalization of at least some types of drugs undermine the profits of these gangs, and therefore possibly reduce violence?
- After reading Chapter 17, return to this case study. Which of the four levels of gangs described in this chapter do the Bacon Brothers fall into? Explain your answer.

Organized Crime and Gangs

LEARNING OBJECTIVES

After reading this chapter, students will be able to:

- Identify various ways in which gangs and organized crime groups have been defined.
- Understand the reasons why it has been difficult to identify a uniform definition of gangs.
- Describe the four levels of gangs and provide examples of each.
- Identify six types of gang violence.
- Discuss the ways in which key criminological theories can be applied to examinations of organized crime and gang behaviour.
- Describe the impact of gang suppression strategies.
- Identify some promising prevention strategies, as well as those that have proven ineffective in reducing gang membership.

Introduction

In recent decades, Canadians have been bombarded with a variety of terms used to identify various forms of organized criminal activity. These terms have been used to capture such phenomena as the Mafia, outlaw motorcycle clubs, Chinese triads, youth gangs, girl gangs, **drug cartels**, hate groups, and even terrorist cells. Canadians have also been confronted with the idea that street gangs are an increasing threat to our society. Indeed, one study found that over 80 percent of Toronto residents feel that street gangs and gang-related violence are on the increase in Canada (Wortley & Tanner, 2007). The question is, How can the general public believe that street gangs are on the rise when no uniform definition of what constitutes a gang or organized crime group exists? (See Ball & Curry, 1995.) As Finn-Aage Esbensen, Thomas Winfree, Ni He, and Terrance Taylor (2001, p. 106) indicate: "There is little, if any, consensus as to what constitutes a gang and who is a gang member, let alone what gangs do either inside or outside of the law."

Thus, before we can even begin to understand the "gang" or "organized crime" issue, we must first address some fundamental questions: What constitutes "organized crime"? What is a "gang"? How do gangs differ from other social groups? How can we identify gang members and gang-related crime? How can we distinguish street gangs from other types of criminal organization?

drug cartel
Criminal organization, often highly organized and with many partnerships, involved primarily in the trafficking of illegal drugs.

Defining Gangs and Organized Crime

Frederick Thrasher (1927/1963) was one of the first criminological researchers to provide a detailed "gang" definition. He argued that gangs were part of normal peer group activity for adolescents and involved behaviours that ranged from the conventional to the deviant. He proposed that gangs can be identified by six characteristics:

1. a spontaneous and unplanned origin;
2. intimate face-to-face relations;
3. a sense of organization, solidarity, and morale that is superior to that exhibited by the mob;
4. a tendency to move through space and meet a hostile element, which can precipitate cooperative, planned conflict, a morale-boosting activity in itself;
5. the creation of a shared esprit de corps and a common tradition or "heritage of memories"; and
6. a propensity for some geographic area or territory, which it will defend through force if necessary. (pp. 36–46)

It is interesting to note that the characteristics identified by Thrasher are neither intrinsically "good" nor "bad" and do not include acts of crime, violence, or delinquency. Thus, at least according to this scholar, we must differentiate between "law-abiding" and "criminal" gangs.

Since Thrasher's (1927/1963) groundbreaking work, the number of distinct gang definitions—within both academia and the criminal justice system—has soared, and these definitions often seem to mirror the needs of the academics or criminal justice organizations that propose them. For youth gangs alone, hundreds of definitions exist within the literature, including the following:

- "A gang is an organized group of three or more individuals, who rely on group intimidation, violence and criminal acts to gain power and recognition and/or control certain areas of unlawful activity" (Halifax Police Service; as cited in Hemmati, 2006, p. 25).
- "A criminal street gang is an ongoing group, club, organization or association of five or more persons formed for the purpose of committing a violent crime or drug offence, with members that have engaged, within the past five years, in a continuing series of violent crimes or drug law violations that affect interstate or foreign commerce" (United States Criminal Code; as cited in Wheatley, 2008, p. 86).
- "A group must be involved in a pattern of criminal acts to be considered a youth gang. These groups are typically composed only of juveniles, but may include young adults in their membership. Prison gangs, ideological gangs, hate groups and motorcycle gangs are not included. Likewise gangs whose membership is restricted to adults and do not have the characteristics of youth gangs are excluded" (Curry & Decker, 1998, p. 6).

In addition to those definitions for street and youth gangs, we can also list some common broader definitions of gangs and organized crime groups:

- "A criminal street gang is a group of people following a common code of conduct, having common beliefs and identifiers, existing in a semi-structured organization or **hierarchy**, and attempting to accomplish their goals through criminal activity" (Howell 1998, p. 1).
- "The gang is a spontaneous, semi-secret, interstitial, integrated but mutable social system whose members share common interests and that functions with relatively little regard for legality but regulates interaction among its members and features a leadership structure with processes of organizational maintenance and membership services and adaptive mechanisms for dealing with other significant social systems in its environment (Ball & Curry, 1995, p. 240).
- "A group or gang that, in the past twelve months, has done reprehensible acts" (Gatti, Tremblay, Vitaro, & McDuff, 2005, p. 1180).

hierarchy
Group structure built around easily identified leaders and followers; in gangs, the hierarchy often determines the roles, obligations, and rewards of members.

These definitions range from the simplistic to the theoretically complex. They also clearly illustrate that considerable disagreement exists in the literature about exactly what constitutes a gang (see Langston, 2003; Petersen, 2000; Short, 2009; Wood & Alleyne, 2010).

Definitions in the Criminal Code
As stated in the *Criminal Code*, section 467.1(1), a "criminal organization" is a group, however organized, that

a) is composed of three or more persons in or outside Canada; and
b) has as one of its main purposes or activities the facilitation or commission of one or more serious offences, that, if committed, would likely result in the direct or indirect receipt of a material benefit, including a financial benefit, by the group or by any one of the persons who constitute the group.

The *Criminal Code* definition does not include a group of persons that forms randomly for the immediate commission of a single offence, nor does it mention how long a group must exist before it can be considered a criminal organization (although it has typically applied to groups that have been existence for at least one month). The *Criminal Code* also explicitly states that one of the main purposes of a criminal organization must be the commission of crime *for material benefit*. This definition could potentially exclude gangs that are involved in crime or violence for status, honour, or excitement. By contrast, the United Nations' definition of an organized criminal group (outlined in article 2 of the United Nations Convention against Transnational Organized Crime and the Protocols Thereto, 2004) refers to a group committing a serious crime "for the purpose of obtaining a financial or other benefit." The use of the term "other benefit" could be used to include gangs that are involved in crimes that do not have a material or financial motive.

The strength of the *Criminal Code* definition is that it is flexible enough to be applied to a variety of criminal groups. Although it was originally developed to deal with such traditional organized crime groups as the Italian Mafia and the Hells Angels motorcycle gang, it has since been used to target the activities of newer, less organized entities, such as street gangs. A similar situation has been documented in the United States where the **Racketeer** *Influenced and Corrupt Organization Act* (RICO), originally enacted to

racketeering
Criminal activity commonly related to gangs that typically involves obtaining money through acts such as extortion, bribery, illegal gambling, and loan sharking.

dismantle the Mafia, has since been used to successfully prosecute the members of street gangs (see Wheatley, 2008).

Classifying the Various Types of Organized Crime and Gangs

Several scholars have attempted to develop a classification system for different types of criminal organization. Robert Gordon's (2000) work in British Columbia, for example, distinguished between criminal business organizations, street gangs, and "wannabe" groups. Similarly, Mercer Sullivan (2005) developed a gang typology that differentiates between action-sets, cliques, and named gangs. Finally, Cheryl Maxson and Malcolm Klein (1995) identify five different types of gang: (1) the classical or traditional gang; (2) the neo-classical gang; (3) the compressed gang; (4) the collective group; and (5) the specialty group. All of these typologies reflect the specific focus of the individual researcher. However, at a basic level, all of these scholars classified gangs according to their size, permanence, level of organization, and level of involvement in criminal activity.

A Gang Classification System

The following represents one of the many possible ways of classifying gangs. It generally moves from the least to the most organized and stable criminal groups.

Level One Gangs

Level one gangs are characterized by fluid friendship groups, usually based on a common neighbourhood and/or cultural identity. Their criminal activity is periodic, opportunistic, unorganized, and unplanned. Gang members often engage in crime for immediate gratification (including fun and excitement) rather than long-term economic interests. Members make no attempt to specialize or control a particular type of illicit activity. They are rarely involved in serious violence. Level one gangs have no leadership or hierarchical organizational structure. These gangs generally do not have a formal gang name or related gang symbols. Gang membership is often temporary. These gangs often form and disband quickly and are similar to what Gordon (2000) termed "wannabe" groups, or what other scholars have called "delinquent youth groups." Few level one gangs remain in existence for more than a year.

Example: A nameless group of teenagers who hang out in a mall or on the street corner during summer vacation. These youth may engage in shoplifting, bullying, drug use, and other minor forms of criminality, but they never develop a permanent identity and disband once the school year begins.

Level Two Gangs

Level two gangs exist for a significant period of time (i.e., one year or longer). Their criminal activity is often planned and deliberate. Although gang members engage in a variety of criminal activities, they show little criminal specialization. These gangs may or may not have a name and may have group symbols, colours, or a unique language. Activities may or may not be based in a particular neighbourhood or territory. Level two gangs are often egalitarian and typically do not have a formal leadership structure. Individual gang members often engage in crime to further their own personal interests rather than the objectives of the group. Gang activity often involves violence. Disputes over honour or reputation are common.

Example: A group of delinquent youth who maintain ties beyond the summer vacation period. Gang members give themselves a name and begin to engage in more serious crimes, including the extortion and robbery of other neighbourhood youth. This type of gang may even begin to sell drugs on the street for more established criminal organizations.

Level Three Gangs

Level three gangs are characterized by a hierarchical organizational structure with easily identified leaders and followers. These gangs exist for a significant period of time (i.e., one year or longer). Gang-based criminal activities are almost always planned and deliberate. These gangs usually have a name and may have group symbols, colours, or a unique language. Level three gangs typically try to control a particular type of illicit activity (e.g., drug trafficking) or all illicit activities within a defined geographical area. Gang activity often involves serious violence—including the use of firearms. Gang violence can occur for both economic reasons and to settle disputes over honour or respect. Gang members are often influenced by an informal or formal gang code. An enforced code of silence means that level three gang members rarely testify against other members. Witness intimidation is common.

Example: Gang sets—sometimes with names such as the Bloods or Crips—traffic in drugs and operate within specific public housing communities.

Level Four Gangs

Level four gangs have a long, stable history (i.e., they have been in existence for at least five years). These gangs have a sophisticated organizational structure with easily identified leaders and followers. Gang-based activities are almost always planned and deliberate.

Members of the Hells Angels motorcycle club attend a funeral for one of their own. They and other outlaw biker gangs have often been the source of the sort of "moral panics" described in Chapter 2, The Media: Shaping Our Understanding of Crime.

Source: Toronto Star/GetStock.com.

These gangs are commonly involved in both the illicit and the licit economy and often engage in international business transactions (often funding legal enterprises with the proceeds of crime). Individual gang members often have specialized skills or tasks. Level four gangs sometimes work with lower level gangs in order to meet their economic goals. Level four gangs will use violence to protect their economic interests. However, lower-level gangs or gang members are often used to perform risky criminal acts as a means of protecting the gang leadership. Violence is used for strategic purposes and rarely involves issues of honour or respect.

Example: Level four gangs include such established criminal organizations as the Italian and Russian Mafia, Asian Triads, Jamaican Posses, Mexican and South American Drug Cartels, and outlaw motorcycle gangs.

Having a distinct gang definition or gang classification system, of course, does not eliminate the problem of gang member identification or questions about how to best identify gang-related crime. For example, how does one distinguish real gang members from other civilians who reside in high-risk, gang-dominated neighbourhoods? A possible solution would be to define a gang member as "any individual who admits gang membership or who is identified as a gang member through expert investigation." However, the specific criteria for "expert" identification still needs to be established.

Criminality as a Gang Criterion

criminality
The state of being criminal; criminal acts or practices.

A significant debate that has emerged within the gang literature is whether **criminality** should be considered a necessary criterion for gang membership. Thrasher (1927/1963), the godfather of gang research, did not include criminality in his gang definition and subsequently argued that we must distinguish between criminal and non-criminal gangs. This stance has also been put forward by a number of contemporary scholars (see Bennett & Holloway, 2004). Others, however, maintain that the absence of criminality makes the definition of a gang too broad. Indeed, without the criminality criterion, the study of gangs, in practice, would become the study of all organized group behaviour—including sports teams, church groups, and youth clubs. Overall, Wood and Alleyne (2010) captured the sentiments of most gang scholars and criminal justice officials when they stated the following:

> [T]he argument that criminality should be a measure criterion for defining a gang is compelling. One of the defining features of an entity is who is interested in it. Those interested in gangs include the police, criminologists, task force agents and more recently forensic psychologists. Thus, it is the criminal activity of gangs that triggers the interest of these parties. As such it makes sense that criminal behaviour should be included as a necessary criterion for defining a gang. (p. 102)

Meanwhile, a growing number of academics have argued that it would be more productive for both scholars and criminal justice officials to focus on all forms of individual and collective violence, and not focus on "gangs" at all (see Sullivan, 2005, 2006).

Yet another perspective holds that violent crime—not crime itself—distinguishes street gangs from other social groups. Should violence be a gang criterion? Or should we consider all groups that engage in a regular pattern of criminal activity? For example, college fraternities often meet the standard of most gang definitions:

Police display a bag of ammonium nitrate, evidence in the case against the Toronto 18, who had been accused of plotting bomb attacks in Toronto and Ottawa in 2006. Several of the politically motivated young Muslim men pled guilty to participating in a terrorist group. Although a very rare phenomenon, the existence of such groups within Canada, the United Kingdom, and other Western nations in the years after the September 11, 2001 attacks and the wars that followed adds yet another variation to the many definitions of what constitutes a "gang" or "organized crime."

Source: Toronto Star/GetStock.com.

1. They involve three or more members.
2. They usually have a name, group symbols, and initiation rituals.
3. They have a clear organizational structure.
4. Research suggests that fraternities are often involved in various criminal activities including illegal drug use, drug trafficking, under-age drinking, illegal alcohol sales, and illegal gambling (see Hickson & Roebuck, 2009; McCabe et al., 2005; Sanday, 1990).

However, fraternities may have been able to escape the gang label because they rarely engage in serious violence (with the possible exception of some extreme examples of hazing) and typically do not have a "street orientation." The same might be said of corporate crime groups. For example, groups of executives who conspire to defraud investors are almost never identified as criminal gangs—even though they often meet the numerical and organizational criteria of most gang definitions. They also engage in serious economic crimes that often have profound consequences for both individual victims and national economies. When defining gangs, therefore, we must be clear about what types of crime to include as gang criteria and provide a clear justification for why some types of criminality are excluded. This is particularly important when developing gang-based sentencing enhancements.

Identifying Gang Members and Gang-Related Crime

Among criminologists and criminal justice authorities, no standard methodology exists for identifying gang members or gang-related crime. Barrows and Huff's (2009) study of American gang member databases, for example, found that only 15 states have a formal gang member definition, many of them quite vague. For example, Wisconsin simply defines a gang member as an individual who participates in criminal gang activity (Barrows & Huff, 2009, p. 685). Barrows and Huff argue that such definitions are fundamentally inadequate and could lead to a significant problem with gang member over-identification.

Following the lead of local police services, the Canadian Centre for Justice Statistics (2008) attempted to develop a national strategy for identifying gang members. According to the Uniform Crime Reporting Survey (UCR), the following conditions confirm street gang membership. First and foremost, a person must be "directly or indirectly" involved in a gang crime. In addition, the person must meet at least two of the following five criteria:

1. Display gang identification marks, engage in initiation rituals or possess gang paraphernalia (e.g., tattoos, weapons, etc.)
2. Be identified as a gang associate by a reliable source (i.e., inside gang member or rival gang member, community resource, school authority, member of the business community, citizen, etc.)
3. Be identified as a gang associate by a police surveillance report
4. Self-report gang membership
5. Be identified as a gang member by a judicial finding (Canadian Centre of Justice Statistics, 2008, pp. 143–144)

Most of the listed criteria are imprecise and open to manipulation. What, for example, constitutes "gang paraphernalia" and information from "a reliable source"? According to the Canadian Centre for Justice Statistics, for example, almost anyone—including average citizens, business owners, and criminals—can confirm to a police service that someone associates with a gang. Without knowing exactly what these concepts mean and how they are measured, it is impossible to determine how gang members are to be identified.

Law enforcement officials have found it equally difficult to come up with a common definition for *gang-related crime*. Some have argued that any crime committed by a known gang member—or former gang member—should be considered a gang crime. Others have argued that gang crimes must be committed within the group context and clearly promote the goals or interests of the gang (see Howell, 1999; Mares, 2010; Rosenfeld, Bray, & Egley, 1999). Overall, few would debate that a gun battle or drive-by shooting between two competing gangs should be labelled a gang crime. But what if a gang member, acting on his own, decides to sell drugs or rob a stranger at gunpoint for his own personal gain? Similarly, what if a known gang member, acting on his own, assaults or kills a relative during a family dispute? Should these incidents also be classified as gang-related? Clearly, how gang-related crimes are defined and measured will dramatically influence the amount of gang-related crime recorded within specific jurisdictions. For example, St. Louis typically records a much higher rate of gang homicide than Chicago. However, the St. Louis Police Department considers any murder that involves a known gang member (as either a victim or an offender) to be gang-related. By contrast, the Chicago police only classify a murder as a gang homicide if clear evidence shows that the incident "grew out of a street gang function" (Mares, 2010, p. 44).

Characteristics of Youth Gangs

An adequate definition of a gang must not only identify core (essential, universal) elements of the gang, but also distinguish it from other social groups that young people might involve themselves in. The various characteristics used to describe and define youth gangs have included the following:

BOX 17.1

Gang Membership, Criminal Offending, and Victimization: A Canadian Example

The Toronto Youth Crime and Victimization Survey illustrates the strong relationship between gang membership and both criminal offending and criminal victimization. This survey, conducted in 2000, involves a random sample of 3,394 high school students from the Toronto region. All respondents were asked if they had ever been a member of a gang. Those who responded in the affirmative were classified as the members of either social gangs (those who did not engage in crime with fellow gang members) or criminal gangs (those who engaged in criminal activity within the gang context). The survey further distinguished been current and former gang members. Overall, 88.8 percent of the sample indicated that they had never been a member of a gang, 2.0 percent are former social gang members, 1.5 percent are current social gang members, 3.4 percent are former criminal gang members, and 4.3 percent identified themselves as current criminal gang members (Tanner & Wortley, 2002, p. 143).

No matter the type of criminal activity—from marijuana use to aggravated assault—current criminal gang members reported much higher rates of criminal involvement than all other groups (see Table 17.1). The potential seriousness of gang involvement is demonstrated by the fact that almost 70 percent of current criminal gang members report that they carried a knife or gun with them during the past year.

Table 17.1   Percentage of Toronto High School Students Who Have Engaged in Various Criminal Activities in the Past 12 Months, by Type of Gang Affiliation

Type of criminal behaviour	Never in a gang	Former social gang member	Current social gang member	Former criminal gang member	Current criminal gang member
Theft from motor vehicles	2.8	4.5	5.8	13.8	45.5
Motor vehicle theft	0.9	6.0	1.9	11.2	37.3
Broke into a home or business	2.0	7.5	2.0	13.8	35.2
Sold drugs 10 or more times	2.1	0.0	0.0	21.6	51.4
Vandalism	18.0	28.4	28.8	44.8	62.0
Minor theft (less than $50)	17.8	15.9	25.0	40.5	69.5
Major theft ($50 or more)	6.6	11.9	5.8	31.0	60.0
Carried a gun or knife	11.2	20.9	11.8	48.2	68.3
Extortion/robbery	5.6	4.5	5.9	21.1	43.0
Aggravated assault	7.4	6.0	5.9	45.6	57.7
Physical fight	26.5	32.8	27.5	58.8	90.8
Gang (group) fight	12.7	19.7	23.5	47.4	79.6
Sexual assault	0.3	3.0	0.0	3.5	11.3
Used marijuana	26.3	31.8	19.6	65. 5	84.6
Used cocaine/crack	1.6	4.5	2.0	11.2	17.5
Used other illicit drugs	5.3	7.6	2.0	26.7	25.2

Source: Tanner and Wortley (2002).

1. age restrictions (the age criteria for inclusion in a "youth gang" ranges from eight to thirty years—depending on the study and/or organization);
2. a group name or identity;
3. the wearing of colours, distinctive group symbols, or defining insignia (i.e., tattoos);
4. the control of or claim to a specific neighbourhood, territory, or turf;
5. evidence of group organization, including a hierarchical structure (i.e., leaders and followers);
6. number of members (most definitions require at least three members);
7. durability or stability (must exist as a social entity for a specified period of time);
8. a gang code (a set of rules or regulations that must be followed by gang members);
9. initiation rituals for new gang members;
10. street orientation (gang activities are conducted away from the home, work, or school);
11. regular and/or continuous group involvement in crime, violence, or delinquency; and
12. common ethnic or racial background.

However, disagreement exists on the relative importance of these and other factors. American studies strongly suggest that how youth gangs are defined will have a major practical impact on how many gangs are identified in a particular community (Bjerregaard, 2002; Kennedy, 2009; Spergel, 2009). For example, if gangs must have a name, display specific colours, engage in criminal activity, and so on, then fewer of them are going to be found than if one concludes that all groups of young people that hang out together are involved in gang activity. In other words, the larger the number of criteria that have to be met, the smaller the gang count is going to be.

The research literature clearly demonstrates that when it comes to violent offending, gang membership matters: gang membership increases violent behaviour, even among those individuals who demonstrate violent traits prior to their gang involvement. Gang members are also much more likely to become the victim of serious violence—including homicide—than youth who are not involved in gangs. **Longitudinal studies** suggest that rates of violent victimization rise significantly during periods of gang membership and decline once gang involvement ends (see Decker & Curry, 2002; Melde, Taylor, & Esbensen, 2009; Spano, Freilich, & Bolland, 2008). This finding is particularly interesting since many youth report that they join gangs for protection (Wortley & Tanner, 2008).

longitudinal studies
Research that involves long-term observation of specific variables, often across decades (*cohort studies*, for example).

Typologies of Gang Violence
Recent Trends

On December 26, 2005, Jane Creba, a 15-year-old student out exploring Boxing Day sales with her mother, was shot to death in the middle of Toronto's busiest shopping district. Six other innocent bystanders were wounded. Creba and the other victims had apparently been caught in the crossfire of a shootout between two rival youth gangs. In July 2012, Toronto experienced its worst-ever mass shooting when gang-related violence erupted at an afternoon picnic on Danzig Street in Scarborough, leaving two dead and dozens wounded. However, these were not isolated incidents. Over the past decade, gang violence has claimed the lives of many other young people in Canada, and a number of disturbing trends have emerged. Although rates of violent crime have dropped over the past two decades, violent crime has become much more concentrated among Canada's youth population (12 to 24 years of age). Violent offending and victimization has also become more concentrated among young, minority males who reside in Canada's poorest communities. Research also suggests that firearms are becoming more and more prevalent in violent incidents involving young people and that an increasing proportion of violent events are taking place in public rather than private settings (see Gartner & Thompson, 2004; Wortley, 2008). These trends are consistent with the rise in gang activity reported by police services across Canada (see Chettleburgh, 2007). Many of these homicides of young minority men—which often go unsolved—have been directly attributed to gang activity. In most Canadian cities, gang-related homicides typically account for one-quarter to one-third of the annual total (Boyce & Cotter, 2013, p. 35). In 2005—still infamously referred to in Toronto as "the year of the gun"—it was estimated that over 50 percent of all Toronto-area homicides were gang-related. Thus, understanding the reasons behind gang-related violence and other criminal activity has become an extremely important issue for both law enforcement officials and policy-makers.

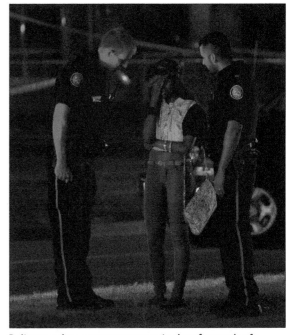

Police speak to a young woman in the aftermath of a gang-related mass shooting at a neighbourhood street party on Danzig Street in Scarborough in July 2012. Two people died and many more were wounded in the crossfire.

Source: Rick Madonik/GetStock.com.

The Toronto Street Gang Pilot Project

The Toronto Street Gang Pilot Project took place in November 2004.[1] It involved detailed qualitative interviews with a large sample of "known gang members" from a variety of backgrounds and neighbourhoods. The term *known gang member* was used to describe individuals who were identified as gang members by police officers, social workers, probation officers, and youth counsellors. The research team completed 209 face-to-face interviews. The vast majority of gang respondents were male (83.3 percent). Almost all came from disruptive family backgrounds: 63.1 percent were raised in a single-parent household, and 13.8 percent grew up within the child-protection system. The majority of respondents were born in Canada (76.1 percent)—a finding that challenges the myth of the alleged link between immigration and gang activity. Nonetheless, the sample was racially diverse: 43.1 percent of respondents self-identified as black, 24.8 percent as white, 12.4 percent as Hispanic, 4.3 percent as Aboriginal, 2.9 percent as Asian, 2.4 percent as of South Asian descent, and 10.0 percent as a mixed-race identity. Interestingly, minority respondents were more likely to be born in Canada (79.6 percent) than white respondents (65.4 percent). A large number of white respondents were immigrants from Eastern Europe. Finally, consistent with previous research, most respondents grew up under circumstances of poverty and social disadvantage (Wortley & Tanner, 2007).

The typical respondent belonged to a gang or "crew" with between 10 and 30 members, and virtually every respondent (98.1 percent) indicated they had been involved in some form of gang violence at some point in their life. That violence generally took one of six forms: (1) economically motivated crime; (2) disputes over territory or turf; (3) involvement in the illicit economy; (4) retaliation for attacks on fellow gang members; (5) conflicts over reputation or honour; and (6) witness intimidation.

1. Economically Motivated Crime

extortion

The crime of demanding money from someone using force or threats.

Many respondents indicated that they engaged in economically motivated crimes, including robbery and **extortion**. This finding is consistent with previous research, which suggests that many youth join gangs for the assumed economic benefits. These crimes may take the form of opportunistic robberies or muggings (Wortley & Tanner, 2008):

> Sometimes we would just be hangin' out, see some kid with something we wanted and we would jump them, give them a couple of shots, threaten the shit out of them and take what we wanted. Like an iPod or some kicks (sneakers). When we did that we usually take their cash too … and tell them that we would fuck them up more if they call the cops. That type of shit we did all the time. Just take what we wanted. (Case number 126, black male, 17 years old)

In other cases, the gang youth planned more complex robberies—usually against rival gang members or individuals within their community who were involved in illegal gun sales or drug trafficking. Gang youth often refer to these types of crimes as "missions":

> We would just go on missions against other, weaker crews. We would find out where they were at and rob them. Sometimes I would play that I wanted to get with one of them so that I could find out what they had. It was easy 'cause those guys like to show off. (Case number 18, white female, 22 years old)

2. Disputes over Territory or Turf

The gang literature often makes direct reference to the issue of gang violence based on territorial disputes. Some contemporary gang activity is linked to the symbolic control of, or emotional attachment to, a particular neighbourhood—often a specific housing project, school, or block. At other times, however, turf disputes were less about neighbourhood control than market control. Having control of the drug trade within a specific area makes good business sense. The buying and selling of drugs is a very lucrative business, but also a very dangerous one:

> Oh yeah we would defend our territory. Yeah, to the fullest. Say somebody was messin' around with my friends, we go there and defend it, you know. Stuff like that. Or, like, if someone came and stole out of our pockets we'd go and retaliate, y'know, defend it. Basically, territory fights too, that happens a lot. So like them wanting to sell drugs where you sell drugs? Yeah. So like, we'd have some out-of-towners, or outsiders we like to call them, come in and try to sell drugs to our people that we sell drugs to already. We didn't like that much, so we'd get into a lot of fights because of that, y'know. (Case number 34, Hispanic male, 23 years old)

3. Involvement in the Illicit Economy

Almost 90 percent of respondents were or had been involved in the illicit drug trade. Many claimed that in order to survive in the drug trade, they had to be ready and willing to use violence. Many respondents stated that they were often the target of predatory criminals, including rival gangs, because (1) they often had large quantities of both cash and drugs in their possession, and (2) the illegal nature of their activities made it impossible for them to rely on the police for protection:

> Like sometimes you had to beat people cause they owed you money man. Like you had spotted them some drugs and they promised to pay you later. Then they like conveniently forget. They say like "What are you talkin about? I don't owe you fuckin anything." Well guys like that you gotta beat their ass and beat them good. Leave some marks, you know what I'm sayin'? If you don't, well people know your soft and they'll just keep ripping you off. (Case number 77, white male, 20 years old)

4. Retaliation for Attacks on Fellow Gang Members

From the interviews, it was clear that a great deal of gang violence is retaliatory—typically against other gangs or crews. Retaliation seems to result when either a robbery has taken place or when a member of the gang has been attacked by another crew. As with failed business transactions, respondents often feel that you need to retaliate in order to prevent future victimizations:

> This guy from our crew named Sticks got the shit kicked out of him by these bouncers at a club. So he just called us and we came with bats. We just waited to the club was closing and then we jumped them and knocked them out. We broke some ribs and shit. Nobody does that shit to one of us and gets away with it. Everybody at the club saw what we did to those guys. We sent all of them a message. Don't fuck with us. Don't show no disrespect. (Case number 122, Asian male, 20 years old)

5. Conflicts over Reputation or Honour

Although some "beefs" (a term used by our respondents to denote individual or group conflict) were motivated by entrepreneurial ambitions and revenge, most did not. Indeed, many violent incidents occurred because a cardinal rule of street life—the need for respect—had been broken. Even relatively minor insults were likely to be met with violence, including the use of weapons:

> On the streets it about reputation, man. You gotta be tough and not take shit from anybody, no matter how big they is or how tough they seem. If somebody dis you, you gotta fight them and show them you don't take that shit. If somebody insult your gang you gotta represent. You can't let anybody punk your crew. If I find out somebody in my crew let our name be disrespected, if I find out that they like did nothin' about it, man I'll beat their ass myself. (Case number 88, black male, 19 years old)

As with business-related violence, several respondents believed that standing up for your honour, and establishing a reputation for using violence, could actually prevent future victimization.

6. Witness Intimidation

Another form of instrumental gang violence involved the intimidation of potential witnesses. Gang members routinely engage in criminal activities that take place in public spaces—including drug trafficking, robbery, and extortion. Community members are often very aware of the gangs in their neighbourhood and the criminal activities they engage in. Gang members often try to create a culture of fear within their community and will use violence against witnesses or former gang members to minimize the risk of them cooperating with the police:

> At school we had to beat this kid who did not come up with the money he owed us. This new kid who transferred from another school saw us do it and told the principal who called the cops. Two of us got arrested. The rest of us waited a while then followed that little snitch home from school one day and beat him till he lost some teeth. We told him that the cops may get one or two of us at one time but never all of us at one time. We told him that the ones on the street always deal with snitches. He won't never snitch again. He also was like an example to other kids 'bout how we deal with snitches. Got to make people afraid so you can go on with your business. (Case number 110, Aboriginal male, 19 years old)

Although the typology of gang violence described above was developed using interviews with street gang members, it could easily be applied to more sophisticated criminal organizations. For example, it is common knowledge that the Italian Mafia, outlaw motorcycle groups, and South American drug cartels all use violence to develop a reputation for ruthlessness, control illicit markets, settle business disputes, and intimidate or eliminate witnesses.

Causes of Gang Crime and Violence

As the interviews above indicate, gang violence can reflect either utilitarian economic motives or more expressive, subcultural values. However, theories explaining the deeper roots of gang formation and gang violence are as varied as the field of criminology. They range from micro-level explanations that focus on individual psychology to macro-level theories that focus on the impact of historical oppression and contemporary structural inequalities (Klein & Maxson, 2006, Wood & Alleyne, 2010). Several of the most relevant theories, as seen in the theory chapters of this book (see Part Three, Theories of Crime), can be applied to gangs and organized crime.

Social Disorganization and the Cultural Transmission of Gang Values

One of the earliest—and most influential—explanations for gang behaviour is provided by *social disorganization theory* (Thrasher, 1927/1963). Social disorganization theory links crime rates and gang activity to neighbourhood characteristics. Gangs and gang violence, it is argued, are most likely to emerge in highly disadvantaged communities that are unable to provide essential services, such as quality education, health care, and housing. Such communities are usually marked by poverty, high levels of unemployment, low family incomes, a high proportion of the population on social welfare, a high number of single-parent families, and a high concentration of public housing units. Within such communities, traditional sources of social control (the family, church, school, social service agencies, etc.) are weak. This, in turn, damages community unity, increases fear, and hinders attempts to solve community problems. It is under these circumstances—when conventional controls are weak and the needs of local youth are unfulfilled—that gangs are most likely to emerge (Thrasher, 1927/1963).

Shaw and McKay (1942) further developed Thrasher's ideas by arguing that when conventional institutions have little functional authority, youth are likely to succumb to deviant norms and values, and will sometimes form gangs to meet their needs for excitement, social support, material goods, and social status. A key component of Shaw and McKay's analysis is that criminal traditions can be *culturally transmitted*, and once firmly established within disorganized communities, pro-gang values can be passed down from generation to generation via normal socialization processes. The idea that criminal behaviour—including gang involvement—is learned through one's social environment has also been proposed by *differential association theory* (Sutherland & Cressey, 1974), *social learning theory* (Akers, 1997), and *subcultural theory* (Anderson, 1999). All of these theories propose that exposure to gang members and pro-gang values greatly increases the likelihood that youth will become gang-involved themselves.

Both social disorganization and social learning theories have greatly influenced subsequent gang research (see Lane & Meeker, 2004; Papachristos & Kirk, 2006; Spergel, 1995). These perspectives are supported by contemporary research results that suggest the following:

1. gangs and serious gang violence are more likely to emerge in economically disadvantaged communities than in middle-class or upper-class neighbourhoods;
2. youth from poor, single-parent families are at the highest risk of gang involvement;
3. peer delinquency and peer pressure are strong predictors of both gang membership and gang violence;
4. youth are often introduced to gangs by close friends or family members;
5. new gang members are commonly socialized into gang culture by peers who teach them the rules and requisite skills of gang life; and
6. compared with non-gang youth, gang members tend to share a belief system that condones violence as a means of dealing with interpersonal conflict (see Brownfield, 2006; Hagedorn, 2008; Mares, 2010).

Critics argue that social disorganization theory does not adequately explain why most poor youth fail to become involved in gangs and why some middle-class youth become active gang members. Such anomalies, however, can be explained by the social learning perspective (i.e., some poor youth are exposed to positive role models while some middle-class youth are exposed to deviant peers).

Strain Theory

The central argument of early *strain theory* is that society sets specific cultural goals—including wealth and status—that are widely accepted by the general population. However, not everyone in society has equal access to legitimate means of attaining these goals. This situation produces *anomie* or status frustration. Some scholars argue that gangs are formed among young people—especially the poor and disenfranchised—because they do not have access to the legitimate means of attaining culturally prescribed goals. Deprived of legitimate economic opportunities, the gang is an "adaption" or "innovation" that provides members with an "illegitimate" strategy for attaining their economic objectives (Merton, 1938).

Subsequent strain theorists (Cohen, 1955) have argued that status frustration sometimes causes lower-class youth to completely reject mainstream norms and establish their own subcultural goals and beliefs. These new goals are attainable for youth from lower-class backgrounds and thus provide an alternative avenue for status achievement. Within this new subculture, gangs often put an emphasis on toughness, courage, criminality, and instant gratification.

The strain perspective is supported by research suggesting that many youth initially join gangs because of the perceived economic benefits (Klein & Maxson, 2006; Wortley & Tanner, 2008). Research further suggests that some gang members believe that they would not be able to make the same amount of money in the legitimate economy because of problems with the educational system and bias in the employment sector (Kemp-North, 2007). Gang members often perceive mainstream institutions, particularly the criminal justice system, as unjust, and engage in crime and violence as acts of defiance (Brownfield, 2006; Wortley & Tanner, 2008).

Impulsivity, Empathy, and Self-Control

Social disorganization, cultural transmission, social learning, and strain theories all argue that gang involvement facilitates or enhances criminal activity and violence. By contrast, *control theorists* maintain that gangs do not cause violence. Rather, violent individuals are drawn to or selected into gangs because of their violent propensities and their lack of alternative friendship choices. In other words, violent individuals create gangs—gangs do not create violent individuals.

Michael Gottfredson and Travis Hirschi's (1990) "general theory of crime" is arguably the most influential theory within this theoretical camp. These authors maintain that the cause of all criminality—including gang-related violence—is low self-control. Low self-control, they argue, is caused by poor parenting and neglect during the first five years of life. Individuals who do not develop self-control by late childhood will never develop it. Gottfredson and Hirschi argue further that people with low self-control

1. are impulsive and desire immediate gratification;
2. have little empathy for others; and
3. cannot anticipate the long-term consequences of their actions.

Crime is attractive to people with low self-control because it is relatively easy and provides immediate gratification. As Gottfredson and Hirschi (1990) state: "crime provides money without work, sex without courtship and revenge without court delays" (p. 46).

Suppression and Prevention

Suppression Strategies

In their thorough analysis of the gang phenomenon in the United States, Judith Greene and Kevin Pranis (2007) argued that once a gang problem has been acknowledged by local politicians, the conversation usually turns to how the police can resolve the problem.

As a result, the policy responses that usually follow the emergence of a gang problem include the following:

1. the formation of a special "gang" or "organized crime" unit within the police service;
2. the creation of a "gang member database" to document gang members and their associates;
3. police crackdowns in "high-crime" neighbourhoods, which includes the addition of special police patrols that aggressively enforce public ordinances; and
4. efforts that target gang "leaders" and "hardcore" gang members through heightened surveillance and harsh sentencing practices (including sentencing enhancements for gang-related crime) (pp. 67–68).

Considerable evidence suggests that a similar model has been adopted within many Canadian jurisdictions. For example, following a rash of gun-related homicides, the Toronto Police Service received additional public funds to develop its own gang unit. The federal government is also supporting new legislation that will produce tougher sentences for gang and gun-related crimes.

The basic objective of most gang **suppression strategies** is to eliminate gangs or significantly reduce gang-related crime through a process of deterrence and incapacitation. Tough enforcement practices, it is argued, will deter people from joining gangs and cause current gang members to reduce or cease their criminal activity. However, the bulk of empirical evidence suggests that despite years of operation, police gang suppression efforts have not produced significant reductions in overall gang activity or gang-related violence (Greene & Pranis, 2007; Hagedorn, 2008; Katz & Webb, 2006; Klein & Maxson, 2006). Indeed, although public spending on police gang suppression strategies is at an all-time high in the United States, research suggests that the number of gangs and gang members has actually increased over recent years (see Egley, Howell, & Moore, 2010). Terrence Thornberry, David Huizinga, and Rolf Loeber (2004) effectively summarize these research results: "The findings of these studies are quite consistent. In general, arrest has little impact on subsequent delinquent behavior, and when it does have an impact, it is most likely an increase in future delinquent behavior. … In addition, those who are arrested and incarcerated as juveniles are subsequently more likely to be incarcerated as adults" (p. 12).

This is not to say that the police have no impact on gangs. Police anti-gang strategies can be very effective at dismantling specific criminal organizations and arresting specific gang members. The evidence, however, suggests that such intervention strategies have little overall impact on reducing gang formation or overall levels of gang-related violence. As Huff (2002) observes: "suppression is a necessary but not sufficient strategy for dealing with gang-related crime" (p. 292). Although effective suppression strategies may temporarily remove violent gang members from a community, gangs and gang violence will ultimately return if we do not address the social factors (poverty, inequality, social disorganization, etc.) that produce gangs in the first place. As a result, many experts believe that we must engage in a coordinated **weed and seed** strategy to reduce gangs (see Bridenhall & Jesilow, 2005; Waller, 2006; Wortley et al., 2008). Police must first remove violent gangs and gang members from our communities (the weed side of

suppression strategies
Efforts to eliminate gangs or significantly reduce gang-related crime through a process of deterrence and incapacitation.

weed and seed
A strategy combining the removal of violent gang members from a community with long-term community development.

the equation). Following the removal of criminal elements, however, the government must also engage in concentrated and long-term community development efforts in order to ensure that gangs do not return (the seed side of the equation). Unfortunately, when it comes to fighting gangs, governments have been much more enthusiastic about funding law enforcement suppression strategies than in-depth community development programs (Bridenhall & Jesilow, 2005).

Prevention Strategies

An increasing number of policy-makers and police officials have recognized the limitations of traditional police gang suppression strategies. As a result, several jurisdictions have sought to develop more community-based enforcement initiatives. These programs tend to share similar characteristics:

1. a focus on reducing gang-related violence rather than efforts to completely eradicate gangs;
2. an attempt to balance gang suppression activities with the provision of social services and other employment/educational opportunities for youth from highly disadvantaged communities;
3. efforts to engage a broader range of stakeholders—including schools, social workers, and grassroots community groups—in the development of gang prevention policies; and
4. efforts to collaborate with researchers on the design and implementation of robust evaluation strategies.

Operation Ceasefire

The Operation Ceasefire model provides a problem-oriented framework for preventing gang-related violence. The approach consists of six basic elements:

1. the selection of a specific crime problem, such as youth homicide;
2. the creation of an interagency working group—including police officials and community leaders—to plan and coordinate an intervention strategy;
3. research to identify key offenders, groups, and behaviour patterns;
4. the development of a deterrence-based response to offenders and groups of offenders that uses various sanctions (known as "pulling levers") to reduce violent behaviour;
5. a coordinated effort to provide social services and opportunities to targeted offenders and groups; and
6. an effort to directly and repeatedly communicate with offenders to make them understand why they are receiving special attention (Kennedy, 2006).

The Operation Ceasefire model was pioneered in Boston and has since been replicated in several other American cities. During the early 1990s, gun-related homicides in Boston increased dramatically. An investigation revealed that this violence was being perpetrated by loosely organized youth gangs. Operation Ceasefire was implemented by the Boston Police Department's Youth Violence Strike Force on May 15, 1996 to address this problem. The assumption behind Operation Ceasefire was that youth violence had resulted in a self-perpetuating cycle where youth resorted to guns and violent behaviour to settle disputes. Fear of reprisals was also causing youth to carry guns to protect themselves (Braga et al., 2002).

The program's primary targets were high-risk youth, serious and violent juvenile offenders, as well as illicit firearms traffickers who supplied youth with guns. The prevention strategy depended on regular meetings between the police and both community groups and gang members. During these meetings the consequences of gang violence were clearly communicated. The program's suppression component used every legal recourse against violent offenders and gun traffickers. Concrete actions included an increase in the number of search and arrest warrants issued, the rigorous enforcement of all probation and parole conditions, and an effort to work more closely with prosecutors to ensure long sentences for chronic offenders (Braga, Kennedy, & Tita, 2002). In Boston, "pulling levers" also meant communicating a direct message to all youth that "articulated explicit cause-and-effect connections between the behaviour of the target population and that of the authorities. Knowledge of what happened to others in the target population was intended to prevent further acts of violence by gangs in Boston" (p. 280). This tactic is known as "marketing deterrence." The authorities also attempted to break the cycle of violence by immediately contacting gang members following violent incidents, thus reducing the risk of retaliation. Importantly, the enforcement effort was complemented by an increase in social services and opportunities available to gang youth and other young people residing in high-risk communities.

Even without the support of a formal evaluation, Boston's Operation Ceasefire was hailed by the media as a great success. However, a US Department of Justice evaluation eventually revealed that at least some of this praise was warranted. Using a quasi-experimental longitudinal design to analyze trends in serious violence between 1991 and 1998, this study found that Operation Ceasefire was associated with a 63 percent decline in the monthly number of homicides in Boston, a 32 percent decrease in gun calls, and a 25 percent decline in gun assault incidents. Analysis suggests that program effects remained after statistically controlling for other explanatory variables (Kennedy, 2006).

In the late 1990s, Operation Ceasefire was successfully replicated in several other US cities. For example, it was associated with a 34 percent reduction in monthly homicides in Indianapolis (National Institute of Justice, n.d.). Similarly, in Chicago, an evaluation of the Ceasefire program found greater reductions in homicides and gun-related violence within treatment communities than control neighbourhoods (Papachristos, Meares, & Fagan, 2007). Finally, an impact evaluation of an Operation Ceasefire program in Lowell, Massachusetts found that the pulling levers strategy significantly decreased both gun-related homicides and aggravated assaults (Braga, Pierce, McDevitt, Bond, & Cronin, 2008).

In sum, the Operation Ceasefire model has shown at least some positive results with respect to reducing gang violence. Supporters argue that the model is successful for a variety of reasons:

1. It focuses on gang violence rather than gang formation.
2. It allows local police and community workers to develop unique, local approaches to gang problems.
3. It provides rewards or incentives to youth who refrain from violence (including reduced police attention and access to social services).

4. It focuses suppression efforts on serious offenders and not all youth who are gang involved.

However, critics argue that the program has not worked in all communities. They also maintain that the Operation Ceasefire model subjugates community interests to those of the police, which can create tension within program committees and ultimately prevent the development of even more effective violence prevention strategies (see Greene & Pranis, 2007; Welford, Pepper, & Petrie, 2005). Nonetheless, compared with traditional suppression strategies, the Operation Ceasefire model has shown promise and may eventually pave the way for greater police–community cooperation.

The Comprehensive Gang Prevention Model

The comprehensive gang prevention model, also known as the *Spergel model*, is designed to provide both social controls and social supports to gang members and other "at-risk" youth from disadvantaged neighbourhoods. The model was first implemented in the Little Village neighbourhood of Chicago during the mid-1990s (Spergel, 2007).

The Spergel model calls for the development of an integrated program team consisting of law enforcement officials, probation officers, youth workers, school officials, and social workers. This committee shares information about individual youth and gang activities and develops specific program strategies. Front-line workers focus on individual youth and family counselling, educational support, job training, and the provision of social services. Besides their traditional law enforcement duties, police and probation officers refer youth to the program and monitor the behaviour of program participants in the community. Youth workers also gather and clarify information about gang crime and help the police identify youth involved in serious gang violence. Information sharing between law enforcement and community workers is thought to improve both suppression and rehabilitation objectives as well as increase opportunities for social development (Spergel, 2007).

An extensive evaluation of the Chicago program produced positive results. At the individual level, participation in the program was associated with a statistically significant reduction in serious violence, fewer arrests for violent crime, fewer arrests for drug offences, and decreased association with known gang members. The greater the level of contact with program workers, the greater the overall reduction in criminal behaviour. Program effects were particularly strong for youth who found employment or re-enrolled in school. At the community level, the program also contributed to a significant drop in gang-motivated crime. Despite these successes, the Chicago police failed to institutionalize this program. The police justification for this decision was that their primary mission was crime suppression—not community development or social work (Spergel, 2007).

Gang Resistance, Education, and Training

Gang Resistance, Education, and Training (GREAT) is another promising gang intervention program. GREAT provides preteen youth from gang-infested communities with a school-based education program that focuses on crime, victimization, prejudice, cultural sensitivity, conflict resolution skills, drugs, and personal responsibility. The program is delivered by police officers working within the school system. The program has been evaluated numerous times. The most ambitious evaluation effort was a study conducted over a four-year period and involving almost 6,000 grade 8 students from 11 different cities. The study found that compared with the control group, GREAT participants had more negative attitudes toward gangs and gang membership, fewer delinquent friends, a greater commitment to pro-social activities, lower levels of impulsivity, better attitudes toward the police, and greater attachment to parents. According to the researchers, program participants also had statistically reduced levels of delinquency and gang affiliation. Overall, the results of the study suggest that, four years after program completion, program participants demonstrated more positive social attitudes and behaviours on 25 of 29 outcome measures (see Esbensen, Osgood, Taylor, Peterson, & Freng, 2001).

The Philadelphia Model

The Philadelphia Youth Violence Reduction Partnership (YVRP) is another multi-agency, wrap-around program that includes various youth-serving organizations and criminal justice agencies. Its aim is to reduce gang activity and violent victimization among young people—14 to 24 years of age—who are currently under court supervision. The program's staff consist of members of more than ten public and private organizations as well as more than 50 police officers, probation officers, and street workers. Staff members are in close contact with program youth and their families through frequent visits. The police and the probation officers also work closely with one another to ensure strict enforcement of probation and parole conditions. The YVRP tries to help participants develop a more productive lifestyle by providing them with increased supervision, vocational counselling, access to job skills and employment training, mentoring, health care, and drug treatment. Street workers play a major role in this program. They are responsible for mentoring participants and helping them with their health care and educational needs. YVRP staff also help the parents of program youth with their employment, health care, and housing needs. They do so to ensure a more stable family life for youth in the program. Preliminary results suggest that the program is working. An evaluation of the YVRP, conducted one year after the program commenced, found that program youth had significantly lower rates of violent victimization than control group subjects and that the homicide rate declined significantly in those areas of Philadelphia in which the initiative was operating (McClanahan, 2004).

The examples above indicate that some targeted gang prevention strategies may be effective. However, most gang prevention programs—especially those in Canada—have yet to be properly evaluated (see Chatterjee, 2006). Furthermore, a growing number of scholars have argued that governments should be paying less attention to programs that focus exclusively on gangs and gang members and more attention to programs that focus on youth violence in general (see Greene & Pranis, 2007; Sullivan, 2005, 2006). After all, gang violence represents only a small proportion of all youth violence. Research also suggests that the risk factors associated with gang violence are very similar to the risk factors associated with other types of youth crime and violence. Indeed, studies reveal that youth often have violent histories long before they become involved in gangs. Finally, while few gang prevention programs have been properly evaluated, a large number of evidence-based practices have been proven to work with violent, delinquent youth (see the review in Wortley et al., 2008).

Ineffective Programs

Along with programs proven to significantly reduce youth and gang-related violence, it is equally important to highlight programs that have been shown to be ineffective and a potential waste of resources. Some high-profile crime prevention programs either have no impact on gang violence or actually have a negative impact. These include the following:

Scared Straight programs

Programs that expose at-risk youth to examples of prison life and other consequences of criminal behaviour, along with testimonials from convicts.

- **Scared Straight programs**
- Gun buyback programs
- Curfews for adolescents
- Instructional programs that do not incorporate cognitive-behavioural techniques
- Peer mentoring programs
- Correctional boot camps using traditional military training
- Harsh sentences for young offenders
- Zero-tolerance programs in school systems
- Heightened security (including the use of metal detectors) within schools (Farrington & Welsh, 2007; Greenwood, 2006; Leschied, 2007; Waller, 2006)

Conclusion

The research literature suggests that gangs, gang members, and gang-related violence are difficult concepts to define. The literature also suggests that gangs are not homogeneous—they vary dramatically with respect to size, organization, durability, and type and level of criminal activity. Nonetheless, the literature suggests that gang-related violence has some common attributes: it often involves disputes over honour, territory, and control over illicit markets. Furthermore, the roots of gang activity seem to stem from common criminological risk factors including social disorganization, social strain, peer deviance, and low self-control. Finally, research suggests that the solution to gangs and gang violence are complex. As such, programs that focus on enforcement alone are bound to be less successful than programs that combine police efforts with community investment and youth development initiatives. The solution will involve all segments of society, not only those charged with enforcing the law.

SUMMARY OF KEY POINTS

- Many urban-dwelling Canadians feel that street gangs and gang-related violence are on the increase, but clear trends can be difficult to determine due to the lack of widely agreed-upon definitions of street gangs.
- Frederick Thrasher, one of the first criminological researchers to examine gangs, argued that gangs were part of normal peer group activity for adolescents and involved behaviours that ranged from the conventional to the deviant.
- Following Thrasher's groundbreaking work, the number of distinct gang definitions—within both academia and the criminal justice system—has soared. There are also numerous ways in which types of gangs have been broadly categorized (in this chapter, four levels or types of gangs are identified).

- As stated in the *Criminal Code*, section 467.1(1), a "criminal organization" is a group that (a) is composed of three or more persons in or outside Canada; and (b) has as one of its main purposes or activities the facilitation or commission of one or more serious offences, that, if committed, would likely result in the direct or indirect receipt of a material benefit by the group.

- A significant debate that has emerged within the literature concerning gangs is whether criminality should be considered a necessary criterion for gang membership.

- An adequate definition of a gang must not only identify essential elements of the gang, but also distinguish it from other social groups that young people might involve themselves in.

- Research of gang members shows that violence generally takes one of six forms: (1) economically motivated crime; (2) disputes over territory or turf; (3) involvement in the illicit economy; (4) retaliation; (5) conflicts over reputation; and (6) witness intimidation.

- An increasing number of policy-makers and police officials have recognized the limitations of traditional police gang-suppression strategies. As a result, several jurisdictions have sought to develop more community-based enforcement initiatives, such as Operation Ceasefire.

- Some high-profile crime prevention programs tend to have little or no impact. These include Scared Straight programs, gun buyback programs, and military-style "boot camps."

NOTE

1. The Toronto Street Gang Pilot Project was funded by a research grant from the Solicitor General of Canada through the Drug and Crime Prevention Strategies Unit.

QUESTIONS FOR CRITICAL DISCUSSION

1. What is a gang? What is an organized crime group? How do gangs differ from other types of social groups?
2. What are the causes of gang activity? Do the causes of gang activity differ from the causes of individual criminal behaviour?
3. Are all gangs or criminal organizations the same? How do gangs differ?
4. Can the police prevent gang activity? Why or why not? Besides policing and punishment, are there any other ways to reduce gangs?
5. Research the "Toronto 18" to find out their motivations, how they came together, and what they were accused of plotting. Of the four levels of gangs described in this chapter, which best describes them, and why?

SUGGESTED FURTHER READINGS

Katz, K. (2011). The enemy within: The outlaw motorcycle gang moral panic. *American Journal of Criminal—Humanities, Social Sciences and Law Justice, 36*(3), 231–249.

Marsden, W., & Sher, J. (2006). *Angels of death: Inside the bikers' global crime empire.* Toronto: Knopf Canada.

Wortley, S., Dorion, J., Levinsky, Z., Owusu-Bempah, A., Marshall, L., Adhopia, R., ... Boyce, A. (2008). Preventing youth crime and violence: A review of the literature. In R. McMurtry & A. Curling (Eds.), *The review of the roots of youth violence* (Vol. 5, pp. 229–561). Toronto: Queen's Printer for Ontario. Retrieved from http://www.children.gov.on.ca/htdocs/English/topics/youthandthelaw/roots/volume5/preventing01_introduction.aspx.

REFERENCES

Akers, R. (1997). *Criminological theories: Introduction and evaluation*. Los Angeles: Roxbury Press.

Anderson. E. (1999). *The code of the streets: Decency, violence and the moral life of the inner-city*. New York: Norton and Company.

Ball, R., & Curry, D. (1995). The logic of definition in criminology: Purposes and methods for defining gangs. *Criminology, 33*(2), 225–245.

Barrows, J., & Huff, R. (2009). Gangs and public policy: Constructing and deconstructing gang databases. *Criminology and Public Policy, 8*(4), 675–704.

Bennett, T., & Holloway, K. (2004). Gang membership, drugs and crime in the UK. *British Journal of Criminology, 44*, 305–323.

Bjerregaard, B. (2002). Self-definitions of gang membership and involvement in delinquent activities. *Youth & Society, 44*(1), 31–54.

Bolan, K. (2013, October 1). Surrey Six murder trial first witness describes grisly scene. *National Post*. Retrieved from http://news.nationalpost.com/2013/10/01/surrey-six-murder-trial-first-witness-describes-grisly-scene-everybody-is-on-the-floor-there-is-blood/.

Boyce, J., & Cotter, A. (2013). *Homicide in Canada, 2012* (Catalogue no. 85-002-x). Ottawa: Canadian Centre for Justice Statistics, Statistics Canada. Retrieved from http://www.statcan.gc.ca/pub/85-002-x/2013001/article/11882-eng.pdf.

Braga, A., Kennedy, D., & Tita, G. (2002). New approaches to the prevention of gang and group-involved violence. In C. Huff (Ed.), *Gangs in America* (3rd ed., pp. 271–286). Thousand Oaks, CA: Sage.

Braga, A., Pierce, G., McDevitt, J., Bond, B., & Cronin, S. (2008). The strategic prevention of gun violence among gang-involved offenders. *Justice Quarterly, 25*(1), 132–162.

Bridenhall, B., & Jesilow, P. (2005). Weeding criminals or planting fear: An evaluation of a weed and seed project. *Criminal Justice Review, 30*(1), 64–89.

Brownfield, D. (2006). A defiance theory of sanctions and gang membership. *Journal of Gang Research, 13*(4), 31–43.

Canadian Centre for Justice Statistics. (2008). *Uniform Crime Reporting Incident-Based Survey: CCJS reporting manual*. Ottawa: Statistics Canada.

Chatterjee, J. (2006). *Gang prevention and intervention strategies*. Ottawa: Research and Evaluation Branch, Community, Contract and Aboriginal Policing Services, Royal Canadian Mounted Police.

Chettleburgh, M. (2007). *Young thugs: Inside the dangerous world of Canadian street gangs*. Toronto: Harper-Collins.

Cohen, A. (1955). *Delinquent boys: The culture of the gang*. New York: Free Press.

Curry, G., & Decker, S. (1998). *Confronting gangs: Crime and community*. Los Angeles: Roxbury Press.

Decker, S., & Curry, G. (2002). Gangs, gang members and gang homicides: Organized crimes or disorganized criminals. *Journal of Criminal Justice, 30*, 343–352.

Egley, A., Howell, J., & Moore, J. (2010, March). Highlights of the 2008 National Youth Gang Survey. OJJDP Fact Sheet.

Esbensen, F.-A., Osgood, D.W., Taylor, T., Peterson, D., & Freng, A. (2001). How great is G.R.E.A.T.? Results from a longitudinal quasi-experimental design. *Criminology and Public Policy, 1*(1), 87–118.

Esbensen, F.-A., Winfree, T., He, N., & Taylor, T. (2001). Youth gangs and definitional issues: When is a gang a gang, and why does it matter? *Crime and Delinquency, 47*(1), 105–130.

Farrington, D.P., & Welsh, B.C. (2007). *Saving children from a life of crime: Early risk factors and effective interventions.* Oxford, UK: Oxford University Press.

Gartner, R., & Thompson, S. (2004). Trends in homicide in Toronto. In B. Kidd & J. Phillips (Eds.), *From enforcement to prevention to civic engagement: Research on community safety* (pp. 28–42). Toronto: Centre of Criminology, University of Toronto.

Gatti, U., Tremblay, R., Vitaro, F., & McDuff, P. (2005). Youth gangs: Delinquency and drug use—A test of the selection, facilitation and enhancement hypothesis. *Journal of Child Psychology and Psychiatry, 46*(11), 1178–1190.

Gordon, R. (2000, January). Criminal business organizations, street gangs and "wanna-be" groups: A Vancouver perspective. *Canadian Review of Criminology,* 39–60.

Gottfredson, M., & Hirschi, T. (1990). *A general theory of crime.* Stanford, CA: Stanford University Press.

Greene, J., & Pranis, K. (2007). *Gang wars: The failure of enforcement tactics and the need for effective public safety strategies.* Washington, DC: Justice Policy Institute.

Greenwood, P.W. (2006). *Changing lives: Delinquency prevention as crime-control policy.* Chicago: University of Chicago Press.

Hagedorn, J. (2008). *World of gangs: Armed young men and gangsta culture.* Minneapolis: University of Minnesota Press.

Hemmati, T. (2006). *The nature of Canadian urban gangs and their use of firearms: A review of the literature and police survey.* Ottawa: Department of Justice Canada, Research and Statistics Division.

Hickson, M., & Roebuck, J. (2009). *Deviance and crime in colleges and universities: What goes on in the halls of ivy.* Springfield, IL: Charles C. Thomas.

Howell, J. (1998, August). Youth gangs: An overview. *Juvenile Justice Bulletin.*

Howell, J. (1999). Youth gang homicides: A literature review. *Crime and Delinquency, 45,* 208–241.

Huff, C.R. (2002). *Gangs in America* (3rd ed.). Thousand Oaks, CA: Sage.

Katz, C., & Webb, V. (2006). *Policing gangs in America.* New York: Cambridge University Press.

Kemp-North, M. (2007). Theoretical foundations of gang membership. *Journal of Gang Research, 14,* 11–26.

Kennedy, D. (2006). Old wine in new bottles: Policing and the lessons of pulling levers. In D. Weisburd & A. Braga (Eds.), *Police innovation: Contrasting perspectives* (pp. 155–170). New York: Cambridge University Press.

Kennedy, D. (2009). Comment on "Gangs and public policy: Constructing and deconstructing gang databases." *Criminology and Public Policy, 8*(4), 711–716.

Klein, M., & Maxson, C. (2006). *Street gang patterns and policies.* Oxford, UK: Oxford University Press.

Lane, J., & Meeker, J. (2004). Social disorganization perceptions, fear of gang crime and behavioural precautions among Whites, Latinos and Vietnamese. *Journal of Criminal Justice, 32,* 49–62.

Langston, M. 2003. Addressing the need for a uniform definition of gang-involved crime. *FBI Law Enforcement Bulletin, 72*(2), 7–11.

Langton, J. (2013). *The notorious Bacon brothers: Inside gang warfare on Vancouver streets.* Toronto: John Wiley & Sons Canada.

Leschied, A.W. (2007). *The roots of violence: Evidence from the literature with emphasis on child and youth mental health disorder.* Prepared for and submitted to the Review of the Roots of Youth Violence by the Ministry of Children and Youth Services (Ontario).

Mares, D. (2010). Social disorganization and gang homicides in Chicago: A neighborhood-level comparison of disaggregated homicides. *Youth Violence and Juvenile Justice, 8*(1), 38–57.

Maxson, C., & Klein, M. (1995). Investigating gang structures. *Journal of Gang Research, 3,* 33–40.

McCabe, S., Schulenberg, J., Johnston, L., O'Malley, P., Bachman, J., & Kloska, D. (2005). Selection and socialization effects of fraternities and sororities on US college student substance use: A multi-cohort national longitudinal study. *Addiction, 100*(4), 512–524.

McClanahan, W.S. (2004). *Alive at 25: Reducing youth violence through monitoring and support.* Philadelphia: Public/Private Ventures.

Melde, C., Taylor, T., & Esbensen, F.-A. (2009). I got your back: An examination of the protective function of gang membership in adolescence. *Criminology, 47*(2), 565–594.

Merton, R. (1938). Social structure and anomie. *American Sociological Review, 3,* 672–682.

National Institute of Justice. (n.d.). Program profile: Indianapolis (Ind.) Violence Reduction Partnership (IVRP). Retrieved from http://www.crimesolutions.gov/ProgramDetails .aspx?ID=65.

Papachristos, A., & Kirk, D. (2006). Neighbourhood effects on street gang behaviour. In J. Short & L. Hughes (Eds.), *Studying youth gangs* (pp. 63–83). Oxford, UK: Altamira Press.

Papachristos, A., Meares, T., & Fagan, J. (2007). Attention felons: Evaluating project safe neighbourhoods in Chicago. *Journal of Empirical Legal Studies, 4,* 223–272.

Peterson, R.D. (2000). Definitions of a gang and impacts on public policy. *Journal of Criminal Justice, 28*(2), 139–149.

Raptis, M. (2013, March 15). Bacon brothers had it made and chose another path. *Province* (Vancouver). Retrieved from http://www.theprovince.com/news/Bacon+brothers+made +chose+another+path/8104495/story.html.

Rizzo, W. (2003). Why do children join gangs. *Journal of Gang Research, 11,* 65–74.

Rosenfeld, R., Bray, T., & Egley, A. (1999). Facilitating violence: A comparison of gang-motivated, and non-gang youth homicides. *Journal of Quantitative Criminology, 15*(4), 495–516.

Sanday, P. (1990). *Fraternity gang rape: Sex, brotherhood and privilege on campus.* New York: New York University Press.

Shaw, C., & McKay, H. (1942). *Juvenile delinquency and urban areas.* Chicago: University of Chicago Press.

Short, J. (2009). Gangs, law enforcement and the academy. *Criminology and Public Policy, 8*(4), 723–732.

Spano, R., Freilich, J., & Bolland, J. (2008). Gang membership, gun carrying and employment: Applying routine activities theory to explain violent victimization among inner city, minority youth living in extreme poverty. *Justice Quarterly, 25*(2), 381–410.

Spergel, I. (1995). *The youth gang problem.* New York: Oxford University Press.

Spergel, I. (2007). *Reducing youth gang violence: The little village gang project in Chicago.* Lanham, MD: Altamira Press.

Spergel, I. (2009). Gang databases: To be or not to be. *Criminology and Public Policy, 8*(4), 667–674.

Sullivan, M.L. (2005). Maybe we shouldn't study gangs: Does reification obscure youth violence? *Journal of Contemporary Criminal Justice, 21*(2), 170–190.

Sullivan, M.L. (2006). Are gang studies dangerous? Youth violence, local context and the problem of reification. In J. Short & L. Hughes (Eds.), *Studying youth gangs* (pp. 15–35). Oxford, UK: Altamira Press.

Sutherland, D., & Cressey, D. (1974). *Criminology.* New York: Lippincott.

Tanner, J., & Wortley, S. (2002). *The Toronto Youth Crime and Victimization Survey: Overview report*. Toronto: Centre of Criminology.

Thornberry, T., Huizinga, D., & Loeber, R. (2004, September). The causes and correlates studies: Findings and policy implications. *Juvenile Justice Journal*.

Thrasher, F.M. (1963). *The gang: A study of one thousand three hundred thirteen gangs in Chicago*. Chicago: University of Chicago Press. Abridged with a new introduction by James F. Short, Jr. (Original work published 1927.)

United Nations. (2004). *United Nations convention against transnational organized crime and the protocols thereto*. New York: Author.

Waller, I. (2006). *Less law, more order*. Westport, CT: Praeger.

Welford, C., Pepper, J., & Petrie, C. (2005). *Firearms and violence: A critical review*. Washington, DC: Committee to Improve Research Information and Data on Firearms and the National Academies Press.

Wheatley, J. (2008). The flexibility of RICO and its use on street gangs engaging in organized crime in the United States. *Policing, 2*(1), 82–91.

Wood, J., & Alleyne, E. (2010). Street gang theory and research: Where are we now and where do we go from here? *Aggression and Violent Behavior, 15*(2), 100–111.

Wortley, S. (2008). A province at the crossroads: Statistics on youth violence in Ontario. In R. McMurtry & A. Curling (Eds.), *The review of the roots of youth violence* (Vol. 4, pp. 1–64). Toronto: Queen's Printer for Ontario.

Wortley, S., Dorion, J., Levinsky, Z., Owusu-Bempah, A., Marshall, L., Adhopia, R., Samuels, K., … Boyce, A. (2008). Preventing youth crime and violence: A review of the literature. In R. McMurtry & A. Curling (Eds.), *The review of the roots of youth violence* (Vol. 5, pp. 229–561). Toronto: Queen's Printer for Ontario. Retrieved from http://www.children .gov.on.ca/htdocs/English/topics/youthandthelaw/roots/volume5/preventing01 _introduction.aspx.

Wortley, S., & Tanner, J. (2007). *Youth gangs in Canada's largest city: Results of the Toronto youth gang pilot project*. Ottawa: Solicitor General of Canada.

Wortley, S., & Tanner, J. (2008). Money, respect and defiance: Explaining ethnic differences in gang activity among Canadian youth. In F. van Gemert, D. Peterson, & I.-L. Lien (Eds.), *Youth gangs, migration and ethnicity* (pp. 181–210). London, UK: Willan.

The Eron Mortgage Fraud: Lessons from a Ponzi Scheme

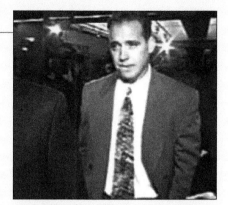

Frank Biller of Eron Mortgage served a short jail term for fraud. His parole board described him as "a prototypical white-collar offender with no previous criminal history who was reportedly motivated by greed and power associated with wealth and a luxurious lifestyle."

In the summer of 1920, Charles Ponzi was the talk of Boston. His seven-month-old business, The Security Exchange Company, was taking in more than a million dollars a week from investors. He had guaranteed them 50 percent interest on their principal in 45 days—an astonishing rate of return. The mechanism for generating this wealth was an international reply postal coupon, a device for facilitating international business. Ponzi told his prospective purchasers that he could buy a postal coupon in Spain for about one cent, and when he cashed it in America, he could buy six one-cent stamps. His plan was to convert on a grand scale—buy millions of dollars of coupons in foreign countries and convert them into five and ten times their value in America. It was all legal, and it was lauded by some commentators as a brilliant plan.

The scheme appeared to work. Early investors did see 50 percent returns on their money and, as a consequence, investments grew exponentially through the spring and summer of 1920. But Ponzi was simply using the money from new investors to enrich himself and pay off earlier obligations; he had created a new variation on the long-standing pyramid deception—a variation that is now termed a "Ponzi scheme." The *Boston Post* questioned the legitimacy of Ponzi's approach in July 1920: Who, after all, would buy the millions of dollars' worth of stamps that Ponzi was said to be collecting? In response to increasing media criticism, Ponzi allowed an auditor to examine his books, and his abrupt decline began. The newspaper learned that Ponzi had previous convictions for forgery and smuggling and had spent time in prison in both Canada and the United States; his books quickly revealed his latest deception. He was convicted of fraud and sent to jail for 14 years, leaving thousands of Americans in financial ruin.

Eron Mortgage of British Columbia was a contemporary, albeit more sophisticated, version of Charles Ponzi's scheme. Like the postal reply coupon, the high returns on investments promoted by Eron Mortgage—real estate developments in Canada and the United States—seemed plausible to investors at the time. Like Charles Ponzi, the principals of Eron Mortgage did not actually carry out the plans that they enthusiastically described to their willing contributors, although their businesses were widely praised by many media commentators. And in both cases, after questions were raised about their businesses, their books were examined and their frauds discovered. But for both Ponzi's investors and the investors of Eron Mortgage, it was too late; the businesses had crashed, their money was gone, and little could be done to retrieve it.

A few years after the 1999 conviction of Eron Mortgage's top officials, a research team based at Simon Fraser University conducted a post mortem of the Eron Mortgage fraud. It focused on more than 550 responses from the 2,200 men and women who invested in Eron Mortgage. The team found that about 60 percent of Eron investors were male and older than the average Canadian investor; most were in their mid-50s or older at the time of their initial investment. The Eron investors were no better educated and no more affluent than the average British Columbian of a similar age. They were not particularly wealthy; approximately two-thirds reported total annual incomes of less than $75,000, and with an average age of 55, their net worth was approximately $200,000.

The purpose of the Eron investment was, for the overwhelming majority of these investors, to fund retirement. These men and women were approaching that time of life without adequate resources, and the post mortem learned that the majority of the investors took their existing retirement funds, borrowed money, and mortgaged their homes to invest in Eron. Additionally, those who described themselves as "highly knowledgeable" investors—typically affluent middle-aged men—lost more than twice as much as the other Eron investors.

The effects of the Eron mortgage losses were devastating to hundreds of investors. More than half of those who lost more than $50,000 reported extreme or major harm to their emotional well-being, their current financial situation, and their retirement security. Between 20 and 30 percent of these investors also reported extreme or major harm to their marital relations, friendships, and physical health.

The story of Eron Mortgage resonates with this chapter: the public, our courts, and our law and policy-makers must better understand the very considerable consequences of investment fraud. In both civil and criminal contexts, the penalties imposed do not adequately reflect the harms created by such activity. The deliberateness of the conduct of the principals and the devastating consequences for hundreds of individuals stand in stark contrast to so much violent crime—the sort of criminal activity that receives considerably more attention and attracts much more substantial penalties.

Before You Read Chapter 18

- Why do you believe "street crime" tends to get relatively more attention and receive harsher sentencing than "white-collar crime" such as that of Eron Mortgage?
- Consider the media's role in dealing with white-collar crime. How are the perpetrators typically portrayed?
- Compare the Ponzi and Eron Mortgage cases described above. How are they similar? In what ways has white-collar crime changed in the century between Ponzi's time and today?

White-Collar Crime

LEARNING OBJECTIVES

After reading this chapter, students will be able to:

- Understand the origins of the term *white-collar crime* and contemporary debates about the concept's scope and content.

- Recognize the principal distinctions between traditional or "street" crime and white-collar crime, including issues concerning criminal liability for corporations.

- Identify the legal frameworks relevant to prominent cases of white-collar criminality across the criminal, regulatory, and civil domains.

- Explain the impact of a number of prominent white-collar cases in Canada and the United States in recent years.

- Appreciate the regulatory, legal, and social-scientific aspects of white-collar investigations and prosecutions.

- Understand the ways corporations are reacting to white-collar crime under corporate governance, including whistle-blowing protocols and corporate social responsibility.

Introduction

Polished floors, cubicle rows, leather-clad boardrooms—these are hardly the first images that spring to mind when we think of the word *crime*. Yet both the incidence of and damage associated with **white-collar crime** today far outstrips that of traditional forms of crime. The first decade of the new millennium began and ended with unprecedented white-collar scandals that shook the public's faith in business: the meteoric fall of Texas-based energy giant Enron in an infamous accounting fraud in 2001 and the unravelling of Bernie Madoff's record-breaking US$65 billion **Ponzi scheme** in 2009. These and other scandals have fuelled demand for stiffer white-collar penalties on both sides of the forty-ninth parallel, as well as demand for tougher quasi-criminal and civil regulation to keep a watchful eye on markets. Far more troubling than the dramatic, economy-wide impact of its worst cases, however, is the extent to which so much white-collar misconduct could lurk behind the veil of legitimate business activities—in Madoff's case, for as many as four decades before prosecutors knocked on his door.

Canada, despite its reputation for politeness and conservative regulation, has never been immune to the patterns of white-collar crime observed in the United States. The accounting misdeeds at Livent, for example, proved to be Canada's own Enron; and former Canadian newspaper magnate Conrad Black proved to be an especially unrepentant example of criminality before the US courts. Indeed, a historically softer enforcement culture may have made Canada a haven for white-collar offenders. A 2007 *Canadian*

white-collar crime
A crime committed by a person, usually of high social status, in the course of his or her occupation.

Ponzi scheme
An investing scam where a fraudster pays returns to existing investors with new investors' funds under the false pretense that returns are being made, sustained by the constant recruitment of new contributors.

Business article titled "A Good Country for Crooks: Canada's Losing War Against White-Collar Crime" noted how, six years after Enron, the 1,200 white-collar convictions racked up by the US Department of Justice were matched by only *two* convictions by the RCMP's special market enforcement teams (Gray, 2007). An *Economist* article likewise refers to Canada's "shockingly slow" approach to white-collar crime and corruption compared with its US neighbour, noting how not only weaker legal tools but also Canada's deference-to-authority culture may be to blame ("White-collar crime," 2009).

In this chapter, we explore the perplexing phenomenon of white-collar crime in a Canadian context. The chapter begins by tracing the term's origins to the work of sociologist Edwin Sutherland and explores how white-collar criminality encompasses conduct broader than the strictly "criminal." The chapter also presents an overview of several of the most prominent white-collar laws in Canada, including those on fraud, money laundering, bribery, embezzlement, tax evasion, insider trading, market manipulation, price fixing, workplace safety, and cybercrime. It also explores the actual enforcement process for white-collar offences from the investigation process through to sentencing. Finally, the chapter discusses the many roles of the corporation in white-collar crime, including the roles of criminal defendant, in-house investigator, and "good corporate citizen."

What Is White-Collar Crime?
The Origins of the Label
The pioneer in the study of white-collar crime was American sociologist Edwin Sutherland, whose work has been discussed previously in Chapters 6 (Theories of Crime: A Brief Introduction) and 12 (Sociological Approaches). Sutherland first conceived of the term in an influential 1939 address to the American Sociological Society titled "White-Collar Criminality" (Sutherland, 1940). He defined *white-collar crime* as "crime committed by a person of respectability and high social status in the course of his occupation" (Sutherland, 1983, p. 7). So jealously guarded was that "respectability" that the companies named in Sutherland's landmark 1949 book on the topic, *White Collar Crime*, used legal threats to successfully keep their references out of its text for 34 years (Beare, 2003).

Sutherland questioned the then-prevailing wisdom that crime was a lower-class phenomenon reducible to low intelligence, mental illness, slum neighbourhoods, and broken homes. Instead, he entertained the notion that samples of criminality might be "biased in that they have not included vast areas of criminal behaviour not in the lower class" (Sutherland, 1940, p. 2). In one paper, Sutherland analyzed 547 legal findings against 70 large US companies under competition law, false advertising, labour, and intellectual property statutes. He found that while only 49 (9 percent) were prosecuted criminally, 473 (87 percent) involved conduct designated as socially injurious for which a penalty was attached—revealing what he saw to be a marked legal double standard in favour of white-collar actors (Sutherland, 1945). Sutherland also speculated that white-collar crime's financial cost was "several times as great" as traditional crime, combined with a reduction in social trust that produced "social disorganization on a large scale" (Sutherland, 1940, p. 5). Sutherland concluded that dominant definitions of criminal conduct were underinclusive, and that "[c]onvictability rather than actual conviction should be the criterion of criminality" (Sutherland, 1940, p. 6).

Edwin Sutherland: The Problem of White-Collar Crime

Pioneering American sociologist Edwin Sutherland's influential 1949 book *White Collar Crime* called for criminology to widen its scope, beyond "street crime," or crime in the lower socio-economic classes. The following excerpt is from the opening chapter, "The Problem of White Collar Crime," in which he points out the inherent bias in the ways crime was defined and prosecuted.

[S]ocial and personal pathologies are not an adequate explanation of criminal behavior. The general theories of criminal behavior which take their data from poverty and the conditions related to it are inadequate and invalid, first, because the theories do not consistently fit the data of criminal behavior; and second, because the cases on which these theories are based are a biased sample of all criminal acts. ...

And much more important is the bias involved in administration of criminal justice under laws which apply exclusively to business and the professions and which therefore involve only the upper socioeconomic class. Persons who violate laws regarding restraint of trade, advertising, pure food and drugs, and similar business practices are not arrested by uniformed policemen, are not tried in criminal courts, and are not committed to prisons; their illegal behavior receives the attention of administrative commissions and of courts operating under civil or equity jurisdiction. For this reason such violations of law are not included in the criminal statistics nor are individual cases brought to the attention of the scholars who write the theories of criminal behavior. The sample of criminal behavior on which the theories are founded is biased as to socioeconomic status, since it excludes these business and professional men. The bias is quite as certain as it would be if the scholars selected only red-haired criminals for study and reached the conclusion that redness of hair was the cause of crime.

The thesis of this book, stated positively, is that persons of the upper socioeconomic class engage in much criminal behavior; that this criminal behavior differs from the criminal behavior of the lower socioeconomic class principally in the administrative procedures which are used in dealing with the offenders; and that variations in administrative procedures are not significant from the point of view of causation of crime. The causes of tuberculosis were not different when it was treated by poultices and bloodletting than when treated by streptomycin.

These violations of law by persons in the upper socioeconomic class are, for convenience, called "white collar crimes." This concept is not intended to be definitive, but merely to call attention to crimes which are not ordinarily included within the scope of criminology. White collar crime may be defined approximately as a crime committed by a person of respectability and high social status in the course of his occupation. ...

The significant thing about white collar crime is that it is not associated with poverty or with social and personal pathologies which accompany poverty. If it can be shown that white collar crimes are frequent, a general theory that crime is due to poverty and its related pathologies is shown to be invalid. Furthermore, the study of white collar crime may assist in locating those factors which, being common to the crimes of the rich and the poor, are most significant for a general theory of criminal behavior.

Source: Excerpted from Sutherland (1949/1983, pp. 5–7).

Subsequent scholars have taken up Sutherland's proposal in full, extending the definition of *crime* to not only civil and regulatory law violations but also "harmful acts for which no legal remedy yet exists" (Brown & Chiang, 1995, p. 32)—a virtually bottomless definition that would confound most lawyers. Others have approached Sutherland more critically, making note of his often transparent anti-corporate bias and deficient methodologies (Clinard & Quinney, 1978). In one departure from Sutherland, Susan Shapiro (1990) calls for "collaring the crime, not the criminal," or for a definition of *white-collar crime* that focuses on the nature of crimes rather than the privileged identity of their perpetrators. Sutherland's suspicion of white-collar crime's low public visibility and staggering financial and human cost, however, has been broadly and consistently sustained through the years.

What Makes White-Collar Crime Distinct?

While white-collar crime can easily be distinguished from street crime—comprising such offences as murder, assault, sexual assault, and robbery—the term's lack of precise boundaries otherwise belies its ubiquity in popular and academic usage. What is it about white-collar criminality that makes it such an enduring concept? The factors below, in our view, provide a useful starting point.

Material Privilege

Class is the fundamental ingredient of Sutherland's definition of *white-collar crime*. One insight supporting a "collar the crime" approach, however, is that conduct close to that which Sutherland targets is often carried out by people of modest means—for example, cheque fraud, unhygienic food-handling, and email schemes. Subsequent research, however, lends an empirical basis to Sutherland's generalization. For example, one US study found that only 21.2 percent of defendants convicted of murder, manslaughter, assault, robbery, burglary, and auto theft ("street offenders") had completed at least some university, while that number rose to 49.7 percent among defendants convicted of fraud, embezzlement, bribery, tax offences, competition offences, and food and drug violations ("white-collar offenders"). Likewise, 78.3 percent of street offenders had a high school education or less, while only 45.8 percent of white-collar offenders had that educational profile (Shover & Hochstetler, 2006, p. 53).

Influence on the System

Related to the privileged status of white-collar offenders is their immensely greater influence on both "the law in the books" and "the law in action." Corporations and professional associations have long invested resources to mould legislation, regulation, and judicial precedents to their interests, including through direct lobbying, advertising, and court or regulatory interventions. Street criminals, in contrast, often lack the means to engage in advocacy in their own court cases. White-collar offenders are also far more likely to share the middle-class or upper-middle-class backgrounds of those doing the enforcing or judging relevant to their conduct—a "class bias" well grasped by Sutherland (Sutherland, 1940, p. 7).

Occupational Context

Most observers share Sutherland's starting point that white-collar crime occurs in workplace environments—hence, of course, the reference to office apparel. The offence of impaired driving, for example, tends not to be regarded as white-collar crime despite the fact middle-class people frequently show up as offenders (including elites such as celebrities, business leaders, and politicians).

Complexity

The dissection of white-collar conduct often engages bodies of complex economic and scientific knowledge, especially in regulated domains such as securities, energy, environmental or competition law. For instance, evidence of the impact of a criminal price-fixing conspiracy on economic efficiency or consumer welfare can significantly impact a corporate offender's sentence. Likewise, an electric utility accused of manipulating power markets may use engineering evidence to show that plant shutdowns were a response to equipment issues, not an attempt to drive up prices. As a result, a "battle of the experts" can take place at trial, with the evidence of a well-credentialed prosecution witness competing against the evidence of an equally well-credentialed defence witness.

Public Ignorance

White-collar crime's complexity can lead the public to "tune out," as the evidence overwhelmingly suggests it does (Cullen, Hartman, & Jonson, 2008; Holtfreter, Van Slyke, Bratton, & Gertz, 2008). Topics such as derivatives trading, for example, hardly lend themselves to attention-grabbing headlines for lay newsreaders. In contrast, the human drama of a local murder case can easily capture front-page coverage for weeks. Yet the abuse of derivatives can entail incredible, even economy-wide risks and repercussions, while "mass panics" about isolated street crime betray decades-long data about its diminishing prevalence.

Wide Impact

While some white-collar crimes impact only a small number of people, others can harm hundreds or thousands in a way that no crime short of a large-scale act of terrorism can. For example, a global price-fixing scheme in the market for now-ubiquitous LCD televisions affected almost all early adopters from 2001 to 2006 by artificially raising sets' prices (FBI, 2012). While few deny that the economic effect of white-collar crime far exceeds street crime, the indirect and diffuse nature of that harm can also make its quantification difficult (Gustafson, 2007).

Corporate Context

White-collar crime's corporate context also makes it a distinct animal in criminology. A far broader range of stakeholders is harmed by corporate misconduct than a traditional offence, including employees, creditors, customers, shareholders, community partners, and even tax-collecting governments. As discussed below, the corporation's separate legal personality also allows it to be sued or charged separately from its managers or employees, giving the corporate investigation or prosecution unique legal and ethical characteristics.

Although the terms often overlap considerably, it may be useful here to distinguish between *white-collar crime*, as it is broadly understood, and *corporate crime*.

White-collar crime:

- is typically committed by *individuals* in positions of trust, for personal benefit;
- commonly takes place within a corporate context; and
- may include crimes such as embezzlement, fraudulent billing, or misrepresentation of financial information.

Corporate crime, by contrast:

- is committed by a corporation, or an individual acting for a corporation; and
- may include crimes such as illegal dumping of toxic waste, price fixing, workplace safety violations, or knowingly selling a hazardous product.

Use of Technology

The modern-day explosion of information technology has produced a concomitant rise in white-collar crime that abuses the Internet's facilitation of long-distance, anonymous commerce. While some forms of cybercrime are relatively simple (such as email scams), others are very sophisticated, such as "cyberterrorism" aimed at undermining government computer networks. Such conduct often reflects a more educated and resourceful offender base.

It should be noted that cyberterrorism is only tangentially related to the standard conception of white-collar crime, as it has been defined above. Similarly, many of the people who engage in "cybercrime" would not be considered white-collar workers and likely do not hold positions of power within companies or organizations. However, it is worth noting these developments here in order to underscore how the high-tech tools for committing significant fraud or theft have now become available to a much broader range of people. It also suggests that the definition of "white-collar crime" may continue to evolve as society itself changes.

BOX 18.2

Green Criminology

green criminology
The analysis of environmental harms from a criminological perspective.

One relatively new area of study that is commonly included within the imprecise boundaries of the term "white collar-crime," and the related field of corporate crime, is **green criminology**. As the name suggests, it is concerned with bringing the tools of criminology to the study of environmental issues. Gary Potter notes:

> As elsewhere in criminology, this means thinking about offences (what crimes or harms are inflicted on the environment, and how), offenders (who commits crime against the environment, and why) and victims (who suffers as a result of environmental damage, and how), and also about responses to environmental crimes: policing, punishment and crime prevention. (Potter, 2010)

Recent environmental disasters, such as the explosion and massive oil spill at BP's Deepwater Horizon rig in the Gulf of Mexico in 2010, have increased interest in this topic. One key consideration in examining such issues through a criminological lens is that, in the case of long-term environmental degradation, or climate change effects, the specific harms may be impossible to quantify with any precision, and in many cases, the victims may not have been born yet. Additionally, for many green criminologists, the "victims" of environmental abuses may not be human beings, but particular species. Consider, for example, the illegal trade in ivory, which threatens the existence of the African elephant. Also at stake are habitats such as the Amazon rain forest. Extensive logging of these forests is not illegal. But on a global scale, the long-term effects of deforestation can result in significant harm to humans and the environment alike.

According to Potter, in 2008 the UK government department responsible for generating the most legislation for "new crimes" (852 of them) was the Department of the Environment, Food, and Rural Affairs. "This message seems clear: if sociologists and criminologists are concerned with crime, then this statistic alone is reason enough to become interested in the environment" (Potter, 2010).

Non-Violence

White-collar crime tends to be associated with guile and the abuse of trust rather than the confrontation and violence seen in street crime. Certain forms of white-collar conduct do affect the physical integrity of others: for example, a doctor's abuse of an anaesthetized patient or a company's non-compliance with workplace-safety standards. The categories explored below, however, more often centre on economic rather than physical forms of harm.

An Overview of White-Collar Offences in Canada

Canada's criminal law presently covers a range of white-collar crime, both in the *Criminal Code* and in other federal, provincial, or territorial statutes. We survey some of the most prominent categories below. While we largely confine ourselves to conventional, legal definitions of *crime*, we also survey some of the conduct Sutherland would have described as "white-collar criminality" more broadly. In particular, a universe of administrative and civil penalties exist in Canada and elsewhere for socially injurious white-collar conduct akin, in many respects, to criminal conduct.

Fraud

The most typical case of white-collar crime is **fraud**—a social wrong as ancient as commerce itself. The Roman poet Phaedrus (15 BCE–50 CE) captured the anti-social connotations of the act when he wrote that "[w]hoever is detected in a shameful fraud is as ever after not believed if even they speak the truth." In modern-day Canada, fraud is addressed in section 380(1) of the *Criminal Code* and applies broadly to

> [e]very one who, by deceit, falsehood or other fraudulent means … defrauds the public or any person … of any property, money or valuable security or any service.

fraud
A dishonest act that deprives, or risks depriving, another person of something.

The Supreme Court of Canada has interpreted "other fraudulent means" to refer to an act that would be "dishonest" in the eyes of a reasonable person. When such an act fuses with a "deprivation" or even a *risk* of deprivation to a person, a fraud exists (*R v. Théroux*, 1993).

Of particular relevance to white-collar fraudsters is the "mandatory minimum" two-year term of imprisonment now in place for frauds over $1 million. Introduced in 2011, the reform was part of the Conservative government's Bill C-21, the *Standing Up for Victims of White-Collar Crime Act*. The bill also toughens the sentencing process for white-collar offenders by, among other things, requiring judges to consider new "aggravating circumstances" and allowing them to order the offender to compensate victims for their losses ("restitution," in legal parlance).

Fraud has also long been a civil wrong, or tort, that can support a lawsuit between two private parties. In civil form, fraud is known as the tort of "deceit" or "negligent misrepresentation," depending on whether the defendant intentionally or negligently misled the plaintiff, respectively. Torts are not found in legislation but in the common law (i.e., the body of law found in judicial precedents from past court decisions); they lead to monetary **liability** for damages caused rather than a conviction; and they are proven to the court on a "balance of probabilities" rather than the criminal level of "beyond a reasonable doubt."

liability
Legal responsibility for an act or omission.

Money Laundering

money laundering
The process of concealing
the source of illegitimately
obtained money.

Money laundering is the process of making "dirty" money obtained from crime (formally referred to as "the proceeds of crime") appear "clean" or legitimately sourced to escape legal scrutiny. Money laundering is specifically prohibited in section 462.32(1) of the *Criminal Code*. While the International Monetary Fund's estimate of the global volume of laundered funds is a staggering US$2 to US$4 trillion, estimates of the inherently concealed practice's prevalence remain unreliable. Money laundering is an indispensable part of large-scale organized crime, and the first laundering operations on record tracked the vast underground liquor economy of the prohibition era (Beare & Schnieder, 2007).

The recommendations of a task force at the 1989 Paris G7 Economic Summit gave momentum to Canada's first money-laundering statute in 1991 and a voluntary protocol between the RCMP and the Canadian Bankers Association in 1993. These initiatives established private sector systems for transaction monitoring, usually based on monetary thresholds or circumstantial triggers of suspicion. In 2000, Canada adopted a mandatory monitoring regime in the *Proceeds of Crime (Money Laundering) Act* of 2000. The Act also establishes the Financial Transactions and Reports Analysis Centre of Canada (FINTRAC), an independent agency that receives and analyzes transaction reports for potential links to criminal behaviour.

The September 11, 2001 terrorist attacks in the United States spurred legislatures to devise laws to thwart "terrorist financing"—a mirror image of money laundering that looks to funds' "dirty" destinations rather than their origins. In the United States, the controversial "war on terror"–era *PATRIOT Act* dedicated a full section to "anti-money laundering to prevent terrorism." Canada's money-laundering statute was likewise amended into the *Proceeds of Crime (Money Laundering) and Terrorist Financing Act* (PCMLTFA) in December 2001, with FINTRAC's responsibilities enlarged in turn.

Bribery

bribery
The practice of illegally inducing a
person, company, or government
to act in one's favour, usually by
transferring money or property.

Another white-collar crime of international scope targets Canadian nationals who bribe foreign officials. For much of the 20th century, **bribery** was the "unspoken rule" of corporate multinationals when operating in developing countries. Perhaps as a response to the post-Watergate uptick in public concern over corruption, the US Securities and Exchange Commission (SEC) launched a voluntary disclosure program in 1975 to encourage companies to admit to bribery in exchange for lenient prosecutorial treatment. The results were striking: over 400 companies responded, accounting for bribes of over US$300 million. Before a congressional hearing, for example, the Lockheed Corporation admitted to spending US$24 million on bribes worldwide, claiming the amounts to be legal and merely a part of its business (Kochan & Goodyear, 2011). On the tail of such revelations, the United States enacted the *Foreign Corrupt Officials Act* in 1977.

In 1999, Canada passed its own *Corruption of Foreign Public Officials Act* to ratify the anti-bribery convention of the Organisation for Economic Co-operation and Development (OECD), signed that year. However, the country's anti-bribery efforts have come under fire since Transparency International recently called out the "little or no enforcement" of the statute (Sher, 2011). In 2013, the Conservative government—acting consistently with its "tough on crime" approach—proposed amendments to increase the Act's penalties and extraterritorial reach.

Embezzlement

Embezzlement involves a person's misappropriation of funds entrusted to him or her. A store clerk, for example, could engage in embezzlement by diverting funds from a cash register on a daily basis. However, given the multitude of professionals legally in possession of far larger sums of client, customer, or corporate funds, embezzlement is an especially significant white-collar crime. An investment adviser, for example, might be found guilty of embezzling client funds transferred to purchase stocks or bonds.

While embezzlement is a specific offence in the United States, Canadian law treats embezzlement as a form of fraud or theft. In the case of certain professionals, however, embezzlement is also likely to be a "fiduciary duty" violation—a violation of a civil duty to act in the best interests of a "principal" he or she serves. A lawyer, for example, has a common-law fiduciary duty to his or her client. Likewise, section 122 of the *Canada Business Corporations Act* sets out the fiduciary duty of corporate board members and officers to "act honestly and in good faith with a view to the best interests of the corporation."

embezzlement
To take money or misappropriate funds that belong to someone else.

Tax Evasion

Taxes are the lifeblood of Canadian government: 82 percent of federal revenues, for example, could be attributed to taxes in the 2011–12 fiscal year (Flaherty, 2013, p. 289). Accordingly, tax evasion criminalizes the illegal circumvention of taxes. Tax evasion can be contrasted with the legal practice of tax *avoidance*: the law generally allows people to strategize to reduce their taxes by legally approved means. For example, a

---

BOX 18.3

Conrad Black

Conrad Black was involved in a notable case of corporate embezzlement. As a director of newspaper conglomerate Hollinger International Inc., he personally received "non-competition" side payments in sale agreements between Hollinger and buyers of its newspaper subsidiaries. Theoretically, these payments would have protected the buyers from Black or his co-directors *personally* setting up competing newspapers in small towns in the United States—a scenario a Chicago court found implausible. The buyers themselves never requested this protection, and Hollinger itself was unaware of this bargain until it was a *fait accompli*. While part of Black's conviction was overturned on extraneous legal grounds before the Supreme Court of the United States, the Chicago court, in reconsidering the case, affirmed Black's convictions for both obstructing justice and fraudulently appropriating money to which Hollinger was legally entitled (*United States v. Black*, 2010).

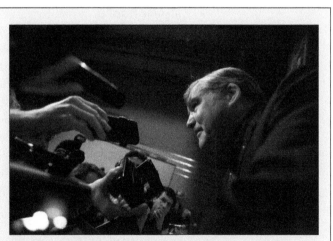

Media baron Conrad Black is perhaps Canada's best-known white-collar felon. He served 42 months in prison in the United States for fraud and obstruction of justice and was released in 2012. He has since returned to public life in Canada, and has also become an outspoken advocate for prison reform.

Source: Peter Power/GetStock.com.

taxpayer concealing income from his second job in his tax filings commits criminal tax evasion; on the other hand, a taxpayer making RSP contributions to deliberately reduce her obligations at tax-time engages in legal tax avoidance. While income earners at all levels can commit tax evasion, the average offender—perhaps owing to the higher payoffs at stake—has a markedly white-collar profile: "male, under age 50 in a high tax bracket with a complex return" (Sabatini, 2007).

History's most infamous tax evader remains Al Capone, who despite escaping prosecution for his organized-crime activities was caught evading taxes amounting to US$2.8 million in today's dollars. Capone was sentenced to 11 years in prison—at the time, the longest tax evasion sentence in US history. Canada's *Income Tax Act* is less punitive: tax evaders can be liable for a fine of between 50 and 200 percent of the amount of the tax sought to be evaded and a prison term of up to two years.

Starting in 1988, Canadian tax authorities began narrowing their view of tax avoidance's legality in line with the enactment of the general anti-avoidance rule (GAAR) in section 245 of the *Income Tax Act*. The non-criminal rule allows the Canada Revenue Agency to target otherwise legal activities incompatible with the spirit of the law, or what it has recently characterized as "aggressive" or "abusive" tax planning (Fleury, 2010). While not extensively used, the GAAR reflects the trend in favour of non-criminal enforcement paths by regulators, both in the interests of enforcement efficacy and to target lesser forms of socially injurious conduct by rehabilitative or compliance means. Reflecting its middle-ground status between criminal evasion and non-actionable avoidance, the GAAR requires taxpayers to include wrongly claimed amounts in their taxes rather than pay a penalty.

Insider Trading

insider trading
The practice of trading in a stock, bond, or other security while possessing material, non-public information about the company in question.

One of the most notorious white-collar crimes is the securities law offence of **insider trading**—not only because its prevalence and difficulty to enforce exemplify Sutherland's thesis but also because many people (sometimes self-servingly) deny that there is anything wrong with the practice. Insider trading is the purchase or sale of stocks or other securities by individuals with access to non-public information about a company. The criminalization of insider trading relates to a core policy aim of securities markets: the maintenance of a level playing field between investors in relation to market information. Separate disclosure rules also serve that end by requiring companies to issue press releases of material events affecting their operations, thus preventing insiders (such as directors, officers, employees, and advisers to the company) from reaping windfalls from large, strategically timed stock purchases or sales.

The first insider-trading law was enacted in the United States after the Great Depression as part of the federal *Securities Exchange Act of 1934*. In Canada, the prohibition can be found in the *Securities Act* in force in each province, although in 2004 a parallel federal prohibition was enacted as section 382.1(1) of the *Criminal Code*. Some academics within the economics and "law and economics" traditions support the legalization of insider trading, including Milton Friedman, Henry Manne, and Frank Easterbrook. These scholars insist that insider trading benefits investors by introducing new information more quickly into the market. While some empirical support exists for that proposition, concerns about distributional fairness to ordinary "mom-and-pop" investors with inferior access to information continue to underpin support for prohibition. The International

Organization of Securities Commissions (2004), for example, cites the protection of investors from insider trading as a "core principle" of securities regulation.

Market Manipulation

Market manipulation is another key securities prohibition, and it can be understood as a specialized branch of fraud aimed at protecting the fair and transparent operation of securities markets. Market misconduct affects not only upper-middle-class investors who hire professional money managers but, for example, working-class pension plan members whose ability to retire comfortably is equally tied to the market. Ontario's *Securities Act* prohibits (in section 126.1(1)) a person or company from "any act, practice or course of conduct relating to securities … that the person or company knows or reasonably ought to know … (a) results or contributes to a misleading appearance of trading activity in, or an artificial price in, a security … or (b) perpetuates a fraud on any person or company." A classic market manipulation device is a "pump-and-dump" scheme, whereby a significant shareholder makes false positive statements about a stock—thereby pumping up its value—before selling his or her holdings at a large profit (dumping) to investors who suffer the inevitable fall in the security's value.

> **market manipulation**
> The practice of interfering with the proper operation of a market, usually by employing or creating misleading or artificial information.

The market manipulation concept has also been transplanted beyond the securities context. For example, the US Federal Energy Regulatory Commission (FERC) enforces an "anti-market manipulation" rule to govern the country's energy markets. In 2013, FERC issued a US$285 million civil penalty under the rule against JPMorgan Chase & Co.'s energy-trading arm for using a strategy of artificial, uneconomic bidding to abuse "make-whole" payments approved by regulators (Wingfield & Kopecki, 2013). These payments resulted in unnecessary hikes to consumers' utility bills. While civil in nature, the rule illustrates the close behavioural linkages Sutherland observed between criminalized and non-criminalized white-collar conduct.

Price Fixing

Direct and indirect forms of consumer predation are also a preoccupation of the enforcement authorities overseeing competition law (known as *antitrust law* in the United States). The quintessential competition law offence is **price fixing**, which refers to the practice by which groups of competing buyers or sellers (together, a "cartel") agree to collude to set prices in a market. The "conspiracy" provision in section 45 of the *Competition Act* criminalizes the act in Canada. Adam Smith grasped the challenges of detecting price fixing when he wrote, in 1776's *An Inquiry into the Nature and Causes of the Wealth of Nations*, that

> **price fixing**
> An agreement between competitors to fix the price for a good or service by buying or selling at an agreed-to price or by manipulating supply or demand.

> [p]eople of the same trade seldom meet together, even for merriment and diversion, but the conversation ends in a conspiracy against the public, or in some contrivance to raise prices. It is impossible, indeed, to prevent such meetings, by any law which either could be executed, or would be consistent with liberty and justice.

Smith's point is well reflected in the scarcity of price-fixing convictions worldwide. At the same time, modern developments—including anonymous tipping from employees and competitors, wiretapping, and the development of immunity guarantees for price-fixing cartel "defectors" that assist in the prosecution of others—have also contributed to major and minor victories. These techniques, for example, enabled the Competition

Bureau's recent string of price-fixing convictions in gasoline cartels in Quebec and eastern Ontario between 2008 and 2012 (Competition Bureau, 2012; Gray, 2012).

Convictions or settlements in price-fixing cases often leave a trail of class action lawsuits that can boost the deterrent effect of a conviction. Class actions are civil lawsuits where a "representative plaintiff" sues a company on behalf of a larger group of persons with closely associated claims. The procedure assists a group of plaintiffs to recover small individual losses that, aggregated together, often scale into the millions. For example, following a guilty plea by Hershey Canada in June 2013 concerning price fixing in the chocolate industry, the company and competitors Cadbury Adams Canada, Nestlé Canada, and Mars Canada settled a class action suit that made $23 million available for payouts to purchasers who bought at least $1,000 in chocolate in the period of alleged price fixing (2005 to 2007) (Zaccagna, 2013).

Health and Safety Breaches

Prior to the advent of modern health and safety legislation, the British common law had evolved to recognize the duty of employers in physically dangerous workplaces "to take all reasonable precautions for the workman's safety" rather than deem employees to have "voluntarily assumed" risks to their safety under their employment contracts (*Smith v. Baker*, 1891). Workplace deaths also spurred on legislation that empowered inspectors to ensure that workplaces adhered to minimum standards, especially in inherently dangerous locations such as mines (Edmonds & Edmonds, 1963). In Canada, the provinces administer the modern successors to these regimes under statutes such as Ontario's *Occupational Health and Safety Act*, with federal workplaces falling under the *Canada Labour Code*.

In Ontario, Ministry of Labour inspectors visit workplaces and, as needed, issue non-compliance orders, resolve disputes, and refer appropriate cases for criminal prosecution. The governing philosophy of modern health and safety laws, however, is a compliance-oriented concept of shared employer–employee responsibility for workplace safety. This concept is manifested in initiatives such as Ontario's Internal Responsibility System, which encourages organizations to give "everyone within an organization direct responsibility for health and safety as an essential part of his or her job" (Plummer, Strahlendorf, & Holliday, 2009). Ontario workplaces with over 20 employees must appoint joint health and safety committees comprising worker and employer representatives who hold regular meetings, inspect the workplace, and recommend measures to improve health and safety.

Despite these developments, corporations have come under scrutiny for a perceived indifference to workplace safety. A particularly tragic safety incident occurred in the case of an explosion at the Westray Mine in Plymouth, Nova Scotia on May 9, 1992, which killed 26 miners. Subsequent legal proceedings failed to yield convictions of two mine managers and a corporation—although that result could, at least in part, be attributed to prosecutorial misconduct. A public inquiry led to a recommendation that the federal government study how to make corporate managers properly accountable for their company's wrongful or **negligent** treatment of workplace safety (Richard, 1997). Part of the federal government's response in Bill C-45 (discussed in greater detail below) included a new section 217.1 of the *Criminal Code*, providing that "[e]very one who undertakes, or has the authority, to direct how another person does work or performs

negligence
A legal intent standard that considers whether a person, regardless of actual intent or knowledge, failed to take reasonable care in doing or failing to do something.

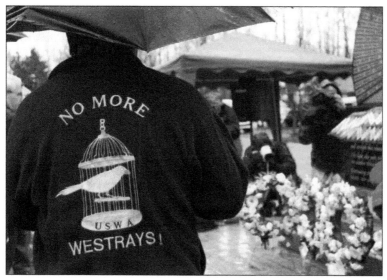

A mourner visits the Westray Miners' Memorial in Nova Scotia. The explosion at the Westray Mine on May 9, 1992 was one of the worst industrial accidents in Canadian history. The tragedy led to a public inquiry that examined the owners' management of the mine and workplace safety, as well as the lack of proper government oversight.

Source: Miles Howe (Halifax Media Co-op).

a task is under a legal duty to take reasonable steps to prevent bodily harm to that person, or any other person, arising from that work or task." While conceptually similar to the common law duty set out above, this change effectively exposes supervisors to conviction under the criminal negligence provisions of the Code, which provides in section 219(1) that "[e]very one is criminally negligent who ... in omitting to do anything that it is his duty to do, shows wanton or reckless disregard for other persons." Such penalties should, at a minimum, provide a personal incentive for directors and officers to invest resources in proper health and safety procedures in the workplace.

Cybercrime

The newest white-collar crimes fall into a nebulous category of conduct known as **cybercrime** (sometimes called *technological crime* or *technocrime*), and capture the growing information-age impact of computers and the Internet on crime. As one scholar puts it, "crooks can con better with technology; paedophiles can lure their victims better; and anyone can harass, defame, threaten or blackmail better with technology" (Leman-Langlois, 2008, p. 2). Cybercrime also includes new forms of criminal activity that cannot be committed without modern technology, such as computer-systems penetration, data alteration, and hacking (RCMP, 2013). While many cybercrimes can be prosecuted using "classical" criminal law (such as fraud), specific computer-related prohibitions can also be found within the *Criminal Code*, such as unauthorized use of computer (section 342.1), mischief in relation to data (section 430(1.1)), and interception of communications (section 184).

Technology has escalated concerns about **identity theft** in particular, where a person uses another's credentials to access information, siphon funds, or even commit fraud. In

cybercrime
Crime committed over the Internet or a computer network.

identity theft
The theft and use of a person's identifying information, usually for monetary gain.

recognition of impersonation's new, "faceless" form, Canada's federal government introduced Bill S-4 in 2010 to create new *Criminal Code* offences prohibiting the following:

- Obtaining and possessing identity information with the intent to use the information deceptively, dishonestly or fraudulently in the commission of a crime;
- Trafficking in identity information, an offence that targets those who transfer or sell information to another person with knowledge of or recklessness as to the possible criminal use of the information; and
- Unlawfully possessing or trafficking in government-issued identity documents that contain information of another person. (Canada, Department of Justice, 2010, para. 3)

Criminal law's increasing attention to identity-theft issues is consistent with a heightened emphasis on privacy law by both federal and provincial governments. Privacy legislation restricts the extent to which public institutions—a prime target of cybercrime—can collect, use, and disclose "personal information" obtained in the course of government business.

White-Collar Crime Enforcement in Canada

A vast regulatory apparatus surrounds the investigation and prosecution of laws relating to white-collar crime such as those outlined above. The following sections provide an overview of the actors, processes, and challenges involved in the battle against white-collar crime in Canada.

Responsible Agencies

The detection and enforcement of conventional crime in Canada overwhelmingly takes place within the jurisdiction of police departments operating at the municipal, provincial, and federal levels. These agencies also play a role in white-collar matters. In particular, the RCMP's ten Integrated Market Enforcement Teams (IMETs) operating in Toronto, Vancouver, Montreal, and Calgary target capital markets fraud offences and include specialized investigators from the RCMP, local police, provincial securities regulators, and other federal and provincial agencies, as well as in-house forensic accountants (RCMP, 2011). However, an account of the enforcement landscape would be incomplete without mention of other governmental and non-governmental oversight authorities associated with particular regulatory regimes and the thousands of officers under them. Federally, these authorities include agencies and departments such as the Competition Bureau, the Canada Revenue Agency, Environment Canada, Fisheries and Oceans Canada, Health Canada, the National Energy Board, the Security Investigations Service of Canada Post, and the Canadian Food Inspection Agency. In the provinces and territories, they include regulators or governments departments overseeing the securities, financial services, health and safety, environmental, transportation, and energy domains. At the provincial and territorial level, the enforcement apparatus also includes the "colleges" and licensing bodies of self-regulated professions such as medicine, nursing, dentistry, and law.

Enforcement staff are frequently drawn from the ranks of industry or its advisers and consultants. For example, securities commissions regularly recruit attorneys from private sector law firms that advise companies selling stocks, bonds, or other securities to the public. While such an approach ensures that the body has sufficient expertise to regulate effectively, it also introduces the risk of **regulatory capture**: a phenomenon, first identified by Nobel Prize–winning economist George Stigler, where public-interest bodies begin to serve the commercial or other interests of those they regulate (Stigler, 1971). In particular, those with industry backgrounds may be more likely to identify with the goals of regulated entities; have personal and professional connections on the other side influencing their judgment; and be inclined to use their experience to cross over to a private sector compliance or defence role later—the so-called regulatory revolving door. Given enforcement agencies' need for deep expertise to function, however, the problem has no easy solutions. An interesting alternative theory to "staffing capture" is that the prospect of private sector job opportunities encourages current enforcers to pursue conduct more—not less—aggressively to showcase their expertise (Kedia, 2012).

> **regulatory capture**
> A theory of corruption whereby regulatory bodies in a sector advance the private interests of the actors they regulate over the public interest.

The Investigative Process

The investigative process for most enforcement bodies is highly consistent—reflecting the legal risks associated with an abundance of officer discretion. These risks include instances of "officially induced error," which involve officers engaging in conduct that appears to bless or even invite the problematic conduct under investigation. At the other end, overzealous enforcement practices may open the investigative agency to a claim of negligent law enforcement, a court challenge based on the "reasonableness" of the agency's decision or even a constitutional attack based on the *Canadian Charter of Rights and Freedoms*. Investigative mistakes can, in other words, imperil an otherwise meritorious case and deny the public the protection or justice it deserves.

The investigative process begins with monitoring for compliance, which is accomplished by varying means. Some agencies are data-heavy, relying on the expertise of economists, accountants, and others to detect anomalies in a market or in documents submitted pursuant to legal reporting or disclosure requirements. Securities and energy market regulators exemplify this style of "behind-the-desk" monitoring. Others, such as health and safety and environmental regulators, rely more heavily on actual "field" visits to workplaces or on obligating companies to inspect and self-report issues themselves.

A conceptual separation exists between "inspections" and "investigations" by enforcement personnel who attend offices and other workplaces. Inspections—common among regulatory agencies—can be scheduled or random and are targeted at monitoring regulated actors' compliance in general. Investigations, in contrast, follow the discovery of specific misconduct or risks, often aim at prosecution, and nearly always involve the gathering of evidence. Legislation often sets up separate powers in relation to each type of visit, with the latter almost always requiring a search warrant authorized by a judge. That warrant is another requirement of the Charter, which protects both individuals and companies against "unreasonable search and seizure." Courts have generally given leeway to investigators to assess the line between a "reasonable" and "unreasonable" search. In so doing, they have drawn a distinction between the invasiveness of searching a home versus an office, where individuals have a lower expectation of privacy (*British Columbia Securities Commission v. Branch*, 1995). A poorly executed search, however, can still derail a case: critically important, yet unconstitutionally obtained evidence can be excluded under section 24(2) of the Charter.

The volume of evidence produced in white-collar cases can be daunting for the regulator and the regulated alike. Investigators will sometimes request companies to provide all "records" relating to the topic under investigation—a broad-ranging term that includes emails. In the information age, such a search will often require thousands of documents to be reviewed in a "regulatory due diligence" process, often by lawyers billing at hourly rates of $400 and above. One reason lawyers conduct the review is that records may be subject to attorney-client privilege, a legal doctrine intended to allow clients to speak freely with lawyers. Unless waived by the client, the doctrine makes communications for the purposes of legal advice permanently inadmissible in a hearing. The amount and complexity of evidence are just two factors behind why it takes so long for white-collar cases to result in convictions. For example, the fraudulent misstatement of financial statements by Canadian entertainment moguls Garth Drabinsky and Myron Gottlieb at the theatre production company they co-founded, Livent, occurred between 1993 and 1998. It took until 2009 for the duo to be convicted (*R v. Drabinsky*, 2009).

Once the police or relevant enforcement body possesses enough evidence to support a criminal charge against the person or company in question, the matter proceeds according to ordinary criminal procedure. For less serious offences, an "information" is sworn by an officer in court; for more serious ones, an "indictment" is used. Both documents outline the allegations against an accused and record the case's history. While police can arrest a white-collar criminal like any other, more common in the case of less serious offences is the issuance of an "appearance notice," which involves a promise to appear in court. Since corporations, plainly, cannot be arrested, a summons or notice pursuant to section 703.2 of the *Criminal Code* is sufficient. The Crown must provide "disclosure" to the accused of the relevant case-related information it possesses—another Charter-protected right (*R v. Stinchcombe*, 1991).

With respect to less serious forms of white-collar conduct, regulatory authorities may opt against criminal enforcement in favour of a more informal and educational response, with the ultimate goal being rehabilitation rather than punishment. Especially where corporations are concerned, avoiding an adversarial, sanctions-based approach can be a more effective method of securing compliance and thus public-interest outcomes. This is especially true where personnel respond to the regulator's feedback, as John Braithwaite has argued in his model of "Responsive Regulation" (Braithwaite, 2011). Cooperative models of regulation involving closer government–industry relations, however, can also invite concerns of regulatory capture as officials begin to personally relate to those on the other side (Snider, 1993).

Another regulatory "half-way house" is civil or administrative enforcement. The British Columbia Securities Commission, for example, can elect to proceed on a criminal or civil track for many violations of the BC *Securities Act*. The former route, set out in section 155 of the Act, allows for jail time up to five years and fines up to $3 million or more, depending on profits earned. The latter, set out in sections 161 and 162, forfeits a "hard time" sanction but allows for a range of orders "in the public interest." These include an order to resign or refrain from assuming a director or officer position; to pay back profits earned from non-compliance; and to account for a financial penalty of up to $1 million per contravention—a so-called **administrative monetary penalty (AMP)**. The increasing use of AMPs has been controversial. In particular, Charter challenges have been brought against AMPs alleged to be so high that they amount to a disguised

administrative monetary penalty (AMP)

A non-criminal penalty issued by a regulatory body, without court approval, for the violation of a law it administers.

criminal fine levied without accompanying criminal law due process standards (Keith, 2011). Likewise, 2009 amendments to the *Competition Act* gave the Competition Bureau a "civil track" alternative to laying price-fixing charges: it can issue AMPs against competitors who engage in collaborations—such as joint ventures or strategic alliances—that, while short of naked price fixing, nevertheless demonstrate an anti-competitive effect (Competition Bureau, 2009).

White-Collar Prosecutions and Hearings

Prosecutions in any white-collar case differ according to forum. Criminal-track prosecutions are heard in court and face the scrutiny of the both the criminal law's traditional "beyond a reasonable doubt" burden of proof and the strict rules of evidence applicable in court settings. The ordinary criminal process applies: accused persons are entitled to a bail hearing where the Crown (the prosecutor) may argue that jail custody pending trial is justified (1) to secure the accused's attendance in court; (2) to protect the public; or (3) to "maintain confidence in the administration of justice" (*Criminal Code*, s. 515(10)). Generally, a white-collar accused will be able to elect to hear his or her case by a judge alone or by a judge and jury, which includes a preliminary inquiry. The inquiry—mandatory in jury cases—determines whether enough evidence exists to stand the accused for trial, and also has the advantage of giving the defence a sneak peek at the Crown's case prior to trial. Corporations "appear in court" through agents or their counsel, as set out in sections 538 and 556 of the *Criminal Code*.

Administrative cases, in contrast, are heard before specialized tribunals or boards. A bewildering number of administrative avenues exist: for example, by one recent count, 235 such bodies (many with their own appeal procedures) existed in Ontario alone, from the Ontario Municipal Board to panels of the Ontario Securities Commission to the Ontario Human Rights Tribunal (Ministry of the Attorney General, 2010). To provide for a more speedy and accessible process relative to a court setting, legislation often provides that these venues are not subject to the strict laws of evidence. For example, "hearsay" evidence—second-hand evidence not tendered through a witness in court—can be accepted without resort to the complex rules governing its admission in court. Moreover, enforcement-body applicants need to prove their case only on a "balance of probabilities," which is a far cry from the criminal "beyond a reasonable doubt" standard. However, administrative hearings in other respects resemble a court process: the adversarial setting; the presence of lawyers; the hearing of evidence; and the procedural formalities involved (such as rules of procedure).

Class actions and civil cases in respect of white-collar cases are heard in court. In securities, pension, corporate fiduciary duty and bankruptcy matters, Ontario has appointed a "commercial list" of judges with specific corporate and commercial expertise to hear cases. Other disputes are heard by more generalist judges whose exposure to complex business matters may be limited. While the civil court process, similar to the criminal court process, requires that various evidentiary and procedural formalities be followed, the burden of proof remains a "balance of probabilities." Civil and administrative hearings can thus result in liability even if a parallel criminal proceeding renders a "not guilty" finding—akin to the famous result in the O.J. Simpson–Nicole Brown murder saga, where the former NFL football player was held criminally "not guilty" for murder, but civilly liable for "wrongful death."

Sanctions in White-Collar Cases

At the end of a criminal trial, the accused is either "not guilty" or "guilty" (and thus an "offender"). At the end of a civil trial or administrative process, "liability" and not "guilt" in the strict sense, is assessed. Many, including Sutherland, were bothered by these distinctions. One might argue that the stigma of being labelled a "fraudster" and penalized before a securities commission is no different than that of being labelled a "fraudster" and fined before a court. Rightly or wrongly, Canadian law reflects the other view. Clearly, however, civil and administrative tracks enable white-collar accountability in cases where the prosecution cannot secure a watertight "beyond a reasonable doubt" case. In such cases, filling the gap with AMPs and public-interest orders, or in lesser cases with warnings and education, may be a better result for the public interest than the elusive trophy of conviction.

Just as the overwhelming majority of civil lawsuits are settled prior to trial, plea bargaining and settlement pervade criminal and administrative disputes between enforcers and those accused of white-collar crime. In the United States, prosecutors have made good use of deferred prosecution agreements (DPAs). DPAs involve a promise by enforcers not to prosecute a criminal charge against a company on the condition that it complies with specified contract-like terms. These terms usually commit the company to substantial internal compliance reforms as well as requirements that personnel cooperate with the government, often to build a criminal case against individual employees (Spivack & Raman, 2008). The result, in one commentator's view, is a brave new world where the corporation becomes, in effect, "the branch office of the prosecutor" (First, 2010). DPAs have not yet spread to Canada.

When an individual or corporate accused pleads guilty or is convicted of a crime at trial, a separate hearing follows whereby a sentence is determined on the basis of factors such as the nature of the offence, the offender's circumstances, and the offence's community or victim impact. The sentence must be guided by the sentencing objectives in section 718 of the *Criminal Code*:

  (a) to denounce unlawful conduct;
  (b) to deter the offender and other persons from committing offences;
  (c) to separate offenders from society, where necessary;
  (d) to assist in rehabilitating offenders;
  (e) to provide reparations for harm done to victims or to the community; and
  (f) to promote a sense of responsibility in offenders, and acknowledgment of the harm done to victims and to the community.

The "fundamental principle" of sentencing is specified in section 718.1 of the *Criminal Code*: "A sentence must be proportionate to the gravity of the offence and the degree of responsibility of the offender." White-collar crimes present competing considerations in light of these criteria. On one hand, white-collar conduct often (but not always) results in predominantly *economic* harm rather than physical harm with the emotional gravity of murder or sexual assault. White-collar offences have been labelled "victimless" crimes by certain academics and judges (Gustafson, 2007). On the other hand, individual white-collar offenders frequently abuse positions of immense social and economic privilege for gains having little to do with passion or desperation, often showing little or no remorse for their actions. Conrad Black, for one, has variously described his criminal conviction as a "persecution"; compared the justice system in the United States to that of North Korea; and described his presiding judge as a "megalomaniac" and "the most tiresome publicity-seeking judge in America" (Black, 2012).

In the Westray Bill, or Bill C-45, additional sentencing factors were enacted into section 718.21 of the *Criminal Code* specific to corporate and other organizational offenders:

(a) any advantage realized by the organization as a result of the offence;

(b) the degree of planning involved in carrying out the offence and the duration and complexity of the offence;

(c) whether the organization has attempted to conceal its assets, or convert them, in order to show that it is not able to pay a fine or make restitution;

(d) the impact that the sentence would have on the economic viability of the organization and the continued employment of its employees;

(e) the cost to public authorities of the investigation and prosecution of the offence;

(f) any regulatory penalty imposed on the organization or one of its representatives in respect of the conduct that formed the basis of the offence;

(g) whether the organization was—or any of its representatives who were involved in the commission of the offence were—convicted of a similar offence or sanctioned by a regulatory body for similar conduct;

(h) any penalty imposed by the organization on a representative for their role in the commission of the offence;

(i) any restitution that the organization is ordered to make or any amount that the organization has paid to a victim of the offence; and

(j) any measures that the organization has taken to reduce the likelihood of it committing a subsequent offence.

These additional factors reflect unique considerations that accompany criminal prosecutions of a corporation: namely, the impact of a sentence on innocent bystanders, such as employees (d); the complexity of prosecution (e); the above-discussed existence of parallel administrative regimes (f and g); and rehabilitative measures such as internal compliance programs (j).

Corporate Criminal Liability and Governance

Corporations are a focal point of any discussion around white-collar crime, especially when the topic of conversation turns to sanction: How, exactly, does it make sense to attach culpability to organizations that have "no soul to damn" and "no body to kick" (Coffee, 1981)? The fact, however, that the largest and most profitable private entities in the world—and those with the greatest potential to impact the economic fortunes and physical well-being of the public—are corporations makes these and other inquiries unavoidable.

The Criminal Liability Debate

Whether the criminal law should seek to punish corporations is a hotly debated topic among criminologists, lawyers, and economists. In Canadian law, however, the matter has been settled: Canada's experience with treating corporations as capable of being convicted dates back to a case that is well over a century old (*R v. Union Colliery Co. of British Columbia*, 1900).

One puzzle is how the requirement of *mens rea*, or intent, attached to most criminal offences sits with purely legal persons that lack a "mind." In a landmark competition law case, *R v. Canadian Dredge & Dock Co.* (1985), the court elaborated on the logic behind its approach to this matter. The court accepted identification theory as the basis for criminal liability. According to this theory guilt can be assigned to a corporation when a crime is committed by senior employees (the "directing mind"), including "the board of directors, the managing director, the superintendent, the manager or anyone else delegated by the board of directors to whom is delegated the governing executive authority of the corporation" (para. 32). When any such person commits a crime while acting "(a) was within the field of operation assigned to him; (b) was not totally in fraud of the corporation; and (c) was by design or result partly for the benefit of the company" (para. 66).

Largely in response to Nova Scotia's Westray Mine disaster and the scathing recommendations of Justice Peter Richard in its inquiry, Parliament enacted significant reforms to this liability framework in 2004 by enacting Bill C-45. In cases where the prosecution must prove the company's negligence, new section 22.1 of the *Criminal Code* provides that "an organization is a party to the offence" if a "representative" is a party to the offence—defined to include a director, partner, employee, member, or even an agent or a contractor of the organization. For offences requiring proof of more than negligence (i.e., an intentional or reckless act), a higher standard is set out in section 22.2: only the actions of a "representative" directed or overseen by senior officers can be attributed to the company. Together, these provisions represent a significant expansion of the Supreme Court's model of liability.

Even if one accepts the logic of corporate criminality as declared by the Supreme Court and Parliament, other idiosyncrasies result from the concept. For one, convicting a corporation financially impacts a wide body of innocent bystanders. In particular, shareholders stand to lose from a decline in the value of their securities. Innocent rank-and-file employees, too, may suffer if the conviction has a lasting impact on the firm's fortunes in the market. For example, the collapse of Enron auditor Arthur Andersen led 27,000 people to lose their jobs—a massive unintended consequence of the prosecution of the company (Meeks, 2007). Another critique of corporate criminal liability is that it breeds an antagonism between government oversight bodies and regulated entities that is incompatible with regulatory law's core goal of promoting compliance rather than punishing actors for anti-social behaviour (Snider, 1993, p. 135). As Shapiro (1985, p. 199) puts it: "Criminal prosecution is associated with regulatory failure. It is a response to offences that are discovered too late to prevent substantial harm." Finally, criminal prosecution is inefficient and unduly involved: "it is too slow, too expensive, and there are too many legal protections for powerful corporations to exploit to circumvent compliance" (Snider, 1993, p. 136).

Still, a compelling case can be made that no AMP can compensate for the sheer moral condemnation of a criminal conviction. While fines or penalties themselves seldom make a lasting dent on a large company's balance sheet, the stigma associated with culpability can have a grave impact on the "reputational capital" required to keep an enterprise afloat—a good reason for high-level personnel to abide by the law. Without parallel prosecutions of individual decision-makers, however, both deterrence and punishment are arguably diminished. The United States' embrace of DPAs is one way around the problem—allowing regulators to pursue individual employee responsibility through the criminal law while leaving corporate responsibility to be dealt with by enforceable conditions (such as employee education and cooperation with investigations) in the DPA, a breach of which opens up the company to prosecution.

Internal Investigations

The progressive expansion of criminal, administrative, and civil liability for corporations has led to a sea change in internal corporate practice. Multinational companies, in particular, now administer substantial internal compliance programs that represent a multi-million-dollar business (Green & Podgor, 2013). Companies hire not only consultants but also specialized, full-time personnel, such as internal investigation attorneys, to manage such processes (Murphy & Dervan, 2005). Having robust procedures around misconduct allows companies to demonstrate due diligence at the corporate and management level. A lack of due diligence is a minimum legal requirement for criminal culpability in Canada, according to the Supreme Court of Canada (*R v. Sault Ste. Marie*, 1978), but also for many forms of civil and administrative liability. Compliance procedures also increase the odds that the company itself, rather than regulators, will discover a "smoking gun" first, allowing it to be proactive in putting out fires.

Companies have increasingly embraced "whistle-blowing" protocols in particular. The term **whistle-blower** refers to a person who exposes actual or potential misconduct at an organization. A notable example is Sherron Watkins, the former vice president of Corporate Development at Enron, who alerted then–Enron CEO Kenneth Lay about accounting irregularities in the company's financial statements in August 2001 and was later named as a *Time* "Person of the Year" in 2002. By the Association of Certified Fraud Examiners' (2012) count, three times as many frauds are uncovered by these "tipsters" than by other means. However, stories of retaliation against whistle-blowers—who may be perceived as disloyal "snitches" within the company culture—have prompted legislators to enact protective legislation. The US *Sarbanes-Oxley Act* of 2002 made retaliation itself a criminal offence punishable by seven to ten years of jail time. In the recent *Dodd-Frank Wall Street Reform and Consumer Protection Act* of 2010, this regime was bolstered by provisions awarding whistle-blowers 10 to 30 percent of the value of any judicial award or monetary settlement obtained by the SEC. These reforms reflect a growing prosecutorial realism about the extent to which white-collar crime can be effectively detected from the outside.

Company investigations that follow misconduct reports typically feature the formation of a "special committee" of the board of directors with its own legal counsel. This institutional device insulates the investigation, at least in part, from pressures to cover up misconduct. Numerous legal and ethical issues arise in such investigations. In particular, the interests of the company in weeding-out misconduct will often diverge from the interests of its managers or employees implicated (or personally aligned with those implicated) in the wrongdoing. External lawyers who normally owe a fiduciary duty to the *company* as client must navigate an awkward terrain: prior working relationships with individuals under investigation may lead to pressures that conflict with their professional duties. A lawyer also has an ethical duty to caution employees during interviews that his or her client is the company, and that the attorney–client privilege blanketing the conversation "belongs" to it—and can be waived if the company reports the matter

whistle-blower

A person who reports misconduct within an organization.

to a regulator. Implicated managers or employees often retain separate counsel from the corporation to preserve their rights. Still, the largely unregulated nature of the internal investigation, combined with imbalances between managerial and employee power, can invite a risk of deception or coercion in the process as employees' interests are shuffled aside in the quest for closure (Green & Podgor, 2013).

Corporate Social Responsibility

corporate social responsibility (CSR)
A theory of corporate self-regulation whereby companies actively pursue compliance with the law and ethical norms as a part of doing business.

The rise of in-house attention to such compliance matters can also be tracked to the growing **corporate social responsibility (CSR)** movement. CSR has been described as "a concept whereby companies integrate social and environmental concerns in their business operations and in their interaction with stakeholders on a voluntary basis" (European Commission, 2001, p. 6). CSR takes matters a step beyond the mere *avoidance* of misconduct by firms: rather, it envisions them voluntarily pursuing higher standards. Companies have increasingly adopted CSR language—such as *sustainability*, *the triple-bottom-line* ("profit, people, planet"), *corporate citizenship*, and so forth—in their disclosure documents, suggesting a discrete awareness of shareholder and customer concern over such issues.

Some critics, however, have charged that companies' CSR initiatives are mere window dressing. For example, Canadian oil and gas firms' "Ethical Oil" campaign—in concert with an award-winning book of the same name by journalist Ezra Levant—has sought to recontextualize criticism of the industry and its oil-sands activities by contrasting the human rights and environmental records of their developing-country counterparts. This argument has won applause from some but raised the eyebrows of David Suzuki, among others, who has called Levant an "apologist" (Suzuki, 2011). To mediate between industry and activist concerns about "greenwashing"—the term used to describe a company's deceptive promotion of an environmentally friendly image or products—the Competition Bureau and the Canadian Standards Association jointly developed a guidance document in 2008 to delineate between legitimate and illegitimate green marketing (Competition Bureau, 2008).

While CSR is essentially voluntary, policy-makers appear to be interested in how law can facilitate a more CSR-engaged corporate sector. In December 2013, the federal government invited comment as to "whether additional measures to promote CSR objectives are warranted" in the *Canada Business Corporations Act*, which governs some 235,000 federally incorporated companies (Industry Canada, 2013).

Judges, too, are taking note. In its landmark corporate law decision in *BCE Inc. v. 1976 Debentureholders* (2008), the Supreme Court of Canada—albeit without much elaboration—described a corporate director's duty "to act in the best interests of the corporation viewed as a good corporate citizen" (para. 66). Such language serves as a marked departure from past, shareholder-focused conceptions of the corporation's mission. It envisions corporate managers as considering a broad range of stakeholders in making important decisions—including "shareholders, employees, suppliers, creditors, consumers, governments and the environment" (para. 39). While CSR claims will continue to require a probing eye, the concept carries some promise as a normative vision of corporate governance—one in which corporate boards are bound more by the "social sanction" of an ethical corporate culture than by legal deterrents.

Conclusion

While blunt in their conclusions and liberal with their facts, Edwin Sutherland's early studies on white-collar crime's prevalence and social impact remain as true today as they were in the 1940s. But what has changed? For one, a series of high-profile scandals—from Enron to the financial crisis and beyond—has made the scourge of white-collar crime more visible, prompting a more sustained legislative focus on the problem from both the business-skeptical left and the tough-on-crime right. The result, in turn, has been a stepping-up of North American white-collar enforcement, using both the traditional tools of criminal law and an array of administrative powers. Private enforcement, too, has played a role, with victims better able to assert multi-million-dollar class-action claims against at-fault companies to recover their losses. Investors recovered $7.2 billion, for example, in a 2008 class-action settlement with banks alleged to be complicit in Enron's accounting fraud (Lozano, 2008). Technology has also changed the landscape of white-collar crime by allowing for more anonymous, high-speed, and cross-border forms of criminality, and by forcing police and regulators to adapt in step. Finally, large corporations are voluntarily joining the battle against white-collar crime, either to limit their liability risks or to fulfill self-imposed CSR commitments. Sutherland saw a "lack of social organization" against white-collar crime as its greatest enabler (Sutherland, 1940). While a cultural tendency to defer to authority aggravates that problem in Canada, US media and regulatory spillover, domestic scandals, and newly popular "tough-on-crime" politics at the federal level appear to have put white-collar crime on the Canadian public-policy agenda as of the early 21st century. Whether that concern can support current resource investments into the longer term will have lasting consequences for the fairness and competiveness of Canada's economy for years to come.

SUMMARY OF KEY POINTS

- The term *white-collar crime* was coined by sociologist Edwin Sutherland in 1939, and it generally describes a category of misconduct defined by either the privileged identity of the offender or the occupational context of the act.

- White-collar criminality is captured in criminal, regulatory, and civil laws, sometimes all at once. Purely criminal offences make up only a fraction of the legal response to white-collar misconduct in Canada.

- Technology is changing the nature of white-collar crime and creating new opportunities for computer-based exploitation. It has also made investigations and prosecutions more complex and document-heavy.

- Regulators are increasingly turning to administrative monetary penalties (AMPs) and compliance-oriented regulation—including the use of deferred prosecution agreements (DPAs)—to overcome the criminal law's limitations in prosecuting white-collar conduct, especially that of corporations.

- Companies are increasingly taking a proactive approach to preventing employee misconduct—both to avoid penalties and protect their reputation—by developing rigorous internal compliance processes. "Corporate social responsibility" envisions a concept of "corporate citizenship" whereby companies serve not only their shareholders, but the broader community.

- Eron Mortgage, Bernie Madoff, and other high-profile business scandals will continue to be the primary impetus for tougher white-collar enforcement by shifting public attitudes away from a "default" complacency. The scandal-plagued 2000s tracked a sustained legislative interest in white-collar criminality.

QUESTIONS FOR CRITICAL DISCUSSION

1. Is Canada unduly "soft" on white-collar crime? If so, why do you think that is?
2. Is the criminal law an effective sanction against corporations?
3. Should white-collar crime be defined by the privileged status of its perpetrators, or the nature of the offences themselves? Does it matter?
4. Is white-collar crime more or less blameworthy than traditional "street" crime?
5. Do you believe Sutherland was right in describing the criminal law's underinclusiveness with respect to white-collar misconduct? Have things changed? What conduct should—or should not—be criminal, and why?

SUGGESTED FURTHER READINGS

Byttle, S. (2012). *Still dying for a living: Corporate criminal liability after the Westray Mine disaster*. Vancouver: UBC Press.

McLean, B., & Elkind, P. (2004). *The smartest guys in the room: The amazing rise and scandalous fall of Enron*. New York: Portfolio Trade.

Puri, P. (2001). Sentencing the criminal corporation. *Osgoode Hall Law Journal, 39*, 611–653.

Sutherland, E.H. (1940). White-collar criminality. *American Sociological Review, 5*, 1–12.

Websites

Competition Bureau: Legal Actions and Opinions: http://www.competitionbureau.gc.ca/eic/site/cb-bc.nsf/eng/h_00020.html

Department of Justice Canada: Backgrounder on White-Collar Crime: http://www.justice.gc.ca/eng/news-nouv/nr-cp/2010/doc_32504.html

FBI: White-Collar Crime. Retrieved from http://www.fbi.gov/about-us/investigate/white_collar/whitecollarcrime

KPMG: Global profiles of the fraudster: White-collar crime—present and future: http://www.kpmg.com/Global/en/IssuesAndInsights/ArticlesPublications/global-profiles-of-the-fraudster/Documents/global-profiles-of-the-fraudster-v2.pdf

White Collar Crime Portal: Law and Practice: http://www.whitecollarcrimeportal.com

REFERENCES

Association of Certified Fraud Examiners. (2012). 2012 Report to the nations. Retrieved from https://www.acfe.com/rttn.aspx.

Beare, M.E. (2003). *Critical reflections on transnational organized crime, money laundering, and corruption*. Toronto: University of Toronto Press.

Beare, M.E., & Schnieder, S. (2007). *Critical reflections on transnational organized crime, money laundering, and corruption*. Toronto: University of Toronto Press.

Black, C. (2012, April 4). Beware an improvident interloper. *National Post*. Retrieved from http://fullcomment.nationalpost.com/2012/04/04/conrad-black-beware-an-improvident-interloper/.

Braithwaite, J. (2011). The essence of responsive regulation. *UBC Law Review, 44*, 475–520.

Brown, S.E., & Chiang, C.-P. (1995). Defining corporate crime: A critique of traditional parameters. In M.P. Blankenship (Ed.), *Understanding corporate criminality* (pp. 29–56). New York: Garland.

Canada, Department of Justice. (2010). Backgrounder: Identity theft. Retrieved from http://www.justice.gc.ca/eng/news-nouv/nr-cp/2010/doc_32471.html.

Clinard, M.B., & Quinney, R. (1978). Corporate crime: Issues in research. *Criminology, 16,* 255–272.

Coffee, J.C., Jr. (1981). "No soul to damn, no body to kick": An unscandalized inquiry into the problem of corporate punishment. *Michigan Law Review, 79,* 386–459.

Competition Bureau. (2008, June 25). What does green really mean?: Competition Bureau and Canadian Standards Association seek greater accuracy in environmental claims [Press release].

Competition Bureau. (2009). Competitor collaboration guidelines. Retrieved from http://www .competitionbureau.gc.ca/eic/site/cb-bc.nsf/eng/03177.html.

Competition Bureau. (2012, September 28). List of Charges and Sentences in the Quebec Gasoline Price-fixing Cartel. Retrieved from http://www.competitionbureau.gc.ca/eic/ site/cb-bc.nsf/eng/03079.html.

Cullen, F.T., Hartman, J.L., & Jonson C.L. (2009). Bad guys: Why the public supports punishing white-collar offenders. *Crime, Law & Social Change, 51,* 31–44.

Edmonds, O.P., & Edmonds, E.L. (1963). An account of the founding of H.M. Inspectorate of Mines and the work of the first inspector Hugh Seymour Tremenheere. *British Journal of Industrial Medicine, 20,* 210–217.

European Commission. (2001). *Green paper: Promoting a European framework for corporate social responsibility.* Retrieved from http://eur-lex.europa.eu/LexUriServ/site/en/ com/2001/com2001_0366en01.pdf.

FBI. (2012). LCD price fixing conspiracy: Taiwanese company, execs sentenced. Retrieved from http://www.fbi.gov/news/stories/2012/november/lcd-price fixing-conspiracy.

First, H. (2010). Branch office of the prosecutor: The new role of the corporation in business crime prosecutions. *North Carolina Law Review, 89,* 23–98.

Flaherty, J. (2013). Jobs, growth and long-term prosperity: Economic action plan 2013. Retrieved from http://www.budget.gc.ca/2013/doc/plan/budget2013-eng.pdf.

Fleury, S. (2010). Abusive tax planning: The problem and the Canadian context. Library of Parliament Background Paper No. 2010-22-E. Retrieved from http://www.parl.gc.ca/ Content/LOP/ResearchPublications/2010-22-e.htm.

Gray, J. (2007, September 18). A good country for crooks: Canada's losing war against white-collar crime. *Canadian Business.* Retrieved from http://www.canadianbusiness.com/ business-strategy/a-good-country-for-crooks-canadas-losing-war-against-white -collar-crime.

Gray, J. (2012, March 21). Canadian Tire pleads guilty in gas price-fixing scheme. *Globe and Mail.* Retrieved from http://www.theglobeandmail.com/globe-investor/canadian-tire -pleads-guilty-in-gas-price-fixing-scheme/article534996.

Green, B., & Podgor, E. (2013). Unregulated internal investigations: Achieving fairness for corporate constituents. *Boston College Law Review, 54,* 73–126.

Gustafson, J. (2007). Cracking down on white-collar crime: An analysis of the recent trend of severe sentences for corporate offenders. *Suffolk University Law Review, 40,* 685–701.

Holtfreter, K., Van Slyke, K., Bratton, J., & Gertz, M. (2008). Public perceptions of white-collar crime and punishment. *Journal of Criminal Justice, 36,* 50–60.

Industry Canada. (2013). Consultation on the Canada Business Corporations Act. Retrieved from https://www.ic.gc.ca/eic/site/cilp-pdci.nsf/eng/h_cl00867.html#p3.10.

International Organization of Securities Commissions. (2004). Objectives and principles of securities regulation. Retrieved from http://www.iosco.org/library/pubdocs/pdf/ IOSCOPD154.pdf.

Kedia, S. (2012, September 19). Does the revolving door affect the SEC's enforcement outcomes? Harvard Law School Forum on Corporate Governance and Financial Regulation [Web log message]. Retrieved from http://blogs.law.harvard.edu/corpgov/2012/09/19/ does-the-revolving-door-affect-the-secs-enforcement-outcomes.

Keith, N. (2011). *Corporate crime and accountability in Canada: From prosecutions to corporate social responsibility*. Markham, ON: LexisNexis Canada.

Kochan, N., & Goodyear, R. (2011). *Corruption: The new corporation challenge*. New York: Palgrave Macmillan.

Leman-Langlois, S. (2008). Introduction: Technocrime. In S. Leman-Langlois (Ed.), *Technocrime: Technology, crime and social control* (pp. 1–13). Portland, OR: Willan.

Lozano, J.A. (2008, September 10). Enron investors to share $7.2 billion settlement. *Washington Post*. Retrieved from http://www.washingtonpost.com/wp-dyn/content/article/2008/09/09/AR2008090903144.html.

Meeks, W. (2007). Corporate and white-collar crime enforcement: Should regulation and rehabilitation spell an end to corporate criminal liability? *Columbia Journal of Law & Social Problems, 40*, 77–124.

Ministry of the Attorney General. (2010, December 10). Guidelines for Administrative Tribunals. Retrieved from http://www.attorneygeneral.jus.gov.on.ca/english/justice-ont/french_language_services/services/administrative_tribunals.asp.

Murphy, P.B., & Dervan, L.E. (2005). Watching your step: Avoiding the pitfalls and perils of corporate and internal investigations. *Attorneys' Liability Assurance Society Loss Prevention Journal, 16*, 2–11.

Plummer, I.M., Strahlendorf, P.W., & Holliday, M.G. (2009). *The internal responsibility system in Ontario's mines*. n.p.: Ontario Ministry of Labour. Retrieved from http://www.labour.gov.on.ca/english/hs/pubs/mining/syn_minirs_2.php.

Potter, G. (2010, November). What is green criminology? *Sociology Review*, 8–12.

RCMP. (2011). IMETs: Frequently asked questions. Retrieved from http://www.rcmp-grc.gc.ca/imet-eipmf/faq-eng.htm.

RCMP. (2013). What is technological crime? Retrieved from http://www.rcmp-grc.gc.ca/qc/services/gict-itcu/crim-tech-eng.htm.

Richard, P.K. (1997). *The Westray story: A predictable path to disaster* (Report of the Westray Mine Public Inquiry). Retrieved from http://novascotia.ca/lae/pubs/westray.

Sabatini, P. (2007, March 25). Tax cheats cost U.S. hundreds of billions. *Pittsburgh Post-Gazette*. Retrieved from http://www.post-gazette.com/businessnews/2007/03/25/Tax-cheats-cost-U-S-hundreds-of-billions/stories/200703250264.

Shapiro, S.P. (1985). The road not taken: The elusive path to criminal prosecution for white collar offenders. *Law and Society Review, 19*, 179–217.

Shapiro, S. (1990). Collaring the crime, not the criminal: Reconsidering the concept of white-collar crime. *American Sociological Review, 55*, 346–356.

Sher, J. (2011, May 24). Canada ranked worst of G7 nations in fighting bribery, corruption. *Globe and Mail*. Retrieved from http://www.theglobeandmail.com/news/politics/canada-ranked-worst-of-g7-nations-in-fighting-bribery-corruption/article592312.

Shover, N., & Hochstetler, A. (2006). *Choosing white-collar crime*. New York: Cambridge University Press.

Smith, A. (1776). *An inquiry into the nature and causes of the wealth of nations*. n.p. Retrieved from http://www.gutenberg.org/files/3300/3300-h/3300-h.htm.

Snider, L. (1993). *Bad business: Corporate crime in Canada*. Scarborough, ON: Nelson Canada.

Spivack, P., & Raman, S. (2008). Regulating the "new regulators": Current trends in deferred prosecution agreements. *American Criminal Law Review, 45*, 159–193.

Stigler, G.J. (1971). The theory of economic regulation. *Bell Journal of Economics & Management Science, 2*, 3–21.

Sutherland, E.H. (1940). White-collar criminality. *American Sociological Review, 5*, 1–12.

Sutherland, E.H. (1945). Is "white-collar crime" crime? *American Sociological Review, 10*, 132–139.

Sutherland, E.H. (1983). *White-collar crime: The uncut version*. New Haven, CT: Yale University Press.

Suzuki, D. (2011, October 6). Can oil be ethical? Retrieved from http://www.davidsuzuki.org/blogs/science-matters/2011/10/can-oil-be-ethical.

White-collar crime in Canada: Too trusting. (2009, April 2). *The Economist*. Retrieved from http://www.economist.com/node/13415555.

Wingfield, B., & Kopecki, D. (2013, July). JPMorgan to pay $410 million in U.S. FERC settlement. *Bloomberg*. Retrieved from http://www.bloomberg.com/news/2013-07-30/jpmorgan-to-pay-410-million-in-u-s-ferc-settlement.html.

Zaccagna, R. (2013, September 19). Settlement could be sweet. *Chronicle Herald*. Retrieved from http://thechronicleherald.ca/business/1155549-settlement-could-be-sweet.

Legislation

Canada Business Corporations Act. (1985). RSC 1985, c. C-44.
Criminal Code. (1985). RSC 1985, c. C-46.
Income Tax Act. (1985). RSC 1985, c. 1 (5th Supp.), s. 239(1).
Securities Act. (1990). RSO 1990, c. S.5.
Securities Act. (1996). RSBC 1996, c. 418.

Cases

BCE Inc. v. 1976 Debentureholders. (2008). 2008 SCC 69.
British Columbia Securities Commission v. Branch. (1995). [1995] 2 SCR 3.
R v. Canadian Dredge & Dock Co. (1985). [1985] 1 SCR 662.
R v. Drabinsky. (2009). 242 CCC (3d) 449 (Ont. Sup. Ct. J.).
R v. Sault Ste. Marie. (1978). [1978] 2 SCR 1299.
R v. Stinchcombe. (1991). [1991] 3 SCR 326.
R v. Théroux. (1993). [1993] 2 SCR 5.
R v. Union Colliery Co. of British Columbia. (1900). 31 SCR 81.
Smith v. Baker. (1891). [1891] UKHL 2 (BAILII).
United States v. Black. (2010). 625 F. 3d 386 (7th Cir. 2010).

Glossary

810.1 order A community prohibition order for sexual offenders deemed to be at a high risk to commit another sexual offence or a serious personal injury crime. It includes a list of conditions designed to monitor and limit the person's movement, accommodations, and social interactions. It also includes certain requirements to meet with a supervising officer (a probation, parole, or bail officer) and attend specific treatment programs. The ultimate objective of the order is to maximize public protection while managing risk for sexual recidivism.

absolute deprivation Low income or poverty in and of itself.

active audiences The concept that audiences are not passive recipients of information or meanings but are instead active in the process of creating meaning.

actual victim A person who is the direct target of victimization.

actus reus The criminal act or personal conduct relating to a crime; it may include a failure to act, but does not include the mental element of a criminal offence.

acute dynamic factors Individual characteristics associated with risk of reoffending that are rapidly changing and include factors such as intoxication and mood.

administrative monetary penalty (AMP) A non-criminal penalty issued by a regulatory body, without court approval, for the violation of a law it administers.

anomie-strain theory Merton's theory describing the state of anomie in American society caused by the disjunction (or dysfunction or strain) between the cultural goals of the "American dream" and the institutional means to achieve those goals.

anomie A term coined by Durkheim to describe periods of lawlessness, normlessness, and unrestrained choice, or a breakdown in social solidarity.

anti-social personality disorder (APD) A personality disorder characterized by a lack of morality, impulsivity, and aggressive behaviour; individuals with APD often have a history of criminal behaviour.

assault Applying force on a person, attempting to or threatening to apply force on a person, or using a weapon (or imitation of a weapon) to accost or impede a person.

atavism A term associated with Cesare Lombroso and the Positivist School of thought; the notion that criminals are less evolved than "normal" humans.

attention deficit hyperactivity disorder (ADHD) A condition that includes a combination of behaviours, such as difficulty sustaining attention, hyperactivity and impulsive behaviour.

behaviourism A learning theory that suggests all behaviour can be shaped by rewards and punishment.

blame continuum The range of blaming possibilities, from total guilt to total innocence, of both the victim and the victimizer.

bounded rationality (limited rationality) Decisions are often made imperfectly as best guesses given available information and time constraints. Decisions are "bounded" by the limits of our knowledge and circumstances, and so our rationality is bounded.

break and enter A type of property crime where the accused trespasses on private property with intent to commit a crime.

bribery The practice of illegally inducing a person, company, or government to act in one's favour, usually by transferring money or property.

card not present fraud A form of fraud usually carried out over the telephone or the Internet when a stolen or forged credit card is used to purchase a good or to acquire a service.

Chicago School The first school of sociology in the United States; contributed to social disorganization theory, cultural transmission theory, differential association theory, subcultural theory, the sociology of deviance, and symbolic interactionism.

choice theory The framework for understanding how decisions are made by individuals by weighing the perceived costs and benefits of an action. The framework includes poor decisions and bounded rationality. The term is used here as synonymous with rational choice theory, while avoiding the ambiguity that sometimes arises over the meaning of "rational."

civil commitment Also known as *involuntary commitment*, the legal process by which a person is detained after serving a sentence due to concerns that he or she will commit further crimes.

civil law A system in which the law is primarily set out in legislation, and judges' discretion is limited to interpretation and application of those written provisions.

Classical School of criminology A body of work that emerged in Europe in the 17th and 18th centuries that argued people have the capacity to think rationally; contemporary deterrence theory is rooted in this school of thought.

clearance rates The proportion of criminal incidents solved by the police. A crime is cleared when the police believe they have found its perpetrator.

collective efficacy A group's shared belief that it can come together and achieve desired goals.

common law A body of law defined primarily through successive decisions of judges, as opposed to through legislation.

community and social support factors The people and resources that support the individual experiencing traumatic stress; that is, community members, family, and friends that serve to insulate the community and its members from traumatizing events through prevention and/or by fostering resilience.

compositional effect The combination of parts that make up something. In neighbourhoods, a compositional effect refers to the aggregate characteristics of individual residents.

CompStat COMPuter STATistics; the name given to New York City Police Department's accountability process that was introduced in the 1990s to facilitate a reduction in crime.

computer tomography A medical technique combining X-rays taken at many different angles and computer technology.

concordance rate In a random sample of pairs, the proportion of pairs that share a certain characteristic.

conditioning factors Factors that shape the impact of a certain cause or correlate of crime. For example, having supportive friends, spiritual coping resources, or physical coping resources (i.e., sports, music outlets) may reduce the impact of emotional and financial strains on criminal offending, and these factors (friends, coping resources) may also vary by gender (e.g., friends may encourage boys to fight or retaliate, while friends may encourage girls to talk through their grievances and avoid confrontations).

conflict theories Theories, originating primarily with Marx, that focus on the unequal distribution of power in society—for example, due to class, race, or gender. Conflicts between classes or groups are driven to a large extent by this unequal power and unequal access to resources.

consensus theories In opposition to conflict theories, consensus theories, which originate with Durkheim, hold that society functions through social bonds and collective beliefs, and is characterized by widespread acceptance of values, norms, and laws.

constructionist Constructionist perspectives emphasize the idea that life does not come with categories and labels, and that we understand and define the world on the basis of our socialization and interactions with others.

contextual effect The influence of environmental factors on human behaviours.

corporate social responsibility (CSR) A theory of corporate self-regulation whereby companies actively pursue compliance with the law and ethical norms as a part of doing business.

correlates In criminology, factors that are associated with or related to crime.

correlation The finding that two measurable phenomena occur together, suggesting a relationship, but not necessarily one of direct cause and effect.

cortical arousal Activation of the reticular formation of the brain.

counterfeiting Producing imitation currency without legal sanction of the government; it is a form of fraud.

crime funnel A model indicating that the actual total quantity of crime is much higher than the decreasing proportion that is detected, reported, prosecuted, and punished.

crime opportunity theory An umbrella term for the set of theories and concepts that are underpinned by the notion that the level of crime opportunities is the main cause of crime—e.g., rational choice theory, routine activity theory, situational crime prevention, and crime pattern theory.

crime pattern theory A theory that helps explain how crime patterns arise; it asserts that crime is not random. Its concepts (e.g., nodes, paths, and edges) describe how offenders move in the urban environment. This theory is closely linked to routine activity theory.

crimes of morality Illegal activities that are against the law because they are regarded as threatening to values.

criminal justice system The various institutions and processes through which an offender passes, such as the police, the courts, and correctional facilities and programs.

criminal law The entire set of principles, procedures, and rules established by governments through the courts and criminal legislation in order to ensure public safety. It includes definitions of crimes, criminal responsibility, and punishments, and defences to a criminal charge.

criminality The state of being criminal; criminal acts or practices.

criminalization To define an act as a crime, and thereby subject that act to formal punishment.

criminology The study of crime and criminal behaviour, which are defined by reference to criminal law.

critical criminology A school of thought with multiple subfields, but largely concerned with social justice and inequality, promoting active opposition to the status quo, and favouring larger-scale societal transformations rather than minor policy changes.

critical race theory A theory that examines the ways in which race and racial power are constructed by law and society, and that sees the law and criminal justice system not as solutions but as part of the problem.

critical thinking The process of evaluating information, claims, or arguments through careful questioning and the application of reason.

culpable Deserving of blame; guilty of wrongdoing.

cultural transmission theory The Chicago School notion that criminal subcultures develop their own subcultural (criminal) values or norms, which are then transmitted from gang member to gang member, and from generation to generation.

cybercrime Crime committed over the Internet or a computer network.

dangerousness The capacity of a person to physically, psychologically, or morally harm oneself or others. It includes an estimation of both the severity and likelihood of harm.

dark figure of crime Refers to the variation between the number of crimes that occur and the number of crimes that are actually reported to the police. This figure highlights the large number of unreported crimes.

decriminalization The removal of criminal penalties, though fines may still apply

demographics Statistical data relating to characteristics of a population, such as relative size of age groups, gender balance, or any other measurable information.

denunciation A formal expression that conduct is unacceptable.

designing-out The concept that crime prevention can start at the design process so that products and places are designed with potential criminal threats or opportunities in mind.

determinism The doctrine that one's will is not the sole cause of choices, but that those choices are conditioned or determined by factors external to one's will.

deterrence A principle of sentencing or punishment intended to discourage citizens from offending or reoffending.

deterrence theory A theory based on the idea that for punishment to be effective, it must be swift, sure, and certain.

deviance Behaviour that differs from accepted social norms; may include acts that violate specific rules (crime), sexual behaviours, or non-criminal acts that challenge accepted values.

differential association theory Sutherland's theory that criminal behaviour is learned through the process of social interaction, and that the process includes the learning of criminal skills, motivations, attitudes, and rationalizations.

direct victim A person who is present at the time of victimization and experiences harm.

discourses Refers to forms of language, representation, and practices and how meaning is created and shared. Discourses take place within specific cultural and historical contexts.

dispositional theories Theories that seek to explain variations between individuals in their tendency or disposition to commit crime. Explanations are usually biological or psychological.

dopamine A neurotransmitter that controls the reward and pleasure centres of the brain.

drug cartel Criminal organization, often highly organized and with many partnerships, involved primarily in the trafficking of illegal drugs.

duress An unlawful threat or coercion used by one person to induce another to perform some act against his or her will.

dynamic factors Individual characteristics associated with the risk of reoffending that are amenable to change and are targets for treatment. These are often referred to as *criminogenic needs* and include characteristics such as attitudes tolerant to criminal behaviour and criminal associates. A reduction in dynamic factors is associated with a decreased risk for recidivism and subsequently plays a larger role in identifying targets for assessment and intervention.

ego An aspect of Freud's theory of personality; the aspect of personality that helps negotiate the demands of the real world.

embezzlement To take money or misappropriate funds that belong to someone else.

empirical That which is understood or verified through experiment, measurement, or direct observation; as opposed to *theoretical*.

environment The external conditions, resources, and stimuli a person interacts with.

environmental criminology A term coined by C. Ray Jeffery; it focuses on the environment (including targets, guardians, and places) as a key area of interest in understanding how and why crime occurs.

etiology The cause of a condition.

eugenics Methods to improve populations by controlling breeding to increase the occurrence of desirable heritable characteristics.

extortion The crime of demanding money from someone using force or threats.

extraversion (E) A person's activity level; people high in extraversion enjoy social interaction and being around groups of people, while people low in extraversion generally prefer solitude and quiet conversations with those close to them.

feeble-mindedness A term used in the 19th century to describe individuals with low intelligence or low IQ.

femicide The act of killing a woman. *Homicide* typically referred to both the killing of men and women. However, in recent years, femicide has emerged as a distinct term to describe the killing of women, while homicide refers to the killing of men.

fetal alcohol spectrum disorder (FASD) The range of disorders that can arise in a child if the child's mother drank alcohol while pregnant. It is a leading cause of preventable developmental disability in Canada.

folk devils Originating in images from folklore, this term refers to people or groups presented in media as deviant outsiders and the cause of social problems.

forensic entomology The study of insects to assist in legal investigations; insects found on a corpse can help identify facts about the time and place of the victim's death.

formal sanctions Punishments or corrections undertaken by official organizations such as schools, the police, and the courts.

Foucauldian Relating to the works of influential French thinker Michel Foucault.

fraud A dishonest act that deprives, or risks depriving, another person of something.

free will A will whose choices are not conditioned or determined by factors external to itself; also, the doctrine that free will exists.

frustration–aggression hypothesis The view that crime is a natural byproduct of aggression and can be explained as a consequence of frustration.

functionalism In sociology, the idea that society is comparable to a functioning organism with interrelated parts and structures to ensure that the parts work together; functionalists believe that society is based on consensus (shared values, beliefs), not conflict.

gender gap The difference between men and women in areas such as social, political, and economic attainment; a persistent finding in criminology is that men commit more crime than women.

gender stratification A society's unequal distribution of wealth, power and privilege between men and women.

gendered The notion that processes (e.g., learning roles) and behaviours (e.g., participation in crime) are gender-based.

general strain theory Explains delinquent acts by teens from relatively affluent families; teens have more immediate strains than adults, such as physical appearance, popularity, parental discipline, academic performance, and peer pressure to join gangs and participate in delinquent behaviour.

generalization problem The question of whether it is possible to explain female criminality with mainstream theories of crime that were originally developed to explain male criminality.

genocide The deliberate and systematic attempt to exterminate an entire population or subpopulation that shares a racial, religious, national, or cultural identity.

geographic profiling A tool that permits police officers to focus on the likely residence of offenders in cases of serial crimes.

goal responses Behaviours meant to achieve particular goals that provide pleasurable outcomes.

green criminology The analysis of environmental harms from a criminological perspective.

habeas corpus The right of an accused (in the form of a *writ*) to appear before a court, and not be detained without just cause.

harm principle A central tenet in the writing of John Stuart Mill, often regarded as the father of moral liberalism. The *harm* principle holds that the actions of individuals should only be limited to prevent harm to other individuals.

harm reduction A public health–oriented policy or program designed to reduce the harmful consequences of behaviours with known risks, which are often illegal, such as prostitution and recreational drug use.

hedonism The view that pleasure is the primary good; the pursuit of pleasure.

hegemonic masculinity A culturally idealized form of masculinity; in contemporary Western societies, for example, hegemonic masculinity involves displays of autonomy, aggressive individualism, a lack of emotion, normative heterosexuality, and the capacity for violence.

heritability The quality of being heritable, via genes.

hierarchy Group structure built around easily identified leaders and followers; in gangs, the hierarchy often determines the roles, obligations, and rewards of members.

homelessness A range of physical living conditions that can include living on the streets or in the open, staying in emergency shelters, or being provisionally housed (couch surfing with friends or relatives).

id An aspect of Freud's theory of personality; the impulsive part of one's personality.

identity theft The theft and use of a person's identifying information, usually for monetary gain.

indictable offence A serious offence, such as murder or rape, which carries a severe penalty. An *indictment* is the formal process of setting out a criminal charge in a document for serious, "indictable" offences.

indictment A formal written accusation, usually reserved for more serious crimes.

indirect victim A person who is not immediately affected by victimization, but nonetheless suffers in some way as a result of it.

informal sanctions The actions taken by others, such as a verbal reprimand, punishment, withdrawal of privileges, and suspension of activities. These actions may lead to shame and embarrassment and may deter individuals from participating in crime.

insider trading The practice of trading in a stock, bond, or other security while possessing material, non-public information about the company in question.

institutional-anomie theory Messner and Rosenfeld's theory that institutional-anomie (institutional imbalance) is caused by the cultural goals of capitalist society and the failure of social institutions to properly integrate and regulate the pursuit of those goals. Institutional imbalance occurs when the economy comes to dominate the political and educational systems and the family, leading to an amoral "ends justifies the means" attitude.

insulators Social and psychological factors that protect an individual from being harmed.

integrationist A combination of structuralist, positivist, and constructionist approaches in criminology facilitating the inclusion of philosophy and sociology of law, the empirical study of crime, and its interpretation by those who control and implement the law.

interactional theory Thornberry's theory that both social bond theory and social learning theory are needed to explain criminal behaviour, because weakening of the social bond and the social learning of criminal values is interactional or reciprocal (not unidirectional).

interactionist perspective A theoretical approach that focuses on relatively small-scale social interactions among individuals or small social groups, as well as the conscious acts of individuals and their interpretation of others' behaviour.

interjurisdictional Relating to crimes, legislation, or other legal issues that cross the boundaries of nations, provinces, or other jurisdictions.

interpersonal violence Violence that is most commonly inflicted by one individual against another, or by a small group of individuals against another.

interventions Strategies intended to shape the physical environment to mitigate crime; also various programs targeting individual offenders, offering alternatives to criminal behaviour.

intoxication A potential defence in which drugs or alcohol may prevent an accused from forming the necessary intent to commit a particular crime.

intra-class crime Crime in which the victim and offender are from the same social group (e.g., an ethnic or racial group); by contrast, inter-class crime takes place between different social groups.

intra-racial Within the same race of people.

IQ (intelligence quotient) A standardized measure of intelligence used by psychologists.

labelling Based on labelling theory, the act of describing someone as deviant.

labelling theory The theory that the stigma (or label) affixed through the criminalization process may lead individuals to develop a deviant self-image and feel separate from the "normal" community, and thus continue with deviant behaviour.

legalization The removal of an existing prohibition against something that is currently unlawful. In the case of drugs and prostitution, the term often implies a regulated system of supply or licensing of services provided.

lethal violence Violent victimization that causes death.

liability Legal responsibility for an act or omission.

life-course-developmental theory Sampson and Laub's theory that individuals can be deflected off of the trajectory toward a criminal career by life events ("turning points") that can lead them to transition out of criminal behaviour.

longitudinal studies Research that involves long-term observation of specific variables, often across decades (*cohort studies*, for example).

magnetic resonance imaging A medical diagnostic technique that uses a powerful magnet, radiofrequency waves, and computer imaging to produce images of tissues.

market manipulation The practice of interfering with the proper operation of a market, usually by employing or creating misleading or artificial information.

Marxism A school of thought developed by Karl Marx (1818–1883) arguing that society must be understood in terms of social conflict, class relations, and the inequalities caused by capitalism; Marxists promote revolution by the working class.

media effects The concept that exposure to media has an effect on behaviour. For example, young people exposed to violent media will behave aggressively.

memory fade The phenomenon whereby a survey participant forgets about a victimization that has taken place.

mens rea The mental element of a criminal offence or the state(s) of mind of the offender; it is the intent to commit a criminal act.

meta-analysis A quantitative statistical analysis of several similar experiments or studies to test for statistical significance.

modelling A form of learning that occurs through observation of others and vicarious reinforcement; also known as *observational learning* or *imitation*.

money laundering The process of concealing the source of illegitimately obtained money.

moral absolutism A philosophical perspective which holds that certain actions are absolutely right or wrong, regardless of other circumstances such as their consequences or the intentions behind them.

moral entrepreneur A person, group, or organization that takes the lead in identifying certain behaviour as deviant and in need of legal sanctions.

moral panic Phenomena—socially constructed by the media, politicians, and "moral entrepreneurs"—in which certain people or groups are labelled or stigmatized as the cause of a perceived social problem, resulting in widespread public alarm. Occurs when there is a gap between people's perceptions of a problem and the "fact" of the problem, and the difference can be explained ideologically (Hall et al., 1978).

moral relativism A perspective on the nature of morality asserting that norms or standards of behaviour are not fixed or absolute.

morals The normative standards, codes, and beliefs governing judgments and values concerning right and wrong action, justice, and fairness.

motor vehicle theft The act of stealing or attempting to steal a motor vehicle.

multi-causal The notion that an event occurs as a result of more than one factor.

negligence A legal intent standard that considers whether a person, regardless of actual intent or knowledge, failed to take reasonable care in doing or failing to do something.

net widening Imposing a form of control on individuals who might otherwise not be subject to such control.

neurotic According to psychoanalytic theory, a condition that results from an overactive superego.

neuroticism (N) A person's excitability level and emotional stability; highly neurotic people tend to be emotionally unstable and overreact to minor situations.

neurotransmitter A substance that carries signals from cell to cell.

neutralization An extension of Sutherland's differential association theory; the notion that criminals learn motivations and rationalizations to justify their criminal behaviour. The five techniques of neutralization are denial of responsibility, denial of injury, denial of the victim, condemnation of the condemners, and appeal to higher loyalties.

obtaining goods under false pretenses Misrepresenting the truth to obtain goods that belong to someone else.

other A person or group of people defined as fundamentally different, or even deviant, by the dominant culture, often through stereotyping.

overcriminalization The intrusion of the law into consensual activities which are relatively harmless to the actor(s) and society.

paraphilia Sexual interest in an activity other than masturbation that does not include mutual consent with another person.

parliamentary supremacy The concept that the legislative body is superior to other institutions, including the executive and the courts.

patriarchy An elitist form of social structure, in which men dominate politics, economics, and other aspects of society, and perpetuate that domination by limiting opportunities for women to exercise power.

penal law A law that imposes punishment, as opposed to (for instance) a law that provides only the right of a victim to compensation.

personal protective factors The characteristics an individual possesses to help deal with stress, including coping skills, the ability to handle new situations, and social skills.

phrenology The study of the shape and size of the skull as a supposed indication of character and mental abilities. This theory has been discredited.

pleasure principle The notion that one should maximize pleasure and minimize pain.

Ponzi scheme An investing scam where a fraudster pays returns to existing investors with new investors' funds under the false pretense that returns are being made, sustained by the constant recruitment of new contributors.

positivism The application of the scientific method to the study of society, including the study of crime and criminals

Positivist School A school of thought that attributed criminal behaviour to biological or psychological factors; often referred to as the "Italian School."

positron emission tomography A recording of body images via a radioactive isotope injected into the blood that can be followed in the body during activities. It is commonly used to study the functioning of parts of the brain.

post-colonial theory The wide-ranging academic study of the social, political, and cultural legacy of colonial rule and its effects on individual and group identities and social power relations. It also examines the domination of other cultures through a discourse of "otherness."

post-structuralism A theoretical perspective concerned with how power operates between and among individuals, groups, and social institutions (as opposed to belonging to the state or power elites alone). Post-structuralists look for differences in power in areas such as language use and social practices.

post-traumatic stress disorder (PTSD) A set of symptoms that emerge as a result of the stress of experiencing severe trauma. Symptoms may include recurring nightmares, jumpiness, agitation, trouble sleeping, trouble concentrating, and social isolation.

power-control theory A theory of crime that emphasizes the socialization by parents in the development of different levels of risk taking and the perceived sanctions among boys and girls. The theory suggests that mothers play a key role in relational and instrumental control, leading girls to experience increased supervision and, as a result, a lower inclination to participate in risky activities such as delinquency and crime.

price fixing An agreement between competitors to fix the price for a good or service by buying or selling at an agreed-to price or by manipulating supply or demand.

primary victim A person who is directly harmed as a result of a victimizing experience.

prison industrial complex Adapted from "military industrial complex"; a term used to attribute increases in incarceration rates to the efforts of private for-profit corporations that build and maintain prisons with the active legislative and financial support of their political allies.

problem frame A narrative that is easily understood because it focuses on the existence of something extraordinary and "bad" that affects many people, and identifies unambiguous solutions that can be implemented in the future.

prohibition A law forbidding a specific act.

psychoanalysis A therapeutic technique in psychiatry and philosophy pioneered by Sigmund Freud.

psychopathy A personality disorder characterized by a lack of empathy and an inability to feel for others.

psychoticism (P) A measure of attributes such as aggression, empathy, and tough-mindedness; those who score high in psychoticism tend to be cold, callous, and manipulative.

punitive turn The move from criminal justice policies and programs aimed at rehabilitating offenders toward those that simply offer punishment for its own sake. This shift occurred despite declining crime rates and evidence that punishment is not always effective.

qualitative The study of phenomena based not on measurement but an exploration of the reasons for human behaviour and the qualities of subjective experience.

quantitative Relating to the measurement of something—its quantity—rather than its qualities.

racial profiling The act or tendency of law enforcement officers and others to consider people suspicious or more likely to commit crime because of the colour of their skin or their ethnicity.

racialized The process of marginalizing a group of people based on perceived physical and socio-cultural differences.

racketeering Criminal activity commonly related to gangs that typically involves obtaining money through acts such as extortion, bribery, illegal gambling, and loan sharking.

rape myths Stories that reflect belief systems that reveal incorrect assumptions about the causes of sexual assault.

rape trauma syndrome (RTS) A set of PTSD symptoms that have been linked specifically to those who have experienced severe violence in the form of sexual assault.

rational choice theory A modern version of Classical School thinking originating in economics; it assumes that humans are rational and have free will, and that offenders make conscious choices to commit crime, based on a cost–benefit analysis.

reality principle The notion that one should assess the demands of the real world and act accordingly.

recidivism Also referred to as *reoffending*, when an offender goes on to commit another crime; general recidivism refers to any new offence, and sexual recidivism refers to another sexual offence.

regulatory capture A theory of corruption whereby regulatory bodies in a sector advance the private interests of the actors they regulate over the public interest.

relative deprivation The perception of unfair disparity between one's situation and that of others.

resilience The ability to successfully recover from trauma.

restorative justice An approach to justice and sentencing, often influenced by Aboriginal culture, that emphasizes the healing and reconciliation of victims, perpetrators, and their communities, and promotes positive social engagement instead of social control.

retribution Punishment for transgressions.

risk The probability that a person will commit future harmful acts.

risk-need-responsivity (RNR) model An assessment and rehabilitation theory that suggests it is possible to accurately predict the likelihood that someone will reoffend and provides principles on how to effectively intervene to reduce the risk.

robbery Stealing property from someone, with or without using violence, threats of violence, or a weapon (or imitation of a weapon).

routine activity theory Felson's theory that everyday routines and legitimate activities are key determinants of crime opportunities. At the centre of the theory is the seemingly simple, yet immensely strong and flexible, concept that "criminal acts require convergence in space and time of likely offenders, suitable targets and the absence of capable guardians against crime" (Cohen & Felson, 1979, p. 588).

rule of law The principle that governments, individuals, and corporations must follow the law; governments may take actions that limit the activities or rights of citizens only in accordance with substantive and procedural requirements prescribed by law.

sampling In statistics, the selection of a subset of the population in such a way that will allow the results of one's research to be generalizable to the population as a whole.

Scared Straight programs Programs that expose at-risk youth to examples of prison life and other consequences of criminal behaviour, along with testimonials from convicts.

script The steps in decision making and the sequence of actions for a particular criminal event.

secondary victim A person who is not directly impacted by the harmful effects of a victimizing event, but may witness the event or have to deal with the after-effects of a victimizing event, such as supporting a victim in recovery.

serotonin A neurochemical that plays an important role in depression, anxiety, and bipolar disorder. Also involved in brain development, serotonin dysfunction could lead to an increase in impulsiveness.

sex offender registry (SOR) A searchable database with information on convicted sexual offenders. Although the details of SORs can vary between jurisdictions and countries, the general process of registration remains the same. SORs require convicted sexual offenders to provide information to local law enforcement (such as name, date of birth, photo, distinguishing physical characteristics) and any changes to that information (such as change in residence).

sexual assault Unwanted sexual activity, including sexual attacks and sexual touching.

single-photon emission computed tomography A recording of body images via a radioactive isotope injected into the blood that provides a 3D image of tissues. It is commonly used to measure brain blood flow.

situational characteristics Factors associated with an incident; in the case of a violent act, location, weapon type, motive, and the victim–offender relationship are situational characteristics.

situational crime prevention (SCP) Measures taken to reduce crime opportunities. SCP takes into account the nature of the crime, the environmental factors that allow for the crime, and the risks and rewards associated with crime.

social bond theory Social control theory by Hirschi (based on Durkheim's concept of the social bond); the four elements of the social bond include attachment, commitment, involvement, and belief.

social control theory Rooted in Durkheim's forces of integration and regulation and the Chicago School concern with the breakdown in informal social controls; includes social bond theory, interactional theory, and life-course-developmental theory. Social bonds and informal social controls act as restraints on teen delinquency.

social disorganization theory The theory that a breakdown of the networks, norms, and trust that facilitate coordination and co-operation among residents of neighbourhoods can lead to greater crime and violence. The prevalence and density of social networks and the level of participation in community-based organizations generate solidarity and mutual trust—or social cohesion—among neighbourhood residents. In turn, social cohesion promotes the neighbourhood's capacity to monitor and manage criminogenic situations. Cohesive neighbourhoods that can effectively mobilize to regulate the behaviour within their boundaries are said to have high levels of collective efficacy. As so-called disorganized neighbourhoods lose control of the behaviours within their boundaries and a clear consensus on appropriate conduct dissolves, crime and violence are predicted to increase.

social forces In sociology, the perspective that elements of society have the capability of causing cultural change or influencing human behaviour.

social justice Movement promoting the need for equality, tolerance, and fairness for all members of society, particularly with regard to different classes and the less privileged.

social learning theory A combination of the Chicago School's symbolic interactionism, Sutherland's differential association theory, Skinner's operant conditioning, and Bandura's observations on imitation and modelling behavior. Definitions (one's values about acceptable and unacceptable behaviour) favourable to criminal behaviour are learned through a process of differential reinforcement. Individuals are more or less likely to engage in criminal behaviour, depending upon whether their behaviour has been reinforced (rewarded) or punished in the past and what consequences they anticipate if they continue.

socialization The process through which children learn language, culture, roles, expectations, and beliefs. It is facilitated by parents, siblings, and relatives, and later by friends and within schools and community organizations.

sociology of deviance Blends Chicago School symbolic interactionism with views on how crime and deviance are used to maintain social boundaries and/or social control; it examines how certain groups or behaviours come to be viewed as "social problems," not because they are necessarily deviant or criminal, but because of the social reaction to these groups or behaviours by "moral entrepreneurs" or "moral crusaders."

somatotyping A research technique that links behavioural characteristics to body types, such as mesomorphy.

sousveillance The recording, by a citizen participant or witness, of an incident or activity, to hold a bureaucratic organization to account. It can be used to record incidents in which police may be seen abusing their power.

spatial inequality The unequal distribution of resources and services from one area to another.

spousal violence Acts including common assault, assault with a weapon, sexual assault, homicide, forcible confinement, uttering threats, criminal harassment, failure to provide the necessities of life, psychological abuse, and financial abuse.

static factors Individual characteristics associated with the risk of reoffending that are immutable to external influences (e.g., age at first offence and offence history). They can be used to determine an overall risk level but are not targets for change.

stereotyping The simplistic and often belittling representation of a person or group, using exaggerations of traits that the larger group supposedly possesses.

stigmatize To strongly disapprove of a person or behaviour; to find disgraceful.

strain theories Theories that state certain societal stressors (e.g., unequal opportunities to achieve success) increase the likelihood of crime.

structural functionalism A sociological theory that explains how society functions according to the structure of a system of interrelated parts.

sub-lethal violent victimization Violent victimization that does not cause death.

summary offence A relatively minor offence, punishable by a fine or a maximum jail sentence of six months.

superego An aspect of Freud's theory of personality; one's moral compass, conscience, and ethical principles.

suppression strategies Efforts to eliminate gangs or significantly reduce gang-related crime through a process of deterrence and incapacitation.

surveillance The monitoring of individuals or populations for the purposes of control and/or care (Lyon, 2001).

symbolic interactionism The Chicago School notion that meaning and reality are socially constructed through the sharing of gestures used to show emotion or to demonstrate how to do something, through symbols such as monetary instruments or university degrees, or through words—which are themselves socially created symbols that convey socially agreed-upon meanings.

systemic racism The belief that racism does not occur only in isolated instances, but is entrenched in and perpetuated by our criminal justice system and other institutions.

telescoping The phenomenon whereby a survey participant recalls events as having occurred more recently than is actually the case.

tertiary victim A person who may suffer repercussions of victimization even though they are not directly involved in or witness to the harmful event.

traits Those attributes or features that distinguish or characterize an individual.

utilitarianism A philosophy that suggests reasoned decisions will produce the greatest good for the greatest number. The actions of governments and individuals should be measured in terms of their utility—how much pleasure they bring, and how many people benefit (derive pleasure) from those actions.

utility maximization Choices are made based on what one perceives will provide the greatest rewards for the lowest costs.

vicarious reinforcement Reinforcement that is experienced indirectly through observing another person's behaviour being rewarded.

vicarious victim A person who does not experience direct victimization but nonetheless responds as if they had been victimized directly after learning of the event.

victim A person harmed, injured, or killed as a result of a crime, accident, or other event or action.

victim blaming A process whereby a victim is found at fault for his or her own victimization, in whole or in part.

victim impact statement (VIS) A written document describing the harm done to the victim as a result of victimization and may include statements about physical, emotional, or financial impact(s).

victim precipitation The problematic assumption that victims can somehow influence or bring about their own victimization by exhibiting behaviours that provoke a victimizer.

victimless crime Actions (often perpetrated consensually) that are ruled illegal but do not directly violate or threaten the rights of other individuals.

victimology The study of victims.

vigilantism When a person or group of people take the law into their own hands, typically in a violent manner, in an attempt to effect justice according to their understanding of what is right and wrong.

warrant expiry date (WED) A correctional option to detain a sexual offender until the very end of his or her sentence. Those who are detained under a WED have been deemed to be a high risk for committing another sexual offence or serious personal injury offence until the very end of their sentence. The rationale for using this option is to keep the offender incapacitated for as long as possible due to his or her high risk to recidivate.

weed and seed A strategy combining the removal of violent gang members from a community with long-term community development.

whistle-blower A person who reports misconduct within an organization.

white-collar crime A crime committed by a person, usually of high social status, in the course of his or her occupation.

Index